HEALTH EDUCATION

Third Edition

HEALTH EDUCATION
Elementary and Middle School Applications

Susan K. Telljohann
University of Toledo

Cynthia Wolford Symons
Kent State University

Dean F. Miller
University of Toledo

Boston   Burr Ridge, IL   Dubuque, IA   Madison, WI   New York   San Francisco   St. Louis
Bangkok   Bogotá   Caracas   Lisbon   London   Madrid
Mexico City   Milan   New Delhi   Seoul   Singapore   Sydney   Taipei   Toronto

McGraw-Hill

A Division of The McGraw·Hill Companies

HEALTH EDUCATION: ELEMENTARY AND MIDDLE SCHOOL APPLICATIONS
THIRD EDITION

ISBN 0–697–29433–1

Vice president and editor-in-chief: *Kevin T. Kane*
Executive editor: *Vicki Malinee*
Developmental editor: *Carlotta Seely*
Senior marketing manager: *Pamela S. Cooper*
Senior project manager: *Jayne Klein*
Associate producer: *Judi David*
Production supervisor: *Laura Fuller*
Coordinator of freelance design: *David W. Hash*
Freelance cover design: *Sarin Creative*
Cover photo: *©Jon Feingersh/The Stock Market*
Senior photo research coordinator: *Lori Hancock*
Photo research: *Connie Gardner Picture Research*
Senior supplement coordinator: *David A. Welsh*
Compositor: *Interactive Composition Corporation*
Typeface: *10/12 Times Roman*
Printer: *Quebecor Printing Book Group/Dubuque, IA*

The credits section for this book begins on page 331 and is considered an extension of the copyright page.

Library of Congress Cataloging-in-Publication Data

Telljohann, Susan Kay, 1958–
      Health education: elementary and middle school applications / Susan K. Telljohann,
Cynthia W. Symons, Dean F. Miller.—3rd ed.
      p.   cm.
   Rev. ed. of: Health education in the elementary & middle-level school / Dean F. Miller,
Susan K. Telljohann, Cynthia Wolford Symons. 2nd ed. © 1996.
   Includes bibliographical references and index.
   ISBN 0–697–29433–1
   1. Health education (Elementary)—United States.   2. Health education (Middle
school)—United States.   I. Wolford Symons, Cynthia, 1953– . II. Miller, Dean F.
III. Miller, Dean F. Health education in the elementary & middle-level school. IV. Title.

LB1588.U6 T45 2001   00–020991
372.3'7'0973—dc21   CIP

www.mhhe.com

CONTENTS

CHAPTER 5

Managing Health Education in the Busy Classroom Environment 80

SECTION III
The Primary Content 101

CHAPTER 6

Skills to Impact the Psychosocial Causes of Negative Health Behavior 102

CHAPTER 7

Safety: Prevention of Unintentional Injury 116

CHAPTER 8

Intentional Injury Prevention: Violence in Families, Schools, and Communities 137

PREFACE

The ideas, concepts, and challenges presented in this textbook have developed out of many different experiences: teaching elementary and middle-level children, teaching a basic elementary/middle-level school health course to hundreds of pre-service elementary early childhood and special education majors, working with numerous student teachers, and serving on a variety of local, state, and national curriculum and standards committees. Two of the authors of this book have taken sabbatical leaves from their university teaching positions and taught for one term in a local elementary and middle school. This has provided opportunities to use the various strategies included in this third edition.

We have written this textbook with several different groups in mind: (1) the elementary and middle-level education major who has little background and experience in health education but will be required to teach health education to his or her students in the future; (2) the health education major who will be the health specialist or coordinator in an elementary or middle-level school; (3) the school nurse who works in the elementary and/or middle-level school setting; and (4) those community health educators and nurses who increasingly must interact with elementary and/or middle-level school personnel.

The book is divided into four sections. Section I, *The Program,* includes chapters 1 and 2 and introduces the coordinated school health program, the relationship between health and learning, national health initiatives, and school health services. Section II, *The Tools of Teaching,* includes chapters 3, 4, and 5. These chapters provide information on developing the elementary and/or middle-level health education curriculum. Information on the basics for effective health education, developmentally appropriate practice, the National Health Education Standards, the use of computers, and instructional approaches is included. Section III, *The Primary Content,* includes chapters 6 through 14. These chapters are organized around the Centers for Disease Control and Prevention health risk priority areas and the skills needed to be a health-literate individual. Each of these chapters includes basic background information related to the content area, developmentally appropriate information and skills, sample teaching activities, related children's literature books, and related Web sites. Section IV, *The Secondary Content,* includes chapters 15 through 17. These are also content chapters that are included in most health education curricula. Each of these chapters also includes basic background information related to the content area, sample teaching activities, related children's literature books, and related Web sites.

FEATURES OF THIS EDITION

Updated Content

As experienced health educators and authors, we realize how important it is to provide students and teachers with the most current information available. Each chapter includes the very latest information. In addition, we have introduced many timely topics (e.g., violence prevention) and issues that are sure to stimulate student interest and class discussion.

Updated Developmental Appropriate Practice Recommendations

Each of the content chapters includes the developmentally appropriate concepts that should be taught at the K–2, 3–5, and 6–8 grade levels. These lists of concepts will help future and current teachers as they prepare their health lesson plans for their students.

Updated Sample Teaching Activities

We have added more sample teaching activities in each of the content chapters. We have also divided many of these activities sets into appropriate developmental levels (e.g.,

K–2, 3–5, 6–8). These activities not only focus on knowledge acquisition, but also on skill development.

Updated Recommendations of Children's Literature Books with a Health-Related Theme

Each content chapter includes an updated list of recommended children's literature books that are relevant for each developmental level. Franki Sibberson, a children's literature expert, assisted with the selection of recommended books for each content area. Special attention was given to books with a multicultural approach. In addition, award-winning books were also included in the recommended reading lists.

Updated Website Lists

Each content chapter also includes an updated website list. These websites are useful resources to current and future teachers in staying up-to-date on a variety of health topics.

ANCILLARIES

There is an accompanying Instructor's Manual and Test Bank to this text. The manual for this edition has been expanded and prepared by one of the co-authors. Learning objectives for each chapter and a lecture outline are included. The computerized test bank package is available to qualified adopters of the text in Windows and Macintosh formats.

ACKNOWLEDGEMENTS

Many people and organizations provided information, photos, and other material during the preparation of the manuscript. We offer our sincere thanks to all of these individuals. In particular, we would like to thank Terry Fell for providing many of the photos in this edition. We would also like to thank Franki Sibberson for developing the lists of related children's literature books that are found in the content chapters. Her insight into children's literature is an asset to this new edition.

The manuscript was greatly enhanced by the thorough review by Beth Pateman from the University of Hawaii. Her new ideas and suggestions were a wonderful contribution to this new edition.

We also want to thank the following reviewers for their helpful comments on various versions of this work:

Robert B. Beavers   *Claflin College*
Michael J. Cleary   *Slippery Rock University*
Carl Hanson   *Montana State University*
Margo Harris   *Western Washington University*
Denise M. Seabert   *University of Florida*
Donna M. Videto   *SUNY College at Cortland*

We hope that you enjoy the changes and additions made to the third edition of this book. We welcome any comments or suggestions for future editions. Best wishes and success when teaching health education to children and preadolescents.

Susan K. Telljohann
Cynthia Wolford Symons
Dean F. Miller

The Program

Section I begins by presenting a case for the importance of school health programs. It outlines the available research on the relationship between health risks of students and their academic achievement. This section then continues to describe the eight components of a coordinated school health program. Elementary and middle-level teachers should find this information to be a helpful orientation for all of the individuals in a school who affect the health of their students. Last, the health services component of the coordinated school health program and the role of the school nurse are highlighted.

1

THE COORDINATED SCHOOL HEALTH PROGRAM

Organization, Structure, and Influence on Student Health and the Academic Environment

OUTLINE

HEALTH: A CONCEPT

When most of us review our understanding of the concept of health, we think only in physical terms. We limit our focus to such issues as preventing or managing illness, participating in fitness activities, or modifying our diets. Importantly however, the elementary and middle-level school classroom teacher must understand that the concept of health encompasses more than the element of physical well-being. Health is comprised of several dimensions.

The definition of health with which most people are familiar was provided by the World Health Organization in 1947. This definition suggested that health is best understood as ". . . a state of complete physical, mental, and social well-being and not merely the absence of disease or infirmity."[1] In this context, we are better able to identify that there are complex elements that influence personal health. More recently, however, definitions have emerged that help us to view the elements that influence our health in more personal terms. Rather than being understood in the context of complete well-being in all areas, more contemporary definitions now suggest that health relates to our ability to function in the context of personal strengths and weaknesses. Bedworth and Bedworth clarified that health ". . . can be defined as the quality of people's physical, psychological, and sociological functioning that enables them to deal adequately with the self and others in a variety of personal and social situations."[2] Current definitions of health that enrich our understand of this complex concept share common integrated elements. In particular, there are five such elements that are foundational to understanding the health of school-age youth. These elements include the physical, emotional, social, spiritual, and vocational dimensions of health.

The *physical* dimension of health is not only the most often considered, but it is the most easy to identify. Frequently, we judge a person's general health status based on appearance, energy level, body weight, or the kind of physical fitness activities in which he or she participates. Our initial, and sometimes lasting, impression of a person's well-being results from observing behaviors in the physical dimension. If people are overweight or use tobacco products, we tend to assume that they are unhealthy. Certainly their general health status could improve by reducing participation in health risk behaviors. However, they may be very healthy in other dimensions.

The *emotional* dimension of health is focused on how individuals feel about themselves and how they express emotions. Emotionally healthy people possess strong coping skills and express their feelings in socially acceptable ways. They tend to have positive feelings about themselves. While this does not mean they never feel sad, angry, or depressed, emotionally healthy individuals express and deal with negative feelings in positive and socially acceptable ways. An individual with compromised emotional health may exhibit manifestations of a negative sense of self, or express feelings by acting out in inappropriate or even abusive ways. In some instances, people keep feelings bottled up, contributing to stress-related illnesses. Unhealthy emotional adaptations can result in a variety of physical and mental health disorders.

The *social* dimension of health is based on the social skills practiced by an individual. We all live and interact in a variety of different social environments—our home, school, neighborhood, and place of work. Socially healthy people feel comfortable in the company of others. They are concerned about others, and usually are well received in social contexts. Such individuals practice appropriate interpersonal skills and view themselves as contributing members of society. On the other hand, there are people who do not function comfortably or effectively in the company of others or whose concern focuses only on themselves. The behaviors of socially unhealthy people have a negative impact on their quality of life and on others with whom they work and live.

The *spiritual* dimension of health includes an individual's philosophy, values, and meaning of life.[3]

Spiritual health is not defined in context of formal religious practice. Usually, it is understood more broadly. Spiritually healthy individuals integrate accepted, positive moral and ethical standards such as integrity, honesty, and trust into their lives. Such people demonstrate a strong concern for others regardless of gender, race, nationality, age, or economic status. A person with compromised spiritual health usually is not strongly motivated by moral or ethical principles. Often, such individuals do not believe that a higher process or being gives meaning to life. For such people, life can become isolated and troublesome.

The *vocational* dimension of health relates to the ability of individuals to collaborate with others in their professional, community, or work relationships. Vocationally healthy people tend to demonstrate a commitment to carrying out their share of responsibility to projects and activities. This commitment is demonstrated when individuals contribute their best effort to tasks to which they make a commitment. The vocational dimension of health is manifested also in the degree to which one's work makes a positive impact on others or the well-being of society. In this context, the behaviors of people with negative vocational health are not limited only to threats to individual goals. Compromised vocational health also can make a negative impact on the well-being of professional associates and the collaborative community or workplace environment.

When thinking about these dimensions of health, it is important to remember that balance among the dimensions is just as important as maintaining an optimal level of functioning within each. An individual who is very healthy in the physical dimension may be ineffective or abusive when expressing emotions. Also, it is quite possible for physically healthy people to demonstrate a poorly developed code of personal moral or ethical standards. Similarly, a person with a physical disability may be very productive, possess strong self-esteem, and interact very effectively and productively with others.

In this context, personal health can be compared to a wheel. The wheel is highly functional as long as all sides perform well independently, contributing to a whole that can operate smoothly and in balance. If the wheel is out of alignment or suffers a blowout, its entire function is compromised. Similarly, in persons with high-level personal well-being, each dimension of their health functions well and is balanced with the other dimensions. Problems, or a "puncture," in one or more of the dimensions of personal health, can render the individual less effective (figure 1.1).

When working with and preparing lessons that focus on promoting healthy behaviors among elementary and middle-level learners, teachers should remember the importance of each of the dimensions of health. In addition, teachers would be wise to develop learning activities that highlight the interrelated nature of these dimensions.

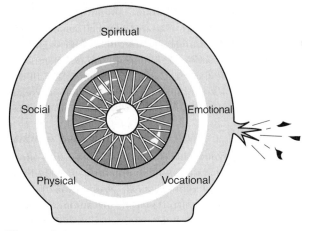

Figure 1.1
When a tire is punctured, the ability of the entire unit to function is impaired. The same is true of health. A malfunction to any of the five dimensions that influence personal health has a negative effect on the other dimensions. Can you think of other ways that this idea could be depicted?

HEALTHY AMERICANS

In 1979, the U.S. government embarked on a multiyear initiative to improve the health status of all Americans. This agenda was started with the publication of *Healthy People: The Surgeon General's Report on Health Promotion and Disease Prevention.* This document confirmed that the leading causes of illness and death of Americans had shifted significantly between the beginning of the 20th and the start of the 21st centuries. In the early 1900s, our leading causes of death were related primarily to infectious or communicable diseases. At this time, influenza and pneumonia, tuberculosis, and diarrhea and related disorders were among the leading causes of death of Americans. Because of improvements in sanitation and waste disposal, changes in public health policy, and medical discoveries including immunizations, Americans now live longer and healthier lives.[4]

Although our length and quality of life have improved significantly since 1900, *Healthy People* confirmed that four major factors continue to influence premature illness and death of Americans. Heredity (20%), exposure to environmental hazards and pollutants (20%), and inadequate access to quality medical care (10%) account for about 50% of our premature morbidity and mortality.[5] These variables largely are beyond the control of the individual.

Importantly, however, all citizens must be aware that approximately 50% of premature illness and death in the United States is related to the effects of our participation in risky health behaviors (figure 1.2).[6] As seen in the Consider This box on the causes of death, research has confirmed the ten most prevalent conditions at the time of death among Americans.[7] Importantly, however, most

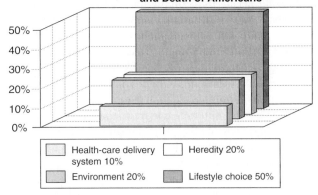

Variables Related to Premature Illness and Death of Americans

- Health-care delivery system 10%
- Heredity 20%
- Environment 20%
- Lifestyle choice 50%

Figure 1.2
Approximately 50% of early death of Americans is related to the cumulative effects of our participation in risky health behaviors.

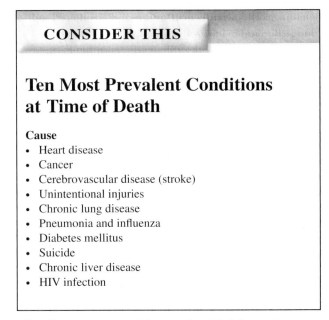

CONSIDER THIS

Ten Most Prevalent Conditions at Time of Death

Cause
- Heart disease
- Cancer
- Cerebrovascular disease (stroke)
- Unintentional injuries
- Chronic lung disease
- Pneumonia and influenza
- Diabetes mellitus
- Suicide
- Chronic liver disease
- HIV infection

Note: The most prevalent conditions at the time of death for most Americans are chronic in nature.

Source: McGinnis and Foege, 1993.

underlying causes of these chronic conditions can be traced to the cumulative effects of participation in risky health behaviors. These are behaviors over which we can exercise significant personal control (table 1.1).[8]

In specific, public health professionals at the Centers for Disease Control and Prevention have concluded that six preventable behaviors have been identified as priority areas for programming and educational intervention. Since most people initiate participation in these risk behaviors in their youth, advocates for student health would be wise to concentrate their efforts in the following areas:

- Tobacco use,
- Poor eating habits,
- Alcohol and other drug risks,

TABLE 1.1	Underlying Risk Behaviors Related to Leading Causes of Death	
Risk Behaviors	**Approximate Number of Annual Deaths**	**Approximate Percent of Annual Deaths**
Tobacco	400,000	19%
Diet/Inactivity patterns	300,000	14%
Alcohol	100,000	5%
Infections	90,000	4%
Toxic agents	80,000	4%
Sexual behavior	40,000	3%
Firearms	35,000	2%
Motor vehicles	25,000	1%
Drug use	25,000	<1%

Note: We can influence the common lifestyle risks related to premature death. Annually, these health risks are the actual leading causes of death among Americans.

Source: McGinnis and Foege, 1993.

- Behaviors that result in intentional and unintentional injuries,
- Physical inactivity, and
- Sexual behaviors that result in HIV infection, other sexually transmitted diseases, or unintended pregnancy.[9]

Healthy People recommended the establishment of national health promotion goals that focus on five different age groups: *infants* (younger than 1 year), *children* (1–14 years), *adolescents and young adults* (15–24 years), *adults* (25–64 years), and *older adults* (over 65 years).[10] To achieve these broad age-group health goals, a national agenda directed at achievement of more than 200 specific measurable health-promotion objectives was formalized. These original health objectives, targeted for achievement by 1990, provided an organizational structure for coordinating program emphasis in health promotion and disease prevention during the decade of the 1980s. By 1990, success in meeting the objectives was mixed—some goals were met; some were not; others were surpassed.

After extensive review of the 1990 Health Objectives for the Nation, three broad health promotion goals were established to continue improving the health status of all Americans by the year 2000. These goals focused on:

1. Increasing the span of healthy life,
2. Reducing health disparities among Americans, and
3. Achieving access to preventive services for all citizens.[11]

To address these goals, 298 specific health promotion objectives were detailed. As a means to continue this national agenda, these goals were published in a document entitled *Healthy People 2000*. Specific activities to

CONSIDER THIS

Health—A Personal Evaluation

As someone who will be teaching health concepts to elementary and middle-level schoolchildren, you will find it helpful to reflect on the status of your own health in the five different dimensions.

With which of the five dimensions that comprise the concept of health do you feel most comfortable from a personal point of view? In what types of activities do you participate to improve your health within each dimension? In what activities do you participate to improve your general health across the dimensions?

On the other hand, what dimension, or dimensions, of health seem to cause you problems? Why? What significant measures and activities might you undertake to strengthen this dimension of your state of health?

Discuss how this understanding of the concept of health will affect your teaching as an elementary or middle-level schoolteacher.

be carried out by national, state, and local agencies were identified to contribute to achieving these objectives by the turn of the 20th century.[12]

Several of the specific objectives to be achieved by the year 2000 identified a role for America's schools in promoting the nation's health. Recommendations specified the integration of planned sequential school health education in at least 75% of the nation's schools in kindergarten through twelfth grade.[13] While this objective has yet to be achieved, an ongoing commitment to promoting health for all Americans has been structured in the nation's health objectives to be achieved by the year 2010.

HEALTH IN THE ACADEMIC ENVIRONMENT

If you were asked to describe the school health program in the community where you attended elementary or middle school, what impressions would you highlight? Unfortunately, the school health program is not a priority in many school communities. When budget deficits occur, it is not unusual for health promotion activities to be cut. Findings from the national School Health Policies and Programs Study, sponsored by the Centers for Disease Control and Prevention, revealed that while many states employ directors to coordinate state-level school health initiatives, such professionals or activities rarely are part of the local district agenda.[14] In fact, the National School Boards Association has confirmed from estimates that full implementation of quality health instruction is found in only a disappointing 5% to 15% of the nation's schools.[15]

TABLE 1.2	National Education Goals

BY THE YEAR 2000

1. All children in the United States will start school ready to learn.
2. The high school graduation rate will increase to at least 90%.
3. All students will leave grades 4, 8, and 12 having demonstrated competence over challenging subject matter, including English, mathematics, science, foreign languages, civics and government, economics, the arts, history, and geography, and every school in America will ensure that all students learn to use their mind well so that they are prepared for responsible citizenship, further learning, and productive employment.
4. U.S. students will be first in the world in science and mathematics achievement.
5. Every adult American will be literate and will possess the knowledge and skills necessary to compete in a global economy and to exercise rights and responsibilities of citizenship.
6. Every school in the United States will be free of drugs, violence, and the unauthorized presence of firearms and alcohol and will offer a disciplined environment conducive to learning.
7. The nation's teaching force will have access to programs for the continued improvement of their professional skills and the opportunity to acquire the knowledge and skills needed to instruct and prepare all U.S. students for the next century.
8. Every school will promote partnerships that will increase parental involvement and participation in promoting the social, emotional, and academic growth of children.

Source: U.S. Department of Education.

Recent attention to child and adolescent health issues in the school setting has evolved in context of a broad national commitment to educational reform. Since the early 1980s, a number of reports, publications, and legislative initiatives have been directed at improving the quality of education for American youth. This educational reform movement has led to a number of new and different initiatives whose primary focus has been on improving educational programming in basic or core academic subjects, including the language arts, mathematics, social studies, and the physical sciences.

Consistent with the ongoing commitment to education reform, the Goals 2000: Educate America Act was passed by the U.S. Congress in 1994. This legislation established eight National Education Goals targeted to be achieved by the year 2000, and mandated that content standards be developed by individual states. In addition, the legislation called for improved measurement of student achievement, and the establishment of voluntary standards in selected content areas, including English, history, science, mathematics, arts, geography, and foreign language (table 1.2)[16].

Unfortunately, academic activities to address the complex health issues confronting students have received little emphasis throughout this education reform movement. This omission was brought into clear focus in *A Nation at Risk,* a 1993 study conducted by the National Commission on Excellence in Education. This prestigious report, sponsored by the United States Department of Education, placed health education in a category referred to as an "educational smorgasbord." The report asserted that American education curricula had become "diluted . . . and diffused . . . ," and recommended that educational programs in this category be either eliminated or significantly reduced in emphasis.[17] Consistent

with this clear message of educational reform, no direct mandate to improve health instruction was included in the specific goal statements of the National Education Goals. There is only one goal in this agenda that makes specific reference to child and adolescent health issues. This goal asserts that, "every school in America will be free of drugs and violence by the year 2000."[18] While this specific goal refers to the negative impact of specific student risk behaviors on the educational environment, the Goals 2000 agenda provided no specific governmental mandate for schools to participate in improving the health outcomes of learners.

At the same time that education reform activists were calling for decreased emphasis on a range of content areas including school health, many reports, including those related to *Healthy People 2000,* documented the poor state of health of American children. Local schools were expected to lead in the battle against student risk behaviors, including teenage pregnancy, alcohol and other drug abuse, adolescent suicide, and youth violence, but were provided with only weak governmental support for any school-based activities that did not directly target improved academic and proficiency test scores.

In response, the Secretaries of Education and Health and Human Services issued a federal interagency position statement in April 1994. This statement provided strong support for the establishment of comprehensive school health programs and the provision of school-related health services. This statement confirmed that a range of health and social problems have had an adverse effect on the culture of schools and the academic outcomes of students.[19] In this spirit, health-related objectives embedded in each of the National Education Goals were highlighted (table 1.3).[20]

TABLE 1.3	**National Education Goals: Health-Related Objectives**

- Children will receive the nutrition, physical activity experiences, and health care needed to arrive at school with healthy minds and bodies, and to maintain the mental alertness necessary to be prepared to learn **(Goal 1 objective)**
- All students will be involved in activities that promote and demonstrate good citizenship, good health, community service, and personal responsibility **(Goal 3 objective)**
- All students will have access to physical education and health education to ensure they are healthy and fit **(Goal 3 objective)**
- All teachers will have access to preservice teacher education and continuing professional development activities that will provide such teachers with the knowledge and skills needed to teach to an increasingly diverse student population with a variety of educational, social, and health needs **(Goal 4 objective)**
- Every school will implement a firm and fair policy on use, possession, and distribution of drugs and alcohol **(Goal 7 objective)**
- Every local educational agency will develop and implement a policy to ensure that all schools are free of violence and the unauthorized presence of weapons **(Goal 7 objective)**
- Every local educational agency will develop a sequential, comprehensive kindergarten through twelfth grade drug and alcohol prevention education program **(Goal 7 objective)**
- Drug and alcohol curriculum should be taught as an integral part of sequential, comprehensive health education **(Goal 7 objective)**
- Every school should work to eliminate sexual harassment **(Goal 7 objective)**

Source: U.S. Department of Education.

Support for broad-based, integrated school and community programs to address student health risks has emerged from another source. A growing body of literature now confirms that student health behaviors and academic achievement are "inextricably intertwined."[21] The American Cancer Society and representatives of over forty national organizations have concluded that "healthy children are in a better position to acquire knowledge," and cautioned that no curriculum is "brilliant enough to compensate for a hungry stomach or a distracted mind."[22] Many publications confirm a direct relationship between student participation in dangerous health behaviors and negative academic outcomes. Specifically, the consequences of student health risks have been linked to compromises in such foundational education elements as attendance, class grades, performance on standardized tests, graduation rates, and feelings of safety while at school.[23] In this context, as a means to improve academic outcomes, elementary and middle-level teachers are turning to this growing body of research as a source of support for integrating health promotion activities across the curriculum.

THE COORDINATED SCHOOL HEALTH PROGRAM

A Foundation for Understanding

Individuals who are concerned about the health status of elementary and middle-grade learners and the impact of their health choices on academic achievement would be wise to assume the role of advocate for a well planned and effective school health program. One might wonder about the value of science, mathematics, language arts, or social studies instructional activities to even the brightest or most talented students if these young people are at risk for alcohol or other drug-related behaviors, pregnancy, or the negative outcomes of violence. In this context, an investment in keeping students healthy must become part of the core responsibilities for which schools must assume leadership. Unfortunately, while it is common for professionals who work with elementary and middle-level students to mobilize to confront complex student health risks only when there is a crisis or when evidence confirms that such risks are having a negative impact on student learning, student advocates must be aware of the limited time that is available for school-based health promotion activities on an ongoing basis.

In the context of such time constraints, child health and education advocates must plan programming that is both effective and consistent with the educational mission of schools. Sound school-based programming is grounded in adapting what research has identified as best practice, to meet local needs. Only in this way can both the health and academic outcomes for students be realized.

The 1979 *Healthy People* initiative provided a starting point for organizing effective school health programs by defining the key concepts of *medical care, disease prevention,* and *health promotion.* Understanding these concepts helps student health advocates by framing boundaries of professional practice, identifying realistic program expectations, and targeting key stakeholders with a shared responsibility for the health of learners.

Medical care is defined with a primary focus on ". . . the sick," and involves activities designed ". . . to keep these individuals alive, make them well, or minimize their disability."[24] Each day, there are children enrolled in

CONSIDER THIS

A Fence or an Ambulance

By Joseph Malins

'Twas a dangerous cliff, as they freely confessed,
Though to walk near its crest was so pleasant;
But over its terrible edge there had slipped
A duke and full many a peasant.
So the people said something would have to be done,
But their projects did not at all tally;
Some said, "Put a fence around the edge of the cliff,"
Some, "An ambulance down in the valley."

But the cry for the ambulance carried the day,
For it spread through the neighboring city;
A fence may be useful or not, it is true,
But each heart became brimful of pity
For those who slipped over that dangerous cliff;
And the dwellers in highway and alley
Gave pounds or gave pence, not to put up a fence,
But an ambulance down in the valley.

"For the cliff is all right, if you're careful," they said,
"And, if folks even slip and are dropping,
It isn't the slipping that hurts them so much,
As the shock down below when they're stopping."
So day after day, as these mishaps occurred,
Quick forth would these rescuers sally
To pick up the victims who fell off the cliff,
With their ambulance down in the valley.

Then an old sage remarked: "It's a marvel to me
That people give far more attention

To repairing results than to stopping the cause,
When they'd much better aim at prevention.
Let us stop at its source all this mischief," cried he,
"Come, neighbors and friends, let us rally;
If the cliff we will fence we might almost dispense
With the ambulance down in the valley."

"Oh, he's a fanatic," the others rejoined,
"Dispense with the ambulance? Never!
He'd dispense with all charities, too, if he could;
No! No! We'll support them forever.
Aren't we picking up folks just as fast as they fall?
And shall this man dictate to us? Shall he?
Why should people of sense stop to put up a fence,
While the ambulance works in the valley?"

But a sensible few, who are practical too,
Will not bear with such nonsense much longer;
They believe that prevention is better than cure,
And their party will soon be the stronger.
Encourage them then, with your purse, voice, and pen,
And while other philanthropists dally,
They will scorn all pretense and put up a stout fence
On the cliff that hangs over the valley.

Better guide well the young than reclaim them when old,
For the voice of true wisdom is calling,
"To rescue the fallen is good, but 'tis best
To prevent other people from falling."
Better close up the source of temptation and crime
Than deliver from dungeon or galley;
Better put a strong fence round the top of the cliff
Than an ambulance down in the valley.

America's schools who are receiving medical care consistent with this definition. These conditions have been diagnosed and treatment has been prescribed by physicians. Care for these students is managed by trained medical care professionals. In the context of this definition, school personnel have not been identified as the principal providers of such diagnostic and therapeutic intervention. Exceptions exist only in the provision of first aid or emergency care by specially trained individuals. The appropriate role for school-based professionals in providing medical care for students is to refer, support, and comply with the prescriptions and proscriptions that have been made by responsible medical care providers. In this way, education professionals participate by helping parents and trained others carry out medical care plans that are developed to respond to diagnosed student needs.

By contrast, *disease prevention* "begins with a threat to health—a disease or environmental hazard—and seeks

to protect as many people as possible from the harmful consequences of that threat."[25] Often, teachers stress hand washing and proper disposal of soiled tissues as part of daily classroom practice. It is common for education professionals to collaborate with school nurses, administrators, parents, and medical care providers during outbreaks of such infectious conditions as chickenpox, head lice, or the flu. School policymakers work with public health officials in screening and enforcing compliance with immunization policies. Whether working independently in the classroom environment, or in collaboration with others on issues of a broader scope, teachers assume a much more active role in disease prevention strategies than in the delivery of medical care.

While school-based professionals should understand their roles with regard to medical care and disease prevention, they must be most comfortable with activities that focus on student *health promotion*. *Healthy People* defined all strategies that begin with "people who are basically healthy" as the target for health promotion activities. Health promotion "seeks the development of community and individual measures which can help," people ". . . to develop healthy lifestyles that can maintain and enhance the state of well-being."[26] Given the confirmed connection between health risks and academic performance and the fact that the great majority of school-age youth are "basically healthy," it is clear that the primary role for school-based professionals lies in developing, coordinating, and collaborating in the implementation of health promotion efforts. "Beginning in early childhood and throughout life, each of us makes decisions affecting our health. They are made, for the most part, without regard to, or contact with, the health care delivery system. Yet their cumulative impact has a greater effect on the length and quality of life than all the efforts of medical care combined."[27]

Unfortunately, such a proactive orientation to the complex health issues that confront learners is not the norm in most school communities. The scope of school health activities often is limited to a reaction to some illness, injury, or complex youth crisis in the community. By contrast, a commitment to health promotion provides a foundation for proactive collaboration by many stakeholders invested in learners and learning. The contrast between conventional school health activities and implementation of a health promotion philosophy in school health practice is highlighted in the Consider This box on page 8. This poem, written in the 1800s, clarifies the value of a commitment to a prevention orientation to student health.

A Program Model for Best Practice

Undergirded with the foundation of a health promotion approach, the next step to managing complex challenges to student health and achievement is to integrate effective school health programming into local school district practice. While most school communities are involved in a range of health related activities, these policies and programs usually are categorical in nature. It is common for schools to provide drug prevention assemblies, school safety activities, physical education classes, and conflict mediation or violence risk-reduction training. Unfortunately, these activities rarely are organized and implemented in a way that capitalizes on communication among the professionals who offer the specific programs. In addition, few school districts organize their health promotion programming to maximize available resources and put academic achievement and student health at the heart of the matter.

By contrast, the coordinated school health program model is organized to capitalize on two key elements:

1. The expertise of many invested advocates, and
2. Their collaborative approach to health promoting activities.

Coordinated school health programming provides a way to improve, protect, and promote the well-being of students, families, and personnel involved in the educational system. This model, depicted in figure 1.3, has been defined as "an organized set of policies, procedures, and activities designed to protect and promote the health and well-being of students and staff which has traditionally included health services, healthful school environment, and health education. It should also include, but not be limited to, guidance and counseling, physical education, food service, social work, psychological services, and employee health promotion."[28] All activities are organized to send consistent messages about many health issues in a way that is reinforced across multiple communication channels. The model implies that there is a commitment to maximizing the resources and talents of many school and community citizens who are dedicated to children and youth. Finally, in the coordinated school health program, student health risks are addressed in context rather than in place of the academic mission of the school.

Comprehensive School Health Education: The Keys to Quality Health Instruction

The foundation of the coordinated school health program is built on the educational or instructional component of the model: comprehensive school health education. This program of studies is organized to include planned, sequential, developmentally appropriate, and cross-curricular activities. A program of quality health instruction is focused on enabling and empowering students to gather accurate health information, evaluate attitudes that influence personal and community health, and practice skills necessary to integrate health enhancing practices into daily living.

In light of the confirmation that the leading causes of death of Americans are related to participation in risky health behaviors, student health advocates must broaden conventional approaches to health education. As with other subjects in the total school curriculum, health education must be approached as any other important academic discipline. While knowing that accurate information provides an important foundation for the practice of health enhancing behaviors, a program of studies developed only in this domain is insufficient to influence complex behavior. Consistent with best practice protocol in other academic subjects, quality health instruction must contain activities that bridge all three domains of learning, including (1) cognitive, (2) affective, and (3) psychomotor or skill domains. In addition health education should incorporate the use of developmentally appropriate learning materials, equipment, and books so that effective learning can take place.

As a means to support improved school health instruction, a collaborative committee representing national health and advocacy organizations published a 1995 document entitled *National Health Education Standards:*

Figure 1.3
The Coordinated School Health Program Model.

Achieving Health Literacy. Consistent with educational reform initiatives in other content areas, this publication outlined national standards for health education. These standards were developed to set ambitious goals for improving health education for all students. In addition to the standards, rationale for each standard and performance indicators to be achieved by students in grades 4, 8, and 11 were specified. Elementary and middle-level teachers are encouraged to examine the appendix to chapter 1, which identifies health education performance indicators for students in grades K–4 and 5–8. Further, table 1.4 confirms that the *National Health Education Standards* were developed to apply to a broad range of

health topics and the three domains of learning. In addition, the standards provide a framework for developing a rigorous health education instructional scope and sequence for students in all grade levels.[29] As a result, over 50% of state departments of education and many local school districts have used the *National Health Education Standards* as a starting point for curriculum update or revision initiatives.

State legislatures or boards of education often mandate that certain time allotments be targeted for health instruction at the local level. In an alternative model, some states have abandoned time-based requirements in favor of identifying outcome competencies or academic

TABLE 1.4	National Health Education Standards

1. Students will comprehend concepts related to health promotion and disease prevention.
2. Students will demonstrate the ability to access valid health information and health-promoting products and services.
3. Students will demonstrate the ability to practice health-enhancing behaviors and reduce health risks.
4. Students will analyze the influence of culture, media, technology, and other factors on health.
5. Students will demonstrate the ability to use interpersonal communication skills to enhance health.
6. Students will demonstrate the ability to use goal-setting and decision-making skills to enhance health.
7. Students will demonstrate the ability to advocate for personal, family, and community health.

This represents the work of the Joint Committee on National Health Education Standards. Copies of the *National Health Education Standards: Achieving Health Literacy* can be obtained through the American School Health Association, Association for the Advancement of Health Education or the American Cancer Society.

targets for students. While there is great variability among states, it is common for more formal instructional time to be devoted to health education in the upper-elementary and middle-level grades than in the primary grades.

In the case of either model, research has revealed important findings about the amount of instructional time necessary for effective health education in the three domains of learning. Scholarly analysis has confirmed that more hours of formal health instruction are necessary to produce changes in the affective domain than in either the cognitive or psychomotor domains of learning. Further, 40 to 50 hours of formal health instruction are necessary to produce stable, improved outcomes across all three domains—knowledge, attitudes, and skills.[30]

In addition to variability in instructional time, there is great variety across local school districts about the content areas included in the health education course of study. Until recently, most school districts built their health education curriculum around ten critical content areas identified by the Education Commission of the States.[31]

Importantly, however, few districts are able to integrate such an extensive instructional program into the limited time constraints of the school day. In addition, it is important to remember that the Centers for Disease Control and Prevention (CDC) has targeted six problem priority areas confirmed to be related to the leading causes of illness and death of Americans. In this context, this book is organized with particular emphasis on these six priority health risk behaviors. Local health educators who are trying to balance issues of instructional quality and time constraints are encouraged to focus classroom practice and district level curriculum revision activities on these six priority health risk behavioral categories. In this way, revised courses of study will be organized to provide sufficient time for effective instruction in all three learning domains in each priority content area. With this foundation, remaining instructional time can be devoted to locally important issues included in the traditional ten health education content areas. The Consider This box on page 12 contrasts the ten traditional health education content areas with the six CDC problem priority areas.

Unlike secondary schools in which content specialists are employed, elementary and middle-level classroom teachers often are expected to deliver the health education program of studies. On occasion, however, a health education specialist will come to the classroom either to provide this instruction or to supplement the efforts of the classroom teacher. Often, the school nurse provides such instructional support.

The basis for this practice is rooted in the fact that many elementary and middle-level teachers have an inadequate academic background to teach health. These professionals may lack the confidence or enthusiasm for health instruction due to limitations in their teacher preparation curriculum. In this context, state departments of education often specify only minimal requirements for teacher certification or licensure for those who will teach health education concepts to younger learners.

In response to this dilemma, competencies have been identified by representatives of professional health education associations for elementary classroom teachers who assume primary responsibility for teaching health education to young students. These responsibilities are focused in five general areas, including (1) describing the discipline of health education within the school setting, (2) assessing health instructional needs and interests of elementary students, (3) planning effective instruction, (4) implementing health instruction, and (5) evaluating the effectiveness of health instruction for young students.[32] Readers are encouraged to use these competencies as a foundation for a self-check of strengths and weaknesses in their expertise. Identified weaknesses should be addressed by participating in staff development or continuing education opportunities for in-service professionals. Such programs focus on helping teachers to update content and develop skills to improve health instruction.

In summary, classroom teachers and curriculum developers are encouraged to review table 1.5. This checklist provides a review of important elements of a comprehensive school health education program—the keys to quality health instruction.

CONSIDER THIS

Contrasting the Ten Traditional Health Education Content Areas with the Six CDC Problem Priority Areas as a Foundation for Health Education Curriculum Development

THE TEN TRADITIONAL CONTENT AREAS:

- Personal health
- Mental and emotional health
- Prevention and control of disease
- Nutrition
- Substance use and abuse
- Accident prevention and safety
- Community health
- Consumer health
- Environmental health
- Family life education

THE SIX CDC PRIORITY AREAS:

- Tobacco use
- Poor eating habits
- Alcohol and other drug risks
- Behaviors that result in intentional and unintentional injuries
- Physical inactivity
- Sexual behaviors that result in HIV infection, other sexually transmitted diseases, and unintended pregnancy

---

Sources: Education Commission of the States; Kolbe

TABLE 1.5 **Keys to Quality Health Instruction: A Checklist of Important Elements that Confirm a Commitment to Comprehensive School Health Education**

- Has your school community developed a planned, sequential, developmentally appropriate pre-K–grade 12 health curriculum focused on the six CDC problem priority health areas?
- Does the curriculum include learning activities that enable learners to actively practice skills common to the adoption of health promoting behaviors?
- Has the health education curriculum been developed with attention to the national school health standards?
- Are parents actively involved in the health instructional program?
- Are certificated health educators employed to deliver the program of health instruction?
- Do community health agencies participate as active partners in health instruction?
- Is an on-going program of health related staff development provided for administration, faculty, and staff?

School Health Services

Laws in the United States provide for universal and compulsory education for all children. Although some parents choose private, charter, or home-schooling options for their children, the majority of American children attend public schools during the formative years of their growth and development. Although they do not reach all children, schools are an appropriate setting for the provision of mandated health services. School health services include a range of policies and programs designed to assess the health status of children. In addition, measures to protect the health of all children are incorporated into the program of school health services. Although various school personnel contribute to the school health service program, it is the school nurse who assumes primary responsibility for leadership in this component of the coordinated school health program. With the support of parents, teachers, administrators, support staff, community agency professionals, and physicians, the school nurse leads the collaborative effort to:

- Assess student health needs and problems,
- Plan school-based activities that respond to identified needs,
- Assure scrupulous implementation of care plans, and
- Evaluate the impact of the intervention on the health status and achievement of the student.

In this way, the school nurse coordinates communication with many people who focus on student health concerns.[33]

The delivery of quality school nursing services is affected by the ratio of nurses to the number of students enrolled in the school district. Caseload assignments are influenced by a number of factors, including:

1. Functions mandated for the school nurse,
2. The number of buildings to be served,

3. Social, economic, and cultural status of the community,
4. Special health problems of students, and
5. Licensed or unlicensed personnel to provide assistance.

In any case, the National Association of School Nurses asserts that to meet the health and safety needs of all students ". . . the maximum ratio of nurse to student should be:

- One school health nurse to no more than 750 students in the general school population,
- One school health nurse to no more than 225 students in the mainstreamed population,
- One school health nurse to no more than 125 students in the severely chronically ill or developmentally disabled population, and
- In the medically fragile population, a ratio based on individual needs."[34]

Debate continues about the kinds and extent of direct medical care services that should be provided at the school site. Consistent with the *Healthy People* definition of medical care, generally it is concluded that elementary and middle-level schools are not the best locations for the provision of primary medical care. However, the school setting is an ideal location for basic screening to identify deviations from normal growth and development and problems that exert a negative influence on the learning process. In the context of the range of students in attendance, and the kinds of learning activities that are part of the school program, many physical, emotional, and social issues are revealed during school-sponsored activities. The classroom teacher is in an important position to participate in initial observation and referral of any student with conditions that make a negative impact on school success. Such reports should be made to the school nurse. In response, the coordinated team of health service providers can plan appropriate intervention protocol to address the problem. Clearly, the program of school health services fills a critical role in advancing the academic mission of the schools.

In addition to the process of ongoing identification of student health problems, school health service professionals participate in a formalized program of student health status assessments. These activities include health examinations and screening practices. In most school districts, a child must have a health examination before enrolling in school. Some school districts require additional periodic health examinations for their students. These requirements vary from state to state.

School nurses collaborate with a range of allied health professionals in providing health screening activities. Most states require vision and hearing screening at some point in the child's schooling experience. Often, vision problems and hearing difficulties are not identified until the child enters school. Scoliosis screening is a

simple, but very effective, procedure to identify spinal curvatures in school children in upper-elementary grades. Additionally, during the elementary school years, the child's weight and height are recorded. These measurements provide a record of basic childhood growth and development. A review of a growth chart can quickly provide evidence that a child's physical development is consistent with his or her chronological age.

School health service professionals also coordinate measures to prevent communicable diseases and participate in activities to protect the health of students, faculty, and staff. To this end, policies must be developed in collaboration with public health officials to exclude children who are infected with contagious conditions from school activities. Such policies should be understood by the teacher, the family, and the child to reduce the risk of spreading infections. Elementary and middle-level classroom teachers must be informed about when and under what circumstances a child who has been absent from school with a communicable disease can be permitted to return.

Health protection activities also include compliance with immunization mandates. Every state has a legislative mandate requiring that children be immunized against certain communicable diseases before they can enroll in school. Although these requirements differ slightly from one state to another, immunization requirements for polio, diphtheria, pertussis, tetanus, measles (rubeola), and German measles (rubella) are common. Accurate record keeping and communication with immunization providers is a very time-consuming, but important, role of the school nurse.

It is imperative that school districts develop written policies for managing sick and injured students. To this end, staff development programming must be implemented to ensure that there is full compliance with universal precautions for handling body fluid spills in the educational environment. Such training should be extended to include playground monitors, bus drivers, and other classified staff.

Finally, policies should be implemented to ensure safe distribution of prescribed student medications. Given the range and complexity of health issues facing students, the responsibility for caring for sick or injured children cannot rest solely on the school nurse, the school secretary, or the principal. School professionals are expected to collaborate with parents, public health officials, and physicians to develop and manage such policies. In summary, table 1.6 provides a checklist of important elements in a quality program of school health services.

Healthy School Environment

The school environment in which a student spends a large part of each day has an impact on health status and achievement. Not only is the physical environment of the school facility important, but there is need for establishing an inviting, safe, and nurturing learning environment

TABLE 1.6	Confirming a Commitment to a Quality Program of Health Services: A Checklist of Important Elements

- Has your school community developed plans and policies concerning:
  - — Prevention and control of communicable diseases?
  - — Provision of emergency care and first aid?
  - — Health status appraisal of all students?
  - — Response to the needs of students with special needs?
  - — Screening, referral, management, and record keeping for students with these areas:

Vision	Hearing
Immunizations	Height/weight
Scoliosis	Blood pressure
Dental health	Physical exams for co-curricular activities?

- Have staff development activities been implemented to promote sanitation and compliance with universal precaution recommendations?
- Are instructional, transportation, and physical activity areas stocked with universal precaution supplies?
- Are plans implemented for safely dispensing of student medications?
- Have interagency networks been established to assure quality and collaborative services for students?
- Do health service professionals participate in the academic program of health instruction?
- Are licensed staff members employed?
- Do employed professionals participate in an ongoing program of staff development?

that extends throughout the school campus. Research has confirmed that students who feel that they are citizens of their school community enjoy their academic experience more than their counterparts in less welcoming environments. These students also demonstrate patterns of higher achievement.[35]

A recent study of fifth grade students confirmed that the environment, or social context, of a school is related to a range of student attitudes and behaviors. In this research, social context was defined to include a school environment that students perceived to be caring. Providing students with opportunities to participate in school activities, development of shared norms, and decision making was shown to be an important component of social context. Importantly, this study reinforced that students attending schools with a stronger sense of community tended to participate in less drug taking and delinquent behavior.[36]

The quality of the learning environment is maintained through adoption and consistent implementation of health promoting policies. The school administration, under the direction of the board of education, assumes primary responsibility for maintaining a healthy school environment. Importantly, however, while the school board and administration provide important direction, it is the responsibility of all school personnel to ensure that children do not become injured from potentially physically or emotionally dangerous conditions in their classrooms or on school campus. Obviously, this does not mean that the classroom teacher must make necessary repairs to school equipment or facilities. Rather, it is important for professionals to report any potential health hazards to the appropriate administrator. Such reports should be made in writing, in a timely manner.

A primary source of concern for school environmental advocates is the management of specific physical health hazards. Physical hazards include such factors as the temperature of the rooms in which the students spend the school day. Rooms that are too warm or too cold can detract from the learning experience and can cause health problems. The physical surroundings of the classroom, including lighting, glare, and room color, affect the attitude of students as well as their ability to function to their full capacity. Noise affects humans both psychologically and physically. The kind of noise that is of most concern in the school setting is distracting, continuing sound that emanates from outside the building. The movement and noise of traffic along the expressway or the noise of construction equipment in surrounding areas can interfere with the learning activities within the classroom.

In addition to attending to health hazards at the school site, school districts also are responsible for the safety of students being transported on school buses or other school vehicles. Students must be provided with safe transportation coming to and going home from all school activities. Because the potential for injury and accident is always present, the vehicles must be in safe operational condition. In addition, bus drivers should be provided with continuing education opportunities concerning the operation of the bus and the management of the behaviors of their young passengers.

The role of the classroom teacher with regard to bus transportation rests in instructing children in appropriate ways to get on and off the bus and appropriate behavior

TABLE 1.7	**Confirming a Commitment to Promoting and Maintaining a Healthy School Environment: A Checklist of Important Elements**

- Does your school district maintain compliance with standards for cleanliness, lighting, heating, ventilation, and managing environmental hazards?
- Does your district participate in periodic health and safety inspections and training for certified and classified staff?
- Are adopted policies consistently implemented to ensure safety and a tobacco-, alcohol-, and other drug-free school campus?
- Are adopted policies consistently implemented to ensure that fundraising and celebration activities do not contradict a health promotion agenda?
- Is a district-wide/community school health advisory council or committee in operation?
- Does the administration demonstrate support for the coordinated school health program?
- Is there a designated coordinator/director of the coordinated school health program?
- What provisions have been made to maintain a supportive and caring emotional climate throughout the educational environment?
- Are health promotion activities extended throughout the district and community?

while riding the school bus. Also, students should receive instruction about how to wait for the bus along the roadways and how to proceed from the bus after getting off. Importantly, a majority of school bus-related fatalities occur during these times.

An integral part of many school programs, is the school safety patrol program. The school safety patrol program is designed to meet the needs of students who attend neighborhood schools within walking distance of their homes. In specific, this program is designed to teach pedestrian safety to students in the elementary grades. Older children in the school usually are chosen on a voluntary basis and instructed to assist younger children across intersections and roadways. One cannot overlook the importance of proper selection and training of school safety patrol members. As an alternative, many districts employ adults to monitor student safety at busy intersections in the district.

Finally, educators are reminded that important maintenance and safety activities do not focus only on the physical facilities and emotional climate of the educational environment. School districts must provide for consistently enforced policies in all six of the CDC problem priority areas. This includes proactive attention to such issues as weapon carrying, tobacco, alcohol, and other drug possession, and management of threatening or inappropriate acting-out behaviors. In addition, policies should be enforced consistently for all students and personnel within the school community. This includes such practices as enforcement of tobacco-free campus policies during all school activities, and elimination of fundraising activities that threaten the nutritional health of students. While such policies can be unpopular, all school personnel share a responsibility for maintaining the highest standards of a health promoting, safe, and nurturing educational environment. In summary, student health advocates are encouraged to review table 1.7, which

reviews important elements that confirm a commitment to a healthy school environment.

School Nutrition Services

The primary function of school nutrition services is focused on promoting student health through two avenues:

1. Serving nutritionally sound, appetizing, and quality meals within budgetary parameters, and
2. Supporting the nutrition education curriculum of the elementary or middle-level school.

The most visible element of this program is to support the nutritional intake of students.

The dietary behaviors of students play an important part in the physical development of elementary and middle-level school students. In addition to the documented impact on growth and development, educators should take particular note of the growing body of literature confirming the strong relationship between nutritional behaviors and student achievement. Researchers have noted that hungry children manifest such behaviors as apathy and shorter attention spans. These students often have lowered energy levels and a compromised ability to concentrate. These factors threaten attention to detail and the general quality of academic work. Importantly, hungry children are at increased risk for infections and tend to be absent from school more often than children who are well-fed. There is little question that students who are absent frequently tend to fall behind in their class work.[37]

In response to the inadequate nutritional status of many students, a variety of federally funded programs have been initiated. These programs include the national school lunch and breakfast programs. School lunch programs began with the enactment of the National School Lunch Act in 1946. This legislation provided surplus agricultural commodities and federal funds to local school districts for the purpose of providing nutritious meals to children through a school lunch program. Management of this program is the responsibility of the U.S. Department of Agriculture.

Educators must remember that the school lunch and breakfast programs in most districts operate under strict budgetary constraints. Importantly, however, research has demonstrated that these school-based activities serve as a significant source of nutrition for many children. Nearly two-thirds of all school students in the United States receive about one-third of their daily nutrients from the school food service program. In addition, the meals served in the school lunch program constitute the majority of the daily food supply for many students.[38]

In addition to the amount and nutritional density of these school-based feeding programs, research has confirmed that students who participate in such programs have better school attendance, greater class participation, and improved achievement than their hungry counterparts.[39] While schools are not mandated to participate in the national school lunch program, there is little question of the value of school-based nutrition programs.

Unfortunately, many school districts do not take advantage of the second purpose of the school food service program: enrichment of nutrition education. Importantly, if there is a kitchen located in the building, it provides the only access to such a learning laboratory for the teachers of most younger students. In this context, the cafeteria has the potential to be used as an important learning laboratory.

Wise teachers have learned to collaborate with food service personnel to enrich nutrition units of instruction for their students. In addition, the food service personnel in some school districts provide nutrition education activities that are developmentally appropriate and meaningful for all students. Some schools have organized student/food service advisory councils that collaborate on special meal planning and nutrition education activities. Special event luncheons, nutrition newsletters, cafeteria bulletin boards or posters, food-tasting parties, and nutritional labeling of breakfast or lunch line food choices are activities with the potential to enrich the nutrition education curriculum.[40]

While the cafeteria in many middle-level schools is used only for large-group study halls, other districts have developed ways to use this area for more academically enriching activities. Special mini-lectures on a range of topics can be targeted to particular students during their lunch meal. In addition, table-tents can be constructed by student organizations, teachers, or administrators to highlight important content matters or upcoming events scheduled on the school calendar.[41]

In this context, nutrition education is enhanced without sacrificing additional valuable classroom instructional time. The use of a valuable instructional space also is expanded. In summary, table 1.8 provides a checklist of key elements that confirm a commitment to quality school nutrition services.

School Counseling, Psychological, and Social Services

School counselors, psychologists, and social workers have the potential to make unique and valuable contributions to the health promotion agenda in a school. Unfortunately, in many districts, the activities of these professionals are limited to assessing, placing, and intervening in the needs of selected students. From this reactive perspective, these professionals have only limited contact with the broader population of enrolled students.

Importantly, however, many of the problems for which children are referred to counseling, psychological, or social service professionals are health related. Examples of such issues include emotional and self-esteem concerns, weight problems, academic stress and test anxiety, and personal adjustment and relationship issues. As a result, many school districts have asked counselors, psychologists, and social workers to extend the range of their services. Many such professionals now participate in more proactive and broader kinds of education and prevention activities. In these school districts, the counselors,

---

TABLE 1.8	**Confirming a Commitment to Quality School Nutrition Services: A Checklist of Important Elements**

- Does your school district provide a breakfast and lunch program consistent with or supported by the U.S. Department of Agriculture?
- Are the meals provided by your school food service program in compliance with the Dietary Guidelines for Americans Initiative?
- Are kitchen and cafeteria facilities used as nutrition education learning laboratories?
- Are qualified personnel employed in the food service program?
- Are only nutritionally sound products sold in all fundraising activities and vending machines throughout the school district?
- Is nutrition information shared with faculty, staff, parents, and students?
- Are students and other stakeholders invited to collaborate with food service staff in menu planning and nutrition education activities (advisory council)?
- Do food service personnel act as resource persons for nutrition education curriculum matters?

psychologists, and social workers assume an expanded role as applied behavioral scientists in the schools.

In addition, it is becoming more common for counselors and social workers to be active participants in the instructional program in elementary and middle-level schools. These professionals often are invited guests who provide classroom instruction in such areas as nonviolent conflict resolution, problem solving, communication, and decision-making skill development. In other districts, counselors, psychologists, and social workers collaborate in curriculum and staff development activities. Under this model, the classroom teacher is better prepared to integrate these important skills across the curriculum.

In particular, the school psychologist can play a unique role in the district health promotion program. In addition to their conventional duties, many districts invite their school psychologists to provide individual and group services for students. These professionals can conduct informational sessions for parents, faculty, and staff. Importantly, school psychologists can coordinate collaboration and referral networks with community service providers.[42]

School personnel trained in the teaching and health professions, but not in guidance and counseling (the teacher, school nurse, and health-education specialist), need to develop various interpersonal and health-counseling skills. Because many counseling activities involve interacting with parents as well as children, teachers need to practice effective communication skills. Acquiring listening skills and other verbal communication and nonverbal communication techniques is useful. Learning the skills of small-group dynamics also is important. School counselors, psychologists, and social workers can also collaborate with their education colleagues to organize an ongoing program of staff development. In summary, readers are encouraged to review table 1.9, which provides a checklist of important elements that confirm a commitment to a quality program of school counseling, psychological, and social services.

Physical Education

A strong link has been established between participation in physical activity and enhanced student academic outcomes. In particular, research has concluded that a consistent and organized program of school-based physical activity is related to increased concentration and improved scores on tests of math, reading, and writing skill.[43] Further, it has been confirmed that people who regularly exercise are more likely to participate in other healthy behaviors, including less cigarette use, better dietary behaviors, and more effective stress management practices.[44] In light of these findings, the American Association of School Administrators has concluded that "children need to be attentive to maximize the benefits of participation in learning tasks. Attention takes energy, and students who are physically fit, well-nourished, and stress-free have more energy."[45]

The physical fitness of students is enhanced by a high-quality physical education program. Such programs are developed to include a range of learning activities targeting cardiovascular health, muscular endurance, flexibility, strength, agility, balance, coordination, and good posture. The emphasis of quality physical education activities is not placed on the development of skills for athletic competition. Rather, emphasis is placed on physical fitness and the development of skills that lead to life-long habits of physical activity. As children learn basic exercise movement skills, they are more likely to develop lifelong activity patterns. Like other content areas, national physical education standards have been developed to provide guidelines for program development.

Physical education experiences that are most effective in addressing these fitness components involve participation in vigorous, aerobic activity. In addition, skills

---

TABLE 1.9	**Confirming a Commitment to a Quality Program of School Counseling, Psychological, and Social Services: A Checklist of Important Elements**

- Are an appropriate number of licensed, credentialed professionals employed to meet the counseling, psychological, and social service needs of all students in the district?
- Has a student assistance program been established?
- Have the school district and community collaborated in the development of an interagency network of counseling, psychological, and social service providers?
- Have interdisciplinary patterns of collaboration been established to identify students at risk in the school community?
- Do students have access to the following school/community-linked services to support academic outcomes?

Individual counseling	Group counseling
Crisis counseling	Tutoring
Developmental programs	

- Do counseling, psychological, and social service professionals provide consultation and staff development to update and inform curricular matters?
- Do students have access to a developmentally appropriate, planned, and sequential guidance and counseling program?

must be introduced that have value in supporting lifelong patterns of physical activity. Unfortunately, research has confirmed that the five activities most commonly incorporated into physical education in the primary grades are movement experiences and body mechanics, soccer, jumping or skipping rope, gymnastics, and basketball.[46] In addition, instructional activities for students in the upper-elementary grades have a primary focus on more team-related activities. Softball, basketball, soccer, volleyball, football, and track and field take on greater emphasis in each higher grade.[47] It is worth questioning the emphasis on competitive team sports and the personal fitness value of skills directly related to them. Importantly, school physical education programs should be developed that emphasize individual fitness and skill development, not team sport participation.

The amount of time allotted for the physical education class varies tremendously. In some schools, the time allotment may be as little as 15 to 20 minutes, or it may be as much as 45 minutes to 1 hour. Research has shown that the average length for elementary school physical education classes is 33.4 minutes.[48]

The amount of vigorous aerobic activity in which each student participates during this time also is worthy of discussion. If you have ever observed an elementary physical education class, you have likely witnessed students standing or sitting while the teacher instructs. The kinds of activities (relays, team games, etc.) tend to result in many of the students watching the participation of others. Research has suggested that in the average physical education class, the typical student may participate in only 2 to 3 minutes of individual exercise.[49] Clearly, this is not an acceptable level of participation if there is going to be any positive impact on the physical fitness or achievement of students.

In addition to physical education class, most elementary schoolchildren are provided with a recess period. Many schools count time spent in recess toward meeting state requirements for participation in physical education. This is an unacceptable policy. This practice implies that the learning experiences of children in physical education classes are less important and valuable than their experiences in other academic subjects. Recess can contribute to the physical well-being of children, but it must not be a substitute for formal physical education instruction. Further, recess should not be eliminated on days when the children have regularly scheduled physical education classes.

In conclusion, advocates for improving student physical fitness and achievement are urged to examine table 1.10. This checklist provides readers with a review of the key elements in a quality program of physical education.

Schoolsite Health Promotion for Faculty and Staff

In recent years, businesses and industries have increased their interest in health promotion initiatives for their employees. A major impetus for this interest has been concern about the rising cost of health care. In addition, long-term hospitalization and an aging American public have led many businesses and industries to seek ways of reducing their costs for hospital, medical, and other types of insurance. Most workplace health promotion initiatives have focused on reducing the incidence of premature illness and death through programs targeted at such unhealthy lifestyle factors as tobacco use, dietary risks, physical inactivity, excessive drinking, and stressful living.

Many in the health promotion and medical care professions feel that with appropriate health promotion and disease prevention initiatives, these long-term episodic care expenses can be reduced by implementing behaviors that will reduce the risk factors. By making health promotion activities available corporations formalize opportunities for their employees and their families to assume more responsibility for their health and well-being. In turn, the employees tend to be more productive, have less absenteeism, and improve their overall attitudes and morale.

TABLE 1.10	Confirming a Commitment to a Quality Physical Education Program: A Checklist of Important Elements

- Has a planned, sequential physical education curriculum been implemented in grades pre-K through 12?
- Has the curriculum been developed with attention to the national physical education standards?
- Are credentialed teachers employed in the physical education program?
- Do all students participate in a program of organized daily physical activity?
- Is the physical education curriculum organized with a focus on lifetime activities rather than acquisition of team sport skills?
- Do students participate in an ongoing program of health related fitness assessments?
- Does the physical education faculty collaborate with health service personnel to record results of fitness assessments on students' permanent health records?
- Are noncompetitive co-curricular fitness activities organized for student participation?
- Is participation in co-curricular fitness activity promoted for elementary and middle-level students?

Importantly, school districts are faced with these same issues. A significant portion of the budget of a school district is spent on health insurance and other related benefits for school employees. With health-care costs increasing, the importance of providing health promotion activities for school personnel will continue. For example, many school systems now provide an employee-assistance program for administrators, faculty, and staff. These programs, which have been available in corporations for years, provide help to individuals who are experiencing alcohol and other drug risks, and other types of stress problems. There is little question that the teaching profession is stressful. Stress management programs often are made available for school personnel to help teachers cope with stressful situations.

School districts are an ideal location for providing work site health promotion programs. The school enterprise constitutes one of America's largest employers. In addition, schools have well-maintained facilities and professional resources to plan and implement quality programs to promote the health of faculty and staff.[50]

Healthy teachers, administrators, and support staff not only cost taxpayers less in health care costs, but also have fewer absences. In this way, the continuity of instruction for students is maintained. In addition, professionals who practice health-enhancing behaviors have the potential to serve as healthy role models for their students. Elementary and middle-level teachers interested in exploring the advantages of such programs in their local district are urged to review table 1.11. This checklist contains a review of key elements in a quality schoolsite health promotion program for faculty and staff.

Family and Community Collaboration with the Schools

The school is an agency of the community that cannot function in isolation. While it is common for the responsibility for student problems to be focused on shortcomings in the school program, there are many health and human service organizations that serve as advocates for children and their families. In addition to the impact of their families, children who attend local schools also are influenced by practices in the neighborhoods, churches, and stores, and by medical care providers with whom they have contact. In this way, no school district is solely responsible when confronted with students who have tobacco, alcohol, other drug, or violence problems. Rather, students who are at risk are members of families that reside in the community, shop in local stores, and participate in chosen religious celebrations. All student advocates must remember that the complexity of today's health and social problems require that no one agency or group be blamed or held responsible for intervening in such matters in the absence of other stakeholders.

As an important step in confronting such challenging issues, the school health literature has confirmed the need for local districts to establish a school health advisory council. Such organizations focus the efforts of school, medical, safety, and advocacy services on health promotion in the school community. Specifically, such coalitions or committees work to increase the quantity and quality of school-based health promotion efforts. In addition, such groups help to reduce duplication of services, and enhance the visibility and potential impact of all participant agencies. With pooled resources, advocacy

---

TABLE 1.11	**Confirming a Commitment to a Quality School Site Health Promotion Program for Faculty and Staff: A Checklist of Important Elements**

- Have health promotion programs for faculty and staff been organized to focus on the following health promoting practices?

Weight management	Physical fitness
Tobacco use cessation	Blood pressure screening
Stress management	Cholesterol screening
Cancer screening	Back injury prevention

- Does health promotion programming include the basic elements of screening, referral, and education?
- Is the expertise of school district and community professionals incorporated into the schoolsite health promotion program?
- Have policies and incentives been developed to promote faculty/staff participation in health promotion activities?
- Do the faculty and staff participate in an ongoing program of health risk appraisals?
- Have recordkeeping and referral protocol been developed to maintain confidentiality of all health information of faculty and staff?
- Do administrators participate in health promotion activities with other district employees?
- Has a relationship been developed among the district, insurance providers, and coordinators of the district health promotion program to help contain health care costs?
- Does the designated coordinator of this program receive release time for organizational, management, and record-keeping tasks?
- Has an oversight committee involving diverse stakeholders been organized?

TABLE 1.12	Confirming a Commitment to High-Quality Family and Community Collaboration with the Schools: A Checklist of Important Elements

- Does an active school/community coalition or committee meet regularly to address student health problems and curricular matters, and to plan health promotion activities?
- Is there conspicuous administrative/board of education involvement or support for integrated school and community health promotion activities?
- Have policies and protocol been established to engage active parental involvement in school health activities?
- Has a pattern of collaborative programming been established between the school district and public and community health agencies and advocates?
- Have protocol and communication networks been established to expedite interagency referral and record keeping concerning student health issues?
- Have policies and communication networks been established to manage controversial health issues that confront the school community?

initiatives and projects that are too large for any one agency become realistic health promotion options.[51]

In addition to addressing more global concerns, the elementary and middle-level classroom teacher would be wise to establish relationships with the different organizations and agencies that are advocates for student health. Many of these organizations also offer support for classroom instruction by providing resource materials developed to focus on a broad range of health content matters. In summary, table 1.12 contains a checklist of key elements that confirm a quality program of family and community collaboration with the schools.

Pulling It All Together

The health status and academic achievement of students who attend elementary and middle-level schools is threatened by many complex variables. While some students are absent frequently because of allergies or communicable infections, others have difficulty maintaining their attention to schoolwork because of dietary risks. The key to confronting such complex issues is to capitalize on the many resources and talents of professionals who promote the health of children and youth.

The coordinated school health program is a model that represents best health promotion practice. The successful integration of this eight component model into the active life of the school community depends on several key elements. As a foundation, all school and community personnel with a commitment or expertise in any aspect of student health must be invited to be active participants in this proactive health promotion agenda. In addition, the likelihood of successful application of the model is related to the extent of cooperation, collaboration, and communication among the stakeholders. Importantly, participants representing the eight component programs of the model must organize their efforts in a coordinated manner.

Many schools offer a range of programs to address individual, at-risk students. In addition, many districts offer diverse activities to prevent participation in any

number of health risk behaviors. Importantly, however, these activities must be offered in a coordinated and intentional manner to increase the probability of their longevity and success. For example, nutrition education is a common content area in health instructional programs of study. Also, the school food service program may try to provide nutritionally sound meals, and students with eating disorders may be referred for intervention counseling. Unfortunately, professionals involved in these nutritional health promotion activities rarely are involved in collaborative planning.

By contrast, the approach to nutritional health promotion in a school district with a coordinated school health program would be very different. Such a district, with an established school health council, might collaborate in planning proactive and well-organized activities, including:

- Health education — Provide a developmentally appropriate nutrition education curricular scope and sequence.

- Health services — Provide consultation and resources for planning a nutritional health week in which cross-curricular instruction about healthy foods is the focus.

- Healthy environment — Review, by administrators and the board of education, all fundraising policies and practices to make sure that none sabotage the district commitment to nutritional health promotion.

- Counseling, etc. — Provide support groups and appropriate referral activities for students with eating disorders or risky dietary behaviors.

- Physical education — Develop exercise prescriptions that feature healthy weight management practices for all students.

- Faculty and staff Organize a "Healthy Nutrition for Life" support group open to all faculty and staff.
- Healthy community Organize "a taste of (name of your community)" event. In this event, local restaurants and food outlets are invited to the school campus to prepare samples of their healthy entrees for school district residents. Proceeds could support a range of activities of the health promotion committee.

Finally, many school health advocates have identified the need for a person or leadership team to coordinate and champion all activities of the school health program. The primary responsibility of this person or group would be to translate the model into specific programming activities to meet local needs. In particular, this program administrator would focus his or her energies on coordination of the school health advisory committee; maintenance of the program budget; and advocacy and liaison activities with district, community, and state agencies. The coordinator would provide direct health promotion activities and services. In addition, the administrator would organize evaluation activities to ensure quality control of the many aspects of the coordinated school health program.[52]

With such a structure, the talents of many can be focused efficiently and effectively on promoting student health while maintaining a focus on the primary mission of schools: to maintain the highest standards of academic achievement.

SUMMARY

Many public health advocates and health promotion professionals have confirmed that the health status and academic achievement of students attending elementary and middle-level schools are threatened by many variables. While some students are absent frequently because of allergies or communicable infections, others have difficulty maintaining their attention to school work because of dietary behaviors. In this context, the Centers for Disease Control and Prevention has suggested that school health professionals place priority attention on the priority health risks that have been confirmed to be related to the leading causes of death among Americans. The key to confronting such complex issues is to capitalize on the many resources and talents of school and community professionals who promote the health of children and youth. Schools are an important setting for coordinating and providing health promotion activities.

The coordinated school health program makes an important contribution to promoting the health and academic achievement of the elementary and middle-level schoolchild. This program model encompasses a range of activities that are designed to improve, protect, and promote the health of schoolchildren, their families, and various school personnel in the educational system. The coordinated school health program includes classroom learning experiences of health instruction, the provision of health services, the provision of a safe and healthy school environment, the provision of school nutrition services, school counseling, psychological and social services, a physical education program, and health promotion activities for school personnel. All should be integrated within the context of a broad-based community health promotion.

DISCUSSION QUESTIONS

1. Discuss the various components that make up the concept of health.
2. What is your understanding of the spiritual dimension of health as presented in this chapter?
3. Discuss the various factors that compose the social dimension of health.
4. What has been the status of the school health program within the overall educational system in this country?
5. Discuss the place of health as noted in various educational reform initiatives in recent years.
6. Explain the significance to school health of the National Health Promotion and Disease Prevention Objectives for the Nation.
7. What is your description of a coordinated school health program?
8. Discuss various ways in which school health instruction takes place within the school curriculum.
9. Explain the difference between incidental health instruction and direct health instruction.
10. What is the role of the school nurse in a coordinated school health program?
11. Identify several screening procedures often found in a school health service program.
12. What role is expected of the classroom teacher in providing a healthy school environment?
13. Explain why providing a school safety patrol program is an important part of a school health program.
14. Why is there concern over asbestos in schools?
15. Discuss several problems that have been associated with the school lunch program.

16. Do you believe that vending machines with candy, carbonated drinks, and flavored ice bars should be permitted in an elementary school? Be able to defend your answer.

17. What are some health counseling skills that the classroom teacher should possess?

18. Identify ways in which a school health program should be a part of a broader-based community health program.

19. Identify some of the services for elementary school health programs that are available from the voluntary health organizations.

20. Discuss the importance of the *National Health Education Standards* in the context of the more broad-based commitment to educational reform in the United States.

21. Review the relationship between participation in priority health risk behaviors and threatened school success.

22. List the six priority health risk behaviors identified by the Centers for Disease Control and Prevention for attention by school health advocates.

23. Why were these six behaviors identified to have such significance for child and adolescent health advocates?

24. Discuss advantages for schools and communities that collaborate in the organization and implementation of a coordinated school health program in local schools.

ENDNOTES

1. World Health Organization, "Constitution of the World Health Organization," *Chronicle of the World Health Organization* (1947): 1.

2. D. Bedworth and A. Bedworth, *The Profession and Practice of Health Education* (Dubuque, IA: Wm. C. Brown Publishers, 1992).

3. K. Mullen et al., *Connections for Health* (Madison, WI: Brown and Benchmark, 1996).

4. U.S. Department of Health, Education, and Welfare, Public Health Service, *Healthy People: The Surgeon General's Report on Health Promotion and Disease Prevention* (Washington, DC: U.S. Government Printing Office, 1979).

5. Ibid.

6. Ibid.

7. J. Michael McGinnis and W. H. Foege, "Actual Causes of Death in the United States," *Journal of the American Medical Association* 270, no. 18 (1993): 2207–2212.

8. Ibid.

9. Lloyd Kolbe, "An Epidemiological Surveillance System to Monitor the Prevalence of Youth Behaviors that Most Affect Health," *Health Education* 21, no. 3 (1990): 24–30.

10. U.S. Department of Health, Education, and Welfare, Public Health Service, *Healthy People,* 14–16.

11. U.S. Department of Health and Human Services, Public Health Service, *Healthy People 2000: National Health Promotion and Disease Prevention Objectives* (Washington, DC: U.S. Government Printing Office, 1991).

12. Ibid.

13. Ibid., 255.

14. Lloyd Kolbe et al., "The School Health Policies and Programs Study (SHPPS): Context, Methods, General Findings, and Future Efforts," *Journal of School Health* 64, no. 8 (1995): 339–343.

15. National School Boards Association, *School Health: Helping Children Learn* (Alexandria, VA: National School Boards Association, 1991), 3–4.

16. U.S. Department of Education, *America 2000: An Education Strategy* (Washington, DC: U.S. Government Printing Office, 1994).

17. National Commission on Excellence in Education, *A Nation at Risk: The Imperative for Educational Reform* (Washington, DC: U.S. Department of Education, 1983).

18. U.S. Department of Education, *America 2000.*

19. Joint Statement on School by The Secretaries of Education and Health and Human Services, April 7, 1994.

20. U.S. Department of Education, *The National Education Goals Report: Building a Nation of Learners* (Washington, DC: U.S. Government Printing Office, 1994).

21. A. Novello et al., "Healthy Children Ready to Learn: An Essential Collaboration Between Health and Education," *Public Health Reports* 107, no. 1 (1992): 3–15.

22. American Cancer Society, *National Action Plan for Comprehensive School Health Education* (Atlanta, GA: American Cancer Society, 1992), 4–7.

23. Cynthia Wolford Symons et al., "Bridging Student Health Risks and Academic Achievement Through Comprehensive School Health Programs," *Journal of School Health* 67, no. 6 (1997): 220–227.

24. U.S. Department of Health, Education, and Welfare, Public Health Service, *Healthy People,* 119.

25. Ibid.

26. Ibid.

27. Ibid.

28. Joint Committee on Health Education Terminology, *Report of the 1990 Joint Committee on Health Education Terminology* (Reston, VA: AAHE, 1990).

29. The Joint Committee on National Health Education Standards, *National Health Education Standards: Achieving Health Literacy* (Atlanta, GA: American Cancer Society, 1995).

30. David B. Connell et al., "Summary of Findings of the School Health Education Evaluation: Health Promotion

Effectiveness, Implementation, and Costs," *Journal of School Health* 55, no. 8 (1985): 316–322.

31. Education Commission of the States, *Recommendations for School Health Education: A Handbook for State Policymakers* (Denver: Education Commission of the States, 1981).

32. "Health Instruction Responsibilities and Competencies for Elementary (K–6) Classroom Teachers," *Journal of Health Education* 23, no. 6 (1992): 352–354.

33. American School Health Association, *Achieving the 1990 Health Objectives for the Nation* (Bloomington, IN: Tichenor Publishing, 1988), 25–26.

34. National Association of School Nurses, *Caseload Assignments Position Statement* (Scarborough, ME: NASN, 1995).

35. V. Battistich et al., "Schools as Communities, Poverty Levels of Student Populations, and Students' Attitudes, Motives, and Performance: A Multilevel Analysis," *American Education Research Journal* 32, (1995): 627–658.

36. Victor Battistich and Allen Hom, "The Relationship Between Students' Sense of Their School as a Community and Their Involvement in Problem Behaviors," *American Journal of Public Health* 87, no. 12 (December 1997): 1997–2001.

37. K. B. Troccoli, "Eat to Learn, Learn to Eat: The Link Between Nutrition and Learning in Children," *National Health/Education Consortium: Occasional Paper* 7 (April 1993): 1–33.

38. Kevin Bushweller, "Health on the Menu," *The American School Board Journal* (July 1993):94.

39. American School Food Service Association, "Impact of Hunger and Malnutrition on Student Achievement," *School Food Service Research Review* 13, no. 1 (1989): 17–21.

40. American School Health Association, *Achieving the 1990 Health Objectives,* 25–26.

41. Ibid., 26.

42. Ibid., 26.

43. Lloyd Kolbe et al., "Appropriate Functions of Health Education in Schools: Improving Health and Cognitive Performance." In N. Krairweger, J. Arasteli, and J. Cataldo, *Child Health Behavior: A Behavioral Pediatrics Perspective* (New York: John Wiley, 1986).

44. C. Bouchard et al., *Exercise, Fitness, and Health: A Consensus of Current Knowledge* (Champaign, IL: Human Kinetics Books, 1990).

45. American Association of School Administrators, *Critical Issues Report: Promoting Health Education in Schools—Problems and Solutions* (Arlington, VA: American Association of School Administrators, 1985).

46. James G. Ross et al., "What Is Going On in the Elementary Physical Education Program?" *Journal of Physical Education, Recreation, and Dance* (November–December 1987): 81.

47. Ibid.

48. James G. Ross et al., "What Is Going On in the Elementary Physical Education Program?" *Summary of Findings from National Children and Youth Fitness Study II* (Washington, DC: U.S. Department of Health and Human Services, 1987), 78–84.

49. Guy S. Parcel et al., "School Promotion of Healthful Diet and Exercise Behavior: An Integration of Organizational Change and Social Learning Theory Interventions," *Journal of School Health* 57, no. 4 (1987): 150–156.

50. American School Health Association, *Achieving the 1990 Health Objectives,* 26.

51. Ibid., 26–27.

52. Ken Resnicow and Diane Allensworth, "Conducting a Comprehensive School Health Program," *Journal of School Health* 66, no. 2 (February 1996): 59–63.

SUGGESTED READINGS

Allegrante, J. P. "School-site Health Promotion for Faculty and Staff: A Key Component of the Coordinated School Health Program." *Journal of School Health* 68, no. 5 (May 1998): 1990–1995.

American Association of School Administrators (AASA). *We Care, We Act.* Arlington; VA: AASA, 1999.

American Cancer Society. *Report of the Gallup Survey on the Values and Opinions on Health Education in the U.S. Public Schools.* Atlanta, GA: American Cancer Society, 1994.

Bushweller, Kevin. "Health on the Menu." *The American School Board Journal* 181, no. 2 (February 1994): 38–40.

Butler, J. Thomas. *Principles of Health Education and Health Promotion.* Englewood, CO: Morton, 1997.

Carnegie Council on Adolescent Development. *Great Transitions: Preparing Adolescents for a New Century.* New York: Carnegie Corporation of New York, 1995.

Cortese, Peter A. "Accomplishments in Comprehensive School Health Education." *Journal of School Health* 63, no. 1 (January 1993): 21–23.

Diaz, David P. "Foundations for Spirituality: Establishing the Viability Within the Health Disciplines." *Journal of Health Education* 24, no. 6 (November/December 1993): 324–326.

Doster, Mildred. "School Health Education: Who, When, Where?" *Journal of School Health* 55, no. 4 (April 1985): 161.

Education Development Center. "Speaking With One Voice." *School Health Program News* 1, no. 2 (1996): 1–2.

Elders, M. Jocelyn. "Schools and Health: A Natural Partnership." *Journal of School Health* 63, no. 7 (September 1993): 312–315.

Essex, Nathan et al. "Handle with Care." *The American School Board Journal* 181, no. 3 (March 1994): 50–53.

Frank, Gail C., Allene Vaden, and Josephine Martin. "School Health Promotion: Child Nutrition Programs." *Journal of School Health* 57, no. 10 (December 1987): 451–460.

"Improving the Health of Youth Through a Coordinated School Health Program." *Promotion & Education* 1, no. 4 (1997): 42–47.

Institute of Medicine. *Schools and Health: Our Nation's Investment.* Washington, DC: National Academy Press, 1997.

Killip, Diana C., Sharon R. Lovick, Leslie Goldman, and Diane D. Allensworth. "Integrated School and Community Programs." *Journal of School Health* 57, no. 10 (December 1987): 437–444.

Lavin, Alison T. "Comprehensive School Health Education: Barriers and Opportunities." *Journal of School Health* 63, no. 1 (January 1993): 24–27

Lawton, Millicent. "Healthy Kids Healthy Learners." *Middle Ground* (August 1999): 10–17.

Marx, Eva, Susan Frelick Wooley, and Daphne Northrop, eds. *Health is Academic: A Guide to Coordinated School Health Programs.* New York: Teachers College Press, 1998.

McClellan, Mary. "Why Blame Schools?" *Research Bulletin.* Phi Delta Kappa, no. 12 (March 1994).

Nelson, Betty Jo. "The Role of the Federal Government in Promoting Health through the Schools: Report from the Department of Agriculture." *Journal of School Health* 62, no. 4 (April 1992): 138–140.

Ravitch, Diane. "The Role of the Federal Government in Promoting Health Through the Schools: Report from the Department of Education." *Journal of School Health* 62, no. 4 (April 1992): 141–142.

Seffrin, John R. "The Comprehensive School Health Curriculum: Closing the Gap between State-of-the-Art and State-of-the-Practice." *Journal of School Health* 60, no. 4 (April 1990): 151–156.

Tomlinson, Janis "Health and Education: A Changing Panorama." *Infobrief: Association for Supervision and Curriculum Development* 17 (May 1999): 1–5.

Tyson, Hariet. "A Load off Teacher's Backs: Coordinated School Health Programs." *Phi Delta Kappan* 80, No. 5 (January 1999): K-1–K-8.

World Health Organization (WHO). *Promoting Health through Schools: Report of a WHO Expert Committee on Comprehensive School Health Education and Promotion.* Geneva: WHO, 1997.

SCHOOL HEALTH SERVICES

Activities to Protect and Promote the Health of Students

O U T L I N E

SCHOOL HEALTH SERVICES

The provision of various health services to students in the United States has been a part of the school health program since the early years of the 20th century. There has been much discussion and difference of opinion as to how many resources, both financial and in terms of personnel, should be allotted to providing direct health services to children at school.

Many people believe that only the study of academic subjects should take place in the school setting, and therefore it is inappropriate to use school staff and taxpayers' money to provide personal health services. Many others point out that it is impossible to separate successful academic achievement from the health status of school-age children, and, therefore, the school health service program is an important contributor to a well-rounded educational experience for all elementary and middle-level schoolchildren. School health services must be considered to be an important component of the coordinated school health program and, therefore, are of concern to all school personnel, including the classroom teacher.

As one visits schools throughout the United States, a variety of different school health service program patterns can be seen. In some instances, health services within the schools are provided principally by personnel employed by the local public health department. Public health nurses are assigned to visit the schools on a regular basis to provide various kinds of health screening services to students. In other instances, such services are made available by personnel employed by the school district. In this model, the school nurse usually is found working in the schools throughout the school day and is an active participant in the total school program.

Another model for providing comprehensive health services within the school setting is the school-based, or school-linked, health center. This type of program, now found in more than 1,000 schools throughout the nation, provides a health-care clinic within, or associated with, the school. These health centers' main objective is to improve the student's access to primary care. They are designed to overcome such barriers to obtaining health care as time scheduling, lack of transportation, and apprehension, which often keep school-age children from getting proper care during the school day.

The *school-based health center,* located within the school, provides a broad range of comprehensive primary health-care services to students within the school environment that are convenient and confidential. The *school-linked health center* is located apart from the school building. However, formal and informal relationships with the school are established. The goal of improving student access to medical services is the same as for the school-based health center. In the school-linked health centers, it is possible to target young people who have dropped out of school but are still living in the area. Year-round services are provided, not just during the school calendar. Operation of a school-linked health center helps to avoid politically sensitive and restrictive issues related to family-planning services.

The majority of school-based or school-linked health centers are located in secondary schools. However, a few are situated in elementary and middle schools.

Regardless of the format, schools that are located in areas where children experience the greatest need for health services often have the least amount of money to support such services. Schools that are located in communities with large enrollments of lower socioeconomic level children who have poor general access to health care are often the schools in which a school nurse is not available or where immunizations and health examinations are inadequate. On the other hand, the school district in an upper-economic, middle-class community often is the school district that can afford to employ a school nurse in every building and to have a well-supplied emergency care nursing room. Increased efforts need to be made in communities across the nation to provide school-based or school-linked health services to children living in low socioeconomic settings.

The types of health services available in school settings vary. Generally, the school health service program includes numerous services that are designed to appraise the health status of schoolchildren. The prevention and control of communicable diseases has been a major focus of most school health service programs. Also, schools should have in place an effective policy for providing care for schoolchildren who become sick or injured while at school.

PROFESSIONAL ROLES

Several school personnel play important roles in a school health service program.

The School Nurse

The most commonly identified individual in a school health service program is the school nurse. This individual, educated in the medical model, can provide a broad range of medical services to the schoolchild. In addition, the school health nurse can be a valuable help to classroom teachers by providing instructional support and serving as a resource person. The school nurse is often called upon to provide supplemental instruction in content areas, including sexuality and disease prevention. The nurse can also act as a resource for the classroom teacher in other units of instruction.

When one thinks about the school health-service program, the school nurse is the first person to come to mind. The presence of a nurse in a school setting had its start at about the beginning of the 20th century. Those early school nurses were employed to reduce the incidence of childhood diseases.

Today's school nurse often has a much broader role. The three activities reported by nurses as consuming the largest percentage of their time are: (1) administering first aid, (2) assessing student health complaints, and (3) carrying out screening procedures.[1] The school nurse provides help to the child who becomes sick or injured while at school. This involves giving emergency care procedures and seeing that appropriate attention is given to the sick child.

The broadened scope of school nursing today involves providing needed assistance to handicapped children enrolled in the elementary and middle-level school classrooms who possess special needs, and managing students' medications during the school day. Also, school nurses are often at the forefront of identifying and referring cases of child abuse and neglect and sexual abuse to the proper authorities. HIV/AIDS, family problems, nutritional concerns, and emotional adjustments are other issues with which a school nurse must cope today. In addition to providing direct services to students at school, the school nurse also provides services and renders help, advice, and counsel to students' families and members of the school staff.

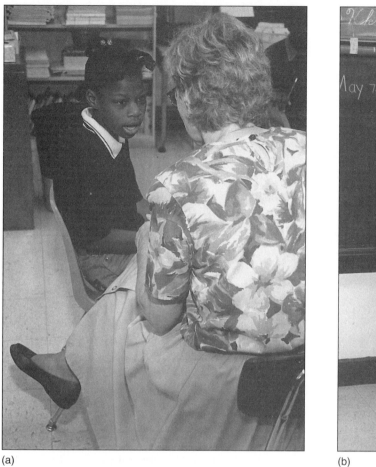

(a)

(b)

The school nurse fulfills a variety of roles, including (a) counseling a student about a health concern and (b) teaching a class about a health concept.

The school nurse, in many cases, has the responsibility for maintaining school health records. However, many school nurses feel their skills, education, and professional abilities could be more effectively used in providing medical assistance and counseling than in recording information on health records.

Many of the school health screening procedures are carried out by the school nurse. For many school nurses, this activity is very time-consuming. After recording the screening results on each child's health record, little time is left for extensive follow-up, and screening activities are only as effective as the appropriate follow-up measures. Where appropriate, the children should be informed of the results of the screening procedures. Parents have a need, and a right, to know what any health screening activity has revealed about their children.

Effective school health screening follow-up measures involve health counseling of the child, the parents, and others about the findings and recommendations that need to be followed. This is particularly important when deviations from normal have been noted and additional medical attention is needed. The school nurse often acts as a liaison between the family and various community health and social agencies; therefore, the school nurse needs to develop good health counseling skills.

The school nurse can be effective not only in individual parent and child counseling, but in developing group sessions to assist children with a broad variety of problems. Divorce can have a very unsettling effect on an elementary or middle-level schoolchild. With the support of school psychology and counseling personnel, the nurse can organize a program about divorce for schoolchildren in which common situations and emotional reactions to divorce can be discussed. Other special-problem needs such as suicide, death, and obesity can be addressed in such a manner.

The school nurse can meet on a regular basis with school guidance counselors to discuss student health-related problems. This team approach can help in identifying children's needs that must be addressed by both the health and the guidance and counseling personnel of the school.

Since passage of PL 94-142 (the Education for All Handicapped Children Act) in 1975, the school nurse has become increasingly involved in managing the medical needs of the medically fragile child. This federal legislation, which mandated that medically fragile children have the right to be enrolled in public school programs in the "least restrictive environment," has led to the inclusion of such children in regular class settings along with regular students. An increasing number of children with serious disabilities now are attending public schools. Many of these children require special health and medical services during the course of the school day.

The school nurse is expected to participate in activities designed to identify children with disabilities and to be involved in the development of educational programs for these individuals. This often involves working with teachers, school administrators, and the child's parents to develop an individualized educational plan (IEP). With the number of medically fragile children who have serious medical problems now attending school, it is not unusual for the school nurse to be expected to provide various types of needed medical care during the school day.

The school nurse is not usually certified to teach health education classes. The certification pattern in some states prohibits the nurse from doing regular health classroom instruction, while in other states the nurse can be involved in direct health teaching. Regardless, the nurse can educate students effectively in informal, one-on-one teaching opportunities. The elementary and middle-level schoolteacher should make use of the knowledge and skills of the nurse in preparing health classes. The nurse can be an excellent resource for information, and should be included in the health curriculum development process, and invited to visit classes from time to time to present information to the students. This will help the students think of the school nurse as an educator about health matters in addition to being a person to whom one goes when ill or injured.

The school nurse works with the school administration to establish policy for all matters relating to the health of the children while they are at school. The nurse often serves on various policy and guideline-establishing committees in this capacity.

The educational preparation of a nurse who works in the schools varies among states. The nurse is principally educated in the medical model, usually spending numerous clinical hours in the hospital and/or health-care delivery setting. Little in this education prepares the nurse for issues he or she will face when working in an educational setting. The school nurse must be better prepared to fulfill the many tasks required in the nonclinical, educational environment. Because of this need, many states today require a school nurse to have a baccalaureate degree before permanent school nurse certification can be obtained. School nurses should be considered professional members of the school, the same as teachers. Salary, fringe benefits, and professional expectations should be determined on the same basis as with the teaching personnel.

Other School Health Service Personnel

In addition to the school nurse, other personnel are employed to provide health services during the school day. These include school nurse practitioners, nurses' aides, and school administrators. School secretaries, sometimes with no formal health care or first-aid training, are often expected to fill the role of health services provider in many schools. This is also true of adult voluntary helpers in some instances.

Special education teachers, speech therapists, school social workers, and psychologists carry out numerous activities of this component of a coordinated school health program. Many special education teachers are trained specifically to provide services to medically fragile children in the schools. In schools that do not have nurses, the special educators can be expected to render assistance to medically fragile students. Also, the classroom teacher assists significantly with the provision of health services to the children. These professionals collaborate to provide the best in school health services for the students.

The Classroom Teacher

In addition to using health service activities as an opportunity to educate students, the classroom teacher can provide much information about the health status of the children through classroom teacher observations. The teacher often prepares the students for screening and appraisal activities through organized instructional units, and is in a position to communicate with the students' families about health problems that are recognized in the school setting.

In addition to their instructional responsibilities, classroom teachers play an important role as child health advocates. Their contact with children in formative developmental years puts them in an advantageous position to recognize child health problems, often in the earliest stages. Since conditions are best managed before advanced symptoms are manifested, teachers are key participants in a comprehensive team approach to student health promotion.

In addition to their important role in responding to such health issues as vision and hearing problems, teachers also come in contact with child abuse and other family and community issues that interfere with a child's ability to gain the most from learning experiences. Their attention to such matters is consistent with their professional training and responsibility. As an advocate for child health, the classroom teacher can play four roles: observation, referral, gathering of information, and follow-up of referrals.

Teacher observation. Teachers are in a position to observe their students in a unique context. Their professional objectivity and training can help them to recognize health concerns in children that may go unrecognized by others. Specifically, teachers can observe students' physical, cognitive, social, emotional, and language performance in comparison to age-cohort peers. While nuances of a problem might not be noticed when the child is alone, developmentally consistent peers can provide an invaluable frame of reference. Further, teachers can observe student performance and behavior on a daily basis over a period of time. Academic performance measures and classroom structure provide a stable backdrop for observing potential health problems in children.

Referral. Teachers do not have the training or expertise to diagnose and treat suspected conditions. However, they must act to ensure that the child's learning is not impaired by a health problem. If teachers suspect, based on their best professional judgment, that a health problem may be a learning impediment, their responsibility extends to making an appropriate referral. Such referrals should be made in the context of school policy. Whenever possible, such referrals should be made in writing. Teachers should recognize that their colleagues are very busy and that verbal referrals can be forgotten by those involved with the case while responding to the needs of other children.

Gathering of information. The involved student, and his or her classmates, can be best served if the teacher gathers information about the condition as observed over a period of time. This can serve to improve the teacher's own comfort level with the health issue, and help him or her to better integrate the affected child into daily classroom activities while the condition is being treated by appropriate professionals.

Follow-up. Referral networks often move slowly. Many more students need support than there are professionals to respond. In the spirit of ensuring that the many needs of students are best served, teachers must be patient and persistent in their follow-up activities. This includes continuing observation and documentation to support the work of intervention specialists who are working with the child.

PROVISION OF MEDICAL CARE AT SCHOOL

Historically, providing medical care to students in elementary and middle schools has not been a part of the school health service program. It was felt that medicines and medical care for children could be provided before they came to school or when they returned to their homes. Rarely did children in regular classrooms have physiological conditions that demanded care during school hours. Teachers, school nurses, and other school personnel were not expected to provide such care.

Today, children are attending school with a number of special needs that necessitate medication administration. These conditions include epilepsy, asthma treatment

with metered dose inhalers, attention deficit hyperactivity disorder, reliance on medication for behavior control, and diabetes.

Another major factor that has resulted in medication administration changes in recent years has been the inclusion of children with disabilities in the regular school classroom. With the passage of federal legislation (Education for All Handicapped Children Act, 1975; Education of the Handicapped Act Amendments, 1986; Individuals with Disabilities Education Act, 1990; and Individuals with Disabilities Education Act, 1997), many new expectations have fallen upon school personnel. The legislation mandated that children with disabilities have the right to be admitted to public schools and their needs met so that they can experience success.

The most recent legislation, the Individuals with Disabilities Education Act (IDEA), 1997, was passed to raise expectations for children with disabilities. It required that education goals for the disabled must relate more clearly to those of children in the regular school curriculum. This legislation mandated involvement of parents in making placement decisions. Also, regular classroom teachers should be involved in the planning and assessment of children's progress. The classroom teacher is to be a part of the team designing and evaluating the student's IEP.

There has been an increase in the number of medically complex (sometimes referred to as medically fragile) students at school who need nursing care. The medically fragile child is that individual in need of a bio-medical device to compensate for loss of body function for which nursing care is needed. Some of these children are in need of daily medical technology nursing care. It is estimated that one child in 1,000 is in need of such care.[2]

For many school nurses, this need for student medical care during the school day has meant a shift from the traditional assessment and referral activities to the provision of various complex procedures at school. It is not unusual for children in schools today to need procedures that in the past were carried out in the hospital or medical center setting, such as catheterizations, tracheostomy care, laryngeal suctioning, gastric tube feedings, or management of oxygen therapy.

School nurses must learn skills not only to assess, but also to manage the care of children with a variety of disabilities. This also involves skill in networking with the families of the students, health professionals, teachers, and others in the community involved in the care of the child. Nurses must make sure that policies are established to ensure that all medically mandated care is provided while the student is at school. This has led to an increase in the continuing education and in-service seminars for school nurses to update their clinical skills in the school setting.

When medications are given during the school day at school, careful documentation and appropriate supervision must be in place. Written permission that includes written instructions from the physician must be obtained from the parents. Planning is essential in determining storage of medicine during the day and delivery procedures.

HEALTH APPRAISAL ACTIVITIES

Several health appraisal activities are a part of the school health service program. These include a health examination in which the complete health history and status of the child is noted and several different screening programs that are designed to identify early problems. Appraisal of the health status of an individual is important for identifying deviations from normal and conditions that may have a negative effect on the learning and everyday functioning of a schoolchild.

The classroom teacher should use the various activities involved in school health appraisal activities as an educational motivation for students. These health appraisal activities should be integrated with the instructional component of the children's school experience.

Health Examinations

Most school districts have adopted policies requiring that children have health examinations before enrolling in school for the first time. Children who transfer from another school district often must provide a record of a previous health examination from a physician or from their former school.

The health examination should provide a history of the health status of the child and identify any health problems that the child might have. Another reason for requiring elementary and middle-level schoolchildren to have a health examination is its educational value. This experience should be used to reinforce the importance of health examinations to the child. Further, this practice can help the child begin to develop a positive attitude toward health-care providers.

During this contact with the health-care provider, a health history is usually obtained prior to the examination. This includes a history of health problems, growth and development, diseases, allergies, nutritional status, immunization status, and other factors related to the health of the child. The health history usually includes information about the family health record, and about relatives who have had such diseases as cancer, heart disease, diabetes, and other chronic conditions. Developing the health history should encourage the child's family to become aware of factors that affect the health status of the student.

Physicians should conduct thorough examinations of schoolchildren. If the examination process is going to be of value to the child and the parents, a follow-up discussion should be conducted between the examining physician and the parents or caregivers (guardians).

It is usually recommended that a health examination be conducted by the child's family physician. Examinations conducted in large-group sessions at the school are rarely used today. When problems and deviations from what has been previously recorded about a child are discovered, prompt follow-up care is most likely to occur if the family physician conducts the exam.

Unfortunately, many children of lower socioeconomic families do not have a family physician because their families cannot afford preventive health care. These individuals often rely on the emergency rooms of hospitals

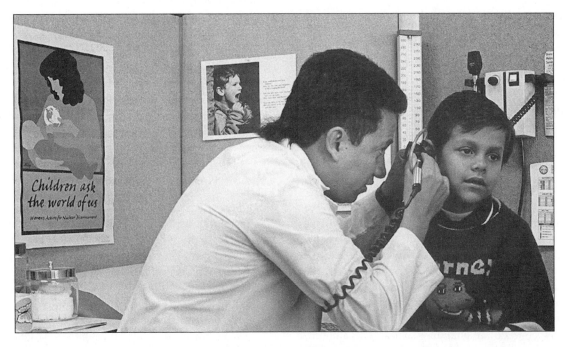

The health examination of elementary and middle-level schoolchildren is usually required for school admittance.
This experience should be an educational opportunity for the children to learn about their physical well-being.

or public health department clinics for both their preventive and emergency health care. It is important that school districts with requirements for health examinations prior to school admittance make provisions to assist children whose families cannot afford such preventive health care. Often this kind of assistance is available at local health department clinics, community centers, or various agencies within the community that have health programming objectives.

Screening Programs

Screening activities conducted within the school setting are usually the responsibility of a school nurse. In some instances, other school personnel, including the classroom teacher, may be expected to carry out these procedures. School districts with limited financial resources often use parent/community volunteers to help organize, record, and gather screening data. The work of these volunteers is carried out under the supervision of a trained health-care provider, usually the school nurse. The health screening activities most commonly carried out within the school are inexpensive, can be conducted on a routine basis, and provide important early information about potential deviations from normal that may need medical attention.

Health screening is particularly important for elementary and middle-level schoolchildren because many parents are not aware of some of their children's problems. Many seemingly minor behavioral patterns are considered normal by parents. Not until a student's condition is seen in relationship to that of developmental peers does a deviation become evident.

A number of different health screening activities are conducted in the elementary and middle-level schools. The most commonly found screening activities are height and weight screening, vision and hearing screening, and screening for scoliosis.

Physical Growth and Development

Several times throughout the school year, elementary and middle-level schoolchildren, particularly those in the primary grades, are likely to have their height and weight measured. These measurements are helpful in ascertaining if the children are experiencing appropriate physiological growth and development patterns.

Recording and charting the measurements over a period of several years provides a composite picture of the child's development. It is possible to identify individuals who are experiencing abnormal weight and/or height by reviewing such charts.

Diagnosis of growth disorder in children can be accomplished only by a physician. However, teachers, the school nurse, and other school personnel can identify those individuals who appear to be growing inconsistently with age-cohort peers. These children should be referred to the appropriate medical personnel for further evaluation.

School programs enable a variety of growth disorders to be identified. For example, malnutrition-related problems, hypothyroidism, and various skeletal dysplasias are often identified as the result of analyzing a child's growth chart.[3]

Vision Screening

The ability to function effectively and learn in school depends significantly on the ability to see. The mechanism of sight is a very precise physiological process. It is particularly important among elementary schoolchildren, in that poor vision can lead to various behavioral problems that can have negative effects on academic performance. Figure 2.1 illustrates the basic physiology of the human eye.

School personnel are in a vital position to observe children and detect early signs of visual problems. By noticing children's behaviors in the classroom and during other activities, the teacher can identify deviations from normal visual patterns. For example, eye strain can be recognized by noting students who squint or frown while reading or looking at the chalkboard. The child with visual problems may hold reading material too close to the face or at arms' length. Tilting or turning the head to one side so as to use the best eye often indicates visual problems. The classroom teacher must be alert to these and other unusual vision-related behaviors and take appropriate measures to see that vision screening is accomplished and that parents are alerted to the problem.

Visual Defects   There are numerous defects of the eyes that can diminish one's ability to see properly and, thus, diminish one's educational experience. Inflammation, injuries, and refractive error, which keeps the light rays from focusing on the retina, are the basic visual defects that affect children of elementary and middle-school age.

Inflammation of the eyes. Inflammation of the eyes can be caused by several different microorganisms. *Conjunctivitis,* an inflammation that affects the white of the eye—the sclera—is caused by bacteria and viruses. This condition is commonly referred to as "pinkeye." It can be easily transmitted to others by rubbing the inflamed eye or by reusing a washcloth or towel used by the

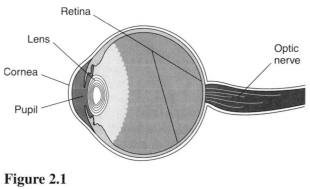

Figure 2.1
The human eye.

infected individual. Consistent with school district policies on causes for exclusion, a student with conjunctivitis should stay at home, be isolated from his or her classmates, and be careful not to share washcloths or towels with others. There are effective antibiotic ointments or drops that will cure bacteria-caused infections. These preparations are prescribed by physicians, to whom infected children should be referred. However, no such ointments are effective with viral-caused infections.

Another inflammation that is often noted among school-age children is a sty: a red, swollen inflammation of the sebaceous gland on the edge of the eyelid. The most effective measure to counter the sty is to apply hot compresses several times a day to the sty. One must be careful that the pus within the sty does not spread and carry the infection to other parts of the eye.

Injuries to the eyes. Even though the eye is anatomically well protected, injury can still occur. Direct blows to the eyeball or penetration of the eye with foreign objects can result in serious problems. Also, one must be careful not to spill dangerous objects into the eye, which can result in permanent damage. Wearing eye-protective devices in high-risk situations is important. In many industrial settings, employees are required to wear eye-protective devices. Many states have mandated requirements that students who use potentially dangerous pieces of equipment or machinery in vocational classes must wear eye-protective goggles.

While prevention is the important factor, the elementary and middle-level schoolteacher must be familiar with appropriate emergency care measures that can be taken when a child's eye is injured or when something splashes into a student's eye at school. School personnel should be able to take whatever measures are appropriate to reduce long-term injury to the eyes.

If a student should get a foreign object on the eye, it is often possible to remove the object by pulling the upper eyelid out and down over the lower lid and having the student blink. The eye will naturally begin to tear, and the object may be washed out in this way. When necessary, an appropriate emergency care measure is to flush the eye with clean water. Should an object become embedded in the eyeball, no effort should be taken to remove the object. Instead, apply a loose bandage to prevent eye movement and get the individual to medical care as quickly as possible.

In cases involving injury to the tissues surrounding the eyes, the wounds should be cared for like any other wound. If a black eye results from a direct, blunt blow to the eye, an ice-cold compress should be applied to lessen the likelihood of swelling and to reduce accompanying pain, and the child should be referred for treatment by medical care personnel.

Refractive errors. Under certain circumstances, the normal procedure by which the light rays enter the eye and focus upon the retina may not function properly. This results in what is known as refractive errors. There are three basic types of refractive errors: nearsightedness (myopia), farsightedness (hyperopia), and astigmatism. These conditions are often observed in schoolchildren and can be identified in school screening programs.

With *nearsightedness (myopia)*, objects at a distance appear to be fuzzy and blurry, but nearby objects are clear. In a case of myopia, the light rays are bent so that they meet short of the retina. This may be caused by an eyeball that is too long or by a sharply curved cornea. Myopia can be corrected by wearing prescription glasses or contacts with concave lenses, which spread the light rays so that they will focus upon the retina.

In other instances, the eyeball may be shorter from front to back and the light rays cannot be bent enough to focus on the retina. This condition is known as *farsightedness (hyperopia)*. It may also be caused by an insufficiently curved cornea. The hyperopic individual has difficulty seeing objects that are nearby clearly. Difficulty in reading is a common indication of farsightedness. Distant objects tend to be in focus. This condition is correctable with a convex lens.

A third type of refractive error occurs when there is an imperfectly shaped cornea. This is referred to as *astigmatism.* Because of the abnormal shape of the cornea, light rays focus at different points short of the retina. As a result, there are various forms of blurring or misshapes. This refractive error often accompanies myopia or hyperopia.

School Vision Screening Procedures   Vision screening is an effective school screening endeavor because deviations from normal vision can be identified easily and refractive errors can be referred for correction by eye-care providers. Early detection identifies children who need prescription glasses, contact lenses, and/or special education assistance.

The first state-wide school vision screening program was established in 1899 in Connecticut. Today, more than half of the states require vision screening during the elementary school years.[4] Children who are enrolled in Medicaid-funded Early and Periodic Screening, Diagnosis, and Treatment (EPSDT) programs are required to have vision screening. Most state mandatory vision screening regulations do not specifically dictate what procedures or conditions are to be part of the screening protocol.

Visual acuity refers to how well an individual sees an object at a specific distance. Students are screened at the standard distance of 20 feet. The screening environment should be in a quiet room with normal light without glare and shadows. The purpose of the school visual acuity screening activity is to identify those children in need of referral to a medical specialist for evaluation and treatment.

Several commercial units are used in school vision screening programs. The Snellen Eye Chart is the most commonly used, the least expensive, and the easiest screening test to perform. Studies have shown that this procedure has a remarkably high degree of success in identifying students with vision problems.[5]

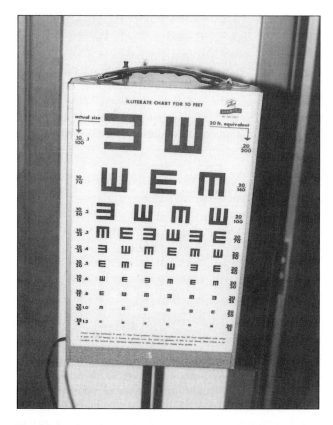

The Snellen Eye Chart is the easiest and most reliable instrument to assess the vision of children in elementary and middle-level schools.

The Snellen Eye Chart screening procedure, developed in the 1860s by Dutch ophthalmologist Herman Snellen, measures a person's ability to see distant objects. With this procedure, the eye chart should be placed at eye level at a distance of 20 feet from where the individual is standing or sitting. The student is then asked to identify the line on the chart at which he/she can read at least 50% of the letters correctly. Both eyes should be checked individually.

The acuteness of vision is reported in the form of a fraction in which the denominator indicates the smallest letters, or symbols, that the individual being tested can see. The numerator indicates the distance at which the test was given. For example, for a reporting of 20/40, the 20 indicates that the individual was tested at 20 feet from the chart and the 40 indicates the value of the smallest line of letters that could be read. A child with a reading of 20/40 or less should be referred for further vision examination by an eye-care professional.

Screening for hyperopia can best be carried out by ascertaining the ability to see near objects. A reading card that is effective for these purposes is available from medical supply houses. The individual is asked to read several paragraphs, each written in successively larger print. It is less effective with primary schoolchildren because of limitations in reading skills.

Screening for astigmatism is more difficult. There is no screening device available for use in the schools for this

CONSIDER THIS

Testing Procedure for Distance Visual Acuity: Use of Snellen Eye Chart

1. Child should stand at a distance of 20 feet from the chart.
2. Cover the left eye and test the right eye, then reverse the procedure.
3. If child wears glasses, test with glasses on.
4. Do not isolate a single symbol; present the whole line.
5. Eye not being tested should remain covered, but relaxed and open.
6. After the second screening, refer children with 20/40 vision or less in either or both eyes to an eye-care professional.

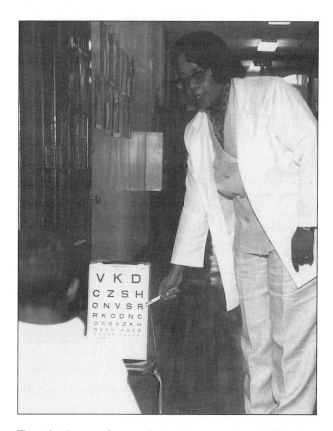

The school nurse often conducts vision-screening activities in most elementary and middle-level schools. Children with glasses should be screened while wearing their glasses.

type of refractive error. Astigmatism must be diagnosed by an eye-care professional. At school, individuals with this condition can best be identified by subjective observations and their own awareness of blurry, unclear vision.

Screening for eye muscle imbalance should be carried out as early in life as possible. The procedure involves having the student look at a small target object held about 15 inches from the face. The individual giving the test moves the object alternately from eye to eye about ten times. The screener watches the eye for horizontal and vertical movement.

Screening for color deficiency is recommended for boys, since one in ten males of school age has some type of color deficiency. Although color deficiency is less common among females, elementary schoolgirls should also be screened. There are several instruments that can be used in screening for color-vision defects. Two of the better instruments used in school programs are the Ishihara plates and the American Optical Hardy-Rand-Rittler Pseudo-isochromatic plates.[6] The former makes use of numbers; the latter uses geometric designs. The individual being tested must identify a number or figure made of colored dots within a background of other colors. These tests are very effective; however, they can be rather ineffective among younger children who lack the ability to identify numbers or figures.

There is no test for color blindness specially designed for children.[7] Probably the best school screening procedure is to ask the student to identify a specific color from among a grouping of colors. The student could be presented with a number of different colors of yarn held together or crayons mixed together and asked to locate a given color. This procedure is only effective among pre- and early-elementary schoolchildren when they have been taught color names.

Hearing Screening

The ability to hear sounds determines how well one can communicate within the environment. (Figure 2.2 illustrates the structure of the human hearing mechanism—the ear.) Hearing is important during all stages of life, but has particular impact during the elementary school years when speech patterns are developing and adaptations first occur outside the home. Hearing loss can interfere with normal speech and language development. This can contribute to poor academic performance. Children with hearing loss often exhibit negative behaviors. The child who has even minor hearing problems can develop speech problems. These communication and language deficiencies often require the professional assistance of a school speech therapist.

Hearing screening for preschool and kindergarten children is mandated in several states.[8] A school auditory screening program is not developed to diagnose or treat hearing disorders, but to identify and refer to a health-care provider those students with hearing impairment severe enough to interfere with learning.

It is not unusual for a child to arrive at the start of elementary school with a hearing disorder that has gone undetected. Often the individual with a hearing disability has learned to adapt and cope with the condition without alerting others, such as parents, to the problem.

Classroom teacher observations often serve as the foundation for identifying potential hearing loss. Failure to hear questions posed by the teacher is an indication of a hearing problem. Inattention, excessive loudness by the child in talking and responding to others, and turning the head to one side to hear are other important indications. The child with a hearing problem may ask to have statements and questions repeated. All too often, the teacher assumes that the child has not been paying attention, when in fact there is an unrecognized hearing disorder.

School Hearing Screening Procedures

Teacher Observation. The daily classroom practice of the elementary and middle-level schoolteacher includes several measures that can help identify children with possible hearing losses. The teacher should not see these

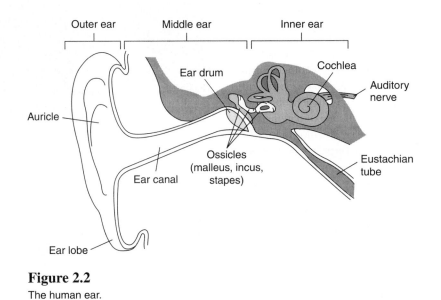

Figure 2.2
The human ear.

measures as another thing he or she must do in an already overcrowded school day, but as a part of the normal observation of children during school activities. These are subjective, unscientific appraisal procedures, but they do assist first-hand hearing screening.

In the case of a sensorineural hearing loss, the ability to understand what is said may be greatly reduced with only a slight increase in distance from a speaker. One screening procedure is to speak in both a conversational tone and in a whisper while standing at a distance of 20 feet from the child. If the child cannot hear, the examiner moves closer. If the child cannot hear at 10 to 20 feet, he or she should be referred to a physician for hearing examinations.

Another measure that has been used is to speak in conversational tones to a child who is facing in the opposite direction, away from the speaker, thus reducing the likelihood of lip reading. Also, listening closely to how the child pronounces certain sounds can provide clues of hearing difficulties. Distortion in children's speech is another important early observation cue for hearing problems.

Audiometer Screening. Hearing screening performed with the pure-tone audiometer is the most reliable procedure for detecting hearing loss in schoolchildren. Training in the operation of this instrument and in the interpretation of the results are usually beyond the education and expectations of an elementary or middle-level classroom schoolteacher. Although the teacher is not expected to be able to do audiometry testing, teachers should be aware of the different kinds of testing and the meaning of the results so that they can help to integrate students with hearing problems into the learning environment.

The audiometer is an electric instrument that emits tones of varying frequencies. The student is seated in a quiet room environment near the instrument. Earphones cover the student's ears. The audiologist, a specialist in the nonmedical evaluation and rehabilitation of persons with hearing disorders, operates the instrument. The student can be screened at each of several frequency levels. Most commonly, screening is carried out at 500, 1,000, 2,000, and 4,000 hertz (Hz). The single most reliable test frequency is 1,000 Hz. A specific level of intensity of sound is presented and then reduced until the person being tested indicates that the sound can no longer be heard. The results of these testing measurements are recorded on an audiogram.

This testing measures the lowest level that can be heard through the earphones, and is referred to as air conduction (AC). Inability to hear normal sound levels by this means of testing indicates a hearing loss in the outer, middle, or inner ear. Should a hearing loss be noted using air conduction screening, the audiologist must ascertain if the loss is a sensorineural loss. A sensorineural loss results from damage to the sensory cells in the cochlea or the neural pathway between the cochlea and the brain. Testing for sensorineural hearing loss is accomplished by bone conduction (BC). An instrument (the conduction

transducer) is placed on the mastoid bone behind the ear. Vibrations of the skull on the basilar membrane are indicated as sound. Failure of this screening test indicates the problem is sensorineural. This type of hearing loss tends to be permanent.

If the hearing loss is not sensorineural, we know that the problem is in the conductive mechanism—the outer or middle ear. A conductive hearing loss can usually be corrected. It may be the result of a buildup of earwax in the ear canal or the presence of a foreign body in the ear canal. Removal of both will return the person to normal hearing. Hearing loss due to problems in the middle ear usually results from infection or otosclerosis, a growth on the little bones of the middle ear that causes them to calcify. Both of these conditions can be corrected: Prescribed medication may eliminate the infection, and otosclerosis may be repaired by microsurgery.

Different kinds of hearing loss have certain characteristics. Understanding these characteristics can help the elementary schoolteacher interpret a child's audiogram. A sensorineural hearing loss usually affects the higher frequencies more than the lower ones. Hence, an audiogram that shows greater loss in the 1,000 to 8,000 Hz range than in the 125 to 1,000 Hz range indicates a sensorineural loss. Conductive hearing losses usually appear as flat losses on the audiogram or as greater losses at the lower frequencies. The importance of this is seen when one realizes that a conductive loss is usually correctable, while a sensorineural loss is most likely permanent. This information can be useful to the classroom teacher's knowledge of the student's hearing condition and the prognosis for correction.

Otitis Media   One of the most common diseases of childhood is otitis media, a common cause of conductive hearing loss. This middle ear infection results in fluctuating

Children with minor hearing problems can be identified through school hearing screening procedures.

hearing loss during the school year. Research has shown that fluctuated hearing loss is correlated with decreased learning skills. The use of tympanometry screening measures the function of the middle ear. Since it is possible that a child can have middle ear disease without hearing loss, it is recommended that both tympanometry and pure tone audiometry screening procedures be carried out.

Scoliosis Screening

Scoliosis is a sidewise (lateral) curvature of the spine that usually begins in the prepubertal and adolescent growth years. In some cases, the cause may be congenital or the result of trauma, but in most instances, the cause is unknown. However, there is a tendency for scoliosis to run in families.

There are two different types of scoliosis: postural and structural. Postural scoliosis is a curve in the spinal column resulting from incorrect relationships between the body and its center of gravity. This type of curvature is usually slight and is correctable with exercise.

Structural scoliosis cannot be corrected actively by an individual. It is observed much more prevalently in females than in males. With this type of scoliosis, there is a fixed rotation of the curve. If left untreated, it can become extremely severe and can result in permanent disability. Initially, the spinal curvatures are flexible; however, the curves become rigid with age. When left untreated, the thoracic and lumbar curvature can increase substantially; however, this condition can be arrested and corrected if it is identified early. Prognosis is not as positive when it is diagnosed after skeletal maturity has taken place. Skeletal maturity for girls is between 13 and 16 years of age and, for boys, between ages 14 and 17.

Human posture is maintained by the spinal column, or the backbone, which is composed of thirty-three vertebrae in children and twenty-six in adults. The structure of each vertebra is relatively the same: There is an opening through which the spinal cord passes, and each vertebra is separated from the next by intervertebral disks, which are composed of soft, elastic, fibrous tissue. These disks allow for movement of the spinal column.

Scoliosis is characterized by lateral curvature of the spine and rotation of the vertebral column around its long axis. This causes the ribs on the side of the curve to become prominent. The scapula—the shoulder blade—is pushed backward, which causes the spine to be out of balance, and the head and shoulders lean to the right or left.

School Scoliosis Screening Procedures   It is estimated that one child in ten will develop some degree of scoliosis. Girls tend to be affected by this condition more than boys. Generally, most children are not taken to a physician for preventive health care. As a result, the school health service program has been identified as a good place to screen children for scoliosis and identify beginning spinal curvatures at an early stage of development.

A relatively easy and effective screening procedure can be conducted in the schools to identify children with scoliosis (figure 2.3). A number of states now require that all children, at certain ages, be screened for

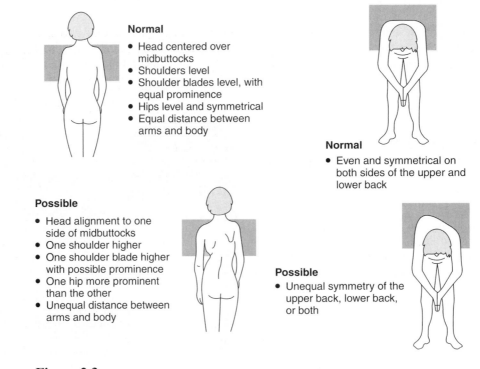

Figure 2.3

School scoliosis screening can detect early spinal curvatures. One in every ten individuals has scoliosis.

this condition. Generally, it is recommended that all children in grades 5 through 10 be screened annually. It is during these years that early signs of spinal curvature are noted.

The basic aim of the school screening program is to observe children just prior to, or beginning, their adolescent growth spurt. Early deviation can be identified and referred to the family physician. The school nurse often conducts scoliosis screening of schoolchildren. However, the physical education specialist and the classroom teacher can easily screen for early identification of scoliosis. Whenever a growing child or teenager is found to have one or more of the physical features that suggest scoliosis, it is important that competent medical investigation and advice be obtained.

Boys and girls should be screened separately. Boys should be asked to remove their shirts; girls should be examined in a location where they can remove their blouses without embarrassment. In screening girls, it is important that those in upper elementary and middle-level grades be permitted to wear their bras during the procedure.

Several questions need to be answered in performing scoliosis screening. What does one look for in carrying out a screening program? Students should be examined from the back and side while standing erect and bent halfway forward. From the back, observe the symmetry of the torso and observe the shoulder, scapula, and hip levels. Is one shoulder or hip higher than the other? Does the scapula protrude or seem to be higher?

Normally, the first thing to note in screening for scoliosis is whether there is any tilt of the shoulders. By looking at the child from a distance of several feet, it is possible to determine whether one shoulder is noticeably higher than the other. A second factor to note is whether there is any evidence of a lateral curvature of the spine. A normal spine is in a relatively straight line; scoliosis is present if the spine is in a *C-* or an *S-*curve pattern. This can also be noted by simply examining the person from a short distance. It might be more clearly noted if each vertebra is marked with a felt pen.

By having the student look directly at the examiner, one can see if the hips are in balance. If one hip is higher than the other, scoliosis may be the cause.

Another screening technique is to have the student bend forward from the waist, with head and arms falling freely, feet flat on the floor and slightly apart, and fingertips touching each other. The chin should be tucked up toward the neck. The examiner looks at the shoulder blades (scapula). If one shoulder blade protrudes higher than the other, it is indicative of a bulge of the rib cage resulting from scoliosis.

Children with scoliosis must be provided with instruction about the condition. Children who have this condition often have a variety of negative reactions. The parents and child are usually uncertain as to what kinds of activities will be permitted. They are also uncertain how medical care can correct the problem. Children with poor

self-concepts to start with are at a disadvantage and need support and encouragement.

The Scoliosis Foundation (5 Cabot Place, Stoughton, MA 02072, 781-341-6333) provides a variety of educational materials that are quite helpful. *Growing Straighter and Stronger,* a 15-minute video presentation that can be used for pre-screening education of students in grades 5 through 7, is available. There is an accompanying teacher's guide and several reproducible worksheets.

Medical Treatment for Scoliosis Although treatment for scoliosis is a medical matter, school personnel should be familiar with the various procedures the affected child is likely to experience. This will help the teacher to integrate the child into classroom activities and to provide support to the student.

If the curve is less than 20 degrees, continual visual observation, inspection, and periodic X rays are all that is usually necessary until the curve stabilizes. Medical examination for scoliosis begins with an X ray, which ascertains the extent of the scoliotic curve. Some physicians recommend exercises for the improvement of this condition. Although exercises will strengthen the surrounding muscular structure, they will not eliminate the skeletal curvature or stop it from continuing to develop. External bracing with a body jacket or plaster techniques is necessary if the curve is between 20 and 40 degrees. There are

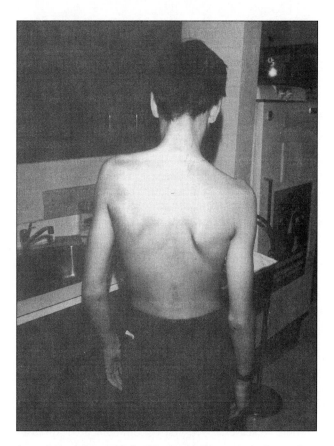

Annual screening at this boy's school led to an early diagnosis and treatment for scoliosis.

Compression apparatus used by the French in the 1770s for straightening the back of a child suffering from scoliosis.

several different kinds of bracing procedures that help to stabilize the spine during the years of physiological growth. A third treatment involves surgically realigning the spine and fusing the vertebrae. Surgical procedures are costly and usually time-consuming, and keep the patient out of school for several months.

DISEASE CONTROL—IMMUNIZATIONS

One of the most significant changes in mortality and morbidity in the United States during the latter half of the 20th century has been the reduction of communicable diseases and the increase of chronic diseases. In the early part of the 20th century, communicable diseases accounted for seven of the ten leading causes of death. Today, five of the leading causes of death result from chronic diseases.[9] The only communicable diseases found on the list of the ten top causes of death in the 1990s were pneumonia/influenza and AIDS.

One of the principal factors in this reduction of incidences of communicable diseases has been the widespread acceptance of immunization. Nowhere has this been more evident than with the diseases often referred to as the *childhood communicable diseases.* Seven major childhood infectious diseases that, in some cases, could cause permanent disability or death have been significantly reduced or eliminated today. All of these diseases are preventable by immunization with safe and effective vaccines.

The schools have been a significant agency in the expanded coverage of immunizations among the American population. Today, immunization is required by law for admission to school in all states.[10] Since education is legally required for all children, the various state immunization regulations for school attendance have had the force of compulsory legislation. These various state mandates that require children to be immunized before they are permitted to attend school have never been successfully challenged in courts of law.[11] As early as 1905, the United States Supreme Court held that state statutes requiring compulsory immunization of schoolchildren for smallpox were constitutional.[12] Such compulsory immunization requirements are considered to be a reasonable measure for the protection of the health of the public.

Several exemptions from compulsory immunization requirements have been ruled to be acceptable. If parents of a child object on religious or philosophical grounds, the child may be exempted. However, if an outbreak of a particular disease occurs, that nonimmunized child can be excluded from school attendance. A child might also be exempted from immunization mandates for medical reasons. In these cases, the child's physician must present a signed exemption request. These situations usually involve allergic reactions or other medical reasons.

Common Childhood Immunizations

It is generally assumed that if 90% to 95% of a population group is immunized against a particular disease, there is little danger of an epidemic outbreak of that disease. With this in mind, the U.S. Department of Health and Human Services has set as a goal that school laws mandating immunization should be expanded to include all children in grades K through 12, plus preschool and day-care children.[13] Most states require immunization for diphtheria, pertussis, tetanus, polio, measles, rubella, and mumps in all children prior to their enrollment in school.[14] Figure 2.4 outlines a recommended immunization schedule.

Diphtheria is a disease caused by a bacillus that usually affects the throat, the tonsils, and/or larynx. The bacilli usually enter the body through the nose or mouth. This disease is often confused in the early stages with tonsillitis; its common symptoms include sore throat, hoarseness, nasal discharge, and accompanying fever. Complications resulting from diphtheria include heart damage, crippling nerve damage, and injury to the throat,

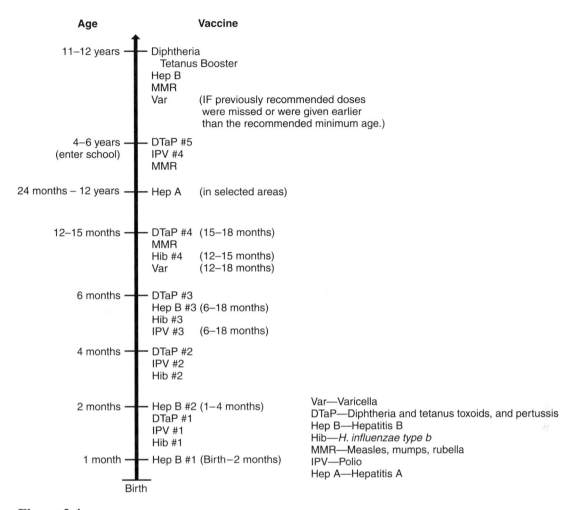

Age   **Vaccine**

11–12 years — Diphtheria
                 Tetanus Booster
               Hep B
               MMR
               Var   (IF previously recommended doses
                       were missed or were given earlier
                       than the recommended minimum age.)

4–6 years — DTaP #5
(enter school) IPV #4
               MMR

24 months – 12 years — Hep A   (in selected areas)

12–15 months — DTaP #4 (15–18 months)
               MMR
               Hib #4   (12–15 months)
               Var   (12–18 months)

6 months — DTaP #3
           Hep B #3 (6–18 months)
           Hib #3
           IPV #3   (6–18 months)

4 months — DTaP #2
           IPV #2
           Hib #2

2 months — Hep B #2 (1–4 months)   Var—Varicella
           DTaP #1   DTaP—Diphtheria and tetanus toxoids, and pertussis
           IPV #1   Hep B—Hepatitis B
           Hib #1   Hib—*H. influenzae type b*
                                       MMR—Measles, mumps, rubella
1 month — Hep B #1 (Birth–2 months)   IPV—Polio
                                       Hep A—Hepatitis A

Birth

Figure 2.4
Recommended childhood immunization schedule—United States, January–December 2000.
Source: Advisory Committee on Immunization Practices (ACIP). Centers for Disease Control and
Prevention, *Morbidity and Mortality Weekly Report,* (January 21, 2000): Vol. 49, No. 2, p. 36.

resulting in choking. Usually a membrane is formed, which, if located in the larynx, obstructs breathing.

This disease, which once caused serious illness to hundreds of children in the United States, has been almost totally eliminated. Immunization for diphtheria is now given as part of a tri-vaccine—the DPT vaccine—which includes immunization for pertussis (whooping cough) and tetanus. Presently, four doses of DPT are required for complete coverage. The immunization, which usually begins within the first 2 to 3 months of life, should be completed by the time a child enters school. The first three shots are given prior to 6 months of age and boosters are given at ages 4 and 6.

Pertussis, a highly contagious infection of the respiratory system that is caused by a bacillus, is popularly known as whooping cough. This disease is characterized initially by an apparently mild cough. Over a period of several days, the cough becomes more pronounced, with a characteristic whoop during inhalation. The disease is particularly dangerous to younger children. The convulsive coughing associated with this con-

dition may result in vomiting or may rupture the lungs, causing a hemorrhage. Pertussis is transmitted through close contact with droplets from secretions of the respiratory tract as the bacillus invades the trachea, bronchi, and bronchioles.

In spite of efforts to immunize the youthful population, there has been an increase of pertussis in all age groups, but it is most common among young children. This has occurred among individuals who have been nonvaccinated or partially vaccinated. The pertussis antigen is included in the combined DPT immunization. It is recommended only for individuals under age 7.[15]

Tetanus (commonly known as lockjaw) is a disease caused by a poison secreted by a microorganism that has an irritating effect on the nervous system. The microorganisms escape from the carrier by way of the feces and enter the body of another individual through an open wound. The spore-forming organism tends to live in soil. Soils of barnyards and fields that have been fertilized with manure are highly contaminated. For this reason, tetanus is found most commonly in rural, agricultural settings.

The initial signs of this disease are irritability and restlessness, followed by stiffness of muscles, development of spasms, and convulsions. The trachea, or windpipe, of tetanus victims may become paralyzed and cause suffocation. The tetanus vaccine is part of the tri-vaccine DPT. It is important that a tetanus booster be repeated every 10 years throughout life. The tetanus vaccine is usually recommended following an injury.

Poliomyelitis is a disease of the central nervous system that is caused by several different viral strains. These can cause paralysis, deformity, and death. Polio is spread through secretions of the respiratory tract and through the feces.

Initially, the disease starts with a slight fever, headache, and general feelings of discomfort. As it progresses, one notices stiffness of the neck, arms, and legs. Eventually, permanent paralysis can result.

For many years, two types of vaccine have been used to protect against polio: the oral polio vaccine (Sabin) and the inactivated polio vaccine (Salk). The inactivated vaccine is now used among children. Four shots of the Salk polio vaccine are necessary to provide complete protection. These are usually recommended to be given at 2 months, 4 months, 6–8 months and 4–6 years.

Measles (*rubeola*) is a respiratory disease that is sometimes referred to as "seven-day" or "red" measles. The indications of this disease are similar to those of a common cold: runny nose, cough, watery eyes, and a fever. An accompanying dark-red, blotchy rash is the specific symptom of rubeola. For most children, this disease is rather mild. However, complications can cause serious illness and death. Pneumonia often follows a case of measles. Also, encephalitis has been known to develop in conjunction with rubeola.

Protection against this disease is obtained by receiving one dose of live measles vaccine after a child has reached 1 year of age. In the past, children were immunized for measles prior to their first birthday. However, there is evidence that when given prior to 12 months of age, long-term protection does not occur.

During the latter part of the 1980s and the early 1990s, there was an increase in measles cases, which caused great concern among public health epidemiologists and physicians. In most cases, these cases occurred in the adolescent and college-age population among individuals who received their immunization prior to 12 months of age. A number of cases were reported among persons who had not been immunized previously for measles. The increase in measles cases was not reported among elementary schoolchildren who received the immunization after 1 year of age.

German measles (*rubella*) is a viral disease that is rather mild in most children. A skin rash accompanied by a mild fever and swelling of lymph glands in the neck are the basic symptoms. The skin rash sometimes is hardly noticeable.

Although this disease is considered a mild condition in most instances, two major complications can occur. On occasion, encephalitis of the brain occurs. Of much greater frequency and of particular importance to young female teachers of elementary and middle-level students is the danger of birth defects resulting to babies born to mothers who have rubella during pregnancy. The earlier in the pregnancy that the mother has rubella, the more serious the damage to the fetus. The woman does not get very sick from rubella, but damage to the fetus can cause serious birth defects, hearing loss, and brain damage. Miscarriages, stillbirths, premature birth, and low infant birthweight also occur. The rubella virus passes through the placenta into the fetus and causes damage to the developing cells. The part of the body that is affected depends on the stage of fetal development at the time of maternal infection.

The incidences of rubella have been significantly reduced in the past two decades with increased immunization. Nearly 12,000 cases were reported in 1979, but only 195 cases were reported by the Centers for Disease Control and Prevention in 1993.[16] The Department of Health and Human Services established a goal of total eradication by the year 2000.[17]

Immunization involves one dose of rubella vaccine. As with the rubeola vaccine, the rubella vaccine must be administered after a child's first birthday. This vaccine is usually administered between the twelfth and fifteenth month of age. It may be administered in combination with the measles and mumps vaccine (MMR) or individually. It is important that a female not be given the vaccine after puberty if there is the slightest possibility that she is pregnant.

One of the most recently developed vaccines for widespread use among elementary and middle-level schoolchildren is for *mumps.* This disease, which is caused by a virus, is characterized by swelling of the glands in front of the ear, and usually by a fever. Although mumps is usually a mild disease, severe inflammation of the brain and infection of the ears, eyes, joints, and other body organs are possible complications. Since the development of the mumps vaccine, its incidence throughout the nation has dropped. The vaccine may be administered in combination (the MMR vaccine) or individually. One dose of live mumps vaccine must be administered after a child's first birthday, preferably at about 15 months of age.

Hepatitis

Hepatitis is a disease that attacks healthy liver cells and causes serious internal destruction. The incidence of this disease has been escalating in recent years. Of particular concern for school programs is the possibility of spread of the disease among school personnel from exposure to blood and other body fluids and the increasing mandate that immunization for hepatitis be included among those requirements for school attendance. Hepatitis is also an increasing threat to young children in schools.

Three different types of hepatitis, *Hepatitis A, Hepatitis B, and Hepatitis C,* are of particular concern among school-age children and educational personnel. Since each type of hepatitis is caused by a different virus, it is important to know with which virus one has been infected. This can only be accomplished by a blood test. Vaccinations are available only for hepatitis A and B.

Hepatitis A. Hepatitis A is found in human waste and is spread by close person-to-person contact or by putting something that is contaminated into the mouth. This condition is often spread by infected food handlers. Washing dishes in hot, soapy water is one of the best preventative measures.

There is no specific treatment for hepatitis A. It simply must run its normal course. Signs and symptoms that develop include fatigue, nausea, abdominal pain, jaundice, and fever. Most people will recover and develop lifelong immunity to additional exposure.

Hepatitis B. The hepatitis B virus is found in blood and other body secretions, such as saliva and semen. The virus causes inflammation of the liver, which can lead to cirrhosis. The virus can survive for up to 7 days and is much more contagious than HIV. It is spread by having unprotected sex, and exposure to needles, razors, toothbrushes, nail clippers, and other personal items. During the acute phase of infection, nausea, vomiting, jaundice, and abdominal pain are experienced by an infected individual.

Most individuals with hepatitis B will recover within 6 months with proper treatment. Interferon therapy administered by injection is the principal treatment for this type of hepatitis. People who have hepatitis B will usually develop lifelong immunity to the virus. Vaccines have been available since 1982 to prevent hepatitis B (HBV). For a number of years, it has been recommended that anyone employed in a vocation in which they are exposed to blood or blood products should be routinely immunized with HBV. This has been directed particularly at those in health-care settings.

Preventative measures include maintenance of good hygiene practices with frequent hand washing. It is important to avoid exposure to blood or blood products by using latex or disposable waterproof gloves.

General classroom contact with children who have hepatitis B is not considered to be a risk factor. However, special concern must be noted for school personnel in classrooms with special needs children. Children who have severe mental handicapping conditions often have poor fluid control, drool, and may have a history of biting and scratching.

The Centers for Disease Control and Prevention recommends that HBV be included in immunization schedules for all children—for newborns and for young people about 11 or 12 years of age. The usual schedule involves administration of three doses: shortly after birth and at 1 and 6 months of age. This usually provides protection for at least 13 years. Nineteen states currently mandate HBV for school admittance and additional states have legislation pending.[18] Opinions differ as to whether teachers, particularly elementary, middle-level, and special education teachers, should be required to be immunized for HBV.

Hepatitis C. The hepatitis C virus is spread by close contact with contaminated blood. At first, it tends to be a mild disease. However, cirrhosis, liver failure, and death can result. The early symptoms of hepatitis C are similar to those of influenza: loss of appetite, fatigue, abdominal pain, and fever. There currently is no vaccine for hepatitis C. Interferon therapy can suppress the virus after it enters the bloodstream.

EMERGENCY CARE FOR SICK AND INJURED STUDENTS

Given the nature of the school experience, students, particularly those in elementary and middle-level grades, are going to become injured or sick while at school. Acute onset or flare-up of medical conditions, such as asthmatic attack, diabetic coma, or epileptic seizures, often occurs unexpectedly, as do unintentional injuries.

School districts should develop written policies that indicate the specific measures to be taken in such circumstances so that school personnel know what actions to take to assist their students. In order for this to occur, school staff members must be educated about the policies and understand their responsibilities.

It has been reported that many school-related injuries are not treated immediately at school. One study indicated that one in six children sent home with an injury was subsequently admitted to a health care trauma unit.[19] Failure to care for a sick or injured child while at school is inappropriate behavior. It is also inappropriate to wait until a circumstance occurs before deciding who should go to the aid of the child.

When there is a nurse available at school, he or she is normally expected to administer emergency care. If the school has a physical education teacher, it is often school policy that any injured child is to be sent to this individual. The policy of relying on a physical education specialist is unacceptable; this person should only be held responsible for his or her own students, not all the children in the school. Also, many elementary schools do not have such specialists in their buildings.

Clearly, relying on the school nurse or the physical education teacher to give first aid is not an acceptable practice. Often, the school nurse is not in the building, since many elementary and middle-level school nurses are assigned to several different buildings. Secretaries and support staff/office personnel often give emergency care to students. One study reported that the person most commonly responsible for taking care of sick or injured children at school was the office secretary.[20] This occurs as they react out of human empathy when there is no other person available to assist the injured or sick student.

School personnel often fail to administer needed care when a student is injured or becomes ill while at school because they fear being sued—a person may be found negligent for performing an act of emergency care. The important factor to remember, however, is that one should take measures that can be considered reasonable and prudent. The legal definition of *negligence* is "the omission to do something which a reasonable man . . . would do, or the doing of something which a reasonable and prudent man would not do."[21] A person can be found to be liable if he or she is negligent. However, following appropriate first-aid measures while at school should not result in a finding of negligence by a court of law.

School personnel are responsible for the health and well-being of students while the students are involved in school activities. This relationship is based upon the legal precedent of *en loco parentis,* which means that the school employee is serving in the place of the parents. A parent would be expected to come to the aid of his or her children when they are sick or injured. Failure to do so would be considered child abuse or child neglect. This legal concept of *en loco parentis* has been followed in court decisions, which have concluded that where injury does occur under the supervision of school personnel, it is important that appropriate emergency care be provided.[22]

School districts need to develop written policies that outline the measures to be taken by teachers and other school staff in cases of injury or sickness while students are under school supervision. These policies need to be developed in consultation with local medical and legal personnel and with parents. All elementary and middle-level schoolteachers should then be informed of the policies and should be expected to follow them.

Rarely is instruction in first aid a requirement for elementary or middle-school teacher certification. As a result, many schoolteachers have inadequate knowledge and skills for assisting a sick or injured child. However, due to the legal expectations and the likelihood of sickness or injury occurring each day, a prospective elementary or middle-level schoolteacher should receive appropriate instruction in first aid, cardiopulmonary resuscitation (CPR), and basic first-aid skills. It is also wise to include this instruction as a regular part of in-service and staff development programs. In this way, the classroom teacher can be kept up to date with the most current developments and changes in emergency care. This instruction can be obtained from various sources in the community; the American Red Cross is the most helpful.

Every elementary and middle-level school should also have appropriate emergency care and first-aid supplies available. This equipment is often located in the nurse's office. This is certainly acceptable if it is available to the teaching staff when needed. Such supplies should not be kept locked in cabinets where they cannot be obtained when needed during the school day. Teachers should have some first-aid supplies in their individual classrooms so that it is not necessary to leave the class unattended while caring for students' minor cuts and scratches.

SCHOOL HEALTH RECORDS

If measures are going to be taken at school to assess the health status of the schoolchild, accurate records must be kept of the findings of these screening procedures. There should be a school health record on file for every elementary and middle-level schoolchild. These records should be kept in an appropriate location that assures confidentiality yet makes them accessible to those who need access to them.

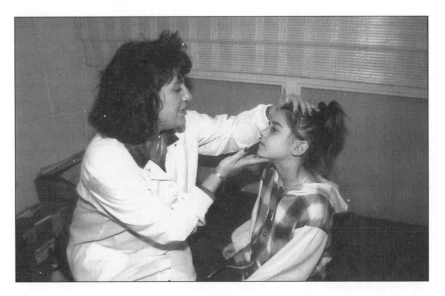

The school nurse provides help to the child who becomes sick or injured while at school.

The kind of information included in school health records varies from one locality to another. The record should be large enough to provide space for health history information, immunization records, the student's measurements during the school years, and substantive information that might be useful to the child's future teachers. If a child moves to another building within the school district or to another district, it is important that these records follow the child.

A number of questions must be answered about the school health records. Who should be responsible for maintaining the records? In many schools, this task is carried out by the school nurse. However, the time spent on record keeping interferes with the other professional activities of the school nurse. As a result, some school districts employ a health aide or health clerk, who records the information on the school health records. In some instances, school secretaries or classroom teachers have this responsibility.

Another concern has focused on who has access to the information on school health records. Certainly, it seems logical that teachers be permitted to see the records. Since passage of the Family Rights and Privacy Act in the early 1970s, parents now can see their children's school records, including health records. The school district is expected to establish guidelines and procedures for this observation.

Under provisions of this legislation, parents have the right to review and confirm the accuracy of school records. If the parents believe that the information in their child's school records is misleading or inaccurate, they may request that changes and corrections be made.

The opportunity for health records to be read, information challenged, and changes requested by parents has created concerns among school nursing and medical personnel. Schoolchildren often come to the school nurse with confidential problems. Medical professionals believe that confidentiality must be maintained in these circumstances. Included in this same category are directions by physicians to the school nurse for providing medication for students. Maintaining the confidentiality of nursing records and third-party information and records within the context of the mandate of the federal legislation has been an ongoing problem. Most school nurse organizations maintain that information of a confidential nature should be kept in a separate file apart from school health records to which parents can have access.[23]

Obviously, it is important that school districts develop written guidelines concerning school health records. A majority of states require that school districts develop such guidelines.[24] The classroom teacher should be familiar with these policy guidelines, if they are available.

SUMMARY

The health service component of the comprehensive school health program encompasses those activities designed to appraise the health status of the schoolchild and school personnel. This includes teacher observations, health examinations, and various screening activities, of which height and weight measurements, vision and hearing screening, and scoliosis screening are the most common.

Several individuals, including the classroom teacher, play a variety of roles in the school health service program. The school health nurse is the most commonly identified person employed in this component of the comprehensive school health program. This individual is prepared to perform a number of different tasks and responsibilities. In addition to numerous health care-related responsibilities, the school nurse is often involved in health counseling and management of the health conditions within the school; the school nurse is also helpful in the health education activities of the school. With the increase of medically fragile children in the schools, the school nurse and the classroom teacher have become more involved in the medical management of these children while they are at school.

Several procedures are taken as part of the school health-service program designed to protect the school community against communicable diseases. The most commonly mandated activity within elementary and middle-level schools is assuring that all enrolled students are completely immunized for the common childhood diseases. Every state has mandates for immunization prior to a child's school enrollment. The most commonly required immunizations include diphtheria, pertussis, tetanus, polio, measles, rubella, and mumps. Protection of both children and school personnel from hepatitis is an increasing concern.

The possibility of students being injured or becoming sick while at school is high. The school must be prepared to provide the appropriate care for students at these times. This includes having appropriate guidelines for how the situation is to be handled.

Keeping useful records concerning the health status of children is part of the school health service program. These records should be available for school personnel involved with each child, particularly the classroom teacher.

DISCUSSION QUESTIONS

1. Explain the different patterns of employment of school nurses in the nation's schools.

2. What are the basic features and differences between the school-based and school-linked health center?

3. What are some examples of ways in which teacher observations can assist in identifying potential health problems of school-age children?

4. What is meant by the concept of school health appraisals?

5. What are some of the components that should be a part of a health examination?

6. What indications of hearing and visual deviations from normal may an elementary and/or middle-level schoolteacher be able to note?

7. Name and briefly explain the function of the various anatomical and physiological structures of the eye and the ear.

8. Explain the characteristics of conjunctivitis and explain what measures can be taken to treat this condition.

9. What are several factors that result in trachoma?

10. What measures should be taken when a student has a foreign object on the eye?

11. Explain the difference between myopia and hyperopia.

12. What is astigmatism?

13. What are the advantages of the use of the Snellen Eye Examination for use in school vision-screening programs?

14. What are the basic characteristics of the two different types of sound?

15. Explain the difference between air and bone conduction testing.

16. What is scoliosis?

17. What procedures can the classroom teacher take to screen for scoliosis?

18. What medical treatment is available for scoliosis?

19. What are the immunizations that are usually required for school enrollment?

20. Why is rubella a particularly dangerous childhood disease?

21. What are the differences among hepatitis A, hepatitis B, and hepatitis C?

22. Why is vaccination with the hepatitis B vaccine particularly important for classroom teachers and school personnel?

23. What is the responsibility of the classroom teacher regarding care for a sick or injured child in the school setting?

24. Explain why there are increasing numbers of medically fragile children in schools today.

25. Explain the impact of the Family Rights and Privacy Act on school health record keeping.

26. Discuss the concern of school nurses about school health record keeping.

ENDNOTES

1. Donna White, "A Study of Current School Nurse Practice Activities," *Journal of School Health* 55, no. 2 (February, 1985): 52–56.

2. *Technology-Dependent Children: Hospital Versus Home Care* (Washington, DC: U.S. Office of Technology Assessment, 1987), n.p.

3. Susan Hall Parker, "Early Detection of Growth Disorders," *Journal of School Nursing* 8, no. 3 (October 1992): 30–41.

4. C. Lovetato et al., *School Health in America: An Assessment of State Policies to Protect and Improve the Health of Students,* 5th ed. (Kent, OH: American School Health Association, 1989), 11.

5. Helen L. Brajkovich, "Dr. Snellen's 20/20: The Development and Use of the Eye Chart," *Journal of School Health* 50, no. 8 (October 1980): 472–474.

6. Arlene Evans, "Color-Vision Deficiency: What Does It Mean?" *Journal of School Nursing* 8, no. 4 (December 1992): 8.

7. David S. Travis, "Color Vision Testing Can Eliminate Misdiagnosis of Cognitive Disability," *Journal of School Health* 58, no. 7 (September 1988): 265.

8. Lovetato, *School Health in America,* 12.

9. National Center for Health Statistics, Centers for Disease Control and Prevention, "Top Ten Leading Causes of Death, 1992," *Chronic Disease Notes and Reports* 6, no. 2 (Fall 1993): 1.

10. Lovetato, *School Health in America,* 15.

11. Dean F. Miller, *School Health Programs: Their Basis in Law* (New York: A. S. Barnes and Company, 1972), 90–101.

12. *Jacobson v. Commonwealth of Massachusetts,* 197 U.S. 11, 255 S. Ct. 358 (1905).

13. Department of Health and Human Services, Public Health Service, *Healthy People 2000: National Health Promotion and Disease Prevention Objectives for the Nation* (Washington, DC: U.S. Government Printing Office, 1991), 52.

14. Lovetato, *School Health in America,* 9.

15. Department of Health and Human Services, *Healthy People 2000,* 514.

16. Centers for Disease Control and Prevention, "Reported Vaccine-Preventable Diseases," 58.

17. Department of Health and Human Services, *Healthy People 2000,* 513.

18. Elizabeth Anthony Mattey, "Hepatitis B Vaccine: For School Staff at Risk," *Journal of School Nursing* 13, no. 1 (February, 1997): 4.

19. Ken Allen, Jana Ball, and Bryna Helfer. "Preventing and Managing Childhood Emergencies in Schools," *Journal of School Nursing* 14, no. 1 (February, 1998): 22.

20. Ibid., 22.

21. Henry Campbell Black, *Black's Law Dictionary* (St. Paul, MN.: West Publishing Co., 1951), 1184.

22. *Pirkle v. Oakdale Union Grammar School District, City of Oakland, County of Stanislaus,* 253 P. 2d 1 (Calif., 1953).

23. Nadine Schwab and Mary Gelfman, "School Health Records: Nursing Practice and the Law," *School Nurse* 7, no. 2 (April 1991): 26–34.

24. Lovetato, *School Health in America,* 14.

SUGGESTED READINGS

Appelboom, Tina M. "A History of Vision Screening." *Journal of School Health* 55, no. 4 (April 1985): 138–141.

Beilenson, Peter, and John Santelli. "An Urban School-Based Voluntary MMR Booster Immunization Program." *Journal of School Health* 62, no. 2 (February 1992): 71–73.

Boyer-Chuanroong, Lynda and others. "Immunizations from Ground Zero: Lessons Learned in Urban Middle Schools," *Journal of School Health* 67, no. 7 (September, 1997): 269–272.

Committee on Infectious Diseases. "Recommended Childhood Immunization Schedule—United States, January–December 1998" *Pediatrics* 101, no. 1 (January, 1998): 156–157.

Cowell, Julia Muennich. "Is the School Nurse a Nurse? *The American School Board Journal* 185, no. 2 (February 1998): 45–46.

Essex, Nathan et al. "Handle With Care." *The American School Board Journal* 181, no. 3 (March 1994): 50–53.

Evans, Arlene. "Color Vision Deficiency: What Does It Mean?" *Journal of School Nursing* 8, no. 4 (December 1992): 6–10.

Fredrickson, Doren D., and others. "Immunization Compliance Among Public and Private School Children." *Journal of School Health* 67, no. 2 (February 1997): 75–77.

Graff, J. Carolyn, and Marilyn Mulligan Ault. "Guidelines for Working with Students Having Special Health Needs." *Journal of School Health* 63, no. 8 (October 1993): 335–338.

Gross, Elaine J., and Marian Passannante. "Educating School Nurses to Care for HIV-Infected Children in School." *Journal of School Health* 63, no. 7 (September 1993): 307–311.

Koenning, Gaye M. et al. "Health Source Delivery to Students with Special Health Care Needs in Texas Public Schools." *Journal of School Health* 65, no. 4 (April 1995): 119–123.

Kosarchyn, Chrystyna. "School Nurses' Perceptions of the Health Needs of Hispanic Elementary School Children." *Journal of School Nursing* 9, no. 1 (February 1993): 37–43.

Lavin, Alison T. et al. "School Health Services in the Age of AIDS." *Journal of School Health* 64, no. 1 (January 1994): 27–31.

Mattey, Elizabeth Anthony. "Hepatitis B Vaccine: For School Staff at Risk," *Journal of School Nursing* 13, no. 1 (February 1997): 4–8.

National Association of School Nurses. *Hearing Screening Guidelines for School Nurses,* Scarboro, ME: NASN, 1993.

Parker, Susan Hall. "The School Nurse's Role: Early Detection of Growth Disorders." *Journal of School Nursing* 8, no. 3 (October 1992): 30–51.

Policy Studies Associates, Inc. "Protecting the Privacy of Student Education Records," *Journal of School Health* 67, no. 4 (April 1997): 139–140.

Schwab, Nadine, and Mary Gelfman. "School Health Records: Nursing Practice and the Law." *Journal of School Nursing* 7, no. 2 (April 1991): 26–34.

Thiel, Thelma King. "Viral Hepatitis: The Quiet Disease," *USA Today* 126, no. 2634 (March 1998): 53–54.

Todaro, Ann Witt et al. "A Model for Training Community-Based Providers for Children with Special Health Care Needs." *Journal of School Health* 63, no. 6 (August 1993): 262–265.

Williams, Richard A. et al. "Evaluation of Access to Care and Medical and Behavioral Outcomes in a School-Based Intervention Program for Attention-Deficit Hyperactivity Disorder." *Journal of School Health* 63, no. 7 (September 1993): 294–297.

INTERNET INFORMATION

Advocates for Youth (formerly Center for Population Options)

Agency of support for school-based and school-linked health clinics

www.advocatesforyouth.org

Immunization

American Academy of Pediatrics

Immunization schedule as recommended by the American Academy of Pediatrics

www.aap.org/family/parents/immunize.htm

Centers for Disease Control and Prevention National Immunization Program

www. cdc.gov/nip/

Scoliosis

Scoliosis Research Society

Provision of information about scoliosis, glossary of terms, and educational material about scoliosis

www.srg.org

National Scoliosis Foundation

Provision of information about scoliosis, resources about the condition; provides interactive capabilities relating to scoliosis

www.scoliosis.org

The Tools of Teaching

Section II begins by reviewing such foundational elements as learning styles, principles of learning developmentally appropriate practice, and the learning domains. The National Health Education Standards also are reviewed as they relate to the health education curriculum. In addition, this section reviews the "hardware of instruction," which includes textbooks, computers, the Internet, and instructional television as they relate to health education. Last, general teaching techniques, instructional models, working with parents, and managing controversy are addressed.

THE INSTRUCTIONAL PROGRAM

Comprehensive School Health Education

O U T L I N E

INTRODUCTION

The responsibility for curriculum development in the United States rests with the local school district. In this way, planning, development, and implementation of curricula can reflect the unique interests and standards of each community. As a result, the body of professional education literature can be interpreted in the context of local needs by informed teachers, supervisors, and administrators.

While there is no federal constitutional mandate for operation of an educational system, the individual states and thousands of individual school districts throughout the nation have been charged with the responsibility for:

- What is taught in their schools,
- What materials are used,
- Who does the teaching, and
- How necessary funding for these activities is provided.

Historically, the American public has been very protective of the notion of local control over its education enterprise. Centralized federal initiatives have been considered by most people to be an interference with local and states' rights. As a result, many people have opposed efforts to impose national education guidelines or national testing practices.

With increasing concern about perceptions concerning the poor quality of American public education, however, many people have become mobilized with an agenda to restructure or reform public education. A number of national education commission reports have called for the establishment of national education standards to be met by all elementary and secondary school students. While such outcry has not resulted in a centralized governmental approach to the planning of health curricula, readers are urged to review information contained in chapter 1 concerning the National Health Education Standards.

While health education usually is not considered to be an important element in the education reform movement, the emerging body of literature that links student health risks to compromised academic outcomes (see chapter 1) confirms that a commitment to student health must be part of any agenda focused on improving academic outcomes. Specifically, many of the goals embedded in plans to restructure schools are consistent with the underpinnings of *effective,* comprehensive school health education, including:

1. A focus on the whole child,
2. Identification of clear goals and student outcomes (making healthy choices and avoiding risk behaviors),
3. Use of relevant curricula that focus on increasing health knowledge, examining health attitudes, and practicing health enhancing skills,
4. Student-centered teaching methods that reinforce active, hands-on, and cooperative learning,
5. Placing a priority on critical thinking/higher-order thinking among students,
6. Teacher training to ensure effectiveness,
7. Formalizing the critical element of parent engagement,
8. Collaboration within the school and between the school and the community, and
9. Establishment and refinement of the Coordinated School Health Program as a way to reinforce consistent health promotion messages throughout the school and community.[1]

Importantly, the commitment to local control over education reinforces the diversity in academic activities in American public schools. The processes of organizing and planning the curricular scope and sequence differ significantly across school districts. This has been the case with curriculum development in health education. Rarely is there consensus among school administrators, teachers, community leaders, and parents in identifying developmentally appropriate health topics (substance abuse, nutrition, sexual health promotion, personal and social skills, and violence risk reduction). Further, once appropriate topics have been selected, additional conflict can arise about the health education instructional scope and sequence.

As a way to provide baseline data, a 1994 national study was sponsored by the Centers for Disease Control and Prevention. Findings from this survey confirmed that all states employ a professional responsible for school health education. In addition, the School Health Policies and Programs Study (SHPPS) confirmed that *nearly* all states require that schools provide some health instruction at the elementary, middle, and high school levels.[2]

Unfortunately, however, SHPPS revealed that it is uncommon for state departments of education to provide specific direction about exact content matters to be covered in designated grade levels at the local level. It is far more common for state education agencies to limit their involvement in local instructional practices. Typically, this commitment to limited involvement in local district practice translates to participation only in such limited activities as *recommending* curricula, guidelines, or frameworks that may dovetail with prescribed tests of student proficiency. In some cases, state education agencies prescribe minimum time allotments for health instruction.

As a result, local education professionals are left essentially on their own to develop curriculum materials. It is not surprising that SHPPS revealed that there is a great disparity in health education programming among the nation's school districts. This study confirmed that 97% of middle/junior and senior high schools require some instruction about health topics. Importantly, only 44% of the required health courses in middle/junior high schools last for one semester, and only 20% of American high schools require a full year of such instruction. The findings from SHPPS summarized that 90% of schools require some instruction in alcohol and other drug risk reduction, 84% include instructional activities about nutrition and healthy eating, and 80% require human sexuality concepts to be addressed, but only 78% include a required instructional focus on physical activity and fitness.[3]

In addition to variability in instructional time and content coverage, it is common for local professionals to struggle when establishing protocol for coordinating health instruction across grade levels. Scope and sequence models that are common in other disciplines often are not applied to health education curriculum development projects. All too often, the material that is covered in a classroom is determined by the knowledge and interests of the individual teacher. If a teacher is particularly interested in nutrition, weight management, and dietary behaviors, these and other related subjects are likely to receive major instructional emphasis. Conversely, those topics with which the teacher has little interest or expertise can be slighted or even omitted. This problem is compounded by the fact that many elementary and middle-level classroom teachers have very weak professional preparation in health education. Often as a result of limited college or university attention to empowering preservice teachers to manage child health issues, these professionals have neither the knowledge nor the confidence to plan effective lessons about a range of developmentally appropriate health topics.

The content of health lessons for elementary and middle-level students also can be influenced by the availability and quality of textbooks. Many school districts do not purchase health texts for younger students. In addition, under the auspices of correlated approaches to instruction, it is common for publishers to attempt to blend health issues into a textbook series that has been developed with primary emphasis on another content area. Often, science texts are marketed as a less-expensive way for a district to address two content areas and purchase only one series of books. Another problem can arise when less-experienced teachers turn to the health book as the sole source of content to be presented to students. Under such circumstances, current or potentially controversial information may never reach students. In this way, textbook authors and publishers can exert significant and sometimes inappropriate influence over the health content to which students are exposed.

These practices can lead to overlap and duplication in the health instructional program. One of students' major criticisms of health instruction is that they were taught the "same thing" previous years. In addition, elementary and middle-level teachers often fail to individualize health instruction to meet students' abilities or interests. All of these situations point to the need for a systematic approach to assessing student needs, planning and implementing developmentally appropriate instructional strategies, and evaluating the effectiveness of the school health curriculum.

One important way to begin to address the problems associated with developing effective curriculum and instructional protocol in health education is to review important elements from the more general body of literature about how students understand and learn. A review of selected issues from education research can be very revealing for local parents, teachers, and administrators who are involved in making decisions about their local health education course of study.

LESSONS FROM THE EDUCATION LITERATURE

In recent years, many educational innovations, including school councils, parent involvement task forces, continuous improvement models, and authentic assessment protocol, have been proposed as ways to improve the quality of instruction and maximize academic success for American students. Many approaches, including those that place students in roles of active or cooperative learners, have been published in the education literature. A great deal of energy has been devoted to developing and refining standards to frame curriculum development, to providing parameters for assessment, and to serving as a foundation for improved instruction. Unfortunately, many proposals to reform education are focused on political, financial, procedural, or technical matters, and not on the fundamental elements of educational quality. Even the highest standards, the most rigorous proficiency testing protocol, or the most academically sound curriculum models can serve to undermine meaningful learning unless such activities are planned and implemented with specific attention to their impact on improving academic outcomes.[4]

Importantly, all educational activities should be directed toward maximizing *authentic* forms of student learning. Newmann and Wehlage use the term "authentic" to distinguish achievement that is significant and meaningful from achievement that is trivial or useless.[5] In specific, authentic achievement is more likely to occur in situations in which:

1. Students construct meaning and produce knowledge,
2. Students use disciplined inquiry to construct meaning, and
3. Student work is directed toward discussion, products, and/or performances that have value or meaning beyond the school.[6]

Teachers and administrators who want to "raise the bar" on their quality of instruction are encouraged to evaluate all instructional activities in the context of five criteria or standards that have been linked to authentic instruction. Following is a list of questions and a clarifying discussion to help with this process:

1. **To what degree are students encouraged to use higher-order thinking?**
   Lower-order thinking occurs when students are asked to receive or recite facts. In addition, they may be called upon to apply rules though repetitive experiences. By contrast, *higher-order thinking* requires students to manipulate, synthesize, explain, or draw conclusions about ideas. The goal of this process is for the student to transform the original meaning of an idea. While higher-order thinking includes the possibility of uncertainty, it implies that students will be engaged in solving problems and discovering new meanings that have applicability or relevance.

2. **What is the depth of knowledge included in the lesson?**
   Depth of knowledge refers to the substantive character of ideas included in a lesson and the level of understanding that students demonstrate as they work with these ideas. Knowledge is characterized as thin or superficial if it does not deal with significant concepts within a discipline. Superficiality results when students have only a trivial understanding of important concepts or they are required to cover large amounts of fragmented information. Knowledge is considered to be deep or thick when it focuses on developmentally appropriate central ideas about a topic or discipline. Students work with deep knowledge when they make distinctions, develop arguments, and construct explanations while covering fewer, but

TABLE 3.1	Six Key Elements that Characterize Understanding

When we truly understand, we:

- Can explain: By providing thorough, justifiable accounts of facts, data, or phenomena
- Can interpret: By telling meaningful stories, providing meaningful personal dimensions to ideas or events, or making issues accessible through images or analogies
- Can apply: By using and adapting what we know in the context of diverse settings
- Have perspective: By demonstrating the capacity to see the "big picture" and other points of view through critical eyes
- Can empathize: By finding value in what others might find odd or implausible
- Have self-knowledge: By demonstrating awareness of personal attributes that shape or limit our capacity for understanding

Source: G. Wiggins and J. McTighe, *Understanding by Design* (Alexandria, VA: Association for Supervision and Curriculum Development, 1998).

systematically connected, topics.[7] To this end, teachers are invited to examine table 3.1, which clarifies six key elements that confirm true understanding.[8]

3. **To what extent do the instructional activities and class content have meaning beyond the confines of the classroom?**

Many class activities include work that has no impact on others or serves only to certify that students have been compliant with the norms of formal schooling. In this case, the educational activities are important only as a foundation for success in school. By contrast, lessons gain *authenticity* when an effort is made to connect instruction to the larger context in which students live. This is accomplished when students address real-world problems, or incorporate personal experiences into learning activities as a framework for understanding or applying knowledge.[9]

4. **How much class time is involved in substantive conversation about the subject?**

It is common classroom practice for teachers to engage students in patterns of classroom conversation that are less than sophisticated. Typically, interaction between students and teachers consists of a lecture, during which the teacher delivers a planned body of information. This part of the lesson is followed by a recitation period in which students respond to predetermined questions in pursuit of short, "correct" answers. This process is the oral equivalent of short-answer or fill-in-the-blank test items. By contrast, high-level, substantive conversation is framed by three characteristics:

- Conversation is focused on higher-order ideas about the topic, including making distinctions, applying ideas, and raising questions rather than simply reporting facts, definitions, or procedures,
- Ideas are shared in a forum that is not scripted— students are encouraged to explain themselves,

ask questions, or respond to comments of classmates, and

- Conversation builds improved collective understanding of lesson themes or topics.

5. **Is there a high level of social support for the achievements of peers?**

Low social support for achievement is demonstrated in classrooms in which the behaviors or comments of teachers or students tend to discourage effort, voluntary participation, or engagement of all students in the learning process. High-level social support is evident in classrooms in which teachers and classmates share high expectations for all students, communicate mutual respect, and reinforce the need for everyone to take risks and work hard to master challenging work.[10]

Professionals who review this information are reminded that authentic instruction is not tied to any specific content area, learning activity, or teaching method. Rather, it is related to the extent to which any activity— new or old, in or out of school—engages students in using their minds to confront issues and solve problems that have meaning or value beyond simple measures of school performance.

Pigg has summarized a collection of ideas from the bodies of literature in learning theory, behavioral psychology, and education into a list of simple conceptual statements about the nature of student learning. Teachers, administrators, and parents are reminded that students learn best when:

1. Information or skills seem relevant to them,
2. Students are actively involved in the learning process,
3. Learning experiences are organized,
4. Learning experiences enable students to derive their own conclusions,
5. Students become emotionally involved with or committed to the topic,

Students learn best when they are actively engaged in the learning process.

6. Students can interact with others,
7. Information can be put to immediate use or skills can be practiced rather than simply discussed,
8. Students recognize the reason or value of the information or tasks to be mastered,
9. Positive teacher-learner relationships are cultivated, and
10. A variety of teaching methods and learning strategies are employed.[11]

It is important to remember that regardless of district grouping practices, all classrooms are comprised of heterogeneous collections of students with regard to ability, interest, background, or health status. In this regard, classroom activities must be diverse if they are to help set students up for success. In this context, Gardner has asserted that intelligence is difficult to reduce to a single number or "IQ" score. Rather, research has confirmed that intelligence has more to do with the capacity of a student to solve problems and fashion products in a natural setting. In this spirit, teachers are encouraged to look to the extensive bodies of research focused on learning styles and Multiple Intelligence theory as a foundation for applying learning theories in specific classrooms. As a practical foundation for planning to meet a range of student needs and interests, table 3.2 presents a brief description and checklist for assessing Gardner's "Intelligences" in students.[12–13]

THE STATE OF THE ART IN HEALTH EDUCATION

Curriculum Recommendations

In 1983, the National Professional School Health Education Organizations defined health education as including several important elements. This group asserted that school health education programs should be undergirded by a planned and well-evaluated sequential curriculum developed for students in grades pre-kindergarten through 12 that is based on:

1. Students' needs,
2. Current health concepts, and
3. Societal issues.

Further, instruction should motivate health maintenance and promote well-being, and not focus only on the prevention of disease. Also, health education activities should enable students to expand their knowledge base, examine health attitudes, and practice decision-making skills and personal responsibility for health maintenance. Finally, a Comprehensive Health Education program of study was defined to integrate the physical, mental, emotional, and social dimensions of health as the basis for the study of ten important health content areas, including: (1) community health, (2) consumer health, (3) environmental health, (4) family life, (5) growth and development, (6) nutritional health, (7) personal health, (8) prevention and control of disease, (9) safety and accident prevention, and (10) substance use and abuse.[14]

As discussed in chapter 1, this list of minimally recommended content areas has been updated by the Centers for Disease Control and Prevention to focus on behaviors most directly related to the leading causes of illness and death in the United States. In this way, schools with limited instructional time for health education are advised to focus academic activities on: (1) nutrition, (2) physical fitness, (3) intentional and unintentional injury, (4) tobacco, (5) alcohol and other drugs, and (6) reproductive health promotion.

Importantly, evidence has emerged to support the effectiveness of such a comprehensive approach to health education. Research suggests that as years of health instruction increase, so does student knowledge, reflections of healthy attitudes, and practice of health-enhancing behaviors. Specifically, the following behavior changes were noted between students with 1 year of health education and their counterparts who completed 3 years of similar study:

- 43% of students with 1 year of instruction reported that they drank alcohol "sometimes or more often," while 33% of their counterparts with 3 years of education reported the same behavior,
- 13% of students with less instruction reported having taken drugs, while 6% reported similar behavior following more instructional time, and
- 72% of students with less health education reported participation in exercise behavior outside of school, while 80% of their counterparts with more instruction reported participating in such exercise behaviors.[15]

In addition to its potential to promote health enhancing student behavior, recent research by the Centers for Disease Control and Prevention has confirmed that health education can contribute to national productivity through cost containment. Estimates suggest that for

TABLE 3.2	**A Checklist for Assessing the "Multiple Intelligences" of Students**

LINGUISTIC INTELLIGENCE—The capacity to use and understand language

Does the student:
- Write better than average?
- Have a good vocabulary for age?
- Enjoy reading and/or word games?
- Tell tall tales, stories or jokes?
- Appreciate tongue twisters or nonsense rhymes?

LOGICAL-MATHEMATICAL INTELLIGENCE— The ability to use numbers effectively or demonstrate sensitivity to logical patterns and relationships

Does the student:
- Enjoy logic puzzles or brain teasers?
- Enjoy math class or math computer games?
- Find pleasure in organizing things in categories or hierarchies?
- Have a good sense of cause-effect for age?
- Compute math problems quickly in head?

SPATIAL INTELLIGENCE—The capacity to perceive and represent visual or spatial ideas or to orient self in space

Does the student:
- Report clear visual images?
- Read maps, charts, and diagrams more easily than text?
- Get more out of pictures than text when reading?
- Enjoy art activities?
- Draw figures that are advanced for age?

BODY-KINESTHETIC INTELLIGENCE—Expertise in using the whole body to express ideas, feelings, or to produce or transform objects

Does the student:
- Excel in one or more sports?
- Mimic the gestures or mannerisms of others?
- Take things apart and put them back together?
- Move, tap, or fidget when seated for a period of time?
- Demonstrate good fine-motor coordination or skill in a craft?

MUSICAL INTELLIGENCE—The capacity to perceive, discriminate, transform, and express musical forms

Does the student:
- Remember melodies of songs?
- Sing or play a musical instrument?
- Express sensitivity to environmental noises or anomalies in music (off-key)?
- Unconsciously hum to self?
- Tap rhythmically while working?

INTERPERSONAL INTELLIGENCE—The ability to perceive and make distinctions in the moods, intentions, and motivations of others

Does the student:
- Enjoy socializing with peers?
- Demonstrate leadership skills?
- Have a strong sense of empathy for others?
- Have others seek out his/her company?
- Appear to be "street-smart?"

INTRAPERSONAL INTELLIGENCE—Self-knowledge and the ability to act on that knowledge

Does the student:
- Display a sense of independence and strong will?
- Have a realistic sense of strengths and weaknesses?
- Play or work well alone?
- Prefer working alone to collaboration with others?
- Accurately express feelings?

NATURALISTIC INTELLIGENCE—Sensitivity to features in the natural world or the ability to discriminate among living things

Does the student:
- Recognize patterns in nature?
- Understand characteristics of different species?
- Demonstrate interest and ability in classification of objects?
- Recognize and name natural things?
- Clarify cultural artifacts?

Source: T. Armstrong, *Multiple Intelligences in the Classroom* (Alexandria, VA: Association for Supervision and Curriculum Development, 1994); C. Checkley, "The First Seven and the Eighth," *Educational Leadership* (September 1997).

every dollar spent on *quality* school health education, society saves more than $13 in direct (medical treatment, addiction counseling, alcohol-related motor vehicle injuries, and drug-related crime) and indirect costs, such as lost productivity associated with premature death and social welfare expenses related to teen pregnancy.[16]

As a result, it should not be surprising that there is broad agreement that schools share an important responsibility for providing health education for children and youth. In 1994, The Gallup Organization conducted a national study that revealed that a majority of school

administrators, families, and students support comprehensive school health education programming. A majority of surveyed parents and administrators asserted that adolescents should receive more health instruction than most districts offer. Interestingly, 55% of student subjects in this study reported the belief that schools should spend more instructional time on health education than on such content areas as English, math, and science.[17]

Importantly, research has identified a number of attributes that distinguish common approaches to health instruction from effective health education curricula.

These findings suggest that the characteristics of effective health education curricula are consistent with previously discussed educational research. Lohrmann and Wooley have summarized that effective health education curricula:

- Are grounded in research and framed by theory,
- Include basic, accurate, and developmentally appropriate information,
- Incorporate interactive, experiential activities that engage learners,
- Provide students with the opportunity to practice relevant social skills,
- Examine the impact of social and media forces on health behaviors,
- Strengthen individual values and group norms that promote health enhancing behaviors,
- Include sufficient instructional time for students to gain information and practice skills, and
- Contain a staff development component to maintain teacher effectiveness.[18]

In 1990, the U.S. Department of Education funded a project to develop criteria for Comprehensive Health Education Curricula. Teachers, administrators, and parents involved in curriculum writing or evaluation projects are invited to review the criteria developed by the funded project professionals. These criteria are summarized in table 3.3.[19]

Regardless of the final form of the local district curriculum document, these valuable materials formalize a specific scope and sequence of content, and in some cases identify suggested learning activities approved by the local board of education for classroom use. Teachers recognize that, just as with other curriculum areas, the formally developed health education curriculum document provides direction for planning meaningful learning experiences for students.

Recommendations for Classroom Instruction

Once the district curriculum writing or selection committee has completed its work, it becomes the job of classroom teachers to translate elements from that general document into teaching strategies and learning activities that will meet the unique needs of their specific students. Unfortunately, few guidelines provide time-management cues for elementary and middle-grade teachers. As a result, these professionals are faced with the challenge of organizing developmentally appropriate learning experiences within significant time constraints.

As a starting point for lesson planning, Seffrin has summarized important characteristics that are common to those teaching strategies and learning activities that are most effective. Teachers seeking to build lessons that are most meaningful are encouraged to:

- Use discovery approaches that include sufficient opportunities for "hands-on" experiences,
- Include learning stations or centers, cooperative learning, and other small-group activities,
- Collaborate with colleagues to develop cross-age and peer tutoring experiences,
- Focus instruction on positive rather than punitive approaches that emphasize the importance and value of good health,
- Include an emphasis on the affective domain with opportunities to build self-esteem and establish self-efficacy, and
- Provide frequent opportunities for students to demonstrate, practice, and master the skills needed to act on health enhancing decisions.[20]

In the context of these recommendations, research has confirmed that there is no direct link between having accurate health knowledge and an increased likelihood of participation in healthy behaviors.[21] Consequently, the National Health Education Standards provide strong support for a skill-based approach to health education. In addition, the following steps have been identified for teachers to help students master health skills:

1. Introduce the skill,
2. Identify the steps involved in developing the skill,
3. Model the elements of the skill,
4. Practice the skill, and
5. Provide feedback and reinforcement.[22]

Developmentally Appropriate Practice

Regardless of the age of students or whether a lesson is focused on increasing knowledge, helping students examine their health attitudes, or practicing skills to live healthier lives, developmentally appropriate practice criteria should serve as the foundation for translating all recommendations in the district curriculum document into sound health education classroom practice. Researchers confirm that "the use of developmentally appropriate practices is one of the best current strategies to ensure that individual children will have opportunities for engaging in meaningful and interesting learning on a daily basis."[23]

Age-Appropriate Activities

The National Association for the Education of Young Children reminds all teachers that planning developmentally appropriate learning activities for any content area includes two important dimensions: strategies that respond to *age-appropriate* and *individually appropriate* student characteristics. As a foundation, teachers in elementary and middle grades are advised to focus their lesson-planning energies on developing age-appropriate activities for students. Such teaching strategies evolve from the research in human development that confirms the

TABLE 3.3	Criteria for Comprehensive Health Education Curricula

1. Goals and Objectives:
   (Goals are the long-range results toward which the curriculum is directed, while objectives list student abilities at the end of the program)

   - Are goals and objectives *realistically* attainable?
   - Do goals and objectives relate to the identified needs of the district?
   - Are the objectives well-defined and measurable?
   - Do the objectives focus on a positive approach to health promotion?
   - Does the program include a balance of cognitive, affective, and behavioral objectives?
   - Do the objectives reflect an appropriate and comprehensive scope and sequence across the grade levels?
   - Are both long- and short-term objectives included?

2. Content:
   (Subject matter included in the curriculum)

   - Does the curriculum contain appropriate continuity, scope, and sequence across the grade levels?
   - Is the content based on the health needs and interests of all students?
   - Is there evidence of cross-curricular or integrated instructional approaches to reinforce the health education program?
   - Does the content address the perspectives of diverse cultural and ethnic groups?
   - Does the content focus at minimum on the six CDC problem priority areas?

3. Teaching Strategies:
   (Activities or strategies used by *the teacher* to facilitate student learning)

   - Does the curriculum rely on a variety of instructional methodologies (simulation, small-group activities, inquiry, cooperative learning, etc.)?
   - Do the instructional methods take into consideration the cultural and ethnic values, customs, and practices of the community?
   - Are teaching strategies interesting and rewarding?
   - Are the instructional strategies developmentally appropriate?
   - Are teaching strategies based on principles of authentic instruction?

4. Learning Activities:
   (Activities in which *students participate* to achieve curricular objectives)

   - Do learning activities enable students to practice skills identified in the National Health Education Standards?
   - Does the curriculum include meaningful homework activities?
   - Do homework assignments provide opportunities for parental engagement?
   - Do activities require higher-order thinking?

5. Materials:
   (Items included in the curricular package to be used by teachers and students)

   - Does the curriculum include the use of effective materials beyond the text (manipulatives, media, learning centers, etc.)?
   - Are materials developmentally appropriate and adaptable for students with special needs?
   - Do materials reinforce program objectives?
   - Are materials available and easy to use?
   - Can materials be updated?
   - Is reference and support available for teachers?

6. Time:
   (Amount of time devoted to implementing the curriculum)

   - Is sufficient time available to meet curricular objectives?
   - Does the amount of time necessary for each lesson fit the scheduling needs of the teacher or school?
   - Is a minimum of 50 hours of instructional time per year allocated for health instruction?
   - Does the curriculum include time for review, reinforcement, and extension of concepts?

7. Evaluation:
   (Student assessments during implementation of the curriculum)

   - Does the curriculum provide teachers with a means to assess student attainment of objectives?
   - Are student assessments linked to all curricular objectives?
   - Is student assessment focused on knowledge, attitudes, and behaviors?
   - Do process evaluations serve as the foundation for revising the curriculum?

(continued)

TABLE 3.3	Criteria for Comprehensive Health Education Curricula *(continued)*
8. Cultural Equity: (Materials reflect cultural equity when diverse populations are represented)	• Are materials free of demeaning labels or stereotypes? • Do instructional materials represent the contributions of diverse ethnic professionals? • Are different cultural customs depicted in a positive light? • Are minorities represented in a range of socioeconomic groups and physical and mental activities? • Are traditional and nontraditional families depicted?
9. Sex Equity: (Balance of gender, roles depicted in traditional and nontraditional settings)	• Do materials contain illustrations of both males and females in traditional and nontraditional roles? • Is language free of gender bias or demeaning labels (doctor = "he," nurse = "she," mailman vs. mailcarrier, etc.)? • Do materials portray both men and women involved in parenting activities? • Do materials show equal representation of men and women involved in mental and physical activities?

Source: J. English, A. Sancho, D. Lloyd-Kalkin et al., *Criteria for Comprehensive Health Education Curricula* (Southwest Regional Laboratory: funded by USDOE, 1990).

universal and predictable sequences of growth and change that occur in the physical, emotional, social, and intellectual or cognitive dimensions of all children.[24] Table 3.4 identifies common growth and development characteristics and the corresponding needs of students in kindergarten through grade 9 that can serve as a foundation for age-appropriate practice.[25]

Knowledgeable teachers can use the general information about the typical developmental sequences of their students in table 3.4 as a foundation for preparing the learning environment and for planning appropriate and effective learning activities.[26] Such a starting place is helpful for teachers who have had limited contact with a particular group of students, such as when the teacher is developing health-education lessons early in the school year. Further, age-appropriate cues are helpful for teachers as they introduce new, potentially emotionally charged, or controversial health education topics.

Individually Appropriate Activities

As teachers become more familiar with students and their likely reactions to the range of issues in health education, they are encouraged to build *individually appropriate learning activities* into lessons. Particularly with regard to child and young adolescent health behavior, teachers should remember to consider the potential impact of the unique personalities, learning styles, and family backgrounds on student learning. Students also have different patterns and timing in personal growth that can influence their reactions and ability to integrate health education concepts into daily behavior.[27] In deciding how to use instructional time effectively, in relation to both age and individually appropriate activities, the teacher should

consider the following attributes of specific groups of students:

• *Physical* abilities and limitations,
• *Mental or cognitive* attributes, including such variables as time on task, attention span, and interests,
• *Social* interaction patterns with family, friends, teachers, and influential others,
• *Emotional* characteristics and reaction patterns, and
• *Language* skills and attributes as a foundation for understanding and communication.[28]

It is important to note, however, that many variables that are not grounded in developmentally appropriate practice criteria can influence the district curriculum development process. This is particularly true of health instruction. Factors such as teacher expertise or comfort levels, the priorities included in a selected textbook series, community traditions, social or cultural values, or parental desires can play a significant role in the development and adoption of the course of study. For example, in many communities, health teachers face pressure to take an approach to tobacco, alcohol, and other drug prevention that is based on the notion that children are "never too young" to receive unconditional messages about abstinence and peer refusal concerning the use of all drug products.

Such an approach might be justifiable with older students, based on their developmental attributes. However, the National Association for the Education of Young Children reminds health educators working with all age groups of students that developmentally appropriate information and learning strategies should serve as the foundation for classroom practice. Instructional time is limited and must be focused on meeting age and individually appropriate student needs. For this reason, tobacco, alcohol, and other

TABLE 3.4	**Growth and Development Characteristics and Corresponding Needs of Students in Kindergarten through Ninth Grade (Ages 5 through 14 Years Old): A Foundation for Age-Appropriate Practice**

Attributes of Students in Grades K through 3 (5–8 Years Old)

PHYSICAL CHARACTERISTICS

Growth relatively slow.

Increase in large muscle coordination, beginning of development of small muscle control.

Bones growing.

Nose grows larger.

Permanent teeth appearing or replacing primary teeth; lower part of face more prominent.

Hungry at short intervals; may overeat and gain inappropriate weight if inadequate physical activity.

Enjoys active play—climbing, jumping, and running.

Susceptible to fatigue and limits self.

Visual acuity reaches normal.

Susceptible to respiratory and communicable diseases.

NEEDS

To develop large muscle control through motor skills.

To have play space and materials.

To use developmentally appropriate instructional tools and equipment.

To establish basic health habits: appropriate use of bathroom facilities, eating, covering nose and mouth when coughing, etc.

To have snack time and opportunity to develop social graces.

To have plenty of sleep and rest, and exercise interspersed with rest.

To have health examinations and follow-up.

To have visual and auditory checks.

To have dental attention.

EMOTIONAL CHARACTERISTICS

Self-centered, desires immediate attention to his/her problem, and wants to be selected first.

Sensitive about being left out of activities.

Sensitive about ridicule, criticism, or loss of prestige.

Easily emotionally aroused.

Can take responsibility but needs adult supervision.

Parent image strong; also identifies with teacher.

Readily express likes and dislikes.

Questioning attitude about sex differences.

NEEDS

To receive encouragement, recognition, ample praise, patience, and adult support.

To express inner feelings, anxieties, and fears.

To feel secure, loved, wanted, and accepted (at home and at school).

To be free from pressure to achieve beyond capabilities.

To have a consistent, cooperatively planned program of classroom control. Must have guidance.

To develop self-confidence.

To have some immediate, desirable satisfactions.

To know limitations within which he/she can operate effectively.

To develop realistic expectations of self.

SOCIAL CHARACTERISTICS

Lack of interest in personal grooming.

Engages in imitative play.

Friendly, frank, sometimes aggressive, "bossy," and assertive.

Generally tolerant of race, economic status, etc.

Gradually more socially oriented and adjusted.

Boys and girls play together as sex equals, but are aware of sex differences.

NEEDS

To have satisfactory peer relationships; to receive group approval.

To learn the importance of sharing, planning, working, and playing together—both boys and girls.

To have help in developing socially acceptable behavior.

To learn to assume some responsibility; to have opportunities to initiate activities, and to lead.

To work independently and in groups.

To accept sex role.

To develop an appreciation of social values, such as honesty, sportsmanship, etc.

INTELLECTUAL CHARACTERISTICS

Varied intellectual growth and ability of children.

Interested in things that move, bright colors. dramatizations, rhythmics, and making collections.

Interested in the present, not the future.

Learns best through active participation in concrete, meaningful situations.

Can abide by safety rules.

Wants to know "why."

Attention span short.

NEEDS

To experience frequent success and learn to accept failure when it occurs.

To have concrete learning experiences and direct participation.

To be in a rich, stable, challenging environment.

To have time to adjust to new experiences and new situations.

To learn to follow through to completion.

To develop a love for learning.

To learn without developing feelings of hostility.

To communicate effectively.

Cues for Teachers Working with this Age Group: Vigorous games emphasizing outdoor play with basic movement patterns and skills, and singing games and rhythms. Parallel play and learning strategies that involve some component of self-selection tend to be more successful among youngest children in this group.

(continued)

TABLE 3.4	Growth and Development Characteristics and Corresponding Needs of Students in Kindergarten through Ninth Grade (Ages 5 through 14 Years Old): A Foundation for Age-Appropriate Practice *(continued)*

Attributes of Students in Grades 4 through 6 (8–11 Years Old)

PHYSICAL CHARACTERISTICS

Growth slow and steady.

Girls begin to forge ahead of boys in height and weight.

Extremities begin to lengthen toward end of this period.

Muscle coordination improving.

Continued small muscle development.

Bones growing, vulnerable to injury.

Permanent dentition continues.

Malocclusion may be a problem.

Appetite good, increasing interest in food.

Boundless energy.

Tires easily.

Visual acuity normal.

Menarche possible toward end of this period.

NEEDS

To develop and improve coordination of both large and small muscles.

To have plenty of activities and games that will develop body control, strength, endurance, and skills/stunts (throwing, catching, running, bicycling, skating).

To have careful supervision of games appropriate to strength and developmental needs; protective equipment.

To have competitive activity with children of comparable size.

To have sleep, rest, and well-balanced meals.

To have health examinations and follow-up.

To have visual and auditory checks.

To have dental attention.

EMOTIONAL CHARACTERISTICS

Seeks approval of peer group.

Desire to succeed.

Enthusiastic, noisy, imaginative, desire to explore.

Negativistic (early part of period).

Begins to accept responsibility for clothing and behavior.

Increasingly anxious about family and possible tragedy.

Increasing self-consciousness.

Sex hostility.

Becomes "modest" but not too interested in details of sex.

NEEDS

To begin seriously to gain a realistic image of self and appreciate uniqueness of personality.

To be recognized for individual worth; to feel self-assurance and self-esteem.

To receive encouragement and affection; to be understood and appreciated.

To exercise self-control.

To talk about problems and receive reasonable explanations.

To have questions answered.

SOCIAL CHARACTERISTICS

Learns to cooperate better in group planning and group play, and abides by group decisions.

Interested in competitive activities and prestige.

Competition keen.

Begins to show qualities of leadership.

Developing interest in appearance.

Strong sense of fair play.

Belongs to a gang or secret club; loyal to group.

Close friendships with members of own sex.

Separate play for boys and girls.

NEEDS

To be recognized and accepted by peer groups; receive social approval.

To have relationships with adults that give feelings of security and acceptance.

To assume responsibilities, have increased opportunities for independent actions and decisions.

To develop appreciation for others and their rights.

To learn to get along with others and accept those different from self.

INTELLECTUAL CHARACTERISTICS

Likes to talk and express ideas.

High potential for learning—in science, adventure, the world.

Eager to acquire skills.

Wide range of interests; curious, wants to experiment.

Goals are immediate.

Demands consistency.

Generally reliable about following instructions.

Attention span short.

NEEDS

To experiment, explore, solve problems, accept challenges, use initiative, select, plan, and evaluate.

To receive individual help in skill areas without harmful or undue pressure.

To have opportunities for creative self-expression.

To have a rich environment of materials and the opportunity to explore it.

To participate in concrete, real-life situations.

To be able to accept one's self with strengths and weaknesses.

Cues for Teachers Working with this Age Group: More formal games with emphasis on body mechanics. Equipment should be appropriately sized and placed at proper height to promote development of sound fundamental skills. Cooperative learning and other supervised group learning strategies contribute to learning and improved interpersonal skills. Students seek attention and reinforcement from both peers and significant adults. Potential tension between norms established by adult authority figures and those of self-selected friends. Emotionally fragile; high need for feeling successful in a variety of areas.

TABLE 3.4 *(continued)*

Attributes of Students in Grades 7 through 9 (11–14 Years Old)

PHYSICAL CHARACTERISTICS

Accelerated and often uneven growth.

Individual differences most prominent; girls continue rapid growth and are taller and heavier than boys in early period.

Muscular growth toward adult size begins toward end of period.

NEEDS

To have adequate nourishment for growth spurt and daily energy.

To understand development change of adolescence.

To recognize wide physical differences among peers as normal.

To have good protective equipment in games.

To have physical activity interspersed with rest.

To have health examinations and follow-up.

PHYSICAL CHARACTERISTICS

Variable coordination.

Bones growing, vulnerable to injury.

Onset of puberty generally at the beginning of this age range for girls, and at the end of this period for boys.

Dental caries common.

Permanent dentition—28 teeth.

Malocclusion may be present.

Appetite ravenous but may be capricious.

Enjoys vigorous play.

Tires easily, particularly girls.

Visual problems may increase.

Variations in development of secondary sex characteristics. Menarche.

Skin problems, voice changes, etc.

Reproductive organs growing.

NEEDS

To have visual and auditory checks.

To have dental attention.

EMOTIONAL CHARACTERISTICS

Emotional instability; sudden and deep swings in mood.

Strong feelings of like and dislike, negative and positive attitudes.

Sensitive, self-critical but vulnerable to criticism.

Overanxious about health; common to think she/he has a gruesome disease.

Over-concerned about physical and emotional changes.

Striving for independence from adults.

Hero worship.

Searching for sensational emotional experiences.

Self-conscious.

Shows growing restraint in expressing feelings.

Unique sense of humor.

NEEDS

To express volatile emotions, grief, anger, disappointment, likes, and dislikes.

To assume responsibility for own conduct.

To achieve more independence.

To feel secure, wanted, loved, trusted, adequate, and capable.

To have privacy respected.

To exercise self-discipline.

To experience success, receive individual recognition.

To identify with a friendly adult (teacher, parent, older friend).

To be alone occasionally.

To feel the support, firm guidance, and assurance of an adult.

To differentiate between reality and fiction; fact and inaccuracy.

SOCIAL CHARACTERISTICS

Interested in competitive sports as participant and spectator.

Developing good sportsmanship.

Socially insecure.

Very peer-conscious.

Desires freedom with security.

Argues against authority but wants it.

Sensitive to appearance (clothes, skin).

Imitative fads in clothing, speech, etc.

Wishes to conform to defined pattern of good school citizenship.

Assumes responsibility for personal and group conduct.

Beginning to discriminate right from wrong.

Aware of opposite sex, chivalry, rivalry, and teasing.

Separating into groups by sex: boys into large groups, girls into small groups, then gradually mixed groups.

NEEDS

To see one's self as a socially accepted, important person.

To relate to members of the same and opposite sex.

To receive recognition from and acceptance by peers.

To work and play with different age groups.

To recognize the importance of leadership as well as being a follower.

To have congenial social settings.

(continued)

TABLE 3.4	**Growth and Development Characteristics and Corresponding Needs of Students in Kindergarten through Ninth Grade (Ages 5 through 14 Years Old): A Foundation for Age-Appropriate Practice** *(continued)*

Attributes of Students in Grades 7 through 9 (11–14 Years Old)   *(continued)*

INTELLECTUAL CHARACTERISTICS	**NEEDS**
Eager to learn, curious, and alert exploring.	To determine individual motives, goals, standard, and ideals.
Reads widely.	To satisfy curiosity, desire to know, and to experiment.
Wider range of abilities and interests.	To express one's self verbally, manually, and through activities
Wants to succeed.	such as dance, music, clubs, debate, etc.
Wants precise assignments and meaningful experiences.	To appreciate the value of work and products of work.
Skeptical, demands facts.	To know the satisfaction of achieving to the extent of one's
Unrealistic in passing judgment.	ability.
Overconfident in own information.	
Increasing span of attention and concentration.	

Cues for Teachers Working with this Age Group: Competitive games with moderate fatigue and emotional stress, involving development of a range of skills. Learning activities and planned repetition to develop conflict resolution, decision making, refusal, communication, and other life skills. Develop opportunities for students to participate in developing rules, codes of conduct, and consequences. Reinforcement for requiring students to identify range of consequences and potential implications for self and others involved in various behaviors. Consistently demonstrate respect for diverse behavioral manifestations common in this stage of development. Provide formal and informal opportunities for discussion of concerns. Protect rights to privacy.

drug prevention instruction for primary-grade children should focus on such developmentally appropriate concepts as:

- Recognizing the differences between medicine and products that are safe for play,
- Safe and adult-supervised use of medication,
- Community health helpers who provide directions and prescriptions for medication,
- Safety risks associated with smoking materials, and
- Fire prevention activities.

While the needs and abilities of the learners become the foundation for planning lessons, other concerns and sources of influence are not disregarded in planning and implementing lessons. However, learner attributes take center stage and other less student-centered concerns provide context. In summary, when organizing learning strategies that are both age and individually appropriate, health educators of elementary and middle-grade students are encouraged to consider the following suggested guidelines:

- The most effective activities tend to be those that help students connect the content issues and health-promoting behaviors to other aspects of their lives. Correlated, integrated, and cooperative learning approaches that will be discussed later in this chapter are likely to be among the more effective instructional approaches.
- Most effective lesson planning is based on a combination of developmental and/or observed

characteristics of students, the body of literature in the content area, and teachers' best professional judgments.
- Learning, particularly about health-promoting behaviors, is rarely successful if teachers approach it as a spectator sport for students. Students of all ages learn best in an active learning environment that encourages exploration and interaction with materials, other children, teachers, and other adults.
- Learning activities and materials should be concrete, real, and relevant to the lives of the students.
- Flexibility, resourcefulness, and humor often are helpful teacher characteristics. Children's interests and

Developmentally appropriate health instruction emphasizes connections between lesson content and life activities outside of the classroom. Student field trips with parents and teachers can reinforce such connections.

abilities often violate developmental rules (think about young children and their fascination with the language and lore of dinosaurs!). As a result, even well-planned lessons flop sometimes. Teachers must be prepared to adapt, adjust, or "think on their feet."

- Responding to human diversity issues is critical in planning all education activities. In particular, given the range of health beliefs and practices, activities should be carefully structured to omit sexist and culturally biased language, examples, and stereotypes (e.g., firefighters vs. firemen, mail carriers vs. mailmen, police officers vs. policemen, flight attendants vs. stewardesses, exclusive male references to physicians, exclusive female references to nurses, etc.).[29]

Involving Children in Curriculum Planning

As an alternative to teacher-developed curriculum models, educators have been exploring the value of involving children in the planning process. Unfortunately, it is not a practice that is widely implemented in elementary and middle-level classrooms. While most administrators and teachers would not want to develop all health curricula this way, there are compelling reasons to supplement conventional instruction with instruction based on children's interests. When students are invited into the process of determining the focus for their learning activities, they become activated in practicing communication skills and connecting health issues to other content areas, including language arts and social studies. This collaborative approach to planning also can bring a richness to classroom instruction because it is based on identified interests of a particular group of students. In this way, it capitalizes on the elements of individually appropriate practice.

Williams has recommended a four-step procedure for teachers interested in engaging students in a collaborative approach to planning. It is recommended that these steps be implemented after the teacher has identified potential instructional topics or themes. Themes can emerge from student comments or questions.[30] The recommended sequence of steps includes involving students in seeking answers to the following specific questions:

Step 1:   What do you wonder?
During this stage of planning, students are given the opportunity to express ideas, questions, or concerns about an identified topic. As questions about the topic emerge, teachers also can gain insight into development, language skills, misconceptions, and thinking processes among students.

Step 2:   What can we do to find out?
This step in this collaborative process is based on the foundation that learning is a social, or collaborative, process. As a result, activities in this phase of planning reinforce that not only are students' questions important, but so is their involvement in finding answers or

solutions. In this context, the teacher and students brainstorm ways in which they could work together to "find out." As an outgrowth of this process, students practice brainstorming and problem-solving skills and are reinforced for creativity when helping to design learning activities.

Step 3:   What materials do we need?
In this step in the process, students are encouraged to make a connection between the methods that they identify to solve problems or answer questions, and the materials with which they will have to work to achieve their goal. As students identify necessary materials, teachers are urged to clarify responses and reinforce the connection between problem-solving methods and necessary materials.

Step 4:   What will you bring (do)? What would you like me to bring (do)?
As concepts and the requisite materials to be explored are clarified, specific contributions to the process are collected from volunteers. Consistent with the tenants of authentic instruction, students reinforce the connection between classroom topics and events or experiences from their own lives. This step also provides fertile opportunities for parent involvement, as "expert" consultation or support can be solicited from the supportive adults.

When children are involved in planning curricula for their classrooms, both teachers and students are rewarded. As curriculum and learning activities emerge from mutual interests, teachers are freed from the constraints of artificial time lines, children are energized by concepts and issues that are of interest to them, parent engagement can be formalized, and the benefits from integrated or cross-curricular instruction can be realized for everyone (see chapter 5). Although unconventional, such a model is a perfect vehicle for implementing a developmentally appropriate practice approach to health instruction.[31]

Recommendations for Implementation

During the last decade, the role of schools in providing comprehensive school health education for students has been under intense scrutiny. Both the *Healthy People* agenda and the Education Goals 2000 federal initiatives call for an increased commitment to reducing the risks associated with student participation in potentially dangerous health practices (see chapter 1).

Unfortunately, many school districts have failed to develop and implement comprehensive health instruction in their graded courses of study. Two primary factors may account for this omission: (1) teachers' discomfort in dealing with sensitive or potentially controversial health issues, and (2) a lack of information available to key decision makers about the availability and effectiveness of health education curricula and resources.[32]

TABLE 3.5	Evaluated School Health Programs

AIDS Education

K–12	CHAMPS HIV/AIDS Prevention Program (Arizona)
6–12	San Francisco AIDS Prevention Education Curricula
7 & 10	AIDS Education Pilot Study (Rhode Island)

Sexuality and Reducing Peer Pressure

7–8	Postponing Sexual Involvement

Pregnancy and Substance Abuse Prevention

6–8	Peer Power (girls)
6–8	Awareness & Development for Adolescent Males (ADAM)

Tobacco, Alcohol, & Other Drug Use

K–7	Growing Healthy
K–12	Here's Looking At You
6–7	Positive Youth Development Program (New Haven, Connecticut)
7	The Television, School, and Family Project (California)

Health Promotion

K–7	Know Your Body
1–6	Changing the Course (New York and Connecticut)

7–12	Teenage Health Teaching Modules (THTM)
8	Project Model Health (Wisconsin)

Heart Disease

6	3 R's and HBP (Georgia)

Nutrition

K–5	Nutrition in a Changing World (elementary students)
3	Hearty Heart (Minnesota and North Dakota)
3–4	Great Sensations (Baltimore)
5–7	Three Intervention Programs (Pennsylvania)
7–8	Nutrition for Life
7–12	Pawtucket Heart Health Program (Rhode Island)

Nutrition and Exercise

4–5	Heart Healthy Eating & Exercise (California)
5–6	The San Diego Family Health Project (California)

Physical Education and Fitness

K–7	Feelin' Good (Jackson County, Michigan)

Safety

PreK–2	Westchester County Occupant Restraint Program (New York)

Source: U. S. Department of Health and Human Services, *School Health: Findings from Evaluated Programs,* DHHS Publication No. 357-637/90247 (Washington, DC: U. S. Government Printing Office, 1993).

In this context, teachers, administrators, curriculum supervisors, and parents will be helped by examining two federal resources. In 1993, the U.S. Public Health Service published a document entitled *School Health: Findings from Evaluated Programs.* "The intended target audience for this publication is health and education officials, including school and community leaders, who are interested in initiating and improving school health programs for students in public and private elementary and secondary schools as well as institutions of higher education." [33] Table 3.5 lists selected programs from this document that have particular relevance for teachers in elementary and middle-level schools. Curricula in this table are organized by health topic area and grade level.[34] For a curriculum model to be positively reviewed for inclusion in this publication, compliance with selected criteria is required. Curricula must:

- Be based or linked to a school,
- Target the developmental needs of school-age children and youth (grades K–12),
- Focus on health and/or educational objectives, and
- Provide process/summative evaluation protocol.[35]

In addition, the Division of Adolescent and School Health (DASH) of the Centers for Disease Control and Prevention has undertaken an activity entitled the Research to Classroom Project. This project began in 1992 and involves an annual review process. These efforts aim to identify curricula that have credible evidence of reducing health risks among youth. Importantly, the CDC does not endorse specific curricula. In addition, schools must determine which models might help to meet the unique needs of local students, and then integrate them into a planned, sequential, and comprehensive program of health instruction.

Several curricula have been identified as showing evidence of reducing sexual risk behaviors associated with HIV, other STDs, and unintended pregnancy. This list includes:

Be Proud! Be Responsible,
Get Real About AIDS, (high school level, 2nd edition),
Reducing the Risk, and
Becoming A Responsible Teen.

Further, in 1997, DASH extended the focus of this project to identify the following curricula that demonstrate evidence of reducing tobacco use among adolescents:

Life Skills Training, and
Project Towards No Tobacco Use (TNT).

Educators interested in these specific curricula will be pleased to know that DASH has prepared a "Programs that Work" evaluation fact sheet for each of the identified risk-reduction curricula. These sheets include information about evaluation outcomes, curriculum objectives, length of optimal instructional time, undergirding theories, and where to get more information about each curriculum. In addition, administrators, teachers, and parents are encouraged to contact the Centers for Disease Control and Prevention in Atlanta, GA ((770) 488-5360) for more general information on the Research to Classroom Project and Programs that Work.[36]

CONCLUSION

Developing and implementing a quality health education program, like health behavior itself, is a very complex matter. In 1990, former President Jimmy Carter provided the following characterization of health education: "The bottom line of what needs to be done in improving American health is through the public elementary and secondary schools in our country. In the past, health has been a kind of appendage, a kind of novelty, forced upon quite often unwilling superintendents, teachers, and administrators in the school system, and part of it is our own fault."[37]

As evidenced in this chapter, successfully managing the complex task of developing and implementing quality health education programs of study requires the efforts of many educators, parents, and community stakeholders. In addition, this process implies a different way of thinking about health, behavior, and learning. In light of the confirmed relationship between student health risks and threats to academic success, and the ever-broadening constellation of health risks to which students are exposed, there is little doubt about the value of hard work in confronting this challenge.

SUMMARY

The foundation for an effective, coordinated school health program lies in the development and implementation of an effective and developmentally appropriate health education program of studies. Although not perceived to be part of the core of basic curricula in many schools and communities, the underpinnings of effective comprehensive school health education are consistent with the national commitment to reforming and improving education for all students.

Importantly, school health educators share many of the same struggles associated with effective curriculum development with their colleagues in other content areas. In this context, health educators are encouraged to consult the rich body of education literature for suggestions about meeting the instructional needs of all students. This body of science has confirmed that, among other conditions, students learn best when:

- The information to be mastered seems relevant to them,
- They are active participants in the learning process,
- They can interact with others while participating in learning activities, and
- There are opportunities for students and teachers to cultivate positive relationships.

The developmental needs of students provide a sound starting point for developing meaningful lessons in health education and other content areas. This developmentally appropriate practice approach considers both general developmental attributes and the individual needs of learners. By attending to the physical, mental, social, emotional, and language characteristics of students, teachers can expedite time management and effective practice decisions.

An alternative curriculum development model has emerged that capitalizes on the developmental needs and interests of students. This approach, which initially targeted the youngest students, has emerged as an effective supplement for conventional approaches to curriculum development for older groups of learners. When students are invited into the process of determining the focus for instruction, they become active participants in practicing communication skills and connecting health issues to other areas of study. This collaborative approach to planning can serve as a foundation for enriching the curriculum and reducing stagnation in classroom practice.

Finally, health educators are encouraged to examine federal agendas and agency-developed curriculum packages as a foundation for improving health education classroom practice. In particular, two federal government activities, *School Health: Findings from Evaluated Programs,* published by the U.S. Public Health Service, and The Research to Classroom Project, sponsored by the Division of Adolescent and School Health (CDC), can help teachers identify curricula that have credible evidence of addressing the health risks of children and youth.

DISCUSSION QUESTIONS

1. Identify ways in which the goals of effective comprehensive health education programming are consistent with the national agenda to reform and improve education in all content areas.

2. Discuss key findings of the School Health Policies and Programs Study that serve as a foundation for improving school health instruction.

3. Identify the key elements of authentic instruction.

4. Discuss differences between age-appropriate practice and individually appropriate practice as they relate to developmentally appropriate practice.

5. What is the importance of attending to physical, mental, social, emotional, and language attributes of learners as a first priority in developing effective lessons?

6. Summarize key age-related developmental differences in primary, upper-elementary, and middle-grade learners.

7. Differentiate between a developmentally appropriate and developmentally inappropriate lesson for a given grade level.

8. Why is it advantageous for teachers to engage students in collaborative curriculum planning?

9. Suggest steps for effectively and efficiently involving students in curriculum development.

10. Discuss the role of the federal government in supporting improved health instruction.

ENDNOTES

1. Deborah Haber and Christine Blaber, "Health Education: A Foundation for Learning," *Content of the Curriculum, 2nd ed.,* A. Glatthorn, ed. (Alexandria, VA: Association for Supervision and Curriculum Development, 1995), 99–129.

2. Janet L. Collins, Meg Leavy Small, Laura Kann, and Beth Collins Pateman, et al., "School Health Education," *Journal of School Health* 65, no. 8 (October 1995): 302–311.

3. Ibid.

4. Fred M. Newmann and Gary G. Wehlage, "Five Standards of Authentic Instruction," *Educational Leadership* (April 1993): 8–12.

5. Ibid.

6. D. Archbald and F. M. Newmann, *Beyond Standardized Testing: Assessing Authentic Academic Achievement in the Secondary School* (Reston, VA: National Association of Secondary School Principals, 1988).

7. Newmann and Wehlage, "Five Standards of Authentic Instruction."

8. Grant Wiggins and Jay McTighe, *Understanding by Design* (Alexandria, VA: Association for Supervision and Curriculum Development, 1998), 44–62.

9. Newmann and Wehlage, "Five Standards of Authentic Instruction."

10. Ibid.

11. R. Morgan Pigg, "20 Concepts of Learning," *Journal of School Health* 63, no. 9 (November 1993): 375.

12. T. Armstrong, *Multiple Intelligences in the Classroom* (Alexandria, VA: Association for Supervision and Curriculum Development, 1994).

13. C. Checkley, "The First Seven and the Eighth," *Educational Leadership* (September 1997): 8–13.

14. National Professional School Health Education Organizations, "Comprehensive School Health Education," *Journal of School Health* 54, no. 8 (1984): 312–315.

15. L. Harris, *An Evaluation of Comprehensive Health Education in American Public Schools* (New York: Metropolitan Life Foundation, 1988).

16. Centers for Disease Control and Prevention, *Is School Health Education Cost Effective? An Exploratory Analysis of Selected Exemplary Components,* Unpublished manuscript (Atlanta, GA: Division of Adolescent and School Health, 1997).

17. The Gallup Organization, *Values and Opinions of Comprehensive School Health Education in U.S. Public Schools: Adolescents, Parents, and School District Administrators* (Atlanta, GA: American Cancer Society, 1994).

18. David K. Lohrmann and Susan F. Wooley, "Comprehensive School Health Education," *Health is Academic,* E. Marx and S. Wooley, eds. (New York: Teachers College Press, 1998), 43–66.

19. Jill English, Anthony Sancho, Donna Lloyd-Kolkin, and Lisa Hunter, *Criteria for Comprehensive Health Education Curricula* (Southwest Regional Laboratory: funded by U.S. Department of Education, 1990).

20. John Seffrin, "The Comprehensive School Health Curriculum: Closing the Gap Between State-of-the-Art and State-of-the-Practice," *Journal of School Health* 60, no. 4 (April 1990): 151–156.

21. M. Pollock and M. Hamburg, "Health Education: The Basic of the Basics," *Health Education* 16 (1985): 105–109.

22. Haber and Blaber, "Health Education: A Foundation for Learning," *Content of the Curriculum,* 116.

23. Sharon L. Ramey and Craig T. Ramey, "The Transition to School," *Phi Delta Kappan* 76, no. 3 (November 1994): 197.

24. Sue Bredekamp, ed., *Developmentally Appropriate Practice in Early Childhood Programs Serving Children from Birth Through Age 8* (Washington, DC: National Association for the Education of Young Children, 1987), 1–2.

25. Jim W. Lochner, "Growth and Developmental Characteristics," *A Pocket Guide to Health and Health Problems in School Physical Activity,* B. Petrof, ed. (Kent, OH: ASHA, 1981), 4–9.

26. Bredekamp, ed., *Developmentally Appropriate Practice,* 2.

27. Ibid., 2.

28. Ibid., 1–3, 5.

29. Ibid., 2–5.

30. Karen C. Williams, "What Do You Wonder? Involving Children in Curriculum Planning," *Young Children* (September 1997): 78–81.

31. Ibid.

32. Michael D. Ballard and Robert W. Grueninger, "Evaluated Health Education Programs," *Kentucky AAHPERD* 31, no. 2 (Fall 1995): 22–24.

33. Office of Disease Prevention and Health Promotion, *School Health: Findings From Evaluated Programs,* DHHS Publication No. 357-637/90247 (Washington, DC: U.S. Government Printing Office, 1993).

34. Ballard, "Evaluated Health Education Programs."

35. Office of Disease Prevention and Health Promotion, *School Health: Findings From Evaluated Programs.*

36. Centers for Disease Control and Prevention, *Research to Classroom Project* (Atlanta, GA: Division of Adolescent and School Health, CDC, 1997).

37. Jimmy Carter, "The Challenge of Education for Health in America's Schools," *Journal of School Health* 60, no. 4(April 1990): 129.

SUGGESTED READINGS

Albrecht, Kay. "Joining the Quality Circle: Developmentally Appropriate Practice in School-Age Care." *Exchange* (January 1993): 19–22.

Allensworth, Diane. "Health Education: State of the Art." *Journal of School Health* (January 1993): 14–19.

Birch, David A. "Improving Leadership Skills in Curriculum Development." *Journal of School Health* 62, no. 1 (January 1992): 27–28.

Bloom, B. S. *Taxonomy of Educational Objectives Handbook I: Cognitive Domain.* New York: McKay, 1956.

Connell, David B., Ralph R. Turner, and Elaine F. Mason. "Summary of the Findings of the School Health Education Evaluation: Health Promotion Effectiveness, Implementation, and Costs." *Journal of School Health* 55, no. 8 (October 1985): 316–323.

Cortese, Peter A. "Accomplishments in Comprehensive School Health Education." *Journal of School Health* 63, no. 1 (January 1993): 21–23.

Darling-Hammond, L. *The Right to Learn: A Blueprint for Creating Schools that Work.* San Francisco: Jossey-Bass Publishers, 1997.

Grace, Marsha. "When Students Create Curriculum." *Educational Leadership* (November 1999): 49–52.

Hausman, Alice J., and Sheryl Burt Ruzek. "Implementation of Comprehensive School Health Education in Elementary Schools: Focus on Teacher Concerns." *Journal of School Health* 65, no. 3 (March 1995): 81–85.

Kohn, Alfie. *What to Look for in a Classroom.* San Francisco: Jossey-Bass Publishers, 1998.

National Middle School Association. *This We Believe: Developmentally Responsive Middle Level Schools.* Columbus, OH: NMSA, 1995.

Robinson, James. "Criteria for the Selection and Use of Health Education Reading Materials." *Health Education* 19, no. 4 (August/September 1988): 31–34.

Simonds, R. L. "A Plea for Children." *Educational Leadership* 51, no. 4 (1993/1994): 12–15.

Smith, D., A. Steckler, L. McCormick, and K. McLeroy, "Lessons Learned About Disseminating Health Curricula to Schools." *Journal of Health Education* 26, no. 1 (January/February 1995): 37–43.

4

TOOLS OF TEACHING

The Hardware of Instruction

O U T L I N E

INTRODUCTION

While the curriculum provides direction to the teacher for organizing the scope and sequence of content in the school health instruction program, there are numerous "tools" available to supplement and enhance lessons. Written materials, including pamphlets, brochures, and booklets, are available from many different community agencies and are useful in the health class. A wide range of audiovisual materials is also available to supplement classroom instruction. Films, slides, videodiscs, and other video presentations are particularly useful to elementary and middle-level schoolteachers in their health classes. A number of creative activities can be designed to encourage student interest and to enhance learning, including experiments, role-playing and drama, and community presentations.

It would be impossible to discuss every strategy that can be employed by the classroom teacher in teaching health within the framework of this chapter. Most teaching methods that the teacher is likely to use are also used in other academic areas of instruction. We select several "tools of teaching" that are particularly relevant to the health education class.

TEXTBOOKS IN HEALTH INSTRUCTION

In the various academic disciplines of the elementary and middle-level school, textbooks play an important instructional role. Even though curriculum guides and courses of study provide direction for instructional decision making, the content in textbooks is very influential in classroom instruction. It has been estimated that between 75% and 90% of the factual information a student learns in a given subject comes by way of course textbooks.[1] If this is so, the evaluation, selection, eventual adoption, and use of textbooks are extremely important.

A basic reference used by teachers in many elementary and middle-level health classes is a health textbook. There are currently two health textbook series available for use in the elementary and middle-level grades.[2] The textbooks have been developed and published as part of a K through 8 series.

In addition, other materials, particularly workbooks, are available for student use.[3] These workbook materials can be used with specific subject material that is identified as part of the locally developed health curriculum for each grade level.

The primary motivation of publishing companies in producing these books is that they sell. As such, teachers must be vigilant in selecting books that support their local school district curriculum and that respond to the needs of their community and the individual students.

Once a text series is adopted by a school district, the classroom teachers should be provided with enough textbooks for all students in the class. It is important that each student in the classroom have and use a textbook because it provides a common starting point and some systematic progression of learning. Unlike other academic disciplines, such as reading, mathematics, and history, the scope and sequence of health content does not usually follow a standard progression recognized in all school districts. As a result, there can be much variance as to what content is expected and appropriate at various grade levels. It is not unusual to hear elementary and middle-level schoolchildren complain about the repetition of health information from grade to grade. By the time students are in middle school, they often assume that they have learned everything about their health status and behavior that they will ever need. This tendency toward duplication can be minimized if a high-quality health textbook series is adopted and used throughout an entire elementary and middle-level curriculum.

Another benefit of using health textbooks is that they provide an excellent source of reliable and accurate information. Current health textbook series are authored by experts in the field of health education, child growth and development, medicine, and reading skills. In the development process, manuscripts receive extensive review. Subject matter and content experts are asked to respond to the manuscript from the point of view of content reliability and the appropriateness of the material. As a result, the text information is relatively current, is appropriate for the age level for which it is presented, and is medically and scientifically reliable.

In addition to containing cognitive information that is applicable to the students, the best health textbooks include a variety of learning activities that are designed to stimulate

children and encourage thinking. Most available textbook series have a number of pedagogical aids to support the learning process. For example, learning objectives are usually provided for each unit, chapter, and section of a text.

In spite of the many positive features of an elementary or middle-level health education textbook, a number of concerns accompany its use. A textbook should not be the sole determiner of a health curriculum. Teachers should not simply follow a textbook from cover to cover. When this happens, the health learning experience often degenerates into a series of reading experiences about facts on health, with little emphasis on application of key concepts to health-attitude formation, skill development, and behavioral change of individual students.

Current Elementary and Middle-Level Health Textbooks

There are currently two elementary and middle-level health textbook series available.[4] These series have books for grades 1 through 8; one has a text for use with kindergarten students. Although they are different in style, approach, organization, and other factors, each series has excellent qualities. One's perception of the quality of each series will differ based on individual school district goals, community criteria, and student needs. An individual who has not been associated with an elementary or middle-level school for more than a decade would be amazed at the significant improvements in health textbooks that have taken place in recent years.

In keeping with the current philosophy in health education in the United States, these elementary and middle-level health texts are designed to encourage individual responsibility for health, starting in the primary grades. The content, organization, and supporting materials of the texts focus on positive health behavior. Learning experiences involve activities outside the classroom, and often include the students' families.

There are differences in content between the health textbook series, but there are also many similarities. The subject content areas most commonly presented include: growth and development, nutrition, diseases, safety and first aid, drugs, exercise and physical fitness, mental health, emotions and stress, family and social health, community health, environmental health, personal health, and body systems. One textbook series includes a feature on careers in the health and safety fields. Students participate in activities that enable them to evaluate the roles and responsibilities of various health and safety professionals, including physicians, dentists, nurses, and medical and dental technicians. These activities stimulate students to appreciate and consider future work in health and safety careers, as well as to "humanize" allied health personnel and to make contact with them more comfortable.

Elementary and middle-level health textbooks are authored by teams comprised of two to five or more individuals. Some of the authors are health educators at the university level, with experience in school health teaching, curriculum, and writing. Others are health teachers with either elementary or secondary school health teaching experience. Medical and nursing specialists and experts in child health and physical fitness are included as authors or as consultants in some texts.

Part of the manuscript preparation process involves a review of the material by content and subject matter experts. Individuals selected to carry out this review process include classroom teachers, school nurses, and college health professors. Therefore, those involved in the writing of textbooks for use in elementary and middle-level school health classes are individuals with appropriate professional backgrounds and experience.

Today, most elementary and middle-level health textbooks are very attractive. Elementary and middle-level schoolchildren usually have an initial interest in the books because they contain many color photographs, attractive artwork, graphs, and charts. On-page material is generally organized to enhance student interest and promote learning. The illustrations usually improve comprehension of the written content.

A number of pedagogical aids parallel the narrative in the various chapters. These aids take the form of boxed information for students to read and respond to. Charts of dental brushing patterns, sleep patterns, and other similar activities are presented for students to use. Thought questions for class and individual discussion are found in most grade-level books. Glossaries help students increase their vocabulary as well as highlight correlated/integrated learning opportunities.

A broad range of resources to assist teachers in using their textbooks is provided. In addition to reproducing the pages from the students' textbooks in the teachers' manuals, teachers' resources include notes, testing materials, and teacher and student masters to be used in preparing tests, quizzes, and assignments. Most of the teachers' materials include chapter notes, with suggestions for class discussion, activities, group projects, and community resources that can supplement the teaching process. Publishing companies often provide large packets of transparencies to support classroom instruction. Regardless of a teacher's experience, the amount and variety of teacher support materials that accompany elementary and middle-level health textbooks can be of tremendous value. In addition, some publishing companies provide other materials to school districts that adopt their books. These may include wall posters, bulletin board materials, overhead transparencies, videotapes, and student activity books. One company provides hand puppets that the teacher can use.

Textbook Selection

Because of the constantly changing nature of the fields of health, science, and medicine, an elementary and middle-level health textbook can become outdated rapidly. A text that is more than 5 years old may contain information that no longer is accurate or may not contain material that is at the forefront of national concern. For these reasons, it is important that school districts select new textbooks on a regular basis, preferably every 3 to 5 years.

School districts may choose not to adopt health texts on a regular basis for economic reasons. In difficult economic times, school boards often choose to make budget cuts by retaining the current texts. When health textbooks are in competition with textbooks for mathematics, science, or language arts, they often take second place. As a result, it is not unusual to see elementary and middle-level teachers using outdated health textbooks that are sometimes more than 10 years old.

Elementary and middle-level classroom teachers who will use the books in their classes should be involved in the selection process. They should be provided with review copies of the series that are approved by the state and local boards of education to examine, analyze, and critique. It is the teachers who must be comfortable with the books that are selected for use by the school board. It is also important that community health agency personnel and staff, along with students' parents, be included in the textbook selection process.

Specific criteria must be considered in the textbook selection process. It is crucial that a text include material that the school district feels is appropriate for the children in its schools. A text should be selected for its ability to support a health curriculum that responds to the individual health needs and interests of the students. These needs and interests can vary from one locality to another.

Most states have various legal mandates as to the subject matter to be included in a curriculum at various grade levels. In reviewing the content of an elementary or middle-level health textbook, it is important to ascertain whether the book satisfies these mandates.

As previously noted, the content of any textbook must include developmentally appropriate approaches to current and relevant material. For example, because of the recent concern and increasing information about HIV/AIDS, elementary and middle-level health textbooks should include information on this topic. If a text has little or no information on this very current issue, the teachers must question the advisability of adopting the series.

Content in an elementary and middle-level health textbook must also be accurate. Older books may use terms and facts that no longer are appropriate. For example, a text that refers incorrectly to a given drug as addictive may prompt both teachers and students to question the credibility of other material in the book. The health textbook that speaks of venereal diseases instead of sexually transmitted diseases or infections is clearly outdated.

There has been increasing concern among textbook developers and education professionals regarding appropriate representation of the many groups in our diverse culture. Fair and equal treatment of races, ethnic groups, and gender is critical. Sexism and racism can be found in elementary and middle-level textbooks.[5] Bias can be depicted in both the illustrative material and in the presentation of content. Sex-role stereotyping is an area of major concern today in elementary and middle-level textbooks. To refer to physicians as only males or to nursing professionals as only females is educationally unsound.

The reading level of a textbook must be developmentally appropriate for the grade for which the book is designed. Children should be challenged by the readability of the book, yet it must not be too difficult. Publishers' promotional materials often indicate the reading level at which a book is written. However, textbook selection committees should evaluate for themselves the reading levels of the books under consideration for adoption. Several standard readability formulas can be used; the most popular formula is the Fry Readability Formula. Most use sentence length and vocabulary load to determine reading level.

The overall design and organization of a textbook are also important in the selection process. A book should be attractive and inviting to students. The summary and introductory sections, the index, the glossary, and the illustrative package all play an important role in final selection of a textbook. The illustrative package usually includes photographs, drawings, charts, and graphs. These visuals should be relevant to the content they accompany.

Both *horizontal* and *vertical* comparisons should be conducted. Horizontal comparison involves examining textbooks published by different publishing companies for the same grade level. For example, if a selection committee is considering books from three publishing companies, the third grade teachers should review and evaluate the third grade textbooks from each publisher. Vertical comparison involves examining books published by the same company at the grade level above and below which an individual will be teaching. If a fourth grade teacher has settled on the textbook from Publisher A, it is important to examine the fifth grade and third grade texts in the same series. This examination should look for repetition from one grade to another, and should provide direction for reinforcement of the concepts and information introduced in the previous grade materials. It should also indicate the foundational materials on which subjects and concepts for study in the next grade will be based.

Health Concepts in Other Subject Textbooks

Health information can be found in other elementary and middle-level subject matter textbooks, particularly in science textbooks. In planning health lessons, a classroom teacher must be aware of the kinds of health related information that the children will be exposed to in science texts. By being so informed, teachers can reduce the repetition between what is taught in science class and in health class. Also, when teachers know what is presented in science classes, they can plan an expanded

focus in health. It is necessary, however, to not consider science as the students' primary source of information about health.

The number of health concepts included varies from one science textbook to another. However, the most commonly found topics include basic anatomy and physiology of the body, the body systems, nutrition, foods and diet, and safety.

In the early primary grades, science texts include instruction about the senses: hearing (the ears) and sound, tasting (the tongue and mouth), seeing (the eyes), smelling (the nasal cavity), and feeling and touching (the skin). Study of the various systems of the human body is included in many elementary science textbooks, particularly in the upper-elementary and middle-level school materials. Discussions of the skeletal, muscular, circulatory, digestive, and respiratory systems are the most common. The nervous and endocrine systems are covered in at least one elementary science textbook.

The reproductive system is not usually discussed in these texts. When it is covered in science books, the emphasis is on reproduction of organisms, particularly low-level, unicellular structures. Nothing is presented about human reproduction. However, material on genetics, with an emphasis on inherited traits, is presented in one upper-elementary science textbook.

Instruction in elementary science textbooks about eating tends to focus on how different foods affect the body's growth and development rather than on enhancing healthy behaviors. There is some emphasis on the basic food groups. Tied in with this is instruction about dental health, the teeth, and their development and care.

A third major topic of emphasis related to health that is found in science textbooks is safety. In addition to information and instruction about general safety concepts, bicycle safety and water safety are areas of particular focus.

Most elementary and middle-level science textbooks have sections devoted to ecology and the environment. These concepts are important from the perspective of the study of health of the environment. However, elementary texts do not usually focus on the impact of environmental concerns on human health.

THE COMPUTER

Anyone who has visited an elementary or middle school in the past several years will have noted the increased use of computer technology in these schools. More than 90% of the schools in the United States have computers.[6] In many instances, computers provide challenging learning experiences for classroom use. It is not unusual today to see children as young as primary school age who are knowledgeable in the use of computers. Elementary, as well as middle-level, children are becoming increasingly computer-literate with skills that surpass those of many adults.

> **CONSIDER THIS**

Textbook Evaluation

Title of Book _____ **Grade Level** _____

Publisher _____

Book Format:

	Good	Satis.	Unsat.
1. Upon initial overview examination, the book appears to be (book size, format etc.)	___	___	___
2. Illustrations:			
Colorful	___	___	___
Varied	___	___	___
Attractive	___	___	___
Relation to content of the book	___	___	___
3. Marginal Material—applicable to the learning process	___	___	___
4. The organization of material in the text	___	___	___

Content:

	Yes	No	Minimal
1. Are subjects mandated by state and local board of education included in the textbook?	___	___	___
2. Are subjects included in local curriculum guide included in the text?	___	___	___
List topics:			
3. Are topics that are controversial in our community included?	___	___	___

Philosophy of Book:

1. Does the book			
emphasize individual health behavior?	___	___	___
emphasize attitude development?	___	___	___
emphasize family relationships?	___	___	___
emphasize scientific thinking?	___	___	___
2. Does the book give appropriate representation of			
various racial groups?	___	___	___
different sexes?	___	___	___
other pertinent groups?	___	___	___

Pedagogical Aids:

	Yes	No	Minimal
1. Are useful study helps available?			
Discussion questions	___	___	___
Word studies	___	___	___
Glossary	___	___	___
Index	___	___	___
2. Do the illustrations contribute to learning?	___	___	___
3. Are there graphs that contribute to learning?	___	___	___
4. Are there charts that contribute to learning?	___	___	___

Teachers' Manual:

1. Does the teachers' manual provide a philosophical overview of the textbook?	___	___	___
2. Is outline material available for teachers' use?	___	___	___
3. Is testing material provided?	___	___	___
4. Does the teachers' manual include suggested learning activities?	___	___	___
5. Does the teachers' manual include a listing of audiovisual aids?	___	___	___
6. Does the teachers' manual include a listing of other appropriate readings?	___	___	___

CONSIDER THIS   *(continued)*

Supplemental Material:

	Yes	No
1. Does the publishing company		
include sample test material?	___	___
include posters for teacher use?	___	___
provide overlays for teacher use?	___	___
provide audiovisual material?	___	___

2. Are other supplemental materials provided by the publishing company?

Final Comments:
This form may be useful in conducting an evaluation of textbooks for use in the health education class by listing specific items in the evaluation process.

As a result, a greater amount of information is now being presented at school by way of computers. The Internet provides access to unlimited amounts of information to both students and teachers.

Microcomputers have played an important role in changing the face of education since the early 1980s. Unfortunately, in many schools, the use of computers is not regularly integrated into classroom instruction.[7] Use of the computer is considered in some schools to be something reserved for the brighter students, or a frill that is not for everyone. This is unfortunate, since the computer should be seen as an aid in instruction for all students across a wide range of content areas, including health education.

The use of computers will increase as developmentally appropriate and content-specific software becomes available. In addition, teachers must develop competence in integrating computer applications into daily classroom practice. It is very unusual for a new elementary or middle-level schoolteacher not to have had at least an introduction to personal computing. However, what may be missing is skill development in using computers with students in the classroom setting. This has become necessary, as many children now have computers in their homes and have developed relatively advanced skills. Computer use will continue to expand in the schools in the years ahead.

Educational and developmentally appropriate computer application is exciting and tends to hold student interest. Computers cannot replace the teacher, but they should assist both teachers and students in the teaching-learning process, particularly in the area of cognitive learning materials. Most school systems have an educational media center where microcomputer software packages are cataloged and available for student and classroom use. These centers are often an expansion of traditional school library services.

The Internet

The Internet has impacted more people in the educational setting than any other technology that has been developed. With the development of the Internet, a global network of thousands of interconnected computer networks, the flow of information has spiraled in the past few years.

Access to information available on the Internet is provided by way of the World Wide Web. To access information on the World Wide Web, it is necessary to use a Web browser. There are an estimated 150 million Web pages today, and the number is increasing daily. Within the next decade, many children in elementary school will never remember when there was no World Wide Web. The Web will be available in most classrooms within that period of time.

The World Wide Web is most useful for the classroom teacher as a provider of information for use in teaching. This is particularly helpful in the health area. It is estimated that more than 10,000 health related websites exist.[8] This information is usually presented by health product advertisers, support groups, governmental agencies, nonprofit health agencies, hospitals, as well as other sources.

Much of this health related information is accurate, current, and on the cutting edge. On the other hand, it must be remembered that anyone can place items of information on the Web. Hence, very inaccurate and biased health related information can be found on the Web. For this reason, teachers must be careful in evaluating health information found on the Internet. The accuracy, recency, and source of the information are most important.

Also, concern must be noted that access to the Internet also provides access to sites that provide unhealthy and unacceptable information for children. Unfortunately, such websites involve certain health education issues, such as sex-related chat rooms, pornography, and so forth. Elementary and middle-level teachers must be alert to what

---

CONSIDER THIS

Evaluating Health Related Websites

According to the Interactive Services Association, an estimated 58 million adults in the United States and Canada are using the Internet. Consumers are accessing a great amount of information from websites. Clinicians and health educators are continually looking for new methods of educating their clientele. In the past, personal counseling, videos, books, and brochures were the patient education methods available. Since the mid-1990s, consumers have referred to the World Wide Web to learn how they can improve their health, prevent disease, and learn details about specific diseases. Unfortunately, there is no formal process of editing or evaluating websites before they are released to the public. As a result, the Office of Health Promotion has developed a reliable and valid instrument to critique the credibility of health-related websites. The instrument's intended users are health educators and clinicians who refer their clientele to websites as an additional source of patient education.

I. Website information
Title of site:

Subject of site:

Website address:

Whom do you think is the intended audience?

What do you think the objective is for this site?

Circle the number that you feel best represents the site: 1 = disagree, 2 = agree, 0 = not applicable (N/A). Add up the total points scored for each page at the bottom of each page.

II. Content

	Disagree	Agree	N/A
1. The *purpose* of the site is clearly stated or may be clearly inferred.	1	2	0
2. The information covered does not appear to be an "infomercial" (i.e., an advertisement disguised as health education).	1	2	0
3. There is no bias evident.	1	2	0
4. If the site is opinionated, the author discusses all sides of the issue, giving each due respect.	1	2	0
5. All aspects of the subject are covered adequately.	1	2	0
6. *External links* are provided to fully cover the subject (if not needed, circle 0).	1	2	0

III. Accuracy

7. The information is *accurate* (if not sure, circle 0).	1	2	0
8. Sources are clearly documented.	1	2	0
9. The website states that it subscribes to *HON code* principles.	1	2	0

Page Score_____

Source: Centers for Disease Control and Prevention, (CDC) Office of Health Promotion, 1998.

Government Document . . . no permission required.

---

the students are viewing within their classrooms and protect children from unacceptable material. To help in evaluating health related websites, the Office of Health Promotion of CDC has published a helpful evaluation instrument.

Computer Software

The term *software* is used to describe computer programs, the sets of instructions to the computer. Software programming involves the organization of material that relates to the specific topic. More than 12,000 educational

software packages are currently available. It is estimated that more than 2,000 new packages are added each year.[9] With this amount of educational computer programming, it is difficult for the classroom teacher to keep current as to what is available and most useful to respond to specific classroom needs.

Among the various types of software available, the compact disk read-only memory (CD-ROM) is most commonly used in classrooms. CD-ROMs are particularly useful because a lot of information—text, graphics, and pictures—can be stored on a small disk and is accessible

Many elementary and middle-level schoolchildren learn to use the computer for classroom instruction. A variety of health concepts can be presented in this manner.

to the students. As much as 650 megabytes of information, a massive storage capacity, are available. Video and film capability is possible on CD-ROM.

Every year, an increasing amount of CD-ROM material is developed for use in the elementary school curriculum. Most of this material is for use in science, language arts, mathematics, and social studies. So far, the amount of CD-ROM material for use with health education has been limited. That which is available is generally designed for use in middle school and secondary school.[10] Educators in health education need to become more involved in exploring ways in which CD-ROM can be used to supplement instruction in the elementary school.

Most elementary and middle-level classroom teachers probably use already-prepared software programs, since most teachers likely do not possess computer programming skills. As available software packages expand, classroom teachers who are interested in health education should request that the school district purchase appropriate health programs. Lists of such software can be found in the media catalogs of various publishing companies. The school media center coordinator, building principal, or school district curriculum director will have access to such materials for the classroom teacher to reference.

Computer-Assisted Instruction

Computer programs are designed to assist in the teaching process. This is referred to as computer-assisted instruction (CAI). CAI has a number of benefits. Students

Computer-assisted instruction provides opportunities for students to study and progress at their own individual rate. Some schools use the computer for classroom instruction for all children; others find that the computer enriches and supports other instruction.

can use it independently at various locations—in the classroom, in learning centers, or at home. CAI permits students to study and progress at their own pace, and microcomputer use reduces instructional time as compared to conventional teaching.[11] Because instruction is individualized, it is possible that increasing amounts of course material can be covered more efficiently. Independent use of the computer can result in challenging enrichment for brighter students and developmentally appropriate remediation and reinforcement opportunities for students who have problems with portions of the material.

Computer-assisted instruction permits interaction between a learner and the material. Instant feedback and reinforcement occur in this interactive process, which facilitates learning. During interaction, the computer software program asks a question, the student responds with specific information, and then the computer feeds back related information. The interactive features of computer instruction create positive attitudes toward the learning situation for many learners.

Computer-assisted instruction is available in several formats. When information is presented in a logical and sequential format, it is referred to as a *tutorial*. A student can be assigned a tutorial at a developmentally appropriate level. A broader range of health education information and concepts needs to be designed in tutorial format.

Other formats of computer-assisted instruction include drill and practice, simulation, and gaming.[12] Drill and practice is often used for reinforcement of material that has already been presented, learned, and understood by students. For example, a question, problem, or word can be presented to the student. The student provides a response. The computer program provides feedback to the student as to whether the answer is correct. Additional information is usually provided. Simulation allows students to decide how they might react to a given situation presented by the computer program. Simulation has been found to be helpful in strengthening decision-making skills. Computer-based educational programs also have been designed using problem-solving strategies.

Health Education Applications

Academic disciplines, such as mathematics and science, are considered prime subjects for computer use in school programs, whereas health education is not. For this reason, there have not been many software programs developed for use in the elementary and middle-level school health curriculum. Nevertheless, the number of software programs on health-related topics is increasing. If health education is to be at the forefront of elementary and middle-level schoolchildren's learning experiences, increasing involvement with computers should be expected.

Software packages have been developed on several health-related topics. Currently, there are limited software programs on diet and nutrition, fitness, drugs, alcohol, and consumer health. However, most health education software developed to date has been designed for adults and adolescents rather than for elementary and middle-level schoolchildren.

Possibly the most widely available software programs on health-related topics are health risk appraisals, which are programmed to take several kinds of basic informational data (age, selected health-behavioral patterns, personal health information such as weight and height and blood pressure, family history, and morbidity and mortality data) and project the likely risks of death over a specified period of time. These health risk appraisals have limited value for young students, particularly those of elementary and middle-school age, who have little perception of their mortality. Most health risk appraisal software programs are designed for adults or young adolescents, although there are health risk appraisal tables for children as young as 5 years of age.[13]

Classroom teachers at the elementary and middle-school levels must be able to evaluate software effectively.

As with any educational technology, teachers must determine how computers are going to be used—for enrichment, for remediation, or to introduce new concepts. Teachers must be able to determine if a software program is developmentally appropriate for their grade level and quickly assess if it meets the specific needs of the students. The objectives of the software program must be evaluated to ascertain if the computer program is consistent with the goals and objectives of the curriculum. The content information presented in the program must be accurate and current. Also, the instructional methodology used should be acceptable and appropriate for the age and grade level of students. In addition, teachers must determine if a program is interesting and understandable to students. The production, the sound and color, and the graphics should be attractive to the students who will be using the material.

Examples of Health Education Programs

The *Body Awareness Resource Network* (*BARN*) software program is a computer-based, health education system designed for adolescents.[14] Although *BARN* was principally developed for secondary school students, it can be used in middle school (grades 6–7). This program includes material on alcohol and drugs, diet and activity, family communication, human sexuality, smoking, and stress management. *BARN* uses gaming, decision-making techniques, and interactive interviewing and provides basic information. Funding for the development of this program was provided by the W. K. Kellogg Foundation.

Several other software packages that are designed for fifth and sixth grades are *Food for Thought, Human Pump, Learning to Cope with Pressure,* and *The Smoking Decision.*[15] The *Food for Thought* program presents gaming activities in which students learn the nutrients of a number of foods. Decision making is built into this program. Information relating to vitamins, calories, protein, saturated and polyunsaturated fats, carbohydrates, iron, sodium, zinc, and fiber is presented. This computer program is designed primarily for adolescents and adults. However, it may have value for upper-elementary and middle-level schoolchildren. *Human Pump* is an information program on the various factors that affect the heart, such as food, smoking, and exercise. *Learning to Cope with Pressure* uses biofeedback to reduce stress; it includes a biofeedback sensor that measures galvanic skin resistance, an indicator of the amount of tension an individual is experiencing. *The Smoking Decision* makes use of the interactive approach in decision making, presenting various situations that involve the smoking of cigarettes and their related effects. A number of colorful graphics are a part of this program.

Several instructional computer packages that build on various aspects of the anatomical and physiological components of the human body have been developed for fifth and sixth grade students.[16] Animated graphics make

CONSIDER THIS

Computer Software Evaluation

Software Title: _____

Publisher: _____

Grade Level Use: _____
(not what is recommended by the publisher,
but as ascertained by teacher preview)

Microcomputer Use:

Useful with:

Apple	_____
IBM-PC	_____
Other	_____

Amount of Memory Required: _____

Instructional Objectives of Content: _____

What health concepts and subjects are the focus of this software package?

Target Group: _____

Accuracy of Content: _____

What formats are used? _____

	Yes	No
Simulation	_____	_____
Graphics	_____	_____
Gaming	_____	_____
Interaction	_____	_____
Programmed instruction	_____	_____
Tutorials	_____	_____
Drill and practice	_____	_____

What supplemental materials accompany the software program?

	Yes	No
Teacher's guide	_____	_____
Student assignment material	_____	_____
Pre- and post-test material	_____	_____
Classroom posters	_____	_____
Other	_____	_____

How can the software package be integrated into the health classroom experience for the students?

Final Comments:

this a particularly valuable educational tool for elementary school health instruction.

Similar computer programs that explain various body systems for children in grades 1 through 6 make use of graphics, humor, and animation.[17] For example, a femur (the long bone of the upper leg) is host to a study of the bones and the muscles of the human body. Stanley the Stomach is host to a study of the digestive system, as is a red blood cell, which takes the students on a trip throughout the circulatory system. Another software package for grades 1 through 6 focuses on the senses: the eyes (sight), ears (hearing), and the nose (smell).

Health Watch[18] is a program designed for grades 3 through 5 that incorporates simulation gaming about dental hygiene, fitness, and nutrition. *Wellness Pursuit*, a gaming activity program designed for grades 4 through 6, provides information on six categories of wellness.[19]

Concern over child abuse has led to the development of the computer instructional program *Keeping Safe*.[20] In this package, simulation is used to help elementary schoolchildren make decisions that relate to abuse.

The American Cancer Society[21] has developed a computer gaming program for grades 4 through 6 called *Healthy Decisions*. Students are required to use decision-making skills in various situations that have an impact on their personal health and well-being. In this program, a visitor from outer space, Starga, helps the students make decisions that influence health. A teacher's guide that accompanies this software includes exercises and assignments that children can take home to involve their families.

Another voluntary health organization, the American Heart Association[22], has a software package that teaches elementary schoolchildren about the heart and circulatory system. *Heart Medley* is a five-part program designed to teach children how the heart functions. Included are various factors that affect the heart's health, such as genetics, nutrition, and personal lifestyle. Gaming activities are a major component of this software package.

Many computer software programs that focus on substance abuse education have been developed in recent years. The majority of these are designed for secondary schoolchildren. One such information program, *Drug Alert*, is designed for children in grades 5, 6, and above.[23] A variety of gaming activities introduce factual information to students. Another software program directed to sixth grade children is *Babysitting Basics*.[24] This interactive program prepares students for the responsibility of child care.

A comprehensive computer software package, *Friend C.H.I.P.*, is designed to focus on nutrition and fitness, self-esteem, safety, and peer relationships.[25] This program, for grades 4 through 6, uses student responses to paper-and-pencil exercises and assesses health-behavioral patterns. A broad range of teacher material accompanies this software package.

Many health instructional computer software programs are designed for grades 7 through 12, the junior and senior high school levels. They cover the broad range of subjects included in most comprehensive school health instructional programs: substance abuse, drugs, smoking, weight control, alcohol abuse, nutrition, health awareness, and sexuality. Although developed for secondary students, some programs may be applicable for upper-elementary students as well as middle-level school students. Teachers of these grades who wish to use computer programs in health instruction should review catalogs of educational computer companies to locate appropriate software.

Effects on Learning

The effects of computer-based education on health behavioral patterns are unclear. There is little evidence to show positive healthful behavioral changes in elementary-age children who have microcomputer experience. One reason for this might be that very few elementary teachers have used the computer in health instruction. Also, most materials designed for use in elementary schools tend to focus on lower-order cognitive learning. There is little application to other higher-order thought.

Almost no research has been conducted to ascertain the outcome of computer learning experiences on the short- and long-term health behavioral patterns of elementary and middle-level schoolchildren. With increasing computer instruction in elementary and middle-level school education, however, it will be necessary for teachers, professors, and researchers to make an effort to ascertain the effects of computer instruction in health education.

INSTRUCTIONAL TELEVISION

There has been a lot of criticism that elementary and middle-level schoolchildren watch too much television. Many believe that such behavior has lessened creative play activities and resulted in less physically active young people. However, television can be used as an effective teaching/learning tool by the classroom teacher in health education. Instructional television broadcasts over public educational television stations provide an exceptional medium for use in the schools. Some type of instructional television is available in most parts of the country, particularly in localities served by public television stations.[26]

The use of instructional television can occur in a variety of ways. Programs that are scheduled for regular broadcast over the public television station can be watched within the classroom when the timing is appropriate. Many public television broadcasting stations have developed lending procedures that permit the teacher to obtain the needed program on videocassette or disc for use at a time that is convenient for the class.

Educational instructional television can meet a number of instructional needs within the school setting. It can enable students to better understand abstract concepts. Students who are experiencing difficulty in the academic program can be helped, particularly those with reading deficiencies. This type of instructional material is effective in presenting controversial or sensitive topics. Instructional television also puts the health message in the context of characters to whom the students can relate in a story they can understand, just as when children are exposed to reading good literature.

The teacher who uses instructional television must integrate the television program with other instruction. For the best results, the teacher must interact with what is being presented on the video. When the television program is being played, the teacher should watch it along with the students and then provide follow-up activities to enhance the experience.

Many programs and series that are designed for use in health instruction are available. Several different approaches are used in each series. For example, drama is used quite effectively with sensitive and controversial topics such as divorce, death, and loneliness. The interactive approach in which the children are able to relate with the person on the screen is very popular. The use of cartoon characters and animation is another effective approach.

It would be impossible to present a description of all of the instructional television series that are available for use in elementary and middle-level school classrooms. Teachers can obtain such a listing from most public television stations in the viewing areas of the individual schools. One nutrition program designed for grades 1 through 4 is *Eat Well, Be Well.* Each 15-minute segment of the eight-part series focuses on a different concept of good nutrition. A very lively and entertaining format is used in this series. A 12-minute program, *Good Touch, Bad Touch,* is designed for use with children in grades 3 through 5, when presenting information to prevent sexual abuse. Children are given information in a very sensitive way that will help them to recognize and avoid abusive situations.

Several instructional television series are designed for use in preschool programs. One popular series is the *Mister Rogers Neighborhood* series. In this series, Mister Rogers talks with children about such topics as death, going to the hospital and to the dentist, wearing a cast, and other health-related topics of concern to preschool children.

Many of the series are prepared for children in the primary-school grades. *All About You* is a series that includes thirty 15-minute programs on a variety of basic health topics of concern to children in grades 1 through 3. Children are encouraged to learn by exploration about the various parts of the body—the skeleton, muscles, skin, brain, and so forth. Fear, friendship, families, safety, and feelings are other topics presented in this series.

A very entertaining, yet informative, set of fifteen-minute programs has been developed with Slim Goodbody. *The Inside Story with Slim Goodbody* series teaches children in grades 3 through 6 about the different systems of the body. Of particular note in this series are two programs that present instruction about substance abuse and AIDS. *The Inside Story of the Immune System and AIDS,* a very effective presentation on this topic, is controversial in the opinion of many parents of elementary schoolchildren. Another series, *All Fit with Slim Goodbody,* includes fifteen 15-minute programs that use music, imaginative sets, and student participation to help develop fitness.

There are also many instructional television programs designed for students in the middle-level schools. Several of these focus on substance abuse, boy-girl relationships, sex roles, teenage pregnancy, and Acquired Immunodeficiency Syndrome (AIDS). Topics that are controversial and sensitive in nature should be previewed by teachers prior to scheduling them for use in their schools.

For every series of instructional television that is available, there is usually accompanying information for the teacher. Although this teacher material varies, there are usually stated objectives for the series, suggestions for follow-up and discussion, and other suggested material that can be used.

Instructional television must not be seen as the principal medium for providing information to children. Teachers must integrate the materials into the health education course of study. Too often, instructional television is used as an adjunct or supplement to the health curriculum, rather than as a reinforcement of the learning objectives of the district-approved curriculum.

SUMMARY

Much of the formal, instructional information to which children are exposed during elementary and middle-level school years comes from their textbooks. The process of selecting textbooks differs from one school district to another. Teachers are often involved in the textbook selection process. Several elementary and middle-level health textbook series are available for use today. These books are designed to encourage individual student responsibility for health. They emphasize development of positive attitudes about health and the development and practice of positive health behaviors.

A broad range of instructional resources is available to assist classroom teachers who use the health-education textbooks. Increasingly, publishing companies provide teachers with supplemental materials such as transparencies, worksheets, handouts, and tests and quizzes for evaluation.

Elementary and middle-level health textbooks have become more attractive and interesting in recent years. A number of pedagogical aids accompany the material presented in most chapters, which include a broad range of topics. Health concepts also are included in other subject matter textbooks. For example, most science texts discuss a number of health concepts.

Computers have taken their place as an important educational tool in most elementary and middle-level schools in the United States. Although educational software has been designed principally for use in subjects other than health, there are a number of health software packages available for instructional purposes. Software packages that have been developed for use in elementary and middle-level schools cover such topics as nutrition, anatomy and physiology, substance abuse, and safety. It is important that elementary and middle-level schoolteachers become familiar with these computer software programs and incorporate them into the learning experiences of their health classes.

The spectacular growth of the Internet and the World Wide Web provides a resource to both teacher and student that was not available just a few years ago. Teachers can have immediate access to hundreds, even thousands, of informational sources to assist their teaching. Numerous teaching materials can be found on the Internet for use in elementary and middle-level health classrooms.

Another technology available for teachers of elementary and middle-level school health education is instructional television.

Numerous programs are useful to the health instructional program of the preschool through middle-school levels. These programs use a number of different approaches and cover a broad range of physical and emotional health topics. They are particularly effective in dealing with controversial and sensitive topics that often occur in the health instructional program.

DISCUSSION QUESTIONS

1. Discuss the role of textbooks in the elementary and middle-level school curriculum.

2. Explain the textbook selection process in a local school district with which you are familiar.

3. Identify some of the features that an elementary and/or middle-level schoolteacher must be aware of in selecting a health textbook.

4. What are some of the pedagogical aids found in elementary and middle-level school health textbooks?

5. In what ways do sexism and racism exist in elementary and middle-level school textbooks?

6. Explain what is meant by vertical and horizontal comparisons of textbooks.

7. What are some health topics and concepts that can be found in elementary and middle-level textbooks other than health?

8. Discuss how the role of computers in the educational process has expanded in the past several years.

9. In what ways has the Internet expanded the sources of information available to classroom teachers?

10. What is the World Wide Web?

11. Identify and explain how you might use some of the health software programs that are now available for use with elementary and middle-level schoolchildren.

12. Why is the CD-ROM particularly important in instructional technology in schools today?

13. What is instructional television as compared with commercial television?

14. Discuss some of the concepts and topics that are included in instructional television programming for use in health instruction.

ENDNOTES

1. M. Jean Young and Charles M. Riegeluth, *Improving the Textbook Selection Process* (Bloomington, IN: Phi Delta Kappa Educational Foundation, 1988).

2. *Health for Life (K–8),* Scott, Foresman and Company, 1900 East Lake Avenue, Glenview, IL 60025; *Health: Focus on You (1–8),* Merrill Publishing Company, 4635 Hilton Corporate Drive, Columbus, OH 43232.

3. ETR Associates; P.O. Box 1830; Santa Cruz, CA 95061-1830.

4. *Health for Life (K–8),* Scott, Foresman and Company; *Health: Focus on You (1–8),* Merrill Publishing Company.

5. Council on Interracial Books for Children, Inc., "Ten Quick Ways to Analyze Children's Books for Sexism and Racism," in *Guidelines for Selecting Bias-Free Textbooks and Storybooks* (New York: Council on Interracial Books for Children).

6. Lois Mayer Nichols, "The Influence of Student Computer-Ownership and In-Home Use on Achievement in an Elementary School Computer Programming Curriculum," *Journal of Educational Computing Research* 8, no. 4 (1992): 407.

7. Karen A. Bosch, "Is There a Computer Crisis in the Classroom?" *Schools in the Middle* (September 1993): 7–9.

8. Lisa N. Pealer and Steve M. Dorman. "Evaluating Health-Related Web Sites," *Journal of School Health* 67, no. 6 (August 1997): 232.

9. Steve M. Dorman, "Evaluating Computer Software for the Health Education Classroom," *Journal of School Health* 62, no. 1 (January 1992): 35.

10. Steve M. Dorman, "CD-ROM Use in Health Instruction," *Journal of School Health* 67, no. 10 (December, 1997): 444–446.

11. Moon S. Chen and Barbara Cornett, "How Effective Are Microcomputer-Based Programs for Health Education?: A Prospective View," *Health Education* 14, no. 6 (October 1983): 88.

12. Donald J. Breckon, "Microcomputer Applications to Health Education and Health Promotion," *The Eta Sigma Gamma Monograph Series* 5, no. 1 (November 1986): 11.

13. J. Hall and J. Zwemer, *Prospective Medicine* (Indianapolis, IN: Methodist Hospital of Indiana, 1979).

14. Kris Bosworth et al., "Adolescents, Health Education, and Computers: The Body Awareness Resource Network (BARN)," *Health Education* 14, no. 6 (October 1983): 58–60.

15. Sunburst Communications, 39 Washington Avenue, Pleasantville, NY 10570.

16. Quere Inc., 562 Boston Avenue, Room S, Bridgeport, CT 06610.

17. Comp Tech Systems Design, P.O. Box 516, Hastings, MN 55033.

18. Ibid.

19. Ibid.

20. Ibid.

21. American Cancer Society, 1599 Clifton Rd. NE, Atlanta, GA 30329.

22. American Heart Association, 7272 Greenville Avenue, Dallas, TX 75231.

23. Narcotics Education, Inc., 6830 Laurel St. NW, Washington, DC 20012.

24. MCE Educational Programming, 157 So. Kalamazoo Mall, Suite, 250, Kalamazoo, MI 49007.

25. Campbell Soup Company, Institute for Health and Fitness, Campbell Place, Camden, NJ 08103.

26. Instructional television programs listed in this section are available through the education services department of the local public television station.

SUGGESTED READINGS

Bosch, Karen A. "Is There a Computer Crisis in the Classroom?" *Schools in the Middle* (September 1993): 7–9.

Caissy, Gail A. *Microcomputers and the Classroom Teacher.* Bloomington, IN: Phi Delta Kappa, 1987.

Daniel, Eileen L. and Joseph E. Balog. "Utilization of the World Wide Web in Health Education," *Journal of Health Education* 28, no. 5 (September/October 1997): 260–267.

Dorman, Steve M. "Evaluating Computer Software for the Health Education Classroom," *Journal of School Health* 62, no. 1 (January 1992): 35–38.

Dorman, Steve M. "CD-ROM Use in Health Instruction," *Journal of School Health* 67, no. 10 (December 1997): 444–446.

Ely, Donald E. "Computers in Schools and Universities in the United States of America." *Educational Technology* 23, no. 9 (September 1993): 53–57.

Gold, Robert S. *Microcomputer Applications in Health Education.* Dubuque, IA: Wm. C. Brown, 1991.

Hunter, Barbara et al. "Technology in the Classroom: Preparing Students for the Information Age." *Schools in the Middle* (Summer 1993): 3–6.

Lee, Jean. "Children, Teachers, and the Internet," *The Delta Kappa Gamma Bulletin* 64, no. 2 (Winter 1998): 5–9.

Nichols, Lois Mayer. "The Influence of Student Computer-Ownership and In-Home Use on Achievement in an Elementary School Computer Programming Curriculum." *Journal of Educational Computing Research* 8, no. 4 (1992): 407–421.

Pealer, Lisa N. and Steve M. Dorman. "Evaluating Health-Related Web Sites," *Journal of School Health* 67, no. 6 (August 1997): 232–235.

Robinson, James. "Criteria for the Selection and Use of Health Education Reading Materials." *Health Education* 19, no. 4 (August/September 1988): 31–34.

Waters, Mae. "The Value of Technology in Teaching Health Education." Proceedings of Six Regional Workshops, Strengthening Health Education for the 1990s. Reston, VA: The Association for the Advancement of Health Education, 1994.

Elementary and Middle-Level Health Textbook Series

Health for Life (K–8)

Scott, Foresman and Company
1900 East Lake Avenue
Glenview, IL 60025

Health: Focus on You (1–8)

Merrill Publishing Company
4635 Hilton Corporate Drive
Columbus, OH 43232

Comprehensive Health for the Middle Grades

ETR Associates, P.O. Box 1830
Santa Cruz, CA 95061-1830

 INTERNET INFORMATION

GENERAL HEALTH-RELATED INTERNET WEBSITES

It is impossible to present all of the Web pages that provide accurate information on all of health topics within the confines of this textbook. In each chapter, selected Web pages are identified that are appropriate to the content of that specific chapter. One Web page that is provided by the government is an excellent source of reference. This website includes sources of information available from United States governmental agencies, nonprofit health organizations, professional health and medical associations, educational institutions, and health and medical libraries. This website is www.healthfinder.gov.

Other websites that have general health-related information include these from governmental agencies:

U.S. Department of Education—**www.ed.gov**

U.S. Department of Health and Human Services—**www.os.dhhs.gov**

U.S. Centers for Disease Control and Prevention—**www.cdc.gov**

U.S. National Institutes of Health—**www.nih.gov**

Administration for Children and Families—**www.acf.dhhs.gov**

5

MANAGING HEALTH EDUCATION IN THE BUSY CLASSROOM ENVIRONMENT

OUTLINE

INTRODUCTION

Although the structure and time frame of the school day have remained relatively stable, the knowledge base in all content areas has grown exponentially. As a result, teachers are challenged to fit an ever-expanding body of knowledge and skills into the time constraints of the school day.[1] Teachers in self-contained classrooms must manage allocation of time resources to accommodate effective instruction in diverse content areas including reading, mathematics, science, social studies, computer literacy, the arts, and health education.

By contrast, the hiring of health education content specialists in the middle grades often is the norm. Health educators in this setting must confront the challenge of organizing meaningful and developmentally appropriate learning experiences in the wide range of health issues associated with the six CDC priority health risk behaviors. This task must be accomplished in context of competing demands on instructional time.

Regardless of the grade level of students, interruptions are common in the school schedule. Activities such as mandated testing and other special enrichment programs can disrupt the continuity of instruction even in classrooms organized around the most developmentally appropriate health education course of study. Time constraints pose significant challenges for all teachers, including those most highly motivated to advance a health promotion agenda.

The unfortunate outcome of this competition for valuable time is that important learning activities, or even whole units of instruction, are sacrificed. In response to community priorities, content matters featured on state tests of proficiency, or the lack of teacher comfort with subject matter, time that should be devoted to instruction with a specific focus on health issues often is compromised. Instructional time is influenced by events on the master schedule of the school. These things are beyond the control of the classroom teacher, and include predetermined recess and lunch periods. In addition, the classroom schedule is influenced by instructional programs in art, music, and physical education, taught by itinerant content specialists. Such demands on time resources have a negative impact on health promotion programming in both elementary and middle-level schools.

This chapter suggests practical ways to support vital, direct instruction about health content matters. "Tools" that can help teachers weave effective health-education activities into the fabric of the school day are discussed. Specifically, learning activities that can be incorporated into a range of health education content areas are described, and cooperative learning applications for health education lesson planning are explored. Beyond direct instructional approaches, correlated and integrated health education strategies are examined, and suggestions for managing potentially controversial health lessons are offered. Finally, this chapter reviews the importance of parent involvement in health promotion activities and suggest ways to engage parents in student health promotion.

Many of the recommendations included in this chapter are techniques with which elementary and middle-grade teachers are familiar. The "tools" in this chapter, however, are applied specifically to comprehensive health instruction. These practical recommendations are offered to help teachers who feel that although health promotion activities are important, they are just "one more thing to add to an already overcrowded school day."

INSTRUCTIONAL APPROACHES FOR EFFECTIVE HEALTH EDUCATION

Chapters 1 and 3 of this text suggested direction for elementary and middle-level teachers in curriculum development. Foundational elements for improving direct instruction in health education also were discussed. This body of information illuminates the many important variables that influence developmentally appropriate health education learning experiences.

Importantly, however, once developmentally appropriate health promotion concepts are identified, corresponding learning activities must be organized to maximize effective use of finite time resources. It is common for education professionals in elementary and middle schools to incorporate three instructional approaches:

1. The traditional model, organized with a specific focus on health issues;
2. A cooperative learning approach; and
3. Individualized instructional strategies.

Teachers are likely to encounter all three curricular approaches in health education courses of study. Teacher comfort and expertise can be enhanced by a review of the foundational elements of each approach.

Instruction Organized with a Specific Focus on Health Issues

The starting point for all discussion about the nature of knowledge is its organization into discrete disciplines. Many education researchers contend that each academic discipline is a form of knowledge with separate and discrete characteristics and a unique set of questions. Further, the motivation for organizing instruction by discrete academic disciplines, particularly in American middle and high schools, is that this model reinforces efficiency.[2] Piaget (1972) defines a discipline as a specific body of teachable knowledge with its own background of education, training, methods, and areas of focus.[3]

Many local district curriculum resources include learning activities that are organized into strictly focused discrete subjects or content areas. In schools that adopt this model, subjects are taught in separate blocks of time. In secondary classrooms, the schedule of time blocks usually is predetermined and identified by a centrally triggered system of bells or other signals. Time blocks in self-contained classrooms usually are more fluid. In these classrooms, teachers have more latitude to respond to the interests, pace, or developmental attributes of the learners.

Instruction that is organized by discrete discipline represents the most common scheduling model incorporated into the United States educational enterprise. This approach is associated with the following advantages for students, teachers, administrators, and parents:

- Parents, teachers, and students are familiar and comfortable with it;
- Courses of study and state goals and mandates are organized in this way;
- Textbooks and supplementary learning materials are readily available;
- Students are empowered with specialized information and skills;

- Secondary teachers are academically prepared as content specialists with a limited range, but with great depth of expertise; and
- All content areas, even those perceived to be of less importance, are afforded some portion of formal instructional time.

Supporters of such instructional approaches for health education base this endorsement on the notion that health education is a discrete body of knowledge that has its own philosophy and, consequently, an integrity worthy of content-specific attention and time allocation.[4]

Instructional Activities with Many Uses

It is not uncommon for teachers to associate a particular learning activity with a specific grade level or health topic area. However, teachers must remember that there are countless instructional activities or learning strategies that have applicability for diverse target audiences. In addition, many activities can be adapted to span a wide range of health related content areas.

Teachers who are interested in activities with applicability for a range of students and health topics are encouraged to examine table 5.1. Each of the activities in the table can be applied to all of the six CDC problem priority areas and can help teachers target the national health education standards. While this figure does not include an exhaustive list of such versatile activities, it provides a starting point for teachers to experiment with cross-topical application of learning activities. Recommendations for using these learning activities to address specific health issues can be found in later content-based chapters of this text. Finally, these activities can be used across the curriculum to reinforce instruction in other academic subjects, including reading, social studies, math, and/or science.

Limitations of Instructional Approaches with a Direct Focus on Health Issues

Although common and familiar, instruction with a discipline-specific content focus can present limitations for teachers and students. The major problem associated with this instructional approach is the fundamental fragmentation of concepts and instructional time. In practical application, as students in secondary schools move from one subject to another, they also change rooms. As a result, teachers are forced to structure learning activities according to time parameters rather than in response to developmental needs of students. Finally, although structuring instruction in discrete content categories is a very common academic approach, it presents an unrealistic perspective of problems and issues that students will confront in the world outside of school. This instructional model implies that students will be required to manage situations and questions one at a time and only within discrete subject areas. This model does not provide formal learning experiences or reinforcement for enabling and empowering students to draw relationships between or across content issues—tasks that they must successfully manage in their daily lives.[5]

In addition, discipline-specific instruction usually is based on a philosophy that reinforces the value of competition. This very common competitive teaching/learning philosophy is implemented in today's classrooms more than 90% of the time.[6] The underpinning of this model implies that all students are expected to do their own work. Classmates are discouraged from seeking assistance from their peers. Further, providing assistance for other students usually is regarded as cheating. As a result of intentional or unintentional teacher behaviors, students are reinforced for working against one another to accomplish personal goals. In this way, the potential benefits from collaborative problem solving and decision making about academic challenges are not maximized for learners.

An undesirable, yet common, example of this competitive classroom environment occurs when the teacher asks students to answer a question. It is common for several students to demonstrate a willingness to respond to the challenge. Interestingly, however, as the selected student is providing a response, classmates who also want to provide an answer often hope that the selected student will fail. In the event that the student who was called upon offers an incorrect response, the remaining volunteers have a chance to be selected and recognized for better work. Even under the best of circumstances, a hierarchy of student performance emerges that can adversely influence academic performance, classroom climate, and student interaction.[7]

Cooperative Learning: An Instructional Alternative

One alternative in managing the competitive philosophy that is often associated with traditional instructional approaches is to incorporate cooperative learning into health education curricula. This alternative currently is used in about 7% of classrooms.[8] Cooperative learning includes both a teaching philosophy and a collection of instructional methods that have broad applicability.[9] This model has been incorporated into language arts, science, mathematics, and social studies units of study. Research has confirmed positive benefits for students who participate in cooperative learning strategies, including improved attitudes toward learning, better retention and achievement, and increased time-on-task and motivation. In addition, critical thinking skills, social support behaviors, and attitudes toward culturally diverse and mainstreamed academically handicapped peers are influenced positively by participation in cooperative learning.[10] Further, these important outcomes are gained in the context of, rather than in addition to, content-based instructional activities. In this way, valuable instructional time is conserved without compromising learning.

Despite this positive and compelling evidence, there has been limited application of cooperative learning

TABLE 5.1	Selected Activities with Applicability for a Range of Health Topics and Grade Levels

Anonymous Cards Strategy

1. Each student receives an identical 3 × 5 inch card or piece of paper. All students must have similar writing implements.
2. Students are instructed to provide no personal identification on the card or paper.
3. Students respond to a series of teacher-developed questions on their card.
4. Questions are reviewed and cards are collected when all students have completed their responses.
5. The teacher shuffles the cards and redistributes them. Students receive a card that is not their own. Students who might receive their own card in this process are encouraged to proceed with the activity as though the responses were provided by a classmate. It is important to assure the presumption of anonymity as cards are redistributed.
6. The teacher cues the discussion with the following: "Who has a card on which someone said. . . " or "What did your classmate who wrote on the card that you received, have to say about. . .?"

(The Anonymous Card activity enables students to compare and contrast their knowledge, beliefs, and self-reported practices with classmates. This activity can be used to explore health issues across all three learning domains while protecting students' anonymity. Nonwriters can use drawings, colors, or shapes to depict responses.)

Human Scavenger Hunts/ People Scrambles

1. Prior to class, teachers construct a handout asking students to conduct a self-assessment of their knowledge, attitudes, or self-reported practices about the health issue on which the unit is focused. Space is provided for student reflections on the handout.
2. One self-assessment sheet is distributed to each student.
3. Developmentally appropriate time limits are set for students to address all questions or items on the sheet.
4. When all students have completed this portion of the activity, they are encouraged to seek classmates with additional knowledge, different beliefs, or alternative health practices. Classmates from whom this information is gathered are asked to place their signature on the sheet confirming that they shared their alternative response.
5. Teachers are encouraged to place strict time limits on this phase of the activity. In addition, the activity may be structured to limit the number of signatures that students may gather from any one classmate.

(This activity works well for any group of students with reading and writing skills. Developmentally appropriate accommodations must be made. The Human Scavenger Hunt is an effective trigger activity, or it can be used to summarize a unit of instruction.)

The Carousel Activity

1. Prior to the class, the teacher prepares a series of trigger questions, phrases, or words about the health topic. Each is placed at the top of large sheet of newsprint paper.
2. Students are organized into appropriately sized groups. Each student has something with which to write. Each group receives a sheet of newsprint for its consideration. For older students, the groups can assemble around sheets that have been taped to the wall. For younger students, it may be appropriate to work on the floor.
3. In carefully monitored time periods, all students are encouraged to provide written feedback to the question or issue on their large sheet of paper. As students respond concurrently, it must be reinforced that no student may write on top of the work provided by any other student.
4. When the time period has elapsed, all students are asked to stop writing. The groups of students are instructed to rotate to another issue or question to which they will respond. When they reach the next sheet, they are to provide as complete a response as possible in the available time. Teachers are urged to remind students to ignore the work of previous responders. This process continues until all students have responded to all items.
5. When groups return to the sheet on which they provided their original responses, they are to read all responses, tally and react to the comments, and prepare to share a summary of the remarks with the class as a whole.

(Structuring developmentally appropriate time blocks for all phases of this activity is imperative. The advantage of this activity is that each student responds independently in relative anonymity to each item before groups process the responses. This activity can be used to introduce, reinforce, or summarize units of health instruction.)

(continued)

TABLE 5.1	Selected Activities with Applicability for a Range of Health Topics and Grade Levels *(continued)*

Fishbone Diagrams

Figure 5.1
The Fishbone diagram.

1. Prior to the lesson, the teacher prepares a blank fishbone diagram for each student (see figure 5.1). This activity also can be used in a group format. In addition, the teacher identifies themes with contrasting points of view.
2. Each student places the theme on which he or she is working in the "head" of the fishbone diagram. Then opposing viewpoints, conflicting information, or alternative practices are brainstormed. Contrasting responses are written on opposing "bones" of the diagram.
3. When completed, responses are shared with partners, small groups, or the whole class.

(This activity can be part of an art or social studies correlation. It has been adapted from the body of literature on total quality management, and also is referred to as Ishikawa Charts, a tool for brainstorming. This brainstorming format has the advantage over its counterparts of enabling students to compare and contrast information, beliefs, or self-reported skills.)

CONSIDER THIS

Identifying the Differences between Traditional and Cooperative Learning Groups

TRADITIONAL LEARNING GROUPS	COOPERATIVE LEARNING GROUPS
No interdependence	Positive interdependence
No individual accountability	Individual accountability
Homogeneous grouping	Heterogeneous grouping
One appointed leader	Shared leadership
Responsible only for self	Shared responsibility for groupmates
Only task emphasized	Task and maintenance emphasized
Social skills assumed	Social skills directly taught
Teacher ignores group function	Teacher observes and intervenes in group process
No group processing following task	Groups process their effectiveness as well as accomplishment to the task

strategies in health-education units of instruction.[11] *Code Blue: Uniting for Healthier Youth* asserts that a new kind of health education be taught, an approach focused on developing student skills in decision making, dealing with group pressure, avoiding fights, and working cooperatively.[12] In this spirit, cooperative learning has been associated with improving the following specific health-related outcomes: self-esteem, conflict resolution, content mastery of HIV/AIDS information, and social and resiliency skills.[13]

While many teachers in elementary and middle grades incorporate group work into classroom practice, coopera-

tive learning involves much more than randomly arranging clusters of students into health-issue discussion groups.[14] Cooperative learning groups are carefully arranged to include students with a range of abilities. The Consider This box above reviews the differences between simple group work and cooperative learning groups.[15] In addition, Gardner's work on the Multiple Intelligences, which was discussed in chapter 3, provides an interesting and effective way to organize cooperative learning groups.[16]

In cooperative learning, students are responsible not only for their own achievement, but also for that of their

TABLE 5.2	An Overview of Selected Cooperative Learning Strategies
Structure	**Brief Description**
Roundrobin	Students take turns sharing information, attitudes, or skills with their teammates.
Corners	Group designees move to a predetermined corner of the room. Students in corner groups then discuss and prepare to paraphrase ideas for their reassembled cooperative learning groups.
Numbered Heads Together	Questions or challenges are posed to groups by the teacher. Group members who have been previously assigned numbers consult on the answer or response, reflecting the best collective wisdom of the group. When the teacher calls a number at random, the student with that assigned number shares the group response.
Pairs Check	Groups of students work in pairs to alternate in the roles of "problem solver" and "coach." After two problems, each pair compares answers with its counterpart in the group.
Think-Pair-Share	Working independently, then with a partner, students identify a solution or response for a teacher-posed challenge. Pairs then share responses with classmates.
Team Word Webbing	Group members respond simultaneously on a large sheet of paper to identify main concepts, supporting elements, and bridges between concepts.
Roundtable	Learners take turns providing responses as a pencil and paper are passed around the group.

groupmates. Such a practice not only reinforces collaboration, but also encourages a more reciprocal status among group members.[17] Specifically, cooperative learning implies that students depend on one another for rewards by contributing to team achievement through participation in peer tutoring.[18] Cooperative learning groups and activities consistently are organized to contain the following common elements:

- *Positive Interdependence.* This is ensured through assigning mutual goals, providing joint rewards, and dividing tasks, materials, resources, and information among group members.
- *Face-to-Face Interaction.* Students seated in close physical proximity are supported in mutual discussion of all aspects of the assignment. Such practices reinforce positive interdependence.
- *Individual Accountability.* Although there is a focus on group outcomes, it is important that individual student achievement is not compromised. To this end, teachers can support individual learning by assigning students to bring individually completed work to the group, picking random students to answer questions, and assigning challenging jobs or roles for each student.
- *Interpersonal and Small-Group Skills.* Rather than assuming that students possess social and collaborative skills, these skills are formally taught as a foundation of cooperative learning. Reinforcement of these skills is enhanced by establishing the following expectations for groups: everyone contributes and helps, everyone listens carefully to others, group members praise good work, and quiet voices are used unless otherwise specified.
- *Group Processing.* Formal acknowledgment is provided for assessing group achievement and

working relationships. This can be accomplished by having students follow group work by identifying at least three group members or specific things that enhanced collaborative success.[19]

A variety of strategies can help teachers maintain fidelity to these fundamental tenets of cooperative learning. Researchers have identified a number of selected cooperative learning structures for use with diverse age groups and content areas. These structures are effective in health education by supporting academic growth in the cognitive, affective, and psychomotor learning domains. Commonly used cooperative learning strategies or structures include "Roundrobin," "Corners," "Numbered Heads Together," "Pairs Check," "Think-Pair-Share," "Team Word Webbing," and "Roundtable." A brief overview of each strategy is found in table 5.2.[20]

Applying Cooperative Learning to Nutrition Education   The following "Jigsaw" structure can be included in a unit on nutritional health promotion. In this example, students in middle-grade cooperative learning groups are challenged to increase their understanding of the *Dietary Guidelines for Americans* developed by the U.S. Departments of Agriculture and Health and Human Services. Group members are responsible for developing expertise in one segment of a similar body of information that is distributed to each group. Students then teach this information to group members. The following steps are suggested for using this "Jigsaw" activity:

1. Teachers provide identical and complete packets of material to each group. Packets for each group are arranged in similarly labeled subsections.
2. Each student receives an individual assignment of one subsection of material.

3. Students then seek out peers from other cooperative learning groups with identical assignments. This temporary group of "experts" reads, discusses, and formulates a plan for effectively presenting the information to their peers.
4. "Experts" then return to their original cooperative learning groups and teach this content to their peers.
5. The "Jigsaw" can be processed by the teacher, who randomly calls on students to explain specifics of the dietary guidelines, has groups prepare model meal posters for classroom display, or tests student content mastery on a written quiz.[21]

In addition to previously discussed advantages, one of the most appealing attributes of a cooperative learning approach is its flexible applicability. Cooperative learning structures or strategies have been incorporated successfully into units of instruction ranging from nutritional health promotion to HIV/AIDS risk reduction. In addition, cooperative learning activities have been used with a wide range of learners from groups of students in the late primary grades to corporate environments.

Teachers are encouraged to explore the extensive body of literature on cooperative learning. Cooperative learning most likely will never completely replace the more traditional or competitive classroom approach to learning. However, when used as an instructional supplement from one-third to one-half of the time, cooperative learning approaches help students benefit from both formats.[22]

Individualized Instruction: An Instructional Alternative

When health instruction is not organized with a discipline-specific focus or with the cooperative learning format, individualized instructional approaches can provide an effective alternative. This much less common instructional format has enjoyed wide use in learning resource centers to better meet the needs of students with learning or developmental disabilities. Individualized learning approaches also are used to remediate or supplement more conventional educational approaches.[23]

One specific application of individualized instruction that holds merit for health education practice is the use of learning centers. Learning centers that focus on timely health issues often add an important individualized dimension to elementary and middle-level classrooms.

Learning Centers   A learning center consists of an organized sequence of child-centered activities, each of which increases knowledge, develops skills, and/or helps children examine their attitudes or beliefs about a health topic. While working at a learning center, students are active and independent learners. They are encouraged to work at their own pace on any number of interesting and multisensory activities organized to supplement more formal instruction.

Learning centers usually are arranged in a compact location in the classroom. To develop a learning center, teachers are encouraged to collect sets of materials, instructions, and/or complete activities in a designated, often separate, classroom space. The physical space of a learning center is often large enough for multiple students to work simultaneously on several self-selected tasks. This reinforces the notion of "parallel play" that is particularly appropriate for students in primary grades. Student work commonly is displayed at the learning center as a model for other students. Projects also can be shared with broader school audiences.

In a traditional classroom setting, learning centers are developed to expand or reinforce particular aspects of the formal curriculum. In addition, a well-designed learning center can extend an educator's effectiveness by providing an independent learning alternative for students. Well-designed learning centers can serve to:

- Organize resource materials for students,
- Encourage students to work independently,
- Respond to individual learning pace,
- Incorporate both independent and collaborative activities,
- Supplement or reinforce basic instruction,
- Provide opportunities for applying higher-order thinking skills and work in multiple learning domains, and
- Combine a well-organized structure and freedom for independent thinking and creative expression.

Although there is great variety in the structure of learning centers, planning should be focused on the following common elements:

1. Developmentally appropriate learning objectives or organizing concepts,
2. Directions for students working at the center,
3. Samples or models of previously completed work,
4. Media or computer applications,
5. Strategies for introducing and sequencing activities, and
6. Evaluation protocol based on the identified objectives.

The Health Fair   An interesting and effective alternative to the conventional use of learning centers in the classroom is to organize multiple student-developed centers into a health fair or health carnival. Students and teachers may be familiar with the format of health fairs from having participated in such events at a hospital, shopping mall, or community center. A health fair can be an exciting, useful trigger or reinforcement activity when it is incorporated into the district's approved health education graded course of study.

When describing a county or state fair, words like fun, excitement, noise, rides, food, booths, games, prizes, music, color, and exhibits often come to mind. These same words have been used to describe health fairs or carnivals. Health fairs provide opportunities to teach health concepts in a hands-on, fun, creative, and exciting way. Learning centers developed for school health fairs focus direct health instruction on topics as diverse as substance abuse prevention, handicap awareness, the senses, and fire safety. Although health screening (including vision and hearing testing, reaction time testing, and blood typing) often is conducted at community health fairs for adult target audiences, it is less developmentally appropriate for use with school students.

While health fairs provide valuable supplemental health education learning experiences, they should not be perceived as the foundation for direct health instruction in any school. Rather, the purpose of a health fair is to stimulate interest in health education and to expose participants to a variety of developmentally appropriate health issues in a compressed period of time. The health fair also can serve as an effective organizational umbrella for collaborative activities among community groups, parents, teachers, and students. As such, health fairs can provide unique and memorable learning experiences.

Types of Health Fairs. Health fairs can be incorporated into an elementary and middle-level school health curriculum in a variety of ways. First, they can be organized for elementary students by college students enrolled in health-education classes, by junior or senior high health classes, or by health agencies in the community. Such collaboration between elementary and middle-level students and their secondary or university counterparts, or local agency professionals can prove to be mutually enriching.

A second way that health fairs can be integrated into the academic program of studies in elementary and middle-level schools is to have students in the upper grades develop learning centers and organize a health fair for their primary-grade counterparts. Teachers who supervise activity planning for such cross-age activities should be cognizant of developmentally appropriate practice issues.

A third application of the health fair format is to have middle-grade students organize a health fair for parents and the local community. When organizing a fair for parents, appropriate topics for adults, including diabetes prevention, tobacco use, cardiovascular disease prevention, and osteoporosis prevention, should be the focus. Such an activity allows students to learn more about their parents' health concerns while promoting the health of adults in the community.

Organization of the Health Fair. In organizing a health fair as part of comprehensive school health instruction, both teachers and students have responsibilities. While the specific division of labor will vary depending upon the age of student planners and target groups for the health fair, the following general planning recommendations will be helpful for teachers of all grade levels:

Time Considerations. When elementary and middle-level students develop and conduct a

health fair for younger peers or for adults in the community, significant preparation is needed to make the activity a success. When conducting a health fair for the first time, appropriate lead time (usually 6 to 8 weeks) is important. In addition, planning should include blocking out a time frame on the master calendar of the school (usually between 1 and 2 hours depending on the age of the target audience) for the actual health fair.

Facilities/Location. Upper-elementary teachers must make arrangements for access to a facility that is large enough to conduct the fair. Typically, a cafeteria or gymnasium provides sufficient wall and floor space.

Supplies and Equipment. Each group of students creating a learning center for the health fair needs access to an appropriately sized table. While 8-foot tables work well, card tables suffice. Supplies to create the topical learning centers, including poster board, newsprint, streamers, and magic markers, can be provided by the school art department or by local merchants.

Publicity. Local radio, newspaper, and television stations should be contacted by the district information official. In addition, promotional materials and press releases should be distributed well in advance of the health fair. Students are reinforced by such publicity, and it serves as a good public relations tool for the school.

Administrative Approval and Invitations. While administrative support is ideal, administrative approval is a critical element for any school activity. Once administrative sanction is granted for the health fair, formal invitations should be made to teachers of invited classes. If the fair is for parents and adults in the community, individual invitations should be mailed or sent home with the students.

Bags/Containers for Collected Materials. Learning center planners should arrange for bags to be available for attendees to collect materials. Health fair participants will gather a number of tokens or mementos to remind them of their participation in the various learning center activities. Teachers can ask local merchants, hospitals, or service agencies to donate developmentally appropriate-sized containers.

Invite Evaluation. Following the health fair, it is a good idea to invite the elementary and middle-level school participants to write reaction paragraphs or draw pictures about what they learned or liked best. This provides important and, usually, positive feedback for developers of the learning centers at the health fair.

In addition to the responsibilities implied for teachers whose students are preparing for a health fair,

---

CONSIDER THIS

Team Request for Health Fair Topics

Group Members' Names:

1.

2.

3.

4.

Topic Choices:
Please list your top three choices for booth topic. Then with each general topic, state the specific theme for your activities (examples: (1) Tobacco—Why people smoke, (2) Alcohol and other drugs—safe use of medicine). General Topic and Specific Theme of Each (in order please):

General Topic   **Specific Theme**

1.

2.

3.

(Having each student group submit such a form is helpful to the teacher. The teacher can then select from among the groups' three choices and inform the students which topic they are to prepare and present at the health fair.)

---

elementary and middle-level students involved in learning center development also must be willing to assume responsibility for a great deal of work in planning and organizing activities. This can serve as an ideal activity for cooperative learning groups.

Once groups have been organized, children should be provided with background information to enable them to select an interesting learning center topic. Groups should be encouraged to develop original ideas. At this point in the planning process, however, they will often need suggestions of general topics.

To increase the range of topics addressed at the health fair, it is helpful to have student groups identify three general topics that interest them. In addition, students should clarify a specific theme or concept within this broader topic, around which their learning center activities will be organized. Once each planning group submits its ideas, teachers can make assignments that maintain fidelity to student interests and increase the variety of topics

addressed. The Consider This box above, suggests elements for a handout to help students with topic selection.

Once topics have been assigned, all planning groups should be provided with a handout that clarifies the names of group members, the topics on which they will be working, and the number assigned to their learning center. At this time, the teacher should clarify for the students the common expectations and specific parameters for organizing learning centers.

Planning groups should prepare colorful and inviting centers that include fun activities for participants. On the day of the health fair, dressing in a costume that matches the theme is often an advantage for planning groups. For instance, students might dress like dentists and allied professionals when focusing on a dental health theme. For older students, balloons, streamers, and colorful posters should be used to decorate the learning center. It is very effective to arrange correlated learning experiences with art education professionals. In this way, specific student

Learning centers at health fairs should be colorful and should include activities in which all children can participate.

planning activities for the health fair are supported by other teachers in the school.

Students may need help with developing trigger activities or organizing effective ways to introduce their learning centers. Trigger activities should consist of a hands-on activity or demonstration that involves multiple senses of the learning center participants. Examples include working with smoking machines to demonstrate tar in cigarette smoke, and food samples to introduce the sense of taste. In addition, students should plan to share accurate information and to provide summary or closure activities. To make learning more fun and interesting, learning center organizers must be reminded of the developmental attributes of the target audience that will be participating in the health fair.

Student planning groups should be prepared to distribute tokens for everyone participating in the activities at their learning center. Tokens are intended to remind the participants of the activities in which they participated at the health fair. Tokens can be handmade by the students who develop the learning center or as an activity completed by students who participate in the health fair. Tokens also can be donated by community health agencies (American Cancer Society or American Heart Association), or by local businesses. Although printed brochures and pamphlets commonly are distributed as tokens at community-based health fairs, often they are not developmentally appropriate for use in school settings.

Younger health fair participants often respond more positively to buttons, stickers, and certificates. Tokens that can be worn are also very popular with younger students. For safety reasons, however, pins should be avoided. Finally, teachers are urged to remember that only healthy treats and products should be distributed at health fairs—no junk food or candy! The following are examples of tokens that are appropriate for distribution at a range of learning centers:

Cardiovascular Health: A balloon in the shape of a heart, a heart crossword puzzle, or a construction paper heart on which students have listed heart healthy snacks.

Dental Health: Dental floss, toothbrushes, student-made tooth powder, toothpaste, or a toothbrush.

Alcohol and Other Drug Prevention: "Just Say No" buttons for primary-grade students, "Red Ribbon" campaign ribbons, bumper stickers, or drug-free contracts/pledges.

Emotional Health: Yarn pom-poms representing warm fuzzies, a mirror, or a card with instructions to do a "random act of kindness" or to give a compliment to a friend or family member.

Fitness: Jump ropes, a certificate indicating resting and exercise heart rate, or sweat bands.

First Aid: Band-aids, a chart showing common pressure points, or rolled gauze bandages.

Growth and Development: A flower seed planted in a cup, or an outline of the participant's hand or foot.

Personal Health: A bar of soap, coloring books about keeping clean, a washcloth, tissue packages, or a self-made certificate that says "I'm Clean."

Nutrition: Paper plate with a picture of the Food Guide Pyramid in the center, a piece of fresh fruit or some other nutritional snack, or a recipe card.

Reducing Unintentional Injuries: Bicycle reflectors, transparent window stickers with safety slogans, or a sticker with important safety telephone numbers including those for the fire and police departments.

Senses: A hand, tongue, nose, eye, or ear shaped out of construction paper, ear plugs, perfume or cologne, a surgical glove, or the participant's name typed in Braille.

Tobacco Prevention: Buttons that say "Kiss Me, I Don't Smoke" from the American Cancer Society, bumper stickers and signs that say "No Smoking" from the American Heart Association, or a certificate that says "I Don't Smoke and I'm Proud of It."

As a final stage of planning, students should complete and submit a written, detailed plan of their learning center. The Consider This box on page 90 includes a sample outline that can serve as the basis for a writing correlation activity for students and as an opportunity for teachers to check group progress. In addition, planned activities and accuracy of student information can be evaluated.

Students should be given time during class to work on their learning centers so that teachers can provide adequate support and supervision. It is a good idea to have groups present their learning centers for their classmates several days before the event. At this time, students can practice their various roles and make final adjustments before the health fair.

CONSIDER THIS

Sample Health Fair Outline

General Health Topic of the Learning Center:

Specific Theme or Concept on Which the Center Is Focused:

Learning Center Number:
Organization or Sequence of Activities (attach on a separate sheet):
  A. Trigger Activity/Introduction

  B. Information to Be Shared

  C. Multisensory Activities Planned

  D. Summary/Closure Activity

Drawing or Diagram of the Layout of the Booth:

List of Equipment and Materials Needed:

Sample of Token (attached):

(This is a model of an outline that the students can be expected to submit to the teacher clarifying plans and procedures for their health fair learning center.)

Evaluation of the Health Fair. Several types of evaluation can occur before, during, and after a health fair. Formative evaluation strategies involve those formal or intentional assessment activities that occur during the planning or developmental process of an activity. One example that is appropriate as a learning activity involves having the teacher and/or group members provide reactions as they develop the learning center. In addition, groups are encouraged to complete a teacher-developed, written, self-evaluation checksheet immediately preceding the health fair. This helpful exercise can solve last-minute problems.

During the health fair, group members formally and/or informally can ask the participants to evaluate the overall health fair activity. In addition, each group can as-

sign one student to be a "roving reporter" who circulates among health fair participants asking a series of predetermined questions. "Roving reporters" can carry "press passes" and can gather information about participant reactions to the event. Although this is not a precise objective evaluation protocol, much worthwhile qualitative information can be gathered from it. Suggestions that are gathered could help improve future health fairs. In addition, such an evaluation offers a structured opportunity for students to practice important communication skills.

Following the health fair, participants can be sent a checksheet on which they indicate their reactions to the health fair and the specific activities in which they participated. In addition, teachers may be asked to have involved students write letters or create artwork indicating their evaluation of the fair. Another type of summative evaluation involves formal teacher feedback about individual and group activities. These comments can focus on both the development and implementation of the learning center. The teacher will need to visit each learning center to record observations while the activities are in progress. This could be followed by the teacher writing a letter summarizing evaluation comments to each group. In response, in a writing correlation activity, cooperative learning groups that planned the health fair learning centers could compose "letters to the editor" summarizing their impressions, concerns, and recommendations about their participation in the health fair and its value as a learning experience.

Interdisciplinary Instructional Approaches

In 1977, Elvin provided an analogy to help educators see the value of examining alternatives to direct instructional approaches. He suggested that when we are walking outside, we are not confronted with 50 minutes of exclusive contact with flowers, followed by a discrete time period of contact with only animals.[24] To support this contention, brain research has indicated that in the process of learning, the brain searches for patterns and interconnections as a way to make meaning from new concepts. If students learn by making such connections between concepts, then educators must explore ways to teach through connections between and across concepts.[25]

Interdisciplinary approaches to instruction are defined as a view of knowledge (and thus, curriculum), that formally applies information, beliefs, and skills from more than one discipline to a problem, topic, theme, or experience.[26] Links between and across content areas serve as the foundation for classroom practice. Interest in interdisciplinary approaches for all grade levels has increased for several reasons, including:

1. The growth of knowledge in fields that often fall between, rather than neatly within, the confines of traditional content areas,
2. Fragmentation of the school day and the associated time-management problems,
3. Concerns about the relevancy of many issues included in the school curriculum, and
4. Preparation of students for multifaceted job expectations in the professional adult world.[27]

Correlated Health Instruction

While educators have identified a variety of interdisciplinary approaches to managing instruction, correlated approaches to education are common in health education practice. In correlated instructional approaches, complementary, discipline-specific units of study or related disciplines are brought together to answer common questions, solve problems, or address complex issues. The advantages of correlated instruction are evident for health education in elementary and middle-level classrooms for the following reasons:

1. Connections between previously unrelated content areas are formally reinforced,
2. More realistically complex health issues can be addressed,
3. Complementary resource materials emerge, and
4. Time-management problems can be eased with such an approach.

Teachers who are interested in correlating health education with another content area are urged to examine the treatment of health concepts in the textbooks of other subjects. This exploration can provide teachers with a starting point for reducing repetition and expanding the use of correlated learning activities with other subjects. Teachers are most likely to find such material in science textbooks. Importantly, however, teachers and administrators must not consider the text developed for science instruction or any other content area as the students' primary source of information about their health.

When attempting correlated instructional approaches that include health education themes, teachers should be aware of the associated potential limitations. Like the previous discussion of conventional instructional approaches, problems can be associated with the use of correlated instructional practice. Any change in organizational structure that deviates from the familiar may be met with resistance from parents, teachers, administrators, or students. In addition, scheduling problems, lack of teacher training and comfort, and lack of clarity about appropriate evaluation protocol are common sources of concern about correlated instructional approaches. Finally, self-contained classroom teachers who attempt correlated instruction can place unintentional emphasis on one content area over another. For example, if a teacher has greater expertise in language arts than in health education, the health issue is unlikely to receive equal attention when the teacher develops and implements learning activities.

Although chapters in this text have been organized by discipline-specific content areas, every effort has been made to feature a list of recommended children's and adolescent literature trade books in each chapter. Many of the books have been selected because they have been recognized with the Newberry Award for their literary merit. Other books have been suggested because they contain multicultural characters, themes, or illustrations. Still others appear on the lists because they have received the Caldecott Award for noteworthy illustrations. Finally, others have been used successfully in classroom applications. These lists are by no means intended to serve as a complete catalog of all appropriate books that address health-related issues. Rather, they are included as a way to reinforce the value of sound, correlated instructional approaches. In addition, these and other trade books can

TABLE 5.3	**Children's Literature with Themes About Children/People with Special Needs**

Grades K–2

Brown, Tricia. *Someone Special Like You*. Henry Holt, 1984.

Martin, Bill. *Knots On A Counting Rope*. Henry Holt, 1987.

Millman, Isaac. *Moses Goes to a Concert*. Frances Foster Books, 1998.

Fleming, Virginia. *Be Good To Eddie Lee*. Philomel, 1993.

Grades 3–5

Byars, Betsy. *Summer of the Swans*. Penguin, 1970. (Newberry Medal)

MacLachlan, Patricia. *Through Grandpa's Eyes*. Harper & Row, 1980.

McMahon, Patricia. *Listen for the Bus: David's Story*. Boyds Mill, 1995.

Polacco, Patricia, *Thank You, Mr. Faulker*. Philomel, 1998.

Peterson, Jeanne Whitehouse. *I Have A Sister. My Sister is Deaf*. Harper Collins, 1977.

Osofsky, Audrey. *My Buddy*. Henry Holt, 1992.

Senisi, Ellen. *Just Kids*. Dutton, 1998.

Grades 6–8

Abel, Samantha. *Reach for the Moon*. Pfeifer-Hamilton, 1993. (International Reading Association Distinguished Book Award, American Library Association Best Books For Young Adults Nominee)

provide a starting place for integrating health education concepts into classrooms and districts that have made a commitment to a whole-language approach to reading instruction. As a place to begin, teachers are urged to examine table 5.3, which contains a list of children's literature with themes about characters with special needs. Consistent with the national school health standards, the characters and stories in these books can provide a foundation for practicing a range of communication and decision-making skills.

As is the case with all children's and adolescent literature, caution is urged to ensure that books selected for classroom use are developmentally appropriate and have received administrative review. Readers of this text who are concerned about the potential for controversy about any curricular approach or student health issue are urged to read the section of this chapter that focuses on managing controversy in health education.

Integrated Health Instruction

In integrated approaches to instruction, the perspectives of multiple discrete disciplines are collected into thematic units of instruction. These theme-based units can last a few days or can emerge over longer periods of time. Thematic, or integrated, instruction is very common in early childhood learning environments. Integrated instruction shares similar, yet exaggerated, advantages and disadvantages with correlated (1:1) instructional approaches. The most compelling reason to incorporate integrated instruction into classroom practice is that it is consistent with real life outside the classroom. Consequently, it is stimulating and motivating for students and teachers. There are, however, time, resource, and evaluation problems associated with integrated instruction. Funding constraints, preparation time, and staff development are practical issues that compromise long-range integrated planning. In addition, parents and taxpayers in the community often need to be educated about the value of integrated educational approaches if such approaches are to have widespread application and acceptance.[28]

Importantly, as with cooperative learning approaches, the developmental needs of students should drive decision making about which curricular approaches are best for students. While teachers are not likely to abandon direct instruction, they may find that interdisciplinary education approaches hold promise in addressing the complex health issues that face elementary and middle-level students.

MANAGING CONTROVERSY IN HEALTH EDUCATION

Controversy involves a conflict of values and beliefs. Such conflict is an inevitable part of life in a pluralistic society. School-based professionals and programs are particularly vulnerable to controversy because of their primary source of funding (public tax dollars). In addition, the U.S. educational enterprise is predicated on manditory participation by all children and youth. While some children attend private or charter schools, controversy about school policies and practices takes two common forms:

1. Conflict about what content and issues are addressed, and
2. Disagreement about proper parameters for implementation of the curriculum.[29]

In the context of both sources of conflict, the subject matter and curricular approaches that undergird effective health education practice can provide fertile ground for dispute. In some school districts, the notion of including a comprehensive school health education program of studies in the approved district curriculum is regarded as an inappropriate use of instructional time. Advocates for a "back-to-basics" approach to education often view attention to anything other than core content as a waste of valuable academic time. Still others view the process of organizing a coordinated school health program as a way to formalize intrusion into family issues or to attempt to usurp parents' rights.

While some health topics are likely to evoke little or no heated response, others, including sexual health promotion, stress management, death education, and some approaches to tobacco, alcohol and other drug risk reduction, can serve as a lightening rod for parental and public concern. In addition, the national school health education standards imply that the primary focus of instruction should be placed on skill development in potentially controversial areas.

Importantly, like education professionals, parents and taxpayers who express concern about curriculum or policy matters in their schools are motivated by a commitment to creating the best possible learning environment for students. Consequently, the best way to avoid controversy is to maintain open and effective communication among all invested stakeholders.[30] The coordinated school health program model discussed in chapter 1 of this text provides an effective mechanism for anticipating discrepancies in values. In addition, the coordinated school health program model formalizes a structure for community and parent review of all curricular and policy matters.

While there is no guarantee that controversy always can be avoided, recommendations have been offered for the school community to manage negative outcry in a way that will reduce its impact on the continuity of instruction. While many such recommendations are taken from the body of research in human sexuality, school personnel also may find them to be helpful when they are confronted with controversy about reading or math curricula or literature selections in the school library.

Anticipation: Proactive Strategies for Administrators

The most effective strategy for managing controversy in a school district is to anticipate the potential for a negative reaction. The following recommendations are provided to help in developing proactive district-wide plan:

- Develop and integrate a coordinated school health advisory committee to serve as curriculum reviewers, support persons, and informed stakeholders (see chapter 1 as a reference to the coordinated school health program model),
- Cultivate a relationship with local media outlets to support fair and balanced treatment of related issues,
- Meet with parents and concerned others to:
  - Examine curriculum materials,
  - Review qualifications and preparation of teachers,
  - Evaluate assignments and class activities,
  - Discuss communication protocol for parents,
  - Assess student evaluation strategies, and
  - Explore options for parents who do not want their child to participate,
- Define the role of parents at district-sponsored public meetings.[31]

School districts that have established school health advisory committees are far more likely to manage controversy successfully than their less proactive counterparts. In addition, the importance of well-planned, developmentally appropriate, and board-approved health curricula cannot be overstated. Finally, administrators must assure classroom-based professionals of their support when delivering controversial content.

Recommendations for Teachers

While most of the previously described activities are beyond the responsibility of the individual classroom teacher, it is these professionals who must translate district policy into instructional practice. As a starting point, many teachers look to district-approved texts and instructional materials. Unfortunately, these materials often provide very little help in teaching potentially controversial topics. A review of currently available elementary and middle-level health textbooks reveals a lack of coverage of certain subjects. Most noteworthy is the omission of information about human reproduction, sexuality, and childbirth. No information can be found in these same texts on the subject of death and dying. Although drug abuse is a major problem in American society today, elementary and middle-level health textbooks provide little developmentally appropriate information about current drugs of choice with which children might be familiar.

As a result, teachers must be prepared to create a safe and nurturing learning environment for all students about all subject matter in the district course of study. As a starting point, chapter 13 of this text provides guidelines for teaching sexuality that can be generalized to address any health education content area. In addition, teachers must be prepared to provide accurate and timely information about classroom content matters. To this end, participation in staff development opportunities is advised. Also, teachers must seek the support of their local administrators and would be wise to consult their colleagues in professional associations to which they belong.

Finally, the following recommendations are offered to help teachers respond to the many questions that children have about their health. In general, the reaction to student questions can be as important as the response that is provided. In this context, professionals are encouraged to:

1. Affirm and clarify questions.
2. Separate personal emotions from their response, and
3. Maintain the lines of communication.

The following types of questions and response strategies are particularly relevant to questions about potentially controversial topics.[32]

Request for Information Questions

Many times, students will be very curious about a subject, or they will need something clarified. If you think the question is appropriate for the grade level you are teaching and you know the answer, then it is certainly appropriate to answer the question. If you do not know the answer, tell the student that you do not know, and ask students to identify a strategy for finding the answer. In addition, it is important for the teacher to make sure that student questions get correct, and developmentally appropriate responses.

If you feel as though the question is inappropriate for the grade level, tell the class that you do not feel comfortable answering that question. However, it is important to find out from the student why he or she asked it. Try to find out more information about what motivated the question before answering it.

"Am I Normal" Questions

These questions generally focus on concerns about students' bodies and the physical and emotional changes that are occurring in them. It is important to validate their concerns by informing them that many young people of their age share those same concerns. Next, provide information about what they can expect as their body continues to change, grow, and develop over the next few years. In addition, it is appropriate to suggest that they can talk to parents, counselors, clergy, and other community resources if they need additional information.

Permission-Seeking/Personal Belief Questions

Generally, these questions are intended to ask your permission to participate in a particular behavior. For example, "Is it normal for kids my age to . . . ?" "Did you participate in . . . activity when you were growing up?" or "Do you think it is okay to . . . ?" are cues for parents and teachers that permission may be being sought. It is important to avoid using the word "normal" or "typical" when answering questions. Morality enters into these questions, and it is not up to you to decide what is right or wrong for students. The exception to this is something that is against the law. Also it is important to establish ground rules at the beginning of the year, and to emphasize that personal sexual behavior is not open for discussion.

Shock Questions

Sometimes students ask questions to shock the teacher. Many questions are shocking because of the vocabulary that is used. To deal with this situation, reword the question using proper terminology. In any case, it is important to stay calm and not act embarrassed.

In conclusion, the keys to managing the potential for controversy lies in having a coordinated school health program in place and anticipating community response to curricular matters. Successful implementation of both of these strategies lies in knowing parents and key stakeholders in the community. Increasing parental engagement in all aspects of the education process in an important goal for all school districts.

PARENTAL INVOLVEMENT: A FOUNDATION FOR HEALTH PROMOTION AND SCHOOL PERFORMANCE

Confirming the value of partnerships between the home and the school has been the focus of intense public debate and the subject of a growing body of scholarly research. Educators and politicians recommend that increased energy be devoted to increasing parent participation in the academic lives of their children. Most major educational reform efforts have identified parent involvement as an important ingredient for improving the education process. To this end, governmental and education agencies have made recommendations to help schools organize parent participation programs. In addition, documents have been published that describe the characteristics of exemplary parent involvement programs.[33] In this spirit, the National PTA has developed standards for parent/family involvement programs. These standards, listed in table 5.4, were developed with three purposes in mind:

- To promote meaningful parent and family participation in the educational lives of children and youth,

TABLE 5.4	**National Standards for Parent/Family Involvement**
Standard I:	**Communicating**—Communication between home and school is regular, two-way, and meaningful.
Standard II:	**Parenting**—Parenting skills are promoted and supported.
Standard III:	**Student learning**—Parents play an integral role in assisting student learning.
Standard IV:	**Volunteering**—Parents are welcome in the school, and their support and assistance are sought.
Standard V:	**School decision making and advocacy**—Parents are full partners in the decisions that affect children and families.
Standard VI:	**Collaborating with community**—Community resources are used to strengthen schools, families, and student learning.

Source: National PTA. *National Standards for Parent/Family Involvement Programs.* Chicago, IL: National PTA, 1998.

CONSIDER THIS

Building a Healthy Child-Parent Tip Sheet for Raising Alcohol- and Drug-Free Children

Know your children's friends and their parents. Call, introduce yourself, and stay in touch with friends' parents to share ideas and support.

Work with your children to counter the media images that glamorize alcohol and other drugs. Guide them in recognizing the manipulative potential of advertising and other media images.

Be a positive role model. Be conscious of how you use prescription and even over-the-counter medicines. Show that you can deal with mild pain or tension without alcohol and other drugs.

Be aware of how your own use of alcohol can influence your children. Your children tend to have the same drinking habits that you have when they grow up.

Show your children that you don't "follow the crowd," but prefer to make your own decisions. Help them practice ways to resist peer pressure about using alcohol and other drugs.

Learn about alcohol and other drug use in your community. Find out what you can do to help in local prevention efforts.

Source: National PTA. *Building A Healthy Child.* Chicago, IL: National PTA, 1997.

- To raise awareness regarding the components of effective involvement programs, and
- To provide guidelines for schools and agencies to improve existing programs.[34]

In addition to their role in influencing improved academic outcomes, research has documented that parents and other significant adults exert significant influence over the health behaviors of young people. A recent longitudinal study confirmed that, among the most basic forces of influence that include the social contexts in which students live and function, ". . . the family and school contexts are among the most critical."[35] Across all health risk domains, the role of the family in shaping the health of adolescents was demonstrated to be significant. Specifically, when students perceive that their parents have high expectations for their success in school, there is decreased likelihood that they will participate in health risk behaviors. This study demonstrated that feelings of warmth, love, and caring from parents were particularly important variables in supporting healthy lifestyle choices. To this end, the importance of parental availability was confirmed as an important component of "family connectedness."[36]

In addition, the home environment has been demonstrated to play an important role in shaping specific health risks. For example, if students have easy access to guns, alcohol, tobacco, and other drugs in their homes, they are at higher risk for suicide, violence, and substance use.[37] In response, the National PTA has offered specific recommendations for parents who are interested in participating in health risk reduction. Tips from this agenda specifically focus on "raising alcohol and drug-free children." The recommendations are summarized in the Consider This box above.[38]

Finally, this growing body of literature has also confirmed the protective value of a sense of connection with the school. Students who have a sense of connection with their school, parents, family, and other adults tend to participate in far fewer health risk behaviors.[39] Consistent with the philosophy and practice of the coordinated school health program model (see chapter 1), collaborative approaches to pooling home, school, and community resources in health promotion agendas can result in very positive outcomes.

While much attention is directed toward increasing the in-school participation of parents, research has identified several types of parental engagement in the educational process that have been linked consistently with improved academic performance.[40] These activities primarily are based in the home and include:

Managing and organizing children's use of time:
Parents of successful students help their children organize their schedules and check to see that their children are following routines.[41] In addition, parents would be wise to stay informed about school activities, performance, and assignments and provide a place and time for homework to be completed. Finally, academic outcomes are improved for students whose parents know where they are, with whom they are spending time, and when they plan to come home. Engaged parents also exercise control over nonschool activities including time devoted to television viewing.

Helping with homework:
Participating in homework provides parents with the opportunity to confirm their interest and take a direct role in children's schooling. Specific

Parents who get involved in homework activities demonstrate their commitment to school success for their children.

suggestions for supporting academic success include making certain that assignments are done, checking accuracy, and asking questions about the nature of assignments.

Discussing school matters with children:

It is important for children and their parents to talk regularly about school activities; the kind of conversation is also important. Parents should be willing to discuss problems as well as successes and reinforce persistence in confronting challenges. In addition, research supports developmentally appropriate collaborative decision making about such matters as participation in activities, projects undertaken, or for older students, course selection.

Reading to and being read to by children:

A large body of research confirms the importance of such activities for developing reading proficiency in younger learners. In addition, there is a connection between school success and living in a home that is literacy-laden; i.e., the presence of newspapers, books, magazines, and a computer or word processor.[42]

While teachers can support parent involvement in student learning by providing engaging and developmentally appropriate assignments, it is important to remember that strong parent-teacher relationships are based on reciprocal elements. The literature is clear that parents tend to have consistent concerns about teacher performance. Specifically, parents are concerned about how well teachers *know and care about:*

1. Teaching,
2. Their children, and
3. Communication with parents.

As a means to evaluate the often unintentional messages they are sending to parents, readers are encouraged to ask themselves the following questions.

CONSIDER THIS

Communication for Parents and Teachers: Recommendations for Improved Student Success from the Education Commission of the States

1. Listen to people first, then talk later.
2. Expect to fail if you don't practice communicating well.
3. Make involving interested parties from the community a top priority.
4. Be clear about what it means to set and meet high standards for all students.
5. Show concerned others how new ideas can enhance, rather than replace, old ones.
6. Educate parents about the choices available to them.
7. Help parents and community residents understand how student progress is evaluated and what the results mean.

Source: Education Commission of the States, *Listen, Discuss, and Act* (Denver, CO:ECS, 1996a), 15–17.

Concerning my teaching:

1. Do I appear to enjoy teaching and believe in the value of what I do?
2. Do I set high expectations and help children reach them?
3. Do I know my subject matter and practice effective teaching methods?
4. Do I create a safe and inviting learning environment in which students are encouraged to pay attention, participate, and learn?
5. Do I deal with behavior problems consistently and fairly?
6. Do I assign meaningful homework that is returned in a timely manner?
7. Do I make learning expectations clear to students and parents?

Concerning my students:

1. Do I understand the diverse ways in which children learn and create correspondingly diverse learning activities?
2. Do I treat students fairly and with respect?
3. Do I contact parents promptly about academic or behavioral concerns?
4. Do I provide helpful information during conferences?

Concerning communicating with parents:

1. Do I provide parents with clear information about expectations?

2. Do I use a variety of tools to communicate with parents?

3. Am I accessible and responsive when contacted by parents?

4. Do I cooperate with parents to develop strategies that are helpful for students?[43]

To support parent engagement, the Education Commission of the States has made seven recommendations for teachers to improve student achievement by reaching out to parents. While not surprising, this list of suggestions, found in the Consider This box on page 96, can help teachers to build bridges and improve communication networks to influence student health and academic performance.[44]

In conclusion, involving parents in the learning process has been demonstrated to influence academic outcomes and student participation in health risk behaviors in a positive way. Developing a strategy to engage these important caregivers depends more on the attitude and personal characteristics of teachers and administrators than on the sophistication of any organizational or recruitment plan. To create mutually rewarding relationships between parents and school personnel requires honesty, humility, and authenticity.

SUMMARY

For various reasons, including teacher preparation and discomfort or district and community pressures, health-education programming in the elementary and middle-level grades does not often have the academic priority of other content areas. However, in response to student needs and district or state instructional mandates, teachers often find themselves challenged to develop and implement effective health-education learning activities within serious time constraints. These professionals can feel as if they are trying to fit one more huge coat into an already overcrowded closet. Recognizing that time constraints affect all content areas, this chapter urges teachers to look at tactics and strategies with which they are familiar to enhance effective health instruction.

Like other content areas, the foundation for health education lies in discipline-specific approaches to instruction. In this model, health issues are addressed in discrete blocks of instructional time. In elementary classrooms, most instructional activities are organized by the classroom teacher or expert guests from the community. By contrast, in middle-level schools, such instruction may be in the hands of a content specialist. In any case, there are many teaching activities or strategies that can enhance health instruction. In addition to the general learning activities described in this chapter, the emerging body of literature on cooperative learning can provide an interesting starting place for enriching, sound health-education practice. Supplementing traditional or competitive classroom approaches with cooperative learning activities enhances students' cognitive, affective, and psychomotor development. Teachers are cautioned about the differences between simple group work and cooperative learning and the related benefits to learners.

Discipline-specific instructional approaches to health education can be enhanced by incorporating individualized learning approaches, including learning centers and health fairs, to health promotion classroom practice. These kinds of activities, which are usually reserved for remedial instruction, can serve as a foundation for cross-age learning. By inviting others to a health fair, diverse groups of students can benefit from participation in learning center activities organized by peers.

As an alternative, teachers who are comfortable with correlated and integrated learning environments are urged to include health-education activities in such interdisciplinary models. In particular, children's literature and health education have a strong relationship. Here, teachers will find fertile opportunity for interdisciplinary learning activities, since many trade books are written about characters who are wrestling with health concerns. Such approaches help connect class activities to life events.

Concern about the potential for controversy remains a significant barrier for health promotion programming at both the school district and classroom teacher levels. As discussed in chapter 1, the coordinated school health program model provides formalized opportunities for soliciting input, communicating concerns, and organizing intervention strategies for addressing the potential for controversy. In addition, teachers should be prepared to address questions posed by their students. Texts rarely address this problem. Recommendations for managing questions about health issues are similar to managing student queries about other content matters: (1) affirm and clarify the question, (2) separate emotions from the issue embedded in the question, and (3) maintain the lines of communication.

Finally, there is little question about the importance of establishing cooperative relationships between educators and parents and other adult caregivers. This is particularly true in the context of reducing student participation in health risk behaviors. Teachers must develop strategies to cultivate effective and collaborative partnerships to support parental engagement in enriching the academic successes of children.

DISCUSSION QUESTIONS

1. Identify variables that contribute to the priority that many elementary and middle-level teachers place on health instruction.

2. Describe the foundation of discipline-specific instructional approaches.

3. Discuss the limitations of traditional and competitive approaches to learning.

4. List the comparative benefits of cooperative learning approaches over traditional, or competitive, learning activities.

5. What are some key health-related benefits of participation in cooperative learning activities?

6. What is the difference between simple group work and cooperative learning?

7. Apply one cooperative learning activity to instruction on a specific health issue.

8. Define the benefits of individualized learning approaches.

9. How can learning centers enhance health instruction?

10. Discuss the benefits of organizing student-developed learning centers into a health fair.

11. How can health fairs be used to enhance health instruction?

12. Suggest teacher and student organizational cues for effective health fairs.

13. Identify the strengths and limitations of direct instruction and interdisciplinary approaches.

14. Provide an example of a correlated learning activity involving health education and language arts for a given group of students.

15. How are correlation and integration similar and different?

16. Discuss the foundation of controversy concerning school-based health promotion programming.

17. Identify ways in which the coordinated school health program can help prevent and manage controversy.

18. List general recommendations for teachers who are confronted with student questions.

19. Discuss the potential meanings behind questions posed by students.

20. What is the relationship between parental engagement and academic achievement?

21. Discuss the importance of the home and school "contexts" in influencing student health risk behavior.

22. Suggest strategies for parents to improve academic outcomes for their students.

23. List three primary concerns that parents express about teacher performance.

24. Suggest ways in which teachers can build bridges to improve relationships with parents and other adult caregivers.

ENDNOTES

1. Heidi H. Jacobs, "On Interdisciplinary Curriculum: A Conversation with Heidi H. Jacobs," *Educational Leadership* (October 1991): 24.

2. H. Jacobs, ed., *Interdisciplinary Curriculum: Design and Implementation* (Alexandria, VA: ASCD, 1989), 7.

3. J. Piaget, *The Epistemology of Interdisciplinary Relationships* (Paris: Organization for Economic Cooperation and Development, 1972).

4. Evelyn E. Ames, Lucille A. Trucano, Julia C. Wan, and Margo H. Harris, *Designing School Health Curriculum,* 2nd ed. (Dubuque, IA: W. C. Brown, 1995), 90.

5. Jacobs, *Interdisciplinary Curriculum,* 1.

6. Stan Friedland, "Bridging the Gap," *The Executive Educator* 16, no. 10 (October 1994): 27.

7. Ibid.

8. Ibid.

9. Bethann Cinelli, Cynthia W. Symons, Lori Bechtel, and Mary Rose-Colley, "Applying Cooperative Learning in Health-Education Practice," *Journal of School Health* 64, no. 3 (March 1994): 99–102.

10. R. Slavin, "Research on Cooperative Learning: Consensus and Controversy," *Educational Leadership* 47, no. 4 (1989/1990): 30–31; D. Solomon, M. Watson, E. Schapps et al., "Cooperative Learning as Part of a Comprehensive Classroom Program Designed to Promote Prosocial Development," *Current Research on Cooperative Learning,* S. Sharon, ed. (New York: Praeger, 1990); G. Gist, "Problem-based Learning: A New Tool for Environmental Health Education," *Journal of Environmental Health* 54, no. 5 (1992): 10–11.

11. Cinelli et al., "Applying Cooperative Learning," 99.

12. National Commission on the Role of the School and the Community in Improving Adolescent Health, *Code Blue: Uniting for Healthier Youth* (Alexandria, VA: NASBE and AMA, 1990), 37–38.

13. Cinelli et al., "Applying Cooperative Learning," 99–100; Gist, "Problem-based Learning," 12; G. Tanaka, J. Warren, and L. Tritsch, "What's Real in Health Education?" *Journal of Health Education* 24, no. 6 (1993): 57–58.

14. Cinelli et al., "Applying Cooperative Learning," 100.

15. Ibid.

16. Ibid., 101.

17. Friedland, "Bridging the Gap," 27.

18. Cinelli et al., "Applying Cooperative Learning," 100.

19. Friedland, "Bridging the Gap," 27.

20. Cinelli et al., "Applying Cooperative Learning," 103.

21. Ibid., 102.

22. Friedland, "Bridging the Gap," 27.

23. Ibid.

24. L. Elvin, *The Place of Common Sense in Educational Thought* (London: Unwin Educational Books, 1977).

25. Susan M. Drake, *Planning Integrated Curriculum* (Alexandria, VA: ASCD, 1993), 3.

26. Jacobs, *Interdisciplinary Curriculum,* 8.

27. Ibid., 3–6.

28. Drake, *Planning Integrated,* 2.

29. Loren B. Bensley and Elizabeth Harmon, "Addressing Controversy in Health Education," *Alliance Update* (May/June 1992): 9–10.

30. Ibid.

31. Irving R. Dickman, *Winning the Battle for Sex Education* (New York: SIECUS, 1982), 4.

32. K. Middleton, B. Hubbard, W. Kane, and J. Taylor, *Contemporary Health Series: Making Health Education Comprehensive* (Santa Cruz, CA: ETR Associates, 1991), 31–33.

33. B. Rutherford, B. Anderson, and S. Billig, *Parent and Community Involvement in Education* (Washington, DC: U.S. Department of Education, Office of Educational Research and Improvement, 1997).

34. National PTA, *National Standards for Parent/Family Involvement Programs* (Chicago: National PTA, 1998), 5.

35. Michael D. Resnick, et al., "Protecting Adolescents from Harm," *Journal of the American Medical Association* 278, no. 10 (September 10, 1997): 823–832.

36. Ibid., 830.

37. Ibid., 831.

38. National PTA, *Building a Healthy Child* (Chicago: National PTA, 1997), 17.

39. Michael D. Resnick, et al., "The Impact of Caring and Connectedness on Adolescent Health and Well-being," *Journal of Pediatric Child Health* 29, (suppl 1): S3–S9.

40. Jeremy D. Finn, "Parental Engagement that Makes a Difference," *Educational Leadership* 55, no. 8 (May 1998): 20–24.

41. R. M. Clark, *Family Life and School Achievement* (Chicago: University of Chicago Press, 1983).

42. R. M. Wolf, "The Measurement of Environments," in *Invitational Conference on Testing Problems,* A. Anastasi, ed. (Princeton, NJ: Educational Testing Service, 1964).

43. Dorothy Rich, "What Parents Want from Teachers," *Educational Leadership* 55, no. 8 (May 1998): 37–39.

44. Education Commission of the States, *Listen, Discuss, and Act* (Denver, CO:ECS, 1996a), 15–17.

SUGGESTED READINGS

Advocates for Youth. *Parent-Child Communication: Promoting Healthy Youth.* Washington, DC: Advocates for Youth, 1995.

Association for Supervision and Curriculum Development. "Making Parental Involvement Meaningful." *Education Update* 40, no. 1 (January 1998): 1, 3, 8.

Birch, David A. "Involving Families in School Health Education: Implications for Professional Preparation." *Journal of School Health* 64, no. 7 (September 1994): 296–298.

Cohen, Elizabeth G. "Making Cooperative Learning Equitable." *Educational Leadership* (September 1998): 18–21.

Fogarty, R. *The Mindful School: How to Integrate the Curricula.* Arlington Heights, IL: IRI/Skylight Training and Publishing, Inc., 1991.

Johnson, D. W., and R. T. Johnson. *Cooperative Learning: Warm-ups, Group Strategies and Group Activities.* Edina, MN: Interaction Book Co., 1991.

Johnson, D. W., and R. T. Johnson. *Learning Together and Alone: Cooperative, Competitive and Individualistic Learning.* Edina, MN: Interaction Book Co., 1991.

Johnson, D. W., R. T. Johnson, E. J. Holubec, and P. Roy. *Circles of Learning: Cooperation in the Classroom.* Alexandria, VA: ASCD, 1984.

Lyman, L., H. Foyle, and T. Azwell. *Cooperative Learning in the Elementary Classroom.* Washington, DC: National Education Association, 1993.

Manna, Anthony L., and Cynthia W. Symons. *Children's Literature for Health Awareness.* Metuchen, NJ: Scarecrow Press, 1992.

Rottier, J., and B. Ogan. *Cooperative Learning in Middle-Level Schools.* Washington, DC: National Education Association, 1993.

Sexuality Information and Education Council of the United States. *Filling the Gaps: Hard to Teach Topics in Sexuality Education.* New York: SIECUS, 1998.

Slavin, R. *Student Team Learning: A Practical Guide to Cooperative Learning.* Washington, DC: National Education Association, 1991.

Spalt, Susan W. "Coping With Controversy: The Professional Epidemic of the Nineties." *Journal of School Health* 66, no. 9 (November 1996): 339–340.

The Primary Content

Section III contains content that relates to the CDC priority risk behavior areas and the skills included in the National Health Education Standards. Teachers should be able to understand the primary content well enough that they can comfortably infuse health skills throughout these primary content areas. Each chapter in this section provides background information about the content area, developmentally appropriate practice recommendations, activities that can be conducted with students at different grade levels, and children's literature and Web sites related to the content area.

6

SKILLS TO IMPACT THE PSYCHOSOCIAL CAUSES OF NEGATIVE HEALTH BEHAVIOR

O U T L I N E

INTRODUCTION

Until the last decade, the acquisition of health knowledge was the primary focus of health instruction. Today, however, personal and social skill development in the area of health education has become a major area of emphasis. There are several reasons for this change in focus. First, administrators and concerned parents are committed to promoting positive health behaviors rather than just increasing health knowledge. For example, it is more important for schools to contribute to reducing tobacco use rather than simply making sure students know the different chemicals in tobacco products. Much of the research conducted in the area of effective health education curricula has found that to promote healthy behaviors, curricula must have a strong skills based component. Specifically, in the area of tobacco prevention, two curricula have been documented to delay the onset of tobacco use.[1,2] These two curricula have a strong skills based component. They have activities that reinforce decision-making skills, resistance skills, and communication skills. Effective health education curricula in other content areas also incorporate a strong emphasis of integrating personal and social skills into content matter.

A second reason the health education profession is focusing more on skill development is because of the enormous amount of new health information produced each year. For example, it is common for teachers to teach a specific fact about nutrition one year and for that fact to be proven wrong soon after. Consistent with the National Health Education Standards covered in chapter 1, it is more important to teach students how and where to access accurate health information. This does not mean the health curriculum should contain no information; however, there should be more of a balance between skills and content.

Third, the National Health Education Standards (see appendix on page 326) focus on several different health promoting skills. Because most states have used the National Health Education Standards to create their own state standards or curricular documents, many local school districts have revised curricula that represent a better balance between content and skills.

The personal and social skills that should be developed in elementary and middle-level students include:

- Accessing valid health information and services,
- Stress management,
- Communication,
- Peer resistance,
- Decision making,
- Goal setting,
- Advocating for personal, family, and community health,
- Conflict management, and
- Self-esteem building skills.

Because self-esteem and stress-management skills (National Health Education Standard 3) are so closely related to emotional health, they are the focus of chapter 15. In addition, conflict resolution (National Health Education Standard 5) is addressed in chapter 8, which focuses on risk reduction for unintentional injury. The remaining personal and social skills are discussed in this chapter; background information and suggested teaching activities are included. In addition, many of these skills are reinforced in later chapters in the suggested teaching activities sections. It is important for teachers to understand that these skills cross all health content areas. Specifically, it is not enough to teach one unit on personal and social skills related to health; instead, it is important to integrate the personal and social skills throughout all of the health content areas and other subjects that are taught (e.g., science, social studies, etc.).

SKILLS TO ACCESS HEALTH INFORMATION, PRODUCTS, AND SERVICES

National Health Education Standard 2

Accessing valid health information and health-enhancing products and services is important in promoting positive health behaviors among youth. Specific skills include the ability to:

- Analyze the validity of health information, products, and services;

- Utilize resources that provide valid health information;
- Locate health-promoting products and community health helpers; and
- Decide when situations require professional health services.

Students are called upon to make many health related decisions in their lives. They must do this in an environment in which they are sometimes bombarded with incomplete and inaccurate information. Students need to be able to identify credible sources of information, and then use the information to make healthy choices. Many times these technology sources are the Internet or health related software packages. Other situations require students to seek advice from community health helpers. This section addresses how students can access products and services. Chapter 4 addressed the "hardware of instruction," health education technology and other information sources. Activities to help improve communication skills can be found on page 104.

COMMUNICATION SKILLS

National Health Education Standard 5

Although speech develops in most children in predictable developmental sequences, effective communication includes a set of skills that do not come naturally. Effective communication includes a range of skills that must be learned. Just as doctors practice medicine or athletes practice their sport, students need structured opportunities to practice effective communication skills. According to Fetro, "a person's ability to communicate can have a direct effect on self-esteem and the quality of relationships with others. Good communication skills can help a person learn more about the self and others. Poor communication can cause misunderstandings, leading to feelings of anger, mistrust and frustration in relationships with teachers, friends, family and others."[3]

In addition to building a child's self-esteem, good communication skills are important in helping a child succeed in the classroom. Success in school depends on listening and speaking skills as much as on intellectual ability.[4] Instructions, feedback, and subject content are all delivered orally. If students have difficulty listening and organizing effective questions and responses, their general academic achievement is threatened.

The importance of good communication follows us beyond childhood and into the adult world of work. Most jobs require good communication skills for the employee to be successful. If a manager has a difficult time listening or speaking, he or she may not do a good job relating to employees. The result could be poor work performance, poor job satisfaction, or a decline in productivity. Oral communication can be defined as the use of words and language to send a message. Most people communicate

ACTIVITIES

Accessing Health Information Products and Services

The following activities are suggestions for teaching children accessing skills.

Grades K–2

1. Ask the school nurse and the school counselor (if available) to be guest speakers for the class to explain to students their roles in the school and the ways they can be of help to students.

2. Utilize community health helpers as guest speakers so that students can learn the types of services they provide. Firefighters, doctors, school nurses, school counselors, dentists, and police officers are a few of the individuals who might be utilized for this activity.

Grades 3–5

1. Review with students different advertising techniques that are used to sell products, including testimonials, quick-and-easy cures, "everyone is using it," famous people, and making products look sexy or fun. Next, ask cooperative learning groups to review an advertisement they brought from home. Each group should then identify the advertising technique and describe a more truthful message about the product or service.

Grades 6–8

1. Place students into cooperative learning groups, each comprised of four students. Give each group a scavenger hunt worksheet and a telephone directory. This worksheet should contain questions that require students to look in the telephone directory and identify the agency/person that could help in a specific situation. For example, who could you call for help if your best friend started drinking alcohol and you wanted to help her? After the students have completed the worksheet, the teacher should discuss the appropriateness of their answers. This activity helps students become familiar with the telephone directory and different agencies in the community.

2. Ask students to create a health education directory of different health agencies in their community. Assign each cooperative learning group a different preadolescent health topic to research. The directory could include the name of the agency, the health issue(s) it addresses, and the agency's address and telephone number. Duplicate the directory and give it to each student as a resource.

3. Assign students to review a health related advertisement to determine its validity. For example, they could review an advertisement about a weight-loss program and determine if factual information is included.

by talking. This means conveying a message that accurately describes to a listener what one feels, thinks, knows, or believes.[5]

As mentioned previously, there are two main types of oral communication skills: speaking and listening skills. Speaking skills include the ability to convey a specific message clearly, such as identifying time, location, feelings, and thought. Many plans have been ruined because a person was not able to convey information to the listener clearly. Another speaking skill that is important to

children is the use of "I statements." Children should be taught to express their feelings by saying, "When you . . . I feel . . . " Also, the way a person says something is very important. Two people can say the same thing, but use a different tone or nonverbal cues, and the statement will have two different interpretations.

Listening is the second skill in oral communication. It is wonderful to talk to a person who you know is listening to you. On the other hand, it is discouraging to try to have a conversation with a person who interrupts or never

---

CONSIDER THIS

Good Listening Skills

- Maintaining eye contact
- Asking questions
- Paraphrasing what the speaker has said
- Providing nonverbal cues such as nodding or smiling
- Complimenting the speaker when appropriate
- Responding in an empathetic manner

---

looks at you. The Consider This box above identifies many of the skills that are important in being a good listener.

People tend to communicate in three ways: aggressively, passively, or assertively. Aggressive communicators do not care about the feelings of the person with whom they are talking. The most important issue for aggressive communicators is the importance placed on getting their ideas, feelings, or messages communicated, regardless of who is hurt in the process. Aggressive communicators have the following qualities:

- They do not like to appear weak or to lose control of the situation.
- They need to win or to get their way all of the time.
- They do not know how else to act.
- They put down other people.
- They do not care about the other person's feelings.[6]

Passive communicators are those individuals who comply with all or most of the demands placed upon them. By contrast, such communicators place a priority on not making anyone angry at them. These individuals are mostly concerned about the other person's feelings, rather than their own. Individuals who are passive communicators generally do not have a positive self-concept. They do not feel good enough about themselves to believe they should be concerned about their own feelings. Passive communicators exhibit the following qualities:

- They do not know how to be assertive.
- They are fearful that others will not support them or like them.
- They want to keep the peace at all costs.
- They are scared to change because they only know how to be a victim.
- They think they are being polite, not passive.
- They succumb to peer pressure.
- They were rewarded for being passive sometime in their life.[7]

Finally, assertive communicators are concerned about their own feelings **and** the feelings of the person with whom they are talking. Assertive communicators

generally have positive self-concepts and can manage negative peer influences effectively. Because passive communicators are prone to succumb to peer pressure, and aggressive communicators put down other people, students should be taught to communicate assertively. Assertive communicators exhibit the following qualities:

- They state their opinion or disagreement clearly.
- They listen to the other person.
- They use a neutral, calm voice.
- They acknowledge other viewpoints and opinions.
- They thank the other person for listening.

Activities to help improve communication skills can be found on page 106.

PEER-RESISTANCE/REFUSAL SKILLS

National Health Education Standard 5

Adolescents report that the most common reasons they begin using drugs or engage in sexual activity is because their friends do, because they want to fit in with others, or because they want to belong to a group. Being accepted into a group is important at every age, but it seems to be even more important during early adolescence. By contrast, primary-age children are developmentally egocentric and family focused. This results in a lack of attention toward other children. Upper-elementary children begin to extend beyond the family unit and begin practicing the appropriate developmental task of establishing their own identity. Although establishing their own identity is developmentally appropriate and necessary, many times children begin to participate in negative behaviors because of peer pressure or because they want to be accepted by a group. For instance, children may be influenced by their friends to cheat on homework, to lie to their parents, and to steal.

A body of research about social influence resistance skills training identifies skills to counteract the peer pressure by friends (normative influences) and by media messages (informational influences) that students experience.[9] This research suggests that teachers should develop instructional activities to expose elementary and middle-level students to the social pressures to use drugs and other negative health behaviors that they may encounter in the future. These activities should be conducted in the controlled environment of the classroom under the supervision of a skilled and nurturing teacher before students are actually confronted by these pressures in "real life." In this context, the teacher might show students videotapes or have students actually role-play some of the social pressure situations they may encounter in the future. Teachers should follow the videos or role-plays with well-planned discussions or demonstrations on how to get out of the pressure situation and still maintain positive peer relationships. Because younger students (grades 4 and 5) admire older students, an excellent strategy is to have older

ACTIVITIES

Promoting Communication Skills

The following activities are suggestions for teaching children communication skills.

Grades K–2

1. Construct a puppet play that demonstrates the appropriate and inappropriate use of listening skills. For example, one puppet is explaining to another puppet how to play a game such as Chutes and Ladders. As the first puppet is explaining the rules, the other puppet is looking around the room and is not listening to the explanation. When they start playing the game, the second puppet does not know how to play. Ask the class the following questions: Why didn't the second puppet know how to play? What could have the second puppet done differently? What do you think would have happened? Ask for a volunteer to play the role of the second puppet, this time using good listening skills. After the teacher led demonstration, encourage children to create their own puppet play during a learning center time.

2. Use "what if" questions to discuss appropriate assertiveness skills. For example, ask "What if you are waiting for your turn on the slide and someone pushes in front of you?"

Grades 3–5

1. Ask students to brainstorm the qualities of a good listener. Structure learning opportunities for students to practice listening, by identifying one student as the talker and one student as the listener. After students have practiced a few times, let them identify at least one listening skill that they really want to work on, such as maintaining eye contact. Children need to practice listening skills many times throughout the school year. Choose a question for children to react to so that students have a starting place for discussion. One good resource for questions is a book entitled *The Kid's Book of Questions* by Gregory Stock.[8]

2. Ask students to role-play different scenarios using poor listening skills, and then repeat the role-play using good listening skills. For example, during the first role-play, children have a conversation about their favorite computer game. One child does not listen and asks things that do not relate to the conversation. The other children might be less likely to include the nonlistening child the next time. Repeat the role-play using good listening skills.

Grades 6–8

1. Structure opportunities for all children to talk or report on the information discussed in their group. Children need practice in talking in front of all sizes of groups. The Jigsaw activity in chapter 5 is a good technique to allow all students to report information.

2. Include role-plays in your lessons. This allows students to practice both speaking and listening.

---

students (grades 6–8) role-play pressure situations and demonstrate successful resistance skills.

It is important for children to be introduced to and given time to practice peer-resistance skills in the classroom beginning in about the third grade. Around this time, children show independence from adults and begin to rely more heavily on their peers. Activities to help promote peer resistance skills can be found on page 107.

DECISION-MAKING SKILLS

National Health Education Standard 6

Decision making is another important social skill with which students should be empowered. Many times, students, and even adults, make decisions without thinking about them. At a very young age, children should be

(continued after Activities on page 109)

ACTIVITIES

Promoting Peer Resistance Skills

The following activities are suggestions for teaching children peer resistance skills:

Grades K–2

Because children at this grade level are more heavily influenced by their family than by their peers, peer resistance activities for this grade level are not presented.

Grades 3–5 and 6–8

All of the following activities can be conducted with students in grades 3–8. Adjustments should be made to account for developmental differences.

1. Organize opportunities for students to discuss with one another the times they have been pressured by their friends to participate in an uncomfortable behavior. These situations do not have to be related to health behavior; peer resistance skills should be developed to enable students to manage a variety of situations effectively.

2. Give students the opportunity to have several peer resistance techniques demonstrated correctly so that they know how the techniques can be used properly. They can be demonstrated for elementary students by the teacher, by older students through cross-age tutoring experiences, by commercially made video-tapes, or by other students in the class.

3. Give students time to practice the skills in a safe classroom environment. Practice should occur multiple times throughout the year within different health education units. Students should be able to successfully demonstrate a minimum of three peer resistance techniques because, generally, that is how many refusals are needed to get out of a peer-pressure situation, as shown in the Consider This box on page 108. In addition, students should have a rationale for refusal instead of learning just to say "no." This means students will need to know why they are refusing, and not just learning how to refuse. The following teaching activity can be conducted to reinforce peer resistance skills with students:

   a. Ask students to write down peer-pressure situations they have been in, such as cheating on a test or homework, skipping school, smoking cigarettes, or drinking beer. Students can list situations in which they have refused or succumbed.

   b. Place students into groups of four and ask them to synthesize their lists on blank newsprint that is hanging on the wall.

   c. After they are finished writing, ask each group to share its list with the class.

   d. Pick a common peer-pressure situation and ask for a volunteer. Play the part of the pressurer and instruct the student to resist. The rest of the class should write down all of the different techniques the student used to resist the pressure. After the role-play, list the techniques on the chalkboard. Repeat the exercise with two or three different students.

   e. Instruct the students to go back to their original group of four. Students will take turns being in the position of resisting pressure from two of the group members, while the last group member acts as a judge. It is best to start and end the role-plays together. The judge should watch for the different techniques that were used and how well they were used. After the role-play, the judge should be given time to give feedback to the person who resisted the pressure. Each student should have an opportunity to play each part.

   f. If time permits, give groups the opportunity to do their best role-play in from of the entire class. This gives students the chance to see good peer resistance skills being demonstrated again.

4. Because the media is another influence or pressure in a student's life, students need to be able to recognize inaccurate messages. Review with students the techniques that are used to sell products

CONSIDER THIS

Peer-Pressure Resistance Techniques

1. Give an excuse or a reason. This is a technique with which students will be familiar because they frequently use it in other types of situations, such as when they forget their homework or when they don't clean their rooms.

   Examples of reasons or excuses:
   a. I promised my dad I would be home after school.
   b. I'm allergic to smoke.
   c. I'm going to the movie with my older brother and his friends.

2. Avoid the situation or walk away. Have students think of ways to leave the situation to avoid being confronted with the peer pressure. This may happen when they think there may be alcohol at a party and they choose not to go, or it may occur when they are already in a pressure situation and decide to leave.

   Examples of avoiding the situation or walking away:
   a. I'm busy right now.
   b. I can't go to the party because I am grounded.
   c. I'm supposed to be home right now.

3. Change the subject. Students can refuse the offer and then change the subject. For example, if a friend offers you a cigarette, say "No thanks. What did you do last night after school?"

Examples of changing the subject:
a. What did you watch on TV last night?
b. Let's go play some basketball.
c. Let's go to my house and get something to eat.

4. Broken record. Students keep repeating the same response over, with no additional response.

   Examples of the broken record response:
   a. I don't want to.
   b. Not right now.
   c. No.

5. Strength in numbers or recruit an ally. Because there is strength in numbers, students find friends who have the same values. When they are in a pressure situation, it will not be as difficult to get out of it if friends are present.

   Examples of strength in numbers:
   a. Do you agree with them?
   b. What do you think I should do?
   c. Do you go along with what they want me to do?

6. Alternatives. Students can try to get their friends to do something that is healthy instead of unhealthy.

   Examples of alternatives:
   a. Let's go watch a video.
   b. Let's go play soccer.
   c. Let's call Sherry and see what she is doing.

CONSIDER THIS

Advertising Techniques

1. Bandwagon—These advertisements make it seem like everyone is "doing it" or using the product.
2. Testimonial—These advertisements use a famous person to sell the product.
3. Snob Appeal—These advertisements show well-dressed, good-looking people using the product.
4. Fun and Friendship—These advertisements show friends having fun while using the product.
5. Just Plain Folks—These advertisements show ordinary people using and talking about the product.
6. Humor—These advertisements use humor to sell the product.
7. Sensitive—These advertisements stir the emotions of individuals watching or reading the advertisement.
8. Statistics—These advertisements use studies and statistics to sell the product.
9. Romance—These advertisements show a romantic situation between two people when they are using the product being advertised.
10. Sex Appeal—These advertisements use "sexy" models/spokespersons to sell the product.

(See the Consider This box above). Give students an assignment to go home and watch television commercials or to look at magazine advertisements and identify the advertising techniques being used. After students understand the advertising techniques, ask them to create their own advertisement (print or commercial) to "sell" a positive health behavior. This could be used for any health-content area.

CONSIDER THIS

Sample Decision-Making Model

1. Figure out and define the decision that needs to be made.
2. Make a list of people who may be able to help in making the decision. It is important that at least one adult be included on this list.
3. List all possible alternatives. Brainstorm and try to find all the different ways this situation could be handled. The more ideas to choose from, the better chance of finding the one that works best. Questions to ask when brainstorming include the following:
   a. What has worked in the past in a similar situation?
   b. What would an adult I look up to do to solve this problem?
   c. What are some things I haven't tried that might work?
4. List pros and cons of each alternative. Consider both short- and long-term positive and negative consequences. Ask questions about each alternative:
   a. What are my responsibilities to my parents?
   b. What are my feelings and fears concerning each alternative?
   c. How does each alternative fit into my value system?
5. Cross out the alternatives that no longer seem logical.
6. Number the remaining solutions in the order you want to try them. (Some decisions will have only one possible alternative, so this step may be eliminated.)
7. Try the alternative chosen.
8. Evaluate the choice. If it did not work out, see if another alternative would work better.

---

encouraged to make some of their own decisions with the help of an adult. They learn two very important lessons if they are allowed to make some of their own choices or decisions. First, they learn that every choice is connected to consequences. Sometimes they will learn that their choices will produce results that are not pleasant or are sometimes even dangerous. If they are allowed to experience these minor, unpleasant results with adult support, they will become more independent adults who understand the importance of decision making. Second, children learn that they will be held accountable for each choice. If parents and teachers hold children accountable for their decisions, they will become more responsible adults because they will understand the concept of consequences for their actions.

When children are young, it is not appropriate for them to be taught a formal decision-making model. Instead, children should be encouraged to make choices and then experience both the negative and positive outcomes of those choices. Older students should be taught a formal decision-making model as a means to organize a process for making more complex decisions that confront them. Numerous decision-making models can be found in various health-education curricula or in other books. See the Consider This box above for an example. Activities that help teach decision-making skills can be found on page 110.

GOAL-SETTING SKILLS

National Health Education Standard 6

Goal setting is another important health skill that children should learn. A goal is something that a person would like to do, to have, or to be. It is something within a person's power to accomplish in the short or long term. Without goals, it is easy for children and adolescents to lose their direction and make bad decisions. One of the important outcomes of good goal-setting skills is the ability to delay gratification or to improve on impulse control.

Delayed gratification and impulse control are important because of the findings from the "marshmallow" study conducted at Stanford University several years ago. Preschool children were brought individually into a room and one marshmallow was placed in front of them. They were told that they could eat the one marshmallow right away, or they could have two marshmallows if they waited until the researcher ran an errand and then came back into the room. About one-third of the children ate the single marshmallow right away, one-third waited a little while and then ate the one marshmallow, and one-third were able to wait 15–20 minutes for the researcher to return. The researchers located these children 14 years later and discovered that the children who waited to eat the marshmallow were more emotionally stable, better liked by their teachers and peers, and were still able to delay gratification in pursuit of their goals. The researchers found that the children who ate the marshmallow right away were more likely to be more emotionally unstable, did not handle stress well, were not liked as well, and still were not able to delay gratification. In addition, the children who waited until the researcher returned scored an average of 210 points higher on the SAT compared to their counterparts who did not wait.[10] Teachers can help students work on their goal-setting skills in specific health-content areas and throughout all academic areas. It is important that children are given the opportunity to improve their goal-setting skills so that they make good decisions and reach their potential. Activities that help teach goal-setting skills can be found on page 111.

ACTIVITIES

Promoting Decision-Making Skills

The following activities are suggestions for teaching children decision-making skills. These activities allow students to practice their decision-making skills and experience the consequences of their decisions in a safe environment.

Grades K–2

1. Allow students to make low-level decisions in the class. These are decisions that do not interfere with your teaching, but allow students to participate in the decision-making process within the classroom. For example:
   a. Let students decide where they are going to sit. (A discussion about the responsibilities of sitting next to a friend should take place before seat selection.)
   b. Let students decide if they want to do math or language arts first.
   c. Let students decide on the way they want to present their book report (e.g., oral report, written report, poster presentation, etc.).

Grades 3–5

1. Ask students for examples of some bad decisions that children their age sometimes make. An example might be deciding to watch television instead of doing homework. Ask students to write down the consequences of that decision. Also ask them to write down better alternatives to watching television. Discuss their answers.

2. There are many good children's books that deal with solving problems or making decisions. The main character is often faced with a problem and must decide what to do. Before reading the ending of the book, ask children to identify the problem, tell what the character is feeling, and give possible solutions to the problem. This

Children listen to their teacher read a book about the main character who has a problem. The teacher asks them what they would do if they were the main character.

will allow children to practice their decision-making skills without facing the consequences. End the lesson by reading the rest of the book and comparing what the character did to what the students chose.

3. Tell students that they will have a "problem box" in the classroom. Students can anonymously write down problems that they are experiencing and then place them into the "problem box." Periodically, read a problem to the class and instruct students to brainstorm solutions to the problem. This activity reinforces the notion that it is important to talk to other people about problems because additional alternatives can be created when more people are involved. (Review the problems before reading them aloud to the class. Some problems may not be appropriate to read in front of the entire class.)

Grades 6–8

1. After introducing the decision-making model, ask students to use the decision-making steps on an actual decision they have had to make. This is more meaningful than giving the students fictitious examples and expecting them to apply the decision-making steps. For a continuous reinforcement activity, ask students to write down in their journal each time they used the decision-making model in their lives.

2. Have students read a book that presents a problem. Instruct students to not read the entire book, but to stop after the problem is presented. Then ask them to complete the decision-making steps and decide what they would do if they were presented with the same problem. This activity allows students to practice the decision-making steps in a nonthreatening environment. Have students track how the characters in the book did or did not use the decision-making process.

ACTIVITIES

Promoting Goal-Setting Skills

The following activities are suggestions for teaching children goal-setting skills.

Grades K–2

It is very difficult for young children to work on long-term goals due to their developmental level and skewed perception of time. "Long-term," to most young children, is one day or at the most one week. To help children work on short-term goals, teachers can do the following activity:

1. Ask the children to choose one specific goal they would like to work on for the day. This goal can be related to their behavior in the classroom or a health behavior. For example, their goal may be to eat five fruits and two vegetables during the day. Create a checksheet to help the students keep track of their goals. For example, design a worksheet that has smiley faces on it. When the students eat one piece of fruit or a vegetable, they color the smiley face. When they color all of the smiley faces on their paper, they can bring it to the teacher, who, in turn, gives students a sticker. If students do not meet their daily goal, ask them to reflect on why they did not and determine how they might meet that goal the next day. If they did meet the goal, encourage them to add on to that goal for the next day.

These children have set a goal to eat at least one fruit and vegetable for lunch.

Grades 3–5

1. Children in grades 3–5 are more capable of working on week-long goals instead of just daily goals. Encourage students to write down their weekly goals. When students reach their goals, give them a reward. Examples of weekly goals include, "I will study 30 minutes every night this week," "I will exercise five days this week," "I will turn in all of my homework this week."

2. Work on class goals. Each week, decide together on one goal for students to achieve for that week. For example, students could try to increase the number of compliments they say during the week and decrease the number of put-downs. Post a chart on the bulletin board to record these statements. Give the class a certain goal to reach for the week, and if the goal is reached, give a reward to the class.

Grades 6–8

1. A long-term project that middle-level students are capable of completing is a health-maintenance or health-behavior change project. Ask students to think of one health behavior they want to improve. Instruct them to write a long-term goal statement that is doable and measurable, for example, "I will jog for 20 minutes, 3 days a week" or "I will eat five fruits and two vegetables every day." Examples of unmeasurable goals include, "I will improve my eating habits" or "I will reduce the stress in my life." Help students refine their long-term goals so they are doable and measurable. After students have written a measurable, long-term goal, have them then write short-term goals to help them meet their long-term goals. For example, "During the first week I will jog 10 minutes, 2 days a week," "During second week I will run 10 minutes, 3 days a week," etc. Encourage students to keep a journal about how well they are meeting their short- and long-term goals. At the end of the project, assign students to write a reaction paper about the process that explains how they felt as they were working toward their goal. The Consider This box on page 112 can be used to help students work toward their goal.

2. As students get more sophisticated with understanding the steps of goal setting, introduce the concept of roadblocks, or obstacles. Explain to students that sometimes goals are not met because of roadblocks or obstacles. Ask students to brainstorm different roadblocks. After several roadblocks are recorded, place students in groups and ask them to brainstorm ways to overcome these roadblocks. This activity can help students the next time they are working on a goal and are faced with one of the roadblocks discussed in class.

CONSIDER THIS

Goal-Setting Steps

1. What long-term goal do I want to accomplish?
   —Think about something you want to improve or do better.
2. Where are you now and where do you want to be in the future?
   —Determine your level of achievement at the present time.
   —Set your goal. It must be doable and measurable.
3. How will you achieve your goal?
   —What resources will you need?
   —Who will support you while you try to reach your goal?

   —What short-term goals can I work on to meet my long-term goal?
   —How long will it take for me to meet my goal?
4. How did you do?
   —Encourage students who reached their goal to acknowledge the success and to thank those who helped.
   —Encourage students who did not reach their goal to evaluate why they did not reach their goal and to think about what they would have to do differently to reach their goal the next time.

ADVOCACY SKILLS

National Health Education Standard 7

Advocacy skills are another important set of health skills to teach children. Advocacy skills in health education are related to teaching children and adolescents to promote and encourage positive health choices for themselves, their family, and their community. This means teaching students how to:

- Convey accurate health information;
- Express their opinions about health issues; and
- Influence others in making positive health choices.[11]

Advocacy skills are very important because many children and adolescents believe and trust their peers more than they trust their parents or teachers.

This trust of peers supports the concept of the social norm theory. The social norm theory states that upper-elementary and middle-level students many times believe that "everyone is doing it."[12] Students at this age also have the strong desire to fit in and be accepted by their peers. Educators first need to convince students that the majority of their peers are practicing positive health behaviors. Secondly, they should teach students how to influence others into making positive health choices. This allows students to use peer pressure in a positive way. Activities that help promote advocacy skills can be found on the page below.

ACTIVITIES

Promoting Advocacy Skills

The following activities are suggestions for teaching children advocacy skills.

Grades K–2

1. Give students specific instructions for a show-and-tell activity. Encourage students to tell the class one way that they help keep their body healthy. For example, students may bring in a jump rope and explain

how they like to jump rope every day. They may bring in a healthy cereal and tell how they eat break-fast every morning. This will allow students to see that practicing positive health behaviors is the norm.

Grades 3–5

1. Teach students how to write a letter. Ask them to write a letter to their favorite restaurant asking management to go completely smoke free.

2. Ask students to make a public commitment or pledge about a specific health behavior. Have them sign a poster that says, "I promise to eat three fruits and two vegetables every day for the next week."

Grades 6–8

1. Teach students how to write a letter to the editor. Have them choose a health topic that needs improvement in the community, do research about that issue, and then write and submit a letter to the editor. For example, they may write a letter to the editor encouraging a smoke-free environment in all restaurants in their town or city. Another example would be to encourage adults to drive the speed limit within school zones.

2. Place students into groups and require them to create a health fair booth on an adult health issue (see chapter 5). Topics may include high blood pressure, osteo-

These children are working together to gather information about a health topic that needs improvement in their community.

porosis, cancer, smoking cessation, diabetes, etc. Present this health fair during an open house or during a special event. This activity allows students to advocate for their parents' health.

3. Teach students how to write an advocacy letter to a city council person or state representative. Introduce a controversial issue that is related to health. Students can decide what they think about the issue and then write a letter to their representative expressing their views.

4. A project for an entire class can be to start a petition advocating for some health issue. The class can create the petition and then collect the signatures needed for a successful petition drive. This can be either a school issue or a community issue. For example, students may want the opportunity to have intramurals before school starts. A petition could be started to promote this practice. Once the majority of students have signed the petition, it can be presented to the school board.

SUMMARY

There are three primary reasons why health instruction should focus on the infusion of health knowledge with personal and social skill development. First, research has shown that the most effective way to positively influence health behaviors is through social skills training. Second, information is constantly changing. It is important to teach students how and where to access valid information. Third, the National Health Education Standards focus on both health knowledge and skills. The primary social skills included in this chapter are communication, peer resistance, decision making, goal setting, advocacy, and accessing skills.

There are two main components of verbal communication: speaking and listening. As with most skills, verbal communica-tion is a skill that must be learned and practiced. Good communication skills can improve self-esteem and can help students succeed in the classroom. In addition, good communication skills help adults succeed in their personal relationships and professional jobs.

Speaking skills include the ability to convey a message clearly, by expressing feelings and thoughts in a specific manner. Listening is the second skill in verbal communication. Good listening skills include maintaining eye contact, asking questions, paraphrasing, giving nonverbal feedback, compli-menting, and showing empathy.

There are three main ways that people tend to communi-cate: aggressively, passively, or assertively. Aggressive communicators do not care about the feelings of the person with whom they are talking. Passive communicators let people walk all over them because they are mostly concerned about the other person's feelings rather than their own. Assertive communicators are concerned about their own feelings and the feelings of the person with whom they are talking. Teachers should help students become assertive communicators.

Peer resistance skills also are important for elementary and middle-level students to learn. One of the most common reasons why adolescents adopt negative health behaviors is because of peer pressure. Social-influence resistance training was developed to help counteract peer pressure. This theory suggests that students be exposed to social pressure in the classroom, so that when they actually encounter negative peer pressure, they will know how to handle the situation positively. Children should be given many opportunities to practice peer resistance skills. Peer resistance skills include making excuses, avoiding the situation, changing the subject, and the broken record.

Decision making is another skill that is important for elementary and middle-level students to learn. Individuals do not always consciously use a decision-making model every time a decision is made. However, it is important for students to know the steps in making healthy decisions so that if they are confronted with a different choice, they will have a better chance at making a positive decision. The steps of decision making are to figure out the problem, make a list of people who may be able to help in making the decision, list all possible alternatives, list the pros and cons of each alternative, cross out the alternatives that do not seem logical, number the remaining solutions in the

order you want to try them, try the alternative chosen, and evaluate the choice.

Goal-setting skills are also very important for elementary and middle-level students. Students who are skilled at setting and completing goals are better at understanding delayed gratification and demonstrating impulse control. Young children can focus on setting and achieving daily goals, while older students can set long term goals. Older students should learn the appropriate steps of goal setting, which are to determine the long term goal, determine their present status toward reaching that goal, determine how the goal will be achieved, and evaluate their progress toward reaching their goal.

Advocacy skills are also important to today's youth. Advocacy skills include teaching children to promote and encourage positive health choices for themselves, their family, and their community. These skills are important because peers have more influence on adolescent behavior than do parents during the middle-level years. Teachers need to use the power of positive peer pressure (advocacy) to help encourage positive health behaviors.

Skills to access information and health-promoting products and services are also important to elementary and middle-level students. This includes teaching students how to utilize community health helpers, to decide when situations require professional help, to locate health products and services, and to find valid health information. Adults will not always be available to help children and adolescents, therefore it is important to teach them these skills so they will be prepared to locate accurate health information, products, and services.

DISCUSSION QUESTIONS

1. Who should be responsible for teaching children personal and social skills?

2. What are the two main verbal communication skills?

3. What are four good listening skills that elementary students should practice and learn?

4. What are three different ways to communicate? Which type of communication is the most desirable?

5. Why is it important for children to learn peer resistance/refusal skills?

6. What are four different ways to resist peer pressure?

7. Why is it important for children to learn the steps of decision making?

8. What are the steps of making a healthy decision?

9. Why is it important for students to improve their goal-setting ability?

10. What are some activities to help students improve their goal-setting abilities?

11. What are advocacy skills?

12. Why are advocacy skills important to students?

13. What are some activities that can be conducted to teach children how to advocate for their personal, family, and community health?

14. What are included in skills to access information and health-promoting products and services?

15. Why are accessing skills important to students?

16. What are some activities that can be conducted with students to help them improve their accessing skills?

ENDNOTES

1. S. Botvin, Schinke, J. Epstein, and T. Diaz, "Long-term Follow-up Results of a Randomized Drug Abuse Prevention Trial in a White Middle-Class Population," *Journal of the American Medical Association* 273, no. 14, (1990): 1106–1112.

2. S. Dent, Sussman, A. Stacy, S. Craig, D. Burton, and B. Flay, "Two-year Behavior Outcomes of Project Towards No Tobacco Use," *Journal of Clinical and Consulting Psychology* 63 (1995): 676–677.

3. J. Fetro, *Personal and Social Skills: Understanding and Integrating Competencies Across Health Content* (Santa Cruz, CA: ETR Associates, 1992), 152.

4. D. Hodzkom, L. Read, E. Porter, and D. Rubin, *Research Within Reach: Oral and Written Communication, A Guided Response to the Concerns of Educators* (St. Louis, MO: Mid-Continent Regional Educational Laboratory, 1984).

5. Ibid.

6. E. Hipp, *Fighting Invisible Tigers: A Student Guide to Life in "The Jungle"* (Minneapolis, MN: Free Spirit Publishing Company, 1985), 71.

7. Ibid., 70.

8. Gregory Stock, *The Kids' Book of Questions* (New York: Workman Publishing Co., 1988).

9. D. Herrman and J. McWhirter, "Refusal and Resistance Skills for Children and Adolescents: A Selected Review, *Journal of Counseling and Development* 75 (1997): 177–187.

10. J. O'Neil, *On Emotional Intelligence: A Conversation with Daniel Goleman.* Educational Leadership 54, no. 1, (1996): 6–11.

11. Joint Committee on National Health Education Standards, *National Health Education Standards* (Atlanta, GA: American Cancer Society, 1995), 23.

12. Fetro, *Personal and Social Skills*, 152.

SUGGESTED READINGS

Danielson, C., and P. Algava. *Getting Along: A Social Skills Curriculum, Primary Edition.* Princeton, NJ: Outcomes Associates, 1989.

Fetro, J. *Personal and Social Skills: Understanding and Integrating Competencies Across Health Content.* Santa Cruz, CA: ETR Associates, 1992.

Hart, S. *Balancing Stress for Success.* Santa Cruz, CA: ETR Associates, 1990.

Herrman, D., and J. McWhirter, "Refusal and Resistance Skills for Children and Adolescents: A Selected Review," *Journal of Counseling and Development* 75 (1997): 177–187.

Joint Committee on National Health Education Standards, *National Health Education Standards* (Atlanta, GA: American Cancer Society, 1995).

Mendler, A. *Smiling at Yourself: Educating Young Children About Stress and Self-Esteem.* Santa Cruz, CA: ETR Associates, 1990.

The National Commission on the Role of the School and Community in Improving Adolescent Health. *Code Blue: Uniting for Healthier Youth.* Alexandria, VA: National Association for State Boards of Education, 1990.

CHILDREN'S LITERATURE WITH SOCIAL AND PERSONAL HEALTH SKILL THEMES

Grades K–2

Grindley, Sally. *What Are Friends For?* Kingfisher, 1998.

Henkes, Kevin. *Lily and the Purple, Plastic Purse.* Greenwillow, 1996.

Hest, Amy. *The Purple Coat.* Macmillan, 1986.

Kroll, Virginia. *Hands.* Boyds Mill, 1997 (Multicultural).

Oram, Hiawyn. *Badger's Bad Mood.* Scholastic, 1998.

Pfister, Marcus. *The Rainbow Fish.* North-South Books, 1992.

Sesisi, Ellen. *Secrets.* Penguin, 1995.

Grades 3–5

Angeloum M. *Life Doesn't Frighten Me.* Stewart, Tabori, and Chang, 1993. (Publisher's Weekly Best Book 1993).

Blos, Joan. *Old Henry.* Scribner's, 1987.

Calmenson, Stephanie. *The Principal's New Clothes.* Scholastic, 1989.

Fletcher, Ralph. *Flying Solo.* Clarion, 1996.

Kroeger, Mary, and Louis Borden. *Paper Boy.* Clarion, 1996.

Naylor, Phyllis Reynolds. *Shiloh.* Antheneum, 1991. (Newbery Medal Book).

Smith, Robert Kimmel. *The War With Grandpa.* Bantam, 1984.

Viorst, Judith. *If I Were in Charge of the World.* Antheneum, 1981.

Estes, Eleanor. *The Hundred Dresses.* Harcourt Brace, 1944.

Grades 6–8

Avi. *Nothing But the Truth.* Orchard, 1991. (Newberry Honor Book).

Brooks, Bruce. *The Moves Make the Man.* Harper & Row, 1984. (Newbery Honor Book) (Multicultural).

Erlich, Amy. *When I Was Your Age.* Candlewick, 1996.

Philbrick, Rodman. *Freak the Mighty.* Scholastic, 1993.

7

SAFETY: PREVENTION OF UNINTENTIONAL INJURY

O U T L I N E

CONCEPTS TO TEACH ABOUT UNINTENTIONAL INJURY IN ELEMENTARY AND MIDDLE-LEVEL SCHOOLS

In grades K–2, students should be able to:

- Explain and practice rules for safety on school bus and school playground.
- Recognize dangerous situations.
- Practice safety as a pedestrian.
- Recognize potentially dangerous situations.
- Demonstrate safety rules to follow at home and at school.
- Know the importance of safe practices around water.
- Demonstrate the stop, drop, and roll techniques in fire situations.
- Seek necessary help when injured.
- Know basic first-aid procedures.
- Know the importance of the use of seat belts.
- Know and practice procedures for safety on bicycles.
- Understand the importance of practicing fire prevention measures.
- Explain the difference between safe and unsafe behaviors.

- Know the universal symbol for poison.
- Recognize helpers in the community for safety and information.

In grades 3–5, students should be able to:

- Learn first-aid measures for minor injuries.
- Practice use of seat belts when riding in a motor vehicle.
- Learn swimming skills and measures to be taken to be safe around water.
- Practice safe behaviors to prevent injuries in a variety of settings—in the home, at school, while outdoors, etc.
- Develop a home safety plan.
- Recognize hazards around the home and yard—poisons, insects, etc.
- Know how to get emergency help when necessary.
- Learn and practice basic skills of bicycle riding and safety.
- Know measures that can be taken to protect oneself in severe weather conditions.

In grades 6–8 students should be able to:

- Become familiar with factors associated with motor-vehicle collisions—speed, alcohol use, seat-belt use, air bags.
- Know the relationship among behaviors, personal responsibilities, environmental factors, and prevention of injury-producing situations.
- Use protective equipment when involved in recreational activities—helmet when cycling, proper equipment when skiing and roller blading.
- Know and practice bicycle safety rules.
- Perform standard first-aid skills.
- Recognize and become familiar with community resources available to provide a safe environment.
- Practice attitudes and behaviors that result in unintentional injury events.
- Develop a safety plan for the family in case of fire or natural disaster.
- Become familiar with and practice safety in boating, swimming, and when involved in any type of water activity.

UNINTENTIONAL INJURY

Instruction in safety and injury prevention is an important component of an elementary and middle-level school curriculum. A major reason for this is the fact that the leading cause of death among schoolchildren of this age, ages 1–14, is unintentional injuries. In a recent year, approximately 2,900 children between the ages of 5 and 14 died from unintentional injuries.[1] Over half of these fatalities result from motor-vehicle accidents. Deaths from drowning, fires and burns, firearms, and falls account for most of the remainder. For this reason, safety instruction cannot be ignored.

In spite of the fact that some safety prevention emphasis has been a part of the school curriculum since the early years of the 20th century, only a few states mandate such instruction today. Several states do require the teaching of fire prevention, and in most states periodic fire drills are required during the school year. In some parts of the country, tornado drills are carried out during the school year. Also, in areas of the country where an earthquake is a possibility, such as in California, earthquake drills are conducted on a regular basis. In addition to such incidental emergency management activities, organized and planned safety instruction should be a priority component of the health education program in the elementary and middle-level school.

The term *unintentional injuries* has become the accepted term among professionals in the field of safety.[2] The term *accident,* historically used, tends to incorrectly imply a circumstance over which one has no control. As a result, many persons do not become involved in programs and activities designed to reduce or even prevent injury-causing situations. This has too often led to a passive or reactive attitude toward reducing unintentional injuries.

All too often, it has been assumed that having an unintentional injury event, an "accident," is an unavoidable circumstance. Many have believed that there is little they can do to reduce the incidences of injury and fatality from accidents. However, it is increasingly evident that education can help develop safety behavioral patterns.

The concept of injury control in current safety education programming involves expanding knowledge about safety prevention, promoting a positive attitude regarding unintentional injury prevention, and learning and incorporating skills that will prevent such occurrences into daily practice.

Numerous factors account for the high incidence of injury among elementary and middle-level schoolchildren. Many situations during the elementary and middle-level school years result in injury because children of this age group tend to be daring rather than cautious. They tend to believe that they are old enough to perform certain activities that they really are unable to do. Children also are curious during these years. They attempt actions because of the interest and excitement of the activity, without considering the chance of injury.

During the upper-elementary and middle-level school years, peer pressure can greatly influence the activities of young people. Children often dare others to take actions that can result in injury. It is difficult for some children to refrain from taking a certain action when one's friends, or a group, is present.

The ultimate objectives of any safety presentation are to develop positive attitudes and establish behavioral patterns that can prevent and protect against unintentional injuries. In addition to establishing safe and nurturing environments, the school must teach students that everyone has a personal responsibility for his or her own safety and well-being. It is important that each person learn and follow procedures that reduce the likelihood of injury-producing circumstances.

Attitude formation begins early in a child's life and has a major impact on safety behavioral patterns. Although innumerable factors influence attitude formation, the actions of parents and respected adults are a major force, particularly among children in the primary grades. Parents must realize that their actions, attitudes, and comments affect the attitudes of their children. The parent who exceeds the speed limit while driving the car, operates a boat while drinking a bottle of beer, or improperly places flammable substances near a fire on the outdoor grill is modeling unsafe behaviors to the child.

Likewise, the school environment can affect the attitude formation and behaviors of elementary and middle-level schoolchildren with regard to injury control. It is difficult to encourage the practice of safe behaviors when the playground equipment is improperly maintained, or the school grounds are littered with bottles and broken glass, or when there are blacktop or cement play areas without proper surfaces under swings and other equipment.

FORMAT OF SAFETY INSTRUCTION

Most elementary and middle-level schools do not set aside a specific time in the day for the exclusive study of safety. Nevertheless, there are numerous curriculum packages, audio and visual materials, as well as written materials to assist the elementary and middle-level teacher in preparing safety instruction that can be used in conducting safety and injury-control learning experiences.

Circumstances that can lead to effective learning in injury prevention occur every day in the life of the elementary and middle-level schoolchild. Teachers must recognize these moments and use them effectively to develop positive attitudes and behavioral practices. For example, there may have been a report on the local news of a train-car crash involving two local teenagers that the children heard their parents talking about over breakfast. This presents an opportunity for an open discussion of the importance of railroad crossing safety and its implications for children.

Students may be aware of events within the community, such as a major fire at a store in the mall. This presents an opportunity to discuss factors in fire safety. On the other hand, a more personal situation may present itself for incidental instruction. A child in the class or school may have been injured in a bicycle accident, an automobile accident, or an all-terrain vehicle collision.

Beyond general circumstances, safety concepts may be related to the content of the various academic subjects of the elementary and middle-level school curriculum. For example, one might find a story in children's literature in which a character or an animal in the story becomes injured. Follow-up of this story could lead to a discussion of injury prevention and improved safety

behavioral patterns. In a science class unit on electricity, it would be appropriate to include material about the potential for injury from contact with electricity. Measures to protect against electrocution would be an expected part of instruction. Each of these incidental circumstances, and literally hundreds more, present opportunities throughout the school year for discussion, class interaction, and learning experiences related to injury prevention and protection.

Safety concepts are often correlated within the elementary and middle-level school curriculum through units of study. A class might be examining the various means of, and development of, transportation in the United States. As types of transportation are studied, opportunities arise to incorporate motor-vehicle safety concepts.

MOTOR-VEHICLE SAFETY

The first recorded fatality resulting from an automobile accident occurred in 1899 in New York City when a man stepped off a streetcar and was struck by an automobile. He was pronounced dead shortly afterward.[3] Since that incident, many persons have been killed as the result of motor-vehicle collisions. Approximately 115 people a day are fatally injured from motor-vehicle collisions; slightly less than half of these accidents involve alcohol use.

Today, motor-vehicle collisions are the leading cause of unintentional injury death in the United States. For the elementary and middle-level school-age population, motor vehicles are responsible for more deaths than the next four causes of death combined.

Motor-vehicle collisions not only result in fatalities, but are responsible for numerous injuries and extensive economic loss. More than 2 million disabling injuries occur from motor-vehicle accidents each year.[4] The estimated cost of motor-vehicle accidents is over $191 billion annually.[5] With safety data like these emphasizing the seriousness of the problem in American society, instruction about motor-vehicle safety must begin early in a child's life. Such instruction should be a part of every elementary and middle-level school safety class. Teachers must be aware of the facts and recognize appropriate information and material for instruction.

Numerous factors can be identified as causes of motor-vehicle accidents. The human element is of primary importance. Errors in judgment, physical conditions such as fatigue and drowsiness, and inattention have been shown to be major causes. Excessive speed and failure to follow traffic regulations also lead to motor-vehicle collisions. There are also a number of environmental factors—road instability due to rain, ice, and snow, and vehicle engineering are just two such conditions.

Alcohol Use

Possibly the one factor associated with the most instances of motor-vehicle fatalities and injuries is the abuse of alcohol; approximately 39% of all motor-vehicle fatalities result from alcohol use.[6] Obviously, elementary and middle-level schoolchildren are not of driving age, and they have little or no control over whether their parents drive while under the influence of alcohol. However, attitudes are developed early in life. Long-term attitudes and practices can be influenced by understanding the dangers associated with drunken driving.

In an effort to reduce the problem of alcohol-caused fatalities and injuries, a number of different initiatives have been introduced in recent years. Several states have introduced legislation that reduces the level of blood alcohol content (BAC) at which motor-vehicle drivers are considered legally intoxicated. In most states, the BAC level at which a driver is considered intoxicated is 0.10; however, at least twelve states have moved to lower the level to 0.08.

Public concern regarding drunken driving has increased significantly during the past decade. Throughout the nation, hundreds of changes in local ordinances and laws have been implemented in an attempt to reduce fatal accidents involving drunken driving.[7] About half of the states permit authorities to suspend the suspect's license, from the time of the arrest until trial, if he or she had a BAC level above 0.10. The suspension of a driver's license following a drunken driving conviction has been supported as an effective countermeasure for reducing alcohol-related accidents. However, courts have been hesitant to suspend a license when doing so causes an economic hardship on the driver.

Many states have increased the penalties for drunken driving. Stiffer fines, suspension of licenses, and jail sentences for repeat offenders and for those involved in traffic accidents resulting in injury or fatality are examples of such legislation. Also, more than half of the states have implemented some type of zero tolerance limit for minors. Generally, this places stiff BAC limits, in some cases as low as .01 and .02 BAC, for anyone under the age of 21.

The public's concern about the problem of drinking and driving in recent years has led to the formation of more than 600 nationwide chapters of the private organization Mothers Against Drunk Driving (MADD). The principal focus of MADD is to work for solutions to drunk driving and underage drinking problems. Among the various initiatives of this organization are public awareness initiatives, special alcohol-related programs directed to young people, and lobbying in the public policy at both state and federal levels.[8]

Preventive Restraints
Seat Belts

A number of preventive measures help to prevent motor-vehicle-related fatalities and injuries. The use of seat belts has received major emphasis. Seat-belt use demands action on behalf of the vehicle occupants, for they must hook the belt in order for the device to function.

As early as 1971, laws were passed in Australia mandating seat-belt use. However, it was not until 1984 that New York became the first state in the United States to pass a mandatory seat-belt use law. Since then, forty-nine states and the District of Columbia have passed similar laws.[9]

There is little question that the use of seat belts helps to reduce fatalities from motor-vehicle collisions. The United States Department of Transportation estimates that seat belts save approximately 4,000 lives annually.

Despite the statistics, legislation mandating the use of seat belts has been controversial. Many people feel that such legislation is an intrusion on personal freedoms. They say that government has no right to require individual behaviors in a private vehicle. Others believe that seat belts are uncomfortable and that they are not effective in reducing injuries and fatalities.

Opponents of this legislation say that, in most jurisdictions, authorities have little ability to enforce such mandates. In several settings, police issue citations for failure to use seat belts only when stopping a vehicle for some other offense. These opponents also suggest that in states with mandatory seat-belt laws, less than half of the vehicle occupants use the belts. Most mandatory provisions apply only to occupants in the front seat. Since elementary and middle-level schoolchildren usually ride in the backseat of a motor vehicle, these laws have little effect in protecting them. In an attempt to help protect individuals who ride in vehicle rear seats, the National Highway Safety Administration has mandated that all cars have lap and shoulder safety belts for riders in the rear seat. This regulation is applicable to all cars, but not to vans, small trucks, and utility vehicles.

It has been generally noted that use of seat belts increases immediately after new laws go into effect. In New York and several others states, fatalities and serious injuries dropped to their lowest level in the first year that the seat-belt law was in effect. However, after a period of time, use of seat belts tends to drop off.

Developing behavioral patterns of seat-belt use among elementary and middle-level schoolchildren is important. It is not unlikely that young children, after studying the value of using seat belts, will encourage their parents to use them. For this reason, instruction about the use of seat belts should be an important part of the elementary and middle-level school health and safety curriculum.

Passive Restraints

The use of a seat belt demands action on behalf of the occupant. The person must take some specific action for the belts to be effective. Many safety authorities feel that passive restraints have a greater potential for reducing fatalities and injuries in motor-vehicle collisions. There are two specific passive restraints that have received much attention: the air bag and automatic safety belts.

Since 1984, the United States Department of Transportation has ruled that all new vehicles must have passive restraints. For a variety of reasons, these controversial mandates have been postponed, modified, or set back. Many feel that it is inappropriate for the federal government to mandate such regulations. The automotive industry has been opposed because of the cost of installing air bags in vehicles. Currently, federal regulations call for the inclusion of air bags to protect the driver and front-seat passenger in all new passenger cars. As of 1999, light trucks must also be installed with air bags.

In spite of opposition, air bags, combined with lap/shoulder belts, offer the best safety protection available in motor vehicles today and save many lives and prevent injuries. The National Safety Council estimates that they save as many as 700 lives annually.[10]

Even though air bags do save many lives, they present a danger to small adults and young children. Air bags deploy at speeds up to 200 miles per hour. Unfortunately, there have been instances in which individuals sitting in vehicle front seats have been fatally injured or suffered disabling injuries by the deploying air bag. Because of this, it is recommended that children 12 years of age and under always ride in the backseat and be protected by appropriately installed shoulder/lap seat belts. Also, small adults must sit at least 10 inches from the air bag.

Other passive measures have been built into motor vehicles. For example, the energy-absorbing steering system that was introduced in 1967 automobiles has proven effective in saving lives and reducing serious injury. In addition, high-penetration-resistant windshields have proven effective in reducing injuries to the face.

Child Restraints

Infants and small children are particularly at risk in a motor-vehicle collision. They should never be allowed to travel unrestrained in a motor vehicle. A sudden stop can thrust the child forward and up into the window or other structure of the interior of the vehicle. The majority of child fatalities occur to children riding in the front seat who are usually not using a seat belt.

In 1978, Tennessee became the first state to require that infants and small children be secured in child restraints. Today, all fifty states and the District of Columbia have legislated similar provisions, and usage rates have increased to the point that today, over 80% of preschool-age children ride in automobiles with child restraints.[11]

Death and injury rates have dropped significantly among children who are in child restraint seats at the time of an accident. Child restraint seats are effective in reducing fatalities and are up to 80% effective in reducing injury.[12]

There are several different types of child safety seats; each is appropriate to the age of the child. Newborns must be placed in a carrier—a tub-shaped bed—that is held securely by a seat harness. The carrier is designed to face toward the rear of the car and is secured to the seat by the

Every elementary and middle-level schoolchild should wear a seat belt whenever riding in a motor vehicle.

adult seat belt. Once children can sit up, they should be placed in a toddler seat. Booster seats are available to serve the child who has outgrown the child safety seat but is not large enough to use the adult seat belt. The basic guidelines, as recommended by the federal government, are that children should ride in a car seat that faces forward when they weigh over 20 pounds and are at least 1 year of age. They should be kept in a booster seat until the regular vehicle seat belt fits—when the child weighs about 40 pounds.

Parents should be encouraged to use child restraint seats in a proper manner. In an effort to encourage new parents to use infant child safety seats, the federal government set as one of the National Health Promotion Objectives for the Year 2000 that all parents of newborns should be instructed in the proper use of infant safety seats.[13]

Child safety restraint information packets are available to parents in various communities. For example, the American Academy of Pediatrics has developed a safety restraint information education program. This program's materials have been distributed to pediatricians and health departments throughout the nation. Another program that is designed to encourage use of infant restraints is the child safety seat loaner program. In some communities, hospitals loan a safety seat to parents of newborns when they leave the hospital with their new baby.

ACTIVITIES

Motor Vehicle Safety

Excellent educational material can be found on the Internet for teaching about motor-vehicle safety.

- The National Highway Traffic Safety Administration (**www.nhtsa.dot.gov**) has several useful activities for classroom use. At the time of writing this book, this agency's Web site had a lot of useful information about air bags. The agency's *Buckle Up* activity focuses on the importance of using seat belts. Another activity—*Safety City*—is designed to encourage children to learn about the proper use of child safety seats. Lesson plans for teachers are available, along with games, art projects, and other material for students.

- The Federal Highway Administration (**www.fhwa.dot.gov**) has two education sites that are useful to elementary and middle-level schoolchildren. The K–5 program includes coloring materials, computer games, quizzes, and the presence of *Otto Club*. The material for use in grades 6–8 is more age appropriate. Children are encouraged to read road maps and compute distances. Various kinds of information about highway safety is included. There are instructional aids for teachers with either package.

- The NHTSA Hotline (1-888-DASH-2-DOT) is a 24-hour-a-day telephone hotline that anyone can access for information about motor-vehicle concerns.

Studies have indicated that use of child restraints among parents as well as elementary and middle-level schoolchildren is most effective when instructional programs include some type of incentive.[14] Monetary awards have been the most common type of incentive.

WATER SAFETY

Aquatic activity, such as swimming and boating, is an important part of life for millions of Americans. Most people take measures to protect against injury and fatality while they are involved in such endeavors. However, drowning constitutes the fourth leading cause of unintentional fatalities in the United States.[15] Among elementary and middle-level schoolchildren, death from drowning is second only to fatalities caused by motor-vehicle accidents: nearly 500 children die each year.[16]

Drowning is a health-related problem that has been recognized in the National Health Objectives for the Year 2000 Initiative.[17] One objective is to reduce deaths from drowning by about one-half. In 1987, there were 2.1 drownings per 100,000 people. By the turn of the century, the objective was to reduce that number to 1.3 drownings per 100,000 people.

Many instances of drowning occur while the victim is participating in activities that are not normally considered dangerous. These activities include fishing from docks or from bridges, or along the shore of a fast-moving river or stream; or playing or wading along the

shore. The important point to remember is that deep water is not needed for a drowning to take place. People drown in very shallow water as well as in deep rivers and lakes. For example, infants have been reported to drown by falling into buckets of water head first. Drownings occur from not recognizing hazardous conditions and from individual practices.

The suddenness of most drownings makes this a particularly difficult kind of fatality with which to cope. Teachers cannot overemphasize the importance and need for supervision of all swimming activities. Young children should never be left alone around water.

Elementary and middle-level schoolchildren must know their swimming abilities, and they must be taught not to overextend themselves. It is during this period of life that swimming skills can be developed most easily. Learning to swim should be encouraged at this age. Not only is it important to possess good swimming skills for safety, but swimming is also an excellent activity for personal fitness.

If possible, elementary and middle-level schoolchildren should be given the opportunity to learn to swim as part of the school program. Even though few schools have swimming pools as part of the school facility, arrangements can be made to collaborate with community agencies to support learn-to-swim programs.

Of particular concern to elementary and middle-level schoolchildren are the dangers associated with home swimming pools. Most pool drownings can be prevented,

Regardless of their ability to swim, children should wear proper flotation devices when in a boat.

and parents need to construct protection measures for their pools. All home pools should be enclosed by a fence that young children cannot climb. Self-latching gates that are out of reach of young children should be used. Children should be taught how to respond to an emergency situation in the pool area.

Among early preschool and primary-age children, injury or drowning occurs from falls in home bathtubs. Young children should be instructed about the potential hazards of bathtubs.

Children should be taught the potential dangers of jumping and diving into water, whether in home pools or at lakes and streams. These actions can result in broken bones, spinal cord injuries, and a variety of other injuries. Children should know not only the depth of the water, but whether there are rocks or other dangerous objects below the surface of the water that can cause serious injury.

Boat safety must be emphasized in instructional programs designed to reduce the incidence of drowning. Children must be taught how to enter and leave a boat. They must be encouraged to develop appropriate behaviors while riding in a boat. Obviously, standing and horseplay in a boat are inappropriate. Emphasis should be on preventative measures such as the presence and use of Coast Guard-approved personal flotation devices for each passenger, and other safety gear such as cushions, flares,

a foghorn, bailing bucket, and paddles. Children should be shown how to use these items.

Care must be taken to keep upper-elementary and middle-level schoolchildren from operating boats that are beyond their capability. Although some states have licensing regulations for the operation of small outboard engines by children, others do not.

It is estimated that more than 50% of boat-related drownings involve the presence and use of alcohol. It is unlikely that alcohol use among elementary and middle-level schoolchildren is a direct contributing factor to drowning. However, children at this age need to begin to be educated and to understand the danger of combining alcohol with boat operation.

Elementary and middle-level schoolchildren can learn to help rescue others who are in danger in the water. A very important rule to follow, particularly when individuals do not have life-saving skills, is not to jump into the water to rescue another person. Instead, an object—a pole, a towel, a ring, a buoy, or a kickboard—should be extended to an individual who is in trouble in the water.

Fire Safety

Another major cause of death and unintentional injury among elementary and middle-level schoolchildren is

ACTIVITIES

Water Safety

S uggested classroom activities with an emphasis on water safety:

1. Bring the following items to class: a ring buoy, a kickboard, a shepherd's crook, a life jacket, and a towel. Explain how each is used in protecting oneself in the water. Have the children practice and demonstrate the use of all five items.

2. Provide a drawing of a home pool. The picture should have a number of items that are unsafe and/or could contribute to injury or drowning. Discuss the dangerous items noted in the picture and explain how the condition noted can be corrected.

3. Bring a fishing boat into the class or improvise with chairs. Demonstrate how to sit and move about in the boat and show other measures that should be taken for safety while in a boat. Put various types of personal flotation devices on each child.

4. Role-play scenarios in which peers are supporting swimming or water-related risk behaviors, such as diving in the shallow end; climbing fences into unsupervised pools or ponds; or horsing around at pools, lakes, or beaches.

fire. More than 500 deaths occur each year among preschool and elementary schoolchildren from fires and burns, most of these occurring in the home.[18] In addition to fatalities, burns often result in pain and long-term debilitation and physical scarring. These circumstances can have long-term psychological effects on the victim.

A fire is created by the presence of three elements: air (oxygen), heat (enough to make fuel burn), and fuel (something that will burn). Fire results from a chemical reaction in which heat and light are produced. Rapid oxidation, combined with some fuel, causes fire. This chemical process is know as *combustion*. The necessary oxidizer in fires is oxygen. Flame and heat can be produced without oxygen, as in the case of combining sodium and chlorine, but only when oxygen is the oxidizer is it referred to as fire.

In order to extinguish a fire, one of the three necessary elements that comprise the fire triangle must be removed. For example, if something is burning and the source of oxygen is removed by smothering the flame, the fire will be extinguished. This can be shown to an elementary or middle-level class by placing a small burning candle in a glass jar and covering the top of the jar. When the oxygen is exhausted, the flame ceases. Since heat is necessary to the production of fire, measures taken to cool the blaze to a point below the ignition temperature will extinguish the fire. This is why water is used to put out fires. Water will absorb the heat and, in the process, extinguish the fire.

Fires fall into one of four different classifications (figure 7.1). A *Class A* fire is probably the best known type. This type of fire involves such combustible materials as wood, paper, textiles, and clothing. Class A fires are usually best extinguished by water. A *Class B* fire includes flammable liquids, such as grease, oil, gasoline, paint, and kerosene. To extinguish this type of fire, it is necessary to smother, or deny oxygen. Water should not be put on this type of fire. Pouring water on this type of fire usually causes the flaming liquids to splash and, in turn, spread the fire.

Class C fires are electrical fires. Water should not be used to put out an electrical fire because water is a conductor of electricity. The fourth classification, *Class D,* is not likely to be of concern to schoolchildren. This classification of fire involves combustible metals and is usually found in industrial settings.

Although fires occur in many different settings, most fatalities that result from fires occur in the home.[19] Home fires can occur anywhere in or around the house, but they are most likely to occur either in the kitchen or in the bedroom. Deaths from home heating fires have decreased during the past decade. This is due to several developments, particularly the increased availability of home smoke detectors and improved emergency medical system services. In spite of the decline in home fire fatalities, there are still numerous risk factors to consider.

Storage of flammable materials presents a potential fire hazard. Greater use should be made of flame-resistant

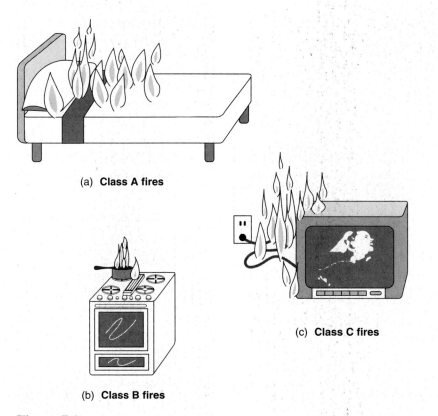

(a) **Class A fires**

(b) **Class B fires**

(c) **Class C fires**

Figure 7.1

(a) Class A fires involve the burning of combustible materials, such as wood, paper, cloth, and rubbish. (b) Class B fires involve flammable liquids or greases, such as those used in a frying pan on the stove. (c) Class C fires involve electrical appliances and are usually caused by faulty wiring.

fabrics in furniture, clothing, bedding, and mattresses as well as flame-retardant construction materials. Cigarette smoking remains a significant cause of many home fires.

A number of interventions can be taken to reduce the possibility of a fire in the home. One major factor has been the increased availability of home smoke detectors, which reduce the likelihood of a residential fire. Since the mid-1980s, home ownership of smoke detectors has increased due to heightened public awareness of the value of such detectors and a decrease in their retail price. Further, a number of states and local jurisdictions have implemented ordinances and legislation mandating the installation of smoke detectors in newly constructed homes and multifamily dwellings. It is recommended that smoke detectors be located on every level of a residence including the basement and outside each sleeping area.[20] The majority of fire deaths occur at night while people are sleeping. Smoke detectors should be checked periodically, preferably monthly, to make sure that they are in proper working order. The National Fire Protection Association recommends that home smoke detectors be replaced after 10 years.[21] The importance of regular maintenance of smoke detectors is noted by the fact that 90%

of fire-related deaths among children occur in homes without a functioning smoke detector.[22]

Children in the elementary and middle-level school should understand the value of a smoke detector and be able to explain what to do in their individual homes when the detector signals that a fire is present. Children should be taught how to safely escape from a burning building. Although one could talk about public buildings such as the school, the theater, or a department store, it is probably best to start by focusing on the home. It is important to know the telephone number of the local fire department and what to say when a call is placed. In many communities, dialing the 911 emergency telephone number or the "0" will reach appropriate emergency services.

Every family should develop a home fire escape plan. This should not be a confusing plan, but one that simply identifies two different ways to get out of each room in the house. It is important to identify two different routes out of each room in case the primary route of escape is blocked by smoke or fire. In a single-floor home, exit will most likely be through the nearest window. On a second floor, the availability of a fire escape ladder is important. The types of materials to use for a ladder in a

Students should be familiar with steps to be taken to use a fire extinguisher in their homes.

home should be planned in advance, before a fire occurs. Some people have purchased a commercial rope or chain ladder. Others have made a makeshift ladder out of rope or bedsheets tied together. Children must be taught that it is dangerous to jump from the upper stories of a burning building. The plan should include a prearranged location at which to gather outside. This will help to determine if and when everyone is safely out of the burning building. Families should not only have a predesignated fire escape plan, but the plan should be practiced so that all the children will know what to do in case of a fire.

Some fire departments provide stickers to be placed in children's bedroom windows. In case of a fire emergency, these stickers help to identify locations where children are sleeping.

When one hears the fire alarm signal, it is important to remain as close to the floor as possible since smoke rises and will not be as thick near the floor. As a result, there will be more oxygen available closer to the floor. Children should be taught to crawl to the nearest door and touch the door to see if there is a fire close to it. If it is hot, they should use another exit. If the door is not hot, they should open it slowly and see if there is any smoke. If not, they should continue to exit the building.

Fires are a particularly serious problem among children of preschool age. Matches should never be left where youngsters have access to them; they are not items to be used for play. Preschool children should understand that serious fires can result from even a very tiny match. Although it is the responsibility of adults and parents to keep matches and lighters out of reach of children, preschool educators should inform the children of the dangers associated with matches.

Serious burns can also result from hot items spilling on small children. Children should be taught to stay away from the stove, and adults should take measures to protect

children, such as keeping pan handles turned in toward the center of the stove and using back burners on the stove where pan handles are out of children's reach.

Young children can suffer death and injury when their clothing catches fire. Federal, state, and local regulations since the mid-1970s that mandate the use of fire-retardant materials in the manufacture of children's clothing have helped to reduce the number of such occurrences. Nevertheless, elementary and middle-level schoolchildren should understand what to do if their clothes catch fire and how they can protect themselves from a fire. Should clothing catch on fire, the individual should not run or even continue standing. Movement will only fan the flames and contribute to the fire's spread. Children should fall to the ground and roll about until the flames are extinguished. This procedure is referred to by safety professionals as *Stop, Drop, and Roll.* Covering the person with a blanket, a coat, or other heavy material will help to smother the flames.

Scalds

Scalding occurs when a person comes into contact with hot liquids. Preschool-age children are at most risk for scalding. All children should be taught to test bath water before getting into the bathtub to assure that the water is not too hot. Putting a little water on the wrist allows one to determine the temperature.

Parents can take preventative measures to protect against tap water scalds. They can lower the water heater thermostat settings to 120 degrees Fahrenheit. Not only will such a measure reduce the possibility of serious injuries, but it also saves energy.

School Fire Drills

The fire drill is an important school activity designed to assist children in knowing what actions to take in case of a fire. State and local regulations usually dictate how many and how often fire drills must be conducted at school. It is important that these drills not be seen as a fun time to get away from the classroom. They must be taken seriously by the teachers and the students and should be designed to help educate the children as to what should take place in case of an actual fire. Although not often implemented, a school fire drill should present some fire simulation. For example, a flashing red light at the end of the hallway to simulate flames at a particular entrance would require the students to take a secondary route out of the building. Fire drills should not be announced in advance, and they should occur at various times during the school day, not just before dismissal when the students have on their coats and jackets.

Internet Teaching Resources

There are a number of excellent teaching resources on the subject of fire safety available on the Internet. The

ACTIVITIES

Fire Safety

Suggested classroom activities related to fire safety:

1. Have the children list as many situations as possible that can cause a fire. For each situation identified, explain how a fire can be caused and discuss measures that the children can take to protect against a fire.

2. Develop an escape plan for getting out of each student's home as well as the school building in case of a fire.

3. Demonstrate the appropriate procedure to follow when one's clothing is ablaze. The emphasis here is in understanding what to do: Stop, Drop, and Roll.

4. Visit the local fire department. At the preschool and primary-school levels, this can be a very educational experience. This visit will help the children understand the role of local firefighters in protecting the community. Most firefighting personnel are interested in explaining fire prevention measures to school groups.

5. Explain that there are three elements necessary for a fire to result. To stop a fire, it is necessary to remove one of these elements. Have students tell appropriate measures for putting out a fire by eliminating each of the elements.

6. Have the class members practice and demonstrate appropriate measures for moving around in a smoke-filled room. Teach the students to remain low to the floor. Practice touching and opening the door in an appropriate manner.

7. Create a homework scavenger hunt requiring the student to collaborate with parents/guardians to find, test, map, and discuss placement of smoke detectors in their homes.

8. Analyze how a smoke detector works to inform a family of fire. Have students create a telephone directory of places in their community to purchase or get free smoke detectors.

9. Have primary-school students dress in firefighter uniforms brought to class by the local fire department. Discuss what each part of the equipment does to protect the firefighter. Draw analogies to prevention messages.

10. Create child and elderly locator stickers for adult and children's bedrooms as a class project. After these stickers are placed in the home in appropriate places, discuss them in the context of one's home fire escape plan.

National Fire Protection Association (**www.nfpa.org**) has a lot of information for teachers, parents, and children. Sparky the Fire Dog, mascot of the National Fire Protection Association, appears on this Web page. Sparky is an adult Dalmatian dog that wears full firefighter clothing.

There are several different activity pages for children taken from the *Sparky Activity Book.* For example, children are taught the basic skills of Stop, Drop, and Roll. Also, *Two Ways Out* teaches children the importance of having an alternative escape route from each room in their home. They are taught to draw a floor plan of their home and to locate possible escape routes. *Know What's Hot and What's Not* teaches children to identify things that are potentially dangerous and can cause burns.

In addition to the material available on the Internet, brochures, coloring books, and fire safety products can be obtained by contacting the National Fire Protection Association (1 Batterymarch Park, Quincy, MA 02269-9101). This association has produced a number of television public service announcements about fire safety.

Another interesting Internet page is Smokey Bear (**www.smokeybear.com**). This Web page is a public service of the United States Forest Service. A lot of interesting and useful information is presented, along with short quizzes, games, and *Smokey's Rules.* This is a very useful resource for teachers of elementary school-age children.

Kid's Page on the United States Fire Administration (**www.usfa.fema.gov/kids/**) provides several educational, interactive activities, including quizzes, word searches, and other games. All are designed to provide information about fire safety to the student.

ELECTRICITY

The current of electricity flowing through an electrical wire is of sufficient energy to both start a fire and to kill an individual. Electrical injuries result when the current of electricity comes into contact with the human body. Most people, particularly elementary and middle-level schoolchildren, do not understand the potential danger of electricity, particularly in their homes. It is important that they not only understand how electricity works, but that they learn to respect its power and be knowledgeable of its proper use.

The flow of electricity is measured in *amperes.* The current that flows through a wire is moved along by a force known as a *volt.* Extremely high voltage is generated at an electrical power plant. By the time the current has reached a home electrical circuit, it has been transformed downward to approximately 120 volts. The rate at which an appliance uses electrical power is measured in *watts,* which is the rate of using amperes pushed along by a certain number of volts. Most electrical appliances list their watt usage. Household light bulbs, for example, range from 25 to 300 watts.

The normal wall outlet in a home is capable of carrying 15 amperes of current. If the current exceeds this amount, the circuit is overloaded. When this occurs, the house wiring becomes overheated and an electrical fire may occur.

The human body is an excellent conductor of electrical current. If an electrical circuit is not grounded adequately, the current passes through the body and into the ground. Passage of current through one's body may produce fatal shock or serious burns along the pathway traversed by the current; this may lead to cardiac arrest.

Elementary and middle-level schoolchildren should be taught to respect the power of electricity. It is important to be instructed in the appropriate ways to plug and unplug an electrical cord, to turn off the power in the home when necessary, and to be aware of the dangers associated with frayed electrical wires.

Electrical appliances are particularly dangerous around water, because water is an excellent conductor of electrical current. If an appliance, such as a radio, curling iron, or hair dryer, should fall into a sink or bathtub containing water, an individual who is in contact with the sink or bathtub could be electrocuted. For this reason, children should be instructed about the dangers of using appliances around water. Children should learn that electrical appliances in a bathroom or around kitchen sinks must be disconnected when not in use and must never be used in the bathtub. Also, electrical appliances, such as hair dryers, can cause shock when they fall into water even when they are turned off.

FALLS

Falls rank second only to motor-vehicle collisions as a cause of death involving unintentional injuries. More than 16,000 fatalities result annually from falls.[23] The greatest number of these occur among the elderly population over 65 years of age and among children of preschool age. Although falls are not a major cause of fatality among elementary and middle-level schoolchildren, they do occur quite regularly and lead to a variety of injuries.

Among the causes of falls among elementary and middle-level schoolchildren is the failure to abide by safety rules and regulations. For example, climbing on and using playground equipment in inappropriate ways often results in a fall and accompanying injury. Young people also have a tendency not to be cautious in potentially dangerous circumstances. Running on stairways or on slippery surfaces can result in a fall. Taking chances and using inappropriate objects as ladders, such as chairs and tables, can result in falls.

Since many unintentional injuries related to falls occur around the home, learning activities within the classroom can center upon identifying potentially dangerous settings within the student's homes. Upon identifying these locations, brainstorming measures that can be taken to eliminate the dangers can be a very useful class activity.

Not only should children be taught to be cautious and take measures to prevent possible falls, they must also be familiar with what to do when a fall occurs. Associated cuts, wounds, and bruises must be attended to by an appropriate person. Bone fractures are a common result of a fall. Children of elementary and middle-level school age need to understand the importance of obtaining appropriate medical care in these circumstances.

POISONING

Throughout life, one is exposed to a number of agents that are poisonous. More than 8,000 deaths occur annually from exposure to various poisonous substances.[24] In addition, more than 500,000 children require emergency medical attention because they have ingested or been exposed to harmful poisonous substances in the home. The elementary and middle-level schoolchild should be aware of potentially hazardous substances and learn to take measures to protect against poisoning.

Many harmful toxic substances are found around the home. Harm comes from inappropriate ingestion of medications and drugs. For this reason, medicines should be stored in locations where young children cannot reach them. Proper labeling of medicines is important in protecting against accidental poisoning. Federal law mandates that medicines be packaged in such a manner that children under 5 years of age are not able to open them. Parents and guardians should keep medication lids closed tightly to protect young children. Never should medication be referred to as candy, or other attractive food. This only confuses the child and leads to improper ingestion of medicines.

Many cleaning agents used around the home can cause serious injury to a person. Such products include bleaching agents, wax remover, and toilet bowl cleansers. These common agents should be stored in places where children, particularly preschool children, cannot reach them. Elementary and middle-level schoolchildren should be instructed of the dangers of these substances.

For example, highly corrosive drain cleaners are found in most homes. These very effective cleansers are particularly dangerous if swallowed or splashed into the eyes. Liquid cleansers spilled onto the skin are difficult to remove and can cause tissue destruction.

Another source of potential harm comes from exposure to petroleum products, particularly gasoline. As with other poisonous substances, gasoline should be kept out of reach of small children, and children should understand the danger of causing a fire by playing with matches around petroleum products.

Many people are not aware of the potential poisonous nature of food extracts found in every kitchen. When taken undiluted, and straight from the bottle, extracts such as almond and vanilla can be toxic to a child.

Elementary and middle-level schoolchildren should not only be taught about the various potentially dangerous substances with which they come into contact, but they need to know what emergency care measures to take when they are exposed. Young children also benefit from instruction in how to wash the exposed area of the skin or in what to do when a poisonous agent has been ingested. Also, upper-elementary and middle-level schoolchildren need to be familiar with the community agencies to contact when an accidental poisoning has occurred.

Throughout the nation, a number of poison control centers have been established for the purpose of providing information on the ingredients, toxicity, expected signs and symptoms, and recommendations for treatment of poisons and medicines. These centers, which operate a 24-hour telephone service, are able to provide information about every poisonous substance—for example, the composition of the poison and measures to neutralize the toxic effect. Poison control centers should be contacted whenever there is a poisoning that one is unsure how to care for. Schoolchildren should be aware of telephone numbers that can be called to reach such help. Within every home, the telephone numbers of the local poison control center, the family physician, and hospital emergency room should be posted near the telephone along with other emergency numbers.

Every family should have syrup of Ipecac in the home. Syrup of Ipecac is useful for getting a person to vomit ingested toxic substances. Most medical personnel

It is important that poisonous products be kept out of reach of all young children.

recommend that syrup of Ipecac be taken only on the advice of a physician or an emergency center at a local hospital or following a call to the local poison control center. This is particularly important because some toxic substances should not be reintroduced into the upper digestive system. Ipecac can be purchased at most local pharmacies.

> Federal law (P. L. 87-319) authorizes the federal government to designate the third week in March as National Poison Prevention Week. During this week, interested agencies, such as schools, are encouraged to include initiatives that inform the public of the need to take active measures to prevent poisoning. Schools should include special programs during this week to educate parents, as well as students, about dangerous poisonous substances.

BICYCLING AND PEDESTRIAN SAFETY

Riding a bicycle or walking and running along, and into, roadways results in many injuries and a number of fatalities each year. Many factors can contribute to injury from both activities: for example, schoolchildren often walk along and/or cross streets in ways that contribute to unintentional injuries. Even though most elementary and middle-level schoolchildren have a bicycle, they are rarely instructed in how to operate it safely in traffic, and the majority do not wear helmets.

Bicycling

Bicycle use among elementary and middle-level schoolchildren is usually a recreational activity. Before being permitted to operate a bicycle, the child should be instructed in its safe care and operation.

For safe operation, the bicycle should be solidly built and have all parts functioning in a safe and effective manner. The bicycle frame should be solid and should be adjusted for individual comfort and safe operation. In ascertaining appropriate "fit," the cyclist should be able to straddle the frame with both feet flat on the ground. The seat should be adjusted to a height that will permit the rider's heel to rest on the pedal with the leg completely extended.

The mechanical functioning of the bicycle is important to protect against injury-causing situations. No bicycle should be used if the braking mechanism is faulty. The wheels and tires must be frequently checked to ensure that the tires are not worn, that they are properly inflated, and that the wheels are properly aligned.

The height and type of handlebars on a bicycle are important. They should be secure and level, with the seat adjusted for individual comfort. Many bicycles purchased for children have high-rise handlebars and often a long, banana-shaped seat with a backrest. It has been shown that some of these types of handlebars can cause more injuries than do conventional models.[25]

All bicycles should have reflectors in order to be seen more easily. If an individual is going to ride a bicycle at dusk or after dark, retro-reflective materials such as vests and sashes should be worn. The rider should also wear white or light-colored clothing that will help him or her to be seen.

All too often, the head is injured in a bicycle collision. Statistics indicate that in 96% of fatalities and nearly two-thirds of all hospital admissions involving bicycle accidents, injury to the head occurs.[26] Only about 18% of all bicyclists wear helmets. Unfortunately, very few elementary and middle-level schoolchildren wear a helmet when riding their bicycles around the neighborhood. Although wearing a helmet is not popular with schoolchildren, they should receive instruction about the importance of wearing helmets when riding a bicycle.

At present, fifteen states and more than fifty local jurisdictions have implemented some form of mandatory bicycle helmet legislation. Most of this legislation is directed toward young riders of elementary and middle-school age.

Parents and teachers should consider teaching preschool children the importance and value of wearing a helmet when bicycling. This should begin when small children are riding with their parents. To encourage the wearing of helmets, it has been recommended that bicycle manufacturers include them with the purchase of a new bicycle. Many believe that if helmets are made

Most children do not wear a helmet when riding a bicycle or roller blading. Serious head injury can be prevented by insisting that such helmets be worn at all times when participating in these activities.

available as part of the purchase, they are more likely to be used.

Children should also be instructed in proper riding procedures. A bicycle rider should never carry another person on the cycle because this makes the bike more difficult to control and may lead to falls and collisions. He or she should also ride the bicycle in a straight line, observe and obey all traffic signs, and use appropriate turn signals. Many people believe that a bicycle should be ridden on the left side of a street facing traffic. Children must be taught that this is inappropriate. A bicycle should be ridden on the right side of a street or road with the flow of traffic.

The school can include several activities in the instructional program to develop safer bicycle riding behaviors. A very popular activity is a bicycle rodeo. Here, the children are given experiences in handling their bicycles in a variety of situations. The students are expected to ride in a straight line for a given distance as well as maneuver the cycle around a set of cones and stop at a specific point. Not only is the rodeo concept fun, but it provides children the opportunity to develop their skills.

The creation of the National Bicycle Safety Network is a current national initiative designed to increase safe bicycle use. This coalition of more than a dozen organizations and agencies works to develop programs and to share information promoting bicycle safety. The organizations involved in this initiative include governmental agencies

ACTIVITIES

Bicycle Safety

S uggested Learning Activities Teaching Bicycle Safety include:

1. Bring in someone from the police department or from a local bicycle shop to show students what to look for in solid, safe bike construction. Note also the appropriate fit of the bike.

2. Display the following traffic signs and ask the class to explain or demonstrate what actions should be taken with each:
   a. Stop sign
   b. Yield sign
   c. Railroad crossing sign
   d. Traffic light

3. Have a bicycle safety poster contest. Assign students to draw a poster emphasizing some aspect of bicycle safety. Have the students explain the particular concept their poster depicts.

4. Have the students, working in groups, write a script that could be broadcast over radio concerning some bicycle safety concept. If possible, contact a local radio station and see if these scripts could be produced and presented as public information announcements. If this is not possible, broadcast them over the school announcement system in the principal's office.

5. Map safe bicycle routes from students' homes to school, to the library, to the homes of their friends, and to other locations within the community where the students are likely to be riding their bicycles.

6. Invite guests from local bicycle shops to teach children to maintain and care for their bicycles. Keep a journal of routine maintenance checks that parallel family car maintenance practices and protocol.

7. Dissect and discuss the components and importance of the parts of a bicycle helmet. Develop a class poster for display in the school about how to select a good-fitting and appropriate helmet.

8. Have the children create a banner supporting a helmet-wearing pledge. Use numbers and categories of names from the banner to review basic math concepts.

(such as the Federal Highway Administration, National Highway Traffic Safety Administration, and the Consumer Product Safety Commission), nonprofit, safety-related agencies (National Safety Council and the American Automobile Association), and medical groups (American Academy of Pediatrics and the Brain Injury Association).[27]

Pedestrian Safety

Many traffic fatalities and injuries involve persons who are not riding in a motor vehicle. They involve people walking along the road, children running out into the traffic, and persons entering the flow of traffic without regard to proper safety. Nearly 6,000 pedestrian fatalities occur each year, with nearly 65% occurring in urban settings.[28]

A pedestrian accident occurs either because the driver fails to see the pedestrian and is unable to avoid a collision or because the pedestrian fails to see the approaching vehicle. No one should ever enter a roadway unless there is a clear field of vision. When walking along a street or roadway, pedestrians should walk on a sidewalk; if there is no sidewalk, they should walk facing the oncoming traffic. Crossing streets at crosswalks helps to protect against injury-producing accidents. Wearing light-colored clothing or reflectorized garments helps visibility.

Pedestrians should watch for turning automobiles. In every state, it is lawful to turn right on a red light after coming to a complete stop, unless there is a posted sign indicating otherwise. Unfortunately, drivers usually look for oncoming motor vehicles but fail to note pedestrians crossing the street with the green light.

Elementary and middle-level schoolchildren are at risk for pedestrian accidents because of play activity that takes them into the pathway of moving vehicles. It is not

ACTIVITIES

Pedestrian Safety

Activities related to pedestrian safety:

1. Ask children of primary-school age to draw a map showing the route they take to come to school. Discuss the various street crossings and possible dangers along the way to school.

2. Have the students observe a busy street intersection where there are many pedestrians. Ask them to identify and record inappropriate actions taken by pedestrians. Discuss with the children why certain actions are dangerous and what other measures should have been taken.

3. With preschool children, design a street intersection on the floor of the classroom. Using teacher-made signs, have the children demonstrate actions they should take. Signs should include a stop sign, walk and wait lights, red and green lights, and a yield sign.

4. Have the children use their bicycles to review traffic patterns around their school and crosswalks and street markings for pedestrian use.

unusual for children to run into the street without looking when chasing a ball or playing a running game. Also, in many urban centers, the streets are used by young people as a place to play. Children need to be instructed from the earliest years about safety-conscious behaviors that can help to reduce the possibility of accidents.

Two specific situations often result in injuries to elementary schoolchildren: the backup accident and the vendor-related accident. Moving a motor vehicle in reverse creates a dangerous situation in that the driver may not see someone behind the car. Among preschool-age children, this type of situation occurs far too often in the home driveway. Children must be taught to keep away from behind vehicles, particularly when the car is occupied.

A vendor-related accident occurs when the pedestrian is hit going out into the street to make a purchase from a street vendor. This situation is a particular problem during the summer months when children, in their excitement to get to the ice cream truck, usually give no thought to oncoming traffic. Some communities require that vendor vehicles have warning devices such as flashing warning lights and/or ringing bells to provide some warning to oncoming motor vehicles.

CURRICULUM PROGRAMS

A number of curriculum packages are available to assist the elementary and middle-level schoolteacher in organizing instructional units about safety. Many of these packages have excellent material for the students' use as well as guides for the teacher. They often include visual material to assist in the learning process. A sampling of such material follows.

The American Red Cross has developed several curriculum programs that have value for elementary and middle-level school safety instruction. A course entitled *Bicycle Safety* is available for use in any of the elementary school grades. *Home Safety is* another program that is designed to help children become aware of the various dangers around the home.

The *First Aid for Children Today (F.A.C.T.)* program is for use in grades K through 3. This health promotion and injury program helps children understand how to manage their health and safety by including study about personal safety, health habits, injury prevention, and road safety. The program's material makes use of multicultural animal characters that will interest primary-grade children.

The *Basic Aid Training program* is for use in grades 3 to 5. This program's material covers topics such as safety, first-aid skills, and accident prevention. Bicycle safety, motor-vehicle safety, and water safety are a major part of this program. There is also instruction about the importance of avoiding substance abuse and building avoidance skills.

Also, a course has been designed by the American Red Cross to help young people be effective baby-sitters. Students are taught how to feed babies and play with and care for youngsters. The program emphasizes safety, and emergencies and illnesses that the baby-sitter is likely to encounter.

The American Automobile Association has developed an elementary school (K–6) alcohol education and traffic safety program. This curriculum includes learning material and lessons for use at each grade level. There are five lessons for each grade, with between 30 and 45 minutes allotted for each lesson. Teachers' guides for each grade, reproducible masters, filmstrips, game charts, as well as reproducible test booklets are available. This program, entitled *Starting Early,* is designed for elementary schoolchildren with the premise that they will be better prepared for alcohol-related situations if they learn how alcohol influences the body and the mind. Students explore attitudes about alcohol consumption. They practice planning and acting out, ahead of time and under guided adult supervision, ways to cope with or avoid alcohol-related situations that may be dangerous.[29]

The American Automobile Association has also developed a program, *Crossroads,* which informs children about the responsibilities of being on the school safety patrol. This material is designed to be used in school safety patrol training programs.

Another program that is available from the American Automobile Association is *See and Be Seen,* which teaches safe street-crossing techniques to children 5 to 7 years of age. *Thinking about School Bus Safety* provides information on proper and safe school bus behavior for children in grades 4 through 6. A bicycle safety program, *Bicycling Visual Skills,* explains the rules of the road as they apply to bicycle riding. This program is designed for use in grades 4 through 6.

The National Safety Belt Coalition [30] has developed *The Buckle Up Game.* This educational board game teaches young children the importance of wearing seat belts and of riding in the backseat.

Teachers should also consult local safety service agencies within their communities to obtain appropriate materials that relate to the specific needs of their local community.

A number of educational packages have been developed to assist classroom teachers in teaching fire safety. The National Fire Protection Association has a *Fire Safety Curriculum* for grades K through 6.[31] Other agencies that offer material on the topic of fire safety include the U.S. Consumer Product Safety Commission (Washington, D.C. 20207), the United States Forest Service, and the International Association of Fire Chiefs (1329 18th St. NW, Washington, D.C. 20036). Several of these programs are also found on the Internet.

THE SCHOOL BUS

Many of the children in the elementary and middle-level grades arrive at school on the school bus. It is estimated that over 22 million children ride to school each day in such vehicles. More than 400,000 school buses travel more than 4 billion miles each year.[32]

With this amount of travel, injury-producing situations are going to occur. Unfortunately, approximately 19,000 people were injured in school bus-related accidents, 11,000 of whom were students, in a recent year. In that same year, 128 persons were killed in accidents involving school buses.[33]

Any injury or fatality resulting from riding on a school bus is tragic. However, considering the numbers of children riding school buses daily, it is somewhat surprising that the statistics are not greater. Regardless, it is the responsibility of the schools to take measures to protect against injury-causing circumstances.

Without a doubt, the most important thing that the school can do is to include instruction about safety measures that need to be taken before, while, and after riding the school bus. Many fatalities and injuries occur while children are waiting for the bus to arrive and after they get off of the bus. Children must be encouraged to understand the importance of following certain rules while waiting for the bus to arrive. They should wait until the bus stops and the door opens before entering the roadway. After getting off of the bus, the child should look both ways before walking across the road or street, in spite of the fact that in every state it is the law that motor vehicles must stop whenever a school bus comes to a stop. When crossing in front of the bus, the student should make eye contact with the school bus driver in order to make sure that the driver knows where the child is and will not start the bus until the child is safely across the roadway.

Children must be clearly instructed in appropriate behavior while riding the school bus. All children riding a school bus must be provided with a seat. They should sit in the seat and never put an arm or their head out of a window while riding the bus. The classroom teacher, in cooperation with the school bus driver, should develop a set of instructions. The children must realize that their behavior while riding the bus is an important individual responsibility and involves more than just following a set of rules put down by the driver.

Most training and in-service instruction of school bus operators is focused on how to control and operate the bus. The maintenance and mechanics of bus operation are the primary emphasis. They receive little instruction or direction in how to manage children on the bus. As a result, there is need to include instruction in behavior management of the children.

Whether states should require school districts to have seat belts on school buses has been a controversial matter. Many suggest that it is inappropriate for states to mandate that automobile occupants wear a seat belt but not provide them on school buses.

In 1989, after conducting a lengthy study, the National Transportation Safety Board of the National Research Council reported that requiring seat belts on school buses is of minimal value. This report indicated that it would be of more value to raise the minimum height of seat backs. Noting that many injury-causing situations occur at loading zones, the National Research Council recommended increased efforts to provide safe loading zones. It also called for better selection and training of bus drivers and for more effective education of students who ride the buses.

Safe school bus transportation demands proper maintenance, selection and instruction of drivers, and continuing instruction of the riders in proper procedures, both while on the bus and after getting off of the bus.

Currently, two states, New Jersey and New York, along with several local jurisdictions, mandate seat belts in large school buses. Unfortunately, it is doubtful that universal, mandated seat-belt usage will become the norm on school buses for some time.

Several new safety features have been manufactured and installed in school buses in recent years. New strobe lights that flash as many as four times per second are now being used. These are easier to see from a distance and are very effective in fog and in minimal sunlight. Also,

new front-mounted crossing gates that jut out from the grill or bumper of the bus are being used. These gates cause children to walk around to where they can be better seen by oncoming vehicle drivers. Another device being used is the automatic braking shield, which provides protection for the child crossing in front of the bus. This braking system is activated if a child comes into contact with the safety shield on the front of the bus, keeping the bus from running over a child.

SUMMARY

Unintentional injuries are the leading cause of death and a major cause of disability among elementary and middle-level schoolchildren. In order to develop a positive safety consciousness and good behavioral patterns, safety instruction must be included in the curriculum. Although safety instruction is not considered a basic part of the educational system, school districts do include different approaches to such instruction.

Every year, several thousand children are killed or seriously injured in motor-vehicle collisions. Research and legislation have focused on measures to reduce the carnage on America's streets and highways from such collisions. A major cause of motor-vehicle collisions is alcohol use. Prevention is important when considering ways to reduce the incidence of motor-vehicle injuries and fatalities. Use of seat belts, passive restraints such as air bags, and child restraints are examples of such measures that can help to reduce death and injury resulting from motor-vehicle collisions.

Other major causes of unintentional injury, disability, and fatality are drowning, falls, and fires. The factors associated with each of these and appropriate preventive measures need to be better understood if improvements are to occur.

Injury also occurs from other activities in which the elementary and middle-level schoolchild participates. Bicycle riding, an important activity to this age group, demands effective educational initiatives. The same is true of pedestrian safety.

There are many curriculum packages and programs available to assist the elementary and middle-level schoolteacher in safety instruction. These usually include material for student use as well as teachers' guides and supplemental learning materials. Increasingly useful teaching materials can be accessed on the Internet on Web pages of safety-related agencies and organizations.

DISCUSSION QUESTIONS

1. How extensive is the problem of unintentional injury among elementary schoolchildren?

2. Discuss the meaning of the term *accident* as it has been used in safety prevention.

3. Discuss the importance of attitude formation and behavior relating to safety practices among young children.

4. Explain why presentation of material on alcohol use relating to motor-vehicle driving is needed in an elementary and middle-level school curriculum.

5. What are the principal program emphases of Mothers Against Drunk Driving?

6. Discuss the various issues involved in mandating the use of seat belts in motor vehicles.

7. Should passive seat belts be required in all automobiles? Defend your answer.

8. Why should children of elementary school age be required to ride in the rear seat of a motor vehicle?

9. Why is drowning a particularly emotional experience for the parents of a child?

10. What preventive measures can be taught to elementary and middle-level schoolchildren to protect against drowning?

11. What rescue skills should be included in a water safety instruction class?

12. What are the three necessary elements that result in a fire?

13. How can a fire be extinguished?

14. Identify some of the measures that can be taken to protect a child from injury by fire, scalds, and burns.

15. To what does the phrase, *Stop, Drop, and Roll* refer?

16. What are the differences among Class A, B, C, and D fires?

17. Why is electricity a danger to humans?

18. Would you include specific instruction about prevention of falls to elementary schoolchildren? Explain the reasons for your response.

19. Should children be required to pass an operator's test to ride a bicycle, drive a boat, or operate an all-terrain vehicle? What is the basis for your answer to each?

20. Discuss measures that might be taken to encourage children to wear helmets while riding a bicycle.

21. What measures can be taken to provide protection from pedestrian injuries?

22. How might you use prepackaged safety curriculum materials in teaching?

23. How can Sparky be useful in teaching young children about fire?

24. Explain the responsibility of the elementary classroom teacher in school bus safety.

25. Should children be required to wear a seat belt when riding a school bus? Defend the reasons for your response.

ENDNOTES

1. National Safety Council, (1999) *Injury Facts. 1999 Edition* (Itasca, IL: National Safety Council), 8.

2. Committee on Trauma Research, National Research Council, *Injury in America* (Washington, DC: National Academy Press, 1985).

3. "First Auto Crash Victim Died 72 Years Ago Today," *Journal of American Medical Association* 217, no. 11 (13 September 1971): 1461.

4. National Safety Council, (1999) *Injury Facts, 1999 Edition*, 2.

5. Ibid.,4–5.

6. Ibid., 86.

7. Ralph W. Hingson et al., "Effects of Legislative Reform to Reduce Drunken Driving and Alcohol-Related Traffic Fatalities," *Public Health Reports* 103, no. 6 (November/December 1988): 660.

8. Information about Mothers Against Drunk driving can be found on the Internet at **www.madd.org**.

9 National Safety Council, (1999) *Injury Facts, 1999 Edition,* 88.

10. Information provided by the National Safety Council is on the Internet at **www.nsc.org.**

11. Department of Health and Human Services, *Healthy People: National Health Promotion and Disease Prevention Objectives* (Washington, DC: U.S. Government Printing Office, 1991), 282–283.

12. Ibid.

13. Department of Health and Human Services, *Healthy People 2000,* 283.

14. Robert D. Ross, "Evaluation of a Community-Wide Incentive Program to Promote Safety Restraint Use," *American Journal of Public Health* 79, no. 3 (March 1989): 304–309.

15. National Safety Council, (1999) *Injury Facts, 1999 Edition,* 8.

16. Ibid.

17. Department of Health and Human Services, *Healthy People 2000,* 277.

18. National Safety Council, (1999) *Injury Facts, 1999 Edition,* 9.

19. Department of Health and Human Services, *Healthy People 2000,* 135.

20. National Fire Protection Association, **www.nfpa.org**.

21. Ibid.

22. Centers for Disease Control and Prevention, **www.cdc.gov/ncipc**.

23. National Safety Council, (1999) *Injury Facts, 1999 Edition,* 8.

24. Ibid., 8–9.

25. A.W. Craft, D.A. Shaw, and N.E.F. Cartlidge, "Bicycle Injuries in Children," *British Medical Journal* 4, no. 5885 (October 1973): 146.

26. Richard C. Wasserman et al., "Bicyclists, Helmets and Head Injuries: A Rider-Based Study of Helmet Use and Effectiveness," *American Journal of Public Health* 78, no. 9 (September 1988): 220–221.

27. Information about the National Bicycle Safety Network is available on the Internet at **www.cdc.gov/ncipc**.

28. National Safety Council, (1999) *Injury Facts, 1999 Edition,* 80.

29. American Automobile Association, Falls Church, VA 22047.

30. National Seatbelt Coalition.

31. National Fire Protection Association, 1 Batterymarch Park, Quincy, MA 02269, telephone 617-770-3000.

32. National Safety Council, (1999) *Injury Facts, 1999 Edition,* 94.

33. Ibid., 94.

SUGGESTED READINGS

Albanese, Craig T. and others. "Single Rope Tree Swing Injuries Among Children." *Pediatrics* 99, no. 4 (April 1997): 548–550.

Dannenberg, Andrew L., and Jon S. Vernick. "A Proposal for the Mandatory Inclusion of Helmets with New Children's Bicycles." *American Journal of Public Health* 83, no. 5 (May 1993): 644–646.

Dannenberg, Andrew L. et al. "Bicycle Helmet Laws and Educational Campaigns: An Evaluation of Strategies to Increase Children's Helmet Use." *American Journal of Public Health* 83, no. 5 (May 1993): 667–674.

DiScala, Carla and others. "Causes and Outcomes of Pediatric Injuries Occurring at School." *Journal of School Health* 67, no. 9 (November 1997): 384–389.

Hollander, Sheila K. "Making Young Children Aware of Sexual Abuse." *Elementary School Guidance and Counseling* 26 (April 1992): 305–317.

Hoskin, Alan F. et al. "The Effect of Raising the Legal Minimum Drinking Age on Fatal Crashes in 10 States." *Journal of Safety Research* 17, no. 3 (Fall 1986): 117–128.

Liller, Karen D. "Teaching Preschoolers Injury Prevention." *Journal of Health Education* 28, no. 1 (January–February 1997): 50–51.

Liller, Karen D. et al. "The MORE HEALTH Bicycle Safety Project." *Journal of School Health* 65, no. 3 (March 1995): 87–90.

National Center for Injury Prevention and Control. "Injury Control Recommendations for Bicycle Helmets." *Journal of School Health* 65, no. 4 (April 1995): 133–139.

Nowesnick, Mary. "Shattered Lives." *The American School Board Journal* 180, no. 10 (October 1993): 14–19.

Pless, I. Barry. "Unintentional Childhood Injury—Where the Buck Should Stop." *American Journal of Public Health* 84, no. 4 (April 1994): 537–539.

Rubel, Robert J., and Peter D. Blauvelt. "How Safe Are Your Schools?" *The American School Board Journal* 181, no. 1 (January 1994): 28–31.

Smith, Gary A. "Injuries to Children in the United States Related to Trampolines, 1990–1995: A National Epidemic," *Pediatrics* 101, no. 3 (March 1998): 406–412.

Stober, Michelle. *Injuries in the School Environment, Second Edition,* Newton, MA: Children's Safety Network, Education Development Center, 1997.

Stover, Del. "These New Devices Aim to Enhance School Bus Safety." *The American School Board Journal* 175, no. 11 (November 1988): 38–39.

Vail, Kathleen. "Unruly Cargo," *The American School Board Journal* 184, no. 11 (November 1997): 34–36.

Waller, Anna E., Susan P. Baker, and Andrew Szocka. "Childhood Injury Deaths: National Analysis and Geographic Variations." *American Journal of Public Health* 79, no. 3 (March 1989): 310–315.

CHILDREN'S LITERATURE WITH A SAFETY EDUCATION THEME

(The following are some of the many books available to teachers related to the topic of safety. This is not a complete list, nor are these the only good books. They are simply examples of children's books that can be used with material presented in this chapter.)

Grades K–3

Baker, Amy C. *It's OK to Say No.* Frederick Bennett Green, Illus. Grosset & Dunlap, 1986.

Beck, M. *The Rescue of Brown Bear and White Bear,* 1990.

Berenstain, Stan and Jan, *Berenstain Bears Learn About Strangers.*

Borden, Louise. *Albie the Lifeguard*, Scholastic, 1993.

Brown, Marc. *Dinosaurs Beware: A Safety Guide.* Little, Brown, 1982.

Carlstrom, Nancy White. *Better Not Get Wet, Jesse Bear.* Macmillan, 1988.

Carrick, Carol. *Left Behind,* Houghton Mifflin, 1988.

Davison, Martine. *Maggie and the Emergency Room.* Random House, 1992.

Franklin, Kristine. *Iguana Beach.* Crown, 1997. (Multicultural)

Gobbell, Phyllis, and Jim Laster. *Safe Sally Seat Belt and The Magic Click.* Illus. Stephanie McFetridge Briss. Children's Press, 1986.

Henkes, Kevin. *Sheila Rae, The Brave.* William Morrow, 1982.

Rathman, Peggy. *Officer Buckle and Gloria.* Putman and Grosset, 1995. (Caldecott Medal)

Wachter, Oralee. *Close to Home.* Jane Aaron, Illus. Scholastic, 1986.

Grades 4–8

Cleary, Beverly. *Lucky Chuck.* Morrow, 1984.

Greenberg, Keith Elliot. *Out of the Gang.* Illustrated with photographs. Lerner, 1992.

Park, Barbara. *Mick Harte Was Here.* Alfred Knopf, 1995.

O'Dell, Scott. *Island of the Blue Dolphins.* Houghton Mifflin, 1960.

Grades 6–8

Hinton, S. E. *The Outsiders.* Viking, 1967.

O'Dell, Scott, *Island of the Blue Dolphins.* Houghton Mifflin, 1960.

Paulsen, Gary. *Hatchet.* Macmillan, 1986.

INTENTIONAL INJURY PREVENTION

Violence in Families, Schools, and Communities

O U T L I N E

INTRODUCTION

Intentional injuries including abuse, homicide, suicide, and other forms of violence have been identified as major contributors to premature death, disability, and injury of Americans. The United States ranks first among the industrialized nations of the world in rates of violent death. Approximately 2.2 million Americans are victims of violent injuries each year. The death rate due to intentional and unintentional misuse of firearms in the United States exceeds the combined total of such deaths among our next closest seventeen

CONSIDER THIS

Incidence and Costs of Violence to Children and Youth (Birth–Age 14)

AGES 0–4   It is estimated that 2.6 per 100 children in this age group are raped, sexually assaulted, physically abused, or neglected each year. The per capita costs of such crimes are estimated to be $1,120 for children birth to age 4. Rape, sexual abuse, assault, and murder account for 25% of the total injury costs of this age group.

AGES 5–9   It is estimated that 3.4 per 100 children in this age group are raped, sexually assaulted, physically abused, or neglected each year. The per capita costs of such crimes are estimated to be $1,780 for children ages 5–9. Rape, sexual abuse, assault, and murder account for 36% of the total injury costs of this age group.

AGES 10–14   It is estimated that 9.8 per 100 children in this age group are raped, sexually assaulted, physically abused, or neglected each year. The per capita costs of such crimes are estimated to be $3,340 for children ages 10–14. Rape, sexual abuse, assault, and murder account for 40% of the total injury costs of this age group.

Source: National Public Services Research Institute. "Child and Adolescent Violence: Incidence and Costs." *Childhood Injury: Costs and Prevention Facts* (July 1997).

counterpart nations.[1] In addition, approximately 1 million American children are reported victims of child abuse each year.[2]

The National Academy of Sciences has defined violence to include those behaviors that intentionally threaten, attempt, or inflict physical harm on others.[3] In addition to the physical consequences of violence, the fear associated with such acts can infringe on our sense of personal freedom and compromise our basic shared need to feel safe.[4] Because this epidemic affects all elements of our society, intentional injury risk reduction has become an American public health priority.

As part of this national agenda, particular emphasis has been placed on confronting the incidence and consequences of intentional injury risk among children and youth. Research has confirmed that even the youngest Americans are not immune from being victimized by child abuse and neglect, murder, and other nonfatal assaults. In addition to the human costs of abuse and victimization of children, there is also an enormous financial burden attributable to acts of violence in our culture. Medical care, mental health treatment, and public programs and policy initiatives are among the often overlooked costs associated with intentional injury risks to children and youth. The Consider This box above summarizes incidence and cost data for acts of violence to children and youth from birth through age 14.[5]

The growing body of literature confirming that the risk of intentional injuries also threatens academic success is of particular interest to educators. Students exposed to violence in their homes, communities, or schools tend to lack interest in academic activities and manifest persistent behavior problems. Typically, these young people earn

While many people think of violence only as a criminal justice matter, educators and parents are reminded that the risk of intentional injuries also threatens school success.

lower grades and have higher truancy and drop-out rates than their nonexposed counterparts.[6] Additional research has documented that children who witness chronic violence tend to exhibit poor concentration and short atten-

---

CONSIDER THIS

Risk Factors Associated with Child and Adolescent Violence

Abuse and Neglect	Almost 20% of violent crime appears to be related to physical abuse and neglect during the childhood of the perpetrator. When young victims of abuse go untreated, violence tends to beget violence.
Witnessing Violent Crime	Estimates suggest that over 50% of young people have witnessed a robbery, beating, stabbing, shooting, or murder. The psychological aftermath of seeing such an incident is rarely treated.
Guns	Murders are over twice as likely to occur in homes with guns than in homes without these weapons.
Alcohol and Other Drugs	Over one-fourth of violent crime is associated with alcohol or other drug use.
Media Influence	Fictional accounts of violence suggest that the body can withstand unrealistic force. Children may be desensitized to such acts, and those who imitate behaviors seen on TV or in movies can underestimate their impact.
Other Complex Factors	Social justice and economic issues, community deterioration, and incarceration have been identified as risk factors for violence.

Source: National Public Services Research Institute. "Child and Adolescent Violence: Risk Factors and Prevention." *Childhood Injury: Costs and Prevention Facts* (July 1997).

---

tion spans.[7] Finally, abuse of children and youth by adult caregivers can cause children to be cautious and withdrawn. Abused children often manifest delayed language development, express feelings of powerlessness, and have a general inability to set goals or plan for a meaningful future.[8]

In addition to the consequences associated with victimization, rates of violent and aggressive acting-out behaviors among youth surge to their highest levels during the adolescent years.[9] In this context, *Healthy People 2000,* the ongoing national agenda to improve the health status of all Americans, highlighted the following programming and policy recommendations targeted at reducing youth violence:

- Reduce homicides,
- Reduce weapon-related deaths,
- Reduce injuries associated with assaults,
- Reduce physical fighting among youth,
- Reduce weapon-carrying by youth,
- Reduce inappropriate storage of weapons,
- Improve school-based programming focused on conflict resolution skill development, and
- Increase violence-prevention programs.[10]

Research has confirmed that several risk factors are associated with child and adolescent violence. Some experts believe that violent images are so common in the media that children have become desensitized to their intense and devastating effects. Others suggest that violence can be linked to more complex social and economic changes that affect families and communities. These scholars attribute youth violence to the actions of overworked and financially strapped parents who vent their frustrations at home. When frequent yelling or other aggressive or abusive acts become common in the home environment, children can receive the message that such behavior is acceptable or even necessary. Also, it has been suggested that when children have not developed skills to exercise control over their impulses and behaviors, they may grow accustomed to using violent acts as a way to resolve conflicts or gain desired possessions. Under such circumstances, students who have not learned that nonviolence is a better, or even possible, option, view violence as an expedient and effective way to gain respect when confronted with frustrating circumstances.[11] In 1997, the Children's Safety Network of the National Public Services Research Institute described a number of risk factors associated with child and adolescent violence. This information is summarized in the Consider This box above.[12]

While educators and community residents may recognize that children are exposed to a constellation of risk factors for intentional injury, it is always horrifying when violence to students or school personnel is manifested on school property. Many can recall recent examples of violence at the school site in which student perpetrators used guns to kill classmates and educators.

TABLE 8.1	Advocacy and Violence Risk-Reduction Strategies for Concerned Adults

- Get to know the interests, hopes, and fears of the youth with whom you have contact.
- Be observant, listen well, and offer to help if you suspect a concern.
- Make official reports or referrals of suspected child abuse to the local children's service, police, or protective service agencies.
- Demonstrate consistent, healthy, and respectful communication, problem solving, and conflict resolution.
- Reinforce contextual examples of healthy and respectful communication, problem solving, and conflict resolution.
- Establish and consistently reinforce rules of nonviolence.
- Integrate use of "I'm sorry" into personal communication.
- Learn to recognize, and do not permit, wearing of local gang colors or symbols.
- Encourage students to seek counsel from a trusted adult or school authority about dangerous activities they are aware of.
- Collaborate, communicate, and volunteer with other adults to reduce the risk of intentional injuries to local youth.
- Participate in local, state, or national violence risk-reduction and youth advocacy activities.

Source: Genesee County Community Mental Health Protection and Information Services. *Parent Talk: Protecting Students From Violence.* Flint, MI: Genesee County Community Mental Health Protection and Information Services.

In the first effort to present an accurate and comprehensive picture of the nature and scope of crime and violence on school property, the U.S. Departments of Education and Justice issued the *First Annual Report of School Safety.* This 1998 publication confirmed that although the number of students carrying guns declined and the victimization rate of violent crime has stabilized, there is a growing gang presence on school campuses. In addition, more of today's students than their counterparts of the past are fearful while they are at school.[13] Specific findings contained in this report confirm the following information about the risks for intentional injury on school property:

- In general, schools are very safe places.
- Despite the concerns of many, schools are not especially dangerous places in most communities. Most crimes at the school site involve theft and are not of a serious, violent nature (physical attacks, fights with a weapon, rape, robbery, murder, or suicide).
- Homicides are extremely rare events on school property.
- The concerns that teachers have about their own safety are not without foundation.
- Today's students are not significantly more likely to be victimized than were their counterparts in previous years.
- It has been confirmed that since 1993, fewer students are bringing weapons to school. In addition, there are formal consequences for carrying weapons on school property.
- The presence of gangs in schools makes students and teachers more vulnerable to the risks of intentional injuries.
- A majority of American schools have implemented some type of campus-security measures (zero-tolerance policies for guns, alcohol, and other drugs; controlled access to buildings and grounds; or required sign-in or escort policies for all guests).[14]

In the *First Annual Report on School Safety,* U.S. Secretary of Education Richard W. Riley urged parents, taxpayers, and school leaders to find some satisfaction in the proof that schools are among the safest places for school-age children and youth. In addition, this research confirmed that tough measures to keep guns and other weapons out of schools seem to be paying off. However, while asserting that even one incident of crime at the school site is too many, Secretary Riley urged parents, education professionals, community leaders, and public health advocates to adopt and implement comprehensive unintentional injury risk-reduction strategies to meet local needs.[15] In this context, concerned individuals are urged to examine table 8.1, which suggests advocacy and violence risk-reduction strategies for all concerned adults.[16]

RECOMMENDATIONS FOR TEACHERS: PRACTICE AND CONTENT

There is a great deal of variability in the kinds of intentional injury risks to which students can be exposed. Such behaviors range on a continuum from bullying and verbal abuse, through physical fighting, to rape and homicide. While it is true that such incidents are relatively infrequent at the school site, weapon possession, gang activity, and serious acts of violence have captured the attention of the national media and many concerned citizens. As a result, education professionals in many communities have been called upon to take a leadership role in implementing effective approaches to violence prevention. Interestingly, however, it is unfortunate that the amount of federal funding allocated to support prevention activities represents only a small fraction of the amount spent for law enforcement activities and prisons. In addition, many school and community leaders have failed to take advantage of the full range of school-based violence prevention strategies that research has documented to be effective.[17]

Intentional Injury Prevention Strategies with Low Potential for Effectiveness

Although conducted with the best of intentions to prevent intentional injuries, many schools and communities participate in activities that are supported by very little empirical evidence. In addition to this lack of demonstrated effectiveness, research has confirmed that some of these practices could actually serve to *increase* the potential for aggression or violent acting-out behaviors among student groups.[18] Following is a summary of common school-based activities that have little documented potential for violence risk-reduction among children and youth:

1. *Using scare-tactic approaches based on pictures or videos depicting violent scenes or consequences.* There is a large body of research that confirms that people who watch violence in the media are more likely than their counterparts to behave violently.

2. *Adding a violence prevention agenda to a school district that is overwhelmed with other activities.* It is important for schools to have an organizational structure and climate that supports violence prevention. Too often, school administrators try to add violence prevention programming to a school/community that has not established intentional risk reduction as a priority. Although common, this practice can increase the burden on teachers, increase stress, and ultimately backfire for students, parents, and education professionals.

3. *Segregating aggressive or antisocial students into separate groups.* Research has clarified that integrating delinquent youth into a positive, nondelinquent peer group can have a positive effect. Importantly, there is compelling evidence that efforts to separate or create exclusive groups comprised of aggressive young people does not contribute to a reduction in problem behaviors. In fact, such a practice may actually contribute to an increase in criminal behaviors.

4. *Implementing brief instructional programs that are not reinforced by school climate variables.* Even instructional programs of sufficient duration to be educationally sound cannot sustain outcomes in a climate that is not supportive. More comprehensive approaches to prevention and intervention have proven to result in better outcomes.

5. *Focusing instructional programming exclusively on self-esteem enhancement.* Narrowly focused self-esteem programs have been determined to be largely ineffective. It is important to note that, many gang-affiliated youths have a very highly developed sense of self-esteem. Those programs in which self-esteem enhancement is contextual to a broader agenda that promotes personal and social competency are more likely to produce desired outcomes.

6. *Focusing instructional programs only on knowledge acquisition.* Intentional injury programs focused on disseminating information, like those that have been evaluated in other health risk content areas, do not succeed. Such programs do not enable students to practice important skills to avoid and manage conflicts.[19]

Characteristics of Programs that Show Promise for Intentional Injury Prevention

In contrast, an extensive review of school-based violence prevention programs conducted by the U.S. General Accounting Office has revealed common characteristics that are associated with the most promising interventions.[20] Educators, community leaders, and concerned parents are encouraged to review *School Safety: Promising Initiatives for Addressing School Violence*, a 1995 publication that identified the following foundational elements of promising intentional injury risk-reduction programs:

1. *Comprehensive approach:* Research has suggested that the most successful programs are undergirded by the recognition that youth violence evolves from a complex set of variables. Like the Coordinated School Health Program (see chapter 1), promising interventions tend to address multiple problem areas and link a variety of services both in the school and community. Figure 8.1 provides specific programming suggestions for such a multidisciplinary approach.[21]

2. *Early start and long-term commitment:* Learning strategies and prevention activities are organized in an instructional scope and sequence designed to help young students learn accurate information, examine attitudes, and practice important skills. This program of studies is reinforced by sustained and effective programming for older students.

3. *Strong leadership and disciplinary policies:* To ensure program quality, principals and other school leaders collaborate with others to sustain funding and hire qualified staff. In addition, student disciplinary policies are reviewed and updated regularly, are made clear to all stakeholders, and are applied in a consistent manner.

4. *Staff development:* This document confirmed that an ongoing program of staff development helps to prepare administrators, teachers, and staff to manage disruptive students, mediate conflicts, and integrate prevention activities into daily routines.

5. *Parental involvement:* In more successful programs, schools work to increase parent involvement by offering parent education activities, making home visits, and engaging parents as tutors or volunteers.

6. *Culturally sensitive and developmentally appropriate materials and activities:* The most

Education and Training
- Conflict resolution
- Peer mediation
- Life skills/self-esteem/leadership
- Handgun/gang prevention
- Mentoring
- Peer, parent, and community education
- Administrator, teacher, clinic, and other school staff training

Environment Strategies
- Overall school climate
- Teacher-student respect & communication
- Dress codes
- Landscaping
- Metal detectors
- Locker searches
- Identification cards
- Lighting policies
- Police security

Health Services
- Diagnosis
- Treatment
- Counseling
- Peer support services
- Referral
- Follow-up

Figure 8.1

A comprehensive approach to violence prevention in schools.

effective program materials and activities are developed to be compatible with students' cultural values, language, and experiences with leadership and role models. In addition, all school/community intentional injury risk-reduction activities and materials must be developmentally appropriate for all grades of participant students.[22]

In this context, table 8.2 summarizes a list of suggestions to better prepare school and community advocates to manage a range of risks for youth violence. These recommendations embrace a comprehensive approach to preventing and intervening in general types of youth violence. In addition, cues are provided for educators to address more specific types of intentional injury risk, including dating violence, sexual assault, and sexual harassment.[23]

Recommendations for Teachers: Suggestions for Developmentally Appropriate Instructional Practice

Regardless of the implementation of a well-planned and collaborative approach to intentional injury risk reduction, many local school districts have established internal policies requiring that related content be covered as part of the instructional course of study. In 1994, the School Health Policies and Programs Study, a survey of school district policies and practices, revealed important information about the extent to which conflict resolution and violence and suicide prevention were being taught in American middle/junior and senior high schools.[24] This national study confirmed that the identified percentages of teachers were involved in organizing instructional activities focused on the following topics:

How to handle stress in healthy ways	72%
How to settle conflicts without physical fighting	65%
What to do if someone is thinking about suicide	52%
Practicing skills for nonviolent conflict resolution	39%
Practicing skills for stress management	39%.[25]

Unfortunately, such instructional approaches may not be delivered in ways that are developmentally appropriate nor as part of an educationally sound instructional scope and sequence. In addition, many classroom professionals resent having to spend valuable instructional time on

TABLE 8.2	**What Schools Can Do:**

About Youth Violence

1. Collaborate with community violence prevention coalitions that support values of nonviolence and teach nonviolent alternatives to resolving conflicts.
2. Provide school-wide training in violence prevention and conflict resolution.
3. Implement comprehensive, age-appropriate curricula focused on enriching student self-esteem and violence prevention (racism, sexism, and homophobia).
4. Create peer leadership and conflict resolution/mediation programs for older students.
5. Develop a violence prevention plan that integrates staff, parent, and student input.
6. Provide counseling and support services for students at risk for being victims, witnesses, or perpetrators of violence.

About Dating Violence

1. Provide staff development for school personnel about the warning signs and management of the range of behaviors associated with dating violence (emotional, verbal, physical, and sexual violence).
2. Identify local resources and referral networks for victims, survivors, and abusers.
3. Develop formal policies to protect the confidentiality of students or staff who disclose suspicion of such abuse. Implement policies to guide decision making about informing parents. Formalize record-keeping protocol about in-school incidents, disclosures, or injuries in the event of legal action.
4. Collaborate with local agencies to integrate prevention activities into comprehensive health education curricula for middle and high school students.
5. Train peer advocates to participate in support programming for at-risk classmates.
6. Collaborate with local agencies to provide on-site support groups for victims.
7. Inform parents, students, and staff about the warning signs and community resources for abused or abusive youth.
   (Note: Mediation is not recommended as an intervention for dating violence.)

About Sexual Assault

1. Provide staff development programming focused on sexual assault issues for all school nurses, health educators, counselors, coaches, and administrators.
2. Formalize school policy to manage sexual assault and harassment, including protocol for reporting, disclosing, referring, and maintaining confidentiality.
3. Develop networks with local rape crisis and battered persons programs.
4. Integrate developmentally appropriate sexual assault content matters into the comprehensive health education course of study.
5. Increase student access to local rape crisis services.
6. Maintain up-to-date information about counseling services for adults, adolescents, and children. Share this information with employee assistance programmers and leadership of teachers' unions.

About Sexual Harassment

1. Take all reports of harassment very seriously.
2. Provide staff development and establish policies and grievance procedures to stop harassment.
3. Develop consistent recommendations for students confronted with threats or experiences of sexual harassment.
4. Provide counseling and support groups for victims and perpetrators as a way to promote a healthier school climate.
5. Provide instruction and counseling activities that help support children in clarifying and expressing what feels safe and what does not.

Source: Massachusetts Department of Public Health. *The Comprehensive School Health Manual.* Boston, MA: Massachusetts Department of Public Health Bureau of Family and Community Health, 1995.

discipline and other violence risk-reduction strategies. In this context, teachers often develop psychological defenses against the need to confront the potential for violence in their classrooms. Following are some common defense mechanisms used by teachers and community residents that actually can enable violence to continue:

Denial—We don't have a problem with violence in our community, but that other school district certainly does.

Minimization—Name-calling, pushing, and shoving are just normal behaviors for kids.

Rationalization—It is important for all kids to learn to stand up for themselves.

Justification—Our classes are just too big to do something about violence.

Blame—Violence is the result of single-parent families and mothers who work outside of their homes.

Avoidance—My job is to teach; managing violence is an administrative responsibility.[26]

In response to the complexity and resistance to such instructional challenges, the National Injury Prevention Task Force of the American School Health Association (ASHA) has provided recommendations to support the efforts of local curriculum directors and classroom teachers. To be an effective component of an interdisciplinary approach to violence prevention, classroom instruction should:

- Be developmentally appropriate,
- Include accurate prevention messages,
- Be free of bias with regard to sex, race, age, and sexual orientation,
- Include learning strategies that actively engage students,
- Require students to practice higher-order thinking skills (critical thinking and problem solving),
- Increase students' abilities to:
  - Build their developmentally appropriate knowledge base about violence prevention,
  - Access violence prevention information and resources,
  - Practice safe, nonviolent behaviors,
  - Analyze the influence of culture, media, and technology on violence and its prevention,
  - Use communication, goal-setting, and decision-making skills to promote nonviolent behaviors, and
  - Serve as advocates for personal, family, and community nonviolence.[27]

In the context of these general cues to frame curriculum and classroom instruction, the following specific recommendations are offered to enhance developmentally appropriate classroom practice that focuses on intentional injury risk reduction for elementary and middle-level learners:

Early Elementary (K–2)
- Recognize all kinds of feelings.
- Realize that anger is a normal and healthy emotion.
- Acknowledge how we feel when we are angry.
- Recognize that there are many ways to "calm down" when we are angry.
- Accept differences in others.
- Celebrate cultural and racial uniqueness.
- Practice expressions of empathy.
- Practice problem solving skills.
- Practice skills to manage bullies.[28]

Upper Elementary (3–5)
- Evaluate reality vs. myth in media depictions.
- Practice nonviolent conflict resolution skills.
- Practice critical thinking skills.
- Celebrate cultural and racial uniqueness.
- Practice skills to reduce tobacco, alcohol, other drug, and gang-related risks.[29]

Middle/Junior High School (6–8)
- Celebrate cultural and racial uniqueness.
- Refine expressions of empathy.
- Refine nonviolent conflict resolution skills.
- Evaluate situations for potential danger.
- Evaluate problem-solving options.
- Evaluate differences in the socialization of males and females.
- Evaluate media depictions of violence.
- Practice basic peer mediation skills.[30]

IMPORTANT CONTENT: CHILD ABUSE RECOGNITION AND REFERRAL SKILLS FOR EDUCATION PROFESSIONALS

Introduction

Child abuse can take several different forms: physical abuse, neglect, emotional abuse, and sexual abuse. Definitions and legal statutes concerning each of these types of abuse vary from one state to another. Generally, it has been revealed that physical abuse occurs more commonly among younger students, including preschool children and those of early-elementary school age. A number of indications of physical abuse can be noted by the classroom teacher. Bruises, burns, skeletal and head injuries, and unexplained wounds and lacerations are the most common indications.

Importantly however, not all cases of child abuse involve physical manifestations. Child neglect, a more difficult condition to identify, is more commonly found among elementary and adolescent ages than among preschool-age children. Neglect may involve social isolation, instigation of antisocial behaviors, or failure to provide for the child's basic needs including food, medical care, proper hygiene, and even abandonment. In some cases, neglect takes the form of withholding necessities when parents or other caregivers attempt to punish or correct the child.

When children are continually degraded, emotional abuse occurs. The child who never is able to perform to the satisfaction of parents or caregivers will often experience emotional problems. Family social patterns often are related to emotional abuse, which is common among single-parent families, or in cases in which other forms of instability are manifested in the home.

Increased reporting of sexual abuse has occurred throughout the nation. One in every three or four girls, and one in every six to ten boys is sexually abused by age 18.[31] The average age for onset of sexual abuse is 6 to 8 years old, and the average length of abuse is about 4 or 5 years.[32] The majority of sexual abuse is committed by a family member or a family friend. Only 20% of perpetrators of sexual abuse are strangers to the child.[33]

Sexual abuse involves an adult or older person who uses a minor child for sexual gratification. Although

(continued after Activities on page 146)

ACTIVITIES

Intentional Injury Risk Reduction Curriculum

Keeping the developmentally appropriate themes in mind, the following curriculum activities are suggested for students in elementary and middle-level grades:

Grades K–2

- *Feelings Faces:* Use language that is associated with feelings to evoke student facial expressions. Once students have responded to a range of facial associations to "feeling words," ask them to draw four "feelings faces" in quadrants of a piece of construction paper. Provide verbal cues to trigger their drawings.

- *Feelings in Music:* Play musical selections to which students can make associations of feelings. Direct students to respond to the music with just their faces, then with their bodies, and finally with the words for the feelings evoked. Integrate "feelings words" into spelling lessons.

- *When I Feel Angry I:* Ask students to brainstorm their sources of anger at home, on the playground, during community activities, and at school. On a pre-drawn outline of a child, have them indicate places in their bodies in which they have experienced physical responses to that anger. Ask students to then write responses to teacher-developed, unfinished sentences, including: When I get angry, I feel . . . , The best way for me to behave when I get angry is to . . . , A way that would not be best for me to act when I get angry would be to . . . , etc.

- *Difference Detectives:* Have students in the class construct a badge indicating that they are a "Difference Detective." The game begins when students return to their room from recess, put on their badges, and find the difference that their teacher made in the room during their absence. The regular instructional activities continue until a student detects the difference and verbally shares it with the class. The game can be modified to enable students to "detect" the differences between adults and children, boys and girls, nondisabled and disabled individuals, etc. The key to the game is to detect and discuss differences, not the superiority of one group or situation over another.

- *Managing a Confrontation with Bully Bob:* In a math correlation activity, ask students to add successive "bully" characteristics to "Bully Bob," a fictional character depicted by a drawing, puppet, or doll. A characteristic can be subtracted, but only as pairs of students contribute a way to safely manage a confrontation with "Bully Bob."

Grades 3–5

- *Hand-Tracing:* As a way to review safe and effective ways to resolve conflicts, have students trace their hand and list strategies that they have learned in each finger of their hand.

- *When and How to Say "No" Carousel Activity:* (See chapter 5 for complete directions for the carousel activity. Applications should be developed with a focus on appropriate situations and skills involved in safe and effective refusal.)

- *Crime Prevention Scavenger Hunt:* After a discussion of crime prevention strategies that have been integrated into homes, schools, and the community, give students a list to check off with a parent or other concerned adult as a homework assignment. Have students then build a classroom model of a safer school, home, and community that integrates the strategies from their assignment and class discussion.

- *Feelings Unfinished Sentences:* Prepare a hand-out that focuses on feelings associated with behaviors of others. Have the students complete the sentences, then role-play the feelings with a partner (Example: When you tell me that I did well, I feel . . . , When you call me a name, I feel . . . , When you push my friend on the playground, I feel . . . , etc.). Extend the activity and encourage students to complete the whole sentences themselves (Example: When you . . . , I feel . . .).

- *Personal Relationship Web:* Ask students to draw a circle in the middle of a page (about the size of a quarter) and label it "Me." Scattered around their "Me" circle, have students draw a minimum of ten other similarly sized circles and label them with the initials of the people with whom they have the most regular contact. Students then connect various types of lines from the "Me" circle to each of the others to depict the nature of the relationship that they most often have with that person (Example: A straight line indicates a very peaceful relationship, a curvy line indicates a relationship with ups and downs, a jagged line indicates a relationship in which problems are common, etc.). For each relationship, ask students to write a three-adjective description and identify one strategy that they could use to maintain or improve the relationship.

Grades 6–8

- *Television Scene Analysis:* Assign students to watch a predetermined number of different television shows that include depictions of conflict resolution. Encourage them to note precipitating incidents, resolution strategies, and outcomes or consequences of both nonviolent and violent conflict resolution scenes. Have groups of students then construct bar or pie charts that represent the data they gathered.

- *Making a Video for Younger Students:* Assign groups of students to write and videotape scenarios that depict precipitating variables and confrontations or conflicts between students about developmentally meaningful issues for younger counterparts. Tape the use of nonviolent and violent conflict resolution skills and potential outcomes separately. With supervision of teachers from both groups, have students share their videos with younger counterparts with the endings omitted. Ask the younger students to discuss the contributing factors, ways to resolve the conflicts, and the consequences of violent and nonviolent resolution strategies.

- *Cross-age Poster Making:* Assign cooperative learning base groups of students in middle-level grades to construct posters that communicate messages of healthy problem solving and conflict resolution for their elementary-age counterparts. Upon completion, display the posters at an art fair in agencies and businesses in the local community. Following this showing, display all posters in the school of the younger students.

- *Socialization Collages:* Ask mixed-sex pairs of students to use magazine images to create split-image collages of the different ways in which boys and girls are socialized to communicate, solve problems, resolve conflicts, and express their sexuality.

- *"Danger Will Robinson Game:"* Ask each student to write three brief paragraphs that depict potentially dangerous situations for a fictional age-cohort character named Will Robinson, the character from the vintage TV show and recent movie *Lost in Space*. Have students then turn their situations into a game in which teams pantomime the situations. Give points to teams that correctly guess the danger depicted, and/or respond with an effective solution or resolution to the danger that has been depicted.

sexual intercourse is often involved, the actions may involve genital manipulation, indecent exposure, or exposure to obscene literature or use of obscene language and literature. Recently, concern about exposure to such depictions has increased as children and youth gain access and expertise in exploring the Internet.

There are a number of physical, behavioral, and environmental indicators associated with child abuse. The physical indicators include cigarette-type burns on the hands, feet, or genitals; bruises occurring in unusual patterns; and missing or loosened teeth at developmentally inappropriate ages. Pain or itching in the genital area, torn or stained underclothes, and bruises or bleeding from the external genitalia are indicators of sexual abuse.

The behavioral indicators of sexual abuse can include poor peer relationships, aggressiveness or delinquency, difficulty walking or sitting, drug usage, reluctance to participate in recreational activities, and confiding or reporting to teachers or authorities. Environmental indicators include prolonged absence of one parent, alcoholism in the family, and social or geographical isolation. Some parent characteristics that indicate a possibility of child abuse, including sexual abuse, are being extremely protective, not allowing the child to have any social contact, and distrusting the child.

A disclosure of sexual abuse by a child is something that teachers hope never to deal with. However, it happens. When a child tells a teacher that he or she is being sexually abused, the teacher should believe the child. Most children do not have a frame of reference for describing sexual abuse unless it has happened to them. After the child has disclosed this information, it is important for teachers to act calm and thank the child for talking. Teachers should not make a big deal about the disclosure or ask questions like, "Are you telling the truth?" or "Did you see that on television?" These reactions tell students that they are not being believed. After thanking the student, it is important for the teacher to contact the proper authorities and report the incident immediately.

Observing Students—A Foundation for Advocacy

There are four important advocacy skills that must be mastered by teachers and other professionals who have been designated as "mandated reporters" of suspected child abuse within their states. To undergird their advocacy for child and adolescent health, teachers and other concerned adults must train themselves to be critical observers of the students with whom they come in contact. Such professionals actually may be more able to notice the more subtle signs or symptoms of abuse than are nonabusive parents or other family members. Because teachers have the opportunity to observe students in the context the child's age-cohort peers, any anomalies, changes, or injuries may be more conspicuous to these professionals. In addition, teachers are charged with the responsibility of keeping records about a range of student performance measures. In this context, changes in student health, social interaction patterns, or academic performance may be noticeable over a period of time. Finally, teachers, physicians, and other mandated reporters often are better able than a child's relatives to maintain professional objectivity about potential problems.

In most states, all medical care providers, educators, criminal justice professionals, and clergy have been identified as "mandated reporters." These designated professionals are required by law to report any suspicion of abuse among the youth with whom they work.

In addition to keeping a vigilant eye for indicators of potential child abuse, teachers would be wise to watch for signs that students are likely to behave in violent ways. While children who manifest one or more of these signs may not necessarily become violent, they constitute a reason for teachers to follow up. If the following behavioral warning signs have been observed, there is reason for concern:

1. Serious physical fighting with peers or family members,
2. Severe destruction of property,
3. Severe rage for seemingly minor reasons,
4. Detailed threats of lethal violence,
5. Possession and/or use of firearms or other weapons, or
6. Other self-injurious behaviors or threats of suicide.[34]

In addition, teachers or other advocates are encouraged to act immediately in cases in which any of the following behaviors are currently evident:

1. The child has presented a detailed plan (time, place, and/or method) to harm or kill others—particularly if the child has a history of aggression or has attempted to carry out such threats in the past,
2. The child is carrying a weapon, particularly a gun, and has threatened to use it, and/or
3. The child expresses extreme fear of others or that someone in particular is "out to get him or her."[35]

In all cases in which teachers have suspicions that students are being abused or that violence is eminent, action must be taken. The best course of action is to make an immediate referral or report of these professional suspicions.

Making Referrals—Reporting Abuse

Children who are being abused need appropriate medical and social services. The principal agency that responds to child abuse in most communities is the Child Protective Services agency. Personnel here provide the counsel, help, and social assistance needed by children who are being treated badly. Many agencies provide assistance to parents of abused children for the purpose of preventing further occurrences.

Schools have a significant role to play in the early identification of children who have been abused. Every state now has a child abuse (including sexual abuse) reporting statute. Most of these laws mandate that teachers report any suspicions of abuse. This is not a particularly easy task for teachers. Importantly, it is not the responsibility of the teacher to determine whether or not the child is actually being abused, or to know who the perpetrator is. Instead, it is the job of teachers and other mandated reporters to report *any suspicions of abuse*. Teachers always have the concern that maybe their "hunch" is wrong. Also, many teachers are afraid that they can be sued for reporting their suspicions by the parents or caregivers of the child. However, in most states, the mandated reporter statutes provide legal immunity from liability for those who report suspected child abuse, neglect, or sexual abuse in context of job responsibilities.

Gathering Information

Many teachers are of the opinion that once they make a referral, they turn the responsibility for problematic issues confronting the child over to protective service professionals. In many cases, however, the child continues to attend the same school and work with the same teacher and classmates while the case is being investigated. Once teacher advocates have made reports of their suspicions in a way that is consistent with current interpretations of state law, it is important to gather information about ways to support the child and to continue to integrate them into daily classroom practice. In this regard, teachers are encouraged to seek the support of school counselors, psychologists, social workers, or others recommended by district administrators.

Following Up

Teachers and other mandated reporters are reminded that referral networks often move slowly. This is due in part to the fact that child protective service professionals often must interface with the legal system. In addition, many departments of child protective services are grossly understaffed and stretched beyond their capacity. Teachers who may become frustrated with delays or concerns that the system may have abandoned a student are urged to pursue follow-up activities. Although tempting, teachers are advised to avoid making contact with family members about such matters. Rather, information can be clarified, and the best interests of children and their families can be preserved through telephone contacts, updates or follow-up reports, made to case workers or other child protective service professionals.

Teaching Sexual Abuse Prevention and Education

Sexual abuse prevention and education is a difficult topic for most teachers to teach because they are uncomfortable or uninformed about sexual abuse. Also, many believe that it is a family issue that should be discussed only at home. However, increasingly teachers are having to include this instruction in their curriculum.

How should teachers teach the topic of sexual abuse to their students? First, it is important for teachers to examine their own feelings about reporting suspicions of abuse. The following information on teaching children to protect themselves from sexual abuse will encourage children to tell someone if they are being abused. Children cannot defend themselves if they are being sexually abused; they can only tell someone. If teachers teach these skills, and then choose not to report a suspicion or a disclosure, they are doing more harm than good.

There are five main points regarding sexual abuse that children should be taught:

1. First, children should be taught about the concept of a problem. The word *problem* should be defined, and children should be given the opportunity to give examples of problems that children may have. Examples typically include fighting, teasing, peer pressure, and homework. Some children may bring up abuse and other problems that occur at home. If they do, teachers should thank the student for sharing that information with the class, and agree that abuse is a problem. The teacher should talk to that student about the abuse in a one-on-one situation at a later time. Teachers should then ask the students how problems make them feel. Typical responses are "sad," "angry," "confused," or "mad." The next issue surrounding the concept of problems is to discuss what children should do if they have a problem. Teachers should emphasize that children should tell someone when they have a problem, or else the problem gets bigger.

2. The discussion of problems leads into the second point of sexual abuse prevention that should be taught, which is the availability of support systems. Teachers should explain the concept of support systems and identify the two categories of support systems that children have: community and family. Teachers should emphasize that people in support systems can help when a problem exists. Students should understand that although other children may be in their support system, it is best to tell an adult when there is a problem. It is also important for teachers to separate family and community support systems because of the high percentage of abusers who are family members. Students should be given the opportunity to determine the adults in their support system.

3. The third point that should be taught to children is the concept of different touches. Teachers should define three different touches: safe, unsafe, and secret. Safe touches are those touches that make a person feel good. Teachers should ask students to give examples of some safe touches. They may include hugging, holding hands, a pat on the back, kissing, and a "high five." Unsafe touches are those touches that make a person feel uncomfortable. Teachers should then ask students for examples of unsafe touches. They may include kicking, hitting, pinching, and tripping.

Some students may ask if sexual abuse is an unsafe touch. If this occurs, teachers can simply tell students that sexual abuse is another type of touch called a secret touch. It is important that teachers define a secret touch in the following way: A secret touch occurs when an adult or older person touches your private parts or when they trick you into touching their private parts. Some school districts will encourage teachers to use correct anatomical terminology for body parts, while other districts are more comfortable using the term *private parts.* After discussing each type of touch, it is important to ask students how each of these touches would make a person feel. For example, most students will respond that safe touches make them feel happy, while secret touches might make them feel weird, confused, or mad.

After the three types of touches have been defined, teachers should then continue with a discussion of what to do if someone tries to give them a secret touch. Students should be taught the following rules: Say no, get away, and tell someone. It is important for teachers to emphasize that children tell someone, because children may be too afraid to say no or to get away, but they can always tell someone. The concept of support systems can be reinforced when discussing whom to tell if sexual abuse is occurring.

4. The fourth point that should be discussed when teaching sexual abuse is the concept of secrets.

Teachers should emphasize that students should never keep a touching problem a secret. It should be stressed that even if students are scared to tell someone, the problem will not go away unless they do tell someone. Teachers can discuss the concept of secrets that are appropriate to keep, such as a surprise birthday party, versus those secrets that are not appropriate to keep, such as sexual abuse.

5. The fifth point that should be discussed with students is the concept of fault with sexual abuse. The concept of fault is very difficult for students to understand, so teachers should spend an adequate amount of time on this topic. Teachers should stress that a touching problem is never a child's fault, even if he or she did not follow the rules of "Say no, get away, and tell someone." Students need to understand that a touching problem is always the adult's fault, and that they should not feel guilty if they have a touching problem.

Many of the concepts, such as problems and support systems, can be applied to other subjects and should be reinforced throughout the school year. Although many teachers may find it difficult to teach sexual abuse prevention and education, it is an important topic because of the number of children being abused every day.

SUMMARY

Intentional injuries that include incidents of abuse, homicide, suicide, and other forms of violence have been identified as a major threat to the public health of Americans. There is no place where violence is more of a concern than at the school site. In addition, approximately 1 million American children are reported as victims of child abuse each year. Finally, there is a growing body of literature that suggests that the risk of intentional injuries threatens academic success.

Importantly, concerned education professionals and citizens often pursue violence risk-reduction practices that research has confirmed to have a low potential for success. These practices include such measures as:

- Using scare tactics based on images of violent scenes or consequences,
- Segregating aggressive or antisocial students into isolated groups, and

- Implementing brief instructional programs that are not reinforced by a safe and healthy school climate.

By contrast, effective programs are comprehensive, developmentally appropriate, and involve strong staff development and parental engagement components.

Finally, teachers and other education professionals must be prepared to serve as effective student advocates concerning education and referral of suspected child abuse. With slight variation, most states define educators as "mandated reporters" who are required by law to make immediate reports of any suspicions of child abuse. In addition to being well-versed in advocacy skills, teachers would be wise to update their skills in planning and delivering developmentally appropriate sexual abuse instruction. Although it is unpleasant to deal with the unfortunate reality of child abuse, skilled teachers are an important link in the chain of reducing the corrosive effects of child abuse.

DISCUSSION QUESTIONS

1. Compare and contrast the incidence of violence in the United States and other nations of the world.

2. Define the term *violence.*

3. List examples of intentional injuries.

4. Clarify the relationship between the risk of intentional injury and threats to academic success.

5. Discuss variables that are associated with child and adolescent violence.

6. What data are available to clarify the risks of violence and other intentional injuries on school property?

7. Contrast violence risk-reduction strategies with low and high potentials for success.

8. In what ways can teachers and community residents actually enable violence?

9. Discuss your feelings about the roles of educators in prevention and referral of child abuse.

10. Clarify the roles of teachers and other education professionals as mandated reporters of child abuse.

11. In what ways can the observation skills of teachers be more objective and revealing that those of many parents?

12. Why is it so important for teachers to provide follow-up for reports of suspected child abuse?

13. Discuss the difficulties associated with sexual abuse prevention and education.

14. Suggest strategies for teachers to help students to examine the issue of "secrets" as they pertain to sexual abuse risk reduction.

ENDNOTES

1. Department of Health and Human Services, Public Health Service, *Healthy People 2000: National Health Promotion and Disease Prevention Objectives* (Washington, DC: U.S. Government Printing Office, 1991).

2. J. Wilson et al., "The Silent Screams: Recognizing Abused Children," *Education* 104, no.1 (1983): 100–103.

3. National Research Council, "Summary," in *Understanding and Preventing Violence* (Washington, DC: National Academy Press, 1993): 1–27.

4. Mohammed Forouzesh, and Daria Waetjen, "Youth Violence," in *Promoting Teen Health* (Thousand Oaks, CA: Sage Publications, 1998):166–168.

5. National Public Services Research Institute, "Child and Adolescent Violence: Incidence and Costs." *Childhood Injury: Costs and Prevention Facts* (Landover, MD: National Public Services Research Institute, July 1997).

6. A.T. Lockwood, *Preventing Violence in Our Schools* (Madison, WI: Wisconsin Center for Educational Research, 1993): 1–12.

7. R. S. Lorion, and W. Saltzman, "Children Exposed to Community Violence: Following a Path from Concern to Research Action," *Psychiatry* 56, no.1 (1993): 55–65.

8. D. Prothrow-Stith, and S. Quaday, *Hidden Casualties: The Relationship Between Violence and Learning* (Washington, DC: National Consortium for African American Children, Inc. and the National Health Education Consortium, 1996).

9. D. C. Gottfredson, "School-based Crime Prevention," in *Preventing Crime: What Works, What Doesn't, What's Promising* (Washington, DC: A Report to the U.S. Congress, 1997).

10. Department of Health and Human Services, Public Health Service, *Healthy People 2000*.

11. Carole Remboldt, "Making Violence Unacceptable," *Educational Leadership* (September 1998): 32–38.

12. National Public Services Research Institute. "Child and Adolescent Violence: Risk Factors and Prevention." *Childhood Injury: Costs and Prevention Facts* (Landover, MD: National Public Services Research Institute, July 1997).

13. U.S. Departments of Education and Justice, *Annual Report on School Safety* (Rockville, MD: U.S. Department of Justice, Office of Justice Programs, 1998).

14. Ibid.

15. Ibid.

16. Genesee County Community Mental Health Protection and Information Services. *Parent Talk: Protecting Students From Violence*. Flint, MI: Genesee County Community Mental Health Protection and Information Services.

17. Linda Dusenbury, et al., "Nine Critical Elements of Promising Violence Prevention Programs," *Journal of School Health* 67, no. 10 (December 1997): 409–414.

18. Ibid.

19. Ibid.

20. U.S. General Accounting Office, *School Safety: Promising Initiatives for Addressing School Violence* (Washington, DC: U.S. General Accounting Office, 1995).

21. Children's Safety Network, *A Comprehensive Approach to Violence Prevention in Schools* (Newton, MA: Education Development Center, Draft, 1997).

22. U.S. General Accounting Office, *School Safety: Promising Initiatives for Addressing School Violence*.

23. Massachusetts Department of Public Health, *The Comprehensive School Health Manual* (Boston, MA: Massachusetts Department of Public Health Bureau of Family and Community Health,1995).

24. Janet Collins, et al., "School Health Education," *Journal of School Health* 65, no. 8 (1995): 302–311.

25. Ibid.

26. Remboldt, "Making Violence Unacceptable," *Educational Leadership*.

27. American School Health Association, *Report of the National Injury Prevention Task Force* (Kent, OH: American School Health Association, 1998): 19–20.

28. Prevention & Training By Design, *Creating Safe Schools: Age Appropriate Suggestions* (Westerville, OH: Prevention & Training By Design.

29. Ibid.

30. Ibid.

31. Ohio Department of Human Services, *Child Abuse and Neglect* (Columbus, OH: Office of Compliance and Review, 1988).

32. Ibid.

33. Ibid.

34. Violent Children Project, *Responding to Violent Children: A Handbook for the Community* (Akron, OH: Summit Cluster for Youth, 1998).

35. Ibid.

SUGGESTED READINGS

Barton, P., R. Coley, and H. Wenglinsky. *Order in the Classroom: Violence, Discipline, and Student Achievement.* Princeton, NJ: Educational Testing Service Policy Information Center, 1998.

Bushweller, K. "Probing the Roots and Prevention of Youth Violence." *Education Vital Signs 1998: A Publication of the American School Board Journal* (December 1998): A8–A12.

Carter, S. *School Mediation Evaluation Report.* Albuquerque, NM: National Resource Center for Youth Mediation, 1995.

Children's Defense Fund. "Ecumenical Intervention Helps Conquer Violence." *CDF Reports* (November 1998): 16.

Elliot, D., B. Hamburg, and K. Williams. *Violence in American Schools: A New Perspective.* New York: Cambridge University Press, 1998.

Farrell, A., and A. Meyer. "The Effectiveness of a School-Based Curriculum for Reducing Violence among Urban Sixth-Grade Students." *American Journal of Public Health* 87, no. 6 (1997): 979–984.

Jenkins, J., and M. Smith. *School Mediation Evaluation Materials: Evaluation Plan and Instruments.* Albuquerque, NM: New Mexico Center for Dispute Resolution, 1995.

Lantieri, L., and J. Patti. *Waging Peace in Our Schools.* Boston, MA: Beacon Press, 1996.

Peterson, G., D. Pietrzak, and K. Speaker. "The Enemy Within: A National Study on School Violence Prevention." *Urban Education* 33, no. 3 (1998): 331–359.

Pietrzak, D., G. Peterson, and K. Speaker. "Perceptions of School Violence by Elementary and Middle School Personnel." *Professional School Counseling* 1, no. 4 (1998): 23–29.

Policy Information Center. *Order in the Classroom: Violence, Discipline, and Student Achievement.* Princeton, NJ: Educational Testing Service,1998.

Price, J., and S. Everett. "Teachers' Perceptions of Violence in the Public Schools: The MetLife Survey." *American Journal of Health Behavior* 21, no. 3 (1997): 178–186.

Rasicot, J. "The Threat of Harm." *The American School Board Journal* (March 1999): 14–18.

Steed. Hammond. Paul. "The Making of Safe and Secure Schools." The Schoolhouse of Quality Magazine (Spring 1999): 10–15.

U.S. Department of Health and Human Services. *The Prevention of Violence: A Framework for Community Action.* Atlanta, GA: Centers for Disease Control and Prevention, 1993.

Vail, K. "Give Peace A Chance: Peer Mediators in Cleveland Choose Nonviolence." *The American School Board Journal* (August 1998): 22–24.

Webster, D., J. Vernick, J. Ludwig, and K. Lester. "Flawed Gun Policy Research Could Endanger Public Safety." *American Journal of Public Health* 87, no. 6 (1997): 918–921.

CHILDREN'S LITERATURE WITH AN INTENTIONAL INJURY RISK-REDUCTION THEME

Grades K–2

Cohn, Janice. *Why Did it Happen?* Morrow, 1994.

Fox, Mem. *Feathers and Fools.* Harcourt Brace, 1989.

Henson, Jim. *My Wish for Tomorrow.* Tambourine, 1995.

Thomas, Shelly Moore. *Somewhere Today: A Book of Peace.* Albert Whitman, 1998.

Grades 3–5

Bunting, Eve. *Your Move.* Harcourt Brace, 1998.

Bunting, Eve, *Smoky Night.* Harcourt Brace, 1995.

Powell, E. Sandy. *Daisy.* Learner, 1991.

Sachs, Marilyn. *The Bears' House.* Puffin, 1971. (School Library Journal Best Book of the Year, New York Times Outstanding Book of the Year, American Booksellers' Pick of the Lists)

Spinelli, Jerry. *Wringer.* Harper Collins, 1995. (Newberry Medal)

Grades 6–8

Coman, Carolyn. *What Jamie Saw.* Front Street, 1995.

Cormier, Robert. *We All Fall Down.* Bantam, 1991.

Lobel, Anita. *No Pretty Pictures.* Greenwillow, 1998.

Magorian, Michelle. *Good Night Mr. Tom.* Harper Collins, 1981.

Myers, Walter Dean. *Scorpions.* Harper Collins, 1988. (Newberry Award, American Library Association Notable

Children's Book, American Library Association Best Book for Young Adults, American Library Association Recommended Book for Reluctant Readers)

Paulsen, Gary. *The Rifle*. Harcourt Brace, 1995.

Tolan, Stephanie. *Welcome to the Arc*. Morrow, 1996.

INTERNET INFORMATION

INTENTIONAL RISK-REDUCTION WEBSITES

For additional information on intentional injury risk-reduction, please refer to the following websites.

Center for the Prevention of School Violence
http://www.ncsu.edu/cpsv

Center for the Study and Prevention of Violence
http://www.colorado.edu/cspv

Children's Safety Network
Educational Development Center, Inc.
http://www.edc.org/hhd/csn

Children's Safety Network Injury Data Technical Assistance Center
npatel@mail.sdsu.edu

Keep Schools Safe
http://www.keepschoolssafe.org

Maternal and Child Health Bureau
Injury and Violence Prevention
www.os.dhhs.gov/hrsa/mchb

National Alliance for Safe Schools
www.safeschools.org

National Child Rights Alliance
http://www.ai.mit.edu/people/ellens/ncra/ncra.html

National Crime Prevention Council
www.ncpc.org

The National Exchange Club
Foundation for the Prevention of Child Abuse
www.preventchildabuse.com

National Institute for Dispute Resolution
www.nidr.org

National School Safety Center
www.nssc1.org

National Victim Center
http://www.ncv.org

Safe and Drug Free Schools Program
www.ed.gov/offices/oese/sdfs

Safe Schools for the Twenty-first Century
http://wwwnyu.edu/education/metrocenter/violence/ssrp.htm

ALCOHOL AND OTHER DRUGS

O U T L I N E

INTRODUCTION

There is a definite need for substance abuse prevention programs in today's elementary and middle schools. The United States has the highest rate of teenage substance abuse of any industrialized country in the world. Not only teenagers are affected by drugs. Surveys of students indicate that pressure to use gateway drugs (tobacco and alcohol) begins around the fourth grade.[1] This pressure and other factors lead to an increasing number of elementary and middle-level school children who use alcohol and other dangerous drugs. The 1997–98 PRIDE survey of grade 6–8 students showed that:

- 14.6% had used alcohol within the last 30 days,
- 7.1% had used marijuana within the last 30 days,
- 1.6% had used cocaine within the last 30 days, and
- 3.3% had used inhalants within the last 30 days.[2]

Americans have consistently identified drug abuse as the number one problem facing our schools. In fact, the great majority of parents believe the problem is much more serious that it was 5 years earlier, according to a recent poll.[3] Students also believe alcohol and other drug use is a problem. One in three students believes that drugs and alcohol are the most serious problem facing his or her high school.[4] The education community also has begun to recognize the relationship between drug use/abuse and learning and education. The *America 2000* agenda has identified eight national education goals, one of which focuses on alcohol and other drugs. Goal 8 states:

> By the year 2000, every school in America will be free of drugs, violence and the unauthorized presence of firearms and alcohol and will offer a disciplined environment conducive to learning.[5]

In addition, several objectives included in *Healthy People 2010* are directly related to drug prevention.[6] One element that is central to achieving Goal 8 from the *America 2000* agenda and the objectives in *Healthy People 2000* goals is for elementary and middle-level teachers to know about the dangers of alcohol and other drugs. By understanding the dangers of these drugs and the relationship between the use of drugs and learning, teachers will hopefully be more likely to incorporate alcohol and other drug prevention into their teaching.

RECOMMENDATIONS FOR TEACHERS: PRACTICE AND CONTENT

This section presents basic information about alcohol and other drugs. Most of this information about illicit drugs will **not** be developmentally appropriate for elementary children (see the Developmentally Appropriate Practice Recommendations section). However, teachers should possess basic literacy about alcohol and other drugs because students may ask questions about these drugs. There are too many different drugs to provide specific information about each one. However, table 9.1 lists the most common drugs along with their street names, how long the drug's effects last, their health effects, and their symptoms. In addition, common terms and their definitions are listed in table 9.2.

Alcohol

Alcoholic drinks contain ethyl alcohol, which is a depressant. Ethyl alcohol is not the same as isopropyl alcohol (rubbing alcohol) or methyl alcohol (wood alcohol). Methyl alcohol, even in small amounts, is dangerous. Isopropyl alcohol is found in antifreeze and some cosmetics and can be dangerous if ingested. In fact, every year, a small number of people die from drinking methyl alcohol, thinking it is the same as ethyl alcohol. There are three main types of ethyl alcohol: beer, wine, and distilled

1 glass of wine	1 can or bottle of beer	1 shot glass with distilled spirits
4 oz. of table wine	12 oz. of beer	1.25 oz. of whiskey or other hard liquor
12% alcohol by volume	4% alcohol by volume	40% alcohol by volume or 80 proof
4 x 0.12 = 0.48 oz. of ethyl alcohol per serving	12 x 0.04 = 0.48 oz. of ethyl alcohol per serving	1.25 x 0.40 = 0.50 oz. of ethyl alcohol per serving

Note: Of course, the above calculations would not apply if a wine cooler or a dessert wine were consumed in place of table wine, if a higher alcohol content beer or a lite beer were drunk instead of regular beer, and if higher proof distilled spirits were used in place of 80 proof liquor.

Figure 9.1

How much alcohol is contained in the typical serving of an alcoholic beverage?

spirits. Although some persons believe beer is a less dangerous type of ethyl alcohol, all forms of ethyl alcohol are dangerous if misused. It is important to note that there is the same amount of ethyl alcohol in a 12-ounce beer, one 4-ounce glass of wine, and a 1-ounce shot of distilled spirits (see figure 9.1).[7]

Alcohol, along with tobacco, is a "gateway" drug. That is, those children who use tobacco and alcohol are more likely to use "harder" drugs later. It is important to delay the onset of alcohol use because it has been found that the younger the age of the beginning drinker, the more likely he or she will later turn to illegal drugs.[8] Currently, the average age at which students take their first drink of alcohol is between 12 and 13 years old. Two-thirds of Americans over the age of 15 drink alcohol in some form. Today, the estimated annual average consumption of alcoholic beverages per person in the United States is the amount of alcohol one would obtain from approximately 90 gallons of beer, 30 gallons of wine, or 10 gallons of distilled spirits. Heavier drinkers, who constitute 10% of the drinking population, drink over half of the alcohol consumed in the United States.[9]

Drinking has acute effects on the body. The heavy, fast-paced drinking that young people commonly engage in quickly alters judgment, vision, coordination, and speech, and often leads to dangerous risk-taking behavior. Because young people have lower body weight than adults, they absorb alcohol into their blood system faster

TABLE 9.1	The Drugs that People Use		
Drug/Street Names	**How Long It Lasts (Hours)**	**Health Effects**	**Symptoms**
Alcohol	1–12	Causes depression, aggression, slurred speech, muscular incoordination. Frequent use can lead to cirrhosis of liver, pancreatitis, brain disorders, vitamin deficiencies, and malnutrition.	Puffiness of face, redness of eyes, depression, disorientation, shallow respiration, nausea, cold and clammy skin. Dehydration.
Marijuana/pot, reefer, grass, THC, hash, hash oil	2–4	Can impair memory perception and judgment by destroying brain cells. Raises blood pressure. Contains more known carcinogens than cigarettes.	Euphoria, relaxed inhibitions, disoriented behavior, staring off into space, hilarity without cause, time distortion. Bloodshot eyes, dry mouth and throat.
Barbiturates, Methaquaione/ Quaaludes, luces, yellow jackets, red devils	1–16	Can cause slurred speech; staggering gait; poor judgment, and slow, uncertain reflexes. Large doses can cause unconsciousness and death.	Slurred speech, disorientation, drunken behavior with no odor of alcohol. Sedation.
Cocaine/coke, snow, blow, gold dust, lady	1/2–2	Causes dilated pupils, increased blood pressure, heart rate, breathing rate and body temperature. Can cause seizures, heart attacks, and death.	Apathy, anxiety, sleeplessness, paranoia, hallucinations, craving for more cocaine. Weight loss. Constant sniffing.
Crack Cocaine/ crack, rock	5–10 minutes	More and stronger cocaine is getting to the brain quicker, increasing risks of cocaine use.	Same as cocaine.
Amphetamines/uppers, speed, black beauties, daxies	1/2–2	Increases heart rate, breathing rate, blood pressure. High doses can cause tremors, loss of coordination, and death from stroke or heart failure. Frequent use of large amounts can produce brain damage, ulcers, and malnutrition.	Decreased appetite, dilated pupils, sleeplessness, agitation, unusual increase in activity.
PCP (phencyclidine)/ angel dust, killer weed, crystal cyclone, elephant tranquilizer, rocket fuel	variable	Increased heart rate and blood pressure. Large doses can cause convulsions, comas, heart and lung failure, and ruptured brain vessels. Users may show long-term effects on memory, judgment, concentration, and perception.	Sweating, dizziness, numbness, hallucinations, confusion, agitation. Violence and aggression or silence and withdrawn state.
Heroin/Mexican brown, Cina white, Persian porcelain, "H"	12–24	Repeated use can lead to infections of heart lining and valves, skin abscesses, and congested lungs. Can lead to convulsions, coma, and death.	Watery eyes, runny nose, yawning, loss of appetite, tremors, irritability, panic, chills, sweating, cramps, nausea.
Gas and Glue/Rush, Locker Room, aerosol cans, amyl nitrate, gasoline, lighter fluid (inhaled through a saturated cloth or in a bag covering nose and mouth)	variable	Brain damage occurs when used over a long period of time. All of these chemicals carry considerable risk, particularly of cardiac arrhythmia.	Very alert, keen senses, hallucinations, dizziness, scrambled words, and disconnected sentences. Smells like whatever the child was doing.

(continued)

TABLE 9.1	The Drugs that People Use *(continued)*		
Drug/Street Names	**How Long It Lasts (Hours)**	**Health Effects**	**Symptoms**
Hallucinogens/LSD, Mescaline, Peyote, mushrooms	3–12	Dilated pupils, nausea, increased blood pressure, hallucinations, stomach cramps, blackouts. Flashbacks, a recurrence of the drug effects, may be a problem for some.	Beady eyes, nervous erratic behavior, laughing, crying, personality changes, "sees" smells, "hears" colors. Marked depersonalization.
MDMA/Adam, Ecstasy, X-TC (a Designer Drug —structural analogs of controlled substances)	variable —up to days	Increased heart rate and blood pressure. Blurred vision, chills, sweating. Believed to cause permanent brain damage.	Confusion, depression, sleep problems, anxiety, paranoia, muscle tension, involuntary teeth clenching, nausea.

Source: *National Institute on Drug Abuse.*

TABLE 9.2	Common Terms Used in Drug Education

1. **Antagonism.** A type of substance that blocks a receptor.
2. **Dependence.** The compulsive use of a drug, which results in adverse social consequences and the neglect of constructive activities.
3. **Synergism.** The ability of one drug to enhance the effect of another.
4. **Tolerance.** Lower sensitivity to a drug so that a given dose no longer has the usual effect and a larger dose is needed.

and exhibit greater impairment for a longer time. Alcohol use not only increases the likelihood of being involved in an accident, but it also increases the risk of serious injury in an accident because of its harmful effects on numerous parts of the body. Motor-vehicle crashes are the leading cause of death for 15 to 20-year-olds, and two out of five of these accidents involve alcohol.[10]

When a person drinks alcohol, it takes time for the body to oxidize it. Alcohol always takes the same pathway in the body (figure 9.2). First, alcohol travels through the esophagus to the stomach. The stomach is able to absorb about 20% of the alcohol, depending on how much and what kind of food is in the stomach. The rest of the alcohol, about 80%, travels to the small intestine and is absorbed into the bloodstream. The bloodstream then carries alcohol to all parts of the body, and it continues to circulate through the body until it is broken down and excreted. The brain is one of the organs influenced by alcohol. The more a person drinks, the more the control centers of the brain become depressed. In the short term, alcohol depresses the following functions in a sequential

fashion: judgment, inhibitions, reaction time, coordination, vision, speech, balance, walking, standing, consciousness, breathing, heartbeat, and finally, life. Alcohol is also transported to the liver, where it undergoes oxidation. The liver is able to oxidize about one-half ounce, or one drink, of alcohol per hour. If there is more than one-half ounce of alcohol in the body, the remainder circulates throughout the body until the liver can oxidize more alcohol. The amount of alcohol that circulates in the body and blood is known as the Blood-Alcohol Concentration, or BAC. As BAC rises in the blood and reaches the brain, predictable changes occur (table 9.3). The last organs to be affected by alcohol are the lungs and the kidneys, where about 10% of the alcohol is eliminated by breath and urine.[11]

Several factors influence absorption of alcohol into the bloodstream:[12]

1. *Concentration of Alcoholic Beverage.* The stronger the concentration of alcohol in the beverage, the faster the rate of absorption. If one person drinks 5 ounces of beer and another person drinks 5 ounces of wine, the person who drinks 5 ounces of wine will have a higher BAC because wine has a higher concentration of alcohol (see figure 9.1).
2. *Number of Alcoholic Beverages Consumed.* The more alcoholic beverages a person consumes, the more alcohol there is in the body to absorb. There is a direct relationship between the amount of alcohol consumed and the BAC.
3. *Rate of Consumption.* The faster alcohol is consumed, the higher the BAC. It is important to remember that the liver can oxidize only about one-half ounce of alcohol per hour, and any additional alcohol stays in the blood and other organs in the body.

1. Stomach
Passes quickly through the stomach, though food can slow it down for a short time. It enters the bloodstream quickly and directly.

2. Small intestine
Goes through the wall of the small intestine almost immediately. It's not food, so it is not digested. Again, most of the alcohol enters the bloodstream.

3. Bloodstream
Travels in the blood to all parts of the body. Circulates through the body until it is oxidized by the liver.

4. Brain
Reaches into and depresses certain areas of the brain. Added drinks reach deeper, knocking out control centers one by one.

Sequence is
1. Judgment
2. Inhibitions
3. Reaction time
4. Coordination
5. Vision
6. Speech
7. Balance
8. Walking
9. Standing
10. Consciousness
11. Breathing
12. Heartbeat
13. Life

5. Liver
Oxidized in the liver at a rate of 1/2 ounce every hour.

6. Lungs and kidneys
About 10% is eliminated here in breath and urine.

Figure 9.2

Pathways of alcohol. How does alcohol work? This diagram shows you what happens to that drink after it's swallowed.

TABLE 9.3	Alcohol Intoxication: Progressive States of Impairment with Increasing Blood-Alcohol Concentration (BAC)
BAC	**Possible Effects of Alcohol**
0.01%	Usually mild effects, if any; slight changes in feeling; heightening of moods.
0.03%	Feelings of relaxation and slight exhilaration; minimal impairment of mental function.
0.06%	Mild sedation; exaggeration of emotion; slight impairment of fine-motor skills; increase in reaction time; poor muscle control; slurred speech.
0.08%	Legal evidence of driving under the influence of alcohol in many states.
0.09%	Visual and hearing acuity reduced; inhibitions and self-restraint lessened; increased difficulty in performing motor skills; judgment is now clouded.
0.10%	Legal evidence of driving under the influence of alcohol in many states.
0.12%	Difficulty in performing gross-motor skills; blurred vision; unclear speech; definite impairment of mental function.
0.15%	Major impairment of physical and mental functions; irresponsible behavior; general feeling of euphoria; difficulty in standing, walking, talking; distorted perception and judgment.
0.20%	Mental confusion; decreased inhibitions; gross-body movements can be made only with assistance; inability to maintain upright position; difficulty in staying awake.
0.30%	Severe mental confusion; minimum of perception and comprehension; difficulty in responding to stimuli; general suspension of sensibility.
0.40%	Almost complete anesthesia; depressed reflexes; state of unconsciousness or coma likely.
0.50%	Complete unconsciousness or deep coma, if not death.
0.60%	Death is most likely now, if it has not already occurred at somewhat lower BACs following depression of nerve centers that control heartbeat and breathing. Such a person is "dead-drunk."

4. *Amount of Food in the Stomach.* The more food in the stomach, especially fatty foods, meat, and dairy products, the slower the absorption rate of alcohol.

5. *Body Weight.* Heavier people have more body fluids, including blood, than lighter people. Therefore, heavier people can drink more alcohol than lighter people can and still have the same BAC.

6. *Body Chemistry.* Fear, stress, condition of the stomach tissue, anger, and fatigue can all cause the stomach to empty faster. The faster the stomach empties, the faster alcohol is absorbed into the bloodstream.

7. *Drinking History.* People who have been heavy drinkers for an extended period of time build a tolerance to alcohol, which means they have to drink more alcohol than before to get the same desired effects.

8. *Type of Alcoholic Drink.* Carbonated alcoholic beverages, such as champagne, and alcohol mixed in warm drinks, such as a hot rum toddy, are absorbed faster than other kinds of alcoholic beverages.

9. *Body Composition.* The greater the muscle mass in a person, the lower the BAC. Because males generally have lower percent of body fat than do women, they can drink more alcohol and still maintain a lower BAC.

Just as with tobacco, drinking alcohol has several negative, short-term side effects. Because students deal with the present, it is important to stress the negative, short-term side effects of alcohol; they will be able to identify better with the immediate consequences.[13]

1. *Perception and Motor Skills.* As indicated in table 9.3, even a BAC of 0.06% (one or two drinks) begins to impair fine-motor skills, reaction time, speech, and muscle control. These perception and motor skills are important in many sport, art, and music skills, as well as in riding a bike or driving a car. In fact, over 50% of the motor-vehicle deaths that occur each year are related to alcohol use. At higher BAC levels, there is a decrease in visual and hearing activities, balance, and estimation of time.

2. *Heart and Blood Vessels.* As with tobacco, alcohol temporarily increases both heart rate and blood pressure. Alcohol also constricts the arteries that supply the heart. Although persons who drink alcohol feel warm, they are actually losing body heat because alcohol causes the peripheral blood vessels to dilate or expand. This can be extremely dangerous in cold weather and can lead to hypothermia, which is the extreme loss of body heat.

3. *Sleepiness.* Because alcohol is a depressant, it does cause one to become tired. Many persons believe alcohol is a stimulant because of the way that

alcohol users act; however, those actions result from alcohol initially depressing the part of the brain that controls inhibitions. Alcohol may help a person fall asleep more quickly; however, the sleep is often light, making the person feel tired and unrefreshed even after 8 hours of sleep.

4. *Emotions.* Alcohol depresses the prefrontal lobe of the brain, which controls judgment. With lack of judgment, persons under the influence of alcohol tend to have poor decision-making skills. This tends to increase a person's risk taking, reduce inhibitions, temporarily decrease fears, and increase feelings of relaxation. Increased risk taking, combined with decreased motor skills and perception, causes many motor-vehicle accidents each year.

5. *Hangovers.* Hangovers can have many signs and symptoms, including headache, nausea, stomach distress, and generalized discomfort. These symptoms are caused by drinking too much alcohol, and only time can take away the unpleasant feelings. Theories attribute hangovers to an accumulation of acetaldehyde, dehydration, depletion of important enzymes, and metabolism of congeners in the alcohol. Congeners are toxins that are found in alcohol. Vodka tends to be low in congeners, while red wine and bourbon are high in congeners. The higher the concentration of congeners, the greater the probability of having a hangover.

6. *Overdose.* Alcohol can depress the central nervous system to the point at which the heart and lungs quit functioning, resulting in cardiac or respiratory arrest. This occurs when large amounts of alcohol have been consumed in a short period of time.

7. *Lack of Nutritional Value.* Alcohol provides only empty calories, which means it does not contain any nutritional value. In fact, alcohol has a high caloric content—9 calories/gram. Persons who are trying to watch their weight should avoid alcohol.

Although many young students have a difficult time dealing with future outcomes, they should know that there are several negative, long-term side effects of prolonged, heavy use of alcohol. For instance, longtime alcohol abusers shorten their life span by 10 to 12 years. Other more common, long-term side effects are explained in the following list:[14]

Cirrhosis of the liver is commonly associated with alcohol consumption. With continued use of alcohol, liver cells are damaged and gradually destroyed. The destroyed cells are often replaced by fibrous scar tissue, which is known as cirrhosis of the liver. This disease is the leading cause of death among alcoholics and is the eighth leading cause of death in the United States.

Heavy drinkers also can experience gastrointestinal system disorders, which cause irritation and inflammation of the esophagus, stomach, small intestine, and pancreas. Alcohol use and cancer have also been correlated. Clinical and epidemiological studies have implicated excessive use of alcohol in the development of cancers of the mouth, pharynx, pancreas, and esophagus.

Another problem with heavy drinkers is that they fulfill their caloric intake from alcoholic beverages instead of from food. Even though alcohol is high in calories, it has few nutritional qualities such as vitamins and minerals. Decreased appetite, vomiting, and diarrhea also contribute to nutritional imbalances. The diuretic properties of alcohol also cause a loss of water-soluble vitamins.

Hypoglycemia is another problem associated with heavy alcohol use. Hypoglycemia is a condition in which blood-sugar levels are lower than normal. Because heavy drinkers put such stress on the liver, it has a difficult time producing glucose and storing it as glycogen. Just as with tobacco use, long-term, heavy use of alcohol can lead to cardiovascular disease. Long-term use of alcohol does damage to the heart muscle, leading to a condition known as cardiomyopathy, which can be fatal. It also can lead to premature heartbeats or total loss of rhythm in the heartbeat.

About 10% of persons who continually use alcohol for long periods of time become psychologically and/or physically dependent on it—a condition called alcoholism. At first, the person becomes psychologically dependent, but within time, the dependency usually becomes physical in this population. At this stage, withdrawal symptoms can occur if the person is deprived of alcohol. The earlier a person starts to drink, the shorter the time it takes to become an alcoholic. For instance, in adults, alcoholism can develop after 2 to 10 years; however, among teenagers, the process can occur in as little as 4 months. This is one reason why it is important to encourage students to delay their first use of alcohol. Alcoholics cannot stop drinking once they start. The alcoholic loses control over when drinking begins and ends. There is still debate as to what causes someone to become an alcoholic, but most researchers agree that it is multicausal. The causes include physical or biological factors (heredity), psychological or behavioral factors, and social factors. It is important that students understand that alcoholism does run in families and that about 10% of the population is predisposed to alcoholism. The letter *A* is not written on the foreheads of those who are predisposed to alcoholism. People find out after they have been drinking, which, unfortunately, is sometimes too late.

Dysfunctional Families

When a family is under chronic stress that goes untreated, the family becomes dysfunctional. A family can become dysfunctional for several reasons, including abuse, divorce, death of a family member, illness, money problems, and alcoholism. When the family is dysfunctional because of alcoholism or any other cause, the children tend to assume survival roles. Each member of the dysfunctional family can get locked into one or more survival roles that cause the least amount of personal stress. These roles work well within the family to offer protection from the growing pain. It is important for teachers to understand the characteristics of the survival roles that children tend to manifest, so they can watch for them in their students and provide appropriate referral and follow-up.

Family Hero   The family hero is the role a child takes on to bring honor to the family. The hero tries hard to make things better for the family and works hard to improve the situation. As a result, the family hero earns good grades, is a high achiever, has many friends, and is good in sports and other extracurricular activities.

Scapegoat   The role of the scapegoat is to provide distraction to the family stressor and to give the family something to focus on. Scapegoats tend to cause discipline problems in the classroom so that the family can focus on those problems and not on the real family problem. Scapegoats tend to feel more pain than anyone in the family.

Mascot   The role of the mascot is to provide fun and humor so that some of the stress of the family is relieved. Mascots are often fun to be around, cute, and able to use charm and humor to survive the family situation. As a student, the mascot is known as the class clown.

Lost Child   The role of the lost child is to offer relief because the family does not have to worry about him or her. In the classroom, the lost child seems invisible and quiet, has no friends, is a follower, and has trouble making decisions. Because the lost child is not a troublemaker, many times the teacher forgets to give any attention to him or her.

Although it seems that every child is represented by one of these survival roles, not every child comes from a dysfunctional family. As a teacher, it is important to understand that it is not just the troublemaker who may be experiencing family difficulties. The teacher should provide each student with a warm, positive learning environment and should observe children for any drastic changes. If drastic changes do occur, it is important to refer the child to the school counselor or psychologist.

Marijuana

Marijuana is a green or gray mixture of dried and shredded flowers and leaves of the hemp plant *Cannabis sativa*. The main active chemical in marijuana is THC (delta-9-tetrahydrocannabinol). All forms of marijuana have immediate, negative physical and mental effects. The immediate short-term effects of smoking marijuana include problems with memory and learning, distorted perception, difficulty in thinking and problem solving, loss of coordination, increased heart rate, anxiety, panic attacks, bloodshot eyes, a dry mouth and throat, and increased appetite. Research also shows that students do not retain knowledge when they are "high." Motivation and cognition may be altered, making the acquisition of new information difficult.

Because users often inhale the unfiltered smoke deeply and then hold it in their lungs as long as possible, marijuana is damaging to the lungs and respiratory system. Marijuana smoke contains more cancer-causing agents than contained in tobacco smoke. Someone who smokes marijuana regularly may have a daily cough and phlegm, symptoms of chronic bronchitis, and an increasing number of chest colds. Regardless of the THC content, the amount of tar inhaled by marijuana smokers and the level of carbon monoxide absorbed are three to five times greater than their levels in tobacco.

A drug is addicting if it causes compulsive, often uncontrollable, drug craving, seeking, and use, even in the face of negative health and social consequences. Marijuana meets this criterion. More than 120,000 people per year seek treatment for their primary marijuana addiction.[15]

Cocaine

Cocaine is a powerfully addictive drug. Once having tried cocaine, individuals cannot predict or control the extent to which they will continue to use the drug. Cocaine is a strong central nervous system stimulant that interferes with the reabsorption of dopamine, a chemical messenger associated with pleasure and movement. Dopamine is released as part of the brain's reward system and is involved in the high that characterizes cocaine consumption. Its immediate effects include dilated pupils and elevated blood pressure, heart rate, respiratory rate, and body temperature. The duration of cocaine's immediate euphoric effects, which include hyperstimulation, reduced fatigue, and mental clarity, depends on the route of administration. The high from snorting cocaine may last 15 to 30 minutes, while that from smoking may last 5 to 10 minutes.

Some cocaine users report feelings of restlessness, irritability, and anxiety. A tolerance to the high may develop, and many addicts report that they seek, but fail to achieve, as much pleasure as they received from their first exposure. Occasional use can cause a stuffy or runny nose, while chronic use can ulcerate the mucous membrane of the nose. Injecting cocaine with contaminated equipment can transmit HIV infection, hepatitis, and other diseases. Preparation of free base, which involves the use of volatile solvents, can result in death or injury from fire or explosion. Cocaine can produce psychological and physical dependency, a feeling that the user cannot function without the drug. In rare instances, sudden death can occur on the first use of cocaine or unexpectedly thereafter.[16]

Inhalants

Inhalants are breatheable chemical vapors that produce mind-altering effects. Inhalants are increasingly the drug of choice for many upper-elementary and middle-level students because they are cheap and easy to buy. Inhalants can be divided into three categories:

Solvents—household solvents (paint thinners, degreasers, gasoline, and glues) and art or office supply solvents (correction fluids, felt-tip markers);

Gases—household gases (butane lighters, propane tanks, aerosol dispensers, spray paints, hairspray, deodorant sprays, etc.); and

Nitrates—aliphatic nitrites (cyclohexy nitrite, which is available to the general public).

Nearly all abused inhalant products produce effects similar to those of anesthetics, which act to slow down the body's functions. When inhaled via the nose or mouth into the lungs in sufficient concentrations, inhalants can cause intoxicating effects. Intoxication can last only a few minutes or up to several hours if they are taken repeatedly. Initially, users may feel slightly stimulated; with successive inhalations, they may feel less inhibited and less in control. Finally, a user can lose consciousness.

Sniffing highly concentrated amounts of the chemicals in solvents or aerosol sprays can directly induce heart failure and death. Other irreversible effects caused by inhaling specific solvents are:

Hearing loss—paint sprays, glues, dewaxers, cleaning fluids, and correction fluids;

Limb spasms—glues, gasoline, whipping cream containers, gas cylinders;

Central nervous system or brain damage—paint sprays, glues, dewaxers; and

Bone marrow damage—gasoline.

Serious but potentially reversible effects include:

Liver and kidney damage—correction fluids, dry-cleaning fluids; and

Blood-oxygen depletion—organic nitrites; e.g., poppers, rush, and varnish removers and paint thinners.[17]

DRUG PREVENTION PROGRAMS

When we hear the word *drugs,* most of us immediately think of cocaine, heroin, and marijuana. In this chapter, the word refers to two groups of substances: alcoholic beverages and illegal drugs, including cocaine, heroin, and marijuana. Before teachers can decide what to do in their classrooms to help prevent substance abuse, they must first understand the history of its prevention and the components of successful drug prevention programs.

History of Drug Prevention Programs

Over the years, educators and health professionals have learned how to be more effective in promoting health-enhancing behaviors with students. Consequently, many changes in teaching strategies have occurred. This is especially true for drug prevention programs. It is important, however, to learn from past mistakes and to understand why some drug prevention strategies were and still are unsuccessful. By consistently incorporating successful drug prevention strategies in our schools and communities, we will likely see a decrease in rates of drug use by our students.

In the 1960s, when there was a tremendous increase in drug usage, many teachers used *scare tactics* to try to deter their students from using drugs.[18] For instance, they would teach their classes that if the students took LSD, they would experience a "bad trip" and either jump off a building or feel as though spiders were crawling all over them. Although this technique might scare some students at first, it took only one student in the class to have a brother or sister who experienced a "good" LSD trip to make that teacher lose all credibility. Other inquisitive students may have read credible information on LSD and learned that "bad trips" did not always occur. Other teachers tried to scare their students by telling them they would become "hooked on drugs" after the first time they used them, or that if they were drinking and driving, they would be involved in an accident. It is important for teachers to be truthful to students so that they remain credible. Once teachers lose their credibility, students become skeptical of anything the teacher says. Another problem with scare tactics is that they tend to have short-lived outcomes. In other words, the effects of scare tactics may last for a few weeks, but then students return to their prior belief system.

In the early 1970s, a very popular component of a drug prevention program was to invite recovering addicts to class and let them discuss the problems they experienced with their addiction. Although this technique is still commonly used and may sound effective, many times students internalize different messages than those intended by the speaker. The intended message from the recovering addicts was not to get involved with drugs. Some students, however, concluded that "If I do get involved with drugs, I can get off of them just like the speaker did." Another misinterpretation was, "I am stronger than the speaker, and I won't get hooked on drugs."[19] Yet another problem with this strategy is that if the recovering addicts were significantly older than the students, they had a difficult time relating the intended message. Many athletes, actors, actresses, and rock stars who are recovering addicts also are used for antidrug commercials. These commercials give students the message that if they use drugs and quit, they can recapture their original goals or become popular.

Later in the 1970s, many health professionals started using a different strategy for drug prevention. They believed that if the students were taught all of the facts about drugs, they would certainly choose not to try them or use them. These programs did increase knowledge about drugs; however, behavior was unaffected.[20] Individuals do not decide how to behave based on information alone, but based on their feelings, values, beliefs, and skills. Even adults do not make decisions based on information alone, even though information is reinforced by law. This is shown by the number of adults who are involved in drinking and driving incidents and who do not wear seat belts. Information is the foundation for health enhancing decisions, but other topics need to be included in effective drug prevention programs.

Another popular initiative is the "Just Say No" television campaign. The "Just Say No" public service announcement campaign is not developmentally appropriate for many upper-elementary and middle-level students and is an ineffective way to deal with the drug problem in our country. In these public service announcements, children and adolescents are told to "Just say no," but are not told how or why to say no to drugs. There are, however, "Just Say No" clubs in many school systems that have components of effective substance abuse prevention programs. They encourage students to say no to drug use and allow students to practice getting out of negative peer-pressure situations by using various peer-resistance techniques. In addition, "Just Say No" clubs provide students with a needed, positive alternative way of meeting and making friends, and provide social support for kids who do not use drugs.

Another popular, though unsuccessful, program that is unfortunately still being used today is the "one-shot approach." In this model, schools organize a school-wide assembly in which an expert addresses all students about the dangers of drugs and the wisdom of abstinence. Drug use, abuse, and refusing drugs, for that matter, are very complex behaviors. Therefore, even the most entertaining or spectacular program cannot begin to have an impact on the use of tobacco, alcohol, and other drugs.[21]

The substance abuse prevention methods of the 1960s and 1970s were unsuccessful because they did not focus on the causes of drug use and abuse. Unfortunately, many teachers are still using these outdated methods. Every profession makes mistakes, but the key is to learn from those mistakes and make the necessary changes to be successful.

Risk Factors for Alcohol and Other Drug Use

Factors that are associated with greater potential for drug use are called *risk factors*. Before school districts can decide on their alcohol and other drug prevention program or curriculum, they first must understand the risk factors associated with alcohol and other drug use.

These risk factors should be interpreted like risk factors for heart disease. That is, if a child or family has one of these risk factors, the child's chance of developing a problem with alcohol or other drug use increases. However, having one of these risk factors does not guarantee that a child will become a drug abuser; only the risk is increased. The fourteen identified risk factors can be categorized into community, family, school, and individual/peer risk factors.[22,23] Teachers should pay special attention to the school and the individual/peer risk factors.

School Risk Factors

Early Antisocial Behavior and Hyperactivity A consistent relationship has been found between adolescent drug abuse and male aggressiveness in kindergarten through second grade. The risk is especially significant when this aggressiveness is coupled with shyness and withdrawal. Hyperactivity, nervousness, inattentiveness, and impulsiveness are also characteristics of early antisocial behavior. Whatever the cause for the antisocial behavior and hyperactivity, students who exhibit these behaviors have an increased risk of abusing drugs as they get older.

Academic Failure There is an increased risk for adolescent drug abuse when a child receives low or failing grades in fourth, fifth, and sixth grades. Poor school performance increases the likelihood of an early start of substance use as well as an increase in subsequent use. Academic failure can have many causes, including lack of parental support, boredom, learning disability, or a poor match between student and teacher. Whatever the cause, those children who have poor school performance are more likely to turn to drugs than those students who succeed in school.

Little Commitment to School Students who are not committed to education are more likely to engage in drug use. Regardless of the reason, students in grades 4 through 7 who lose interest in school have a greater risk of getting into trouble with drugs. By way of confirmation, students who expect to attend college have significantly lower usage rates of "strong" drugs such as cocaine, stimulants, and hallucinogens.

Ambiguous, Lax, or Inconsistent Rules and Sanctions Regarding Drug Use and Student Conduct Ambiguous messages in the school climate concerning alcohol and other drug use increase the risk of use by students.

Individual/Peer Risk Factors

Alienation, Rebelliousness, Lack of Social Bonding In middle or junior high school, students who do not adhere to the dominant values of society and who have a low religious affiliation tend to be at higher risk for drug abuse than students who are bonded to societal institutions of family, school, and church. In addition, students who rebel against authority, particularly parents and school officials, are also at increased risk for substance abuse.

Antisocial Behavior in Early Adolescence This risk factor includes a wide variety of antisocial behaviors, including school misbehavior and a low sense of social responsibility. Fighting, skipping school, and general aggressiveness have been shown to be related to drug abuse. A consistent pattern of inappropriate classroom behaviors, including "acting-out" behaviors, are related to increased abuse of alcohol and other drugs.

Friends Who Use Drugs Association with drug-using friends during adolescence is among the strongest predictors of adolescent drug use. Associating with friends who are involved in drug use operates independently of other risk factors. The evidence is clear that friends, rather than strangers, influence children to experiment with and continue to use drugs. This means that even children who grow up without other risk factors, but who associate with children who use drugs, are at an increased risk for drug use and/or abuse.

Favorable Attitudes Toward Drug Use Specific favorable attitudes toward drug use is a risk factor for initiation of use. Having negative attitudes toward the use of alcohol or other drugs inhibits initiation. When children are in elementary school, they may carry strong, adult-supported feelings against drugs, but by the time they reach middle school, many have developed more favorable attitudes. This shift in attitude often comes just before children begin to experiment with tobacco, alcohol, and other drugs.

Early First Use of Drugs Abusers of alcohol and other drugs tend to begin drinking at an early age. Generally, students begin using "gateway" drugs (tobacco and alcohol), and then progress to other illegal drugs. Early initiation into drug use increases the risk of extensive and persistent involvement in the use of other dangerous drugs. Children who begin to use tobacco, alcohol, or other drugs before age 15 are twice as likely to develop problems with drugs as are children who wait until they are older. Delaying first use until children are age 19 or older dramatically decreases the risk for subsequent abuse.

Family Risk Factors

Family History of Alcoholism Well-documented research continues to demonstrate a link between family drinking problems and adolescent alcohol and other drug abuse. Boys, in particular, have a high risk of abusing alcohol when they have alcoholic fathers. Alcoholics are more likely to have a history of parental or sibling alcoholism. In fact, 50% of today's alcoholics are the children of alcoholics.

Family Management Problems Family management problems have been a consistent predictor of adolescent alcohol and other drug abuse. These problems include poorly defined rules for behavior, poor monitoring of children's behavior, inconsistent consequences for breaking rules, excessively severe discipline, negative communication patterns including constant criticism, and absence of praise. In order to make good decisions about their own behavior, children need to be given clear guidelines for acceptable and unacceptable behavior by their families. They need to be taught basic skills, and they need to be provided with consistent support and recognition for acceptable behaviors as well as consistent, but appropriate, punishment for unacceptable behaviors.

Parental Drug Use and Positive Attitudes Toward Use Research not only confirms that child behaviors are related to family alcohol addiction, but that there is an increased risk that children will initiate drug use when their parents are users of alcohol and other drugs. If the parents involve their children in drug use, such as asking them to get a beer from the refrigerator, to light their cigarette, or to mix them a drink, the likelihood that the children will use drugs increases.

Ambiguous, Lax, or Inconsistent Rules and Sanctions Regarding Alcohol and Other Drug Use Ambiguous messages in the family concerning alcohol and other drug use increases the risk of use by students.

Low Expectations of a Child's Success Children whose parents have low expectations for them have a greater chance of drug use. It is important for parents to have high and realistic expectations for their children.

Community Risk Factors

Economic and Social Deprivation Children from families who experience social isolation, extreme poverty, and poor living conditions are at elevated risk of delinquency. When poverty is extreme and accompanies childhood behavior problems, there is an increased risk for drug problems and alcoholism.

Transitions and Mobility Transitions, such as residential moves and the move from elementary to middle school, are associated with increased rates of drug use and abuse. This is important for teachers who teach in transitional grades. For example, if a middle school begins at grade 5, fifth grade teachers should focus more attention on drug abuse prevention. In addition, if a new child enters a class during the middle of the year, teachers should make sure that he or she has positive support from classmates.

Community Laws and Norms Favorable Toward Drug Use Communities with laws that are favorable to drug use, such as low taxes on alcohol, have higher rates of alcohol consumption and alcohol-related traffic fatalities. In addition, the availability of tobacco, alcohol, and other drugs is associated with higher rates of use. Greater availability of drugs in schools, combined with inadequate policies against alcohol and other drug use, leads to a higher use of drugs among students.

Components of a Comprehensive Drug Prevention Program

When developing a successful drug prevention program, it is necessary to direct specific activities at preventing risk factors for child and adolescent drug abuse. Successful drug prevention programs must contain the following three components: (1) school, (2) family, and (3) community. Within each of these components, specific elements need to be included to help increase the chance of success.

The following three protective, or resiliency, factors also are essential to include throughout each of the components: caring and supportive relationships; high expectations for appropriate choices and behaviors; and the availability of a variety of opportunities to participate and contribute in meaningful ways. Although elementary and middle-level teachers will be most interested in the elements of the school component, it is important to understand the comprehensive approach that is needed when trying to prevent alcohol and other drug use.[24,25] As you read the following elements for each component, try to think of specific examples of how elementary and middle-level schools and teachers could incorporate these elements into their teaching.

Education

A K–12 comprehensive drug prevention curriculum should contain the following components (see the next section for a list of effective commercial drug prevention curricula):

- Personal and social skills training (peer resistance, decision making, etc.),
- Changes in the perception of social norms (students need to be taught that the majority of elementary and middle-level students do not use alcohol and other drugs),

A mother and son work on a drug prevention homework assignment together.

- Focus on short-term effects of drug use,
- Homework assignments with parents,
- Promotion of positive peer influence,
- Adequate time—It is best to incorporate drug prevention into every grade level. However, if this is not possible programs must cover necessary prevention elements in at least ten sessions a year with a minimum of three to five booster sessions in two succeeding years. It is best to focus on late elementary and middle-level years. Educators should know that research has shown that youth who have been exposed to more drug prevention in elementary, middle-school, and high school have lower rates of drug involvement.[26]
- Interactive teaching activities (role-play, cooperative learning, etc.),
- Lessons that are developmentally appropriate (see the Developmentally Appropriate Concepts section),
- Curriculum that contains materials that are easy for teachers to implement and are culturally relevant for students,
- Staff development in drug prevention so that teachers are skilled at teaching in this content area,
- A clear no-use policy for all students with consistent consequences when broken (see table 9.4 for minimum elements for a school drug policy),
- Academic achievement programs that are available to all students so they have a better chance at succeeding in school,
- New student transition programs to help students entering a new school feel connected to other students and teachers,
- Drug-free alternatives and activities for students (clubs, intramural sports, after-school enrichment programs, etc),
- Encouragment of student participation in community service projects (cleaning up parks, adopting a family, adopting a grandparent, etc.),

TABLE 9.4	Minimum Elements for a School Drug Policy Statement

A school's policy statement ought to contain at least the following elements:

A clear definition, based on state law, of what types of drugs and drug use are covered by the policy (making clear, for example, that prescribed medication is not covered, but that drinking alcohol is).

A clear statement that the defined drugs and drug use are prohibited on school grounds, at school-sponsored functions, and while students are representing the school.

A description of the consequences to be expected upon violating the policy.

Explanation of the process for referral to treatment—with a guarantee that self-referral will be treated in confidence, and will not result in punishment.

Source: *Drug Prevention Curricula: A Guide to Selection and Implementation*, U.S. Department of Education, 1988.

- Intervention programs for students who have used alcohol and other drugs. Table 9.5 describes signs and symptoms of drug use. Teachers should be aware of these signs and symptoms so they know when to refer students to their school counselor.

Family
- Parents should set clear rules and follow consistent consequences regarding alcohol and other drug use. Research has shown that the more parents talk to their children about their expectations regarding alcohol and other drug use, the less likely they will become involved with drugs.
- Parents should create open lines of communication with their children.
- Parents should spend quality time with their children (e.g., eating meals together, helping with homework, reading books together, etc.).
- New parents should attend parenting classes to learn how to raise their children in a caring and nurturing environment.
- Parents should encourage shared family responsibility.
- Parents should encourage religious affiliation. Children who attend church on a regular basis are at lower risk for alcohol and other drug use.
- Families should participate in rituals and traditions.
- Parents should express clear and challenging expectations for their children.

Community
- Communities should establish a drug prevention task force. This task force should be charged with overseeing all community-based drug prevention efforts.

TABLE 9.5	**Signs of Drug Use**

Changing patterns of performance, appearance, and behavior may signal use of drugs. The items in the first category listed below provide direct evidence of drug use; the items in the other categories may indicate drug use. Adults should watch for extreme changes in children's behavior, changes that together form a pattern associated with drug use.

Signs of Drugs and Drug Paraphernalia

Possession of drug-related paraphernalia such as pipes, rolling papers, small decongestant bottles, eye drops, or small butane torches.

Possession of drugs or evidence of drugs, such as pills, white powder, small glass vials, or hypodermic needles; peculiar plants or butts, seeds, or leaves in ashtrays or in clothing pockets.

Odor of drugs, smell of incense or other "cover-up" scents.

Identification with Drug Culture

Drug-related magazines, slogans on clothing.

Conversation and jokes that are preoccupied with drugs.

Hostility in discussing drugs.

Collection of beer cans.

Signs of Physical Deterioration

Memory lapses, short attention span, difficulty in concentration.

Poor physical coordination, slurred or incoherent speech.

Unhealthy appearance, indifference to hygiene and grooming.

Bloodshot eyes, dilated pupils.

Dramatic Changes in School Performance

Marked downturn in student's grades—not just from Cs to Fs, but from As to Bs and Cs; assignments not completed. Increased absenteeism or tardiness.

Changes in Behavior

Chronic dishonesty (lying, stealing, cheating); trouble with the police.

Changes in friends, evasiveness in talking about new ones.

Possession of large amounts of money.

Increasing and inappropriate anger, hostility, irritability, secretiveness.

Reduced motivation, energy, self-discipline, self-esteem.

Diminished interest in extracurricular activities and hobbies.

- Communities should provide drug-free alternatives and activities for youth (Boys and Girls clubs, recreation programs, latch-key programs, etc.).
- Youth should be encouraged to volunteer and participate in community service projects.
- Communities should work with the media to provide public service announcements on the dangers of the use of alcohol and other drugs.
- Communities should work on making access to alcohol and other drugs difficult.

Commercial Drug Prevention Curricula

There are several existing commercial alcohol and drug prevention programs available to school districts. These curricula should complement, not replace, a comprehensive school health education curriculum. Some of these curricula have been evaluated and have been shown to be effective in reducing the number of students who use alcohol and other drugs, or at reducing the number of students who intend to use alcohol and other drugs. This section provides a description of only those effective elementary and middle-level programs and a summary of the evaluation results.[27,28,29]

Life Skills Training

The Life Skills Training curriculum focuses on resistance skills training within the context of broader personal and social skills. There are fifteen core sessions in sixth or seventh grade with eight to ten booster sessions in the following two grades. The program focuses primarily on tobacco, alcohol, and marijuana, and uses interactive activities to teach the skills and content. It has more published evaluations than any other curriculum.

The evaluations of the program showed a reduction in smoking, alcohol, and marijuana use by 50–75% at the end of seventh grade. By the end of high school, the results slightly eroded to a 44% reduction in tobacco, alcohol, or marijuana use and a 66% reduction in all three.

Alcohol Misuse Prevention Project

The Alcohol Misuse Prevention Project is a curriculum for grades 6–8 that focuses on alcohol use prevention. This program includes normative education and influences and refusal skills. It also has a parent component involving homework. The curriculum has eight sessions in sixth grade, five sessions in seventh grade, and four sessions in eighth grade. Interactive activities such as role-plays are used throughout the curriculum.

The evaluation of this program showed that it reduced the misuse of alcohol in high-risk students 2 years after the completion of the program.

Project Northland

Project Northland is a curriculum for grades 6–8 that focuses on alcohol use and abuse. This program has eight sessions a year, and emphasizes resistance skills and decision making. The whole program sets the norm that it is not cool to drink. The curriculum presents many opportunities for role-plays. In addition, the sixth grade curriculum includes many family take-home assignments.

The evaluation of this program showed a reduction in tobacco and alcohol use by 27% and a reduction in marijuana use by 50% 3 years after the completion of the program.

Students Taught Awareness and Resistance (STAR)

The STAR curriculum is written for students in grades 5–8. It is a 2-year program with ten to thirteen sessions the first year and five sessions the second year. This program focuses primarily on the development of resistance skills, the short-term effects of drug use, and normative education. Role-plays and other interactive techniques are used.

The evaluation of this program showed a reduction of tobacco, alcohol, and marijuana use by 30% 3 years after the completion of the program.

Project Alert

The Project Alert curriculum is a 2-year curriculum for grades 6–8 that covers information on alcohol, tobacco, and other drugs. It has eleven sessions the first year and three sessions the second year. This program emphasizes the development of resistance skills (both perceived or internal pressure and overt peer pressure) and normative education.

The evaluation of this program showed a reduction in drinking up to 50% at post-test. It also reduced marijuana use 33–60% in eighth grade; this evaluation was made only 15 months after the administration of the curriculum. No longer term evaluation has been conducted.

Social Competence Promoting Program for Young Adolescents

This thirty-six-session curriculum is for students in grades 5, 6, or 7. It teaches a strong, interpersonal, cognitive, problem-solving model and has additional sessions on drug abuse prevention.

This curriculum has a weak evaluation that showed a reduction of heavy alcohol use immediately after the completion of the curriculum. No long-term evaluation has been conducted.

Drug Abuse Resistance Education (DARE)

This curriculum is included in this section because 10% of the Drug-Free Schools and Communities Act money is allocated for the DARE program. DARE curriculum is available for students in grades K–12, and is taught by a uniformed police officer. There are seventeen core lessons in fifth or sixth grade, ten lessons in middle school, and nine lessons in high school. The lessons cover important prevention elements, including skill development.

Numerous studies conducted on this curriculum have yielded inconsistent findings. In addition, the evaluations that have been conducted have not been over the long term.

Developmentally Appropriate Practice Recommendations

It is often difficult for teachers, administrators, and parents to know what is developmentally appropriate for children and preadolescents in the area of alcohol and other drugs. Following is a list of concepts that elementary and middle-level students should understand about substance abuse.[30,31,32]

Early Elementary (K–2)

Drug prevention lessons and activities at this age should:

- Keep information simple and direct;
- Focus on life skills, such as decision making and problem solving;
- Not glamorize or instill inappropriate fear about drugs;
- Emphasize that most people do not use drugs;
- Emphasize the development of responsibility for self and others;
- Encourage the development of self-confidence; and
- Emphasize information and skill development over evaluation and testing.

Specific objectives that should be achieved by the end of second grade include the following:

- Describe the differences among foods, poisons, medicines, and illicit drugs.
- Explain that some medicines may help during illness, when prescribed by a doctor and administered by a parent, nurse, or other responsible adult, but that medicines are drugs that can be harmful if misused.

- Demonstrate how to avoid unknown and possibly dangerous objects, containers, and substances.
- Be aware that people can become dependent on alcohol, tobacco, and other drugs, but there are ways to help them.
- Explain that each individual is ultimately responsible for his or her own health and well-being, and that, for young children, this is a shared parent/child responsibility.
- Tell which adults, in school and out, are responsible persons to whom one may go to ask questions or to seek help.
- Explain what the school and home rules are regarding drug use.
- Describe why rules exist and why people should respect them.
- Explain that each individual is unique and valued.
- Describe how one's actions affect others.
- Demonstrate how to avoid strangers.
- Say no to things that one has been taught are wrong, and know how to do this.
- Explain one's responsibility to tell appropriate adults about strangers, about unknown things or substances, and problems.

Upper Elementary (3–5)
Drug prevention lessons and activities at this age should:

- Focus on the drugs children are apt to use first—tobacco, alcohol, inhalants, and marijuana;
- Encourage open and frank discussions of concerns about drugs and drug use;
- Not glamorize drug use through accepting the drug-using behavior of some heroes such as musicians, actors, or athletes;
- Emphasize that most people, including the majority of people their own age, do not use drugs;
- Emphasize the development of personal and civic responsibility; and
- Emphasize the development of health leisure activities, such as sports, music, art, clubs, and volunteering.

Specific objectives that should be achieved by the end of fifth grade include the following:
- Realize that growing up is a great adventure, one best enjoyed through safe, healthy, positive, and drug-free habits and attitudes.
- Explain what drugs are, with specific reference to alcohol, tobacco, marijuana, cocaine, and inhalants.
- Develop a sense of responsibility toward younger children, beginning with siblings.
- Explain what the school and home rules are regarding drug use.
- Explain how drugs affect different parts of the body, and why drugs are especially dangerous for growing bodies and minds.

- Explain that alcohol, tobacco, and other drugs are illegal, either for minors or all persons, and that they are against school rules.
- Demonstrate how to recognize and respond to both direct and indirect social influences and pressure to use alcohol, tobacco, or other drugs.
- Explain that some social influences such as the media, peer pressure, family influences, and the community sometimes promote drug use.
- Describe how to get help or talk over questions and problems while in school.
- Explain that most people, including the majority of people their own age, do not use drugs.
- Describe the potential risk of choosing friends who use drugs.
- Demonstrate ways to encourage friends not to use drugs.

Middle Level (6–8)
Drug prevention lessons and activities at this age should:

- Encourage frank discussions about concerns related to drugs and drug use;
- Focus on life skills such as problem solving, resisting peer pressure, developing healthy friendships, coping with stress, and communicating with adults;
- Not glamorize drug use through the acceptance of drug-using behavior by some heroes such as musicians, actors, and athletes;
- Emphasize that most people, including the majority of people their own age, do not use drugs;
- Emphasize the development of personal and civic responsibility;
- Emphasize the development of self-esteem;
- Emphasize the development of health leisure activities, such as sports, music, art, clubs, and volunteering;
- Emphasize the establishment of positive life goals, such as continuing education and developing work skills that will permit a legal income source; and
- Emphasize the law and its consequences.

Specific objectives that should be achieved by the end of eighth grade include the following:
- Explain how to identify specific drugs, such as alcohol, tobacco, marijuana, cocaine, inhalants, hallucinogens, and stimulants in their various forms.
- Describe how and why the effects of drugs may vary from person to person, especially immediately after use.
- Explain that some social influences such as the media, peer pressure, family influences, and the community sometimes promote drug use.
- Describe what addiction is, and how it can affect the sufferer and others, such as family members.

(continued after Activities on page 171)

ACTIVITIES

Alcohol and Other Drug Prevention Activities

S everal activities can be conducted with elementary and middle-level students to give them a better understanding of the many topics included in alcohol and other drug prevention education. A sampling of activities that instruct in the areas of knowledge, attitudes, and skills at the K–2, 3–5, and 6–8 grade levels follows.

Grades K–2

1. *Storage of Medication.* Ask students to draw a large picture of places where it is safe and appropriate to store medicines. Encourage them to include medicine-taking rules on their picture.

2. *Safe and Unsafe Products.* Explain to students that some household items are safe and some are unsafe. Ask students to name some unsafe items (bleach, gasoline, pills from a medicine cabinet, etc.). Next, provide pictures or empty containers of safe and unsafe items, and two large boxes: Label one box "safe" and the other "unsafe." Have each child take a picture or an object and place it in either the safe or unsafe box.

3. *Poison-Proof Your Home.* Figure 9.3 is a homework assignment that can be sent home for parents and children to do together. This activity will help families reinforce medicine and product safety at home.

NAME_____ DATE_____

Note to Parents

Dear Parent or Guardian,

Today in my class we learned about SAFE things and UNSAFE things. I have several "SAFE" and "UNSAFE" labels for us to properly label various substances in our home. I also have a checklist to help us keep our home safe.

Please help me complete the checklist and sign this form so I can return them both to school tomorrow.

Thank you very much.

_____
signature of parent or guardian

WE'RE PUSHING FOR A DRUG-FREE STATE
TEXAS EDUCATION AGENCY

Figure 9.3

A homework assignment to be done by parents and children together to teach medicine and product safety.

NAME _____ DATE _____

Poison Proof Your Home

With your parents' help, check your house for unsafe areas.

☐ Keep drugs, poisons, and other dangerous substances (such as paint, charcoal lighter fluid, gasoline, and cleaning supplies) out of reach of children and pets. If possible, store these items in locked cabinets.

☐ Read all labels carefully.

☐ Clearly label all poisonous substances.

☐ Store poisonous substances away from food or food containers.

☐ Protect utensils and food when spraying chemicals such as bug spray and cleaning solutions.

☐ Date all drug supplies when you buy them.

☐ Keep medicines in original labeled bottles; do not transfer them into unlabeled bottles.

☐ Clean out the medicine cabinet regularly to remove outdated medicines and prescriptions.

☐ When you throw away drugs and medicines, flush them down the toilet or discard them in containers that cannot be reached by children or pets.

☐ Keep a poison control kit in the house in case an accidental poisoning happens.

☐ Make sure that all family members know what to do in case of a poisoning emergency.

WE'RE PUSHING FOR A DRUG-FREE STATE
TEXAS EDUCATION AGENCY

Figure 9.3 *(continued)*

4. *Things That Help Me Grow.* Ask students to look through magazines for pictures of products that are healthful and products that are harmful. Ask them to divide a piece of paper in half, labeling one side as healthful and the other side as harmful. Ask them to glue their pictures on the appropriate side of the paper. Give students an opportunity to share their pictures while you give feedback. Students will probably cut out pictures of tobacco and alcohol advertisements to glue on their harmful side.

Grades 3–5

1. *Analyzing Alcohol Advertising.* As with tobacco advertising, it is important to analyze alcohol advertisements. Although the alcohol industry claims that it does not try to make its advertisements appeal to young people, adolescent boys seem to disagree. A group of adolescent boys were asked which commercials on television they enjoyed and remembered the most. The majority of them responded that beer commercials were their favorite, and many of them could correctly imitate the beer commercials. A *Weekly Reader* survey found that television and movies had the greatest influence on fourth through sixth graders in making drugs and alcohol seem attractive.[33] The average American

teenager watches 24,000 hours of television by the time of high school graduation—double the amount of time spent in the classroom. Much of what is watched on television is commercials, and many of those are beer commercials. Students need to be aware of the different ways that advertisers try to get them to buy their products.

Version 1 Ask students to watch television for 1 hour, count the number of beer commercials they see, and write down the theme of the commercials. The next day, ask students to identify the techniques that were used in the commercials to try to get them to buy the product. Continue the discussion by asking the students to identify unrealistic claims that were made in the commercials, and to explain how they could change the commercials to make them more truthful.

Version 2 Ask students to bring in magazine advertisements for alcoholic products. Again, discuss the techniques used to try to get them to buy the product. Ask why the advertisements might be appealing to young people. Next, ask the students to make their own advertisements that better depict the outcomes of drinking alcohol. For example, students might show a drinking and driving accident instead of a party scene.

Version 3 Ask students to make video commercials that depict the negative side effects of alcohol. This will allow students to apply the information that they have learned about the short- and long-term effects of alcohol use/abuse. Students can use rap music, skits, singing, or any other method they are comfortable with.

2. *Interviewing an Adult.* It is important for young people to know how the important adults in their lives would feel if they started drinking alcohol. Ask students to go home and interview a parent or guardian about drinking alcohol. Include the following questions on a worksheet for the interview:
   - How would you feel if I started drinking alcohol?
   - What are our family rules and consequences about drinking alcohol?
   - What advice can you give me about how to deal with the pressure to drink alcohol?

3. *Short-term Effects of Alcohol Use.* Ask students to write in their journal some things they like to do (e.g., play sports, draw, play a musical instrument, etc.). Next, ask for a volunteer to come to the front of the room and ask him or her to try to walk a straight line. Place a 15-foot piece of masking tape on the floor to help guide the student. Next, spin the student around several times and then ask him or her to try to walk a straight line again. Because of balance difficulties, the student will not be able to succeed at this task. Explain to students that one of the short-term effects of alcohol use is the loss of balance. Ask them to write in their journal how alcohol use would affect the things they like to do.

Two students work together to create a poster illustrating a drug-free message.

4. Have students work in partners to design posters that effectively illustrate a drug-free message. Encourage students to create posters depicting:
   - Healthy alternatives to drug use, and
   - Consequences of illegal drug use.

Grades 6–8

1. *Breaking a Habit.* As a long-term project to help students understand how difficult it is to change a behavior, such as drinking alcohol, ask them to change a habit. Although it is much more difficult for an alcoholic to stop drinking alcohol than it is for students to stop biting their fingernails, the students will at least begin to understand that it is better to prevent a negative behavior than to try to change it once it has begun.

2. *Cost of Drinking.* Ask students to figure out how much it costs to support a drinking habit for a week, a month, and a year. Also, ask what they would do with the money they save from not drinking.

3. *Locating Community Support Systems.* Although this is an intervention strategy, it is still an important skill for students. Bring in several local telephone directories. Place students in small groups and ask them to look through their directory to locate agencies that could help them if they or a family member had a drug or alcohol problem. Examples might include Alcoholics Anonymous, Alateen, or an alcohol hotline.

4. *The Law and Alcohol.* Invite a police officer to class to discuss the laws related to alcohol use. Discuss laws such as drinking alcohol under the legal age or using fake identification. This is especially valuable for middle-level students.

5. *Current Events.* Ask the class to bring in newspaper articles that are alcohol related. Over a 2-week period, students will find articles related to accidents involving alcohol and some of the negative side effects of alcohol.

6. *Social Norms.* Middle-level students like to feel they are part of the "in" crowd, so if they believe everyone is drinking alcohol, they will be more inclined to want to drink. Youth tend to grossly overestimate the prevalence and acceptability of alcohol use among their peers. It is important to help upper-elementary and middle-level students understand how many people their age do actually drink alcohol.

   - To do this, ask students to anonymously write down on a piece of paper whether they currently drink alcohol. (If teachers feel uncomfortable asking their students about personal behaviors, they can use local or state statistics.)
   - Next, ask the students to write down the percentage of students in class that they think currently drink alcohol. In most cases, students will write down a much higher percentage than the actual percentage of alcohol users in the class. Discuss why students overestimate the number of people their age who drink.

7. *Short-term Effects of Alcohol Use.* Before starting this activity, obtain some old eyeglasses or sunglasses. Smear vasoline over both lenses. Next, ask students to write down things they enjoy doing. Ask several volunteers to try to pour a glass of water from a pitcher. This should be easy for them to perform. Next, have the students put on the glasses and then try to perform the pouring task again. This will be very difficult because their vision will be distorted. Explain that drinking alcohol affects a person's vision. Instruct students to write down how drinking alcohol would affect the things they like to do.

8. *Refusal Skills.* See chapter 6 for peer-resistance skill activities.

9. *Carousel Activity.* (See chapter 5.) Divide the students into five groups. The newsprint headers for the carousel activity should be social, family, education, financial, emotional. In groups, ask students to brainstorm negative consequences that might occur if they were caught drinking alcohol or smoking marijuana.

- Explain that there are specific people and institutions available to help people resist negative influences and to assist those in trouble, and how to contact them.
- Explain that breaking rules and laws about substance abuse can have serious consequences.
- Explain that it is important to get help as soon as possible for anyone who has a substance abuse problem.
- Identify how to recognize and respond to both direct and indirect social influences and pressure to use alcohol, tobacco, or other drugs.
- Demonstrate how to use refusal skills.
- Explain that most people, including the majority of people their own age, do not use drugs.
- Explain the short-term and some long-term effects of commonly used drugs.
- Explain how using drugs affects activities that require motor coordination, such as playing sports or a musical instrument.
- Explain how media pressures and advertising influence young people to use alcohol and other drugs.

SUMMARY

Because the United States has the highest teenage drug abuse problem in the industrialized world, there is a definite need for drug prevention programs in our schools and communities. Although a variety of unsuccessful drug prevention programs have been used in the past, successful programs are currently being used by schools and communities. Components of these successful school and community programs include providing drug information, and teaching personal and social skills, alternatives, intervention, and discipline to students.

Teachers need to present information and activities about tobacco, alcohol, and other drugs to students. Because tobacco and alcohol are gateway drugs, they need to be emphasized in the elementary and middle-level curriculum. One of the more popular types of tobacco among young people, especially males, is smokeless tobacco. Although many persons believe smokeless tobacco is not dangerous, its negative side effects include nicotine addiction, oral cancer, and gum and teeth problems. Cigarette smoking is also common among adolescents and is the number one preventable cause of premature death in the United States. The short-term side effects of smoking, which include increased heart rate, blood pressure, and carbon monoxide levels, and decreased skin temperature and hand steadiness, should be stressed to elementary students. Long-term side effects of cigarette use include cancer, cardiovascular disease, chronic obstructive lung disease, and aesthetic consequences. While there are numerous tobacco prevention activities that can be used in the elementary classroom, teachers should focus on using real-life, relevant activities.

Like tobacco, alcohol has acute effects on the body. Because young people weigh less and have little experience with alcohol, their judgment, vision, coordination, and speech can be altered with a small amount of alcohol. Other short-term side effects of alcohol use include impaired perception and motor skills, increased heart rate and blood pressure, tiredness, unpre-

dictable emotions, and hangovers. Long-term use of alcohol can result in cirrhosis of the liver, gastrointestinal system disorders, cancer, malnutrition, hypoglycemia, cardiovascular disease, and alcoholism. Families with an alcoholic family member often become dysfunctional. Children of dysfunctional families assume certain survival roles. Teachers should be familiar with the characteristics of these roles, which include the family hero, the scapegoat, the mascot, and the lost child. There are numerous alcohol prevention activities for use in the classroom. Just like tobacco prevention activities, alcohol prevention activities should focus on real-life concepts that elementary and middle-level students can relate to.

Adolescents use numerous other drugs: marijuana, cocaine and crack, other stimulants, and inhalants. It is not necessary for elementary and middle-level students to memorize drug charts or for teachers to provide too much information about some of the other drugs. Elementary students should be given information about some of the more common drugs used in their communities, but teachers should remember that drug prevention does not work by just providing drug information to students.

Social and personal skills are also important in drug prevention programs (see chapter 6). Two of the most important are peer-resistance skills and decision-making skills. When teaching these skills to students, teachers should allow students to use personal situations, should demonstrate proper use of the skills, and should allow time to practice the skills.

Drug prevention programs should be in place at every grade level and at every school. Pressure to use drugs has not only increased, but it is now more evident in lower grades. Elementary teachers have a tremendous opportunity and responsibility to impact the drug problem in the United States. Some school systems have adopted commercial drug prevention programs, but if they have not, teachers can still provide information and skills to students to help impact the drug problem.

DISCUSSION QUESTIONS

1. What are some of the unsuccessful drug prevention strategies that have been used in the past?

2. What are the five components of drug prevention programs? Who is responsible for each component? Why is each component important?

3. What are some of the negative side effects of using smokeless tobacco?

4. What are some of the negative side effects of smoking cigarettes?

5. Describe three tobacco prevention activities that are real and relevant.

6. Describe the concept of gateway drugs.

7. Why is it important to try to prevent elementary-age children from using alcohol and tobacco?

8. Describe the process of how alcohol travels through the body.

9. List and explain the factors related to absorption of alcohol into the bloodstream.

10. What are some of the short-term side effects of alcohol use?

11. What are some of the side effects from extended alcohol use?

12. List and explain the characteristics of the survival roles assumed by children from dysfunctional families.

13. What are some alcohol prevention activities that can be used in the classroom?

14. How has drug use affected your community?

15. What are some of the short- and long-term side effects of using some of the more common drugs such as marijuana and cocaine?

16. Why social and personal skills are important to include in a drug prevention program?

17. Describe some of the commercial drug prevention programs available to schools. What are some of the similarities and differences between the programs?

18. Describe a child who is at high risk for drug abuse. What are some steps that teachers can take to help assure that a high-risk student will not abuse drugs?

19. Describe the differences in the information, values, and skills about drug prevention that a younger elementary student should know and the information, values, and skills that a middle-level student should know.

ENDNOTES

1. Drug Strategies, *Keeping Score* (Washington, DC: Author, 1997).

2. PRIDE, Inc., "PRIDE Survey Results," www.drugs.indiana.edu/drug_stats/pride97.html, 1998.

3. Drug Strategies, *Keeping Score: We Can Reduce Drug Abuse* (Washington, DC: Drug Strategies, 1997).

4. Ibid.

5. National Education Association, "Goals 2000: Is This the Most Important Federal Education Legislation in a Generation?" *NEA Today* (May 1994).

6. U.S. Department of Health & Human Services, "*Healthy People 2010:* Understanding & Improving Health," web.health.gov/healthy people/Document/HTML/ (January, 2000).

7. G. Hanson and P. Venturelli, *Drugs and Society* (Sudbury, MA: Jones and Bartlett Publishers, 1998).

8. J. Hawkins, J. Grahm, E. Maguin, R. Abbott, K. Hill, and R. Catalano, "Exploring the Effects of Age of Alcohol Use Initiation & Psychosocial Risk Factors on Subsequent Alcohol Misuse," *Journal of Studies on Alcohol* 58, no. 3, 280–290, 1997.

9. P. Insel and T. Roth, *Core Concepts in Health* (Mountain View, CA: Mayfield Publishing Company, 1996).

10. National Center for Health Statistics, *Vital Statistics Mortality Data–1994, Multiple Cause of Death File,* Atlanta, GA: Centers for Disease Control and Prevention, 1996.

11. Hanson and Venturelli, *Drugs and Society.*

12. J. Kinney and G. Leaton, *Loosening the Grip: A Handbook of Alcohol Information* (Chicago, IL: Mosby, 1995).

13. Hales, D. An Invitation to Health (8th ed.), Brooks/Cole Publishing Company, 1999.

14. Ibid.

15. National Institute on Drug Abuse, *NIDA Infofax, Marijuana, 015* (Washington, DC: National Institute of Health, 1998).

16. National Institute on Drug Abuse, *NIDA Infofax, Crack and Cocaine, 011* (Washington, DC: National Institute of Health, 1998).

17. National Institute on Drug Abuse, *NIDA Infofax, Inhalants, 013* (Washington, DC: National Institute of Health, 1998).

18 R. Towers, *How Schools Can Help Combat Student Drug and Alcohol Abuse.* (Washington, DC: National Education Association, 1987).

19. U.S. Department of Education, *Drug Prevention Curricula: A Guide to Selection and Implementation.* (Washington, DC: U.S. Government Printing Office, 1988).

20. R. E. Glasgow and K. D. McCaul, "Life Skills Training Programs for Smoking Prevention: Critique and Directions for Future Research," in *Prevention Research: Deterring Drug Abuse among Children and Adolescents;* C. Bell and R. Battjes, eds. NIDA Research Monograph No. 63, DHHS Publication Number (ADM) 85-1334 (Washington, DC: 1985).

21. M. Goodstadt, "School-Based Drug Education in North America: What is Wrong? What Can be Done?" *Journal of School Health* 56, no. 7 (1986): 278.

22. Hawkins, Catalano, and Miller, "Risk and Protective Factors for Early Alcohol and Other Drug Problems in Adolescence and Early Adulthood," *Journal of Studies on Alcohol* 58, no. 3, 280–290, 1997.

23. S. Gardner, P. Green, and C. Marcus (eds). *Signs of Effectiveness II—Preventing Alcohol, Tobacco, and Other Drug Use: A Risk Factor/Resiliency-Based Approach* (Washington, DC: U.S. Department of Health and Human Services, Substance Abuse and Mental Health Services Administration, 1994).

24. National Institute on Drug Abuse, *Preventing Drug Use Among Children and Adolescents: A Research-Based Guide,* (Washington, DC: U.S. Department of Health and Human Services, 1997).

25. Drug Strategies, *Keeping Score: We Can Reduce Drug Abuse* (Washington, DC: Drug Strategies, 1997).

26. J. Donnermeyer and R. Davis, "Cumulative Effects of Prevention Education on Substance Use Among 11th Grade Students in Ohio," *Journal of School Health,* 68, no. 4, (1998).

27. L. Dusenbury, M. Falco, and A. Lake, A Review of the Evaluation of 47 Drug Abuse Prevention Curricula Available Nationally, *Journal of School Health* 67, no. 4 (1997).

28. A. Evens and K. Bosworth, "Building Effective Drug Education Programs," *Phi Delta Kappa Research Bulletin,* 19, (1997).

29. Drug Strategies, *Making the Grade: A Guide to School Drug Prevention Programs* (Washington, DC: Drug Strategies, 1997).

30. U.S. Department of Education, *Drug Prevention Curricula: A Guide to Selection and Implementation* (Washington DC: Office of Educational Research and Improvement, 1988).

31. U.S. Department of Education, *Learning to Live Drug Free: A Curriculum Model for Prevention* (Washington, DC: U.S. Department of Education, 1992).

32. Texas Education Agency, *Education for Self-Responsibility: Prevention of Drug Use* (Austin, TX: Texas Education Agency, 1992).

33. U.S. Department of Education, *What Works: Schools without Drugs* (Washington, DC: U.S. Government Printing Office, 1989); U.S. Department of Education, *Drug Prevention Curricula.*

SUGGESTED READINGS

The American Council for Drug Education. *Drug-Free Schools and Children: A Primer for School Policymakers.* Rockville, MD: 1990.

American Medical Association. *Healthy Youth 2000: National Health Promotion and Disease Prevention Objectives for Adolescents* Chicago, IL: American Medical Association, 1990.

Botvin G., and E. Botvin. "Adolescent Tobacco, Alcohol, and Drug Abuse: Prevention Strategies, Empirical Findings, and Assessment Issues." *Developmental and Behavioral Pediatrics* 13, no. 4 (1992).

Cecil, N., and P. Roberts. *Developing Resiliency Through Children's Literature: A Guide for Teachers and Librarians K–9.* Jefferson, NC: McFarland and Company, 1992.

Donnermeyer, J., and R. Davis, "Cumulative Effects of Prevention Education on Substance Use Among 11th Grade Students in Ohio." *Journal of School Health* 68, no. 4, (1998).

Dusenbury, L., M. Falco, and A. Lake, "A Review of the Evaluation of 47 Drug Abuse Prevention Curricula Available Nationally." *Journal of School Health* 67, no. 4 (1997).

Drug Strategies. *Making the Grade: A Guide to School Drug Prevention Programs.* Washington, DC: Drug Strategies, 1997.

Drug Strategies. *Keeping Score: We Can Reduce Drug Abuse.* Washington, DC: Drug Strategies, 1997.

Evans, B., and S. Giarratano. *Into Adolescence: Avoiding Drugs.* Santa Cruz, CA: Network Publications, 1990.

Hanson, G., and P. Venturelli. *Drugs and Society,* Sudbury, MA: Jones and Bartlett Publishers, 1998.

Hawkins, J., R. Catalano, and R. Miller. "Risk and Protective Factors for Early Alcohol and Other Drug Problems in Adolescence and Early Adulthood: Implications for Substance Abuse Prevention." *Psychological Bulletin* 112, no. 1 (1992).

Towers, R. *How Schools Can Help Combat Student Drug and Alcohol Abuse.* Washington DC: National Education Association, 1987.

U.S. Department of Education. *Drug Prevention Curricula: A Guide to Selection and Implementation* Washington, DC: U.S. Government Printing Office, 1988.

U.S. Department of Education. *Reaching the Goals: Goal 6— Safe, Disciplined, and Drug-Free Schools.* Washington, DC: U.S. Government Printing Office, 1993.

U.S. Department of Education. *What Works: Schools without Drugs.* Washington, DC: U.S. Government Printing Office, 1989.

U.S. Department of Health and Human Services. *Preventing Tobacco Use Among Young People: A Report of the Surgeon General.* S/N 017-001-00491-0. Washington, DC: U.S. Government Printing Office, 1994.

Villarreal, S., L. McKinney, and M. Quackenbush. *Handle With Care: Helping Children Prenatally Exposed to Drugs and Alcohol.* Santa Cruz, CA: ETR Associates, 1992.

CHILDREN'S LITERATURE WITH AN ALCOHOL AND OTHER DRUG PREVENTION THEME

Grades K–2

Langsen, R. *When Someone in the Family Drinks Too Much.* Penguin, 1996

Thomas, J. *Daddy Doesn't Have to Be a Giant Anymore.* Clarion, 1996.

Grades 3–5

Birdseye, T. *Tucker.* Holiday, 1990

Byars, B. *The Pinballs.* Harper Collins, 1977.

Daly, N. *My Dad.* McElderry, 1995.

Hughes, D. *The Trophy.* Alfred Knopf, 1994.

Vigna, J. *I Wish Daddy Didn't Drink So Much.* Albert Whitman, 1988.

Grades 6–8

Brooks, B. *No Kidding.* Harper Collins, 1989.

Bunting, E. *A Sudden Death.* Harcourt Brace, 1990.

Osborne, M. *Last One Home.* Dial, 1986.

Service, R. *The Shooting of Dan McGrew.* David Godine, 1995.

Taylor, C. *The House That Crack Built.* Chronicle, 1992. (American Bookseller Pick of the Lists; American Library Association Best Books for Young Readers; American Library Association Best Books for Reluctant Readers).

Voigt, C. *Izzy Will Nilly.* Ballantine, 1986.

Wood, J. *A Share of Freedom.* Putman, 1994. (School Library Journal Best Books, 1994).

Zindel, P. *The Pigman.* Harper and Row, 1968.

INTERNET INFORMATION

ALCOHOL AND OTHER DRUG PREVENTION WEBSITES

For additional information on alcohol and other drug prevention, please refer to the following websites.

Indiana Prevention Resource Center
www.drugs.indiana.edu/

The National Clearinghouse for Alcohol and Drug Information
www.health.org/index.htm

National Institute on Drug Abuse
www.nida.nih.gov/

National Institute on Alcohol Abuse and Alcoholism
www.niaaa.nih.gov/

10

TOBACCO

OUTLINE

INTRODUCTION

Each year, more than 420,000 people die of smoking-related illnesses. Tobacco kills more people than alcohol abuse, auto accidents, AIDS, fires, suicides, homicides, and substance abuse **combined**[1] (figure 10.1). There is a definite need for tobacco prevention programs in today's elementary and middle schools because nine out of ten adult smokers began smoking at or before the age of 18[2] (figure 10.2). More than 3,000 children become regular smokers every day, with one-third eventually dying as a result of their addiction.[3] Although only 5% of high school seniors who smoke daily think they definitely will be smoking in 5 years, the fact is that almost 75% of them still smoke 5 to 6 years later.[4] Unless current trends are reversed, more than 5 million children who are alive today will eventually die from smoking-related diseases.[5] Even with all of the negative information about the health consequences of tobacco use documented through research, smoking among eighth and tenth grade students has increased by nearly 50% since 1991.[6]

There are many reasons why children and preadolescents begin to smoke. Three major reasons are related to:

1. Advertising;
2. Easy access; and
3. Lack of policy enforcement.

The tobacco industry spends over $6 billion a year, or about $15.5 million a day, to advertise cigarettes. In addition, $119 million a year is spent on advertising smokeless tobacco products.[7] This is a tremendous amount of money spent on advertising, considering that tobacco companies are not permitted to pay for commercial time on television. The tobacco companies claim they do not target their advertising toward youth, however, the

Number of deaths per years, 1990

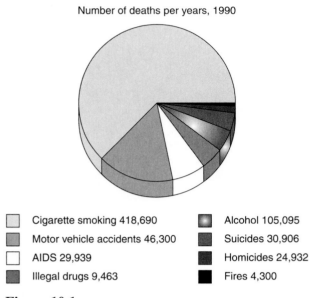

☐ Cigarette smoking 418,690   ☐ Alcohol 105,095

☐ Motor vehicle accidents 46,300   ☐ Suicides 30,906

☐ AIDS 29,939   ☐ Homicides 24,932

☐ Illegal drugs 9,463   ☐ Fires 4,300

Figure 10.1

Cigarettes kill more Americans than AIDS, alcohol car accidents, murders, suicides, drugs, and fires combined.

evidence does not support their claim. Cigarette companies tend to emphasize appealing, youthful qualities such as vigor, sexual attraction, and independence in all of their advertisements.[8] Eighty-six percent of kids who smoke choose either Marlboro, Camel, or Newport, which are the three most heavily advertised brands of cigarettes. Only one-third of adult smokers use these brands.[9] The industry has become even more creative in its advertising techniques over the past few years and is now shifting from easily regulated mass media forms of advertising to alternative media that are more targeted toward youth and are virtually impossible to track. Some of these techniques include sponsoring concerts, sporting events, and other public entertainment; distributing specialty items bearing product names and logos; passing out free samples at events; and issuing coupons.[10] For example, during a Marlboro Grand Prix telecast, the Marlboro logo was seen or mentioned nearly 6,000 times and was visible 46 out of the 94 minutes the race was broadcast.[11] With the amount of money and creative techniques being used by the tobacco industry, it is no wonder there has been a significant increase in youth smoking over the past 6 years.

Easy access of tobacco products is another reason why youth begin to smoke. Among the estimated 2.6 million U.S. smokers who are between 12 and 17 years old, about 1.5 million (58%) usually buy their own cigarettes.[12] About 85% of them often or sometimes buy their cigarettes from a small store, 50% buy them from a large store, and 15% buy them from a vending machine.[13] In fact, children succeed in purchasing cigarettes from vending machines placed in "adult only" areas such as bars 77% of the time.[14] Each year, tobacco products that are il-

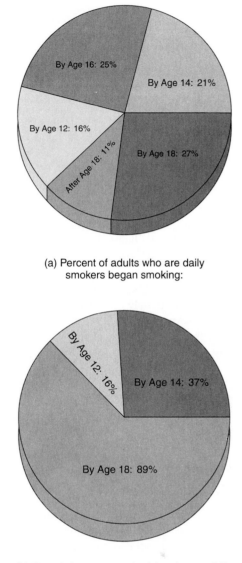

(a) Percent of adults who are daily smokers began smoking:

(b) Cumulative percent of adults who are daily smokers who began smoking by age 18

Figure 10.2

Tobacco use begins early. Note that 11% of adults who are daily smokers began smoking after age 18.

legally sold to minors are estimated to be worth $1.26 billion, and they generate $221 million in profits for the tobacco industry.[15] In addition, 62% of the 13.9 million 12–17-year-olds who have not smoked a cigarette believe it would be easy for them to get cigarettes.[16]

Another major reason why children and adolescents begin to smoke is the lack of policy or policy enforcement for purchasing and using tobacco products. In 1996, the Food and Drug Administration (FDA) instituted new regulations at the national level to prevent the sale of all tobacco products to minors. The following regulations went into effect on February 28, 1997: First, no tobacco sales are permitted to anyone under the age of 18. And second, clerks must check a photo ID for anyone who appears to

CONSIDER THIS

Current Cigarette Users

	9TH GRADE	10TH GRADE	11TH GRADE	12TH GRADE
MALE	34.2%	35.6%	40.7%	40.0%
FEMALE	32.6%	35.1%	31.7%	38.8%

Source: U.S. Department of Health and Human Services, Morbidity and Mortality Weekly Report (1998), 47, SS–3.

More than 3,000 children become smokers every day.

be younger than 27 years old.[17] There are a number of other regulations that are being discussed; however, as of 2000, no other federal legislation has passed. Even though the aforementioned regulations are good, children and adolescents can still buy cigarettes from vending machines. In addition, if state and local enforcement agencies ignore these new regulations, they will do little to deter young people from purchasing cigarettes.

The use of tobacco is the number one preventable cause of death in the United States today. Elementary teachers can play a tremendous role in preventing young people from starting to use tobacco products. The information in this chapter will help teachers decide what and how to teach about tobacco prevention.

RECOMMENDATIONS FOR TEACHERS: PRACTICE AND CONTENT

Before teaching tobacco prevention to young people, it is important for teachers to understand appropriate concepts to teach and to have general knowledge about the dangers of tobacco.

Developmentally Appropriate Practice Recommendations

As with teaching other health topics, tobacco prevention education should be developmentally appropriate based on the physical, cognitive, social, emotional, and language characteristics of specific students. In addition, tobacco prevention should be real, relevant, and right now, which means it should focus on the immediate effects on a student's life. For instance, it is difficult for elementary students to identify with cardiovascular disease because, in their minds, it affects "old" people. Therefore, elementary and middle-level students need to see how tobacco can affect them in a week, a month, or a year. They often have a difficult time identifying with any disease that takes 15 to 30 years to develop, such as lung cancer, cardiovascular disease, or emphysema. Although the long-term side effects of tobacco use should be discussed with elementary students, they will better identify with the short-term side effects. Following is a list of developmentally appropriate

concepts that the Centers for Disease Control and Prevention (CDC) has created to help teach tobacco concepts in elementary and middle-level schools.[18]

Early Elementary (K–2)*

- A drug is a chemical that changes how the body works.
- All forms of tobacco contain a drug called nicotine.
- Tobacco use includes cigarettes and smokeless tobacco.
- Tobacco use is harmful to health.
- Stopping tobacco use has short-term and long-term benefits.
- Many persons who use tobacco have trouble stopping.
- Tobacco smoke in the air is dangerous to anyone who breathes it.
- Many fires are caused by persons who smoke.
- Some advertisements try to persuade persons to use tobacco.
- Most young persons and adults do not use tobacco.
- Persons who choose to use tobacco are not bad persons.
- Make a personal commitment not to use tobacco.
- Take pride in choosing not to use tobacco.
- Communicate knowledge and personal attitudes about tobacco use.
- Encourage other persons not to use tobacco.

Upper Elementary (3–5)*

- Stopping tobacco use has short- and long-term benefits.
- Environmental tobacco smoke is dangerous to health.
- Most young persons and adults do not use tobacco.
- Nicotine, contained in all forms of tobacco, is an addictive drug.
- Tobacco use has short-term and long-term physiologic and cosmetic consequences.

*The authors inserted the specific grade levels for these developmentally appropriate tobacco concepts.

- Personal feelings, family, peers, and the media influence decisions about tobacco use.
- Tobacco advertising is often directed toward young persons.
- Young persons can resist pressure to use tobacco.
- Laws, rules, and policies regulate the sale and use of tobacco.
- Make a personal commitment not to use tobacco.
- Take pride in choosing not to use tobacco.
- Support others' decisions not to use tobacco.
- Take responsibility for personal health.
- Communicate knowledge and personal attitudes about tobacco use.
- Encourage other persons not to use tobacco.
- Demonstrate skills to resist tobacco use.
- State the benefits of a smoke-free environment.
- Develop counterarguments to tobacco advertisements and other promotional materials.
- Support persons who are trying to stop using tobacco.

Middle/Junior High (6–8)*
- Most young persons and adults do not smoke.
- Laws, rules, and policies regulate the sale and use of tobacco.
- Tobacco manufacturers use various strategies to direct advertisements toward young persons, such as "image" advertising.
- Tobacco use has short- and long-term physiologic, cosmetic, social, and economic consequences.
- Cigarette smoking and smokeless tobacco use have direct health consequences.
- Maintaining a tobacco-free environment has health benefits.
- Tobacco use is an unhealthy way to manage stress or weight.
- Community organizations have information about tobacco use and can help persons stop using tobacco.
- Smoking cessation programs can be successful.
- Tobacco contains other harmful substances in addition to nicotine.
- Make a personal commitment not to use tobacco.
- Take pride in choosing not to use tobacco.
- Take responsibility for personal health.
- Support others' decisions not to use tobacco.
- Have confidence in the personal ability to resist tobacco use.
- Take responsibility for personal health.
- Support others' decisions not to use tobacco.
- Have confidence in the personal ability to resist tobacco use.
- Encourage other persons not to use tobacco.
- Support persons who are trying to stop using tobacco.

- Communicate knowledge and personal attitudes about tobacco use.
- Demonstrate skills to resist tobacco use.
- Identify and counter strategies used in tobacco advertisements and other promotional materials.
- Develop methods for coping with tobacco use by parents and with other difficult personal situations, such as peer pressure to use tobacco.
- Request a smoke-free environment.

DANGERS OF TOBACCO

Tobacco is addictive and is responsible for more than one out of every five deaths in the United States. Because the use of tobacco is related to so many health problems, preventing that use has been a major focus over the past few years. The 1994 report entitled "Preventing Tobacco Use Among Young People" is the first Surgeon General report to focus on tobacco as it relates to adolescents. Following are some of the major conclusions of this report:[19]

1. Tobacco use usually begins in early adolescence, typically by age 16.
2. Most young people who smoke are addicted to nicotine and report that they want to quit but are unable to do so.
3. Tobacco is often the first drug used by young people who use alcohol and illegal drugs.
4. Among young people, those with poorer grades and lower self-images are most likely to begin using tobacco.
5. Cigarette advertising appears to increase young people's risk of smoking by conveying that smoking has social benefits and is far more common than it really is.

These conclusions highlight the importance of beginning tobacco prevention education at a young age. Teachers must understand background information about tobacco before they can teach about the dangers of tobacco use. Depending upon the grade level, not all of this information is developmentally appropriate for all elementary and middle-level students, but teachers should still have a basic understanding of the negative side effects of tobacco use.

Smokeless Tobacco

The use of smokeless tobacco is a problem for many of today's youth. For example, about one-third of American high school seniors, and more than half of male high school seniors, have tried smokeless tobacco.[20] Of those high school seniors who are smokeless tobacco users, almost three out of four began using by ninth grade.[21] Because young people begin using smokeless tobacco at a young age, it is important for elementary and middle-level teachers to focus on all forms of tobacco use.

*The authors inserted the specific grade levels for these developmentally appropriate tobacco concepts.

Examples of smokeless tobacco.

There are three principal methods of using tobacco: chewing, dipping snuff, and smoking. Chewing tobacco is made of tobacco leaves that are either dried and shredded and sold in a pouch, or made into plugs or strands that are mixed with molasses, sugar, licorice, and other products. As its name suggests, a portion of the loose leaf, plug, or strand is placed in the mouth and chewed, while excess juices are periodically spit out. Chewing tobacco is the least popular form of tobacco among today's youth. The dangers of chewing tobacco are similar to those of snuff.

Snuff is made from finely cut tobacco leaves and mixed with various products. There are two kinds of snuff: dry snuff and moist snuff. Dry snuff is made from finely ground, dried tobacco leaves and is usually sniffed through the nose. This type of snuff is not popular in most parts of the United States. Moist snuff is also made of finely ground tobacco leaves, but it is packaged while it is still damp. A small amount of moist snuff, known as a "pinch," is held between the lip or cheek and gum and sucked, while excess juices are periodically spit out. This activity is commonly referred to as "dipping." Although many persons believe smokeless tobacco is a safe form of tobacco, it has numerous dangerous side effects. Some of the more common negative side effects are as follows:

Nicotine Addiction. Nicotine is a powerful, addictive substance found in all tobacco products. When a person uses smokeless tobacco, it takes just 5 minutes for nicotine to enter the bloodstream, thus raising a user's heart rate and blood pressure. The 1986 Surgeon General's report suggested that nicotine may contribute to

cardiovascular disease, high blood pressure, ulcers, and fetal problems. As with most stimulants, tobacco users build a tolerance for nicotine, resulting in the person having to use more of the drug to get the same effect.[22]

Oral Cancer. The 1982 Surgeon General's report stated that snuff tobacco contains high levels of nitrosamines.[23] Nitrosamines are highly carcinogenic, or cancer causing. Because snuff stays in the mouth for relatively long periods of time, the nitrosamines may contribute to the high risk of oral cancer for tobacco snuff users. Many snuff users first experience a white, thick, hard patch of tissue in their mouths. This tissue is known as leukoplakia and is considered to be a precancerous lesion. The likelihood of getting oral cancer increases significantly for persons who use smokeless tobacco every day for 3.5 years or more.[24] In addition, long-term snuff users are fifty times more likely to develop oral cancer than nonusers. Oral cancer also has a tendency to spread to the body's lymph system, where cancer becomes very difficult to treat.

Gum and Teeth Problems. Many gum and teeth problems can occur with long-term smokeless tobacco use. Receding gums at the site of tobacco placement are common among smokeless tobacco users. Gum recession exposes the teeth to disease, and because the gum will not grow back, this condition can be corrected only by surgery. The enamel and the biting surfaces of the teeth may also be worn down.[25] Because sugar is added to smokeless tobacco, and the tobacco is held in the

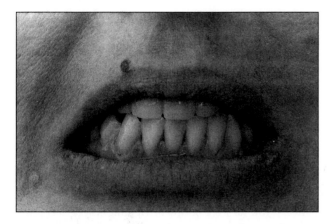

Receding gum lines are a common problem among smokeless tobacco users.

mouth for long periods of time, users also tend to have more dental caries.

Smoking Tobacco

Smoking tobacco is another form of tobacco use. There are three ways that persons smoke tobacco: pipes, cigars, and cigarettes. Because cigarettes are the most popular way for adults and adolescents to smoke tobacco in the United States, the majority of tobacco information in this chapter focuses on cigarettes.

Every day, 3,000 American teenagers begin smoking. The problem with more adolescents beginning to smoke is that tobacco is a "gateway" drug. That is, those young people who use tobacco are more likely to progress to using other drugs. Nearly 95% of all drug abusers follow a progression from one drug to another, typically beginning with tobacco and/or alcohol.[26] This does not mean that cigarette smoking causes other drug use, but rather that cigarette smokers are more likely to use other drugs such as marijuana and cocaine. If the number of teenagers who begin smoking can be reduced through educational prevention programs, then the prevalence of smoking and other drug use among adults can be decreased.

When tobacco is burned or smoked, it produces hundreds of toxic chemicals. When these chemicals are condensed, they form a brown, sticky substance called tar. Some of the chemicals in tar are carcinogens, or cancer-causing agents. Nicotine is another chemical or drug found in tobacco. It is the addictive part of tobacco that causes increased heart rate, blood pressure, and breathing rate, as well as constriction, or narrowing, of the blood vessels. Cigarette smoke also contains carbon monoxide, which is the deadly gas found in automobile exhaust. It is considered to be one of the most harmful components of tobacco smoke. When carbon monoxide is inhaled, it quickly bonds with hemoglobin and reduces the red blood cell's ability to transport oxygen. Because of the reduced oxygen, smokers tend to experience shortness of breath.[27] Because of tar, nicotine, carbon monoxide, and many of the other chemicals and gases in tobacco, its use has many negative short-term consequences, including the following:

Increased Heart Rate. After smoking just one cigarette, the heart rate increases by as many as thirty-three beats per minute. Although the heart rate will decrease in time, smokers generally have a higher resting heart rate than nonsmokers. This means that every day a smoker's heart has to work harder than does a nonsmoker's heart. A higher heart rate is attributed to the increased carbon monoxide levels and the constricted blood vessels caused by nicotine, which make it harder for the heart to pump blood throughout the body.[28] The resting heart rate for young adult smokers is two to three beats per minute faster than that of nonsmokers.[29]

Increased Blood Pressure. After smoking just one cigarette, blood pressure also increases. This increase is caused by the constricted blood vessels.[30]

Decreased Skin Temperature. When persons smoke, their skin temperature quickly decreases. This is caused by nicotine, which reduces blood flow to the peripheral vessels.

Decreased Hand Steadiness. Although some smokers believe that smoking relaxes them, it actually increases nervousness and tension and reduces their hand steadiness. This is the result of the stimulant effect of nicotine. Decreased hand steadiness can affect athletic and art ability and other activities that require fine-motor skills.

Carbon Monoxide Levels. Only about 5% of the smoke a person inhales is carbon monoxide; however, even this amount can be dangerous. When excess carbon monoxide is inhaled into the lungs, the oxygen-carrying capacity of the blood is reduced. The reduced amount of oxygen in the blood makes it more difficult for organs, such as the heart and brain, to do their work. This is why many smokers get out of breath easily, which can affect athletic and musical performance.[31] In fact, teen smokers suffer from shortness of breath almost three times as often as teens who do not smoke.[32]

Bad Breath. Smoking also causes bad breath. This should be one short-term effect that is stressed, especially when older elementary and middle-level students become more interested in social interactions with classmates.

Fires and Burns. Other short-term effects of smoking cigarettes are fire and automobile fatalities related to smoking. Each year there are between 1,500 and 2,000 deaths associated with fires started by cigarettes or traffic accidents related to smoking. Most of these fatalities are caused by smokers who are careless about how, when, and where they smoke. Another short-term effect of cigarette smoking is burns—over 5,000 accidental burns are associated with smoking cigarettes each year.

While students should understand all of the effects associated with smoking cigarettes, attention to the short-term side effects of smoking is more developmentally appropriate for younger learners than is considerable time spent on the long-term consequences. However, some students will be curious about the long-term effects of smoking, and therefore it is important to have some general knowledge about this topic. Although smoking has numerous long-term effects, only the most common are included in this section.

Lung cancer, the leading cancer killer for both men and women, is believed to be caused by smoking in 75–85% of the cases. Breast cancer used to be the highest cancer killer among women; however, today lung cancer kills more women than any other cancer. The increase in lung cancer among women is due to the increase of female smokers during the 1960s through the 1990s. The risk of developing lung cancer increases with the number of cigarettes smoked per day, the number of years smoking, and the age at which the person started smoking. If a person decides to quit smoking, however, the risk of lung cancer decreases significantly after 1 year. Ten years after quitting, the incidence of lung cancer approaches the incidence of those who never smoked. If a person stops smoking before cancer has started, lung tissue tends to repair itself, even if changes leading to cancer are already present.[33] Smoking also increases the long-term risk of getting cancer of the bladder, esophagus, pancreas, pharynx, and mouth.

Smokers have a 70% greater rate of death from cardiovascular disease than nonsmokers. Cigarette smoking is the most important known, modifiable risk factor for cardiovascular disease. Thirty percent of all cardiovascular disease can be attributed to smoking.[34] These alarming statistics are related to many of the chemicals and gases found in tobacco smoke. Young people who smoke already show greater deposits of fat in the blood vessels leading to and from the heart. Cardiovascular diseases that are related to long-term smoking behaviors include heart attacks, high blood pressure, strokes, arteriosclerosis, and atherosclerosis.

Chronic obstructive lung disease includes two related diseases: chronic bronchitis and emphysema. Both of these diseases are related to cigarettes because of the damage smoking does to the airways and the alveoli sacs. Alveoli sacs are the site of carbon monoxide and oxygen exchange in the lungs. Although chronic bronchitis predisposes the smoker to emphysema, it does not mean that the smoker will acquire emphysema. Chronic bronchitis is a persistent inflammation and infection of the smaller airways within the lungs. Emphysema is an irreversible disease in which the alveoli are destroyed. Once the alveoli are destroyed, even quitting smoking will not regenerate them. Healthy adults have about 100 square yards of interior lung surface, created by the lungs' thousands of alveoli sacs. When a person gets emphysema, the walls between the sacs break down, creating larger and fewer sacs, thus gradually diminishing the interior lung surface. Eventually, the lung surface is so small that people with emphysema spend most of their time gasping for air and carrying an oxygen tank with them. Emphysema is a crippling disease that kills over 16,000 Americans each year, and it is caused almost exclusively by cigarette smoking.[35]

Secondhand tobacco smoke has a long-term effect on children and adults who live in homes with smokers. A recent study found that secondhand tobacco smoke kills about 3,000 nonsmokers a year through lung cancer.[36] In addition, children who are exposed to secondhand smoke are at an increased risk of developing pneumonia and bronchitis. Also, children exposed to secondhand tobacco smoke have a greater chance of developing respiratory problems, such as wheezing, asthma, and chest colds.[37] It is important that teachers not scare children with this information, but let parents know about the dangers of secondhand smoke.

There also are numerous aesthetic problems associated with long-term use of cigarettes. First, smokers generally have bad breath and stains on their teeth and fingers. Smoking also destroys much of one's sense of smell and taste, meaning that foods do not taste as good, and flowers and other nice scents do not smell as good. Smoking also causes the skin to wrinkle because of the constant constriction and relaxation of the surface blood vessels, which eventually makes people look much older.

GUIDELINES FOR TEACHERS AND SCHOOLS FOR TEACHING TOBACCO PREVENTION

Guidelines for Schools

Before providing specific teaching ideas, we think it important that elementary and middle-level teachers understand what should be included in a successful school-wide smoking prevention program. The Centers for Disease Control and Prevention has examined all of the current research about successful smoking prevention programs and developed the following seven recommendations for school health programs to prevent tobacco use and addiction:[38]

1. Develop and enforce a school policy on tobacco use.
2. Provide instruction about the short- and long-term negative physiologic and social consequences of tobacco use, about social influences on tobacco use, about peer norms regarding tobacco use, and about refusal skills.
3. Provide tobacco-use prevention education in kindergarten through twelfth grade; this instruction should be especially intensive in middle school and should be reinforced in high school.
4. Provide program-specific training for teachers.
5. Involve parents or families in support of school-based programs to prevent tobacco use.
6. Support cessation efforts among students and all school staff who use tobacco.
7. Assess the tobacco-use prevention program at regular intervals.

Guidelines for Teachers

It is not only important to know what concepts to teach at each grade level, it is equally as important to know what *not* to teach. Following are some guidelines for teachers to follow when teaching tobacco prevention:

1. Do not imply that kids are "bad" if they smoke. Although this might work with some youth, it has been found that this approach tends to backfire, especially with high-risk students. The more smoking is labeled "bad" by authority figures, the more some high-risk students want to rebel.
2. Do not say that smoking is "dumb." Children need to maintain respect for their parents and other adults in their life, whether they smoke or not.
3. Do not encourage children, even indirectly, to denounce smoking at home. Smoking remains a personal choice. If the school is perceived as intruding in the home, parents may become alienated from the school's smoking prevention efforts.
4. Do not tell young children that smoking leads to deadly diseases. This can provoke anxiety in children whose parents or relatives smoke. This information should be taught in later elementary grades when it can be understood that these risks are generally long-term, and that quitting can reverse this trend.
5. Do not warn older students that they will die an early death if they smoke. This "threat" approach is not effective. If is far more effective to focus on immediate consequences.
6. Do not give mixed messages. If you smoke, don't try to hide this fact from your students. Let them know that you want to help them to avoid some of the unhealthy decisions that you have made. The concept of nicotine addiction can also be discussed during this time.

SUCCESSFUL TOBACCO PREVENTION PROGRAMS

There are currently two middle-level tobacco prevention programs that the Centers for Disease Control and Prevention (CDC) has concluded are effective for reducing tobacco use among students who participated in the program. The Life Skills Training (LST) program is ideally designed for students in sixth or seventh grade and focuses on tobacco, alcohol, and other drug prevention. The curriculum impacts on social risk factors including media influence and peer pressure, as well as personal risk factors such as anxiety and low self-esteem. The topics in the curriculum include resistance skills, knowledge, attitudes, self-management skills, and general social skills. Results of the studies that have been conducted on the LST program showed that it had a significant impact on reducing cigarette use after 3 years for those students whose teacher taught at least 60% of the program. Results of the 6-year follow-up indicated that the effects of the program lasted until the end of twelfth grade. To purchase LST materials or to arrange for training, contact Princeton Healthpress at (609)921-0540.[39]

The second program, the "Projects Towards No Tobacco Use" (Project TNT), is designed for minority students in seventh grade. The focus of Project TNT is to make students aware of misleading social information that facilitates tobacco use, to teach skills that counteract the social pressures to achieve approval by using tobacco, and to encourage appreciation of the physical consequences that tobacco use may have on children's lives. The results of the studies show that Project TNT reduced initiation of cigarettes by 26% over a 2-year period, reduced the initiation of smokeless tobacco use by approximately 60%, and reduced weekly use of smokeless tobacco and cigarettes by 30%. To purchase Project TNT material or to arrange for training, call Sandra Craig at the University of Southern California at (213)342-2586.[40]

Tobacco Prevention Strategies for Elementary and Middle-Level Students

Several activities can be conducted with elementary and middle-level students to give them a better understanding of the many topics included within tobacco prevention education. The following activities instruct in the areas of knowledge, attitudes, and skills at the K–2, 3–5, and 6–8 grade levels.

ACTIVITIES

Tobacco Prevention Activities

Grades K–2

Safety and Cigarette Smoking

Introduce the concept of staying away from matches, lighters, and cigarettes using the following story. This story can be acted out by using puppets, by role-plays, or by reading the story to students.

1. Susan and Alex are visiting James at his house. James's dad is a smoker and they find his lighter and matches in the living room. They know they are not supposed to touch these items, but Susan picks up the lighter and begins to play with it.

2. After reading or acting out the story, ask the class what Alex and James should do.

3. Have the students brainstorm all possible solutions and then vote on the best way for the problem to be solved. Also ask the students to brainstorm different ways to avoid the situation.

4. Ask students to draw pictures depicting what children should do when they find matches, lighters, or cigarettes. Display the pictures at PTA meetings or in the classroom.

Grades 3–5

Smoking Machine

One of the most popular tobacco prevention teaching activities, particularly for upper-elementary and middle-level students, is the smoking machine. The purpose of the smoking machine is to show students how tar can accumulate in the lungs after just a few cigarettes. There are numerous ways to make a smoking machine, and several commercial smoking machines can be purchased. Following are the directions on how to make and how to use a smoking machine in class:

1. Use a thoroughly rinsed, clear plastic dish-soap bottle.

2. After the soap bottle is clean and dry, insert loosely packed cotton balls into the container and put the cap in place.

3. Next, remove the nozzle from the cap of the bottle.

4. Insert a cigarette into the opening of the cap, and make an air-tight seal around the cigarette with clay or putty.

5. The smoking machine is now ready for use. It is best to do the smoking machine demonstration outside so the classroom does not get filled with smoke.

6. Explain that the cotton balls represent the lungs of a smoker. Ask the students to watch what happens to the cotton balls after smoking just one cigarette.

7. Press firmly on the plastic container to force out the air before lighting the cigarette. After lighting the cigarette, proceed with a slow and regular pumping action.

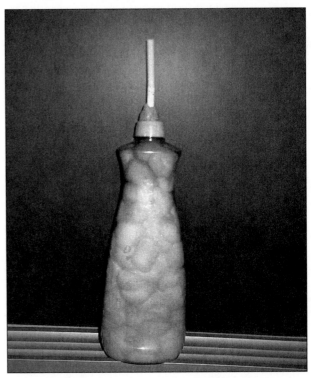

This type of smoking machine is easy to make and is helpful in demonstrating the short-term effects of smoking.

8. After the cigarette is completely smoked, remove the filter and unscrew the cap. The students will notice the tar buildup on the cap and on the cotton balls.

9. Emphasize the difference between the clean cotton balls and the tar-filled cotton balls.

10. Discuss the problems that tar causes in the lungs and cilia.

11. An additional activity that can be completed prior to the smoking machine demonstration is to place some cotton balls in a smoking environment for about 1 week. These cotton balls that were exposed to secondhand smoke can then be compared to the cotton balls from the smoking machine and to clean cotton balls.

This is a sample tobacco advertisement that a sixth grade student completed for an assignment.

Analyzing Tobacco Advertising

Another activity that is important to include in a tobacco prevention unit is to analyze tobacco advertisements. Because approximately 3,000 smokers die every day in the United States, the tobacco industry needs to find 3,000 new smokers every day to make up for the loss. Although the tobacco industry claims that it does not try to appeal to young people, it does use techniques that are attractive to adolescents. For instance, the tobacco industry tries to make smoking look fun, clean, sophisticated, and sexy. In addition, it was recently found that Joe Camel, from Camel cigarettes, is as familiar to 6-year-old children as Mickey Mouse. Students need to be aware of the different ways that advertisements try to get them to buy tobacco products.

1. Ask students to bring in cigarette advertisements from magazines.

2. Discuss the different techniques that tobacco companies use to try to make their product attractive to young people.

3. Next, ask students to make their own advertisement that better depicts the outcomes of smoking. For instance, instead of the famous cigarette slogan, "You've come a long way baby," it might be more appropriate to use the slogan, "You've come the *wrong* way baby." Students could include a graph depicting the rising rates of lung cancer among women.

4. Have students do their own video commercials depicting the negative side effects of smoking.

5. Ask students to write a class letter to a cigarette advertiser, indicating their knowledge of the advertising techniques that are currently being used on them to buy cigarettes.

Demonstration of the Short-Term Effects of Smoking

As mentioned previously, students relate best to what happens after smoking just one cigarette, not to what happens after 30 years of smoking.

1. Ask a smoking parent, staff person, teacher, or administrator to volunteer to come to the class.

2. Ask the school nurse to take the volunteer's heart rate, blood pressure, and skin temperature before the volunteer smokes a cigarette. Record these numbers on the chalkboard so that students can see them.

3. Ask the volunteer to step in the hallway and smoke a cigarette. Ask the nurse to retake the volunteer's heart rate, blood pressure, and skin temperature, and record these numbers on the chalkboard.

4. Two other short-term measurements, carbon monoxide levels and hand steadiness, can be taken if the measuring instruments are available through the American Lung Association. The ecolyzer measures carbon monoxide levels, and the tremor-tension tester measures hand steadiness.

5. The last part of this activity is perhaps the most important step. Ask students to indicate what activities they like to do that would be affected by even the short-term effects of smoking. This way students will

be able to relate the effects to their own life. For example, if their hands are not steady, they may not play a musical instrument as well.

Tar Visualization

Sometimes a picture is worth a thousand words. If students can see how much tar passes through the lungs, they might think twice about smoking.

1. Hold up a 1-quart container of molasses. Explain to the students that when a person smokes one pack of cigarettes a day for 1 year, 1 quart of tar passes through the person's lungs.

2. You could also use this as a guessing game. Hold up the quart of molasses and ask students how many packs of cigarettes a person would have to smoke to have that amount of tar pass through the lungs in 1 year.

Reasons not to Smoke

Many times health education strategies focus around what students should *not* do, instead of what they *should* do. A simple activity of asking students to brainstorm reasons not to smoke focuses the emphasis from the negative to the positive. Use this list to counteract all of the reasons young people give for starting to smoke.

The teacher is showing her students the amount of tar that enters the lungs of an average smoker in one year.

Creating Banners, Kites, T-Shirts, Buttons

Students can be taught to use the same techniques the tobacco industry uses when it promotes the use of tobacco products. Ask students to make their own anti-tobacco use banners that can be posted around the schools and businesses. Have students also make home-made kites that can be flown all at the same time. Ask the media to attend the kite-flying demonstration. Another activity is to have students create buttons and t-shirts that promote tobacco-free lives.

Grades 6–8

Cost of Smoking

Another smoking prevention technique is to have the students determine the cost of smoking for a week, a month, and a year. (The typical smoker spends about $700 a year on cigarettes.) After this is determined, ask the students what they would buy with that amount of money. Most people like to dream about what they would do with extra money. Many times students cannot relate to the health risks of tobacco use, but they can relate to the cost of the habit.

Analyzing Cigarette Smoke

Introduce the topic of tobacco prevention by analyzing the main ingredients of tobacco, instead of looking at the end product.[40] Materials needed for this lesson include two balloons, a small glass jar of flour, a small glass of molasses, and a small glass of clear syrup.

1. Begin the tobacco unit by telling the students that they are going to break down a "mystery" product (tobacco) by looking at a few of the main ingredients. Do not tell the students that tobacco is the product being analyzed; instead, let them guess the mystery product after all of the ingredients have been described.

2. Explain to the students that sometimes products are viewed differently after all of their ingredients are known.

3. Explain that this mystery product is associated with over 500 gases and several thousand chemicals. Hold up one of the balloons and explain that one of the gases, called carbon monoxide, is in the balloon and is one of the gases associated with the mystery product. Explain that carbon monoxide is odorless, colorless, and can be deadly by depleting the amount of oxygen in the body.

4. Hold up the other balloon and explain that one of the other gases that is produced by this mystery product is called hydrogen cyanide. Hydrogen cyanide is a gas that is sometimes used in the gas chambers where prisoners are executed.

5. Hold up the jar of flour and explain that one of the chemicals found in the mystery product is arsenic. Arsenic is used as a rat poison and is dangerous if ingested in large amounts.

6. Hold up the jar of syrup, and explain that this ingredient found in the mystery product is too dangerous in its pure form, so it has been mixed with syrup. (Although the syrup represents nicotine, it is a good idea not to tell the students that the ingredient is nicotine because they will probably be able to easily guess the mystery product.) Explain that two or three drops of this ingredient can kill a person instantly, and it also causes the heart to beat fast and the blood vessels to constrict.

7. Hold up the jar of molasses and explain that this ingredient, found in the mystery product, can cause cancer. (Again, do not tell the students that the molasses represents tar, because it will be too easy for them to guess the mystery product.)

8. Ask the students if they know what the mystery product is. After the students have guessed the mystery product, discuss each of the ingredients in more detail.[41]

Emphysema Simulation

As mentioned previously, emphysema is a crippling, debilitating disease that is primarily caused by smoking. Although students cannot easily identify with getting a long-term disease, this activity allows students to understand how it would feel to have emphysema.

1. Give every student a cocktail straw. It is important that the straw has a small opening.

2. Instruct the students to put the straw in their mouth, hold their nose, and breath in and out of the straw for 1 minute.

3. Tell them that if they feel dizzy, they do not have to keep the straw in their mouth for a full minute.

4. After 1 minute, ask the students how they felt during the experiment. Many of them will say they felt nervous, scared, panicked, and trapped. These are the same adjectives that emphysemic patients use to describe their condition.

Personal Commitment

It is important for youth to make a public, personal commitment not to smoke. This can be accomplished in the following ways:

1. Have a blank piece of newsprint with the title "I promise not to use any tobacco products for the rest of my life" written on the top of it. Instruct the students who want to sign the newsprint to come to the front of the room and sign their name in magic marker. Post in the classroom so that students can see their classmate's commitment for the entire school year.

2. Another type of commitment activity is to give each student an individual paper that has the following statement, "I pledge to stay tobacco free from now until eternity because_____
_____."

   Signed _____

   This encourages students to make a commitment not to use tobacco, and to think about *why* they won't use tobacco. These can be posted in the classroom, hallway, or sent home to parents/guardians.

This class is participating in the emphysema simulation.

Social Norms

Middle-level students like to feel that their behaviors are respected by the people whose opinions they value—usually, their peers. If they believe that everyone smokes cigarettes, they will be more inclined to smoke. Youth tend to grossly overestimate the prevalence and acceptability of tobacco use among their peers. It is important to help students understand how many people their age do actually smoke.

To do this, ask students to anonymously write down on a piece of paper whether they currently use tobacco. (If teachers feel uncomfortable asking students about their smoking behaviors, they can obtain local or state statistics.) Next, ask the students to write down the percentage of students in class that they think currently use tobacco. In most cases, students will write down a much higher percentage than the actual percentage of tobacco users in the class. The teacher can discuss why students overestimate the number of people their age that smoke.

Interviewing an Adult

It is important for young people to know how the important adults in their lives would feel if they started smoking. An effective homework assignment is to ask students to go home and interview an adult about smoking. Include the following questions on a worksheet for the interview:

1. Do you currently use tobacco? If yes, why? When did you start using tobacco? Would you like to quit? If yes, why?

2. If you have never smoked, why not?

3. What advice would you like to give to me about using tobacco?

Creating Health Warnings

Show the different health warnings that are on tobacco products. Discuss with students the effectiveness of these warnings with young people. Most students will think these warnings are not very effective to deter young people from smoking. Ask students to create their own warnings that they think would be effective in deterring youth from smoking. Display these warnings in the hallways throughout the school.

Letters To The Editor

Have students write letters to the editor thanking those restaurants that are totally smoke-free.

SUMMARY

Because tobacco use is the number one preventable cause of death in the United States, there is a definite need for tobacco prevention programs in our schools and communities. Each year, more than 420,000 people die of smoking-related illnesses. In addition, tobacco use rates among young people have been increasing over the past 5 years. Because of the major health and financial implications of tobacco use, schools should devote time and effort to deter young people from using tobacco. School districts should follow the CDC's suggested guidelines for tobacco prevention. In addition, elementary and middle-level teachers should have an understanding of the developmentally appropriate concepts to teach at each grade level and have some background information about the dangers of tobacco.

One of the more popular types of tobacco use among young people, especially males, is smokeless tobacco. Although many persons believe smokeless tobacco is not dangerous, its negative side effects include nicotine addiction, oral cancer, and gum and teeth problems. Cigarette smoking is also common among adolescents and is the number one preventable cause of premature death in the United States. The short-term side effects of smoking, which include increased heart rate, blood pressure, and carbon monoxide, and decreased skin temperature and hand steadiness, should be stressed to elementary students. Long-term side effects of cigarette use include cancer, cardiovascular disease, chronic obstructive lung disease, and aesthetic consequences. While there are numerous tobacco prevention activities that can be used in the elementary classroom, teachers should focus on using real-life, relevant activities.

DISCUSSION QUESTIONS

1. What are some of the negative side effects of using smokeless tobacco?

2. What are some of the negative side effects of smoking cigarettes?

3. Describe three tobacco prevention activities that are real and relevant.

4. Why is it important to try to prevent elementary-age children from using tobacco products?

5. What are the key developmentally appropriate tobacco prevention concepts that should be taught at each grade level?

6. What are some guidelines that schools and teachers should follow when trying to prevent the use of tobacco products among young people?

7. What are two effective tobacco prevention curricula available today?

8. What are some activities that can be used to teach young people the knowledge, skills, and attitudes to deter them from using tobacco products?

ENDNOTES

1. Centers for Disease Control and Prevention. "Cigarette Smoking-Attributable Mortality and Years of Potential Life Lost-United States, 1990" *Morbidity and Mortality Weekly Report* 42:33 (27 Aug. 1993): 645–649.

2. Institute of Medicine, *Growing Up Tobacco Free* (Washington, DC, National Academy Press, 1994).

3. Centers for Disease Control and Prevention. "Projected Smoking Related Deaths Among Youth-United States" *Morbidity and Mortality Weekly Report* 45:44 (8 Nov. 1996).

4. National Institute on Drug Abuse, National Survey Results on Drug Use from Monitoring the Future Survey, 1975–1992, Vol. 2 (Bethesda, MD: U.S. Department of Health and Human Services).

5. Centers for Disease Control and Prevention. "Projected Smoking Related Deaths Among Youth-United States."

6. Monitoring the Future Study, University of Michigan, 1999, http://www.isr.umich.edu/src/mtf/index.html/

7. Federal Trade Commission Report to Congress, *1996 Federal Trade Commission Report to Congress for 1994, Pursuant to the Federal Cigarette Labeling and Advertising Act* (Washington, DC: Federal Trade Commission, 1996).

8. Department of Health and Human Services, *Prevention Tobacco Use Among Young People: A Report of the Surgeon General,* S/N 017-001-00491-0 (Washington, DC: U.S. Government Printing Office, 1994).

9. Centers for Disease Control and Prevention. "Changes in the Cigarette Brand Preferences of Adolescent Smokers— U.S. 1989–1993" *Morbidity and Mortality Weekly Report* 43:32 (19 Aug. 1994): 577–581.

10. Federal Trade Commission Report to Congress, *1996 Federal Trade Commission Report to Congress for 1994, Pursuant to the Federal Cigarette Labeling and Advertising Act* (Washington, DC: Federal Trade Commission, 1996).

11. A. Blum, "The Marlboro Grand Prix—Circumvention of the Television Ban on Tobacco Advertising, *New England Journal of Medicine* 324 (1991): 913–917.

12. Centers for Disease Control and Prevention. "Accessibility of Cigarettes to Youth Aged 12–17

Years—U.S., 1989" *Morbidity and Mortality Weekly Report* 41 (1992): 485–488.

13. Ibid.

14. J. L. Forester, M. Hourigan, and P. Mcgovern, "Availability of Cigarettes to Underage Youth in Three Communities, *Preventive Medicine* 21 (1992): 320–328.

15. J. R. Difranza and J. H. Tye, "Who Profits from Tobacco Sales to Children?" *Journal of the American Medical Association* 263 (1990): 2784–2787.

16. Centers for Disease Control and Prevention. "Accessibility of Cigarettes to Youth Aged 12–17 Years—U.S., 1989," 485–488.

17. FDA Regulations, 1996. http://www.fda.gov/opacom/campaigns/tobacco/execrule.html.

18. Centers for Disease Control and Prevention, "Guidelines for School Health Programs to Prevent Tobacco Use and Addiction," *Morbidity and Mortality Weekly Report* 43, No. RR-2 (1994).

19. Ibid.

20. Department of Health and Human Services, *Preventing Tobacco Use Among Young People: A Report of the Surgeon General,* S/N 017-001-00491-0 (Washington, DC: U.S. Government Printing Office, 1994).

21. Ibid.

22. Indiana State Board of Health, *The Spittin' Image: A Smokeless Tobacco Teaching Guide, Grades 4–7* (Indianapolis, IN: Indiana State Board of Health, 1989).

23. *The Health Consequences of Smoking for Cancer: A Report of the Surgeon General,* DHHS Publication No. (PHS) 82-50179 (Washington, DC: U.S. Government Printing Office, 1982).

24. S. Perry, "Recognizing Everyday Addicts," *Current Health* 2(16) (1990).

25. O. Ray and C. Ksir, *Drugs, Society, and Human Behavior* (St. Louis, MO: Times Mirror/Mosby Publisher, 1987); Indiana State Board of Health, *The Spittin' Image.*

26. Department of Health and Human Services, *Smoking and Health—A National Report: A Report to Congress,* 2nd ed., DHHS Publication No. (CDC) 87-8396 (Rockville, MD: 1989).

27. Ray and Ksir, *Drugs, Society, and Human Behavior.*

28. Southwest Ohio Rural Health Promotion Cooperative, *Smoking and Smokeless Tobacco Resource Guide* (Columbus, OH: Southwest Ohio District Office, Ohio Department of Health, 1988).

29. Department of Health and Human Services, *Preventing Tobacco Use Among Young People: A Report of the Surgeon General.*

30. Ibid.

31. Ibid.

32. Ibid.

33. P. Insel and T. Roth, *Core Concepts in Health* (Mountain View, CA: Mayfield Publishing Company, 1993).

34. Southwest Ohio Rural Health Promotion Cooperative, *Smoking and Smokeless Tobacco Resource Guide.*

35. American Cancer Society, "Fifty Most Often Asked Questions about Smoking and Health . . . and the Answers," Publication Number 82-500M-No. 2023-LE (Atlanta, GA: American Cancer Society, 1982); W. Payne and D. Hahn, *Understanding Your Health.* St. Louis, MD: Times Mirror/Mosby Publisher, 1995.

36. R. Tollison, *Cleaning the Air: Perspectives on Environmental Tobacco Smoke* (Lexington, MA: Lexington Books, 1988).

37. C. D'Onofrio, *Tobacco Talk: Educating Young Children About Tobacco* (Santa Cruz, CA: Network Publications, 1991): 61.

38. Centers for Disease Control and Prevention, "Guidelines for School Health Programs to Prevent Tobacco Use and Addiction."

39. G. Botvin, S. Schinke, J. Epstein, and T. Diaz, "Long-term Follow-up Results of a Randomized Drug Abuse Prevention Trial in a White Middle-Class Population," *Journal of the American Medical Association* 273, no. 14, (1990): 1106–1112.

40. C. Dent, S. Sussman, A. Stacy, S. Craig, D. Burton, and B. Flay, "Two-year Behavior Outcomes of Project Towards No Tobacco Use, *Journal of Clinical and Consulting Psychology* 63 (1995): 676–677.

41. D. White and L. Rudisill, "Analyzing Cigarette Smoke," *Health Education* 18, no. 4 (August/September 1987): 50–51.

SUGGESTED READINGS

American Medical Association. *Healthy Youth 2000: National Health Promotion and Disease Prevention Objectives for Adolescents.* Chicago, IL: American Medical Association, 1990.

Botvin G., and E. Botvin. "Adolescent Tobacco, Alcohol, and Drug Abuse: Prevention Strategies, Empirical Findings, and Assessment Issues." *Developmental and Behavioral Pediatrics* 13, no. 4 (1992).

Centers for Disease Control and Prevention. "Guidelines for School Health Programs to Prevent Tobacco Use and

Addiction." *Morbidity and Mortality Weekly Report* 43, No. RR-2 (1994).

D'Onofrio, D. *Tobacco Talk: Educating Young Children About Tobacco.* Santa Cruz, CA: Network Publications, 1991.

Institute of Medicine. *Growing up Tobacco Free.* (Lynch, G. and Bonnie, R. eds.) Washington, DC, National Academy Press, 1994.

Indiana State Board of Health. *The Spittin' Image: A Smokeless Tobacco Teaching Guide, Grades 4–7.* Indianapolis, IN: Indiana State Board of Health, 1989.

Scheer, J. *Into Adolescence: Living Without Tobacco.* Santa Cruz, CA: Network Publications, 1990.

U.S. Department of Health and Human Services. *Preventing Tobacco Use Among Young People: A Report of the*

Surgeon General. S/N 017-001-00491-0. Washington, DC: U.S. Government Printing Office, 1994.

CHILDREN'S LITERATURE WITH A TOBACCO PREVENTION THEME

Grades K–2

Dutton, C., *Not In Here, Dad.* Barron, 1989.

Muhsil, J. *Where There's Smoke.* Annick, 1993.

Grades 3–5

Tobias, T. *The Quitting Deal.* Viking, 1975.

 INTERNET INFORMATION

TOBACCO PREVENTION WEBSITES

For additional information on tobacco prevention, please refer to the following websites.

Action on Smoking and Health (ASH)
http://ash.org

American Cancer Society
http://www.cancer.org

American Heart Association
http://www.amhrt.org

American Lung Association
http://www.lungusa.org

Centers for Disease Control and Prevention's (CDC) Tobacco Information and Prevention Sourcepage
http://www.cdc.gov/nccdphp/osh/tobacco

Food and Drug Administration
http://www.fda.gov/opacom/campaigns/tobacco

The National Center for Tobacco-Free Kids
http://www.tobaccofreekids.org

NUTRITION EDUCATION

OUTLINE

INTRODUCTION

Nutritional health promotion is among the most important health issues to address with students in elementary and middle-level schools. Poor nutritional habits developed in youth are associated with a number of short- and long-term negative consequences. Obesity has been demonstrated to be related to poor nutritional habits and a lack of vigorous physical activity in childhood. Although not all obese children become obese adults, there is a great likelihood that obesity that begins in early childhood will persist across the life span.[1] Research has confirmed that an increase of 20% or more over desirable weight is associated with higher rates of cancer, hypertension, hypercholesterolemia, and diabetes in adults.[2] Importantly, as many as 10–30% of today's children are obese.[3] Childhood obesity has been linked to changes in behavior, lower self-esteem, and depression—variables that have the potential to affect school performance.[4]

The amount of time that children spend watching television and the associated lack of vigorous physical activity are of particular concern. This combination of factors has been linked to obesity in children. The average child spends 24 hours a week watching television—a pattern of behavior that is related directly to the prevalence of obesity in children.[5]

There are other dietary risks that confront today's children and youth. Preadolescents and their teenage counterparts often eat outside the home and skip meals. In addition, a growing number of young people engage in unhealthy dietary practices as a means to help maintain weight or improve perceived appearance.[6] While such unhealthy behaviors can compromise the health of school-age youth, these practices tend to continue into adulthood. Over time, such behaviors have been demonstrated to contribute to many chronic diseases.

Importantly, health promotion professionals and education advocates would be wise to examine the extensive body of literature confirming the impact of poor nutrition on the academic performance of all students. Specifically, researchers have noted that when children go hungry or are undernourished, they tend to be irritable and apathetic. In addition, these students often have little energy and have difficulty concentrating. Finally, hungry children are at increased risk for infection and are absent from school more frequently than their well-fed counterparts. As a result, such students tend to fall behind in their academic work.[7]

Because nutrition knowledge, attitudes, and behaviors are formalized during the elementary and middle-level years, school-based activities can make an important and positive impact on the nutritional practices of children. Teachers can serve as positive nutritional role models by eating well-balanced lunches. In addition, professionals can provide healthy snacks and encourage their students to try new and healthy foods. Also it is important that school policies reinforce healthy nutritional habits. It is counterproductive for teachers to discuss positive nutritional habits during a health lesson, when those same students are encouraged to sell candy for fundraising activities. As described in chapter 1, it is important for nutritional health promotion to be reinforced by professionals, policies, and practices across the eight components of the Coordinated School Health Program. In this context, the Centers for

Many children spend several hours a day watching television and eating junk food.

Disease Control and Prevention has developed a set of *Guidelines for School Health Programs to Promote Lifelong Healthy Eating.* These guidelines reinforce that school-based nutritional health promotion programs are most likely to be effective when they:

- Help students learn skills (not just the facts),
- Give students repeated chances to practice healthy eating,
- Make nutrition education activities fun, and
- Involve teachers, administrators, families, community leaders, and students in delivering strong, consistent messages about healthy eating as part of a coordinated school health program.[8]

In support of a commitment to an intentional and coordinated approach to nutritional health, school and community advocates are encouraged to review table 11.1, which includes a summary of seven recommended school programming strategies that will support the promotion of lifelong healthy eating.[9]

Although many elementary and middle-level schools include some nutrition instructional activities in their health-education curriculum, it is important that updated and developmentally appropriate, student-centered activities serve as the foundation of any curriculum. Sound elementary and middle-level nutrition education programs exist that can produce positive results.[10] Professionals and parents who are engaged in nutritional health promotion no longer can afford to emphasize simple mastery of nutrition information. In addition to knowledge acquisition and attitude evaluation, nutrition learning activities must be developed to enable students to practice skills that are consistent with those identified in the *National Health Education Standards* (see chapter 1). In this context, sound learning activities are developed to focus on such skills as analyzing the influence of television on food choices, and practicing decision making and advocacy skills to enhance healthy dietary behaviors.

TABLE 11.1	Recommendations for School Health Programs: Promoting Healthy Eating

1. Policy:

Adopt a coordinated school nutrition policy that promotes healthy eating through classroom lessons and a supportive school environment. This policy should include a commitment to:
- Provide adequate time for nutrition education,
- Provide healthy and appealing foods (fruits, vegetables, and low-fat grain products) when these foods are available,
- Discourage availability of foods that are high in fat, sodium, and added sugars (soda, candy, and fried chips) on school grounds and as part of fundraising activities,
- Discourage teachers from using food to discipline or reward students,
- Provide adequate time and pleasant and safe space for consumption of meals, and
- Formalize links with professionals who can provide counseling for nutrition problems, refer families to nutrition services, and plan health promotion activities for faculty and staff.

2. Curriculum:

Implement a sequential, comprehensive nutrition education curriculum to help students in preschool through grade 12 adopt healthy eating behaviors. This instructional program should:
- Help students practice nutrition-related skills (planning healthy meals and comparing food labels), and
- Ensure that students practice general health promotion skills (assessing health habits, setting goals, and resisting pressures to make unhealthy eating choices).

3. Instruction:

Integrate cross-curricular nutrition education strategies that are fun, developmentally appropriate, culturally relevant, and learner-centered into classroom practice. These teaching methods should:
- Emphasize health enhancing and appealing aspects of eating rather than the long-term, harmful effects of unhealthy dietary behaviors,
- Present the benefits of healthy eating in the context of what is important and relevant to involved students, and
- Give students many chances to taste healthy foods (low in fat, sodium, and added sugars and high in vitamins, minerals, and fiber).

4. Program Coordination:

Coordinate school food service and nutrition education with other components of the school health program to reinforce messages about healthy eating.

5. Staff Training:

Provide pre-service and in-service nutrition education staff with training focused on strategies that promote healthy behaviors.

6. Family and Community Involvement:

Involve families and the community in reinforcing nutrition education.

7. Evaluation:

Integrate regular evaluation and modification into nutritional health promotion programming.

Source: Centers for Disease Control and Prevention, "Guidelines for School Health Programs to Promote Lifelong Healthy Eating," MMWR 1996; 45(No. RR-9).

RECOMMENDATIONS FOR TEACHERS: PRACTICE AND CONTENT

Nutrition education is a mandated content area in the graded course of study for the public schools in many states. In the great majority of elementary and middle-level classrooms, however, classroom teachers are responsible for providing nutrition instruction. Because these individuals are not professionally prepared as dietitians or health education content specialists, it is important to note that nutrition education can succeed only when students believe that it is relevant to their lives.[11]

In this context, the *Guidelines for School Health Programs to Promote Lifelong Healthy Eating* confirm that students are more likely to adopt healthy eating behaviors when:

1. They learn about these behaviors through activities that are fun and participatory rather than through lectures,
2. Lessons emphasize the positive and appealing aspects of healthy eating patterns rather than the negative consequences of risky dietary behaviors,

3. The benefits of healthy dietary practices are presented in the context of other issues that are important to students, and

4. Students have repeated opportunities to taste foods that are low in fat, added sugars, and sodium, and high in vitamins, minerals, and fiber during lessons.[12]

In all nutrition education activities, teachers are cautioned to follow hygienic food-handling practices. Further, educators are urged to consider possible food allergies and religious or cultural prohibitions in their lesson planning. To this end, classroom practitioners would be wise to collaborate with or seek the counsel of the school food service director or colleagues from the department of family and consumer sciences in that school district.

Developmentally Appropriate Practice Recommendations

Many teachers, administrators, and parents find difficulty in identifying specific nutrition concepts that are developmentally appropriate for inclusion in a sound nutrition education curricular scope and sequence. Fortunately, the *Guidelines for School Health Programs to Promote Lifelong Healthy Eating* clarify key instructional elements to help teachers create developmentally appropriate lessons for lower- and upper-elementary students and their middle-level counterparts. Although not exhaustive, these recommendations include many of the concepts that are critical to improving the diet, health, and related academic outcomes for youth.[13]

Early Elementary (K–2)

Regardless of the amount and quality of teaching, the youngest students generally do not fully understand abstract nutritional concepts, including:

* The nutrient content of foods, and
* Classification of foods into groups.

Rather, nutrition education for young children should focus on more concrete experiences. Specifically, developmentally appropriate instructional activities for this target audience should focus on the following themes:

1. General recommendations:
   * Increasing exposure to many healthy foods, and
   * Practicing skills necessary to choose healthy foods.
2. Strategies to make the food environment more health enhancing:
   * Making healthy foods widely available, and discouraging the availability of foods that are high in fat, sodium, and added sugars,
   * Involving parents in meaningful homework experiences that focus on eating behaviors and nutrition concepts,

* Providing role models for healthy eating (teachers, parents, other adults, older children, celebrities, or fictional characters),
* Providing cues and reinforcements (posters and marketing activities) for healthy eating and physical activity,
* Using incentives (verbal praise and tokens or gifts) to reinforce healthy eating and physical activity, and
* Avoiding the use of food for rewards or punishments of any behaviors.

3. Strategies to enhance personal characteristics that will support healthy eating:
   * Making connections between food and health ("You need food to feel good and grow"),
   * Reinforcing the importance of balancing food intake and physical activity,
   * Identifying healthy snacks, and
   * Increasing student confidence to make healthy eating choices (practice activities that gradually build up their food selection and preparation skills).
4. Strategies to enhance behavioral capabilities that will support healthy eating:
   * Providing many healthy foods for students to taste in enjoyable social contexts,
   * Structuring opportunities for students to prepare simple snacks, and
   * Having students taste unfamiliar and culturally diverse foods that are low in fat, sodium, and added sugars.[14]

Upper Elementary (3–5)

More abstract associations between nutrition and health emerge more clearly for students in upper-elementary grades. By this age, children are able to understand and act on the connection between eating behaviors and general health status. Professionals and parents who work with these learners are encouraged to develop learning activities that include planned repetition and reinforcement of the concepts identified for K–2 students. In addition, however, teachers should develop lessons that focus on the following additional developmentally appropriate themes and issues:

1. Strategies to make the food environment more health enhancing:
   * Evaluating the impact of social support for making healthy changes in eating and physical activity on personal behavior (discussions and small-group activities).
2. Strategies to enhance personal characteristics that will support healthy eating:
   * Evaluating the effects of diet and physical activity on immediate and long-term health status,
   * Learning the principles of the *Dietary Guidelines for Americans* and the Food Guide Pyramid,

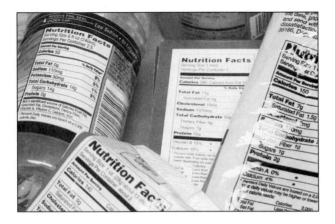

The *Guidelines for School Health Programs to Promote Lifelong Healthy Eating* suggest that it is developmentally appropriate for students in the upper-elementary grades to begin to read food labels.

- Evaluating feelings associated with healthy meals and snacks that are consistent with the *Dietary Guidelines for Americans* and the Food Guide Pyramid,
- Identifying foods that are high and low in fat, saturated fat, cholesterol, sodium, added sugars, and fiber,
- Reviewing the importance of eating adequate amounts of fruits, vegetables, and whole grains,
- Evaluating the personal value placed on health and the sense of control over food selection and preparation, and
- Analyzing food preferences and factors that trigger eating behaviors.

3. Strategies to enhance behavioral capabilities that will support healthy eating:
- Selecting healthy foods from a fast-food restaurant menu,
- Reading nutrition labels to evaluate fat, sodium, and fiber content in foods,
- Recording and evaluating food intake,
- Using the Food Guide Pyramid to assess diet for variety, moderation, and proportion,
- Setting simple goals, devising strategies, and monitoring progress for changing eating and physical activity patterns,
- Using role-playing strategies to support healthy eating and fitness behaviors at home,
- Evaluating the media and social influences on eating and physical activity, and
- Practicing techniques for responding to pressures that support unhealthy eating and exercise behaviors.[15]

Middle-Level School (6–8)

Research has suggested that nutrition instruction for middle school students should begin to focus on empowering

students to assess their own eating behavior and to set goals for improving food selection. Lessons for older students also should begin to emphasize personal responsibility, decision-making skills, and resisting negative social pressures to participate in risky eating and fitness behaviors. In addition to appropriate planned repetition of concepts and activities identified for their younger counterparts, teachers are encouraged to develop learning activities for older students that introduce a focus on:

1. Strategies to make the food environment more health enhancing:
- Using peers as models for healthy eating and fitness behaviors, and
- Participating in peer-led nutrition education activities.
2. Strategies to enhance personal characteristics that will support healthy eating:
- Identifying reasons to adopt healthy eating and physical activity patterns,
- Identifying foods that are excellent sources of fiber, complex carbohydrates, calcium, iron, vitamins A and C, and folate,
- Balancing food intake and physical activity,
- Evaluating the characteristics of a safe weight-loss program and the risks associated with unsafe weight-loss plans, and
- Examining motivations for eating habits through use of food diaries.
3. Strategies to enhance behavioral capabilities that will support healthy eating:
- Planning and preparing simple healthy snacks and meals,
- Selecting healthy foods from cafeteria and restaurant menus,
- Using nutrition labels to enhance food choices,
- Modifying recipes to reduce fat and sodium and increase fiber content,
- Identifying incentives and reinforcements for personal eating and fitness behaviors,
- Analyzing environmental barriers to healthy eating and physical activity,
- Comparing and contrasting diets with recommendations in the *Dietary Guidelines for Americans* and the Food Guide Pyramid,
- Monitoring, modifying, and establishing meaningful rewards for healthy dietary goals, and
- Evaluating nutrition claims from advertisements and nutrition-related news stories.[16]

In conclusion, developmentally appropriate practice guidelines for any grade level must be translated into specific learning activities that are designed to meet the specific needs of a given group of learners. It is important to review, however, that regardless of grade level, the most successful nutrition instructional programs are based

---

CONSIDER THIS

Objectives to Undergird a Sound Nutrition Curricular Scope and Sequence

In addition to increasing student knowledge, sound nutrition education also emphasizes:

- Raising the value that students place on good health and nutrition and identifying the benefits of adopting healthy eating patterns (both short- and long-term),
- Giving students repeated opportunities to taste healthy foods, including those that they have not yet tasted,
- Collaborating with parents, school personnel, public health professionals, and others to overcome barriers to healthy eating,
- Using influential role models, including peers, to demonstrate healthy eating practices,

- Providing incentives to reinforce healthy nutritional messages (ex., verbal praise, small prizes, etc.),
- Helping students develop practical skills and self-confidence to plan meals, prepare foods, read food labels, and make healthy food choices (through observation and active practice experiences),
- Enabling students to critically analyze sociocultural influences, including advertising, on food selection, resisting negative social influences, and developing social support for healthy eating, and
- Helping students analyze their own eating patterns, set realistic goals, monitor progress, and reward themselves for achieving healthy changes in their eating behaviors

Source: Centers for Disease Control and Prevention, "Guidelines for School Health Programs to Promote Lifelong Healthy Eating," *MMWR* 1996;45(No. RR-9).

---

on a series of objectives that go beyond increasing student knowledge. In this context, teachers are encouraged to look at the Consider This box above, which summarizes nutrition objectives beyond content mastery, to undergird a sound curricular scope and sequence for all grade levels.

IMPORTANT TEACHER CONTENT

The following review of basic nutrition information is provided to reinforce teachers' working knowledge of basic nutrition concepts. In addition, it is intended to increase the confidence of elementary and middle-level teachers in integrating developmentally appropriate nutritional health promotion activities into daily classroom practice. Importantly, not all of this information is relevant to all grade levels of elementary or middle-level students. The major concepts that serve as a foundation for teacher effectiveness include the following: (1) nutrient needs, (2) the U.S. Department of Agriculture Food Guide Pyramid, (3) *Dietary Guidelines for Americans,* and (4) common nutritional problems of children and adolescents.

Nutrient Needs

In addition to tasting good, food contains nutrients or chemical components that perform one or more of the following important functions:

1. Providing energy,
2. Supporting proper growth and maintenance of body tissue, and
3. Helping to regulate body temperature.

Recommended Dietary Allowances (RDAs) for nutrient intake have been established by the Food and Nutrition Board of the National Resource Council and the National Academy of Science. The RDAs represent the levels of essential nutrients that will meet essential physiological needs of healthy people. These recommendations were developed to help in planning healthy diets for individuals and groups of people. Also, the RDAs can serve as a foundation for evaluating the nutritional adequacy of the foods that have been eaten. They are the best guide for designing and evaluating the diets of children (table 11.2).

There are six major nutrients that support these life-sustaining functions:

1. Carbohydrates,
2. Fats,
3. Proteins,
4. Vitamins,
5. Minerals, and
6. Water.

Carbohydrates, fats, and proteins are classified as macronutrients, which provide energy (calories) in the diet. A calorie is defined as a unit that is used to measure the energy that is supplied by food, and the energy used by the body. In contrast, vitamins, minerals, and water are called micronutrients. Although micronutrients do not add calories to the diet, they enable the body to use the energy derived from the macronutrients—carbohydrates, fats, and proteins.

Carbohydrates

The main functions of carbohydrates are to provide energy and to maintain normal elimination of wastes from the body. Carbohydrates contain 4 calories per gram.

TABLE 11.2	Food and Nutrition Board, National Academy of Sciences National Research Council Recommended Dietary Allowances,[a] Revised 1989

Designed for the maintenance of good nutrition of practically all healthy people in the United States

Category	Age (years) or Condition	Weight[b] (kg)	Weight[b] (lb)	Height[b] (cm)	Height[b] (in)	Protein (g)	Fat-Soluble Vitamins				Water-Soluble Vitamins							Minerals						
							Vitamin A (μg R.E.)[c]	Vitamin D (μg)[d]	Vitamin E (mg α-T.E.)[e]	Vitamin K (μg)	Vitamin C (mg)	Thiamin (mg)	Riboflavin (mg)	Niacin (mg N.E.)[f]	Vitamin B_6 (mg)[b]	Folate (μg)	Vitamin B_{12} (μg)	Calcium (mg)	Phosphorus (mg)	Magnesium (mg)	Iron (mg)	Zinc (mg)	Iodine (μg)	Selenium (μg)
Children																								
	1–3	13	29	90	35	16	400	10	6	15	40	0.7	0.8	9	1.0	50	0.7	800	800	80	10	10	70	20
	4–6	20	44	112	44	24	500	10	7	20	45	0.9	1.1	12	1.1	75	1.0	800	800	120	10	10	90	20
	7–10	28	62	132	52	28	700	10	7	30	45	1.0	1.2	13	1.4	100	1.4	800	800	170	10	10	120	30

[a]The allowances, expressed as average daily intakes over time, are intended to provide for individual variations among most normal persons as they live in the United States under usual environmental stresses. Diets should be based on a variety of common foods in order to provide other nutrients for which human requirements have been less well defined. See text for detailed discussion of allowances and of nutrients not tabulated.

[b]Weights and heights of Reference Adults are actual medians for the U.S. population of the designated age, as reported by NHANES II. The median weights and heights of those under 19 years of age were taken from Hamill et al. (1979) (see pages 16–17 of reference 1). The use of these figures does not imply that the height-to-weight ratios are ideal.

[c]Retinol equivalents. 1 retinol equivalent = 1 μg retinol or 6 μg B-carotene. See text for calculation of vitamin A activity of diets as retinol equivalents.

[d]As cholecalciferol. 10 μg cholecalciferol = 400 I.U. of vitamin D.

[e]α-Tocopherol equivalents. 1 mg d-α tocopherol = 1 α-T.E. See text for variation in allowances and calculation of vitamin E activity of the diet as α-tocopherol equivalents.

[f]1 N.E. (niacin equivalent) is equal to 1 mg of niacin or 60 mg of dietary tryptophan.

Reprinted with permission from *Recommended Dietary Allowances, 10th Edition* © 1989 by the National Academy of Sciences. Published by the National Academy Press, Washington, D.C.

There are three groups of carbohydrates:

1. Simple sugars,
2. Double sugars, and
3. Complex carbohydrates.

When simple sugars enter the body, they are quickly changed into energy because they do not need to be broken down. Once simple sugars enter the small intestine, they are immediately absorbed into the bloodstream. The three groups of simple sugars include glucose, fructose, and galactose. Simple sugars are found in such common foods as honey, milk, and ripe fruit.

When double sugars are eaten, they quickly are changed into simple sugars. These substances also are absorbed into the bloodstream quite quickly. The three groups of double sugars include:

1. Sucrose (table sugar),
2. Maltose, and
3. Lactose.

Double sugars are found in many common foods including sweet breakfast cereals, cookies, pies, cakes, milk, and ice cream.

The third type of carbohydrates, complex carbohydrates, take much longer to break down than their simpler counterparts. These foods are digested and absorbed by the body at a slower rate. This is beneficial, however, because the body is able to use the energy and nutrients contained in these foods over a longer period of time. In addition, complex carbohydrates contain more nutrients than do simple and double sugars. The three groups of complex carbohydrates include:

1. Starch,
2. Glycogen, and
3. Cellulose (fiber).

Common foods that contain complex carbohydrates include breads, some cereals, fruit, potatoes, rice, and vegetables. It is recommended that carbohydrates should supply approximately 50–55% of the calories, or about

(continued after Activities on page 202)

ACTIVITIES

Nutrition Education Curriculum

As mentioned previously, there are numerous nutrition education activities that can enhance classroom practice. Effective learning activities are developed to reinforce developmentally appropriate knowledge, attitude, and skills, and should engage parents whenever possible. The following nutrition education activities can be used with elementary and middle-level students.

Grades K–2

1. *Food-tasting Parties.* As a way to reinforce the importance of celebrating special events in the lives of students, integrate food-tasting parties into regular classroom practice. Invite parents to help students create healthy celebration foods and snacks. In addition, have students taste culturally diverse foods.

2. *At-home Food Explorer.* Give students a list of foods to find at home or in grocery stores. Encourage students to discuss the sources of the foods with a parent or caring adult. Encourage parents to check off items once they are found and discussed. Students then return the sheet to school for discussion with classmates on an appointed day. Focus the discussion and correlation on where foods are found and from where they come.

3. *Sorting Healthy Foods.* Provide two boxes, one labeled "Healthy Foods" and the other labeled "Less Healthy Foods," and a collection of food boxes, cans, and other containers. Organize teams of students for a timed challenge to see which team can sort the most foods correctly within previously identified time constraints. Add other elements, including analyzing labels, to this gross-motor activity with older students.

4. *Holiday Food as Art.* Ask students to draw pictures of several foods that are part of their family celebrations for various holidays and commemorations. Collect and display the drawings on a holiday foods bulletin board. Have older students sort and make substitutions for less-than-healthy selections. Periodically, make holiday meals in the classroom or in conjunction with age-cohort peers from other classrooms.

5. *Plant a Garden.* Plant a class garden as a continuous class project. Assign groups of students to different sections of the garden and make them responsible for planting, watering, weeding, and harvesting. As a culminating activity, make a salad out of the foods produced from the garden.

6. *Trying New Foods.* Challenge students to try new, healthy foods that fit into one of the food groups. When they try a new food, ask them to place a picture of it on a bulletin board with their name beside it. They can either cut out a picture from a magazine, or they can draw a picture of the new food item. Students enjoy having their names posted where their classmates can see them.

7. *Food in Poetry.* Ask students to create food poems using their favorite or least favorite foods. This can be completed as an individual or a cooperative learning activity. Have students illustrate their poems and share them with the class.

8. *Peanut Butter à la Play Dough.* This is an activity to allow children to make and decorate a food item, and then eat it. *Caution is urged concerning children with allergies to nut products with this activity.* Teachers and children should mix the following items together:

Ingredients

1 18-oz. jar of smooth/creamy peanut butter

6 tbsp. honey

Nonfat dry milk

Pretzel sticks and sunflower seeds

Procedure

Mix the peanut butter and honey together. Add as much dry milk as needed to form a claylike consistency. Once the batter is mixed together, give each child a plate and a portion of the batter. Instruct the children to make a shape out of the batter and then decorate it with pretzel sticks and sunflower seeds. After they have shared their design with the class, they can eat their creation.

Grades 3–5

1. *Unfinished Sentences.* Create a list of developmentally appropriate, unfinished sentence stems. Invite individual students to complete the sentences in the writing correlation activity. Finally, encourage students to find a partner or group of students with whom they must come to a consensus about their responses.

2. *Twenty Questions.* This is an activity to review the five food groups and/or nutrients. Prepare index cards that have one food item written on each card, such as *apple, steak, milk, chicken, bread,* or *fish.* To begin this activity, tape one of the index cards on each student's back so he or she does not know which food item is identified on the card. Have the students go around the class and ask "yes" or "no" questions to determine which food is written on the card. For example, a student may begin by asking classmates, "Is my food item in the meat group?" or "Is my food item high in vitamin C?" If students know what food items belong in each food group, they should be able to systematically narrow the range and guess the food item identified on the card that is taped on their back.

3. *Test Tube Demonstration.* Visuals are very important to use with elementary students because students at this age are such concrete thinkers. For example, when discussing the amount of fat, sugar, and salt content in fast foods, it is helpful to show students what 5 tablespoons of fat and 10 teaspoons of sugar look like. An easy way to do this is to measure certain amounts of salt, fat, and sugar, and place them in test tubes. This allows students to see the exact amount of those ingredients in the foods they are eating. Convert these measurements to grams, because most food labels indicate the number of grams instead of teaspoons. For a math correlation, have students weigh the amount of fat, salt, and sugar in fast foods.

4. *Healthy Snacks or Banquet.* While studying nutrition, it is important to introduce students to new and healthy foods. Many upper-elementary students are willing to try new foods when given the opportunity. Ask different parents to bring materials to make a healthy after-school snack to class. Have students practice making the healthy snacks as alternatives to less-healthy alternatives that may be available to them.

5. *Grocery Store.* Have teachers, students, and parents save empty food containers and labels from different food items. Then set up a grocery store learning center, where students can practice reading labels, buying healthy foods, and seeing different food items. Instruct students on how to read a label. Food label requirements changed in 1994, and manufacturers are now required to include information on calories, fat, cholesterol, sodium, carbohydrates, proteins, and more. Show students where to find the number of calories, protein, carbohydrates, fat, and sodium on the food labels. The American Heart Association curriculum has information and activities on how to read food labels.

6. *Favorite Foods.* Ask students to list their ten favorite foods, place them into the five food groups, and also determine how healthy their food choices are. Ask students to substitute healthier foods for those that are in the fats, oils, and sweets group.

7. *Dietary Guidelines for Americans.* Have students write letters to their parents, informing them about each of the *Dietary Guidelines for Americans.* Letters could feature hints for supporting healthier eating for each child's family. In addition, have children highlight health problems associated with not following the guidelines.

8. *Fast-Food Detective.* Place students in cooperative learning groups for this activity. Provide each group with a prepared packet about the total weight and fat grams in their selected fast food. Ask each group to complete the steps to determine how much fat is in their fast food. A *sample*

handout follows:

Be a Fast-Food Fat Detective. The food that your group is investigating is a Wendy's single hamburger with cheese.

- For your information, this product weighs a total of 210 grams. Your first job is to set your scale for 210 grams.
- Now, weigh clay or play dough and mold it into a 210-gram ball that looks like a hamburger.
- This has 21 grams of fat in it.
- Now, set your scales for 21 grams and weigh out a lump of clay or play dough that weighs 21 grams.
- Figure out how much of your sandwich is not fat: 210 grams minus 21 grams.
- What does your group think about this food? Is it healthy for students your age? Why?

Grades 6–8

1. *Creating a Balanced Diet.* After learning about the Food Guide Pyramid, ask students to cut out pictures of foods from magazines and create a balanced meal or meals. If teachers and students have a difficult time finding pictures of food items, they can use grocery store advertisements that have colored pictures of foods. Meals should have at least one food item from each of the five food groups. Glue these pictures on paper plates and display them in the classroom or send them home to be discussed with parents. As students get older, instruct them to do the same activity but instead identify specific nutrients, or focus on the *Dietary Guidelines of America.*

2. *Analyzing a Diet.* Ask older elementary and middle-level students to write down the foods they ate the previous day. Instruct them to analyze their diets in terms of the Food Guide Pyramid or the amount of nutrients in their diet. If there are any problems in their diet, instruct them to indicate how they could make their one-day food intake a balanced diet. For example, if they were low in the milk group, they might substitute milk for soda. Have students take this information home and share it with their parents.

3. *Nutrition Behavior Change Project.* After learning about nutrition, ask students to choose one negative nutrition habit they are currently engaged in. For instance, they might not eat breakfast, they might always eat candy for a snack, they might not get enough servings from one of the food groups, or they might consume high amounts of soda each day. After identifying the habit they want to change, ask students to keep a diary indicating how their project is progressing. Give students the opportunity to share how their behavior change project is going with a selected support group within the class.

4. *Analyzing School Lunches.* Ask students to analyze a school lunch and indicate if it contains foods from each of the five food groups. Have the cafeteria staff assist in this assignment by labeling the foods in the lunch line. For example, food from the fruit group could be identified with a red label, and foods from the vegetable group could be identified with a green label. If the meal does not contain foods from each of the groups, have students suggest substitutions so that the meal is well balanced and appealing. Ask the school dietician to come to class and discuss the menu and changes with the students.

5. *Analyzing Commercials.* Instruct students to watch food commercials and analyze how the commercials are trying to get them to buy products. Have a discussion about how to be smart consumers when buying food products. In addition, have students develop a series of videotaped commercials that reinforce healthy dietary behaviors. Show these public service commercials on the school's closed-circuit TV system.

6. *Effects of Cholesterol on Arteries.* Before class, take clear plastic tubing and melt colored wax inside of the tube to represent cholesterol and fat deposits in the arteries. Holding a burning candle over the tube and letting the wax drip inside seems to work best for this demonstration. This can tie in nicely when discussing fat and cholesterol.

7. *Rap Songs.* Some children relate to music, and a popular type of music today is rap. Ask students to write their own rap songs about a particular nutrient, the five food groups, or the *Dietary Guidelines.*

8. *Food Pyramid of My Diet.* Assign students to keep a food log for a minimum of 3 days. For each day, have them construct a food pyramid that reflects their actual eating habits. Focus a follow-up discussion on variables that influenced differences in eating behaviors across days, and deviations from the USDA Food Guide Pyramid.

9. *Analyzing Magazine Photos.* Have students collect color ads from magazines that depict men and women of all ages. Ask each student to write a one-paragraph summary of what the photos tell us about cultural criteria for attractiveness for both sexes. Assemble groups to collapse ideas from all individual paragraphs into a group consensus statement. Enrich the follow-up discussion by including student reactions to photos from international magazines or Internet outlets.

300 grams, in a child's daily diet of 2,400 calories. Although most Americans consume an adequate amount of carbohydrates, it is unfortunate that most are in the form of simple and double sugars. At least one-third of the carbohydrates consumed should be in the form of complex carbohydrates that are high in starch and fiber.[17]

Fats

The primary functions of fats are to delay hunger, insulate the body, provide energy, and carry fat-soluble vitamins for important body functions. While carbohydrates contain 4 calories per gram, fats contain 9 of these units of energy per gram. Fats contain more than twice the calories of proteins and carbohydrates.

There are three main types of fats:

1. Saturated fats,
2. Monounsaturated fats, and
3. Polyunsaturated fats.

Saturated fats are found primarily in foods developed from animal sources, including whole milk, cream, butter, cheese, poultry, and meat. Saturated fats are solid at room temperature, and are found in some vegetable oils such as coconut and palm oil.[18] Some cookies, cakes, candy, and other sweets contain high levels of these hidden saturated fats. High amounts of saturated fats in the diet have been linked with cardiovascular disease, because they seem to raise blood cholesterol levels.[19] Other health problems associated with a high intake of saturated fats include cancers of the breast, uterus, prostate, colon, and rectum.

Monounsaturated fats are usually found in foods that are developed from plant sources. These fats are found in olive oil, peanut oil, peanut butter, some margarines, vegetable oils, and salad dressings.[20] Unlike saturated fats, monounsaturated fats tend to decrease blood cholesterol levels.[21]

Polyunsaturated fats also are found in foods that are derived primarily from plant sources. Polyunsaturated fats are found in sunflower, corn, cottonseed, and safflower oils and some fish.[22] Like the monounsaturated fats, polyunsaturated fats also tend to decrease blood cholesterol levels.[23]

Fats should supply 30% or less, or about 72 grams, of a child's daily diet of 2,400 calories. It is common, however, for Americans to consume about 40% of their total calories in the form of fat. Further, it is recommended that saturated fats should constitute only about one-third of the total fat intake. Two-thirds of fat intake should be supplied from unsaturated fat sources.[24]

Cholesterol is the focus of much conversation, but many people are confused about it. Although not a true fat, cholesterol is a fat-like substance that is found in the cells of all humans and other animals. Cholesterol helps the body form cell membranes, hormones, and other important substances. In healthy people, the body is capable of producing sufficient amounts of cholesterol for these important functions. As a result, most people do not need to supplement their diets with additional foods that are high in cholesterol. Even though there has been much publicity about the dangers of such practices, Americans tend to consume diets that are high in cholesterol.

A dangerous link has been confirmed between elevated blood cholesterol levels and increased risk for heart disease and stroke. Cholesterol is carried in the bloodstream by lipoproteins (protein and fat complexes). Some cholesterol may be deposited in the form of fatty streaks in artery walls. If these fatty deposits build up, they form plaque. This process results in a thickening of the artery walls. As the artery walls thicken and become less flexible, it becomes more difficult for blood to flow freely. This process is related to increased blood pressure. Over the long term, arteries can become completely blocked, restricting blood flow to life-sustaining organs. In particular, if blood supplies to the heart or brain are blocked, a heart attack or stroke may occur.

To decrease the buildup of fatty deposits in arteries, the amount of cholesterol in the diet should be reduced. A good rule of thumb suggests that the more saturated the fat, the higher the percentage of cholesterol in that food product.[25]

The buildup of fat deposits also is influenced by the amount of high-density lipoprotein (HDL) and low-density lipoprotein (LDL) in the body. HDLs are considered to be the "good guys" because they carry cholesterol away from artery walls. By contrast, LDLs are known as the "bad guys" because they help carry and deposit cholesterol in the walls of the arteries. The levels of HDLs can be raised by exercising, staying lean, and avoiding the use of tobacco products.

Proteins

Proteins are the third macronutrient. The main function of proteins is to aid in the growth and repair of all body tissues. Like carbohydrates, proteins supply 4 calories per gram and are found in all body cells. Protein should comprise approximately 12%, or about 70 grams, of a child's daily diet of 2,400 calories. When proteins enter the body, they are absorbed into the gastrointestinal tract and are broken into amino acids. Amino acids are substances that make up proteins, and typically are compared to building blocks because they connect together in endless ways to form a variety of protein molecules. Amino acids then are absorbed into the bloodstream and carried throughout the body to help build and repair tissue.[26]

There are two types of amino acids: essential and nonessential. The human body cannot produce essential amino acids. Rather, these substances must be supplied by the foods that we eat. By contrast, the body can produce nonessential amino acids from essential amino acids. These products do not need to be included in the diet. Foods that supply all of the essential amino acids are called complete proteins and include such foods as meat, milk, eggs, fish, cheese, and poultry. All of the essential amino acids also are provided by some combination foods, including beans and rice, cereal and milk, and macaroni and cheese.[27]

The body can use only a limited amount of protein at one time. Because excess protein is stored in the form of fat, it is important to eat protein on a daily basis. Without sufficient intake of protein, tissue building and repair will not occur.

Because of the high intake of meat, poultry, and eggs, most Americans consume at least 12% of their calories from protein. Vegetarians represent the only group that may have a problem achieving sufficient protein intake. Vegetarians can consume an adequate amount of complete proteins if they are careful to consume a diet containing proper combinations of foods.[28]

Vitamins

Vitamins are micronutrients that do not provide energy. Rather, they are needed to transform foods into energy and to help with body maintenance. Vitamins also help regulate body functions and help the body resist infections. There are two types of vitamins:

1. Fat-soluble (vitamins D, E, A, and K), and
2. Water-soluble (B-complex and C vitamins).

Fat-soluble vitamins can be stored and transported by the body's fat cells. Water-soluble vitamins cannot be stored in the body. Any excess water-soluble vitamins are passed through the body. Table 11.3 lists all of the

TABLE 11.3	Fat-Soluble and Water-Soluble Vitamins		
Fat-Soluble Vitamins			
VITAMIN	**WHY NEEDED**	**IMPORTANT SOURCES**	**DEFICIENCY SYMPTOMS**
A	Helps keep eyes healthy and able to see in dim light. Helps keep skin healthy and smooth. Helps keep lining of mouth, nose, throat, and digestive tract healthy and resistant to infection. Aids normal bone growth and tooth formation through proper utilization of calcium and phosphorus.	Liver, butter, fortified margarine, whole milk, vitamin-A fortified milk, deep yellow and dark leafy green vegetables, cantaloupe, apricots, other deep yellow fruits, cheese.	Night blindness, impaired growth of bones and tooth enamel, eye secretions cease, infection of mucous membranes. Deficiency seldom seen in the United States.
D	Helps promote normal growth. Helps body use calcium and phosphorus for the building and maintenance of strong bones and teeth.	Fish-liver oils, vitamin-D fortified milk, liver, egg yolk, salmon, tuna; sunlight produces vitamin D from a form of cholesterol in the skin.	Rickets, a softening of the bones leading to bow legs and other bone abnormalities.
E	Helps prevent red blood cell destruction. Helps prevent damage to cells from oxidation.	Vegetables, vegetable oils, wheat germ.	Anemia due to increased red blood cell destruction.
K	Helps with blood clotting.	Green leafy vegetables, liver, vegetable oil, tomatoes, potatoes, produced by intestinal bacteria.	Severe bleeding, poor blood clotting.

(continued)

TABLE 11.3	Fat-Soluble and Water-Soluble Vitamins *(continued)*		

Water-Soluble Vitamins

VITAMIN	WHY NEEDED	IMPORTANT SOURCES	DEFICIENCY SYMPTOMS
C (ascorbic acid)	Helps bind body cells together through the production of connective tissue. Aids normal bone and tooth formation, maintenance, and repair. Aids in healing wounds. Helps the body utilize iron. Helps resist infection.	Citrus fruits and juices, tomatoes, green peppers, strawberries, cantaloupe, watermelon, cabbage, potatoes, broccoli, brussels sprouts.	Scurvy—degeneration of bones, teeth, and gums, anemia, rough skin, wounds that don't heal.
B_1 (thiamine)	Helps the body change carbohydrate foods into energy. Promotes normal appetite and digestion. Helps to maintain a healthy nervous system.	Pork, liver, dry beans and peas, whole-grain and enriched breads and cereals, nuts.	Beriberi—muscular weakness, mental confusion, cardiac abnormalities.
B_2 (riboflavin)	Helps release energy from carbohydrates, fat, and protein. Helps keep skin healthy.	Milk, liver, eggs, green leafy vegetables, lean meats, dried beans and peas, enriched breads, cereals, and pasta.	Skin sores around the nose and lips, cracking of the corners of the mouth, eyes sensitive to light.
B_3 (niacin)	Helps release energy from carbohydrates, fat, and protein. Helps maintain all body tissues.	Tuna, poultry, lean meat, fish, liver, peanuts, peas, whole-grain or fortified breads, cereals, and pasta.	Pellagra—diarrhea, mental disorders, skin rash, irritability.
B_6 (pyridoxine)	Helps the body to use protein to build body tissue. Helps the body to use carbohydrates and fat for energy.	Whole grains, meat, liver, fish, wheat germ, bananas, spinach, green leafy vegetables.	Skin disorders, mental depression, weakness, irritability.
B_{12} (cyanoco-balamin)	Helps the body form red blood cells. Aids in normal function of all body cells.	Lean meat, liver, eggs, milk, cheese (animal products).	Pernicious anemia, nervous system malfunctions, soreness and weakness in arms and legs.
Folacin (folic acid)	Aids in the formation of hemoglobin in the red blood cells. Necessary for the production of genetic material.	Liver, green vegetables, dried beans and peas, nuts.	Anemia, diarrhea, smooth red tongue.
Pantothenic acid	Helps release energy from carbohydrates, fat, and protein. Helps form hormones.	Liver, whole-grain cereal and bread, green vegetables, eggs, nuts.	Nausea, headache, muscle cramps, low blood sugar.
Biotin	Helps release energy from carbohydrates. Helps the body synthesize fatty acids.	Liver, kidney, egg yolks, green beans.	None known under normal conditions.

fat-soluble and water-soluble vitamins, their functions, sources, and associated deficiency symptoms.[29]

Minerals

Like vitamins, minerals are micronutrients that do not provide energy. Rather, they are tissue-building materials that help regulate body functions. There are two types of minerals: macrominerals and trace elements. Healthy people need more than 100 milligrams of macrominerals, per day including calcium, phosphorus, potassium, sulfur, sodium, chlorine, and magnesium. By contrast, people need less than 100 milligrams of trace elements per day including iron, manganese, copper, iodine, cobalt, and zinc. Just as each vitamin serves a different purpose, so does each mineral. Table 11.4 lists the functions and sources of each mineral.[30]

TABLE 11.4	Functions and Sources of Various Minerals

Major Minerals and Trace Elements

MINERAL	FUNCTIONS	SOURCES
Calcium (Ca)	Structure of bones and teeth, essential for nerve-impulse conduction, muscle-fiber contraction, and blood coagulation, increases permeability of cell membranes, activates certain enzymes.	Milk, milk products, leafy green vegetables.
Phosphorus (P)	Structure of bones and teeth, component in nearly all metabolic reactions, constituent of nucleic acids, many proteins, some enzymes, and some vitamins, occurs in cell membrane, ATP, and phosphates of body fluids.	Meats, poultry, fish, cheese, nuts, whole-grain cereals, milk, legumes.
Potassium (K)	Helps maintain intracellular osmotic pressure and regulate pH, promotes metabolism, needed for nerve-impulse conduction and muscle-fiber contraction.	Avocados, dried apricots, meats, nuts, potatoes, bananas.
Sulfur (S)	Essential part of various amino acids, thiamine, insulin, biotin, and mucopolysaccharides.	Meats, milk, eggs, legumes.
Sodium (Na)	Helps maintain osmotic pressure of extracellular fluids and regulate water balance, needed for conduction of nerve impulses and contraction of muscle fibers, aids in regulation of pH and in transport of substances across cell membranes.	Table salt, cured ham, sauerkraut, cheese, graham crackers.
Chlorine (Cl)	Helps maintain osmotic pressure of extracellular fluids, regulates pH, and maintains electrolyte balance, essential in formation of hydrochloric acid, aids transport of carbon dioxide by red blood cells.	Same as for sodium.
Magnesium (Mg)	Needed in metabolic reactions that occur in mitochondria and are associated with the production of ATP, plays role in conversion of ATP to ADP.	Milk, dairy products, legumes, nuts, leafy green vegetables.

TRACE ELEMENT	FUNCTIONS	SOURCES
Iron (Fe)	Part of hemoglobin molecule, catalyzes formation of vitamin A, incorporated into a number of enzymes.	Liver, lean meats, dried apricots, raisins, enriched whole-grain cereals, legumes, molasses.
Manganese (Mn)	Occurs in enzymes needed for synthesis of fatty acids and cholesterol, formation of urea, and normal functioning of the nervous system.	Nuts, legumes, whole-grain cereals, leafy green vegetables, fruits.
Copper (Cu)	Essential for synthesis of hemoglobin, development of bone, production of melanin, and formation of myelin.	Liver, oysters, crabmeat, nuts, whole-grain cereals, legumes.
Iodine (I)	Essential component for synthesis of thyroid hormones.	Food content varies with soil content in different geographic regions, iodized table salt.
Cobalt (Co)	Component of cyanocobalamin, needed for synthesis of several enzymes.	Liver, lean meats, poultry, fish, milk.
Zinc (Zn)	Constituent of several enzymes involved in digestion, respiration, bone metabolism, liver metabolism, necessary for normal wound healing and maintaining integrity of the skin.	Seafoods, meats, cereals, legumes, nuts, vegetables.

Water

Water constitutes roughly 60% of a person's body weight. The functions of water include transporting usable materials to and wastes away from cells, regulating body temperature, and helping with digestion, absorption, circulation, excretion, and building tissue. A person can live for days and even weeks without food, but can last only a few days without water. It is recommended that a person consume 48 to 64 ounces of water a day. Children who are physically active should be especially careful to consume enough water every day. Importantly, teachers should not restrict the intake of water

---

CONSIDER THIS

How to Use the Daily Food Guide

WHAT COUNTS AS ONE SERVING?

Breads, Cereals, Rice, and Pasta
One slice of bread
1/2 cup of cooked rice or pasta
1/2 cup of cooked cereal
1 ounce of ready-to-eat cereal

Vegetables
1/2 cup of chopped raw or
　　cooked vegetables
1 cup of leafy raw vegetables

Fruits
1 piece of fruit or melon wedge
3/4 cup of juice
1/2 cup of canned fruit
1/4 cup of dried fruit

Milk, Yogurt, and Cheese
1 cup of milk or yogurt
$1\frac{1}{2}$ to 2 ounces of cheese

Meat, Poultry, Fish, Dry Beans, Eggs, and Nuts
$2\frac{1}{2}$ to 3 ounces of cooked lean meat, poultry, or fish
　　Count 1/2 cup of cooked beans, or 1 egg, or 2 tablespoons
　　of peanut butter as 1 ounce of lean meat (about 1/3 serving).

Fats, Oils, and Sweets
LIMIT CALORIES FROM THESE
especially if you need to lose weight.

The amount you eat may be more than one serving. For example, a dinner portion of spaghetti would count as two or three servings of pasta.

---

for children, especially in warm weather. In this context, it is not uncommon to see water bottles or other closed containers of water on the desks in many classrooms. Water is consumed in the form of tap water or is derived from foods. Milk contains about 87% water, meat has between 40–75% water, and bread contains about 35% water.[31]

THE U.S. DEPARTMENT OF AGRICULTURE FOOD GUIDE PYRAMID

In the past, as many teachers know, the United States Department of Agriculture (USDA) classified foods into the basic four food groups. This protocol has been modified, and the USDA now categorizes foods into a Food Guide Pyramid. This model is based on USDA's research about:

1. What foods Americans eat,
2. What nutrients are in these foods, and most importantly,
3. How to make the best food choices.[32]

The five food groups in the Food Guide Pyramid include the following:

1. The bread, cereal, rice, and pasta group,
2. The fruit group,
3. The vegetable group,
4. The milk, yogurt, and cheese group, and
5. The meat, poultry, fish, dry beans, eggs, and nuts group.

Each food group represents a good source of specific nutrients. By eating a variety of foods from each group, people can get all the nutrients that they need to stay healthy. In addition, the Food Guide Pyramid system is an excellent starting point for nutrition education for elementary and middle-level students. It provides a relatively easy visual structure for elementary and middle-level schoolchildren to learn what groups of foods are good sources of specific nutrients. Figure 11.1 shows the Food Guide Pyramid, while the Consider This box above identifies the amount of food contained in one serving from each of the pyramid categories.

The bread, cereal, rice, and pasta group contains foods that are made from corn, oats, wheat, buckwheat, barley, rye, and rice. This food group is located at the base of the pyramid because healthy people need to eat the most food from this group. These foods are good sources of carbohydrates, thiamin, iron, and niacin. It is recommended that children consume nine servings from the bread, cereal, rice, and pasta group every day.[33]

The fruit group contains all fresh, canned, dried, and frozen fruits and their juices. The main nutrients that the fruit group provides are vitamins A and C and potassium. Fruits are also low in fat and sodium. Good sources of vitamin A include yellow fruits, while good sources of vitamin C include citrus fruits and strawberries. Children should consume three servings from the fruit group each day. Teachers are reminded that although many "fruit drinks" look healthy, typically they contain large amounts of water and sugar. Instead, children should be encouraged to drink fruit juice.[34]

Food Guide Pyramid
A GUIDE TO DAILY FOOD CHOICES

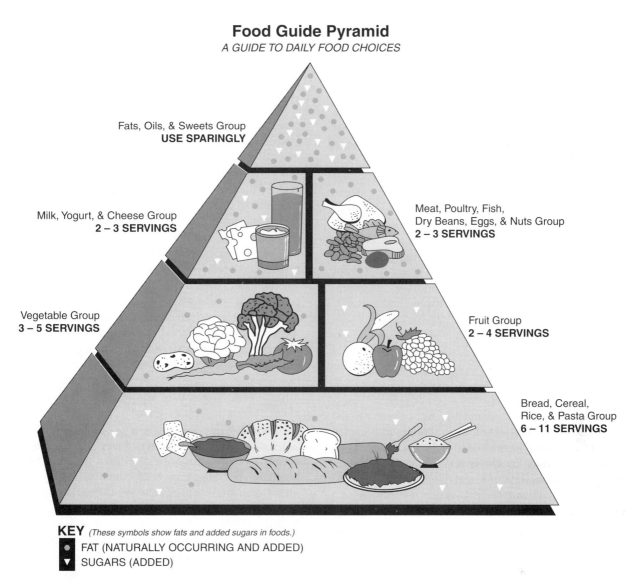

Fats, Oils, & Sweets Group
USE SPARINGLY

Milk, Yogurt, & Cheese Group
2 – 3 SERVINGS

Meat, Poultry, Fish,
Dry Beans, Eggs, & Nuts Group
2 – 3 SERVINGS

Vegetable Group
3 – 5 SERVINGS

Fruit Group
2 – 4 SERVINGS

Bread, Cereal,
Rice, & Pasta Group
6 – 11 SERVINGS

KEY *(These symbols show fats and added sugars in foods.)*
● FAT (NATURALLY OCCURRING AND ADDED)
▼ SUGARS (ADDED)

Figure 11.1
Use the Food Guide Pyramid to help you eat better every day—the Dietary Guidelines way. Start with plenty of breads, cereals, rice, and pasta; vegetables; and fruits. Add two to three servings from the milk group and two to three servings from the meat group. Each of these food groups provides some, but not all, of the nutrients you need. No one food group is more important than another. For good health you need them all. Go easy on fats, oils, and sweets.

The vegetable group contains all fresh, canned, dried, and frozen vegetables and their juices. Vegetables are a good source of vitamins A and C and folate. In addition, these foods are high in the minerals iron and magnesium. Vegetables also provide fiber and are naturally low in fat. It is recommended that children consume four servings of vegetables a day.[35]

The milk, yogurt, and cheese group includes all types of milk, cheese, ice cream, yogurt, cottage cheese, and foods such as pudding that are made with milk. Foods in the milk group are good sources of calcium, riboflavin, and protein. Children need at least two to three servings a day from the milk group.[36] Unfortunately, many children substitute soft drinks for milk in their daily diets. When

discussing the milk group, teachers should stress the importance of consuming healthy milk servings. Due to the potentially high fat content in many foods in this pyramid group, skim and low-fat milk are recommended instead of whole milk for all except the youngest children. In this context, low-fat cheeses, ice milk, and frozen yogurt are healthier milk-group choices.

An adequate amount of calcium not only helps with growth and development, but also increases peak bone mass. A high peak bone mass will help prevent porous bones or osteoporosis later in life. Osteoporosis is a disease that afflicts older persons, especially women. When a person has osteoporosis, he or she is prone to bone fractures and curvature of the spine.[37] The number of osteoporosis cases is increasing among American adults, making it even more important that teachers encourage children to establish healthy dietary habits during formative years.

The meat, poultry, fish, dry beans, eggs, and nuts group includes a variety of foods from sources such as beef, pork, chicken, fish, and eggs. It also includes foods from plants, such as nuts, lentils, beans, peas, and peanut butter. The foods in this group are good sources of iron, protein, niacin, and thiamin. Protein is needed to build and maintain body tissue, to supply energy, and to regulate body processes. Children need at least two servings from the meat group every day.[38]

Other foods, which nutritionists categorize into fats, oils, and sweets, are found in the small, upper tip of the Food Guide Pyramid. Foods in this category do not contain enough nutrients to be placed into any food group. They include candy, cakes, pies, salad dressings, mustard, butter, gravy, potato chips, alcohol, and soft drinks. These foods should be consumed only in moderation and should not replace servings from other food groups.

DIETARY GUIDELINES FOR AMERICANS

In 1985, the U.S. the Department of Agriculture and the Department of Health and Human Services established seven dietary recommendations for healthy Americans. In 1990, these guidelines were revised to reflect current findings in nutrition research, and to make them easier to understand. The *Dietary Guidelines* were established as a foundation for healthy decision making for currently healthy people who have no dietary restrictions. Teachers would be wise to develop learning activities for elementary and middle-level students that focus on these guidelines as a foundation for developing healthy habits during childhood and adolescence. In addition, communication with parents and other caregivers explaining each guideline and offering suggestions for integrating healthy dietary practices into daily practice is an important step to reinforce a commitment to parent engagement.[39] The *Dietary Guidelines for Americans* are described in the following section.

Guideline 1—Eat a Variety of Foods

The first guideline is closely related to the recommendations of the Food Guide Pyramid. It is important to eat a variety of foods to obtain all of the nutrients the body needs to function properly. By eating a variety of foods, children and adults can be sure that they have met all nutrient needs. Physicians may recommend that some adult patients, including pregnant women, take nutritional supplements. Importantly, however, it is recommended that children get their range of necessary vitamins and minerals from foods rather than through supplements. In conclusion, the USDA recommends that children and adults acquire the many nutrients they need by consuming different foods that they enjoy from the food groups identified in the Food Guide Pyramid.[40]

Guideline 2—Maintain a Healthy Weight

Maintaining healthy weight is important for good health. People who have a high percentage of body fat or other individuals who are too thin, increase their chances of developing health problems. Obesity is associated with such medical problems as heart disease, high blood pressure, diabetes, and some cancers. Many elementary and middle-school students have developed problems that are associated with obesity as a result of overeating and a lack of physical activity. It is not uncommon for children to snack on cake, chips, or other high-fat foods while watching television. Because obesity in schoolchildren is a significant risk factor for obesity in later years, it is important to promote the concept of maintaining a healthy weight during childhood.[41] Risks associated with fad diets should be the focus of instructional activities. In addition, students should understand the relationship between caloric intake and output as a basis for weight management. The role of vigorous physical exercise in maintaining a healthy weight also is an important instructional element.

Unhealthy and excessive weight loss related to anorexia and bulimia is a problem for some children and young adolescents. This is especially true of young females. Numerous studies have found that dieting is popular among average-weight girls. A study of Michigan and Indiana schoolgirls found that 18% of underweight girls and 60% of average-weight girls were trying to lose weight. Findings also revealed that even some 9-year-old girls were on drastic and potentially dangerous diets.[42]

When teaching about nutrition, it is important for teachers to avoid the practice of identifying foods as being "bad" or "good." Rather, it is more educationally sound to reinforce the concepts of variety, healthy, less-than-healthy, and moderation. This is important because it has been demonstrated that many people with eating disorders are absolute in their thinking. For example, things are either right or wrong, good or bad, and big or small. If foods are presented as "bad," students who have anorexic tendencies may stop eating those foods. In addition, teachers are reminded that younger students associate the concepts of "good" and "bad" with taste and flavor or preference of foods, rather than with their health risk.

To help detect eating disorders and other risky dietary practices, elementary students consistently should be measured for height and weight. In addition, those measurements should be recorded on school records that follow the students through their developmental years. In conclusion, children need calories to grow and develop normally. In this context, weight-reducing diets are usually not recommended for them. Rather, overweight children may need help to choose physical activities that they enjoy and nutritious diets with adequate, but not excessive, calories.[43]

Guideline 3—Choose a Diet Low in Fat, Saturated Fat, and Cholesterol

A major risk factor for cardiovascular disease is a high blood cholesterol level. As previously discussed, higher amounts of saturated fat and cholesterol in a person's diet have been associated with a greater likelihood for developing a high blood cholesterol level and related medical problems. The following suggestions to reduce fat intake are appropriate to discuss with elementary and middle-level students (table 11.5).[44]

- Choose lean meat, fish, poultry, and dry beans and peas as protein sources.
- Check labels on foods to see how much fat and saturated fat are in a serving.
- Use skim or low-fat milk and milk products.
- Use fats and oils sparingly in cooking.
- Choose liquid vegetable oils most often because they are lower in saturated fat.
- Trim the fat off of meat.
- Moderate the use of egg yolks and organ meats.
- Choose broiled, baked, or boiled foods instead of fried foods.

All Americans are encouraged to include plenty of fruits and vegetables in their daily diets.

TABLE 11.5	Substitutions to Reduce Fat, Cholesterol, and Calories
High Fat	**Reduced Fat**
Milk, evaporated milk, or cream	Skim, 1%, or 1/2% milk.
Sour cream	Nonfat yogurt; low-fat cottage cheese blended until smooth.
Creamed cottage cheese (4%)	Low-fat cottage cheese (2%).
Hard cheeses: cheddar, swiss, muenster	Cheese made with part skim milk (6 grams of fat or less per ounce).
Butter or margarine	Spreads, whipped, lite, or diet margarines.
Shortening or bacon drippings	Vegetable oil or margarines (listed above).
Mayonnaise	Lite mayonnaise or Miracle Whip.®
Salad dressing	Low-calorie dressings with less than 20 calories per tablespoon; homemade dressings using vinegar, lemon or tomato juice, etc.
Eggs	Cholesterol-free egg substitutes (Egg Beaters or egg whites).
Canned soups	Homemade with skim milk; white sauce or tomato juice base.
Ice cream	Frozen yogurt, sherbet, ice milk, popsicles, frozen juice bars, pudding pops.
Potato chips, cheese curls, corn chips	Pretzels, popcorn, bread sticks, crackers.
Pastry, cake	Graham crackers, angel food cake, gingersnaps, Fig Newtons, vanilla wafers, animal crackers, Jello pudding, fruit.
Luncheon meats	Turkey and other lunch meats 90–99% fat free, turkey breast.
Cream cheese	Blend 4 teaspoons margarine spread with 1 cup low-fat cottage cheese.

- Have cooked dry beans and peas instead of meat occasionally.
- Reduce the intake of coconut and palm oil.
- Remove the skin from fish and poultry.

Guideline 4—Choose a Diet with Plenty of Vegetables, Fruits, and Grain Products

This guideline was included so that persons would eat foods that are high in starch and fiber, including vegetables, fruits, and grains. As discussed previously, complex carbohydrates are excellent food choices because of their nutritional value. Starch and fiber are types of complex carbohydrates that should be consumed daily. Foods that are high in starch include breads, rice, potatoes, pasta, and such vegetables as corn, peas, and lima beans.

Fiber is the part of plants that cannot be digested by humans. Even though it cannot be digested, it is still important to consume because it helps to reduce symptoms of chronic constipation and some types of bowel disorders.

The USDA concludes by recommending that children, adolescents, and adults be encouraged to choose foods that are good sources of fiber and starch, such as whole-grain breads and cereals, fruits, vegetables, and dry peas and beans. In addition, it is advised that starchy foods be substituted for those that are high in fats and sugars.[45]

Guideline 5—Use Sugar Only in Moderation

A health problem that affects many Americans, especially children, is tooth decay. The more often a person eats sugar and foods containing sugar, the greater chance of tooth decay. This is especially true if such foods are consumed between meals and if they are foods that stick to teeth. Simple sugars, such as sucrose (table sugar), glucose, and fructose seem to offer the highest risk for tooth decay. Examples of foods that contain simple sugars are cakes, candies, pastries, and soft drinks.

A high intake of simple and double sugars has other consequences. Nutrient density refers to the level, or concentration, of nutrients in any given food compared to the amount of calories it supplies. For example, very low nutrient-dense foods include sugared breakfast cereals, chocolate, pastries, candy, chips, and other less healthy foods. High-density foods include many foods out of the five food groups such as liver, fish, dairy products, vegetables, and poultry. It is important to encourage students to eat foods of high nutrient density instead of those that supply many calories but few nutrients.

Some people believe that a high-sugar diet causes obesity. Obesity, however, results from eating too many calories, regardless of their source. If the amount of sugar consumed is decreased, one will probably lose weight, if one does not increase the intake of other types of food. Several diseases, such as diabetes, heart disease, and cancer, are linked to obesity, but may or may not be linked directly to sugar intake.

Another misconception about sugar is that it is correlated with hyperactivity in children. In fact, there has been no consistent evidence to connect sugar intake with hyperactivity.[46]

The following suggestions are appropriate to share with elementary and middle-level students to help them avoid too much sugar:[47]

- Use less of all sugars and fewer foods containing large amounts of sugars, including white sugar, brown sugar, honey, and syrups. Examples include soft drinks, candies, and cookies.
- How often a person eats sugar is as important to the health of teeth as how much sugar is eaten. It helps to avoid eating sweets between meals.
- Read labels for clues on sugar content.
- Select fresh fruits instead of fruits that are packed in heavy syrups.

Guideline 6—Use Salt and Sodium Only in Moderation

Sodium is found in table salt and is present in many foods and beverages, including processed foods, sauces, pickled foods, condiments, and sandwich meats. High sodium intake is hazardous for people who already have high blood pressure. The suggested sodium intake per day is 1,100–1,300 milligrams. One teaspoon of salt is equal to 2,000 milligrams of sodium. Much of the sodium that Americans consume is hidden. Table 11.6 identifies the amount of sodium found in some commonly consumed foods. It is not known if lowering sodium levels can help prevent high blood pressure (hypertension), but in populations in which sodium intakes are low, high blood pressure is rare. Children should be made aware of the connection between high blood pressure and sodium intake, and should be taught what foods and beverages are high in sodium. Unfortunately, children between the ages of 10 and 13 get almost one-third of their daily sodium intake from school lunches. The following suggestions are appropriate to share with elementary and middle-level students to help them avoid consuming too much sodium:[48]

- Learn to enjoy the flavors of unsalted foods.
- Add little or no salt to food at the table.
- Limit the intake of salty foods such as potato chips, pretzels, salted nuts, popcorn, condiments, pickled foods, cured meats, some cheeses, and some canned vegetables and soups.
- Look at labels to determine the amount of sodium in foods.

Guideline 7—If You Drink Alcoholic Beverages, Do So in Moderation

This guideline was definitely written for adults and not for children. It is important to establish a no-alcohol-use

TABLE 11.6	A Short Guide to Sodium Content of Foods

Foods	Approximate Sodium Content (in milligrams)
BREADS, CEREALS, AND GRAIN PRODUCTS®	
Cooked cereal, pasta, rice (unsalted)	Less than 5 per 1/2 cup
Ready-to-eat cereal	100–360 per oz.
Bread, whole-grain or enriched	110–175 per slice
Biscuits and muffins	170–390 each
VEGETABLES	
Fresh or frozen vegetables (cooked without added salt)	Less than 70 per 1/2 cup
Vegetables, canned or frozen with sauce	140–460 per 1/2 cup
FRUIT	
Fruits (fresh, frozen, or canned)	Less than 10 per 1/2 cup
MILK, CHEESE, AND YOGURT	
Milk and yogurt	120–160 per cup
Buttermilk (salt added)	260 per cup
Natural cheeses	110–450 per 1 1/2-oz. serving
Cottage cheese (regular and low-fat)	450 per 1/2 cup
Process cheese and cheese spreads	700–900 per 2-oz. serving
MEAT, POULTRY, AND FISH	
Fresh meat, poultry, finfish	Less than 90 per 3-oz. serving
Cured ham, sausages, luncheon meat, frankfurters, canned meats	750–1,350 per 3-oz. serving
FATS AND DRESSINGS	
Oil	None
Vinegar	Less than 6 per tbsp.
Prepared salad dressings	80–250 per tbsp.
Unsalted butter or margarine	1 per tsp.
Salted butter or margarine	45 per tsp.
Salt pork, cooked	360 per oz.
CONDIMENTS	
Catsup, mustard, chili sauce, tartar sauce, steak sauce	125–275 per tbsp.
Soy sauce	1,000 per tbsp.
Salt	2,000 per tsp.
SNACK AND CONVENIENCE FOODS	
Canned and dehydrated soups	630–1,300 per cup
Canned and frozen main dishes	800–1,400 per 8-oz. serving
Unsalted nuts and popcorn	Less than 5 per oz.
Salted nuts, potato chips, corn chips	150–300 per oz.
Deep-fried pork rind	750 per oz.

Source: U.S. Dept. of Agriculture.

policy for children and adolescents. Children, however should understand that this is one of the *Dietary Guidelines for Americans,* as alcoholic beverages supply calories but little or no nutrients (see chapter 10). When discussing alcohol prevention, discuss the importance of this guideline with the class. Also, this guideline provides an excellent opportunity for parent engagement— children can be encouraged to relay the information from this guideline to their parents or other concerned adults.[49]

COMMON NUTRITIONAL PROBLEMS FOR CHILDREN AND ADOLESCENTS

In general, children between the ages of 6 and 12 do not have major nutritional problems unless they are living in poverty. They are not in a rapid growth period, nor are they generally preoccupied with body size. In addition, food selection becomes broader for children in this age group. As a result, nutrient intake in this age group usually is adequate.

TABLE 11.7	Nutritional Contents of Selected Fast Foods		
McDonald's	**Calories**	**Fat Grams**	**Sodium (mg)**
Hamburger	260	9	580
Chicken McNuggets (6-piece)	290	17	510
Filet-O-Fish	450	25	870
Big Mac	560	31	1,070
Arby's			
Roasted Chicken Club	503	27	1,143
Roast Beef Regular	383	18.2	936
Mushroom & Cheese Potato	515	26.7	923
Chicken Breast Filet	445	22.5	958
Chocolate Shake	451	11.6	341
Taco Bell			
Soft Taco	220	10	580
Nachos BellGrande	770	39	1,310
Mexican Pizza	570	35	1,040
Burger King			
Whopper Sandwich	660	40	900
Bacon Double Cheeseburger	620	38	1,230
Chicken Sandwich	710	43	1,400

Sources: McDonald's Corp., Oakbrook, IL, 1998; Arby's, Miami Beach, FL, 1993; Taco Bell, Louisville, KY, 1997; Burger King, Miami, FL, 1998.

As children become adolescents, however, their nutritional demands are greater, and many times they are deficient in specific nutrients. In addition to the physical changes occurring at this time, adolescents experience psychological changes that involve their independence and identity. This combination of variables can influence the way these students eat. It is important for elementary and middle-level teachers to know the common nutritional problems that emerge during adolescence as a foundation for developing coordinated risk reduction strategies.

Eating on the Run

As children become adolescents, they begin to eat less with their families and more with their friends. They become more involved with after-school and social activities. As a result, fast-food restaurants, convenience stores, and vending machines become popular sources of food for teens.

Upper-elementary and middle-level teachers should include the topics of food choices and snacking in nutrition curriculum to focus on developmentally relevant nutrition concerns. For example, teachers could bring fast-food menus to class to feature correlated math/health instructional activities. In addition, teachers could create learning activities that reinforce the number of calories and how much fat and salt are in selected fast foods

(table 11.7). The concept of healthy snacking is important to promote while children are still in elementary school. Snacks such as pizza, frozen fruit juices on a stick, yogurt with fresh fruit and nuts, fresh fruit kabobs, low-fat cheese, dried fruit, and popcorn can become the basis for healthy snack activities. Finally, teachers should encourage students to share their ideas of nutritious snacks through a range of activities.

Skipping Meals

Although few elementary-age children miss breakfast, the percentage increases as children become adolescents. In addition, many families cannot afford nutritional breakfast selections for their children. It has been found that poor children who attend school hungry perform significantly below their counterparts on standardized test scores. In contrast to younger students, adolescents often skip meals, especially breakfast. Recent studies conducted in this area suggest that students who do not eat breakfast are more likely to perform poorly on school tasks and may suffer from nausea and fatigue.[50] The School Breakfast Program was established in 1966 to help reduce this problem; however, because of budget decreases, in 1988 only 3.9 million children participated in the school breakfast program compared to 24 million children who participated in the school lunch program.[51]

The School Breakfast Program was established in 1966 to support school success among students who come to school without eating breakfast.

Elementary teachers should emphasize the importance of eating breakfast because of the role it plays in health and academic success. When students go to bed at night, they may get 7 to 10 hours of sleep. If they then do not eat breakfast, they might be going without food for 12 to 15 hours. The body needs a consistent intake of nutrients to run efficiently. If teachers notice unusually tired students in the morning, it is important to ask them about their breakfast habits. In addition, it may be appropriate to refer at-risk students to the coordinator of the local school breakfast program.

Drinking Soft Drinks

Soft drinks contribute calories, sugar, sodium, and no nutrients to the diet. Many adolescents choose soft drinks over milk. This practice can be especially unhealthy for girls due to their increasing need for calcium. Large intakes of soft drinks can also contribute to obesity, because of the high calorie content. Teenagers drink between 9 and 13 ounces of soft drinks per day.[52] Even if children drink diet soft drinks that contain aspartame or other artificial sweeteners, they still are consuming beverages of very low nutrition density. Teachers can serve as positive role models by not drinking soft drinks in front of their students. In addition, school professionals must encourage their administration to furnish juice machines instead of soft drink machines in their schools. In addition, nutritionally risky fundraising practices should be changed (see chapter 1). Only in this way will the nutritional health of students be reinforced by advocacy and sound policy decisions.

As with any health-education topic, the emphasis should be on establishing and reinforcing health-promoting behaviors. Elementary and middle-level teachers have a wonderful opportunity to structure learning activities to help reduce poor nutrition behaviors in their students.

TEACHING NUTRITION EDUCATION

When teaching nutrition education to elementary and middle-level students, it is important to focus not only on nutrition knowledge, but also on positive nutrition attitudes and behaviors. Parents should be engaged in as many homework assignments as possible. Without their support, it is difficult for children to make dietary changes. As with all elementary and middle-level teaching activities, there should be many developmentally appropriate, student-centered, hands-on activities. During nutrition education, students should be exposed to as many different healthy foods and snacks as possible. The following sections describe existing nutrition education curricula and are followed by a series of activities that elementary and middle-level teachers can use to teach nutrition education.

Nutrition Education Curricula

National Dairy Council Nutrition Curriculum

The National Dairy Council is an excellent source for nutrition curriculum materials. The National Dairy Council has developed a range of materials that incorporate current educational theory on how children learn best. Each program uses a variety of developmentally appropriate teaching methods that encourage thinking skills, help students succeed, and aid in retention.

The preschool (ages 4–5) curriculum is called *Chef Combo's Fantastic Adventures in Tasting and Nutrition.* This program of study is designed to provide young children with nutrition and tasting activities to increase their awareness of a variety of foods. All learning activities are organized around eleven developmentally appropriate themes for children, such as seasons, senses, shapes, transportation, and colors. The National Dairy Council preschool program also contains a parent component that is available in both English and Spanish, which helps extend nutrition education to the home.[53]

The National Dairy Council has updated its curriculum materials for students in the primary grades. The *Pyramid Café* materials, targeted for second grade students, have been developed around the story of five friends who open a café to teach other children about sound nutritional practices. In addition to a range of experiential learning activities and a personal workbook for each student, the *Pyramid Café* materials also contain take-home activities to increase parent engagement in the learning process.

Finally, *Pyramid Explorations* focuses six lessons on meeting the nutrition education needs of students in the intermediate grades. Learning activities targeted for students in fourth grade are organized around the theme of friends from space who share food adventures from around the globe. Importantly, all materials in this drama-based program have been developed to be consistent with the national standards in science and health education. In addition, the National Dairy Council learning materials are structured to provide cross-curricular reinforcement of concepts.[54]

American Heart Association

The American Heart Association has a nutrition education component in its curriculum entitled *HeartPower!* Released in 1996, the *HeartPower!* program includes teacher-tested and scientifically documented materials to help students, their families, and teachers practice heart-healthy behaviors. There are four key concepts reinforced throughout this program:

1. Leaning about the heart,
2. Healthy eating choices,
3. The importance of physical activity, and
4. Living tobacco-free.

HeartPower! teaching materials are organized into the following grade-level kits:

- Preschool,
- Spanish Preschool—Grade 1,
- Kindergarten—Grade 2,
- Grades 3–5, and
- Grades 6–8.

All *HeartPower!* materials have been developed with correlated and integrated instructional approaches in mind and focus on the themes of:

> "You can have a healthy heart,
> It's easy as 1, 2, 3!,
> Eat healthy stuff,
> Move around enough, and
> Live tobacco-free!"[55]

SUMMARY

Poor nutrition in the United States contributes to many health problems, such as heart disease, osteoporosis, high blood pressure, diabetes, and some cancers. Once dietary habits are established, they are very difficult to change. For this reason, it is important for elementary and middle-level schools to include nutrition education in their health-education curriculum. Through hands-on activities, positive teacher role models, and good attitudes toward healthy foods, children can begin healthy nutritional habits.

Background nutritional information that elementary and middle-level teachers should understand before beginning to teach nutrition includes nutrient needs, the Food Guide Pyramid, the *Dietary Guidelines for Americans*, and the nutritional problems of adolescents. The Food Guide Pyramid is an important concept for elementary and middle-level students to grasp. When children eat the number of recommended servings from each of the food groups, the chance of a good nutritional diet increases. Following the Food Guide Pyramid approach does not guarantee that all of the *Dietary Guidelines for Americans* are followed, but it is a positive starting point. For instance, children may follow the Food Guide Pyramid recommendations but

still be eating a diet that is high in fat, sugar, and salt. This approach, however, is an excellent building block to comprehensive nutrition education.

Teachers should also be familiar with the six major nutrients: carbohydrates, fats, proteins, vitamins, minerals, and water. Teaching older elementary and middle-level students about the different nutrients is a natural continuation of the Food Guide Pyramid concept.

Older elementary and middle-level students also should be introduced to the *Dietary Guidelines for Americans*. Adults find many of these guidelines difficult to maintain because of their already established dietary habits. If children can begin to practice these guidelines at a young age, they will not have to make drastic changes in their diets as they get older.

When teaching nutrition education to elementary and middle-level students, it is important to focus on knowledge, attitudes, and behaviors. Students should be involved in the learning process as much as possible, instead of being passive learners. It is not enough for students to memorize the five food groups and nutrients. Students and parents must be encouraged to establish positive nutritional habits.

DISCUSSION QUESTIONS

1. What are some negative outcomes of poor nutrition?

2. Are elementary students in a fast or slow growth spurt? How should this affect their nutritional needs?

3. What are the five food groups within the Food Guide Pyramid? What are some common foods in each of the groups? How many servings from each food group should elementary students eat?

4. What is the fats, oils, and sweets category, and how do foods from it affect the diet?

5. What are some ways to reinforce the Food Guide Pyramid concept?

6. What are some ways to encourage students to try healthy foods?

7. What are the macronutrients, and what are their functions?

8. What are the micronutrients, and what are their functions?

9. What are the *Dietary Guidelines for Americans* and how should they be included in an elementary and middle-level nutrition curriculum?

10. What is a calorie?

11. What are some common nutrient problems in the United States?

12. What are some ways to get parents involved in nutrition education?

13. What are some nutrition education teaching activities for elementary and middle-level students?

ENDNOTES

1. L. Epstein, R. Wing, R. Koeske, and A. Valaski, "Long-term Effects of Family Based Treatment of Childhood Obesity," *Journal of Consulting and Clinical Psychology* 55, no. 1 (1987): 91–95.

2. C. Strauss, K. Smith, C. France, and R. Forehand, "Personal and Interpersonal Characteristics Associated with Childhood Obesity," *Journal of Pediatric Psychology* 10 (1985): 337–343.

3. A. Tershakovee, S. Walker, and P. Gallagher, "Obesity, School Performance, and Behavior of Black, Urban Elementary School Children," *International Journal of Obesity* 18 (1994): 323–327.

4. Strauss, Smith, France, and Forehand, "Personal and Interpersonal Characteristics Associated With Childhood Obesity."

5. W. H. Dietz and R. Gortmaker, "Do We Fatten Our Children at the Television Set? Obesity and Television Viewing in Children," *Pediatrics* 75, no. 5 (May 1985): 807–812.

6. J. Touliatos et al., "Family and Child Correlates of Nutrition Knowledge and Dietary Quality in 10–13 Year Olds," *Journal of School Health* 54, no. 7 (1984).

7. K. Troccoli, "Eat to Learn, Learn to Eat: The Link Between Nutrition and Learning in Children," *National Health and Education Consortium: Occasional Paper,* no. 7 (1993): 1–33.

8. Centers for Disease Control and Prevention, "Guidelines for School Health Programs to Promote Lifelong Healthy Eating," *MMWR* 1996; 45 (no. RR-9).

9. Ibid.

10. S. Crockett, R. Mullis, and C. Perry, "Parent Nutrition Education: A Conceptual Model," *Journal of School Health* 58, no. 2 (1988): 53–57.

11. Centers for Disease Control and Prevention, "Guidelines for School Health Programs to Promote Lifelong Healthy Eating," 18.

12. Ibid.

13. Ibid.

14. Ibid., 18, 37, 38.

15. Ibid., 18, 37, 39.

16. Ibid., 18, 40, 41.

17. U.S. Department of Agriculture—Human Nutrition Information Service, "Nutrition and Your Health: Dietary Guidelines for Americans—Eat Foods with Adequate Starch and Fiber," Bulletin Number 232–4 (Hyattsville, MD: U.S. Department of Agriculture, HNIS, 1986).

18. U.S. Department of Agriculture—Human Nutrition Information Service, "Nutrition and Your Health: Dietary Guidelines for Americans—Avoid Too Much Fat, Saturated Fat, and Cholesterol," Bulletin Number 232–3 (Hyattsville, MD: U.S. Department of Agriculture, HNIS, 1986).

19. United States Department of Agriculture, *Nutrition and Health: Dietary Guidelines for Americans* (Washington, DC: Government Printing Office, 1990).

20. U.S. Department of Agriculture—Human Nutrition Information Service, "Nutrition and Your Health: Dietary Guidelines for Americans—Avoid Too Much Fat, Saturated Fat, and Cholesterol."

21. P. Long, "Olive Oil: Sweetheart of the Arteries," *Hippocrates* (July/August 1987).

22. U.S. Department of Agriculture—Human Nutrition Information Service, "Nutrition and Your Health: Dietary Guidelines for Americans—Avoid Too Much Fat, Saturated Fat, and Cholesterol."

23. Long, "Olive Oil: Sweetheart of the Arteries."

24. U.S. Department of Agriculture—Human Nutrition Information Service, "Nutrition and Your Health: Dietary Guidelines for Americans—Avoid Too Much Fat, Saturated Fat, and Cholesterol."

25. M. Boyle and G. Zyla, *Personal Nutrition* (St. Paul, MN: West Publishing Co., 1992).

26. Ibid.

27. Ibid.

28. Ibid.

29. U.S. Department of Health and Human Services, "Some Facts and Myths of Vitamins," HHS Publication No. 79-2117 (Rockville, MD: 1983).

30. U.S. Department of Health and Human Services, "A Primer on Dietary Minerals," HHS Publication No. 77-2070 (Rockville, MD: 1981).

31. C. Lecos, "Water: The Number One Nutrient," HHS Publication No. 84-2180 (Rockville, MD: U.S. Department of Health and Human Services, 1983).

32. U.S. Department of Agriculture, *The Food Guide Pyramid* (Hyattsville, MD: United States Department of Agriculture, 1992).

33. Ibid.

34. Ibid.

35. Ibid.

36. Ibid.

37. U.S. Department of Health and Human Services, Public Health Service, National Institutes of Health, *Osteoporosis: Cause, Treatment, Prevention,* NIH Publication No. 86-2226 (Washington, DC: 1986).

38. U.S. Department of Agriculture, *The Food Guide Pyramid.*

39. U.S. Departments of Agriculture and Health and Human Services, "Nutrition and Your Health: Dietary Guidelines for Americans" (Washington, DC: Government Printing Office, 1990).

40. Ibid.

41. Epstein, Wing, Koeske, and Valaski, "Long-term Effects of Family Based Treatment of Childhood Obesity."

42. University of California Berkeley, Wellness Letter, "Fascinating Facts," 3, no. 9 (New York: Health Letter Associates, June 1987), 1.

43. U.S. Departments of Agriculture and Health and Human Services, "Nutrition and Your Health: Dietary Guidelines for Americans."

44. Ibid.

45. Ibid.

46. National Dairy Council, "Nutrition and the School-Age Child," *Dairy and Nutrition Council* 59, no. 2 (1988).

47. U.S. Departments of Agriculture and Health and Human Services, "Nutrition and Your Health: Dietary Guidelines for Americans."

48. Ibid.

49. Ibid.

50. L. Parker, *The Relationship Between Nutrition and Learning* (Washington, DC: National Education Association, 1989).

51. P. McConnell, "Good Mornings Begin with School Breakfast," *Nutrition News* 52, no. 2 (Fall 1989).

52. National Dairy Council, "Nutrition and the School-Age Child."

53. National Dairy Council, *1998 Nutrition Education Materials* (Rosemont, IL: National Dairy Council, 1998).

54. Ibid.

55. American Heart Association, *Teacher Resource Guide: American Heart Association Scholastic Program* (Dallas, TX: American Heart Association, 1996).

SUGGESTED READINGS

American Cancer Society. *Choices for Good Health: Guidelines for Diet, Nutrition, and Cancer Prevention.* Atlanta, GA: The American Cancer Society, 1996.

Bagby, R., and S. Woika. *Nutrition Smart: Ready to Use Lessons and Worksheets for the Primary Grades.* West Nyack, NY: The Center for Applied Research in Education, Business and Professional Division, 1991.

Baxter, S. "Are Elementary Schools *Teaching* Children to Prefer Candy But Not Vegetables?" *Journal of School Health* 68, no. 3 (1998): 111–113.

Boyle, M., and G. Zyla. *Personal Nutrition.* St. Paul, MN: West Publishing Co., 1992.

Crockett, S., R. Mullis, and C. Perry. "Parent Nutrition Education: A Conceptual Model." *Journal of School Health* 58, no. 2 (1988): 53–57.

Geiger, B. "Using the Food Guide Pyramid to Teach Elementary Students about Nutrition." *Journal of School Health* 29, no. 5 (1998): 319–321.

Hamilton, E., E. Whitney, and F. Sizer. *Nutrition: Concepts and Controversies.* St. Paul, MN: West Publishing Co., 1991.

Nicklas, T., Johnson, L. Myers, P. Farris, and A. Cunningham. "Outcomes of a High School Program to Increase Fruit and Vegetable Consumption: *Gimme 5*—A Fresh Nutrition Concept for Students." *Journal of School Health* 68, no. 6 (1998): 248–253.

Rose, A. "1990 Dietary Guidelines: Implications for Health Educators." *Journal of Health Education* 23, no. 5 (1992): 293–295.

U.S. Department of Agriculture. *Building for the Future: Nutrition Guidance for the Child Nutrition Programs FNS-279.* Alexandria, VA: U.S. Department of Agriculture, 1992.

U.S. Departments of Agriculture and Health and Human Services. "Nutrition and Your Health: Dietary Guidelines for Americans." Washington, DC: Government Printing Office, 1990.

Wechsler, H., N. Brener, and M. Small. "Measuring Progress in Meeting National Health Objectives for Food Service and Nutrition Education. *Journal of Health Education Supplement* 30, No. 5 (1999): 5-12-5-20.

Whitney, E., and S. Rolfes. *Understanding Nutrition.* St. Paul, MN: West Publishing Company, 1993.

CHILDREN'S LITERATURE WITH A NUTRITION THEME

Grades K–2

Carle, Eric. *The Hungry Caterpillar.* Philomel, 1969.

Ehlert, Lois. *Eating the Alphabet: Fruits and Vegetables from A–Z.* Harcourt Brace, 1989.

Goldstein, Bobbeye. *What's on the Menu?* Penguin, 1992.

Jackson, Allison. *I Know an Old Lady Who Swallowed a Pie.* Penguin, 1997.

McMillan, Bruce. *Eating Fractions.* Scholastic, 1991.

Polacco, Patricia. *Thundercake.* Philomel, 1990.

Wells, Rosemary. *Bunny Cakes.* Penguin, 1997.

Wood, Audrey and Mark Teague. *Sweet Dream Pie.* Scholastic, 1998.

Grades 3–5

Aliki. *A Medieval Feast.* Crowell/Harper, 1983.

Barrett, Judi. *Cloudy With A Chance of Meatballs.* Simon and Schuster, 1978.

Barrett, Judi. *Pickles to Pittsburgh.* Antheneum, 1997.

Burns, Marilyn. *Spaghetti and Meatballs for All.* Scholastic, 1997.

Gilson, Jamie. *Can't Catch Me, I'm the Gingerbread Man.* Beech Tree, 1997.

Kovalski, Maryann. *Pizza for Breakfast.* Morrow, 1991.

Priceman, Marjorie. *How To Make Apple Pie and See the World.* Alfred A. Knopf, 1994. (Multicultural)

Rosen, Michael. *The Greatest Table*. Harcourt Brace, 1994. (Multicultural)

Zabar, Abbie. *Alphabet Soup*. Stewart, Tabori, and Chang, 1990.

Grades 6–8

Adoff, Arnold. *EATS: Poems*. William Morrow, 1979.

Crutcher, Chris. *Staying Fat For Sarah Byrnes*. William Morrow, 1993. (American Library Association Best Book for Young Adults)

O'Brien, Robert. *Z for Zachariah*. Antheneum. 1975.

 INTERNET INFORMATION

NUTRITION EDUCATION WEBSITES

For additional information on nutrition education, please refer to the following websites.

American Cancer Society
> **www.cancer.org**

American Dietetic Association
> **www.eatright.org**

American Heart Association
> **www.americanheart.org**

National Dairy Council
> **www.nationaldairycouncil.org**
> **www.nutritionexplorations.org**

International Food Information Council Foundation
> **http://ific.info.health.org**

American School Food Service Association
> **www.asfsa.org**

National Cancer Institute, 5 A Day for Better Health
> **www.dcpc.nci.nih.gov/5aday/**

Nutrition Education Services Oregon Dairy Council
> **www.oregondairycouncil.org**

National School Boards Association, Physical Activity, Nutrition, and Tobacco-use (PANT) Resource Database
> **www.nsba.org/services/federation/paint.html**

Center for Nutrition Policy and Promotion, U.S. Department of Agriculture
> **www.usda.gov/fcs/cnpp.html**

Chef Combo's Fantastic Adventures, National Dairy Council
> **www.chefcombo.com**

Team Nutrition, U.S. Department of Agriculture
> **www.usda.gov/fcs/team.html**

National Center for Chronic Disease Prevention and Health Promotion, Centers for Disease Control and Prevention
> **www.cdc.gov/nccdphp/dash/index.html**

Cancer Information Service, Office of Cancer Communications, National Cancer Institute
> **www.icic@aspensys.com**

Food and Drug Administration
> **http://www.fda.gov/**

Office of Food Labeling, Food and Drug Administration
> **http://vm.cfsan.fda.gov/label.html**

12

PHYSICAL ACTIVITY

OUTLINE

INTRODUCTION

In recent years, a growing body of literature has emerged confirming the public health benefits of increasing physical activity and reducing the effects of a sedentary lifestyle. These findings were summarized in the 1996 Surgeon General's Report on Physical Activity and Health. Research has documented that regular physical activity helps to build and maintain healthy bones and muscles, reduces feelings of depression and anxiety, and promotes psychological well-being. Further, such participation helps control weight, build lean muscle mass, and reduce fat. The Surgeon General's report concluded that regular participation in moderate physical activity is an essential element of a healthy lifestyle for all Americans.[1]

Although more research is necessary to fully define the relationship between physical activity and health among young people, the following specific benefits have been identified for school-age children and youth who participate in regular physical activity:

- Improved aerobic endurance and muscular strength,[2]
- Reduced risks for cardiovascular disease (blood pressure and body mass index),[3]
- Decreased body weight among obese youth,[4]
- Improved self-esteem and self-concept, and decreased anxiety and stress,[5] and
- Increased bone mass density related to weight-bearing exercise.[6]

Of particular interest to education professionals and parents is the growing body of literature confirming that participation in physical activity also is associated with improved academic outcomes for students. Participation in school-based physical activity programs has been linked to improved concentration; better scores on tests of math, reading, and writing skills; and reduced disruptive behaviors. Participation in vigorous physical activity also has been associated with improved student attitudes toward themselves and school.[7]

Interestingly, although science has confirmed that many positive outcomes are associated with consistent patterns of physical activity, many American adults remain inactive. While children and youth are more physically active than their adult counterparts, nearly half of all youth in the 12–21 age group do not engage in physical activity on a regular basis.[8,9] In addition, participation in all types of physical activity declines dramatically throughout the adolescent years. While regular participation in vigorous activity has been reported by 69% of students in the 12–13 age group, only about 38% of their 18–21-year-old counterparts report similar physical activity patterns.[10]

For the purpose of defining healthy levels of physical activity for young people, the International Consensus Conference on Physical Activity Guidelines for Adolescence has suggested that "all adolescents . . . be physically active daily, or nearly every day, as part of play, games, sports, work, transportation, recreation, physical education, or planned exercise, in the context of family, school, and community activities."[11] In addition, experts have encouraged adolescents to "engage in three or more sessions per week of activities that last 20 minutes at a time and that require moderate to vigorous levels of exertion."[12]

As a foundation for promoting student health, understanding the scientific literature, and supporting their professional physical education colleagues, elementary and middle-level classroom teachers would be wise to review the distinctions among the concepts of *physical activity, exercise,* and *physical fitness.* Physical activity is defined as:

- Any body movement produced by skeletal muscles that results in the expenditure of energy.

In this context, exercise is defined as:

- A subset of physical activity that is planned, structured, and repetitive, and is done with the purpose of improving or maintaining physical fitness.

Consistent with this definition, physical fitness includes:

- A set of attributes that are either health-related or motor skill-related.

The elements of physical fitness that are health-related or have been demonstrated to have health benefits include:

1. Cardiorespiratory (aerobic) endurance,
2. Muscular strength and endurance,
3. Flexibility, and
4. Body composition.

Further information about each of the four elements of health-related fitness is clarified in table 12.1. By con-

trast, motor skill-related fitness activities are those that are more closely associated with the attributes of sports or elements of physical performance, and include balance, agility, power, reaction time, speed, and coordination.[13]

In this context, students are likely to participate in a range of specific forms of physical activity and exercise, including walking, bicycling, unstructured play activities, organized sports, dancing, household chores, or physical tasks associated with after-school jobs. Also, students participate in physical activity and exercise in a range of settings, including their homes, schools, playgrounds, public parks and recreation centers, private clubs or sports facilities, hiking/biking trails, summer camps, dance studios, and religious facilities.

RECOMMENDATIONS FOR TEACHERS: PRACTICE AND CONTENT

Schools and communities have the potential to improve the health of school-age children and students through provision of instruction, programming, and services to promote lifelong physical activity. Schools are an important location for the provision of physical activity programs because of the link between such activity and school success. In addition, school-based programming is efficient, as schools touch the lives of most children and adolescents.[14] As discussed in chapter 1, school-based efforts to promote physical activity among young people should be formalized as part of the coordinated school health program. In addition, community-based physical activity programs also are essential because most physical activity among young people occurs away from the school setting.[15] In this context, schools and communities would be wise to coordinate efforts to make the best use of personnel and resources.

Developmentally Appropriate Practice Recommendations

Administrators, teachers, and parents are reminded that models used to identify appropriate types and intensity of physical activity for adults do not provide a developmentally appropriate foundation for such program development for children and young adolescents. A more prudent approach is grounded in the literature concerning exercise and its relationship to characteristics of the age group. Rather than attempting to adapt adult activity models, parents and professionals are encouraged to start program planning with a review of the following elements that influence children's interest and fidelity to participation in physical activity programs:[16]

1. **Young animals, including humans are inherently active.**
   Young children are considerably more active than teens and adults. The most dramatic drop in activity

TABLE 12.1	Clarifying the Elements of Health-Related Fitness

Cardiorespiratory (aerobic) Endurance

1. Ability of the cardiovascular system (heart, blood, blood vessels, and lungs) to transport and utilize oxygen efficiently.
2. Aerobically healthy people can perform required tasks for extensive periods of time.
3. Inefficient cardiovascular fitness results in shortness of breath, fatigue, and the inability to work at normal tasks over time.
4. Long-term chronic diseases, such as diabetes, obesity, high blood pressure, and heart disease, are associated with poor cardiorespiratory fitness.
5. The process of cardiorespiratory disease starts in early childhood.
6. Aerobic endurance is enhanced by regular participation in such activities as running, bicycling, swimming, fast walking, and aerobic dance.

Muscular Strength and Endurance

1. Muscular strength = the amount of force one can exert to accomplish a task.
2. Endurance = the ability to use muscles over time without fatigue.
3. The likelihood of injury is reduced with increased muscle strength.
4. Muscular strength and endurance are developed through use of the muscles.
5. While weight training may be appropriate for adolescents and adults, weight lifting is not recommended for students in elementary grades.
6. Younger children are encouraged to participate in such activities as push-ups (strengthens the triceps and chest muscles) chin-ups (biceps), and curl-ups (back and abdominal muscles).
7. Proper instruction is important to achieve the greatest benefit.

Flexibility

1. Flexibility is the range of movement of body joints and involves the ability to bend, stretch, and twist.
2. Inactivity can result in loss of flexibility, which is associated with risk of injury, poor posture, or discomfort.
3. Healthy levels of flexibility increase the ability to perform daily tasks and reduce injury risks.
4. Flexibility can be improved by slow, sustained stretching of the muscles and joints.
5. Quick, bouncing, or ballistic stretching exercises should be avoided.
6. Developmentally appropriate flexibility exercises include toe touches, sitting and curling the back with the head between the knees, trunk-twists, and reach-and-stretch exercises.

Body Composition

1. Definition—the percentage of fat present in the body.
2. Risk factors associated with high body fat can be reduced by modifying body composition through diet and exercise.
3. School screening activities are helpful in early identification of children with potential weight problems (weight/growth charts and triceps skinfold thickness testing).

levels occurs in the teen years. Importantly, however, young children will take full advantage of opportunities to be active. Conversely, if opportunities for physical activity among children decrease, a drop in activity levels for all age groups is a likely outcome.

2. **When compared to their adult counterparts, children have a relatively short attention span.**
   As children get older, the length of time that they can maintain interest in any one activity increases. As a result, parents, teachers, and physical activity programmers are reminded that activities that are long in duration are not likely to capture the attention of younger learners.

3. **Children are more likely to be concrete rather than abstract thinkers.**
   Children need concrete reasons, feedback, and evidence of success to persist at an activity. To

increase the likelihood that children will participate in physical activity consistently, professionals must offer tangible rationale and benefits beyond the potential for improved health at some future time.

4. **Children need frequent periods of rest following bursts of intermittent activity.**
   Alternating bursts of activity followed by periods of rest or recovery are developmentally appropriate for children. This pattern may persist over a long period of time, and may be necessary for stimulating growth and development.

5. **There is not a strong relationship between physical activity and measures of physical fitness in young children.**
   High scores on measures of physical fitness among children and youth are influenced by many variables, including chronological age, physiological age (maturation), and hereditary

potential. Although consistently physically active, some children may not receive high fitness scores. The associated frustration experienced by some children may become a disincentive for persisting in physical activity.

6. **Physical activity provides a significant medium for learning among children and youth.**
Children and youth are highly intrinsically motivated to seek control over their physical environment. Young children gain mastery of their physical environment through successful performance of physical tasks. Learning to walk leads to mobility and increased control over the environment, and manipulating objects is related to feelings of power and achievement for young children.

7. **Numerous skills involved in adult recreation and leisure are learned during the school-age years.**
While it is never too late to learn, most motor skills used in adult recreation and leisure are learned during youth. People who do not acquire requisite skills early in life are less likely to learn and use them during adulthood.

8. **Although high-intensity physical activity has benefits, it may be associated with reduced persistence in many adults and children.**
Both moderate and high-intensity physical activity are associated with many short- and long-term benefits. Importantly, however, high-intensity activity may reduce exercise adherence in some people. This is particularly true of children who have little time to rest and recover and those who perceive such activities to be too difficult for the benefits that they receive.

9. **Inactive children and youth are much more likely to be sedentary adults than are their active counterparts.**
Childhood activity patterns tend to be related closely to physical activity practices in adulthood. While a high level of childhood activity is not a direct predictor of adult behaviors, inactivity in childhood is very closely associated with inactivity in adulthood.

10. **Self-efficacy (feelings that one can be successful) is a powerful predictor of lifelong participation in physical activity.**
People who believe that they can experience success in physical activity are more likely to pursue such activities than are their counterparts. Consequently, parents and teachers would be wise to organize activities that reinforce feelings of self-efficacy about exercise participation.

11. **Youth who have active parents and family members with whom they can participate in consistent exercise are more likely to be physically active than are their counterparts.**

Children who participate in physical activity with parents or other adult family members are more likely to be active than other children.

Parental and family engagement and reinforcement are critical elements for establishing regular physical activity patterns for children and youth.

12. **Just as habits of regular physical activity can be established, inactivity also can become habitual if youth are not provided with developmentally appropriate opportunities for activity.**
Parents and teachers must integrate ongoing physical activity into daily routines as a foundation for establishing health enhancing exercise habits.[17]

In context of this research on physical activity patterns of children and youth, experts have established five general guidelines to provide a foundation for decision making and development of physical activity programs for children in elementary and middle-level grades. Table 12.2 summarizes these guidelines for physical activity for children.[18]

Examination of these guidelines will reveal to parents, teachers, and administrators that achieving optimal levels of physical activity for children in elementary and middle-level grades presents a significant challenge for families, schools, and communities. It is clear that these goals cannot be achieved through student participation in self-directed recess or leisure activities, or even in the most educationally sound, but infrequently scheduled, physical education classes.

To better meet the fitness needs of children, classroom teachers must integrate developmentally appropriate and cross-curricular physical activity into daily classroom practice. To expedite this process, the following kinds of activities are recommended for students in early- and upper-elementary and middle-level classrooms.

TABLE 12.2	Guidelines for Physical Activity for Children

- Elementary school children should accumulate *at least 30–60 minutes* of developmentally appropriate physical activity in all, or most, days of the week.
- An accumulation of *more than 60 minutes, and up to several hours per day,* of developmentally appropriate activities *is encouraged* for children.
- Some of the child's activity each day should be in periods lasting 10–15 minutes or more, that include moderate to vigorous activity. Typically, this activity will be intermittent and should alternate with *brief periods* of rest and recovery.
- *Extended periods of inactivity are discouraged* for children.
- *A variety of physical activities (selected from the Physical Activity Pyramid) is recommended.*

Reprinted from *Physical Activity for Children: A Statement of Guidelines* (1998) with permission from the National Association for Sport and Physical Education (NASPE), 1900 Association Drive, Reston, VA 20191-1599.

Physical activities should enable children to practice independent discovery of solutions to problems or challenges. This boy is experimenting with dynamic balance; the process of aligning his body during movement.

Although not exhaustive, these suggestions focus on developmentally appropriate elements for improving participation in physical activity and, thus, the academic outcomes of students.

Early Elementary (K–2)

1. The greatest portion of physical activities for young children should be lifestyle activities:
   - Activities that require the child to relocate the body in space, like climbing, tumbling, and lifting, should be included.
   - Activities should be intermittent rather than continuous, and
   - Activities should be simple, with few rules and little formal organization.
2. Young children should be encouraged to participate in some aerobic activities:
   - Aerobic activities should not be continuous,
   - Aerobic activities should last for only short periods of time, and
   - The most appropriate activities are those that are recreational or are part of family or lifestyle activities.
3. Active sports are appropriate only for children who choose to participate:
   - Family recreation activities are advised for young children,
   - Many recreation activities do not provide opportunities for high levels of energy expenditure,
   - Key—Activities that support practicing basic skills (prerequisites for sport performance), should be included, and
   - Activities like catching, throwing, walking, jumping, running, and striking objects should be included.
4. Young children have only limited need to participate in formal flexibility exercises:
   - Young children are much more flexible than are older adolescents and adults,
   - Flexibility activities are easy for young children,
   - Exercises should illustrate and reinforce the importance of flexibility, and
   - Flexibility activities should be integrated into play.
5. There is little need for young children to participate in exercises that are targeted at improving muscular strength and endurance:
   - Strength should be developed through participation in a range of other activities,
   - Muscular strength should be developed without formal calisthenics in physical education and family fitness activities, and
   - Formal resistance training is not recommended.

6. Play should include a range of activities that include alternatives to large muscle exercise:
   - Private play (not gross-motor) is encouraged, and
   - Long periods of inactivity are not characteristic of young children.[19]

Upper Elementary (3–5)

Although similar in type and duration to the recommended activities for their younger counterparts, students in grades 3–5 are capable of a broader and more sophisticated range of exercise participation.

1. The greatest portion of physical activities for children in upper-elementary grades also should be lifestyle activities:
   - More advanced activities like climbing, tumbling, lifting, and relocating the body in space should be included,
   - Activities should be intermittent rather than continuous,
   - Activities should be confined with few rules, and
   - Walking or biking to school and appropriate family chores are advised.
2. Children in the upper-elementary grades should be encouraged to participate in a range of aerobic activities:
   - Aerobic activities should not be continuous,
   - Aerobic activities should last for only short periods of time, and
   - The most appropriate activities are those that are recreational or are part of family or lifestyle activities (walking or biking to school or in the neighborhood).
3. Active sports are most appropriate for children over the age of 9:
   - Many children in this age group choose to participate in organized sports,
   - Sports should be modified to correspond with developmental abilities,
   - Family recreation activities are reinforced,
   - Caution—Recreation activities that do not provide opportunities for high-energy expenditure should be supplemented,
   - Key—Activities that support mastery of basic skills (prerequisites for sport performance) should be included,
   - Expanded practice opportunities of sport prerequisites like catching, throwing, walking, jumping, running, and striking objects should be included.
4. Children in upper-elementary grades also have limited need for formal flexibility exercises:
   - Children are much more flexible than are older adolescents and adults,
   - Flexibility activities are relatively easy,
   - Instructional activities should illustrate/reinforce the importance of flexibility, and
   - Flexibility activities should include tumbling and climbing.
5. There is little need for upper-elementary children to participate in muscular strength and endurance exercises:
   - Strength should be developed through participation in a range of other activities,
   - Strength should be developed in physical education classes and through family fitness activities, and
   - Formal resistance training is not recommended.
6. Play should include a range of activities, including those that do not involve the large muscles:
   - Alternative forms of play should be encouraged, and
   - Long periods of inactivity should not be reinforced.[20]

Middle-Level School (6–8)

1. A majority of the minutes of physical activity for older students should be lifestyle activities:
   - Active play and games that involve large muscles of the body should be encouraged,
   - Activities should be intermittent,
   - Students have a greater ability to participate in continuous activities, and
   - Activities in the context of daily tasks (walking or biking to school, household tasks) should be encouraged.
2. Young adolescents are capable of participation in aerobic activities of longer duration than are their younger counterparts:
   - Continuous participation of long duration should not be emphasized,
   - Reasons for continuous aerobic activity (fitness tests) should be formalized,
   - Intermittent aerobic activity often is preferred by students,
   - Compliance with adolescent fitness guideline (3 days per week, 20 minutes of continuous moderate to vigorous activity) should not be required for all young adolescents, and
   - Some young adolescents may choose to meet adolescent guidelines.
3. More children in this age group are involved in sports:
   - Many will dedicate a great deal of time to sports,
   - Sport activities should be modified to meet developmental needs,
   - Conditioning for sports should be de-emphasized,
   - Skill development and game play should be emphasized,
   - Recreational activities should have a lifetime focus, and
   - Recreation with family and friends is a priority.

Many middle level students dedicate a great deal of time to participation in organized sports.

4. More emphasis on flexibility activities is appropriate for this group than for their younger counterparts:
   - Flexibility for all begins to decrease,
   - There is a particular loss of flexibility for boys, and
   - Promotion of flexibility through other activities (tumbling and stunts) is advised.

5. There is a stronger emphasis on strength and muscular endurance activities for this age group than for their younger counterparts:
   - Importance of strength activities should be reinforced,
   - Activities other than formal weight training are advised,
   - Active play and games that require moving own body weight are advised,
   - Successful participation should be a priority, and
   - Some may be highly motivated to do strength activities.

6. While the range of activities in which young adolescents participate should include rest and recovery, the time between activity periods can be shorter than such periods are for younger students.[21]

IMPORTANT TEACHER CONTENT

The Physical Activity Pyramid

Upon examining the recommendations for developmentally appropriate practice, advocates for student health and academic success will notice that suggestions within grade-level groups are organized by different types of activities. As a foundation for reinforcing developmentally appropriate participation in a range of physical activities, scholars have developed the Physical Activity Pyramid. Like the Food Guide Pyramid discussed in chapter 11, the Physical Activity Pyramid provides a visual representation of the recommended types and amounts of healthy exercise behavior. Five types of physical activities make up the first three levels of the pyramid, including:

1. Lifestyle activities (Level 1),
2. Active aerobics (Level 2),
3. Active sports and recreational activities (Level 2),
4. Flexibility exercises (Level 3), and
5. Exercises for strength and muscular endurance (Level 3).[23]

Within the levels of the pyramid are identified activities that are important elements for inclusion in any personal physical activity regimen. Also, it is important to participate in a variety of activities within each of the activity categories. Finally, Level 4, the uppermost tip of the pyramid, reinforces the importance of periods of rest and inactivity. As depicted in figure 12.1, the Physical Activity Pyramid can serve as an excellent starting point for developing educational activities for students in elementary and middle-level grades. Not only does it provide direction for teachers, but this visual model can help children learn the kinds of activities that are necessary to maintain health.

The base, or Level 1, of the Physical Activity Pyramid is formed by recommended participation in *lifestyle activities*. These activities form the foundation of the pyramid because research has confirmed the positive health benefits of daily participation in them. Activities done as part of a typical daily routine that require involvement of the large muscles of the body are considered to be lifestyle activities. In this context, such activities as walking to school, climbing stairs, raking leaves, and doing vigorous household chores fit into this category. Active play involving the large muscles is a common form of lifestyle activity in which children participate. Adults whose daily routine includes physical work such as digging or lifting are participants in lifestyle activities.[24]

As evidenced in figure 12.1, Level 2 of the Physical Activity Pyramid includes two categories of activities. The *active aerobics* category includes those activities that can be done for long periods of time without stopping.

(continues after Activities on page 227)

ACTIVITIES

Physical Activity Curriculum

Research confirms that many elementary and middle-level schoolchildren are not exposed to a daily, planned period of fitness-related instruction and activity. Although most children participate in some type of physical education activity, the frequency is often minimal. In addition, the activity level of many such classes is open to question. Class activity should not involve continuous activity or lengthy times when children are standing around watching while other children are participating.

In many elementary schools, the recess period is used to fulfill the need to provide time for physical activity. Recess is a most important school activity. It should serve as a time for relaxation, fun, and social freedom. Importantly, however, recess never should be used as a substitute for planned physical education instructional activities.

Fortunately, many elementary schools employ trained physical education specialists. In those districts in which no such professionals are employed, the elementary or middle-level classroom teacher is charged with the responsibility of developing motivational and effective fitness activities. It has been shown that because they lack sufficient background in physical education, classroom teachers tend to emphasize game-type activities during designated physical education class times. This practice places less emphasis on motor skill development, health-related fitness, and health promotion.[22]

In any case, physical activities conducted in the classroom can provide valuable reinforcement for the physical education curriculum. In addition, many fitness activities can enrich classroom practice by providing gross-motor reinforcement of academic concepts. Importantly, such activities should engage parents and other family members as much as possible. Following is a sample of physical activities that meet the developmental needs of elementary and middle-level students. These recommended activities are not intended to replace formalized physical education programming. Rather, as a way to reinforce collaboration with physical educators, these activities are intended to be used on the playground or within the confines of classroom space. In light of safety concerns, it may be wise to move desks and chairs to create a more open space for activity.

Grades K–2

1. *Numbers, Letters, and Shapes:* Have students use body parts and movements to replicate numbers, letters, and/or shapes that have been newly learned.

2. *Changing Speeds:* Use changing musical cues to reinforce moving at different speeds. Invite students to move in any way that they like in rhythm to the music. As an alternative, use sounds made by different animals or modes of transportation as cues for changing the speeds of movement patterns.

3. *Stop and Go:* Use musical cues to structure practice of "going" and "stopping." Have students find a space on the floor where they are not in contact with any other student. While music is being played, encourage students to move with the pace of the beat. Importantly, have students stop and freeze immediately when the music stops. Students must remain still and quiet until the music begins again.

4. *Physical Activity "Simon Says":* Use "Simon Says" cues to direct students moving in place. Have students continue with the activity (arm circles, marching in place, hopping on two feet, etc.) until "Simon Says" differently or another cue is provided. Repeat this activity with children sitting, and then lying, on personal space on the floor.

5. *Physical Activity Story Play:* While reading or telling a story, have students replicate the movements required of characters in the story (bear hunt, a trip to the zoo, a jungle adventure, exploring for dinosaurs, etc.).

6. *Teaching a New Skill to a Classmate:* Ask students to pretend that there is a new student in class. This student has never seen many basic physical skills, including throwing, catching, skipping, running, etc. Have students take turns explaining the steps of selected skills. Next, ask students to imagine the skill

themselves, and then shadow-practice each skill as it is described. Make appropriate modifications to the verbal directions. Finally, ask students to draw a picture of themselves practicing the identified skill. As an opportunity for a writing correlation, have students write a caption to the picture describing their performance of the activity.

7. *Spider Web—Heart-Healthy Activities:* Organize students in a circle seated on the floor. The teacher or a selected student begins the activity with a ball of string or yarn in his or her hand. The leader holds the end of the string in one hand, and rolls the ball of string/yarn to a classmate. As the ball is rolling, the student states an example of a "heart-healthy" activity for classmates. As the string makes a spider web pattern on the floor, students who receive the ball must state a different example of a heart-healthy activity. The process is reversed as students take turns rolling up the string/yarn while identifying activities that are fun, but less heart-healthy. The activity also can focus on identification of activities from the health-related fitness categories (second grade alternative).

8. *Story Writing—My Family's Favorite Activities:* Have students write and illustrate a story depicting the most common physical activities in which they and their family participate. As an alternative, feature students' physical activities while they were on vacation or while they were visiting relatives.

Grades 3–5

1. *Let's Go Shopping for Fitness:* In preparation for the activity, print the names of different activities on strips of paper (10 jumping jacks, 10 toe touches, touch 4 different walls, 10 self-toss and catches of a beanbag, 10 sit-ups, 10 hops on each foot, etc.). As the activity is repeated, encourage students to add to the collection of activity strips. Then scatter the activity strips in an open space on the floor. Organize students into teams of five to six individuals. Give each team a grocery bag. On teacher signal, have each student pick up a piece of paper, complete the indicated activity, and place the slip in the team's grocery bag. The game ends on a signal indicating completion of a prearranged time period or when all slips of paper are picked up. The team with the most slips in its grocery bag is the winner.

2. *Colors, Shapes, or Numbers:* This activity begins with all students seated on the floor. Flash a color, shape, or number card. All students must touch three objects of that shape, color, or number in the room before returning to their designated starting place. There is no scoring process to this activity. Rather, the activity is focused on participation in the activity of finding the objects.

3. *Fitness Spelling:* Split students into teams of no more than four students behind a line of tape on the floor. At an equal distance from each team, place a box of cards containing many letters on the floor. Hold up a card containing a spelling word on which the students have been working. Have the first student run to the box, find the first letter of the word, return to the team, and tap the hand of the next student. Repeat the process until the team has collected all letters to correctly spell the word. Reinforce team cooperation by encouraging teams to identify correct spelling of the word before giving a "go" signal.

4. *Physical Activity Learning Stations:* Tape cards that indicate a range of physical activities in widely-spaced locations around the room (or playground). Play music as a cue to rotate to a new station. Students participate in the activity until the music begins again. As participation matures, have students construct the task cards. As an alternative, center the tasks around a theme (jumping activities, activities at different levels, etc.).

5. *Taking Pulse—A Math Correlation:* As a foundation, teach all students the correct technique for taking their carotid pulse. Have each student take and record his or her resting pulse. Have students participate in a predefined interval of aerobic activity (jumping, running in place, etc.), and then take and record their post-exercise pulse. Basic math concepts are practiced using the numbers from various trials of different kinds of activity or time intervals following bouts of exercise.

6. *Differences in Resting Heart Rates:* Have students take and record their resting heart rates. As a homework activity, have them collaborate with at least six family members of different ages to record their resting heart rates. In addition, have students research resting heart rates of different animals. Following class discussion, instruct students to write or graph variables that influence resting heart rates (size, age, weight, health status, etc.).

7. *Fist Fatigue:* Have all students place the back of one hand on their desk. On a "go" signal, ask students to open and close their fist as many times as they can in an identified time period (2–3 minutes). When completed, ask them to record the number of fists they made, write words to describe the muscle fatigue, and list activities in which they participate that cause them to feel such fatigue in other parts of their body. Organize teams of students and contrast and synthesize the groups' lists. Each team must come up with three reasons why muscular endurance is important for children and adults. Have the groups then explain their reasons to the class.

Grades 6–8

1. *Walking to . . . :* As a preliminary activity, have students walk at a brisk, but comfortable, pace for 10 minutes in a location where distance can be determined. Compute the distance that students were able to walk during that time. Have students record the time and calculate the distance that they walked each day. Using a map, ask students to calculate how far from their school they were able to walk as a class. As an alternative, have teams of students compete to see which team walks the greatest distance in a week, or covers the distance to a specified location first.

2. *Strength Collage:* Have students go through newspapers and magazines to find pictures of people who are involved in activities that require muscular strength. Assign individuals or groups of students to develop a collage depicting strength in various body parts. Attach a paragraph summary of the collage and display in the halls for other students to see.

3. *Skills for Sports Fishbone Diagrams (see chapter 5):* Have teams of students draw a card from a box on which the name of a sport has been written. Ask them to identify that sport in the "head" of a fishbone diagram. Their task is to identify as many skills as possible that are necessary for successful participation in that sport. List the skills on the fishbone diagram. Next, have students identify each skill that corresponds with a health-related fitness category. Finally, have teams share their diagrams with the class before mounting the diagrams in the room.

4. *Fitness and Math Circuit:* Divide students into six groups in six stations in the room. Give each group a task card that indicates a fitness skill. In addition, give students a list of 12 math problems that review developmentally appropriate concepts. Place math sheets and pencils on students' desks. On a "go" signal, have teams at stations complete the number of repetitions of the fitness activity indicated on the card. When all students have completed the physical task, have them return to their seats to solve two problems. When all students have solved the first two problems, rotate the teams to the next station to complete the task indicated on the card. The activity is completed when all rotations and final problems are completed. As an alternative, have teams of students complete math problems, work on spelling words, or answer social studies questions.

5. *Gymnasium Obstacle Course:* Have teams of students participate in obstacle courses that feature aerobic, flexibility, muscular strength, and balance, skills, etc.

For optimal health benefits, activities such as walking, jogging, biking, swimming, and hiking should be done at least at moderately vigorous levels. Also, Level 2 of the pyramid includes *active sports and recreational activities.* Common examples include tennis, soccer, basketball, and racquet ball. In addition, vigorous recreational activities like canoeing and water skiing are included in the *active sports and recreational activities* category. While activities like bowling and golf generally require relatively low energy output, they are considered to have health benefits when they are part of a more comprehensive physical activity program. Importantly, however, because they involve very little calorie expenditure, many recreational or leisure activities (playing cards or chess) do not fit into this physical activity category.[25]

Level 3 of the Physical Activity Pyramid is also comprised of two categories of physical activities. Exercises and physical activities performed to increase the length of muscles and connective tissue are identified as *flexibility exercises.* Flexibility exercises increase the range of motion of joints and help to reduce the likelihood of injury. In general, children are more flexible than their adult counterparts. While many activities in other categories of the pyramid may contribute to increased

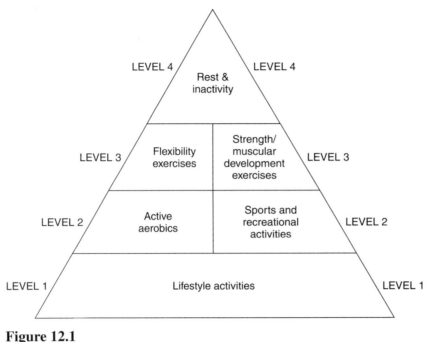

Figure 12.1

The Physical Activity Pyramid.

flexibility, even the most active adults must participate in specific exercises to gain the benefits associated with improved flexibility.[26]

The second category of activities in Level 3 of the pyramid is *strength and muscular endurance exercises.* Activities in this category are designed to improve two elements: (1) strength, or the amount of weight that can be lifted, and (2) muscular endurance, or the ability to persist in muscular effort. While formal resistance training is not advised for the youngest children, most adults will need to participate in specific additional activities to enhance their muscular strength and endurance.[27]

Level 4, the *rest and inactivity* category of the Physical Activity Pyramid, includes two kinds of practices: total sedentary living (no activity) and those pursuits that require very little large-muscle activity (playing computer games). It must be noted that activities such as reading and television viewing have been shown to have health benefits. It is not necessary for students to abstain from such activities unless they limit participation in other physical activities. In this context, rest and inactivity are valuable only as a supplement to participation in activities from the other three levels in the Physical Activity Pyramid.[28]

In summary, parents, teachers, and administrators are encouraged to examine table 12.3, which clarifies recommended emphases for student participation in each category of the Physical Activity Pyramid. This counsel is provided to meet the developmental needs of students in two age groups: 5–9 and 10–12. Importantly, these suggestions embrace all forms of physical activity in which students are likely to participate, including both in- and out-of-school pursuits.[29]

Factors that Influence Participation in Physical Activity

Research has identified many factors that are associated with the patterns of physical activity among children and youth. In specific, demographic variables including sex, age, and race or ethnicity have been demonstrated to account for variations in students' exercise behaviors. In this context, girls are less physically active than boys, and adolescents are less active than their younger counterparts. Research also has confirmed that blacks tend to be less physically active than their white counterparts.[30]

In addition to the influence of identified demographic variables, a number of individual factors have been shown to influence participation in physical activity. Students who perceive benefits from engaging in physical activity or sports (having fun, learning or refining new skills, staying in shape, improving appearance, and improving strength, endurance, or flexibility) are more likely to participate in a range of physical activities. Conversely, those students who perceive barriers to participating in physical activities, particularly a lack of time, are less inclined to engage in exercise behaviors.[31]

Also, exercise participation among children and adolescents is influenced by interpersonal and environmental factors. In particular, both the support and physical activity behaviors of friends, siblings, and parents have been shown to influence the exercise behaviors of youth.[32] Finally, having convenient play spaces, well-functioning sports equipment, and transportation to sports or fitness activities also have been demonstrated to influence student participation in physical activities positively.[33]

			Activity Category		
AGE	**LIFESTYLE**	**AEROBICS**	**SPORTS/ RECREATION**	**FLEXIBILITY**	**STRENGTH/ MUSCULAR ENDURANCE**
5–19	•••••	••	•	•	•
10–12	••••	•••	•••	••	••

TABLE 12.3 Recommendations for Student Participation in Each Fitness Category

Key:
- ••••• Greatest emphasis
- •••• Considerable emphasis
- ••• Moderate emphasis
- •• Some emphasis
- • Little emphasis

Reprinted from *Physical Activity for Children: A Statement of Guidelines* (1998) with permission from the National Association for Sport and Physical Education (NASPE), 1900 Association Drive, Reston, VA 20191-1599.

TABLE 12.4 Content Standards in Physical Education

A Physically Educated Person:
1. Demonstrates competency in many movement forms and proficiency in a few movement forms.
2. Applies movement concepts and principles to the learning and development of motor skills.
3. Exhibits a physically active lifestyle.
4. Achieves and maintains a health-enhancing level of physical fitness.
5. Demonstrates responsible personal and social behavior in physical activity settings.
6. Demonstrates understanding and respect for differences among people in physical activity settings.
7. Understands that physical activity provides opportunities for enjoyment, challenge, self-expression, and social interaction.

Reprinted from *Moving Into the Future: National Standards for Physical Education* (1995) with permission from the National Association for Sport and Physical Education (NASPE), 1900 Association Drive, Reston, VA 20191-1599.

Guidelines for Teachers to Promote Physical Activity in Schools and Physical Education Classes

Although research has confirmed that many variables can influence students to participate in healthy amounts and types of physical activity, many parents, teachers, and administrators remain convinced that the responsibility for such programs in schools rests solely in the hands of physical education professionals. In this context, like other content areas, the National Association for Sport and Physical Education has developed content standards to improve school-based physical education programs for students. These content standards are listed in table 12.4.[34] While a sound physical education program taught by qualified instructors is a critical foundational element, advocates of such a categorical approach are reminded of the complexity of promoting any health enhancing behavior.

Research has demonstrated that the ways in which fitness activities are taught and reinforced contribute to student attitudes about the value of being active for a lifetime. Since children spend a large percentage of their waking hours at school, it is far more educationally sound to develop a coordinated approach to promoting participation in physical activities. In this way, the formalized physical education curriculum, planned recess, and short activity periods are supplemented by a range of opportunities for activity throughout the school day. In addition, classroom teachers should integrate physical activities into cross-curricular instructional approaches. Through such an agenda, many professionals are invested in sending a consistent message about the value of daily physical activity.[35]

As a foundation, researchers have identified the following guidelines to support ways in which physical activity can be promoted in the physical education setting. Importantly, however, classroom teachers are encouraged to examine ways in which they can collaborate with their physical education colleagues to extend this agenda beyond the confines of the gymnasium. In specific, professionals are encouraged to:

1. Provide time for activity in the school setting.
2. Provide opportunities in which activities can be individualized.
3. Expose students to a variety of activities.

Conditions that Reinforce Lifelong Physical Activity

Long-term participation in activities is increased if activities:

- Are noncompetitive and selected and enjoyed by the student,
- Do not require a great deal of mental effort,
- Are able to be done alone,
- Are believed by students to have value in improving health or general welfare, and
- Are believed by students to get easier and more meaningful with persistence.

Note: Research suggests that a minimum of 6 months of participation is necessary for an activity to become "addictive."

Reprinted from *Physical Activity for Children: A Statement of Guidelines* (1998) with permission from the National Association for Sport and Physical Education (NASPE), 1900 Association Drive, Reston, VA 20191-1599.

4. During instruction, focus feedback on the value of regular participation and personal accomplishment rather than on such products as how fast, how many, or how difficult.
5. Reinforce physical skills.
6. Be an active role model.
7. Pay attention to student attitudes about the value of a lifetime of activity.
8. Reinforce successful accomplishment and minimize self-criticism.
9. Promote participation in activities outside the school environment.
10. Encourage participation in activities that can endure for a lifetime.[36]

With these recommendations in mind, teachers are encouraged to review an emerging body of research that suggests that if certain conditions are met, physical activity may become positively "addicting," or a necessary part of one's life. The Consider This box above includes a review of conditions that tend to reinforce a lifelong pattern of physical activity.[37]

Guidelines for School and Community Programs to Promote Lifelong Physical Activity

While the efforts of physical educators and classroom teachers are critical, the Centers for Disease Control and Prevention has published ten broad recommendations for school and community programs to promote physical activity among young people. This comprehensive agenda is based on four key principles that suggest that physical activity programs for young people are more likely to be effective when they:

- Emphasize enjoyable participation in physical activities that are easily done throughout life,
- Offer a diverse range of competitive and noncompetitive activities that are developmentally appropriate for different ages and abilities,
- Provide the skills and confidence that young people need to be physically active, and
- Promote physical activity throughout all elements of the coordinated school health program (as discussed in chapter 1), and cultivate links between school and community programs.[38]

To support program development and coordination, the following recommendations and clarifying elements have been identified:

1. Establish policies that promote enjoyable, lifelong physical activity:
   - Require daily physical education and comprehensive health education (including lessons on physical activity) for all students in grades K–12.
   - Provide adequate funding, equipment, and supervision for programs that meet the needs and interests of all students.
2. Provide physical and social environments that encourage and enable young people to engage in safe and enjoyable physical activity:
   - Provide access to safe spaces and facilities and implement measures to prevent activity-related injuries and illnesses.
   - Provide school time, such as recess, for unstructured physical activity, such as rope jumping.
   - Discourage use or withholding of physical activity as punishment.
   - Provide health promotion programs for school faculty and staff.
3. Implement sequential physical education curricula and instruction in grades K–12 that:
   - Emphasize enjoyable participation in lifetime physical activities including walking and dancing, not just competitive sports.
   - Help students develop the knowledge, attitudes, and skills they need to adopt and maintain a physically active lifestyle.
   - Follow the National Standards for Physical Education.
   - Keep students active for most of class time.
4. Implement health education curricula that:
   - Feature active learning strategies and follow the *National Health Education Standards*.

- Help students develop the knowledge, attitudes, and skills they need to adopt and maintain a healthy lifestyle.

5. Provide extracurricular activity programs that offer diverse, developmentally appropriate activities (competitive and noncompetitive) for all students.

6. Encourage parents and guardians to support their children's participation in physical activity, to be physically active role models, and to include physical activity in family events.[39] In this context, teachers are encouraged to examine the Consider This box, which includes recommendations from the National PTA to help parents promote physical activity in their children.[40]

7. Provide training for teachers, coaches, recreation and health care personnel, and other school and community professionals to enable them to promote enjoyable, lifelong activity to young people.

8. Assess the physical activity patterns of youth, refer them to appropriate physical activity programs, and advocate for physical activity instruction and programs for young people.

9. Provide a range of developmentally appropriate community sports and recreation programs that are attractive to all young people.

10. Evaluate physical activity instruction, programs, and facilities regularly.[41]

In conclusion, coordinated school and community programs that promote a pattern of ongoing physical activity among young people are regarded as health promotion strategies that are highly effective. Such collaborative initiatives have shown promise in reducing the public health burden of chronic diseases that are associated with sedentary lifestyles. Attributes of the most successful programs include a focus on equipping students with knowledge, attitudes, motor and behavioral skills, and the confidence to be physically active during youth. With this foundation, life long physical activity patterns are likely to be established.[42]

CONSIDER THIS

Recommendations for Parents: Promoting Physical Activity in Children

- Expose children to a variety of sports and activities. Many children are inactive because they have not found activities that interest them.
- Teach children that while winning is nice, it is not necessary. In addition, encourage noncompetitive, individual, or team activities that can be done throughout life.
- Encourage children to participate in aerobic activities, which are essential for building healthy bodies.
- Make physical activity part of the family routine by taking walks after dinner or planning family hiking trips.
- Set a healthy example for children by taking the stairs or joining a gym. Reinforce that physical activity is fun and not just for athletes.

Source: National PTA, *Building a Healthy Child: A Collection of Interactive Health Activities Compiled by the National PTA* (Chicago, IL: National PTA, 1997), 14.

SUMMARY

In recent years, the health benefits of a lifelong commitment to physical activity have been confirmed. Research has documented that regular physical activity can help to build and maintain healthy bones and muscles and reduce the effects of stress. These benefits are as important for children and youth as they are for adult Americans. In addition, participation in regular physical activity has been demonstrated to improve student school success.

There are important elements that undergird developmentally appropriate physical activity programs for children and youth. Programmers would be wise to remember that among children and youth, participation in physical activity is related to such variables as:

- Activities should conform to the shorter attention span of children,
- Children need frequent periods of rest following bursts of activity,
- Feelings of success and accomplishment are an important foundation for an ongoing commitment to participation in physical activity, and
- Exercising with parents and other family members can reinforce a commitment to exercise participation.

To help teachers organize and implement developmentally appropriate physical activity programs for children and youth, teachers are encouraged to review the five types of activity elements included in the Physical Activity Pyramid. With the foundation of lifestyle activities, this pyramid, like the Food Guide Pyramid, suggests activity types that are recommended for inclusion in any personal activity regimen. In addition, schools and communities should collaborate to reinforce the value of physical activity for all children, youth, and adults.

DISCUSSION QUESTIONS

1. List the health benefits for adults who participate in regular physical activity.

2. Identify the health benefits for children and youth who participate in regular physical activity.

3. Suggest ways in which participation in physical activity can enhance academic success.

4. Clarify the differences among the concepts *physical activity, exercise,* and *physical fitness.*

5. Contrast important elements of physical activity programs for children, youth, and adults.

6. Compare the value of the Physical Activity Pyramid and the Food Guide Pyramid as foundational elements for developing instructional activities.

7. Suggest ways in which schools and communities can collaborate to improve access to and quality of physical activity participation among children and youth.

8. Discuss the importance of parental and family involvement in supporting participation in physical activity among children and youth.

9. What are the reasons suggested for elementary and middle-level schoolchildren not being physically fit?

10. Develop a program of fitness evaluation for children in an elementary class of your interest.

11. What are the components of health-related physical fitness?

12. What role can the classroom teacher play in a school fitness program?

ENDNOTES

1. U.S. Department of Health and Human Services, *Physical Activity and Health: A Report of the Surgeon General* (Atlanta, GA: U.S. Department of Health and Human Services, Centers for Disease Control and Prevention, National Center for Chronic Disease Prevention and Health Promotion, 1996).

2. J. F. Sallis, T. McKenzie, and J. Alcaraz, "Habitual Physical Activity and Health-related Physical Fitness in Fourth-grade Children," *American Journal of Disabled Children* 147 (1993): 890–896.

3. S. Shea, C. Basch, and B. Gutin et al. "The Rate of Increase in Blood Pressure in Children 5 Years of Age in Relation to Changes in Aerobic Fitness and Body Mass Index," *Pediatrics* 94, no. 4 (1994): 465–470.

4. K. Brownell and F. Kaye, "A School-based Behavior Modification, Nutrition Education, and Physical Activity Program for Obese Children," *American Journal of Clinical Nutrition* 35 (1982): 277–283.

5. K. Calfas and W. Taylor, "Effects of Physical Activity on Psychological Variables in Adolescents," *Pediatric Exercise Science* 6 (1994): 406–423.

6. R. McCulloch, D. Bailey, and R. Whalen et al. "Bone Density and Bone Mineral Content of Adolescent Soccer Athletes and Competitive Swimmers," *Pediatric Exercise Science* 4 (1992): 319–330.

7. L. Kolbe, L. Green, and J. Foreyt et al. "Appropriate Functions of Health Education in Schools: Improving Health and Cognitive Performance. In: N. Krairweger, J. Arasteli, and M. Cataldo, eds. *Child Health Behavior: A Behavioral Pediatrics Perspective* (New York: John Wiley, 1986).

8. U.S. Department of Health and Human Services, *Physical Activity and Health: A Report of the Surgeon General.*

9. P. Adams et al. "Health Risk Behaviors Among our Nation's Youth: United States, 1992," *Vital Health Statistics* 10 (192) (1996): DHHS publication no. (PHS) 95-1520.

10. Ibid.

11. J. Sallis and K. Patrick, "Physical Activity Guidelines for Adolescents: Consensus Statement," *Pediatric Exercise Science* 6 (1994): 434–447.

12. Ibid.

13. C. Caspersen, K. Powell, and G. Christenson, "Physical Activity, Exercise, and Physical Fitness: Definitions and Distinctions for Health-Related Research," *Public Health Reports* 100, no. 2 (1985): 126–131.

14. J. McGinnis, L Kanner, and C. DeGraw, "Physical Education's Role in Achieving National Health Objectives," *Res Q Exercise Sport* 62, no. 2 (1991): 138–142.

15. B. Simons-Morton, N. O'Hara, G. Parcel et al. "Children's Frequency of Participation in Moderate to Vigorous Physical Activities," *Res Q Exercise Sport* 61, no. 4 (1990): 307–314.

16. C. Corbin and R. Pangrazi, *Physical Activity for Children: A Statement of Guidelines* (Reston, VA: National Association for Sport and Physical Education, 1998).

17. Ibid., 6–8.

18. Ibid., 8.

19. Ibid., 10–13.

20. Ibid.

21. Ibid.

22. N. Faucett and S. B. Nillidge, "Research Findings—PE Specialists and Classroom Teachers," *Journal of Physical Education, Recreation, and Dance* 60, no. 7 (September 1989): 51–52.

23. Corbin and Pangrazi, *Physical Activity for Children: A Statement of Guidelines,* 10.

24. Ibid.

25. Ibid., 11.

26. Ibid., 12.

27. Ibid.

28. Ibid., 13.

29. Ibid.

30. CDC, "Youth Risk Behavior Surveillance—United States," *MMWR* 45(SS-4) (1994).

31. M. Tappe, J. Duda, and P. Menges-Ehrnwald, " Personal Investment Predictors of Adolescent Motivational Orientation Toward Exercise," *Canadian Journal of Sport Science* 15, no. 3 (1990): 185–192.

32. J. Zakarian, M. Hovell, and C. Hofstetter et al. "Correlates of Vigorous Exercise in a Predominately Low SES and Minority High School Population," *Prev Medicine* 23 (1994): 314–321.

33. R. Stucky-Ropp, and T. DiLorenzo, "Determinants of Exercise in Children," *Preventive Medicine* 22 (1993): 880–889.

34. National Association for Sport and Physical Education, *Moving Into the Future: National Standards for Physical Education* (St Louis, MO: Mosby, 1995), 1.

35. Corbin and Pangrazi, *Physical Activity for Children: A Statement of Guidelines*, 14–16.

36. Ibid.

37. Ibid., 16.

38. Centers for Disease Control and Prevention, "Guidelines for School and Community Programs to Promote Lifelong Physical Activity Among Young People," *MMWR* 46 (No. RR-6) (1997).

39. Ibid.

40. National PTA, *Building a Healthy Child: A Collection of Interactive Health Activities Compiled by the National PTA* (Chicago, IL: National PTA, 1997), 14.

41. Centers for Disease Control and Prevention, "Guidelines for School and Community Programs to Promote Lifelong Physical Activity Among Young People."

42. Ibid., 24.

SUGGESTED READINGS

Cooper, Kenneth H. *Kid Fitness: A Complete Shape-Up Program from Birth Through High School.* New York: Bantam Books, 1991.

Dorman, Steve. "Enhancing School Physical Education with Technology." *Journal of School Health* 68, no. 5 (1998): 219–220.

Fox, K. "Motivating Children for Physical Activity: Toward a Healthier Future." *Journal of Physical Education, Recreation, and Dance* 62, no. 7 (1991): 34.

Grimmett, D. "Physical Activity and Fitness," in Henderson, A. and Champlin, S. eds. *Promoting Teen Health: Liking Schools, Health Organizations, and Community.* Thousand Oaks, CA: Sage Publications, 1998.

Hannaford, C. *Smart Moves: Why Learning is Not All in Your Head.* Arlington, VA: Great Ocean Publishers, 1995.

Hopper, C. et al. "A Family Fitness Program." *Journal of Physical Education, Recreation, and Dance* 63, no. 7 (1992): 23.

Karp, G. G. et al. "Using Play Structures to Enhance Health and Skill-Related Fitness." *Journal of Physical Education, Recreation, and Dance* 64, no. 4 (1993): 83.

Pangrazi, Robert P., and Charles Corbin. "Physical Education Curriculum," in Glatthorn, ed. *Content of the Curriculum,* 2nd ed. Alexandria, VA: Association for Supervision and Curriculum Development, 1995.

The President's Council on Physical Fitness and Sport. "Economic Benefits of Physical Activity." *Physical Activity and Fitness Research Digest* 2, no.7 (September 1996).

Ross, James G. et al. "New Health-Related Fitness Norms." In *Summary of Findings from National Children and Youth Fitness Study II,* Public Health Service, Office of Disease Prevention and Health Promotion, U.S. Department of Health and Human Services, 1987.

Ross, James G. et al. "What is Going On in the Elementary Physical Education Program?" In *Summary of Findings from National Children and Youth Fitness Study II,* Public Health Service, Office of Disease Prevention and Health Promotion, U.S. Department of Health and Human Services, 1987.

Simons-Morton, Bruce, et al. "School Physical Education: Secondary Analysis of the School Health Policies and Programs Study." *Journal of Health Education Supplement* 30, No. 5 (1999): S-4–S-11.

The Society of State Directors of Health, Physical Education, and Recreation. *School Programs of Health Education and Physical Education: A Statement of Basic Beliefs,* Reston, VA: SSDHHPER, 1998.

CHILDREN'S LITERATURE WITH A PHYSICAL ACTIVITY THEME

Grades K–2

Ackerman, Karen. *Song and Dance Man.* Alfred A. Knopf, 1988. (Caldecott Medal)

Harwayne, Shelley. *Jewels: Children's Play Rhymes.* Mondo, 1995. (Multicultural)

Lazebnik, Ken and Steve Lehman. *A is for At Bat.* Culpepper, 1988.

Martin, Bill and Michael Sampson. *Swish.* Henry Holt, 1997.

Patrick, Denise. *Red Dancing Shoes.* William Morrow, 1993. (Multicultural)

Thayer, Ernest. *Casey at the Bat.* (Illustrated by Patricia Polacco). Putman and Grosset, 1988.

Rice, Eve. *Swim!* Greenwillow, 1996

Sampson, Michael. *The Football that Won.* Henry Holt, 1996.

Grades 3–5

Adler, David. *Lou Gehrig: The Luckiest Man.* Harcourt Brace, 1997.

Adler, David. *A Picture Book of Jesse Owens.* Holiday House, 1994.

Golenbock, Peter. *Teammates.* Harcourt Brace, 1990. (Multicultural)

Hopkins, Lee Bennett. *Song and Dance.* Simon and Schuster, 1997.

Janeczko, Paul. *That Sweet Diamond: Baseball Poems.* Antheneum, 1998.

Spinelli, Jerry. *Maniac Magee.* Harper Collins, 1990. (Newberry Medal) (Multicultural)

Yamaguchi, Kristi. *Always a Dream.* Taylor, 1998.

Grades 6–8

Adoff, Arnold. *Sports Pages.* Harper Collins, 1986. (Multicultural)

Crutcher, Chris. *The Crazy Horse Electric Game.* William Morrow, 1987.

Voigt, Cynthia. *The Runner.* Antheneum, 1995.

INTERNET INFORMATION

PHYSICAL ACTIVITY WEBSITES

For additional information on physical activity, please refer to the following websites.

American Alliance for Health Physical Education, Recreation, and Dance
www.aahperd.org

National Association for Sport and Physical Education
http://www.aahperd.org/naspe.html

American Cancer Society
www.cancer.org

American Heart Association
www.americanheart.org

National School Boards Association
Physical Activity, Nutrition, and Tobacco-use (PANT) Resource Database
www.nsba.org/services/federation/paint.html

American College of Sports Medicine
http://www.acsm.org

National Center for Chronic Disease Prevention and Health Promotion Centers for Disease Control and Prevention
www.cdc.gov/nccdphp/dash/index.html

P.E. Central
www.pe.central.vt.edu

Fitnessgram
The Cooper Institute for Aerobic Research
www.cooperinst.org

Gamekids
www.gamekids.com

Games Kids Play
www.corpcomm.net/~gnieboer/gamehome.htm

P.E. Integrated Learning
www.est.gov.bc.ca/curriculum/irps/pek7/petoc.htm

Human Kinetics
http://www.humankinetics.com/

Aerobics and Fitness Association of America
http://www.afaa.com/

Fitness Sites of Note
http://www.turnstep.com/links.html

Shape Up America
http://www2.shapeup.org/sua/

National Association of Governor's Councils on Physical Fitness and Sports
http://www.fitnesslink.com/govcouncil

National Recreation and Park Association
http://nrpa.org

President's Council on Physical Fitness and Sports
http://www.dhhs.gov/progorg/ophs
and
http://www.indiana.edu/~preschal

American School Health Association (Physical Activity Information Resource List)
http://www.ashaweb.org

SEXUALITY EDUCATION

O U T L I N E

INTRODUCTION

Today's children and adolescents are faced with many serious issues and decisions regarding their sexuality. Unfortunately, they often receive mixed messages about sexuality, which can contribute to confusion about their sexual development and related behaviors. Mixed messages can come from a variety of sources, including approximately 65,000 television references to sexual behaviors, which equates to an average of 27 sexual references per hour for all programs on television combined.[1] These confusing messages may contribute to the fact that preadolescents and adolescents are participating in sexual intercourse at a young age. For example, 7.2% of students have had sexual intercourse before the age of 13, and 48.4% of all high school students in grades 9–12 have had sexual intercourse.[2] The result has been an increase in teen pregnancy and HIV/AIDS and other sexually transmitted diseases for sexually active adolescents. In fact, the United States has more than double the teenage pregnancy rate of any western industrialized country, with more that 1 million teenagers becoming pregnant each year.[3] In addition, teenagers have the highest rates of sexually transmitted diseases (STDs) of any age group, with one in four adolescents contracting a STD by the age of 21.[4]

CONSIDER THIS

Percentage of Students Whose First Sexual Intercourse Was Before Age 13

Grade	Males, %	Females, %
9	14.7	6.5
10	9.7	5.1
11	8.2	3.5
12	6.0	2.9

Although problems regarding sexual activity are well documented, it is estimated that only 5% of students in the United States receive comprehensive, K–12 sexuality education that lasts for a total of at least 40 hours.[5] In addition, only 48.9% of states require instruction on human sexuality, which is typically taught at the secondary level, not at the elementary level.[6] Most states and school districts wait and teach one unit of sexuality education during a one-semester ninth or tenth grade health class. Do these school districts assume that their students do not need developmentally appropriate sexuality education until this time? Studies show that sex education begun before youth are sexually active helps young people stay abstinent and use protection when they do become sexually active.[7]

With all of the sexuality issues and decisions facing young people today, why don't school districts mandate a K–12 sexuality education program? A number of reasons emerge as obstacles to such programming.

First, there typically is a great deal of controversy regarding sexuality education. A handful of vocal parents opposed to such instructional activities often have succeeded at keeping developmentally appropriate, quality, comprehensive sexuality education out of many school districts. Studies show that the 90% of parents are in favor of sexuality education, but parents usually do not get upset if sexuality education is *not* being taught in the schools.[8] If the majority of parents are supportive of sexuality education in the schools, why are quality, comprehensive programs reaching only 5% of the students? The main issue is that many administrators are nervous about the political and practical implications of teaching such a sensitive issue.

A second reason why schools do not consistently teach sexuality education is because some teachers feel uncomfortable teaching the subject, and therefore do not campaign to have it included in the curriculum. Elementary and middle-level teachers typically do not receive adequate training in sexuality education during their undergraduate preparation. A recent survey found that of the 169 colleges surveyed, only 14% require pre-service teachers to take a health education course, which may or may not include sexuality education. Only 2% of colleges require elementary education majors to take a course on sexuality.[9] Just as teachers need to be trained to teach children about math concepts and reading skills, they also need to feel comfortable with their repertoire of skills to teach children about developmentally appropriate sexuality concepts. Most teachers want training in this area so they can help their students understand important concepts and that will help them make health decisions in this area.

Another reason why comprehensive sexuality education is not typically included in the school curriculum is that some people misunderstand the scope of sexuality education. Many times educators make the mistake of using the term *sex education* instead of *sexuality education* or *family life education*. The word *sex* is usually linked with the act of intercourse and, thus, the public sometimes connects sex education with teaching children only about sexual intercourse behaviors. Sexuality, however, implies a much broader scope and is associated with:

1. The ability to participate in warm and loving relationships,
2. Celebrating the self-esteem and self-identity of individuals, and
3. Practicing responsible decision making regarding the physical, emotional, and social aspects of personal sexual health.

Sexuality education, therefore, encompasses topics such as relationships, families, puberty, growth and development, sexual health promotion, and reproduction. Hence, there is a big difference between the concepts implied by the terms *sex education* and *sexuality education*.

Sexuality education, or family life education, encompasses a broad scope of concepts. Strategies include acquiring information about sexual development, reproductive health, interpersonal relationships, affection, body image, and gender roles and identity. It also includes skill development in areas such as communication, decision making, refusal skills, and goal setting. Sexual health promotion programming is grounded in the premise that sexuality is a natural, ongoing process that begins in infancy and continues through life. Regardless of formal instruction about such concepts at home or school, children and adolescents obtain information about these topics. From the moment of birth, children are learning about themselves as sexual people through the unintentional and informal messages of parents and caregivers. As children grow and explore more of their environment, they can learn about sexuality through television, friends, books, and newspapers. Given the speed of communication networks and information transfer, it is not realistic to presume that students can be placed in a vacuum and shielded from all information about sexuality until they reach adulthood. Parents and teachers cannot control a child's curiosity and desire to learn about sexuality. They can, however, empower children with formal, developmentally appropriate sexuality education experiences in the classroom environment that give students accurate, quality, and comprehensive information. Sexuality education should be a planned, intentional, and specific program of instruction that encourages parents and educators to identify the kinds of information, skills, and attitudes that are developmentally appropriate for children of different ages.

If school districts in the United States continue to be held captive by a few, but vocal, minority groups who oppose such instruction, students will likewise be forced to make sexual decisions without the benefit of the best information, skill, and support available to them. There will continue to be high teenage pregnancy rates and sexually transmitted disease problems resulting from a lack of information, healthy attitudes, and appropriate skills regarding sexuality. Research shows that sexuality education programs do not hasten the onset of intercourse, nor do they increase the frequency of intercourse or the number of sexual partners. In fact, skill-based programs have been shown to significantly delay the onset of sexual intercourse and increase contraceptive and condom use among sexually experienced adolescents.[10]

REASONS TO INCLUDE SEXUALITY EDUCATION IN ELEMENTARY AND MIDDLE-LEVEL SCHOOLS

It is important for teachers to have a solid understanding of why sexuality education is important to include in an elementary and middle-level health education curriculum. It is not uncommon for parents to contact teachers about their concerns on this topic. The following reasons should help teachers formulate their own rationale for teaching sexuality education.

1. Attitudes regarding sexuality are formulated early in life, which makes them difficult to change once a person has internalized them. Children begin forming opinions about their bodies, their gender identity, and their feelings about sexuality at a young age. If parents and teachers provide children with negative messages about their sexuality when children are young, these messages generally stay with them through adulthood. For instance, if a 6-year-old girl is taught to use slang terms for body parts, such as *boobs* and *pee pee,* she will probably continue to use that terminology as she gets older. Some parents and teachers feel this is not a problem, but it does give children a message that something is wrong with those body parts.

    Another example occurs when children ask adults questions regarding sexuality, and the adults respond "I never want to hear you talk like that again," or "Wait until you get older." Children quickly get the message that there must be something wrong with their concerns or questions about their sexuality. By contrast, when children grow up in an open and honest environment regarding sexuality and are reinforced for seeking information from significant adults rather than from peers, they have a better chance of developing healthy attitudes and appropriate sexual communication skills as they get older.

2. If factual information and skills are presented in a positive manner throughout the elementary and middle-level grades, negative attitudes, apprehensions, and fears regarding sexuality may be reduced and superseded by a positive understanding that people live as sexual beings. Unfortunately, many school districts teach sexuality education by discussing puberty and the menstrual cycle through a 1- or 2-day presentation during the fifth or sixth grade. The presentation is sometimes given by "outside experts," with the girls and boys in separate classrooms. At this age, many students have already begun going through puberty, making it a developmentally inappropriate presentation. Also, students may feel uncomfortable with an outsider, may not have a question concerning puberty on that day, or may be more curious about what is happening in the opposite genders' presentation. Again, the message that students get from this type of presentation is that there is something wrong or embarrassing about sexuality because the classroom teacher is too embarrassed to talk about puberty. Further, such a strategy sends messages about communication between girls and boys on sexual issues. How is mutual respect and appropriate sexual communication to be reinforced if boys and girls are not allowed to listen to the same presentation?

    If student questions are not answered by trained professionals during that 1- or 2-day presentation during the fifth or sixth grade, students typically have to wait until sexuality is again formally discussed during a high school health class. Again, that gives students the message that sexuality is not important enough to discuss or that there is something wrong with developmentally appropriate curiosity and concern about the topic.

3. Information and skill development are the greatest defenses against the negative aspects of sexuality, such as promiscuity, teen pregnancy, sexually transmitted diseases, and sexual abuse. Sexuality knowledge does increase when students are instructed on this topic. Also, skill-based programs can significantly delay the onset of sexual intercourse and increase contraceptive and condom use among sexually experienced youth. No studies have revealed evidence that sexuality education leads to earlier or increased sexual experience, and several indicate that it is associated with delay of sexual intercourse.[11]

4. Schools can provide a unique opportunity for students to have exchanges of ideas and thoughts about sexuality with their peers, under the guidance of a trained teacher. Sexuality education should take place at home because parents can add love, security, and values to the factual information being taught. Without usurping this pivotal role of the family, school-based programs can add the unique dimension of formalizing student interaction with their peers about sexuality issues. Many students talk about sexuality with their friends, but in an unsupervised arena. Encouraging students to share thoughts, feelings, and questions about sexuality with their peers and a trained teacher complements the learning taking place at home.

5. Students receive a distorted view of sexuality through the mass media. In television shows, commercials, and movies, sexuality is often portrayed in a distorted way. For example, soap operas typically show sexual encounters taking place between unmarried couples. An evaluation of ten popular television programs found that for each hour of the shows, there was a total of 24.5 touching behaviors, including kissing, hugging, and other affectionate touching; 16.5 suggestions and innuendoes involving flirtatious behavior or general allusions to sexual behavior; 2.5 suggestions of sexual intercourse; 6.2 suggestions of discouraged sexual practices such as sadomasochism and exhibitionism; and only 1.6 occasions of educational information about sex.[12] The realistic information about sexuality provided in sexuality education can help counteract the messages that students receive through the mass media.

6. Many parents feel uncomfortable talking to their children about sexuality. Many parents do a wonderful job of teaching formal sexuality education to their children. Unfortunately, other parents feel too uncomfortable talking to their children about sexuality, and therefore they ignore or avoid the topic. Every student is entitled to formal sexuality education as a means to learn correct information and develop health enhancing attitudes and skills.

Within this chapter, factual information about sexuality and ideas about teaching this topic to elementary students is presented. Even with accurate information and suggested teaching activities in hand, it is perhaps most important for teachers to explore their own attitudes and beliefs about sexuality before trying to teach the subject.

RECOMMENDATIONS FOR TEACHERS: PRACTICE AND CONTENT

Before trying to teach sexuality education to elementary and middle-level students, teachers should have some general knowledge about how children grow and change regarding their sexuality. Elementary students in the primary grades (K–3) should be introduced to sexuality topics that can be presented concretely. Young children are egocentric, but as they get older, they do become aware of influences other than their primary caregivers. Children have varying levels of knowledge and skills during this period, depending on their family and preschool experiences. Children at this age may:[13]

- Be very curious about pregnancy and birth.
- Have strong same-sex friendships.
- Show strong interest in male/female roles that are often stereotyped.
- Have a basic sexual orientation by this time.
- Have a new awareness of authority figures.
- Compare their own situations with those of peers.
- Begin to conform to peer group styles of dress and speech.
- Engage in name calling using sexual terms.
- Participate in sex play and masturbation.

Some appropriate sexuality topics for early-elementary students are the proper naming of body parts, discovering the differences between boys and girls, increasing their understanding of the role of the family and different kinds of families, discovering gender differences, and learning how babies are made and born.[14]

The middle-level sexuality education curriculum (grades 4–7) should focus more on preparing students for the emotional, physical, and social changes that occur during puberty. Children at this age may:[15]

- Begin the process of puberty.
- Become more modest and desire privacy.
- Experience emotional ups and downs.
- Develop romantic crushes on friends, older teens, music and TV idols, and sometimes teachers and counselors.
- Continue to attach importance to same-sex friends.
- Feel awkward and wonder "Am I normal?"
- Masturbate to orgasm.
- Be strongly influenced by peer groups, although parents remain the main source of values.
- Continue to learn society's expectations about appropriate behavior for boys and girls.
- Begin to enter the mysteries of the adult world by using sexual language and enjoying romantic and sexual fantasies.
- Face decisions about sex and drugs.
- Initiate sexual intercourse as early as age 12.
- Experience sexual harassment.

Physical changes such as hormonal changes, sperm production, menstruation, and rates of growth and development are developmentally appropriate topics for middle-level students. Emotional and social changes such as friendships, the changing family role, emotions, decision making, feelings, and sexual desire are appropriate topics for discussion at the middle-grade level.[16]

Developmentally Appropriate Practice Recommendations

It is often difficult for teachers, administrators, and parents to know what is developmentally appropriate for children and preadolescents in the area of sexuality. There are a variety of resources that can help school districts decide on the appropriate content for each grade level. For example, the Sexuality Information and Education Council of the United States (SIECUS) has created a comprehensive list of sexuality concepts that are developmentally appropriate for students in grades K–12.[17] A condensed list of those concepts follows.

Early Elementary (K–2)
- Roles and responsibilities of different family members,
- Functions, purposes, and types of families,
- Differences and similarities between boys and girls, and between men and women,
- How babies are born,
- Not all men and women choose to or are able to have children,
- How animals and other forms of life reproduce; the differences between reproduction in animals and humans,
- The correct terms for external parts of the body,
- Adjusting to a new brother or sister,
- Growth and development of babies,
- Privacy associated with body parts and body functions,
- Making and maintaining friendships,
- Bodies change as children grow older, and
- People can only produce children after they go through puberty.

Upper Elementary (3–5)
- Equal opportunity regardless of race, gender, religion, physical or mental ability, or cultural background,
- Prejudice, discrimination, and sexism,
- Heredity influences on growth,
- Puberty and changes in the body during preadolescence, including menstruation and nocturnal emissions,
- Assertive affirmation of beliefs as a part of the growth process,
- Biology of human reproduction,
- Myths about masturbation,
- The importance of responsible social behavior that is consistent with moral and ethical values,
- The family as the origin of personal value systems; the role that schools play in providing supplementary facts and ideas that can help in making decisions,
- Emotions that preadolescents and adolescents may experience,
- Healthy decision making,
- Relationships (with family members, friends, etc.),

- Major family life events including breakup of a marriage, birth of a child, death, adoption, stepparents, stepchildren, serious illness, and new job requiring family relocation,
- Individual differences associated with the rate and timing of physical and emotional changes,
- The birth of a baby,
- Peer refusal skills,
- Sexual harassment, and
- Abstinence.

Middle/Junior High School (6–8)
- Healthy decision making,
- Male and female reproduction systems, intercourse, and conception,
- Social and cultural influences on sexuality and sex roles,
- Relationship building, based on mutual respect, trust, and caring,
- The need to belong and to be normal,
- Respect for self and others,
- Risks associated with sexual intercourse: unplanned pregnancy, sexually transmitted diseases, emotional problems, and conflict with parents or society,
- Interpersonal relationships including readiness, dating, commitment, going steady, and responsibilities,
- The concept of love and how people know if they are in love,
- Principles of birth control,
- STDs and HIV/AIDS including causes, diagnosis, prevention, and control,
- Abstinence as a means of preventing diseases and unwanted pregnancies and promoting a positive lifestyle for adolescents,
- Peer refusal skills/negotiation,
- Sexual orientation, and
- Masturbation.

Depending on the grade level, not all of the information presented in the following sections will be relevant to all elementary and middle-level students, but teachers should have background knowledge about relationships, families, male and female reproductive systems, and puberty.

Relationships

Students develop many different relationships throughout their elementary and middle-level years. For instance, relationships with family members, same-age friends, relatives, and teachers begin to change as children continue through elementary and middle school. It is vital that teachers have a basic understanding of the importance children place on friends as they advance through elementary and middle school.

When children first enter school at age 5, they are very self-centered and more concerned about their own needs and identity than with the needs or characteristics of others. As they progress through kindergarten, they begin to develop an increasing awareness of others. They start to understand that other people have needs and rights too. This recognition might conflict with their early attitudes of self-gratification and might be displayed by throwing temper tantrums and not wanting to share. Friends, and their behaviors, are not that important to students at this age.[18]

Children from age 6 to 8 begin to redirect their personal concerns to intellectual concerns and group activities. They begin to expend more energy on friendships and the community around them. Children in this age group also become less dependent on their parents, although their parents are still important to them.[19] Nine- and 10-year-old children accept sexuality education as they do other subjects. Many children this age do not yet feel self-conscious about their bodies, making it an ideal time to discuss the reproductive system. At this age, boys and girls begin to regard the opinions of their friends as more important than those of their parents. Although same-sex friendships are most popular in this age group, children begin to become interested in the opposite sex. This interest is typically exhibited in the forms of teasing and aggressive behavior.[20]

Between the ages of 11 and 13, children become even more independent from their parents. Their friendships are increasingly more important as they try to emancipate themselves from their parents and other adult authority figures. This is a means to explore the parameters of their own unique identity. Peer pressure becomes a major issue during this time because they are struggling with developing their own code of morals and ethics. Preadolescents also are beginning to become more self-conscious about the physical changes to their bodies. Teachers may find it more difficult to discuss sexual issues with children of this age because of the students' self-consciousness. They also become more interested in the opposite sex as they get older.[21]

Another relationship issue that sometimes arises with preadolescents is homosexuality. Teachers are sometimes nervous and anxious about addressing this topic because of fear of how parents and students will react. In addition, many teachers are uncomfortable with this subject themselves. As with all areas of sexuality, it is important that the teacher know what is in the course of study or curriculum before teaching about a specific topic. If the issue of homosexuality is included in the curriculum, teachers should have some background information on the topic. *First,* students should understand that homosexuals are people of the same sex who have a sexual and an emotional relationship. Many times female homosexuals are referred to as lesbians and male homosexuals as gays. *Second,* it is important for young people to understand that homosexuality is normal because gay and lesbian adolescents need to feel that they are OK, and also to help

prevent violence against gay and lesbian youth.[22] *Third,* sometimes preadolescents have attractions toward individuals of the same sex. It is important for teachers to discuss that sometimes this means that their sexual orientation is homosexual and sometimes it means that these feelings of sexual attraction are transitory. If a student has concerns about his or her sexual orientation, it is important for teachers to be supportive and to refer the student to a gay/lesbian-friendly counselor within the school district. In addition, students should be encouraged to discuss their feelings with supportive family members. *Last,* teachers should feel secure in knowing that discussions about homosexuality will not make someone be gay or lesbian.

Families

When discussing the family structure and the role of the family during sexuality education, the teacher should not be judgmental about different types of families and the way they function. Today's families are quite different from the families of 50 to 100 years ago. For example, in the past, extended families were common. This meant that parents, children, grandparents, and other relatives lived in the same house or in close proximity. Children had several adult role models they could depend on for love, support, understanding, and protection. Various factors have contributed to the changing structure of the family. For example, the increased mobility of families has made it difficult to maintain extended families. It was once common to grow up in a town, marry someone from that same community, and raise a family in that same locale. Today, many people move often because of career changes and do not live close to the town in which they were raised.

Some people believe that the "typical" or "normal" family of today is the nuclear family. A nuclear family consists of children living with both of their natural parents. Of course, many nuclear families exist, but there are many other types of families. People can no longer assume that the nuclear family is the "normal" or "typical" family. Because of the high divorce rate and teenage pregnancy, today's families are more diverse.

Other types of families include single-parent families and families that include stepparents and half-siblings. There are many single-parent families because of the high divorce rate, teenagers who become pregnant and decide not to marry, homosexuals who are raising children, and never-married single people who are raising children. It is important for elementary and middle-level teachers not to assume that all students are being raised in a nuclear family, and that some students might have special needs because of their family situation. Students also should be taught that members of a family do not have to be blood related, such as in an adoption, a remarriage, or when a parent dies. It is important that children believe they belong to a family regardless of its structure.

Children should also be taught that family members have responsibilities to one another and to the overall functioning of the family unit. For example, certain tasks need to be accomplished by a family, such as buying groceries, cooking, cleaning, and helping each other. Teachers should discuss the concept of family roles and responsibilities with their students so they understand that each person must contribute if the family is to be a nurturing, mutually supportive, and happy one.

Another issue when discussing families is sex-role stereotypes. Some families still establish and reinforce clear gender roles for boys and girls; that is, the boys mow the yard and the girls wash the dishes. It is not the teacher's role to judge the ways that different families

Boys and girls should be encouraged to participate in opposite-gender activities and to play with opposite-gender toys.

function. Teachers can, however, try to eliminate sex-role stereotyping in their classrooms. For example, certain chores should not be identified as being for boys or for girls. Textbooks should also be reviewed with sex-role stereotyping in mind. These activities can help balance students' attitudes about sex-role stereotyping. Allowing students to participate in all types of activities also allows them to explore options and talents without fear of negative judgment.

Male and Female Reproductive Systems

As mentioned previously, sexuality education consists of more than just focusing on the physical aspects of sexuality. A general understanding of the male and female reproductive systems is important. The reproductive system is the only system in the body that has different organs for the male and female. The following information should provide enough background for the elementary and middle-level teacher about the male and female anatomy and physiology of the reproductive system.

The Male Reproductive System

The function of the male reproductive system is to produce sperm, which is the male cell that unites with a female egg to form a fertilized egg. Both external and internal organs make up the male reproductive system (figure 13.1).

The external part of the male sex organs is called the genitalia, which is composed of the penis and the scrotum. The penis is a tubelike organ composed mainly of

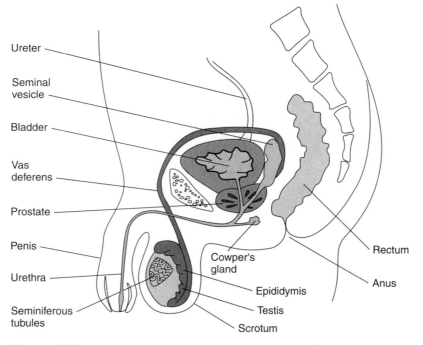

Figure 13.1
Male reproductive system (side view).

erectile tissue and skin and is used for urination and sexual intercourse. When a male becomes sexually excited, the erectile tissue in the penis becomes filled with blood, which makes it become enlarged and erect.

The scrotum is the pouchlike structure hanging behind and slightly below the penis. The scrotum contains the testes and acts like a thermometer. By keeping the testes at a constant temperature, viable sperm can be produced. For example, if the body temperature rises, muscles in the scrotum relax to lower the testes away from the body.

The major internal organs of the male reproductive system include the testes, vas deferens, seminal vesicles, prostate gland, Cowper's glands, and the urethra.

Sperm are produced in a section of the testes called the seminiferous tubules. These tubules produce about 500 million sperm a day and can produce billions of sperm throughout a lifetime. After the sperm are produced, they are stored in another part of the testes called the epididymis. After about 64 days, the sperm reach maturity and are capable of uniting with a female egg.

The vas deferens are two tubes that are connected to the epididymis and are used to store and transfer sperm to the seminal vesicles during ejaculation. The seminal vesicles are two little pouches near the prostate gland. Their function is to secrete a fluid that mixes with the sperm. This fluid contains nutrients for the sperm, helps make the sperm mobile, and provides protection for them.

The prostate gland is about the size of a chestnut and is located near the bladder. It produces a thin, milky, alkaline fluid that mixes with sperm to make semen. The alkaline fluid acts as an acid neutralizer and a coagulant.

The two Cowper's glands are about pea-sized and open up into the urethra. These glands secrete a clear fluid prior to ejaculation that helps to neutralize the urethra. This fluid can contain some sperm, and its release is not felt by the male.

The urethra is a tube that runs the length of the penis. The urethra allows both urine and semen to leave the body, but not at the same time. When semen enters the urethra, the internal and external urethral sphincters close the connection between the bladder and the urethra.

The Female Reproductive System

The function of the female reproductive system is to release a mature egg that unites with a sperm to make a fertilized egg. Both external and internal organs make up the female reproductive system.

The external part of the female sex organs is called the vulva. It is composed of the clitoris, vaginal opening, the hymen, and the labia (figure 13.2).

The clitoris is a knob of tissue located in front of the vaginal opening. It contains many nerve endings and blood vessels. When the female gets sexually excited, the clitoris becomes engorged with blood and enlarges. The clitoris is the only part of the female sexual anatomy that does not have a reproductive function, but it does produce sexual arousal.

The hymen is a flexible membrane that partially covers the vaginal opening. It has no known function and is different in every female. For example, some females have a hymen that covers a larger portion of the vaginal opening, while some have a hymen that is barely visible.

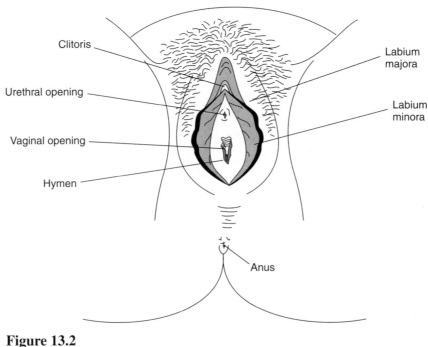

Figure 13.2
External female reproductive system.

A common myth about the hymen is that if it is intact, it is a sign of virginity. This is not true, because every female's hymen is unique and, in fact, some females do not have a hymen at birth.

The labia are folds of skin that protect the female genitals from germs entering the body. There are two labia: the labia majora and the labia minora. The labia majora are large folds of skin that surround the opening of the vagina. The labia minora are smaller folds of skin located between the labia majora.

The internal reproductive organs in the female are the vagina, uterus, fallopian tubes, and ovaries (figure 13.3). The vagina is a muscular tube that goes from the outside of the body to the uterus. It has three main functions: it receives the penis during intercourse, it is the opening for menstrual flow to exit the body, and it serves as the birth canal. It is also called the birth canal, because during birth, the baby is pushed from the uterus through the vagina and out of the mother's body.

The uterus is an elastic muscle that is the size of a fist and the shape of a pear. The tip of the uterus, which leads to the vagina, is called the cervix. The role of the cervix is to help keep the baby inside the uterus until the time of delivery. The uterus has a lining that is composed of many blood vessels. About once every month, this lining thickens and turns into a nourishing place for a fertilized egg to develop into a baby. If an egg is not fertilized, the thickening material disintegrates because it is no longer needed. The fluid and membrane then leave the body through the vagina, which is called menstruation.

There are two fallopian tubes that curl around each ovary and connect to the uterus. The fallopian tubes are narrow and are lined with tiny hairlike projections called cilia. After an egg is released from an ovary, it travels through the fallopian tube for a few days where it waits to be fertilized. If the egg is fertilized, it travels to the uterus where it attaches itself. If the egg is not fertilized while it is in the fallopian tube, it disintegrates.

There are two ovaries, located on either side of the uterus and next to the fallopian tubes. The functions of the ovaries are to house the egg cells for maturation and to produce estrogen and progesterone. While males manufacture sperm following puberty, females are born with all the potential egg cells they will ever have.

Puberty

Puberty is not a single event, but a long process that includes many physical and emotional changes. Regardless of the age at which puberty begins, it takes 4 to 5 years for boys and 3 to 4 years for girls to complete.[23] Puberty has been reached when males and females have the physical capability to reproduce.

Teachers should remember that not all students reach puberty at the same time. That is why some older elementary and middle-level students might seem both physically and emotionally mature for their age, and others might seem very immature. Puberty changes can

occur as early as age 7 and as late as age 18. However, about 50% of all boys and girls reach puberty before age 13. The emotional changes that preadolescents experience are diverse because of their changing hormone levels and the developmentally consistent feelings

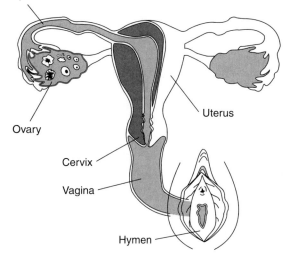

Figure 13.3
Female reproductive system.

Children grow at different rates while going through puberty.

of wanting to be independent. Shifts in certain hormones can trigger feelings of irritability, restlessness, anxiety, happiness, excitement, and frustration. For instance, one day students going through puberty might be happy and sensible and the next day they might seem depressed and irrational. These mood swings are normal and should be expected throughout puberty. Whatever emotion is expressed by the students, teachers should be patient and understanding when interacting with this target audience.

Boys and girls are also curious about the physical changes that are happening to them during puberty. The physical changes that occur throughout puberty are called secondary sex characteristics. These changes occur because different hormones are being released in males and females.

Female Changes During Puberty   For girls, the secondary sex characteristics produced by the release of estrogen that teachers and peers may observe include (figure 13.4):

1. A gain in height and weight,
2. Breast enlargement,
3. Growth of pubic and underarm hair,
4. Onset of menstruation, and
5. Widening of hips.

Females will notice the external changes that happen throughout puberty gradually, such as breast enlargement and pubic hair growth. During this time, internal changes also occur that the female cannot see. The reproductive organs develop so that a female is able to bear children. Part of this internal process is menstruation. Menarche, which is the first period, or menstruation, is a sign that a female's reproduction system is beginning to function so that she can produce a baby.

The menstrual cycle begins at puberty and continues until a woman is in her middle to late 40s. Before the cycle has begun and after it is ended, a woman is usually unable to bear children.

The number of days for the complete menstrual cycle varies from female to female. For adolescents, it is usually 27 to 31 days, although it can last from 20 to 42 days. Teenagers generally have an irregular cycle during the first year of menstruation.

The purpose of the menstrual cycle is to produce a mature egg and to develop the lining of the uterus so that it is ready to receive and nourish a fertilized egg. The menstrual cycle is complex because many hormonal and physical changes occur each month. It is not necessary for the elementary and middle-level teacher to understand every detail in the menstrual cycle, but instead to have a general knowledge of the changes that

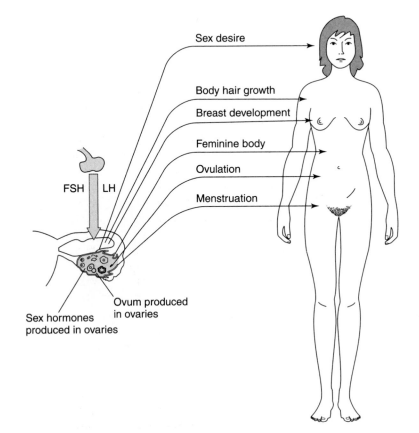

Figure 13.4

Female secondary sex characteristics.

occur (figure 13.5). The cycle begins when one egg in one of the ovaries develops, becomes larger, and is mature enough to produce a baby if it is joined by a sperm. This mature egg is called an ovum. An ovum is produced every month, usually in alternating ovaries. While the egg is growing, the lining of the uterus becomes thick with blood and other materials in preparation for a fertilized egg. As the uterine lining continues to thicken, the egg breaks through the wall of the ovary (which is called ovulation) into the fallopian tube, where it travels toward the uterus for a few days. If the egg is to be fertilized, it must be joined by a sperm while it is in the fallopian tube. While the egg is traveling through the fallopian tube, the uterine lining continues to get thicker and filled with blood.

If the egg does not meet the sperm while it is in the fallopian tube, it disintegrates. The buildup in the uterus is no longer needed, and so it begins to shed. The actual shedding of the uterine lining (menstruation) lasts for 3 to 7 days. The cycle then continues, with the maturing of another egg and the buildup of the lining of the uterus.

Male Changes During Puberty   Boys also go through many physical changes during puberty. Their secondary sex characteristics, produced by the release of testosterone, that teachers and peers may observe include (figure 13.6):

1. Gain in height and weight,
2. Growth and added muscle strength,
3. Growth of body hair around the penis and scrotum, under the arms, on the face, arms, legs, and chest,
4. Increase in the size of penis and scrotum,
5. Broadening of the shoulders,
6. Deepening of the voice,
7. Increase in metabolic rate, and
8. Possible nocturnal emissions (wet dreams).

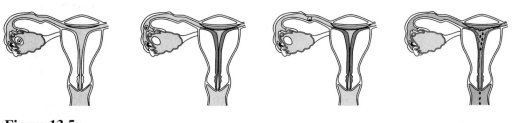

Figure 13.5
The stages of menstruation.

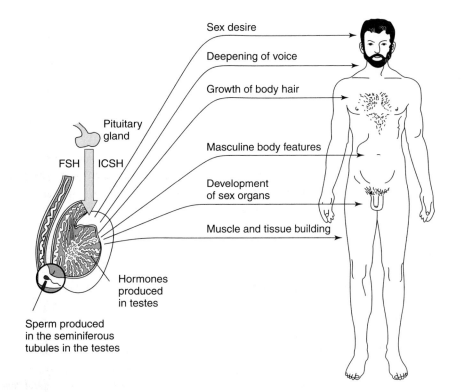

Figure 13.6
Male secondary sex characteristics.

As with girls, boys will notice some of the physical changes occurring in their bodies throughout puberty gradually. During this time, internal changes also are happening that the male cannot see. Hormones are being released, making it possible for the male to produce sperm in the reproductive organs.

Before sperm are being produced, males can become sexually excited and have orgasms; however, no semen is ejaculated. Once a male is able to produce sperm, he ejaculates semen. When males go through puberty, many times they experience ejaculation while they are sleeping. This is called a nocturnal emission or a wet dream. There is no warning when this will occur, and it cannot be prevented. Wet dreams are natural, and boys should be informed about wet dreams before they go through puberty so they are not frightened by this event.

When teaching students about the changes that accompany puberty, it is important to emphasize that these changes can begin anytime from age 7 to 18. When teachers say, "The average age of puberty is at 13," students tend to remember the number *13* and not the word *average*. It should be emphasized that there is no best time to go through puberty and that everyone will experience these changes when his or her body is ready.

GUIDELINES FOR SCHOOLS AND TEACHERS FOR TEACHING SEXUALITY EDUCATION

Several guidelines are important to consider when teaching sexuality education. These guidelines can help school districts make decisions about their sexuality education. The teacher guidelines can help teachers not to be defensive with parents and students when teaching sexuality education.

Guidelines for Schools

1. School districts should establish their own sexuality education guidelines and policies with the input of parents, teachers, administrators, community members, and support staff. This will help school districts determine their philosophy and their curriculum. Policies may include topics such as the omission of students from sexuality education classes, how teachers should respond to questions about specific sexuality topics, or what teachers should do if a student questions his or her own sexual orientation. Without these established guidelines and policies, teachers will have a difficult time determining how to manage these situations.

2. After creating a K–12 sexuality curriculum, it is important to determine if it includes the information and skills that will help children and adolescents make positive sexual choices. The following nine characteristics describe successful sexuality and family-life education programs and will help school districts create their curriculum:[24]

- Focus clearly on reducing participation in or factors related to one or more sexual behaviors that lead to unintended pregnancy.
- Maintain age-appropriate and culturally relevant behavioral goals, teaching methods, and materials that coincide with the sexual experience level of the participants.
- Utilize theoretical approaches that have demonstrated effectiveness at reducing other health-related risky behaviors, such as social learning theory, social inoculation theory, and cognitive behavioral theory.
- Allow sufficient time for presentation of information and completion of activities.
- Involve the participants to personalize the information being presented.
- Provide basic and scientifically accurate information about the risks of engaging in sexual intercourse without protection and about ways to avoid participating in unprotected sexual intercourse.
- Address social pressures to engage in sexual activity.
- Model communication, negotiation, and refusal skills.
- Select teachers or peers who are committed to the program and provide training to help them facilitate the program.

3. Some states and school districts have ignored the nine characteristics just listed and have adopted abstinence-only curricula. The research clearly shows that these programs will not result in young people delaying sexual intercourse.[25] States and school districts have opted for these programs because of pressure from minority groups and because of new legislation at the federal level. In 1996, the federal government added a new formula grant program to Title V of the Social Security Act. Its purpose is to enable the states to provide funding for abstinence-only education. Although some individuals may perceive this as support for sexuality education, it is very limiting in terms of how the grant money can be used.[26]

Guidelines for Teachers

1. Teachers should encourage proper terminology in the classroom. Beginning in kindergarten, students should learn proper terms for their external body parts, including their reproductive organs. At that age, it is not important for students to know the names of their internal body parts (such as fallopian tubes or epididymis) because they are concrete thinkers and have a difficult time imagining what the inside of their body is like. However, as students get older, they *should* learn the proper terminology for internal reproductive body parts. If students are taught proper terminology at an early age, they will

not be as embarrassed to say words such as *penis, testes, vulva,* and *vagina* when they get older. This will allow students to communicate about sexuality in a more comfortable manner.

2. Teachers should not feel as if they have to know all of the answers to every sexuality-related question. Students are capable of asking a variety of questions about sexuality. Because most elementary and middle-level teachers do not receive adequate training in this area, they cannot be expected to know all of the answers about this subject. It is appropriate for teachers to say "I don't know" to a question, as long as they find out the answer and relay that information to the student as soon as possible. The teacher could also ask students to find the answer to the question. Perhaps a student could volunteer to find the correct answer.

3. Although teachers cannot be prepared for all questions asked by children, it is important for them to understand that students are capable of asking unexpected questions. If teachers act shocked when students ask questions about sexuality, the students will be less likely to ask another question in the future. A good way to overcome a shocked look is to practice answering common questions that children ask about sexuality. A sample list of questions with suggested answers can be found in the following section.

4. Teachers should teach only those topics in sexuality education that have been approved as part of their graded course of study by their board of education and administrators. Many teachers have felt so strongly about teaching all aspects of sexuality education that they have jeopardized their jobs because they did not have administrative support for teaching certain sexuality topics. Such a practice can jeopardize the credibility of the entire health-education program. If teachers feel more sexuality education should be included in their curriculum, they should seek the support of their administrators, boards of education, and parents in the community.

5. Teachers should not use hand-made drawings of the reproductive system. Students have a difficult time imagining what the internal male and female reproductive systems look like. When teachers use hand-made drawings, there is a better chance that the proportions or specific organs will be incorrect. There are enough good professional drawings of both the male and female reproductive systems that hand-drawings are not necessary.

6. Activities should be structured to include parents whenever possible. When teaching sexuality education topics, teachers should encourage students to discuss the information taught that day with parents. This will help bridge the gap among children, parents, and schools. Teachers may even want to have specific questions written out on a handout for parents and children to discuss.

These guidelines and common sense should help teachers when teaching sexuality to their students.

COMMONLY ASKED QUESTIONS ABOUT SEXUALITY

A list of some commonly asked questions about sexuality and some suggested answers follows. It is not enough to just read the suggested answers—actually practice saying them out loud. Teachers are encouraged to think of other questions that children may ask and to practice answering them, too.

Sample Questions that Younger Elementary Students Commonly Ask

1. *Where Do Babies Come From?* Babies come from their mother's body. The baby grows inside the mother's body in a place called the uterus. (Do not tell the child that a seed has been planted in the mother's body, because they may imagine a plant starting to grow.)

2. *How Does a Baby Eat and Breathe Before It Is Born?* Before a baby is born, it gets food and air from its mother's blood through a long tube called the umbilical cord. One end of the cord is attached to the inside of the mother's uterus and the other end is attached to the baby's navel, or belly button.

3. *Why Do Grown-ups Have Hair on Their Body, But I Don't?* When children grow up and go through puberty, many changes happen in their bodies. One of these changes is for hair to grow in different places on the body. As you get older, hair will grow on you, too.

4. *How Long Does a Baby Grow Inside the Mother?* About 9 months.

5. *How Does a Baby Get in a Mother's Body?* A man and a woman make a baby. (If this answer does not satisfy the child, the teacher may have to give more detail.) When a man and woman want to have a baby, they put their bodies very close together. This feels

(continued after Activities on page 252)

Children generally have many questions regarding sexuality.

A C T I V I T I E S

Sexuality Education Strategies for Elementary and Middle-Level Students

There are several activities that can be conducted with elementary and middle-level students to give them a better understanding of the many topics included within sexuality education. A sampling of those activities that instruct in the areas of knowledge, attitudes, and skills at the K–2, 3–5, and 6–8 grade levels follows.

Grades K–2

1. *Hatching Chicks.* When discussing reproduction with elementary students, a popular activity is to get chicken eggs and an incubator and allow the children to watch the eggs hatch. This activity can continue after the eggs hatch with a discussion on growth and development. One common problem with this activity, however, is that sometimes the eggs do not hatch. Be prepared to explain this to children; the discussion might lead to a discussion on death and dying.

   Teachers may also have guppies or other animals for classroom pets. If they reproduce, it is a teachable moment to discuss reproduction with students.

2. *Family Members.* This is an activity to teach the concepts of family members to children in the primary grades. Start the discussion by asking children to volunteer to tell how many people are in their families. As they tell who is in their family, have other children stand up to represent each of the family members. Next, ask children to draw and color a picture of one of their family members on pieces of newsprint or butcher paper. As a summary, have different children volunteer to tell a story about the person they drew.

3. *Animal Families.* When discussing different types of families with younger elementary students, discuss the different types of families in the animal kingdom. For example, some animals keep the same mate for life, some males take care of their newborn, and some animals mate and then leave their partner. This discussion will help students understand that there are different types of human families, too.

4. *Body Parts.* Children in early elementary grades are concrete thinkers and therefore have a difficult time visualizing things they cannot see. When teaching early elementary students about body parts, it is important for children to know the correct names and functions of all exterior body parts. For example, a picture similar to the one in figure 13.7 could be used to help students identify the eyes, ears, nose, penis, hand, vulva, and so on. This encourages the use of proper terminology for *all* body parts and reinforces the concept that there is nothing wrong with using the correct names for reproductive body parts. Make sure that administrators support using correct terminology for reproductive organs before doing this activity in class.

5. *My Family.* Instruct children to draw and then color pictures of their family. Have the students then share their pictures with the class. This will help students understand that there are many different types of families and that all families are OK.

6. *Tour of Rest Rooms.* Early elementary students are very curious about the opposite sex's rest room. It is not uncommon for elementary students to sneak into the opposite sex's rest room before or during school hours to see what it looks like. When teachers are discussing the external reproductive body parts with students, a rest room tour is a good opportunity to reinforce the male and female differences. Stress that girls do not use urinals because they do not have a penis.

Grades 3–5

1. *Body Outline.* Pair students and provide each child with one piece of butcher block paper. Ask one student to lay down on the butcher block paper while the other student traces the outline of the partner's

Boy   **Girl**

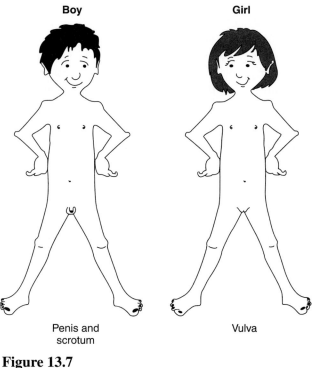

Penis and   Vulva
scrotum

Figure 13.7
Pictures similar to these can be used to help students use the
proper terminology for *all* body parts.

body. Instruct them to then switch roles. After both partners have an outline of their own body, ask them to draw their face, hair, clothes, etc., and then hang the pictures around the room. Lead a discussion about how we all have different body sizes and shapes. Continue the discussion by asking students how their bodies will change as they get older.

2. *Qualities of a Friend.* An activity that is appropriate at this age level is to divide students into small groups and ask them to brainstorm the qualities of a good friend. The importance of friendship increases as children get older, and so their responses will change through time. Ask the groups to share their responses with the rest of the class. Also ask students to identify one way they could improve on being a good friend, and then encourage them to try to improve that quality.

3. *Friendship Story.* When discussing the topic of friendship with elementary students, use this writing activity as a foundation for discussion with students. Ask students to write a short story entitled "What Would It Be Like to Live in a World Without Friends?" Ask students to share their stories with the rest of the class. After the students read their stories, have a discussion with the students about ways to help everyone have friends.

4. *Sharing Traditions.* Allow students to choose one of the following topics and ask them to write about it.

    • A way that your family celebrates a specific holiday,

    • A traditional food or eating pattern in your family,

    • How household chores are assigned in your family,

    • Traditional family trips or vacations, or

    • Cures for the cold or flu in your family.

Place students into small groups and have them share their answers. Assign students to write a follow-up paragraph about how their family is different from another family.

Grades 6–8

1. *Different-Sized Role Models.* Many students feel uncomfortable about their height or weight while they are in elementary and middle-level school. An assignment that can help students understand that all sizes and shapes of people can succeed in life is to ask them to identify famous people who are different sizes and shapes. Follow with a discussion about what makes these people popular and successful. Reinforce the notion that these peoples' size or shape did not stop them from succeeding.

2. *Advantages of Being Different Sizes.* This is another activity that reinforces the concept that we all grow at different rates and that size does not make or break the person. Place students in small groups and ask them to brainstorm the advantages of being short, medium height, or tall. Then ask them to report their responses to the rest of the class. Students may not have thought of the advantages of being the height they are.

3. *Advantages of Different Types of Families.* When discussing different types of families with older elementary students, it is important to focus on the positive aspects of all kinds of families. Ask students to identify different types of families, such as single-parent families, stepfamilies, nuclear families, interracial families, and adopted families. After different families have been identified, place students in small groups and ask them to brainstorm the advantages of being in a particular type of family unit. Ask students to report their responses to the entire class. They can recognize that there are positive aspects about all types of families.

4. *Family Tree.* The family tree activity is a commonly suggested teaching activity when discussing the family. It can be a positive learning experience for some children, but teachers need to be sensitive to the diversity of students in their classes. There may be students who are adopted, some living with stepparents or grandparents, and some might not know who their fathers are. Forcing these students into doing a family tree may make them feel negative toward their family. We suggest that the family tree be an optional assignment for students.

   Another way to reinforce the concept of family members begins with distributing paper plates and crayons/markers to the students. Ask them to draw a circle in the center of the plate and write their name in the circle. Next have the students make bicycle spokes or pie wedges for each of the family members that they know and place their names in the spaces created. Ask students to share their paper plates with the class.

5. *Body Parts.* As students get older, it is important for them to learn the internal and external organs of the reproductive system, just as they learn about the circulatory and respiratory systems. Diagrams, such as those in figures 13.1 and 13.2, are appropriate to use for this lesson.

6. *Matching Game for the Reproductive System.* After teaching older elementary students the names and functions of the reproductive organs, this activity is a good way to reinforce that information. Write the name of one reproductive organ on an index card, and write its function on another card. For example, one index card may have *fallopian tube* written on it, and another card may have *a tube-like structure connected to the uterus where fertilization takes place.* Complete cards for every reproductive organ discussed in class. Give one index card to each student. Instruct students that half of the cards have the names of the reproductive organs written on them, and the other half of the cards have the functions of the reproductive organs written on them. Instruct students to find the person who has the index card that matches the correct organ to its

Children enjoy participating in the Matching Game for the reproductive system.

function. This activity allows students to say the reproductive organ names aloud, and it encourages students to interact with a variety of classmates. Repeat the activity several times so that students receive a different organ or function each time.

7. *Journal Entry.* Children at this age are typically self-conscious about their physical appearance. It may be helpful to ask students specific questions or provide sentence stems related to physical appearance that they can complete in a journal entry. Some sample questions/sentence stems may be:

   a. Two things I like about my body are . . .

   b. How has your body changed in appearance over the past 6 months?

   c. How do you think your body will change over the next 6 months?

   d. My changing body makes me feel . . . .

8. *Interviewing a Parent about Dating/Relationships.* Parents are often uncomfortable initiating conversation with their preadolescents about dating and relationships. Encourage this by assigning an interview between a parent and child. Some questions might include:

   a. When was the first time you went out on a date?

   b. How did you feel about going on your first date?

   c. In what activity did you and your date participate? (movie, eating, etc.)

   d. How do you know when you are really in love?

   e. What things can I do to make dating safe and fun?

9. *Friendship Advertisement.* Place four students into each cooperative learning group. Assign roles like writer, reporter, task master, and leader. Explain that their job is to create an advertisement that explains the characteristics of a good friend. The advertisement can be a poem, skit, jingle, or a song. After students are given time to create their advertisement, let them perform them for the rest of the class. Continue the activity by asking them about the similarities and differences in the friendship characteristics in the commercials. Instruct students to then choose one of the friendship characteristics that needs improvement and to write in their journal how they will try to improve that characteristic over the next month.

10. *Carousel Activity—Negative Outcomes of Becoming a Teen Parent.* This is an activity that can be conducted after discussing that one of the negative outcomes of becoming sexually active is becoming a teen parent. This carousel activity is a way to get students to think about how becoming a teen parent would personally affect them. Place students into small groups and ask them to brainstorm about how their life would change in each of the following five categories: financial, family, social, education, and emotional, if they became a teen parent. After each group returns to its original piece of newsprint, instruct students to circle the four answers that would be the worst consequences of becoming a teen parent.

These students are participating in the negative outcome of becoming a teen parent in the Carousel Activity.

11. *Role-Play.* An activity that helps with skill development is to place students into small groups and allow them to role-play situations in which they may find themselves in the future. Examples include pressure to engage in sexual activity or pressure to brag about how many times a person has had sex.

good to both of them. When they are close, the man's penis becomes hard and is put into the woman's vagina. This is called sexual intercourse. In time, a fluid called semen comes out of the man's body. The semen has sperm cells in it. When one sperm meets with a woman's egg, the beginning of a baby is formed.

6. *What Is Gay?* Gay is a term used to describe homosexuals. Homosexuals are people of the same sex who have a sexual and an emotional relationship.

7. *When Is a Boy Old Enough to Make a Baby?* When he is old enough to ejaculate (ejaculation may have to be discussed). When a boy is able to ejaculate, it is called puberty. Boys go through puberty around ages 10 to 15. Just because a boy can physically make a baby at this age does not mean he is responsible enough to take care of a baby.

8. *When Is a Girl Old Enough to Make a Baby?* Girls are old enough to make babies when they begin to have their menstrual cycle. This usually happens when girls are around 9 to 16 years old. A girl may be physically ready to have a baby when she begins to menstruate, but she is probably not emotionally ready to care for it.

Sample Questions that Older Elementary and Middle-Level Students Commonly Ask

1. *What Is a Rubber?* A rubber is a type of contraceptive that is also called a condom. It is a rubber sheath that covers the penis when it is hard and keeps the sperm from getting into the vagina.

2. *What Makes Puberty Happen?* Glands in the body become more active and begin making different hormones. These hormones have specific functions that make the body change and develop.

3. *Can Urine and Semen Come Out at the Same Time?* No. When semen comes out of the urethra, muscular contractions shut off the valve that allows urine to leave the body.

4. *How Does a Girl Know When She Will Start Her Period?* Nobody knows when a girl will have her first period. When it happens, she may feel a dampness in the vaginal area. When she goes to the bathroom, she will notice some menstrual blood in her panties. This means menstruation has begun.

5. *Does a Penis Have to Be a Certain Size to Work?* No. There are different sizes to all body parts, including the penis; however, most erect penises are about the same size.

6. *Do Boys Have Menstrual Periods?* No. When a boy goes through puberty, his sex glands begin to produce sperm cells. At night, some of the sperm may pass out through the penis during sleep. When this happens, it is called a wet dream or a nocturnal emission, because it is often associated with a sexually exciting dream.

7. *Can a Woman Have a Baby Without Being Married?* Yes. A woman can have a baby when she is able to produce an egg and that egg meets with a sperm.

8. *Is Wet Dream Another Term for Masturbation?* No. Masturbation is performed when a person is awake, but a wet dream happens involuntarily while a person is asleep.

9. *How Do the Sperm and Egg Get Together?* When a man puts his penis into a woman's vagina, some fluid, called semen, is released through the penis. There are many sperm in the semen. If one of them finds and fertilizes an egg in the woman's fallopian tube, a new life can begin to grow. This is called intercourse and should be done only by mature individuals who are ready to raise a child.

SUMMARY

Sexuality education is often viewed as a controversial topic in the public schools. Because of its controversy, fewer than 5% of students receive comprehensive, K–12 sexuality education that lasts for at least 40 hours. Recent surveys, however, indicate that 90% of all adults support sexuality education.

Sexuality education encompasses a broad scope of topics, such as families, sex-role stereotyping, relationships, puberty, and the male and female reproductive systems. It is important for teachers to have a general understanding of the developmentally appropriate concepts of these topics so they can better meet the needs of their students in these areas.

Children change drastically in the relationships they emphasize as they progress through elementary and middle school. For example, when children enter kindergarten, their parents are very important to them and same-age friendships are not as important. As children get older, the need for same-age friendships grows, while dependence on parents weakens. Middle-level students also become more interested in the opposite sex. Teachers should focus their lessons on friendships and families with these changes in mind.

The family is another important topic in sexuality education. The family structure has changed over the past 50 to 100 years, and it is important for teachers to understand these changes. The nuclear family can no longer be considered the "normal" family. Instead, all types of families must be accepted and viewed without prejudice. When discussing the family unit in class, teachers should use different types of families as examples, instead of always using the nuclear family.

Teachers also should have a general understanding of the male and female reproductive systems. The reproductive system should be taught as any other system in the body is taught. It should be emphasized that the reproductive system is the only system that is different between males and females. Teachers should be familiar with the following organs and their functions in the male reproductive system: penis, scrotum, testes, vas deferens, seminal vesicles, prostate gland, Cowper's glands, and the urethra. The female reproductive organs include the clitoris, labia, hymen, vagina, uterus, fallopian tubes, and ovaries.

Teachers of middle-level children should be especially familiar with the changes that occur throughout puberty. The emotional fluctuations during puberty are diverse because of the children's changing hormone levels and feelings of wanting to be independent. Preadolescents also experience many physical changes that can be categorized as secondary sex characteristics. Teachers should be prepared to discuss these emotional and physical changes with their students openly.

Teachers should also understand why sexuality education is important to include in the elementary and middle-level health-education curriculum, because it is not uncommon for parents to contact teachers about this topic. Some of the following reasons may help teachers formulate their own rationale for teaching this topic. First, attitudes regarding sexuality are formulated early in life. Second, if factual material about sexuality is presented in a positive manner, negative attitudes and fears about sexuality may be reduced. Third, information and skill development are the greatest defenses against the negative aspects of sexuality. Fourth, schools can provide a unique opportunity for students to have a formal exchange of ideas about sexuality with their peers. Fifth, students receive a distorted view of sexuality through the mass media. Last, many parents feel uncomfortable talking to their children about sexuality.

There are also many guidelines for teaching sexuality education with which schools and teachers should be familiar. Schools should understand what the researchers suggest for including in sexuality education. Teachers have more specific guidelines to follow. For example, teachers should encourage students to use proper terminology when discussing the reproductive systems. Teachers should also not feel that they have to know all the answers to some of the unexpected or shocking questions that students ask about sexuality. To protect themselves, teachers should teach only those sexuality topics that are supported by the administration.

There are many creative ideas for teaching students about the many aspects of sexuality. Activities should be hands-on and student-oriented as often as possible. Activities should be conducted to reinforce concepts related to friendships, growth and development, families, male and female reproductive systems, and reproduction.

Teachers should also be prepared to answer the many questions students may ask regarding the topic of sexuality. Teachers cannot be prepared for every question, so it is a good idea to practice answering some of the more common questions that children ask.

DISCUSSION QUESTIONS

1. Why do some school districts keep sexuality education out of their curriculum when the majority of parents are in favor of it?

2. What is sexuality education?

3. What are the key developmentally appropriate concepts in sexuality education?

4. What relationship changes occur as children progress through elementary and middle school?

5. What changes have occurred in the family unit over the past 50 to 100 years?

6. List several different types of families and describe several positive aspects of each type of family.

7. What is sex-role stereotyping? How should teachers try to eliminate sex-role stereotyping in their classrooms?

8. List and describe the different male reproductive organs and their functions.

9. Describe the path that sperm take when leaving the body.

10. List and describe the different female reproductive organs and their functions.

11. What is the path the egg takes after it leaves the ovaries?

12. What are the female secondary sex characteristics?

13. What are the male secondary sex characteristics?

14. Describe the stages of the menstrual cycle.

15. What are some reasons to include sexuality education in the health education curriculum?

16. What are some guidelines for teaching sexuality education for both schools and teachers?

17. Describe several activities that could be used to teach sexuality education.

18. What are some questions about sexuality that children commonly ask, and how would you answer them?

19. What would you do if a student asks you questions regarding his or her sexual orientation?

20. What would you do if a parent called you and was upset about what you were teaching about sexuality?

ENDNOTES

1. Family Planning World, "Switching Channels: TV stations Suddenly Tune in to Contraceptive Ads." *Family Planning World* 4 (1994). (Santa Cruz, CA: Network Publications, 1991): 8–12.

2. Centers for Disease Control and Prevention, Youth Risk Behavior Surveillance—United States, 1997, *MMWR* 47 (No. SS-3) (1998):1–89.

3. Ibid., 1–89.

4. Department of Health and Human Services. *Healthy People 2000: National Health Promotion and Disease Prevention Objectives.* (Washington, DC: U.S. Government Printing Office, DHHS Publication No. 91-50212, 1990).

5. Sexuality Information and Education Council of the United States, *Guidelines for Comprehensive Sexuality Education, 2nd Edition* (New York: Sexuality Information and Education Council of the United States, 1996).

6. J. Collins, M. Small, L. Kann, B. Pateman, R. Gold, and L. Kolbe, "School Health Education," *Journal of School Health* 69, no. 8, (1995): 302–311.

7. D. Kirby, L. Short, J. Collins, and D. Rugg et al. "School-based Programs to Reduce Sexual Risk Behaviors: A Review of Effectiveness," *Public Health Reports* 109, No. 3, (1994): 339–360.

8. Sexuality Information and Education Council of the United States, *Guidelines for Comprehensive Sexuality Education, 2nd Edition.*

9. M. Rodrigues, R. Young, S. Renfro, M. Ascencio, and D. Haffner, "Teaching Our Teachers To Teach: A SIECUS Study on Training and Preparation for HIV/AIDS Prevention and Sexuality Education," *Siecus Report* 28 No. 2, (1995/1996).

10. D. Kirby, *No Easy Answers: Research Findings on Programs to Reduce Teen Pregnancy* (Washington, DC: The National Campaign to Prevent Teen Pregnancy, 1997).

11. Ibid, 26–28.

12. D. Workman, "What You See Is What You Think," *Media and Values* 46 (Spring 1989).

13. P. Wilson, *When Sex Is the Subject: Attitudes and Answers For Young Children,* 12. Santa Cruz, CA: ETR Associates, 1991, p. 3.

14. Ibid., 12.

15. Ibid., 13.

16. Ibid., 13.

17. Sexuality Information and Education Council of the United States, *Guidelines for Comprehensive Sexuality Education, 2nd Edition.*

18. Ibid., 15.

19. Ibid.

20. Ibid., 15.

21. Ibid.

22. B. Strong and C. DeVault, *Human Sexuality: Diversity in Contemporary America, 2nd Edition,* (Mountain View: CA, Mayfield Publishing Company, 1997).

23. Ibid., 165–166.

24. D. Kirby, *No Easy Answers: Research Findings on Programs to Reduce Teen Pregnancy.*

25. Ibid., 25.

26. D. Daley, "Exclusive Purpose: Abstinence-Only Proponents Create Federal Entitlement in Welfare Reform," *Siecus Report,* 25, No. 4, (1997): 3–8.

SUGGESTED READINGS

The Alan Guttmacher Institute. *Facts in Brief: Teenage Sexual and Reproductive Behavior.* New York: The Alan Guttmacher Institute, 1993.

American School Health Associates. *Sexuality Education Within Comprehensive School Health Education.* Kent, OH: The American School Health Association, 1991.

Black, Susan. Facts of Life. *American School Board Journal.* August, 1988: 33–36.

Drolet, J., and K. Clark, eds. *The Sexuality Education Challenge: Promoting Health Sexuality in Young People.* Santa Cruz, CA: ETR Associates, 1994.

Kirby, D. *Looking for Reasons Why: The Antecedents of Adolescent Sexual Risk Taking, Pregnancy, and Childbearing.* Washington, DC: The National Campaign to Prevent Teen Pregnancy, 1999.

Kirby, D. *No Easy Answers: Research Findings on Programs to Reduce Teen Pregnancy.* Washington, DC: The National Campaign to Prevent Teen Pregnancy, 1997.

Miller, B. *Families Matter: A Research Synthesis of Family Influences on Adolescent Pregnancy.* Washington, DC: The Nationship Campaign to Prevent Teen Pregnancy, 1998.

Strong, B., and C. DeVault. *Human Sexuality: Diversity in Contemporary America, 2nd Edition,* Mountain View: CA, Mayfield Publishing Company, 1997.

Wilson, P. *When Sex Is the Subject: Attitudes and Answers for Young Children.* Santa Cruz, CA: Network Publications, 1991.

CHILDREN'S LITERATURE WITH A SEXUALITY THEME

Grades K–2

Cooper, M. *I Got a Family.* Henry Holt, 1993. (American Bookseller Pick of the Lists, Booklist Editors' Choice)

Cousins, L. *Za Za's Baby Brother.* Candlewick, 1995.

Curtis, J. *Tell Me Again About the Day I Was Born.* Harper Collins, 1996.

Davis, J. *Before You Were Born.* Workman, 1997.

Hausherr, R. *Celebrating Families.* Scholastic, 1997. (Multicultural)

Henkes, K. *Julius, the Baby of the World.* Mulberry, 1990.

Hoberman, M. *Fathers, Mothers, Sisters, Brothers.* Puffin, 1991.

Numeroff, L. *What Mommies Do Best/What Daddies Do Best.* Simon and Schuster, 1998.

Say, A. *Allison.* Houghton Mifflin, 1997. (Multicultural)

Williams, V. *"More, More, More," Said the Baby.* Greenwillow, 1990 (Caldecott Honor)(Multicultural)

Grades 3–5

Blume, J. *The Pain and the Great One.* Bradbury Press, 1984.

Conrad, P. *Staying Nine.* Harper Collins, 1988.

Graves, D. *Baseball, Snakes, and Summer Squash: Poems About Growing Up.* Boyds Mill, 1996.

Hoffman, M. *Boundless Grace.* Penguin, 1995. (Multicultural)

MacLachlan, P. *Journal.* Bantam, 1991. (American Library Association Notable Book for Children, American Library Association Best Book for Young Adults)

Stickland, D. and M. Strickland. *Families: Poems Celebrating the African-American Experience.* Boyds Mills, 1994. (Multicultural)

Vigna, J. *My Two Uncles.* Albert Whitman, 1995.

Willhoite, M. *Daddy's Roommate.* Alyson, 1990.

Willhoite, M. *Daddy's Wedding.* Alyson, 1996.

Grades 6–8

Blume, Judy. *It's Not the End of the World.* Candlewick, 1995.

Fletcher, R. *Room Enough for Love.* Simon and Schuster, 1998.

Holbrook, Sara. *I Never Said I Wasn't Difficult.* Boyd Mills, 1996.

Myers, W. *Won't Know Till I Get There.* Puffin, 1988. (Multicultural)

Rosen, M. *The Heart is Big Enough.* Hartcourt Brace, 1997.

INTERNET INFORMATION

SEXUALITY EDUCATION WEBSITES

For additional information on sexuality education, please refer to the following websites.

Sexuality Information and Education Council of the U.S. (SIECUS)

http://www.siecus.org

Planned Parenthood

http://www.plannedparenthood.org/

Tambrands

http://www.bodymatters.com/teachers/

Centers for Disease Control and Prevention

http://www.cdc.gov/necdphp/dash/

The Alan Guttmacher Institute

http://www.guttmacher.org/

14

HIV AND AIDS PREVENTION AND EDUCATION

OUTLINE

INTRODUCTION

Twenty years ago, the public had never heard of the acronyms HIV and AIDS. Today, they are commonly seen in newspapers and magazines and heard on television and radio programs. Although what these acronyms stand for may be misunderstood, almost everyone in the United States is familiar with them, including elementary students. When discussing such an important health topic, it is critical, that teachers and students use and understand proper terminology. In 1988, the Presidential Commission on the Human Immunodeficiency Virus (HIV) eliminated some confusion between HIV and AIDS by stating:

> The term AIDS is obsolete. HIV infection more correctly defines the problem. The medical, public health, political, and community leadership must focus on the full course of HIV infection rather than concentrating on later stages of the disease. Continual focus on AIDS rather than the entire spectrum of HIV disease has left our nation unable to deal adequately with the epidemic.[1] (See figure 14.1.)

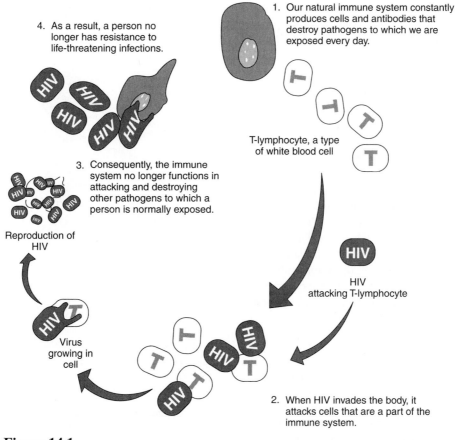

1. Our natural immune system constantly produces cells and antibodies that destroy pathogens to which we are exposed every day.

T-lymphocyte, a type of white blood cell

HIV attacking T-lymphocyte

2. When HIV invades the body, it attacks cells that are a part of the immune system.

Virus growing in cell

Reproduction of HIV

3. Consequently, the immune system no longer functions in attacking and destroying other pathogens to which a person is normally exposed.

4. As a result, a person no longer has resistance to life-threatening infections.

Figure 14.1
HIV attack.

Although this statement was issued in 1988, there is still confusion between these two terms. As a way to reinforce the use of correct terminology, this chapter has been entitled "HIV and AIDS Prevention and Education," and not the more common "AIDS Education and Prevention." We have tried to use the term *HIV* exclusively in this chapter; however, when referring to the disease AIDS, or specific curricula or official documents that use the term *AIDS,* the original terminology is used. While it may be appropriate to use the term *AIDS* with younger elementary students until the concept of HIV has been introduced to them, teachers should be comfortable using correct terminology with their students.

To provide necessary clarification for teachers, a complete chapter in this book is dedicated to HIV education. For instructional purposes, however, this topic should be integrated into other units of study. For instance, HIV/AIDS concepts could be contained in discussions of family life and sexuality education, drug prevention, school health services, life and death education, or personal hygiene. In fact, we discourage teachers from teaching a unit focused exclusively on HIV education. A better practice is to integrate these concepts into already existing health content areas. We felt, however, that a complete chapter dedicated to

HIV and AIDS was needed for teachers because of the complexity, severity, and the relatively recent development of HIV and AIDS.

HIV/AIDS TERMINOLOGY AND DEFINITIONS

HIV: Human immunodeficiency virus (a small germ), which causes the disease AIDS.

HIV Infection/Positive: Being infected by HIV. Individuals can be tested to determine if they have been infected by HIV. HIV antibodies in a person's body are clear-cut evidence that the HIV virus is in that person.

HIV-Disease: A condition in which a person has been infected with HIV and has a set of specific symptoms, but has not yet developed AIDS.

AIDS: Acquired immunodeficiency syndrome. A severe condition that results from years of HIV infection and is life threatening. This is a full range of diseases caused by HIV infection and is characterized by the collapse of the body's immune system. A person with AIDS cannot fight off infection and is vulnerable to unusual infections and cancers that eventually lead to death. A person has AIDS when the CD4 cells (a type of white blood cell) in the blood drop below 200/mm^3 and one of the conditions defined as a marker for AIDS develops.[2]

RECOMMENDATIONS FOR TEACHERS: PRACTICE AND CONTENT

Currently, 79% of states and 83% of school districts require HIV prevention/education to be taught.[3] Classroom teachers are typically responsible for providing HIV and AIDS information for their students at the elementary and middle levels. Unfortunately, only 31 states require elementary education majors to have any heath-education coursework.[4] It is likely that minimal HIV education is taught during that limited health-education coursework. This section, therefore, presents basic HIV and AIDS information. Depending on the grade level, not all of this information will be developmentally appropriate for all elementary and middle-level students. However, teachers should possess basic literacy about HIV and AIDS concepts.

The Disease and the Immune System

Acquired immune deficiency syndrome (AIDS) is not a single, distinct disease, but rather a disorder characterized by a severe suppression of the immune system. AIDS is caused by a tiny germ called a virus, which is a tiny particle with the ability to infect cells. Viruses are thousands of times smaller than cells and millions of times smaller than humans. When cells become infected with viruses, they often die. When many cells become infected and die, the organism (person) becomes sick.

The virus that causes AIDS is the human immunodeficiency virus (HIV). When a person becomes infected with HIV, this particular virus attacks the immune system. The immune system is the body's defense mechanism that provides protection from infection. Barriers, such as the skin and mucous membranes that help prevent various infectious agents from entering the body, are an important part of the immune system. Another part of the immune system is the white blood cells, which are microscopic and circulate throughout the body's bloodstream. There are several types of white blood cells called lymphocytes (B cells and T cells), each with a different function. The functions include engulfing bacteria or producing antibodies, which are substances that help kill viruses (figure 14.2). Because HIV attacks the immune system and kills white blood cells, HIV-infected people eventually cannot fight off even minor infections. Even relatively harmless germs that normally exist in the body are able to cause life-threatening illnesses. When this happens, the person has HIV disease or AIDS (figure 14.3).[5]

People living with AIDS constitute only the tip of the iceberg of HIV-infected individuals. Because many individuals who are HIV-infected do not know their HIV status, it is very difficult to determine the exact number of HIV-infected individuals in the United States. As of 1998, 500,000

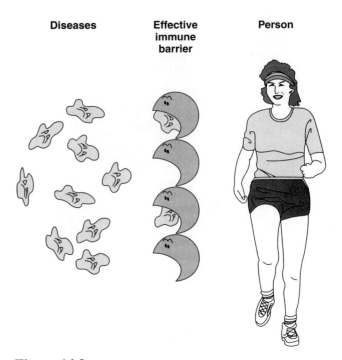

Diseases   Effective immune barrier   Person

Figure 14.2
A healthy person's immune system can fight off disease.

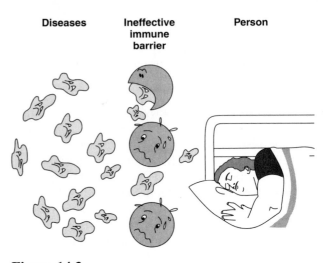

Diseases   Ineffective immune barrier   Person

Figure 14.3
A person living with AIDS (PLWA) has an ineffective immune system.

people in the United States have been diagnosed with AIDS, while there are an estimated 1 million HIV-infected individuals in the United States.[6] It is estimated that 40,000 new cases of HIV infection occur each year in the United States.[7] Individuals 14–19 years old have the highest rates of new HIV infection.[8] As previously mentioned, many HIV-infected persons do not know they are infected (figure 14.4). They may be tired or mildly ill, but they still might not know they are HIV infected. This is crucial to understand, because HIV-infected individuals who are not showing specific HIV disease or AIDS signs and symptoms may, unknowingly, be passing the virus to uninfected individuals.

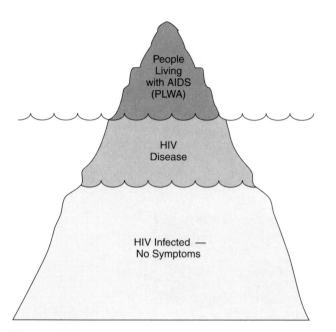

Figure 14.4
HIV infection iceberg.

Coughs/   Insects
sneezes

Food   Handshakes

Figure 14.5
AIDS is *not* spread by casual contact.

Through unsafe   Through blood
sexual contact

From mother   From mother to
to fetus   baby via breast milk

Figure 14.6
AIDS *is* spread . . .

Modes of Transmission/Prevention

In the early to mid-1980s, HIV infection and AIDS were new conditions that were surrounded by myths. There was abundant speculation about how people contracted HIV infections. Due to a lack of research and scientific information, many people were scared to be around HIV-infected persons. People who were HIV infected and those living with AIDS were therefore often mistreated. At that time, many persons erroneously believed that HIV could be transmitted through casual contact. Research, however, has since confirmed that there are no documented cases of HIV transmission among those living with an HIV-infected person, except for the sexual partners of infected persons, children born to infected mothers, and those individuals sharing needles with HIV-positive persons. The risk of transmission in social settings, such as in schools, is probably lower than in household settings.[9] There is no evidence of transmission through mosquito bites, tears, saliva, or by sitting next to a person with AIDS, holding hands, or using a public telephone or rest room (figure 14.5). Because HIV has been documented to have been transmitted in blood, semen, breast milk, and vaginal secretions of infected individuals, only direct contact with one of these fluids can cause HIV infection.

Scientists have identified three ways for HIV transmission to occur: through unsafe sexual activity, blood exchange, and from infected mother to fetus or child (figure 14.6). The two most common methods of transmission for HIV in the United States are through sexual contact and by using contaminated needles to inject

drugs. In addition, infected women can pass HIV infection to their newborns.

Sexual contact with an HIV-infected person, including sexual intercourse (vaginal or anal) from male to female, female to male, and male to male, and oral sexual contact can transmit HIV. Because HIV is found in blood, semen, and vaginal fluids, it can enter the bloodstream through small cuts or sores on the vagina, penis, rectum, or possibly the mouth. These cuts or sores may be so small as to be unnoticeable. Because many infected individuals do not show any signs or symptoms, it is impossible to be sure who is infected with HIV unless a person is tested (figure 14.7).[10]

Another way that HIV can be transmitted is through exposure to infected blood and blood products. Today, the most common exposure to infected blood is through sharing needles or syringes used to inject intravenous (IV)

Low-Risk

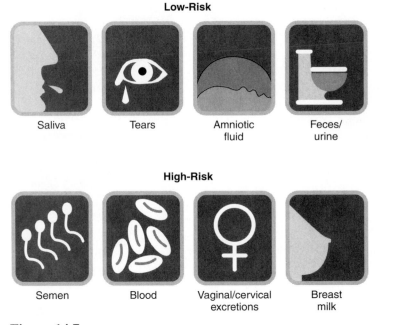

High-Risk

Figure 14.7
Low-risk and high-risk body fluids.

drugs. Blood from an HIV-infected person can remain in a syringe and be injected into the bloodstream of the next person using the needle. Injecting steroids, using needles to pierce ears, and using needles for tattooing are also ways of transferring HIV, if needles are shared. Before 1985, it was also possible to become infected with HIV through blood transfusions. This was especially true for hemophiliacs who needed large amounts of blood. Today, careful screening tests for blood donors are used and an HIV antibody test is conducted on all donated blood. Blood that is found to be infected is discarded and not used. Because it takes anywhere from 1 to 6 months or longer for HIV antibodies to develop after infection occurs, there is still a *slim* chance (1 out of 40,000 transfusions) that HIV can be transmitted through a blood transfusion.[11]

HIV can also be transmitted through the blood of an infected mother to her unborn child, and in some cases infected mothers can also transmit HIV through breast milk. There is about a 25% chance that an infected mother will transmit HIV to her unborn child if the mother gets no treatment during pregnancy. This percentage can be decreased to an 8% chance if the mother takes the drug zidovudine (AZT) during pregnancy.[12]

Once scientific research confirmed the modes of HIV transmission, it was easy to identify preventative measures for HIV infection (figure 14.8). Prevention measures for blood contact include not sharing needles under any circumstance. Preventative measures for sexual contact are not as clearly defined. Of course, the safest practice is abstinence. If individuals do not have sexual and/or intimate contact with other individuals, they will not be-

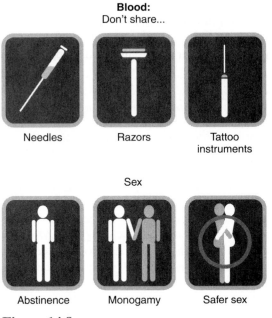

Figure 14.8
Preventative measures.

come HIV infected through such means. If an individual is sexually active, however, the best way to avoid HIV infection through sexual contact is to establish and maintain a monogamous relationship. A monogamous relationship is defined as one partner, all the time, for a lifetime. If neither partner is HIV-infected going into the relationship, then there is no chance that the two become

HIV infected through sexual contact with each other. If individuals are sexually active with more than one partner, however, or if they are unsure of their partner's sexual history, the safest practice is to use a latex condom during every sexual act. Although a condom is not foolproof, its use is better than engaging in high-risk behavior or being unprotected. Condoms provide a barrier and, if used consistently and correctly in conjunction with a water-based lubricant, can greatly decrease the risk of HIV infection and other sexually transmitted diseases among sexually active individuals.[13]

Risks for Young People

Many elementary and middle-level teachers believe they should not have to teach HIV and AIDS education because they perceive this to be a disease that affects only adults. Unfortunately, the number of AIDS cases reported annually among U.S. adolescents from ages 13 to 19 has increased from 53 in 1986 to 2,953 through June, 1997.[14] These data do not include the number of adolescents who are HIV positive. In addition, approximately 50% of new HIV infections in the United States occur among people under age 25, while 25% of new cases of HIV infection occur among young people under age 20.[15] Many elementary and middle-school teachers will respond that 20–25-year-olds are adults, and they are correct. However, because a person can be HIV infected for 10 or more years before signs or symptoms of AIDS appear, a significant number of these young people were infected when they were adolescents. Many teenagers engage in behaviors that will increase their risk of HIV infection. For instance, the average age for a girl to have sexual intercourse for the first time is 16, and for a boy it is 15.5.[16] In addition, 16% of high school students in a recent survey indicated that they had already engaged in sex with four or more partners.[17]

It is imperative for an elementary and middle-level health education curriculum to address the prevention measures for HIV and AIDS, instead of waiting until students are engaging in high-risk behaviors and then trying to change those behaviors.

HIV-Infected Children in the Classroom

Because of new and better treatment, HIV-infected children will live longer and healthier lives. There currently are approximately 7,300 children under the age of 12 who are HIV infected or have AIDS. Most of these children will attend school. Teachers may or may not know a child's HIV status. A recent study found that slightly half of families of children who were HIV positive had informed school personnel of the child's HIV status.[18] Classroom teachers should therefore treat all children equally, respecting their privacy and focusing on their individual educational and emotional needs. In addition, teachers should use universal precautions for handling blood or body fluids of all children, not just the children they suspect of being HIV positive (see the Consider This box below). Some HIV-positive children may be absent

---

CONSIDER THIS

Recommendations for the Handling of Blood and Body Fluids in Schools

While HIV infection has not been transmitted through fluids such as saliva or urine, any body fluids may harbor a number of other organisms that are potentially infectious. All schools should therefore evaluate current procedures for handling spilled blood and body fluids to ensure proper cleaning and disinfection. It is recommended that:

1. Surfaces soiled with *blood, semen* or *other fluids containing blood* should be thoroughly washed with soap and water, then disinfected with a solution of freshly prepared household bleach and water (1/4 cup bleach per gallon of water) or any other Environmental Protectional Agency (EPA)-approved disinfectant.
   a. Personnel who clean the spill should wear gloves and wash hands thoroughly when finished.
   b. Disposable towels should be used whenever possible.
   c. Mops should be thoroughly rinsed in the disinfectant solution.

2. *Other bodily fluids such as urine, feces, vomitus, etc. that have no visible blood* should be contained with paper towels or other absorbent material and discarded. The surface can be cleaned with any detergent solution.
   a. Good sanitation practices consist of avoiding direct contact with body fluids when possible.
   b. Mops should be thoroughly rinsed in the detergent solution.

For an injury that results in bleeding, such as nosebleeds, cuts, lacerations, etc., the person assisting the child should wear gloves whenever possible. Direct contact with blood is, remotely, potentially infectious when there are breaks in the skin, as in severe chapping or eczema. Proper handwashing (soap and running water for 15 seconds) significantly reduces the risk of infection from contact with all potentially infectious body fluids, whether or not gloves are worn.

For questions regarding this information contact: Ohio Department of Health, AIDS Activities Unit Communicable Disease Division, P.O. Box 118, Columbus, OH 43266-0118.

for extended periods of time. Teachers should avoid speculating aloud about the reasons for a child's absences.[19]

The Maternal and Child Health Bureau coordinated the efforts to establish guidelines to support HIV-infected children in school. Following are their established guidelines.[20]

Supports for Children With HIV Infection in School: Best Practices Guidelines

I. Preparation of the School Setting

1. An advisory committee on HIV-related issues shall be established for the school district and commissioned by the Superintendent. Membership shall be comprised of health professionals (community physicians, school nurses, and other child and adolescent health workers), parents, teachers, students, persons with HIV infection, attorneys, advocates, and persons representing diversity in the community. At regular meetings, matters shall be discussed concerning HIV that relate to administrative practices, legal and policy questions, educational programs, universal infection control standards, and student welfare. Consultants shall be used as appropriate.

2. The school district shall adopt policy statements of relevance to students with HIV infection, in collaboration with the advisory committee. These shall conform with state and federal laws and regulations, and draw on state-of-the-art medical and scientific information from appropriate government sources, model documents from national organizations, research studies, and expert consultation. It may be helpful to use public hearings to gain input into these matters. The policy statements shall then be disseminated to all administrative levels, made available to staff, students, parents, and community leaders, and included in student and parent handbooks. They shall be reviewed at yearly intervals.

3. Staff education and inservice training concerning the issues of HIV infection, including transmission, prevention, civil rights, mental health, and death and bereavement, shall be carried out at least annually for all school personnel, including the school board. The program content shall be determined by a multidisciplinary team of appropriate individuals that shall include families of children with HIV infection and also persons with HIV infections. It shall aim to affect staff members' knowledge, feelings, attitudes, behavior, and acceptance of people who are HIV positive. For new employees, this education shall be built into the orientation program, and offered within three months of hire. Teachers responsible for instruction of students regarding HIV infection shall receive specific inservice training.

4. Universal precautions relating to blood-borne infections, as adapted for schools, shall be in effect. School clinics and nursing offices shall follow OSHA guidelines for health care facilities. It is the responsibility of the school district to ensure adequate gloves, bleach, sinks, and disposal containers. There shall be systems of quality assurance or monitoring to document compliance with universal precautions in all school settings. These matters shall be featured in the staff education program.

5. The school district shall provide education relating to the prevention of HIV infection for students in grades K–12, within the context of a quality comprehensive school health program. Delivered by trained teachers, health educators, and nurses, it shall be developmentally, culturally, and linguistically appropriate. It shall actively promote abstinence as the best protection, and shall also offer explicit information about the use and availability of condoms. Acknowledgement shall be given to the special needs of adolescents regarding emerging sexual orientation. An additional effect of this effort should be to enhance understanding of the needs of students, staff, and others who are infected with HIV.

II. The Enrollment Process

6. The parent, guardian, or student shall decide whether or not to inform the school system about HIV status or other health conditions. They may support the transfer of this information by another professional or person, including a personal physician or a case manager, but only in the context of strict informed consent procedures. It shall be recognized that disclosure of HIV status often involves revealing related facts, such as medication, parent condition, transmission, and other matters. Under no circumstances shall parents, guardians, or students be required by school personnel to obtain HIV testing or to release

information about HIV test results on the student or other family members.

7. Few, if any, personnel in the school or school district shall receive information about the HIV status of a student. Determination of those who are to be informed is the prerogative of the parents, guardian, or student, and shall be made in the setting of consideration about special health care or social services that are needed while the student is in school. The terms "need to know" and "right to know" are usually not applicable for school staff, and are best eliminated. Specific release of information by the family as they wish it is obviously acceptable, but such material should then be treated confidentially regarding further dissemination.

8. Information about a student's HIV status shall not be included in the educational record, usual school health records, or any other records that are accessible to school staff beyond those the parents, guardian, or student has determined should know. Documentation about specific health care given by school nurses, counselors, clinicians, or other personnel to students with HIV infection shall be put in special health records kept in locked files. If the child changes schools, a plan for the transfer of these records shall be developed with the family and student.

III. Assurance of Appropriate Services

9. The design of an individual student's program shall be based on educational needs and not the status regarding HIV infection. The curriculum and other activities of a student with HIV infection shall be modified only as required per developmental and/or personal health needs. Exclusion or segregation of students solely on the basis of HIV infection is never appropriate.

10. In-school health services shall be provided as needed, including special regimens required because of HIV infection, but the origin of these programs shall not be identified at the classroom level. Specific "health care plans" may be formulated by school health personnel for students with symptomatic HIV infection. Notification for families about the presence of other communicable diseases at school (e.g., chicken pox) that place students at risk shall be forwarded universally. Particular notification will be given to families who have informed key school personnel about HIV infection. School nurses, and others with appropriate training, shall participate in counseling for students regarding HIV matters, including the availability of testing. They shall establish quality linkages with youth-serving HIV programs in the community that can provide culturally sensitive, age-appropriate medical, mental health, social, and drug treatment services.

IV. Other Elements

11. School administrators shall provide culturally sensitive information, technical assistance/consultation, and access to resources on HIV issues to the school's parents and families through PTAs and other parent organizations. Appropriate issues for discussion include prevention, confidentiality, classroom educational services and related supports, and community resources.

12. Relevant to existing federal and state statutes, teachers, school health professionals, and other qualified employees shall have the right to employment and confidentiality regardless of their own HIV status or other health conditions. If they choose to disclose their HIV status to students or other staff this shall not have ramifications regarding employment.

TEACHING HIV AND AIDS PREVENTION AND EDUCATION

When teaching about HIV and AIDS, it is important to use teaching activities that are developmentally appropriate for elementary and middle-level students, as well as to identify reasons to teach this topic, to address commonly asked questions about HIV and AIDS, and to know the federal government's guidelines for this topic. The information that follows addresses all of these issues.

Reasons for HIV and AIDS Education in the Elementary and Middle-Level Grades

There are several reasons to provide developmentally appropriate HIV education in the elementary and middle-level grades. Although the authors feel teaching HIV prevention to elementary and middle-level students is extremely important, it is crucial that teachers follow their district and/or state guidelines when teaching this or any other controversial topic.

1. Children may be scared about getting HIV. HIV information is in the news weekly. Children hear or

see this information and may become frightened. A part of the elementary and middle-level HIV and AIDS education program should include information about the difficulty of acquiring HIV. Children need to understand that they have the power to prevent this disease and that very few children actually become HIV infected.

2. Children are curious about HIV and AIDS. Because children hear about HIV and AIDS so often, many of them will have questions about the disease. It is important to answer these questions in a developmentally appropriate and direct way. If we delay answering them, we can increase the fear that children have about the disease.

3. An increasing number of people are becoming HIV infected; therefore, the chance of knowing an infected person is increasing. In all probability, within the next 5 to 10 years, many children will know someone with HIV disease or AIDS. It is important for children to know that they cannot get infected through casual contact, and that people with HIV infection and AIDS need compassion and care just like persons with other illnesses.

4. Attitudes about drug use and sexuality are formed early in life. Even if elementary and middle-level teachers do not address drug and sexuality issues in their classes, the students are still formulating attitudes about these topics. The majority of children will receive persistent and developmentally inappropriate information from television, magazines, and their friends. It is important that elementary and middle-level students receive accurate information about drugs and sexuality, and the classroom is an ideal place for that to happen with the help and support of a caring and informed teacher.

Developmentally Appropriate Practice Recommendations

Many teachers already feel there is too much information and too many topics within the elementary and middle-level health-education curriculum. Instead of creating a complete unit on HIV and AIDS prevention and education, teachers can incorporate it into existing health units.

For instance, it could be added to the drug prevention unit. Information about IV drugs and HIV infection are certainly related, and HIV may provide another reason not to get involved with drugs. HIV prevention and education could also be added to a mental health unit when discussing why sick people need friends and how to treat someone with HIV disease or AIDS. Yet another area in which these topics could be added is a disease prevention unit. Information about germs, viruses, communicable diseases, and HIV could be provided. It is important to try

to include HIV and AIDS information into as many health-education units as possible because the more students hear about it, the more information and understanding they will acquire.

It is often difficult for teachers, administrators, and parents to know what is developmentally appropriate for children and preadolescents in the area of HIV prevention. There are a variety of resources that can help school districts decide on the appropriate content for each grade level. A synthesis of developmentally appropriate content for each grade level using different resources follows.[21, 22]

Early Elementary (K–2)

1. HIV is virus that is causing some adults to get very sick, but it does not commonly affect children.
2. HIV is very hard to get. You cannot get it just by being near or touching someone who has it.
3. Germs cannot be seen by the human eye, but there are ways to avoid them.
4. All people need friends, including those who are HIV infected.

Upper Elementary (3–5)

1. Scientists all over the world are working hard to find a way to stop people from getting HIV and to cure those who have it.
2. Viruses are living organisms that are too small to be seen by the unaided eye.
3. HIV disease and AIDS can have an emotional impact on the individual and family.
4. HIV cannot be spread through casual contact.
5. HIV can be transmitted by sexual contact with an infected person, by using needles and other injection equipment that an infected person has used, and from an infected mother to her infant before or during birth.
6. There have only been a small number of medical personnel who have been infected when they were directly exposed to an HIV-infected person's blood.
7. AIDS is an abbreviation for "acquired immunodeficiency syndrome" and is caused by a HIV, a virus that weakens the ability of infected persons to fight off disease.
8. HIV weakens the infected person's immune system.
9. HIV infection has limited signs and symptoms.
10. All students need to understand the signs and symptoms of HIV infection.
11. HIV-infected people can infect other people, even though they do not look or feel sick.
12. HIV affects males and females and people of all races.
13. Universal precautions should be used with all body fluids.

Middle-Level (6–8)

1. People who have AIDS often develop a rare type of severe pneumonia, a cancer called Kaposi's

sarcoma, and/or certain other diseases that healthy people normally do not get.

2. People who are HIV infected live in every state in the United States and in most other countries of the world. Infected people live in cities as well as in suburbs, small towns, and rural areas. Although most infected people are adults, teenagers can also become infected. Females as well as males are infected. People of every race are infected, including whites, blacks, Hispanics, Native Americans, and Asian/Pacific Islanders.

3. HIV can be transmitted by sexual contact with an infected person, by using needles and other injection equipment that an infected person has used, and from an infected mother to her infant before or during birth.

4. It sometimes takes several years after becoming HIV infected before symptoms of the disease appear. Thus, people who are infected with the virus can infect other people—even though the people who transmit the infection do not feel or look sick.

5. There are new drugs available today to help HIV-infected people live longer.

6. HIV can be transmitted by sexual contact with an infected person, by using needles and other injection equipment that an infected person has used, and from an infected mother to her infant before or during birth.

7. All students need to understand ways to prevent HIV infection.

8. Abstinence from drugs and risky sexual activity are the most effective ways to prevent HIV infection.

9. The use of condoms can help reduce the spread of HIV during risky sexual activity.

A Checklist for an HIV and AIDS Curriculum for Elementary and Middle-Level Schools

There are some state and commercial HIV and AIDS curricula available for elementary and middle-level schools, and more are being developed all the time. Whether using a packaged program or integrating HIV prevention and education into an already existing health-education curriculum, it is important that specific information about HIV and AIDS be presented. The following checklist may be helpful when deciding on an HIV prevention curriculum in the elementary and middle-level school.

1. Does the curriculum help students acquire the necessary self-esteem and assertiveness to choose healthy behaviors?

2. Does the curriculum focus on teaching how to make healthy decisions, and not just on the medical aspects of HIV and AIDS?

3. Does the curriculum help eliminate young children's fears of HIV and AIDS?

4. Are several classes provided to give students multiple opportunities to rehearse making decisions based on the information they have learned about HIV and AIDS?

5. By emphasizing high-risk behaviors rather than high-risk groups, does the curriculum strongly support the message that anyone can become HIV infected regardless of race, age, gender, or sexual orientation?

6. Does the curriculum give younger elementary students a foundation for more detailed information on sexuality and health during later grades?

HIV AND AIDS POLICY

Although it is not the responsibility of elementary and middle-level teachers to develop an HIV and AIDS policy for their school, it is important that one exists and that all teachers know its content. Two policies that elementary and middle-level teachers should be familiar with are the policy regarding HIV-infected students and school staff and the policy for handling blood and body fluids in schools.

Policy Regarding HIV-Infected Students and School Staff

There are many policy issues regarding HIV-infected students and school staff, such as confidentiality, due process, testing, and employment issues. Ten to 15 years ago, many school districts did not have HIV-infected students or HIV-infected staff. A policy regarding HIV-infected students and staff was never developed because administrators did not think they would ever have anyone in their school district who was infected. But today, because of the large number of HIV-infected persons in the United States, most school districts will likely have a policy regarding HIV-infected students and staff. It is not the intention of this section to decide what is a fair HIV-infected student and school staff policy, but rather to encourage teachers to know what their district policy is. A sample policy for HIV-infected children can be found in the Consider This box on page 268.

Policy for Handling Blood and Body Fluids in Schools

Every school district should have a policy for handling blood and body fluids so it can help reduce the risk of HIV infection. In addition, every school should provide staff development on handling blood and body fluids in schools. Although the risk of transmission through helping a child with a bloody nose is extremely low, it is still important to take appropriate measures to reduce the risk of transmission. A sample policy can be found in the Consider This box on page 261.

ACTIVITIES

HIV and AIDS Activities for Early Elementary and Middle-Level Students

Many of the activities used in the early elementary grades are designed to lay the foundation for HIV and AIDS prevention and education in later grades. Although some of the K–2 activities presented may not seem directly related to HIV and AIDS, they will be helpful to the students' understanding of HIV and AIDS information presented during the later elementary grades.

Unlike the HIV and AIDS teaching activities for early elementary students, the activities for late elementary and middle-level students should be more directly related to HIV and AIDS. Activities for these grades should focus HIV infection, AIDS, the immune system, and about how students can protect themselves.

Grades K–2

1. *Proper Handwashing to Reduce the Spread of Germs.* At a young age, children should learn the proper way to wash their hands. This skill should be practiced and reinforced consistently throughout the earlier elementary grades. This concept is important when discussing how germs cause disease and how they are spread, and could be included in a disease prevention and control unit. Children often put their hands in their mouth, and unless their hands are washed often, germs from their hands can easily enter their body.

   The following activity will help children visualize the germs on their hands. Place a small amount of vegetable oil on the students' hands, and then sprinkle cinnamon on their palms to represent germs. Ask the students to wash their hands with cold water only. Students will notice that the "germs" remain on their hands. Then instruct the students to use warm water and soap, and the students will then see that the "germs" wash away easily.[23]

   Children should have the opportunity to practice washing their hands the proper way.

   Although HIV and AIDS are not directly mentioned in this activity, it gives the students the opportunity to discuss germs, and to understand how they can prevent germs from entering their body.

2. *Communicable versus Noncommunicable Diseases.* This concept would be appropriate to include in a disease unit. It is important for students to understand that some diseases can be passed from one person to another by germs and viruses, while other diseases cannot be transferred from person to person.

   In this activity, place a variety of names of diseases, such as asthma, colds, measles, flu, diabetes, cancer, heart disease, and HIV, on the chalkboard. Ask students to identify which diseases can be passed from one person to another. Inform students that these diseases are called communicable diseases, and that they can help prevent them through certain behaviors. After students have identified which diseases can be transferred from person to person, ask the students how they are transferred. For instance, colds can be spread by coughing, sneezing, or sharing a glass with someone. Prevention behaviors for colds include covering the mouth when sneezing or coughing and not sharing cups or glasses with anyone. When discussing how HIV is passed, students should understand that it cannot be passed by coughing, sneezing, or sharing a glass with someone, but through using drugs and having sex with someone. At this age, it is not important to go into specific detail about HIV and AIDS transmission, but to emphasize that students can help protect themselves from communicable diseases through their behaviors.

3. *Sick People Need Friends.* This concept can be included in a mental or emotional health unit and can include the idea that people with AIDS need friends too. To begin teaching this concept, ask the students how they feel when they are sick. Responses might include feelings such as bad, hurting,

lonely, and sad. Continue by asking students to brainstorm how they like to be treated when they are sick. Responses might include things such as being spoiled, getting cards or presents, getting to eat their favorite food, and having their chores done for them. Continue the lesson by asking students what they can do to help someone feel better. Responses might include sending a card, calling, helping with homework, visiting, and buying a present. After all of these topics are brainstormed, tell students that all people need special attention when they are sick. This includes people with AIDS because they have a disease that can be very painful and that there is no cure for. The class may even want to adopt a PLWA (Person Living with AIDS) and do nice things for him or her, such as sending cards or letters.

Grades 3–5

1. *Responding to Bleeding.* Students at a young age should be taught the universal precautions about handling blood. This includes not touching other people's blood because of the remote chance of HIV transmission. Because bloody noses, cuts, and scrapes are common occurrences in elementary schools, this concept should be discussed with children at a young age and can be included in a first-aid and safety unit when discussing what to do in an emergency. Students can be taught how to handle their own bleeding injuries. Instruct students to get help from an adult when another child is hurt or is bleeding. Teach students about the dangers of picking up things in and around trash cans, because old syringes can be discarded in community trash cans.

2. *Infection Control Measures for Communicable Diseases.* This concept could be included in a disease prevention unit. To help reinforce the concept that measures can be taken to prevent communicable diseases, allow students to choose one communicable disease on which they would like to become the "prevention expert." Ask students to pair up and trace their partner's body on a piece of newsprint. After all outlines are completed, instruct students to write their disease at the top, along with "Infection Control Measures." Have the students write next to the appropriate body part the infection control measure that could be used so as not to catch the disease. For instance, some students may write about measures such as vaccinations or covering the mouth when sneezing and coughing. The student who chooses HIV would need to address sexual contact and IV drug use.

3. *HIV Prevention.* After discussing prevention measures for HIV and AIDS, instruct students to create a poster about protecting themselves from infection. The posters should incorporate the concept of casual contact and the ways that HIV is spread.

4. *HIV Is Not Spread Through Casual Contact.*[24] Display two clear plastic bottles. Fill one bottle with dark-red water and the other with pale-green water. Explain that the plastic bottles represent our skin. Show that holding the bottles close to one another does not cause the mixing of fluids. Even when the bottles touch or bump into each other, the fluids still do not mix. Explain that HIV must enter the body of a person in order to cause HIV infection.

Grades 6–8

1. *Support Agencies.* Students should know whom they can call or write for information about HIV and AIDS. Ask students to watch television, listen to the radio, read newspapers and magazines, and look at billboards for HIV and AIDS resources. Ask students to write down the names of as many places they have heard about or seen to get information about AIDS. Bring in a local telephone directory so that students can look up further resources. At the end, students should have a list of about seven to ten addresses and phone numbers of agencies where they can find out more information about HIV and AIDS.

2. *Reducing the Risk.* Place students into small groups and ask them to identify as many ways as they can to reduce the risk of HIV infection. After 5 to 10 minutes, ask each group to report the suggestions from their list. Make sure the prevention measures are accurate and clarify any misconceptions on the list.

3. *Identifying Infected People.* Ask students to cut out five pictures of different people in magazines. After each student has five pictures, instruct students to get into small groups and ask them to select from the pictures the ten people they consider most likely to become HIV infected. After they have selected their pictures, ask them to develop a rationale for the pictures they picked. After the students

have reported to the class, explain that there are stereotypes and misinformation about HIV and AIDS. It is impossible to tell who is HIV infected just by looking. Explain that there are large numbers of people in the United States who are HIV infected, but who are not showing any signs or symptoms of HIV disease or AIDS.

4. *Casual Contact versus Risky Behavior.* Pass out an index card with a behavior printed on each card. The cards should have either a casual contact behavior (e.g., sharing a glass with someone, hugging someone, shaking hands, etc.) or a risky HIV-transmission behavior (sharing IV drug needles, unprotected sexual activity, etc.). Place three different signs in the front of the room: no risk, medium risk, and high risk. One row at a time, ask students to stand at the sign that best represents the amount of HIV-transmission risk the behavior on their card represents.

CONSIDER THIS

Ohio Department of Health Guidelines and Recommendations for Elementary and Secondary Schools (K–12) Regarding Children with Acquired Immunodeficiency Syndrome (AIDS)

In 1981, when Acquired Immunodeficiency Syndrome (AIDS) was first reported, specific populations were identified as "high-risk groups" for developing and transmitting the disease. These risk groups include homosexual/ bisexual men, intravenous drug abusers, persons transfused with contaminated blood or blood products, and sexual contacts of persons infected with HTLV-III virus, the causative agent of AIDS.

Relatively few children have been diagnosed with AIDS in the United States. In Ohio, only three cases have been reported in children under age 19 since 1981. Two were hemophiliacs and one was infected either during pregnancy or at birth.

The Centers for Disease Control have reported that "none" of the identified AIDS cases have been contracted in the school setting, or through other casual person-to-person contact. However, exposure of teachers and children to potentially infectious body fluids from children with AIDS has raised several issues regarding school admission. The following information and guidelines have been prepared to assist Ohio's schools in the formulation of policies to protect both children and faculty from AIDS or any other disease transmitted through direct contact with blood and other body fluids. It is prudent to treat all blood and body fluids with caution regardless of the apparent health of a person.

AIDS is transmitted by two mechanisms: sexual contact (genital-oral, vaginal and anal intercourse) and inoculation of blood components from one individual into the bloodstream of another. Transmission of AIDS through casual contact such as kissing, sharing of food, or sharing eating utensils has not occurred. No family members of AIDS cases other than sexual contacts have developed AIDS.

School Admission Recommendations—Based on current evidence, casual person-to-person contact, as would occur among schoolchildren and staff, poses no risk in the transmission of AIDS. Children with AIDS should be allowed to attend school in a regular classroom setting provided:

1. The health status of the child, as determined by his/her physician, allows participation in regular school activities.
2. The child behaves acceptably, i.e., does not bite other individuals or exhibit other violent behaviors. Although very unlikely, significant human bites may inoculate trace amounts of blood directly into the bloodstream.
3. The child does not have open sores or skin eruptions that cannot be covered.

Experience with other communicable diseases suggests that the potential for AIDS transmission would be greatest through contact between younger children and neurologically handicapped children who lack control of their bodily secretions and/or exhibit violent behavior. Decisions to exclude handicapped children who have AIDS from a public school setting should be made only after careful evaluation of each child's individual risk of transmitting the disease. Decisions regarding the type of educational setting for children with potentially infectious diseases should be based on the behavior, neurologic development, and physical condition of the child and the expected type of interaction with others in the school setting.

Due to the small number of children with AIDS anticipated in Ohio within the next few years, individual evaluation of each case is possible. School officials, the private physician, and parents are encouraged to consult public health officials to assist in this process.

When a child with AIDS is admitted to school, personnel who are aware of the child's condition should be the minimum necessary to assure proper care of the child. The number of informed staff should be sufficient to observe the child for behavioral and/or medical problems that could heighten the potential for AIDS transmission.

Source: Ohio Department of Health.

SUMMARY

When discussing HIV and AIDS with students, it is important that proper terminology be used. Since 1988, the acronym HIV has been used instead of AIDS when discussing infection. The term *AIDS* refers to a disease, while *HIV* refers to the virus that causes AIDS.

When a person becomes HIV infected, the virus attacks the immune system. Eventually an HIV-infected person cannot fight off even harmless germs, and then develops HIV disease and then AIDS. People living with AIDS constitute only the tip of the iceberg of the HIV-infected population. A person who is HIV infected probably will not show any signs or symptoms of HIV disease or AIDS for several years. This is crucial to understand because HIV-infected people who are not showing signs and symptoms may, unknowingly, pass the virus to uninfected persons.

There are three ways that HIV can be transmitted: through sexual contact; by exposure to infected blood and blood products; and perinatally. Although many people still believe that HIV can be transmitted through casual contact, there are no documented cases that reinforce this idea.

Prevention measures for HIV infection include not using IV drugs and/or not sharing needles. Preventative measures for sexual contact include abstinence, monogamy, or using a condom during every sexual act.

It is important for HIV and AIDS education to be included in an elementary and middle-level health curriculum. Because the incubation for HIV is around 10 years, many of the young adults who have already died of AIDS may have become infected when they were 12 to 19 years old. It is important to teach prevention measures before students are participating in high-risk activities. Other reasons to teach HIV and AIDS prevention and education during the elementary years include children may be scared about getting AIDS; children are curious about HIV and AIDS; an increasing number of people are becoming HIV infected so that the chances of knowing an infected person are increasing; and attitudes about drug use and sexuality are formed early in life.

Teachers should also be prepared to support children who are HIV infected and attending school. There are several guidelines with which school administrators and teachers should become familiar.

There are developmentally appropriate practice recommendations regarding HIV prevention content for elementary and middle-level students. These recommendations should help school districts decide what to include in an HIV prevention curriculum. A variety of teaching activities can be used in the classroom to help reinforce these recommendations.

Elementary and middle-level teachers should also understand their school's HIV and AIDS policy regarding infected students and school staff, and how to handle blood and body fluids in schools. Although individual teachers may not be responsible for developing the policies, they should know the expectations of the school district in which they work.

DISCUSSION QUESTIONS

1. What do the acronyms HIV and AIDS stand for and what are they?

2. What is AIDS caused by?

3. When a person becomes HIV infected, what body system is affected and how?

4. Describe the three ways that HIV can be transmitted.

5. Describe examples of casual contact for which HIV transmission is not a concern.

6. What are the ways to prevent HIV infection?

7. Why is it important to teach HIV and AIDS prevention and education in elementary and middle-level schools?

8. Where should HIV and AIDS prevention and education be included in the elementary and middle-level curriculum? Why?

9. How can a school district be prepared to provide support for HIV-infected students in the school?

10. What are developmentally appropriate practice recommendations regarding HIV prevention/education?

11. Describe several teaching activities that can be used with younger elementary students to help reinforce the HIV and AIDS objectives of the Centers for Disease Control and Prevention.

12. Describe several teaching activities that can be used with older elementary students to help reinforce the HIV and AIDS objectives of the Centers for Disease Control and Prevention.

13. What two HIV policies should elementary teachers be familiar with?

ENDNOTES

1. U.S. Government, *Report of the Presidential Commission on the Human Immunodeficiency Virus Epidemic* (Washington, DC: U.S. Government Printing Office, 1988).

2. R. Biggar and P. Rosenberg, "HIV Infection/AIDS in the United States During the 1990's," *Clinical Infectious Diseases* 17 (1993).

3. J. Collins, M. Small, L. Kann, B. Pateman, R. Gold, and L. Kolbe, "School Health Education," *Journal of School Health* 96, no. 8, 1995.

4. E. Stone and C. Perry, "United States: Perspective on School Health," *Journal of School Health* 60, no. 7, 1990.

5. Centers for Disease Control and Prevention, *Surgeon General's Report to the American Public on HIV Infection*

and AIDS (Washington, DC: U.S. Government Printing Office, 1993), 5.

6. American Foundation for AIDS Research, *An Ounce of Prevention,* www.thebody.com/amfar/ounce.html, 1998.

7. Centers for Disease Control and Prevention, *Facts about Adolescent and HIV/AIDS,* www.thebody.com/cdc/hivteen.html, March 1998.

8. A. Waley "Preventing the High-Risk Sexual Behavior of Adolescents: Focus on HIV/AIDS Transmission, Unintended Pregnancy or Both?" *Journal of Adolescent Health,* 24, 376–382, 1999.

9. U.S. Department of Health and Human Services, *CDC HIV/AIDS Prevention: Facts About the Human Immunodeficiency Virus and Its Transmission* (Rockville, MD: CDC National AIDS Clearinghouse, 1993).

10. American Association of Colleges for Teacher Education and Centers for Disease Control and Prevention, *HIV Prevention in Teacher Education: Facts About HIV/AIDS and Hepatitis B—Info Guide 1,* (Washington, DC: Author, 1998).

11. Sexuality Information and Education Council of the United States, *Some Basic Facts About HIV/AIDS,* www.siecus.org/ 1998.

12. Y. Bryson, "Advances in the Prevention and Treatment of Perinatal Infection," *Improving the Management of HIV Disease* 4, no. 3, 1996.

13. American Foundation for AIDS Research, *An Ounce of Prevention.*

14. Centers for Disease Control and Prevention, *Facts about Adolescent and HIV/AIDS.*

15. Office of National AIDS Policy. *Youth and HIV/AIDS: An American Agenda.* Washington: DC: Author, 1996).

16. U.S. Department of Health and Human Services, *CDC HIV/AIDS Prevention: Facts About Adolescents and HIV/AIDS* (Rockville, MD: CDC National AIDS Clearinghouse, 1993).

17. L. Kann, S. Kinchen, B. Williams, J. Ross, R. Lowry, C. Hill, J. Grunbaum, P. Blumson, J. Collins, L. Kolbe, and State and Local YRBSS Coordinators, "Youth Risk Behavior Surveillance—United States, 1997," *Journal of School Health* 68, no. 9, 1998.

18. J. Cohen, C. Reddington, D. Jacobs, R. Meade, D. Picard, K. Singleton, D. Smith, M. Caldwell, and A. Hsu. "School-related Issues Among HIV-Infected Children," *Pediatrics* 100, no, 1, 1997.

19. American Association of Colleges for Teacher Education and Centers for Disease Control and Prevention, *Schools and HIV, Info Guide 3,* (Washington, DC: Author, 1998).

20. A. Crocker, A. Lavin, J. Palfrey, S. Porter, D. Shaw, and K. Weill, "Supports for Children with HIV Infection in School: Best Practices Guidelines," *Journal of School Health* 64, no. 1, 1994.

21. Centers for Disease Control, "Guidelines for Effective School Health Education to Prevent the Spread of AIDS," *Morbidity and Mortality Weekly Report* 37, no. S-2 (Atlanta, GA: U.S. Department of Health and Human Services, 29 January 1988).

22. J. Scheer, *HIV Prevention Education for Teachers of Elementary and Middle School Grades* (Reston, VA: Association for the Advancement of Health Education, 1992).

23. M. Quackenbush and S. Villarreal, *Does AIDS Hurt?: Educating Young Children about AIDS* (Santa Cruz, CA: Network Publications, 1992), 70–73.

24. Scheer, *HIV Prevention Education for Teachers of Elementary and Middle School Grades.*

SUGGESTED READINGS

American Association of Colleges for Teacher Education and Centers for Disease Control and Prevention, *HIV/AIDS Prevention in Teacher Education.* Washington, DC, Author, 1998.

American Association of Colleges for Teacher Education. *Teacher Educator's Resource Guide to HIV/AIDS Prevention.* Washington, DC, Author, 1998.

American Association of Colleges for Teacher Education. *Building a Future Without HIV./AIDS What Do Educators Have To Do With It?* Washington, DC, Author, 1997.

Centers for Disease Control. "Guidelines for Effective School Health Education to Prevent the Spread of AIDS." *Morbidity and Mortality Weekly Report* 37, no. S–2. Atlanta, GA: U.S. Department of Health and Human Services, 29 January 1988.

Centers for Disease Control and Prevention. *Surgeon General's Report to the American Public on HIV Infection and AIDS.* Washington, DC: U.S. Government Printing Office, 1993.

Council of the Great City Schools and National Association of State Boards of Education. *Effective HIV Education in Urban Schools: A Policymaker's Guide.* Washington, DC: Council of the Great City Schools and National Association of State Boards of Education, 1991.

Crocker, A., A. Lavin, J. Palfrey, S. Porter, D. Shaw and K. Weill, Supports for Children with HIV Infection in School: "BEST PRACTICES GUIDELINES," *Journal of School Health,* 64 no. 1, 1994.

DiClemente, R., ed. *Adolescents and AIDS: A Generation in Jeopardy.* Newbury, CA: Sage Publications, 1992.

Fumia, M. *Honor Thy Children.* Berkeley, CA: Conari Press, 1997.

Kann, L., S. Kinchen, B. Williams, J. Ross, R. Lowry, C. Hill, J. Grunbaum, P. Blumson, J. Collins and L. Kolbe, "State and Local YRBSS Coordinators, Youth Risk Behavior Surveillance—United States, 1997." *Journal of School Health* 68, no. 9, 1998.

Louganis, G. *Breaking the Surface.* New York: Random House, 1995.

The National Education Association Health Information Network. *Responding to HIV and AIDS.* Washington, DC: The National Education Association Health Information Network, 1992.

National School Board Association. *Reducing the Risk: A School Leader's Guide to AIDS Education.* Washington, DC: National School Board Association, 1990.

Peace Corps. *Alternative Techniques for Teaching About HIV/AIDS in the Classroom,* Report No. R0086. Washington, DC: Peace Corps, Information Collection and Exchange, 1994.

Quackenbush, M., and Villarreal S. *Does AIDS Hurt?: Educating Young Children about AIDS.* Santa Cruz, CA: Network Publications, 1992.

Scheer, J. *HIV Prevention Education for Teachers of Elementary and Middle School Grades,* Reston, VA: Association for the Advancement of Health Education, 1992.

Silin, J. *Sex and Death and the Education of Our Children in the Age of AIDS.* New York: Teachers College Press, 1995.

U.S. Department of Health and Human Services. *CDC HIV/AIDS Prevention: Facts About the Scope of the HIV/AIDS Epidemic in the United States.* Rockville, MD: CDC National AIDS Clearinghouse, 1993.

U.S. Department of Health and Human Services. *CDC HIV/AIDS Prevention: Facts About the Human Immunodeficiency Virus and Its Transmission.* Rockville, MD: CDC National AIDS Clearinghouse, 1993.

U.S. Department of Health and Human Services. *CDC HIV/AIDS Prevention: Facts About Condoms and Their Use in Preventing HIV Infection and Other STD's.* Rockville, MD: CDC National AIDS Clearinghouse, 1993.

U.S. Department of Health and Human Services. *CDC HIV/AIDS Prevention: Facts About Adolescents and HIV/AIDS.* Rockville, MD: CDC National AIDS Clearinghouse, 1993.

Zaccone-Tzannetakis, P. "We Can Protect Ourselves: A Rhyming Puppet Show about HIV Prevention." *Journal of School Health* 65, no. 4, 1995.

CHILDREN'S LITERATURE WITH AN HIV/AIDS THEME

Grades K–2

Alexander, E., S. Rudn, and P. Sejkora. *My Dad Has HIV.* Fairview Press, 1996.

Quinlan, P. *Tiger Flowers.* Dial, 1994.

Verniero, J. *Your Can Call Me Willy.* Magination Press, 1995.

Weeks, S. *Red Ribbon.* Harper Collins, 1995.

Grades 3–5

Fox, P. *The Eagle Kite.* Orchard, 1995.

Girard, L. *Alex, the Kid with AIDS.* Albert Whitman, 1991.

Jordan, M. *Losing Uncle Tom.* Whitman, 1987.

Newman, L. *Too Far Away to Touch.* Clarion, 1995.

Showers, P. *No Measles, No Mumps for Me.* Crowell, 1980.

Wiener, L., A. Best, and P. Pizzo *Be a Friend: Children Who Live With HIV Speak.* Albert Whitman, 1994.

Grades 6–8

Bantle, L. *Diving for the Moon.* Macmillan, 1995.

Draimin, B. *Working Together Against AIDS.* Rosen Publishing Group, 1995.

Durant, P. *When Heroes Die.* Macmillan, 1992.

Kerr, M. *Night Kites.* Harper Collins, 1986.

Miklowitz, G. *Good-Bye Tomorrow.* Delacorte, 1987.

Shire, A. *Everything You Need to Know About Being HIV-Positive.* Rosen Publishing Group, 1994.

Wolf, Bernard. *HIV Positive.* Dutton, 1997.

 ## INTERNET INFORMATION

HIV/AIDS WEBSITES

For additional information on HIV and AIDS education, please refer to the following websites.

Sexuality Information and Education Council of the United States
http://www.siecus.org/

American Foundation for AIDS Research (AmFAR)
http://www.amfar.org/

The Body
http://www.thebody.com/index.shtml

National PTA
http://www.pta.org/programs/hivlibr.htm

Centers for Disease Control and Prevention
http://www.cdc.gov/nchstp/hiv aids/dhap.htm

Healthfinder
www.healthfinder.gov

American Red Cross
http://www.redcross.org/hss/HIV AIDS/basic/prevskil.html

AIDS Education and Research Trust
http://www.avert.org/

The Center for AIDS Prevention Studies (CAPS)
http://www.caps.ucsf.edu/

IV

The Secondary Content

Section IV contains health content that is not directly related to the CDC health risk behaviors, but is still important for elementary teachers to have a basic understanding. Teachers should be able to understand the secondary content well enough that they can comfortably infuse health skills throughout these secondary content areas. Each chapter in this section provides background information about the content area, developmentally appropriate practice recommendations, activities that can be conducted with students at different grade levels, and children's literature and web sites related to the content area.

15

EMOTIONAL HEALTH

INTRODUCTION

Emotional health is commonly understood as the ability to express emotions comfortably and appropriately. It also encompasses such concepts as trust, self-esteem, self-acceptance, and self-confidence. As mentioned in chapter 1, emotional health is related to the other four dimensions of health. For example, an individual who does not know how to express feelings appropriately may experience physical health problems related to stress.

Perhaps the most important aspect of emotional health is self-esteem. Self-esteem can be defined as appreciating one's own worth and importance, having the character to be accountable for one's own actions, and acting responsibly toward others.[1] Youth who have high self-esteem are more likely to be protected from emotional distress.[2] Positive self-esteem can also impact several of the causes of negative health behaviors. For example, alienation, insecurity, rejection, and inadequacy all can be lessened when teachers plan and implement strategies to improve the self-esteem of students. When children feel comfortable, confident, and supported, they typically manifest characteristics that are consistent with high self-esteem.

These are the same characteristics that Abraham Maslow described as the basic human needs. He developed a hierarchy of needs that can lead to being self-actualized (figure 15.1). In addition to the basic survival needs of food, clothing, and shelter, Maslow believed that healthy individuals need security/protection, love/belonging, and self-esteem.

Additionally, there is a direct relationship between school success and self-esteem. Numerous studies conducted at a variety of grade levels concluded that cognitive learning increases as self-esteem improves.[3] Although it does take time and effort for teachers to structure activities that are designed to improve their students' self-esteem, the cognitive gains made by students when this variable is positively influenced confirm the value of such efforts.

A high self-esteem has also been related to practicing positive health behaviors and the intentions to do so in the future.[4,5] For example, it has been demonstrated that the rate of

Figure 15.1
Maslow's hierarchy of needs.

exercise is highest among those students with consistently positive self-esteem.[6] Another study found that positive self-esteem decreased the likelihood for elementary children to engage in alcohol and drug use.[7] In summary, low self-esteem can become a precipitating factor for adoption of unhealthy behaviors.[8]

The book *100 Ways to Enhance Self-Concept in the Classroom: A Handbook for Teachers and Parents* clarifies several principles about self-concept and strategies for teachers and students.[9] Three are especially important from the standpoint of elementary health education:

1. *It is possible to change self-esteem, and it is possible for teachers to affect the changes either positively or negatively.* Because teachers can have an impact on their students' self-esteem, they have to conscientiously work toward the most positive impact possible. Their daily interactions with and between their students will determine the nature and degree of that impact. The self-fulfilling prophecy is a factor to consider when discussing the teacher's ability to help change a child's self-esteem. The self-fulfilling prophecy contends that students who receive consistent verbal and nonverbal messages about being stupid, dumb, or a behavior problem will eventually believe and

internalize these characteristics. Teachers who listen to their colleagues talk about certain "behavior problem" students may believe what they hear and treat those students as if they will act accordingly. It is important for teachers to treat all children as though they are good, bright, and well-behaved so that students can begin to erase those internalized negative messages and replace them with positive messages.

2. *It isn't easy. Change takes place slowly, over a long period of time.* It has been estimated that students experience an average of eight negative events to every one positive event while they are at home. This estimate includes experiences with parents and siblings. Events or experiences include verbal statements and nonverbal gestures. It has also been estimated that students experience an average of sixteen negative events to every one positive event while they are at school. This estimate includes experiences with teachers, staff, and peers. When considering home and school environments, students experience an average of twenty-four negative events for every one positive event. It has also been estimated that it takes approximately six to twelve positive experiences to overcome the

negative outcomes associated with every one negative experience. This information demonstrates how difficult it is to promote a positive change in a student's self-esteem. It takes time and consistent effort to make an impact. Don't give up! It seems to take a short period of time to gain weight, but a very long time to lose weight. The same is true with self-esteem.

3. *Peripheral experiences are helpful.* The more positive and varied experiences that students have, the better. Any time students can be given positive feedback or compliments, the teacher should take the time to do so. Homework, their test improvement, a new outfit, their nice smile, or their good behaviors are all appropriate outlets for compliments and positive reinforcement. Compliments do not have to be related to the students' academic performance, as people respond well to a wide range of compliments. The ways that teachers interact with students and the activities they conduct in the classroom can help respond to safety needs, the need for love and belonging, and the need for self-esteem. Helping students increase self-esteem involves more than focusing on activities that promote the "I'm O.K., you're O.K." philosophy. It includes the acquisition of identified skills to help students feel good about facing challenges, setting goals, making decisions, handling feelings, making new friends, and much more.

THE CONDITIONS OF SELF-ESTEEM

Reynold Bean has categorized self-esteem into four conditions:[10]

1. The sense of connectiveness,
2. The sense of uniqueness,
3. The sense of power, and
4. The sense of models.

All of these conditions are important for a child to have a high self-esteem. If one condition is lacking, such as a sense of power, a child could suffer negative consequences because he or she lacks the skills to succeed in completing a variety of activities. It is important for teachers to focus on all four conditions of self-esteem so that children will gain the knowledge and skills they need to help increase their self-esteem. In the following sections each condition is explained in detail, accompanied by specific classroom strategies and activities to help promote that condition of self-esteem. These activities can be used with most children throughout the elementary and middle-level years. Teachers should use their best judgement to determine what modifications should be made to make the activity developmentally appropriate for their students.

Sense of Connectiveness

According to Bean, children with a high sense of connectiveness:[11]

Feel they are a part of something.

Feel related in important ways to specific people, places, or things.

Identify with a group of people.

Feel something important belongs to them (feel a sense of ownership).

Feel they belong to something or someone.

Feel good about the things they are part of (feel satisfied).

Know the people or things they feel connected to are thought well of by others.

Feel they are important to others.

Feel comfortable with their bodies and trust them to work well (feel connected to themselves).

Teachers can have a tremendous impact on the sense of connectiveness for children.

Sense of Uniqueness

The second condition of self-esteem is a sense of uniqueness. According to Bean, children with a high sense of uniqueness:[17]

Feel there is something special about themselves.

Feel they know things or can do things that no one else knows or can do.

Know that other people think they are special.

Are able to express themselves in their own unique way.

Feel creative and imaginative and have opportunities to express their creativity safely.

Feel respect for themselves.

Are able to enjoy feeling different or unusual.

Feel they are being affirmed for what they are rather than being judged for what they are not.

Teachers can have a tremendous impact on the sense of uniqueness by the way they treat children and the activities conducted in the classroom. Every student is capable of doing at least one thing well. It may be playing a sport or a musical instrument, telling jokes, reading, doing math, drawing, or juggling. Teachers have the responsibility to bring out the talents and uniqueness of their students. Teachers should also work hard at incorporating the interests of students into their curriculum. This will keep students more interested in their academic work.

Sense of Power

The third condition of self-esteem is a sense of power. According to Bean, children with a high sense of power:[18]

Believe they can do what they set out to do.

Feel confident they can handle, one way or another, what is put before them to do, including things that might be risky or challenging.

Feel they are in charge of their own lives, despite having to depend on others some of the time.

Feel comfortable when they have a responsibility to fulfill.

Feel others can't make them do things they really don't want to do.

Feel confident they can make decisions in order to solve their problems.

Know they're not going to lose control of themselves, despite the pressures they may experience.

Are able to use the skills they have in situations for them, and are comfortable about acquiring new skills.

Teachers can have a tremendous impact on the sense of power in students by the way they treat children and the activities conducted in the classroom. Skills discussed in chapter 6, such as decision making, communication, and peer-resistance skills, are very important in developing a sense of power.

Sense of Models

The sense of models is the fourth condition of self-esteem. According to Bean, children with a high sense of models:[20]

Know people they feel are worthy of being emulated.

Feel confident they can tell right from wrong and good from bad.

Have consistent values and beliefs that guide and direct their actions in different situations.

Can depend on prior experiences to help them avoid being intimidated by new ones.

Feel a sense of purpose and know where they are headed.

Are able to make sense of what's going on in their lives and of the circumstances in which they find themselves.

Know the standards being used to judge them, and have a sense of their own standards.

Know how to go about learning what they need to know.

Have a sense of order, enabling them to organize their environment so they can accomplish their tasks.

Experience satisfaction from intellectual activity.

Teachers can have a tremendous impact on the sense of models by the way they treat children and the activities conducted in the classroom. To help develop a sense of models, it is important for teachers to be fair and consistent throughout each day. For example, if it is okay to sharpen a pencil at any time on Monday, the same rule should apply for Tuesday. Standards also should be high and organization should be a priority. Students need organization in their lives so that they can learn how to accomplish the goals that they set for themselves.

ACTIVITIES

Emotional Health Activities

Teacher Characteristics

The following activities can help increase students' sense of connectiveness.

Think back to your favorite teachers and write down some adjectives to describe them. Perhaps words like *warm, caring, fair, challenging, easy to talk to, funny, enthusiastic, interesting,* and *interested* appear on your paper. These teacher characteristics help create a sense of connectiveness with students. Although there are activities that teachers can conduct with their classes to help create a sense of connectiveness, it is the consistent positive attitude of teachers toward their students that means the most.[12]

It is also important for teachers to display these attitudes consistently, regardless of their mood. Elementary students find it difficult to know how to deal with a moody teacher. Let's imagine students are typically allowed to go to one of the learning centers in the classroom once their work is completed. But because the teacher is in a bad mood, he or she disciplines them that day for moving around the room without asking. This is inconsistent behavior that sends mixed messages to students. The teacher's behavior has to be consistent. Teaching is a profession, and therefore teachers have to act professionally, regardless of what is going on in their personal lives.

In the book *Self Concept and School Achievement*, William Purkey lists several questions that teachers can ask themselves about their teacher characteristics:[13]

1. Do I learn the name of each student as soon as possible, and do I use that name often?
2. Do I share my feelings with my students?
3. Do I practice courtesy with my students?
4. Do I arrange some time when I can talk quietly, alone with each student?
5. Do I spread my attention around and include each student, keeping special watch for the student who may need extra attention?
6. Do I notice and comment favorably on the things that are important to students?
7. Do I show students who return after being absent that I am happy to have them back in class and that they were missed?

If teachers can consistently answer yes to these questions, they are on the right track in developing a sense of connectiveness with their students.

Icebreakers

Icebreaker activities are a way to help students get connected to one another. During the first few weeks of school, it is important for teachers and students to learn one anothers' names and to learn more about one another. Students feel more comfortable and connected when they are called by name. There are several icebreaker activities that can be used during the first week of class to help achieve this objective.

First, an activity called *clustering* is a fast way to get students to interact with one another. The objective of this activity is to get the students and teacher to cluster in different groups, several times, so they can have a chance to interact with many different students during a short period of time. This activity needs enough space to allow students to walk around the classroom freely. This can be accomplished by pushing the chairs toward the walls, which allows space in the center of the room. To begin clustering, explain to students that they will be given directions that will allow them to form small groups. Once they get in their small groups, have them introduce themselves to each other and try to learn every person's name. As an example for forming groups, use the category of "favorite color." As soon as the category is announced, everyone begins saying his or her favorite color and tries to find everyone else who has the same favorite color. This will result in all the reds, blues, greens, and so on being grouped together. Give the groups enough time so they can learn one anothers' names.

Use several different categories so that the students and teacher have the opportunity to meet the majority of the class. It is important that teachers cluster with their students each time so that they begin to learn the names of the students and so that students begin to feel comfortable interacting with the teacher. Other categories that can be used include favorite sport, season of the year in which you were born, number of brothers and sisters, favorite brand of toothpaste, favorite animal, last digit of the students' phone number, and a group of three people that you have not been clustered with yet.

Another icebreaker that can be used to help learn names quickly is called *whip around*. Whip around works best when the class is sitting in a circle so the students can see one another. To begin whip around, explain that the students will be asked to say their names and something about themselves. It is best if the teacher begins the activity, followed by one of the students seated next to the teacher, and continuing around the circle until everyone has had the opportunity to introduce herself or himself. Specify what topic the students should talk about, such as their favorite subject, their favorite activity during the past summer, or what they want to be when they grow up. A favorite topic that elementary students like to talk about during whip around is their claim to fame. In claim to fame, students again say their name, followed by something they are famous for or hope to be famous for in the future. The students become creative during this activity. Although whip around takes only a short time to complete, many names and additional information can be learned about the students.

Another icebreaker activity is to have the students participate in a *scavenger hunt*. Every student and the teacher gets a list with incomplete statements on it, similar to the sample in table 15.1. Have the students complete the list by finding one person per item to sign their sheet. They should be encouraged to have as many different people sign the sheets as possible. This takes a short period of time to complete but will help the students to get to know one another better. Make sure that there is a variety of statements on the scavenger hunt so everyone has the chance to put his or her name on at least one person's sheet. Using health statements during this activity is also a way to introduce different health topics to students.

Another icebreaker that can be used to develop connectiveness and communication skills is called *boundary breaking*. In boundary breaking, everyone in the class is asked to choose a partner. If there is an uneven number of students in the class, the teacher should participate with one of the students. One person should be the listener, the other the talker. Instruct the talkers that they will be given 1 minute to answer a question. Provide questions or ask students to volunteer questions. During this time, instruct the listener to be quiet and listen. If the talker runs out of things to say, the listener is allowed to ask the talker questions. After going through this once, the talker and listener should switch roles and repeat the activity. Encourage students to choose new partners every time the question changes. Boundary breaking not only helps class members get

Two students participating in boundary breaking.

TABLE 15.1 Scavenger Hunt
What student in this group . . .
_____ Has the longest hair?
_____ Really feels good today?
_____ Has the nicest smile?
_____ Has the longest name?
_____ Has never smoked a cigarette?
_____ Has a pet cat?
_____ Has lived in the most states?
_____ Has the biggest dimples?
_____ Knows someone who has heart disease?
_____ Is your friend?
_____ Was born in another state?
_____ Is allergic to something?
_____ Plays a musical instrument?
_____ Has flown in an airplane?
_____ Brushes and flosses every day?

to know one another better, but it also helps the students develop their listening and speaking skills. This activity can be conducted throughout the entire school year so that every student has the opportunity to interact with everyone in the class. The following are sample questions that can be used:

1. What was the title of the last book you read, and what was it about?
2. What is your favorite hobby and why?
3. What is your favorite subject and why?
4. How do you select your friends, and what is the most important characteristic in a friend?
5. If you could be any animal other than a human, what animal would you choose and why?
6. What is your favorite television show and why?
7. What do you like about yourself?
8. Who is your hero and why?
9. If you could meet any person in the world today, who would you meet and why?
10. What was the most fun thing you have ever done in your life?
11. What worries you the most?
12. What is one thing you wish for and why?
13. How could the world be a better place?
14. What do you like to do on Saturday?
15. What makes you happy and why?

The list of questions that can be used is endless. A good resource for questions is the book *The Kids' Book of Questions* by Gregory Stock.[14] It contains 260 questions that are developmentally appropriate for elementary and middle-level youth. Students can also make up some of the questions that are used for boundary breakers.

These are just a few of the icebreakers that can be used during the first week of class. The important thing to remember is that icebreakers are a quick and fun way for class members to become acquainted at the beginning of the year, and they are also a way to begin developing a sense of connectiveness.

Greetings Before School Begins

Before school begins, send a postcard to each new student. Indicate your excitement about working with the student throughout the next school year.

I Am Lovable and Capable (IALAC)

IALAC[15] is the acronym for the activity *I Am Lovable and Capable,* which was created by Sidney Simon and Merrill Harmin. This activity will help students understand the importance of being kind to one another, which will also help them become connected to one another. To begin this activity, write the letters *IALAC* on a sheet of paper and hold it in front of the class. Explain to the class that IALAC stands for I Am Lovable and Capable, in other words, their self-esteem. Tell students that every time someone is nice to us, a piece is added to our IALAC, and every time someone gives us a put-down, a piece is torn away from our IALAC (demonstrate this with the IALAC sign you are holding). Everyone's IALAC is a different size, depending on how many positive and negative interactions each person experiences and on how each person feels about himself or herself. Then explain to the students that they will be told a story about a student who is about their same age. Encourage the class to watch what happens to the student's IALAC sign as the day goes on. At this point, tell a story about a "typical" student's day, making sure that each time something negative happens to the student, you tear a piece of paper from the IALAC sign you are holding. Try to use examples of negative statements and gestures that are common for the age of students in the class. Examples include:

Being chosen last for the kickball teams at recess.

Dropping a food tray during lunch and everyone laughs.

Failing a test.

Not being able to work out a math problem on the board.

Getting teased during recess.

Classmates making fun of an art project.

Classmates making fun of the brand of shoes worn.

Mispronouncing words when reading aloud in class.

End the story by having only a small piece of the IALAC sign left and ask the students the following questions:

1. How does your IALAC sign get torn? How do you feel when it does get torn?

2. How does your IALAC sign get bigger? How do you feel when it grows?

3. How can we help make other people's IALAC sign bigger?

4. How can we make other people's IALAC sign smaller?

A student displays his IALAC.

After the class has discussed the answers to these questions, explain to them that they are going to make their own IALAC sign and wear it for the next day. After the signs are made and the students are wearing them, instruct them that they are to tear off a piece of their IALAC sign every time they are put down and to add a piece of paper to their IALAC sign every time they are complimented. Implement as many strategies as possible to make sure that every student's IALAC sign is growing—for example, by giving extra compliments to those students with small IALAC signs. It is important to explain to the class that if they see someone's IALAC sign shrinking, they should try to do something to make it grow. Some classes have even worn their IALAC signs home and explained the concept to their parents.

As can be expected, parents have a variety of reactions to the activity. Many times we don't realize we are putting students down; the IALAC activity really helps one to visualize the put-downs. As one elementary teacher who did this activity with her class for 2 days said: "I always thought I gave mostly positive feedback to my students, but after doing this activity and having many students rip their IALAC sign in front of me, I realized that I needed to work on giving more compliments to my students. I guess I thought my students could read my mind when I was thinking positive things about them."

Positive Letters and Phone Calls

Typically, the only time that parents hear from teachers is if their child has done something wrong or has a problem. Another way to help connect with students is to either call or write to your students' parents when their children have done something well. You may tell parents that their child is improving his or her behavior or performance in a certain subject, or that you enjoy the creativity their child brings to the class. It is important to call or write to every student's parent in the class some time during the school year. Some teachers choose to send home a monthly class newsletter, indicating all the positive things that took place in the class during the last month. Whichever method you choose is fine, but it is important to have positive interactions with your students' parents.

The Compliment Activity

The compliment activity can also help students become connected with one another and to the teacher. It is a fun activity that can be accomplished in a relatively short amount of time. Ask students to tape a blank piece of paper to their back and then go around to each student and write one compliment on his or her back. After everyone is finished, have students take their papers off their back and read them. It is wonderful to see the students' faces light up when they read all the nice comments written to them. Students do not know who wrote each comment, which adds some mystery to the activity. As usual, teachers are encouraged to participate in this activity with the students. Besides helping to increase student/teacher connectiveness, it is important for teachers to be complimented also. This activity should *not* be conducted until students understand the difference between compliments and put-downs and until there is a sense of trust in the class.

Read the following story of "Love and the Cabbie" by Art Buchwald to the class prior to this activity to show students the power of compliments.

Love and the Cabbie

I was in New York the other day and rode with a friend in a taxi. When we got out my friend said to the driver, "Thank you for the ride. You did a superb job of driving."

The taxi driver was stunned for a second. Then he said, "Are you a wise guy or something?"

"No, my dear man, and I'm not putting you on. I admire the way you keep cool in heavy traffic."

"Yeh," the driver said and drove off.

"What was that all about?" I asked.

"I am trying to bring love back to New York," he said. "I believe it's the only thing that can save the city."

"How can one man save New York?"

"It's not one man. I believe I have made the taxi driver's day. Suppose he has twenty fares. He's going to be nice to those twenty fares because someone was nice to him. Those fares in turn will be kinder to their employees or shopkeepers or waiters or even their own families. Eventually the good will could spread to at least 1,000 people. Now that isn't bad, is it?"

"But you're depending on that taxi driver to pass your good will to others."

"I'm not depending on it," my friend said. "I'm aware that the system isn't foolproof, so I might deal with ten different people today. If, out of ten, I can make three happy, then eventually I can indirectly influence the attitudes of 3,000 more."

"It sounds good on paper," I admitted, "but I'm not sure it works in practice."

"Nothing is lost if it doesn't. I didn't take any of my time to tell that man he was doing a good job. He neither received a larger tip nor a smaller tip. If it fell on deaf ears, so what? Tomorrow there will be another taxi driver whom I can try to make happy."

"You're some kind of nut," I said.

"That shows you how cynical you have become. I have made a study of this. The thing that seems to be lacking, besides money of course, for our postal employees, is that no one tells people who work for the post office what a good job they're doing."

"But they're not doing a good job," I said.

"They are not doing a good job because they feel no one cares if they do or do not. Why shouldn't someone say a kind word to them?" he said.

We were walking past a structure in the process of being built and passed five workmen eating their lunch. My friend stopped. "That's a magnificent job you men have done. It must be difficult and dangerous work." The five men eyed my friend suspiciously.

"When will it be finished?" he asked. "June," a man grunted.

"Ah. That is impressive. You must all be very proud."

We walked away. I said to him. "I haven't seen anyone like you since *The Man from La Mancha.*"

"When those men digest my words, they will feel better for it. Somehow the city will benefit from their happiness."

"But you can't do this all alone!" I protested. "You're just one man."

"The most important thing is not to get discouraged. Making people in the city become kind again is not an easy job, but if I can enlist other people in my campaign. . . ."

"You just winked at a very plain looking woman,"

I said.

"Yes, I know," he replied. "And if she's a schoolteacher, her class will be in for a fantastic day."

Catch Somebody Doing Something Good

Catch somebody doing something good is a wonderful year-long activity to help class members become connected to one another.[16] It also is useful if you have a class that specializes in put-downs and tattling. There are many ways to do this activity, but the philosophy behind it is to encourage only positive comments and gestures among students. Instruct students to write down their classmates' names along with any positive gestures performed by those students. These can be handed in to the teacher, and then displayed in some way. This will encourage students to concentrate on the positive, instead of the negative, activities of the class.

Cooperative Learning

Cooperative learning is another way to help develop a sense of connection. Chapter 5 describes cooperative learning in detail and provides examples of different cooperative learning activities.

Interviews

Interviews can help students become connected to classmates and/or family members, and can help improve communication skills. Ask students to either interview a classmate or a family member. Interviewing a family member may help them get more connected to their heritage, while interviewing a classmate may help them make a new friend. Either assign students a list of questions they are to use when interviewing a person, or have the class brainstorm questions that they think would be good to ask. Regardless of the questions, students will get to know the person they interview better, and hopefully feel more connected to him or her. The following questions can be used for a classmate interview:

1. What is your favorite activity to do at home?
2. What is your favorite activity to do outside?
3. What is your favorite TV show?
4. What is your favorite thing to eat?
5. What is your favorite subject?
6. How would you describe yourself?

Class Picture Inspection

Using a class picture on a daily basis is a way to ensure that teachers will connect with every student. At the end of each day, look at your class picture and try to remember at least one positive comment you said to each student. For those students who did not receive a positive comment for the day, begin the next day by saying a positive comment to them. It is easy to forget the quiet students who never cause trouble, but they can be remembered by using the class picture every day. Remember, positive comments do not always have to relate to school work; instead they can be associated with the student's personality, looks, or other skills.

Permission granted by Mr. Art Buchwald.

ACTIVITIES

Sense of Uniqueness

The following activities can help increase students' sense of uniqueness.

Student of the Week

Every week of the school year, allow one different student to be the student of the week until everyone in the class has had a chance. When a child is the student of the week, he or she is responsible for bringing in items from home or making items to be placed on the student-of-the-week bulletin board. Categories for the student of the week could include favorite food or sport, things I am good at, or things I enjoy doing. The bulletin board allows the other students in the class to learn more about the featured student's interests and capabilities, and it allows the student of the week to think about his or her capabilities while preparing the bulletin board.

I Am Unique Icebreaker

This icebreaker allows students to state their name and one thing that makes them unique. If this description fits another student in the class, the original student has to state an additional unique feature about himself or herself until no one else matches the description. For example, if Susan raises her hand, states her name, and says that she knows how to ride a unicycle, her turn is complete if no one else in the class knows how to ride a unicycle. If someone in the class does know how to ride a unicycle, Susan will continue to say something else that makes her unique until this quality, skill, or experience does not apply to someone else in the class. This activity allows the teacher and students to learn interesting things about one another.

Student Collage

A personal collage is an art project that can help students increase their sense of uniqueness. Instruct students to make a collage that represents things they like to do and things they do best. They can draw, write, or cut pictures out of magazines to make their collage. After the collages are completed, they display them in the classroom so that everyone has an opportunity to learn more about one another.

Graffiti Wall

Another activity that teachers can use to help promote a sense of uniqueness is using a graffiti wall. Cover a bulletin board or a wall in the classroom with newsprint or any plain paper. Allow students to write on the graffiti wall whenever their work is completed or during any free time. Teachers may want to have specific themes for graffiti walls, such as what spring means to me, nice things about classmates, favorite activities, or draw your favorite food. Instruct students that only positive comments are allowed on the graffiti wall. If negative comments are written, use the class meeting (described in the Sense of Power section) to allow students to decide how to handle this or other problems with the graffiti wall.

Journal Writing

Ask students to keep a journal throughout the entire class year. Journal writing not only helps to improve their sense of uniqueness, but enhances their writing skills. Ask students to respond to activities in class, write creative stories or poetry, or just write about their feelings for the day. It is important to collect the journals every few weeks and respond to the entries that each child has written. Although this takes time, it is an excellent way for teachers to get to know their students.

Role-Playing

Role-playing is an activity that should be used with students to help promote their sense of uniqueness. Acting allows students to be creative while also practicing a skill. For example, an excellent time to use role-playing is when practicing peer-resistance skills, communication skills, friendship skills, and decision-making skills.

ACTIVITIES

Sense of Power

The following activities can help increase students' sense of power.

Success of the Day

At the end of each day, instruct students to write down a success they experienced that day. Students can keep these successes in a journal or separate notebook so they can look back at them whenever they are feeling bad. Another way to do this activity is to have students share their success with the class at the end of each school day. This activity will help each school day end on a good note and also will help students remember the good things about themselves.

Class Contracts

When promoting a sense of power, it is important to promote the idea that this is the students' class, not the teacher's class. Allowing students to have input into the rules of the class, through a class contract or a positive behavior contract, will help build this concept. Although there are several ways to develop a class contract, a suggested format follows.

First, introduce the concept of a contract (e.g., everyone has to give something to get something back in return). Different jobs that have contracts can also be discussed. Next, ask students to discuss the meaning of the word *privilege*. Ask them to think of privileges that they have liked in other classes. Explain that they will be able to have some of those privileges by creating a class contract. List these privileges on the chalkboard or on newsprint under the category "Students Get." It is the responsibility of the teacher to go through that list and decide or negotiate what items can be given to the students. For instance, a student might suggest that there should be no tests. Although most teachers have to give tests, they might suggest that they will not give any tests on Monday. Actual suggestions from elementary students for the "Students Get" column include interesting activities, field trips, sitting with friends, being allowed to chew gum, good grades, and fun. It is up to teachers, through negotiation, to decide which of the items they can give to students.

Next, explain to the students that very few things in life are free, and if they want to get these things during the school year, they must give something in return. Ask students what they would be willing to give, and write these suggestions on the chalkboard or on newsprint under the category "Students Give." Some actual suggestions from elementary students for the "Students Give" column have been good effort, cooperation, attention, positive attitude, participation, don't talk while others are talking, treat classmates nicely, and respect. Ask the students if they can live up to the items on the "Students Give" list. If a student cannot live up to a certain item on "Students Give," then it must be removed. Remember, this is a *class* contract.

Then share your list of "Teacher Gives." To save time, it is best if you have a list preprinted. Some sample "Teacher Gives" are time, energy, knowledge, humor, kindness, fairness, extra help, and listening to student ideas. Students appreciate this part of the contract, because they feel the teacher is also willing to give to make the class succeed.

Then share a preprinted list of "Non-negotiables." It should be explained that there are always some rules that must be followed, such as laws that are decided by government. Some "Non-negotiables" that have been used with elementary students are follow all school rules, never say "I can't," and no put-downs allowed.

Next, discuss the consequences of breaking a rule in the contract, in case either side does not live up to the contract. Most of the time the students come up with stiffer consequences than those of the teacher. It is important to list only those consequences that are not humiliating to any class member. Some consequences that have been suggested by elementary students in the past are staying after school, apologizing to the class, and doing extra homework.

Probably the most important part of the contract is to also have a built-in reward system. For example, if the class follows the contract for a week, it is important to reward them for good behaviors. Proactive reward systems always work better than reactive punishment systems.

After all of the students have agreed on the contract, it is important to make a copy for everyone in the class and send it home to the parents so they know what is expected of their child. Have the parents and child sign the contract and return it to the teacher. Post a contract in the room for the entire school year. If there is a student in the class who does not agree with the contract, suggest that an individual contract be made for that student.

Most students create a class contract with the "rules" that most teachers would initiate without student input. Students, however, are more willing to follow the rules if they initiated them. Many less-experienced teachers who have tried to use class contracts have been unsuccessful because students do not automatically respond to them. These teachers feel it is easier to throw out the contract and come up with their own rules and consequences. This may appear easier at first; however, as the school year progresses, it typically becomes increasingly difficult to use this as a discipline technique. When teachers use a classroom contract, it is important to remember that it usually takes about 3 or 4 weeks of the teacher reminding the students about "their" classroom contract. Once the students get accustomed to the idea that this is their class and their rules, they will begin to hold other students accountable for their contract. Table 15.2 shows a sample contract that a third grade class used for its school year.

TABLE 15.2	Class Contract
Students get	**Students give**
1. Field trips	1. Try hard
2. No Friday tests	2. Study
3. Good grades	3. No talking when others are talking
4. Fun	4. Pay attention
5. Friends	5. Be prepared
6. Extra help	
7. To learn	**Nonnegotiables**
	1. Follow school rules
Teacher gives	2. No put-downs
1. Fairness	
2. Understanding	**Consequences**
3. Extra help	1. Apology to class
4. Humor	2. Stay after school
5. Enthusiasm	3. Go to principal
6. Praise	
7. Kindness	
8. Good explanations	

I agree to this contract for the school year.
Student signature:_____
Parent signature:_____

Class Jobs

Another way to help develop a sense of power in students is to assign or let students apply for class jobs. Some examples of class jobs include line leader, lunch money collector, chalkboard cleaner, attendance taker, plant caretaker, or animal caretaker. Students who are given a class job feel they have a responsibility to the class to help it function effectively. It is important to be conscientious about not using sexist stereotypes when assigning class jobs, such as boys always being assigned to carry the books.

Low-Level Decisions

Another way to develop a sense of power in students is to let them make low-level decisions in the class. Letting students decide which book they are going to read and what skit they are going to perform are examples of low-level decisions. Low-level decisions allow practice in decision making, and they also allow students to experience the consequences of those decisions.

Class Meetings

Class meetings, which occur by having the class sit in a circle and openly discuss current class issues, is another way to help increase a sense of power. The rules of the class meeting might include only one person speaks at a time; stick to the topic; and speak only for yourself. Discuss the rules with the students before each class meeting. Throughout the class meeting, act as a facilitator by sitting outside the circle, answering questions or clarifying comments when necessary, and summarizing the meeting when needed.

Various topics can be discussed during a class meeting. One topic for a class meeting is having the

The class participates in a class meeting.

students discuss a specific project. For instance, if the class recently conducted a health fair for parents, a class meeting could be used for students to express both the positive and negative aspects of the health fair and to make suggestions on how to improve it for the future. Another topic that could be used for a class meeting is the most and least favorite activities of the week. A good time to have a weekly class meeting is on Friday afternoon, so that students have the opportunity to evaluate the entire week. It will take time for the students to get used to doing this, but after a few meetings, students begin to give useful feedback about the week's activities.

Reinforce the notion that students will *not* be punished for discussing negative aspects of the class, but rather are encouraged to suggest ways to improve activities. Teachers who use the class meeting as a way to promote a sense of power among students must feel secure with themselves and view the negative comments as feedback that can be used to improve their teaching. Teachers will be surprised at how many creative ideas students will suggest during a class meeting. The class meeting not only helps teachers understand their students better, but helps students feel comfortable, confident, and wanted.

Question Box

Another way to help create a positive learning environment is to provide a question box for students. Instruct students that they can write anonymous questions about topics discussed in class, but the questions need to pertain to class issues and not be personal questions about the teacher or other students. This allows those students who are too embarrassed to ask questions a way to find out the answers to their questions. Although this activity is often used just for sexuality questions, it is important to have this option available to students throughout the entire school year.

Involving Students in Curriculum Planning

Involving students in curriculum planning works well when thematic units are used throughout the year. Thematic units are defined as the study of one main topic or theme for a period of time and the integration of all subjects into that one topic. For example, a theme might be the senses. Math, language arts, science, health, social studies, music, and art are all be taught using the senses as the main theme. To give children a sense of power, ask students for input about what themes they would like to learn about for the year. Four important questions should be asked:[19]

1. What do you wonder? What do you want to know about the senses? Children will ask many interesting questions that should be addressed during that thematic unit.

2. What can we do to find out? Children can then brainstorm how they might find out answers to the questions they brainstormed in #1.

3. What materials do we need? Children again are asked to brainstorm what materials they need to find out the answers to their questions.

4. What will you bring? What will you need me to bring? Allowing children to bring resources or information from home makes them an active participant in the learning process.

Teaching thematically allows children to learn about specific subjects in depth. Allowing students to be involved in creating the curriculum or the thematic unit gives students a sense of power.

ACTIVITIES

Sense of Models

The following activities can help increase students' sense of models.

Guest Speakers

It is important to expose students to a variety of respected individuals in the community to discuss specific information, skills, or careers. Students will have an opportunity to learn about new careers that are available to them in the future. This will help them to develop a sense of models by getting to know people they feel worthy of emulating.

Journal Writing

As mentioned previously, it is important to use journal writing to help children develop a sense of uniqueness. But journal writing also can help develop a sense of models. This can be accomplished by asking students to respond to different scenarios. For example, present a scenario of a girl named Sarah who had dilemma of stealing to impress her friends. Instruct students to write what they think Sarah should do, and why. This helps students develop their value system, which is a component of a sense of models.

Integrating Heroes and Language Arts

Assign students to read about different heroes throughout history. Ask them to identify a "local" hero (parent, older brother or sister, etc.) and then write a short story using their hero as a main character in their story.

Peer Tutoring/Cross-Age Teaching

To help students develop positive role models, have older elementary and middle-level students tutor or help teach younger elementary students. Not only can younger students learn from older students, but older students can become role models for younger students.

Goal Setting

Another skill that helps students develop a sense of models is goal setting (see chapter 6). Younger elementary students should learn what the word *goal* means, and be encouraged to work on short-term, daily goals. Examples of daily goals are giving five compliments to classmates, completing a math lesson, or cleaning out their desks. Older elementary and middle-level students can be encouraged to set weekly, monthly, or even longer-term goals. A goal project that older students can work on is a positive health behavior project. Ask students to decide what positive health behavior they want to incorporate into their lives, and then develop a plan on how to reach that goal.

Community Service

Ask students to brainstorm different community service projects in which they could participate. Community service projects allow students to develop a sense of models by reinforcing a value system of helping and contributing to better the total community. Ideas can include cleaning up parks or playgrounds, bringing in food for a needy family, visiting a nursing home, or raising money to help a family in need.

SUMMARY

Emotional health refers to trust, self-esteem, self-confidence, and the ability to express emotions comfortably and appropriately. Perhaps the most important aspect of emotional health is self-esteem. Self-esteem can be defined as the attitudes and beliefs that individuals have about themselves and their judgment of their skills and abilities. Having a positive self-esteem can help impact negative health behaviors. There are four themes or conditions of self-esteem: the sense of connectiveness, the sense of uniqueness, the sense of power, and the sense of models. Children with a high sense of connectiveness feel they are a part of or feel related to specific people, places, or things. Activities that teachers can use to help promote a sense of connectiveness include icebreakers, IALAC, positive letters and phone calls, the compliment activity, catch somebody doing something good, interviews, and class picture inspection.

Children with a high sense of uniqueness feel there is something special about themselves and know that other people feel they are special too. Activities to help increase a sense of uniqueness include student of the week, the I am unique icebreaker, student collage, graffiti wall, and journal writing.

Children with a high sense of power feel confident they can do what they set out to do. Activities to help increase the sense of power include student of the day, class contract, class jobs, low-level decisions, class meeting, involving students in curriculum planning, and question box.

Children with a high sense of models have consistent values and beliefs that guide and direct their actions in different situations. They also have positive role models in their lives. Activities to help increase the sense of models include guest speakers, journal writing, peer tutoring/teaching, and goal setting.

DISCUSSION QUESTIONS

1. What is emotional health and how is it related to the other dimensions of health?

2. What is self-esteem?

3. Describe Abraham Maslow's hierarchy of needs and explain how they are related to self-esteem.

4. What is the self-fulfilling prophecy and how does it affect children? What can teachers do to counteract the negative aspects of self-fulfilling prophecy?

5. What is the relationship between self-esteem and school success?

6. What is the relationship between self-esteem and positive health behaviors?

7. Describe each of the themes or conditions of self-esteem.

8. What are several activities that can be conducted to help promote a sense of connectiveness in students?

9. What are several activities that can be conducted to help promote a sense of uniqueness in students?

10. What are several activities that can be conducted to help promote a sense of power in students?

11. What are several activities that can be conducted to help promote a sense of models in students?

ENDNOTES

1. A. Mendler, *Smiling at Yourself: Educating Young Children About Stress and Self-Esteem* (Santa Cruz, CA: ETR Associates, 1990), xvi.

2. R. Blum and P. Rinehart, *Reducing the Risk: Connections That Make a Difference in the Lives of Youth* (University of Minnesota, Minneapolis, MN: Division of General Pediatrics and Adolescent Health, 1997).

3. L. Silvestri, M. Dantonio, and S. Easton, "Enhancement of Self-esteem in At-Risk Elementary Students," *Journal of Health Education* 25, no. 1, (1994).

4. T. Dielman, S. Leech, A. Larenger, and W. Horvath. "Health Locus of Control and Self-Esteem as Related to Adolescent Behavior and Intentions," *Adolescence* 19, no. 76 (1987).

5. J. Petersen-Martin and R. Cottrell, "Self-Concept, Value and Health Behavior," *Journal of Health Education* 18, no. 5, (1987).

6. Louis Harris and Associates, *An Evaluation of Comprehensive Health Education in American Public Schools* (New York: Metropolitan Life Foundation, 1988).

7. R. Miller, "Positive Self-esteem and Alcohol/Drug Related Attitudes Among School Children." *Journal of Alcohol and Drug Use* 33, no. 3, (1988).

8. D. Hays and S. Fors. "Self-esteem and Health Instruction: Challenges for Curriculum Development." *Journal of School Health* 60, no. 5, (1990).

9. J. Canfield and H. Wells, *100 Ways to Enhance Self-Concept in the Classroom: A Handbook for Teachers and Parents* (Englewood Cliffs, NJ: Prentice-Hall, 1976).

10. R. Bean, *The Four Conditions of Self-Esteem: A New Approach for Elementary and Middle Schools* (Santa Cruz, CA: ETR Associates, 1992), 27.

11. Ibid., 29.

12. William W. Purkey, *Self-Concept and School Achievement* (Englewood Cliffs, NJ: Prentice-Hall, 1970), 49.

13. Ibid., 54.

14. G. Stock. *The Kids' Book of Questions* (New York: Workman Publishing, 1988).

15. Canfield and Wells, *100 Ways to Enhance Self-Concept in the Classroom.*

16. C. Patterson and L. Fine, "Catch Somebody Doing Something Good," *Health Education* 4, no. 2 (1973).

17. Bean, *The Four Conditions of Self-Esteem,* 30.

18. Ibid., 32.

19. K. Williams, "What Do You Wonder? Involving Children in Curriculum Planning," *Young Children* 52, no. 6, (1997).

20. Bean, *The Four Conditions of Self-Esteem,* 34.

Suggested Readings

Bean, R. *The Four Conditions of Self-Esteem: A New Approach for Elementary and Middle Schools.* Santa Cruz, CA.: ETR Associates, 1992.

Blum, R., and P. Rinehart. *Reducing the Risk: Connections That Make a Difference in the Lives of Youth.* University of Minnesota, Minneapolis, MN: Division of General Pediatrics and Adolescent Health, 1997.

Borba, M., and C. Borba. *A Classroom Affair: 101 Ways to Help Children Like Themselves.* Minneapolis, MN: Winston Press, 1978.

Borba, M., and C. Borba. *A Classroom Affair: More Ways to Help Children Like Themselves.* Vol. 2. Minneapolis, MN: Winston Press, 1982.

Canfield, J. *Self-Esteem in the Classroom: A Curriculum Guide.* Pacific Palisades, CA: Self-Esteem Seminars, 1986.

Canfield, J., and H. Wells. *100 Ways to Enhance Self-Concept in the Classroom: A Handbook for Teachers and Parents.* Englewood Cliffs, NJ: Prentice-Hall, 1976.

Eaton, M. "Positive Discipline: Fostering the Self-esteem of Young Children." *Young Children* 53, no. 6, (1997).

Gibbs, J. *Tribes: A Process for Social Development and Cooperative Learning.* Santa Rosa, CA: Center Source Publications, 1987.

King, K. "Self-concept and Self-esteem: A Clarification of Terms." *Journal of School Health* 67, no. 2 (1997).

McDaniel, S., and P. Bielen. *Project Self-Esteem: A Parent Involvement Program for Elementary Age Children.* Rolling Hills Estates, CA.: B.L. Winch and Associates, 1986.

Mendler, A. *Smiling at Yourself: Educating Young Children About Stress and Self-Esteem.* Santa Cruz, CA: ETR Associates, 1990.

Purkey, W., and J. Novak. *Inviting School Success.* Bellmont, CA: Wadsworth Publishing Co., 1984.

Shandler, N. "Just Rewards: Positive Discipline Can Teach Students Self-respect and Empathy." *Teaching Tolerance* 5, no. 1, (1996).

Silvestri, L., M. Dantonio, and S. Easton, "Enhancement of Self-esteem in At-Risk Elementary Students." *Journal of Health Education* 25, no. 1, (1994).

Stock, G. *The Kids' Book of Questions.* New York: Workman Publishing, 1988.

Williams, K. "What Do You Wonder? Involving Children in Curriculum Planning." *Young Children* 52, no. 6, (1997).

Wilson, J. *The Invitational Elementary Classroom.* Springfield, IL: Charles C. Thomas, Publishers, 1986.

Children's Literature with an Emotional Theme

Grades K–2

Andrews, J. *The Very Last First Time.* Atheneum, 1986.

Brown, M. *Arthur's Nose.* Little, Brown, 1976.

Browne, A. *Willy the Wimp.* Knopf, 1985.

Carlson, N. *I Like Me.* Penguin, 1988.

Fox, M. *Whoever You Are.* Harcourt Brace, 1997. (Multicultural)

Henkes, K. *Chrysanthemum.* Mulberry, 1991. (American Library Association Notable Book).

Lattimore, D. *The Flame of Peace.* Harper & Row, 1987.

Margolis, R. *Secrets of a Small Brother.* Macmillan, 1984. (Multicultural)

Schwartz, A. *Anabelle Swift, Kindergartner.* Orchard, 1988.

Viorst, J. *Alexander and the Terrible, Horrible, No Good, Very Bad Day.* Antheneum, 1972.

Zolotow, C. *I Like to Be Little.* Crowell, 1987.

Grades 3–5

Asher, S. *Everything Is Not Enough.* Delacorte, 1987.

Carew, J. *Children of the Sun.* Little, Brown, 1980.

Fradin, D. *Remarkable Children: Twenty Who Made History.* Little, Brown, 1987.

Greene, C. *Monday I Love You.* Harper & Row, 1988.

Greenwald, S. *Give Us a Great Big Smile, Rosy Cole.* Little, Brown, 1981.

Hoffman, S. *Amazing Grace,* Dial, 1991. (Multicultural)

Holbrook, S. *Nothing's the End of the World.* Boyds Mills, 1995.

Little, J. *Hey World, Here I Am.* Harper & Row, 1989.

Moss, M. *Amelia's Notebook.* Tricycle Press, 1995.

Moss, T. *I Want to Be.* Puffin, 1993. (Multicultural)

Park, B. *Beanpole.* Knopf, 1983.

Saltzman, D. *The Jester Has Lost His Jingle.* Jester Books, 1995.

Say, A. *Grandfather's Journey.* Houghton Mifflin, 1993. (Caldecott Medal) (Multicultural)

Grades 6–8

Lowry, L. *Anastasia, Ask Your Analyst.* Houghton Mifflin, 1984.

Paterson, K. *Jaco Have I Loved.* Harper Collins, 1986. (Newbery Medal)

Soto, G. *Baseball in April.* Harcourt, 1990. (Multicultural)

DEATH AND DYING

OUTLINE

INTRODUCTION

Dying, death, and grief are processes that affect everyone, regardless of race, gender, or age. Yet they remain taboo topics of discussion in our society. In order to change this attitude, formalized instruction and informal discussion, particularly of critical incidents or events related to dying, death, and grief, need to be included in the elementary and middle-level health-education curriculum. There is a tendency to try to protect children and preadolescents from some of these topics. However, this prevents those young people from obtaining accurate information, which in turn can exacerbate their fears and anxieties about these natural life processes.

Teaching about dying, death, and grief helps students to deal effectively with their feelings when a loved one does die. It is necessary for schools to become involved in teaching about dying, death, and grief because many adults find it difficult to discuss, particularly with children. Parents sometimes find it easier to evade the issue or even lie about a death because they want to protect their children from any uncomfortable feelings. Although parents who react to a death in this way are trying to help their children, in the long run this avoidance can cause problems. For instance, there are parents who use euphemistic language with their children, such as "Grandma is taking a long vacation" or "Grandpa is sleeping." Although the parents' intention is to ease the pain of loss, children at a more concrete developmental stage may be frightened to take a vacation or go to sleep because they are confused about what happened to Grandma or Grandpa. Parents also may replace a dead pet immediately with a new one. Children typically do not want their pet replaced, but parents sometimes feel it will help the children forget the loss and get over the death.

Teachers who have researched the subject and have been trained in the various aspects of dying, death, and grief are able to satisfy the natural and developmentally consistent curiosities of young children. They can help children understand that their feelings about death are normal and even healthy; teachers also can deal professionally and truthfully with other important issues of dying, death, and grief.

At the elementary and middle-level grades, professional instruction is important because this is the time when students first experience death and dying, whether it is seen on television, or experienced with a pet or a family member. It is estimated that one out of every twenty children will lose a parent by death during childhood and that almost every child will experience the death of a pet, a friend, or a relative.[1] Children need to know the facts and issues surrounding death and dying so that any false impressions they have formed can be dispelled and so that they can deal with death in a healthy manner.

This chapter presents information about dying, death, and grief and ideas on teaching these topics to elementary and middle-level students. Even with accurate information and suggested teaching activities in hand, it is perhaps most important for teachers to explore their own attitudes about dying, death, and grief before trying to teach the subject. If teachers have pronounced death anxiety or fears, these beliefs might be conveyed to their students. Such well-meaning professionals can do more harm than good.

RECOMMENDATIONS FOR TEACHERS: PRACTICE AND CONTENT

Before trying to conduct instructional activities with elementary and middle-level students concerning dying, death, and grief, certain aspects of the topic should be understood. Information about dying, death and grief follows, as well as teaching ideas about this topic.

Information

There are a variety of topics about dying, death, and grief with which teachers should be both familiar and comfortable. These include a basic knowledge about the developmental stages of understanding death, the stages of grief, and the stages of dying. Depending on the grade level, not all of this information will be developmentally appropriate; however, all teachers should have a basic understanding of these concepts.

Developmental Stages of Understanding Death

Several studies have been conducted with children to determine the developmental stages of understanding death. Perhaps the most widely cited study was published in 1948 by Nagy.[2] Nagy maintained that children's ideas about death develop in three age-related stages. Although her work has become the standard for this topic, more current research suggests that the age of a child is not the best predictor of the child's understanding of death. Rather, individual development and experience more heavily influence how a child will understand the concept of death.[3] For instance, terminally ill children have a much more sophisticated understanding of death than do their healthy, same-age counterparts. Likewise, children who have experienced the death of a pet or a relative seem to have a more mature understanding of death than do age-cohort peers. Deaths portrayed in the media and literature also influence a child's understanding of death. Although there are disagreements about Nagy's age-graded developmental model of understanding death, it still provides a foundation for elementary and middle-level teachers as they work with their students.

Stage One (ages 3 to 5 years) During this developmental stage, children do not understand the finality of death. They see death as a sleeplike, reversible state because their conceptions of time are concrete. They view the dead person as being able to still eat, work, laugh, and cry as if alive. Because of this view, children often seem matter-of-fact or callous to death. This is often demonstrated at funerals, when children in Stage One show no signs of grief and in fact enjoy themselves with other Stage One cousins and relatives. Parents are sometimes embarrassed when this type of behavior occurs; however, because these children believe the dead person will eventually return and continue to function, there is no reason for them to grieve. Children may also act this way if the person who died is not in their immediate circle of contact or support. It is not uncommon for children in this stage to ask questions such as "When is daddy coming back?" It is especially important for adults not to explain death in terms of sleep or a vacation because that reinforces some inaccurate beliefs. Although young children do not understand the finality of death, that lack

It is healthy to allow children to attend funerals.

of understanding does not negate the sense of grief that children may experience with any type of separation. Depending on experiences and maturity, many children in kindergarten through second grade will still view death as not final.

Stage Two (ages 5 to 9 years)   Nagy found that children ages 5 to 9 did have an understanding of finality; however, they believe that an outside source such as the "bogeyman" or "death man" causes death. Children will often "communicate" with the "bogeyman" by asking him to leave their family alone or to go away. Many guilt feelings are associated with death during this stage because Stage Two children believe the "bogeyman" is watching their actions. For instance, if a 7-year-old boy asks his grandfather to buy him a toy and the grandfather refuses, the boy may think negative thoughts about the grandfather. If the grandfather then dies, the boy may think that the "bogeyman" heard his negative thoughts about his grandfather and therefore he caused his grandfather's death. During this stage, it is important for teachers to be aware of potential guilt feelings and to try to alleviate them.

Stage Three (ages 9 and above)   During Stage Three, children fully understand the finality of death and know that it operates from within the body, not from some external force. They are more likely to understand that death is universal and an inevitable end to everyone's life, including their own. Children in Stage Three, however, do not associate death with themselves, but rather associate death with other "old" people.

Although these stages have been identified, it is important to remember that they are not prescriptive but rather should serve as guidelines. Children's behavior, depending on their personal experiences with death, may not conform to the suggested age parameters.

Stages of Grief

Grief is the psychological and sometimes physical response to the death of a loved one. It refers to the feelings of sorrow, anger, depression, guilt, confusion, shock, and despair that occur after someone dies. Two terms are used to describe the intensity of grief: *low-grief death* and *high-grief death*. A low-grief death results from a prolonged illness, an anticipated death, or the death of someone with whom there is little emotional connection. Following a low-grief death, the survivors may not show as many emotions because they have already grieved prior to the death. A high-grief death is an unexpected adult death or one that occurs to a child or young person. Following a high-grief death, the grieving process may be more emotional and last longer because there was no preparation for the death.[4]

Just as children go through developmental stages of understanding death, each person typically experiences

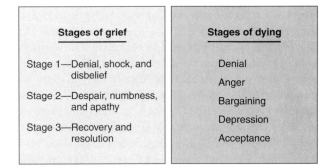

Figure 16.1
Dying and grieving individuals have some similar feelings.

stages of grief following the death of a loved one (figure 16.1).[5] Adults and most schoolchildren follow these stages of grief. It needs to be emphasized that these are patterns, not strict steps that people *should* follow when they are grieving. Although time lines are included with these stages, they are rough estimates and are not prescriptions for appropriate behavior. Various factors, including how close a person was to the deceased and whether the death was expected, affect the length of time and the intensity for each stage.

Stage One—Denial, Shock, and Disbelief   This stage begins after hearing about the death of a loved one. Possible manifestations include crying, confusion, stress, and not believing the death has occurred. This stage typically lasts up to 2 weeks after the death. Some persons stay in this stage for a longer time, which may become unhealthy. Because part of this stage includes denial, it may explain why survivors, many times, can act as though they are "in control" during the funeral or other commemorative ceremonies. Friends of the survivors should not mistake this calmness as an acceptance of the death, and should not assume that the survivors do not need support or help after the funeral. After they accept the death, survivors desperately need support from their friends and loved ones.

Stage Two—Despair, Numbness, Guilt, and Apathy   This stage begins after the survivors have recognized the reality of the death and usually continues up to 1 year. Because this stage generally expands over a long period of time, many feelings and degrees of feelings can be experienced: sadness, depression, guilt, preoccupation with thoughts of the deceased, anger, apathy, and numbness. It is not uncommon for survivors to experience loss of appetite, insomnia, crying spells, restlessness, and to deny themselves pleasure because of the guilt they feel over the death of loved ones. Children are more likely to express their grief in the form of anger, because they are angry that the person died and left them behind. Sometimes adults find these expressions of anger difficult to accept because the children appear to be selfish and egocentric. Because anger is a major part of grief for children, adults can help them by accepting their feelings and not scolding them if they do express anger. It is important that survivors have the opportunity to share all feelings of grief and not be asked to "hold them in" or "be brave." It is particularly true to stress this to boys, who may feel that they have to live up to the stereotype that "boys don't cry." During this stage, children also may experience feelings of loneliness, isolation, and abandonment. Children who feel this way need help in identifying significant people in their lives with whom they can talk.[6] Another behavior sometimes exhibited by children during this stage is assumed mannerisms. This occurs when the grieving child begins to model mannerisms of the dead person as if to take the place of that person. In addition, children tend to idealize the dead person by describing him or her in terms of perfection and excellence.

Stage Three—Recovery and Resolution Recovery and resolution occur approximately 1 year to 15 months after the death. The title of this stage may suggest that the survivor is completely over the trauma and related emotions of the death; however, there are still times of depression during this stage. Sadness will occasionally occur, especially during holidays and on anniversaries and birthdays. Sometimes this sadness occurs at an unconscious level. The person may not realize right away why he or she is feeling so bad. When individuals are taught that this sadness may be stronger during certain special times, they can prepare themselves to cope better when they know the source of the sadness. Survivors should be allowed to express their grief and not be asked to "hold it in." During this stage, the survivor has decreased episodes of sadness and depression, recalls positive memories of the deceased, and is able to return to normal activities and form new friendships. During this stage, the survivor accepts the death and tries to move on with life.

As mentioned previously, children who understand that death is not reversible typically follow these stages of grief. These stages of grief can also occur during divorce or separation. Besides the feelings associated with the stages of grief, children may experience other emotions and behaviors as they go through the grieving process.[7] For instance, children may become isolated or withdrawn from the family because they cannot stand to see their parents' pain. Another common reaction is for children to become hostile toward the deceased or any person whom they feel was responsible for the person's death. Children may also try to find a replacement for the deceased so that they can maintain some of their normal routine. However children express grief, the most important things for adults to remember are to allow them to grieve and to provide them with as much support as possible.

Many times teachers are concerned about what is normal or abnormal grieving. The distinction is not an easy one to determine. It is not so much the emotions or behaviors that are distinctive, but their intensity and duration. What should be of concern is the continued denial or avoidance of reality, prolonged bodily distress, persistent panic, extended guilt, enduring anxiety, and unceasing hostility. If there is any doubt about whether a child needs professional attention, it is best to ask the school counselor for professional advice.

Stages of Dying

It is also important for teachers and students to understand the stages of dying (see figure 16.1). There may be students in school who have a relative who is dying, and it would be helpful for those students to understand why their relative acts the way he or she does. Elisabeth Kübler-Ross is the person who is most associated with research on the emotions of the dying. She interviewed about 200 terminally ill patients and found that most of them went through five psychological stages.[8] It should be noted that not everyone with a terminal illness will experience all of these stages, and not everyone progresses through these stages in the stated order. Some people fluctuate between two stages at the same time, while others skip various stages. These stages should not be valued as being good or bad, but as guidelines to help interact with the dying.

Denial The first emotion that most persons experience when they are told they have a terminal illness is denial. This is a healthy response to a stressful situation, and it acts as a temporary buffer to help protect the individual. It is not uncommon for the terminally ill to return periodically to the denial stage, even after progressing to other stages. This stage becomes dangerous only when the terminally ill person seeks third and fourth opinions about an illness or spends money on "quack" cures.

Anger After terminally ill persons can no longer deny their approaching death, they typically become angry, resentful, and hostile. This is perhaps the most difficult stage for loved ones to deal with because the anger is sometimes directed at them. Anger may be expressed through shouting, complaining, and bitterness. For instance, the person may say something like, "I don't want to see anyone—go away." These emotions are understandable but not always easy to deal with. This is an especially important stage for children to understand because a terminally ill grandparent may yell or express meanness to a child while in this stage. Children need to understand that the grandparent was not angry at them but at the situation.

Bargaining Bargaining typically occurs throughout most of the dying process. This stage is characterized by the terminally ill person bargaining with someone in power, such as the physician or God, to prolong life. For instance, a terminally ill person may think, "If you let me live until my next birthday, I promise I will always be a kind person." An outsider might not be aware of this stage because many patients keep these bargains a secret.

Depression   Many terminally ill people will bounce back and forth from the bargaining stage to the depression stage. After they determine that the bargaining did not work, they become depressed. They begin to understand that death is certain, and feelings of sadness and depression become overwhelming. Although it may be frightening for a child to visit a terminally ill person, children should not be discouraged from visiting a terminally ill relative. Many times children can really help the patient deal with or temporarily forget about death. When visiting a terminally ill relative, children should be encouraged to bring a small present, like an art project from school. This can give the patient and the child something to talk about. The opportunity to bring some happiness to a dying person might also help children feel useful and helpful.

Acceptance   The last stage of the dying process is when the person accepts the outcome of death. It does not mean that the person is happy; rather, there is a lack of feelings. During this stage, the dying person wants to make psychological and practical arrangements, such as funeral arrangements or writing a will. Those arrangements become difficult and frustrating if the relatives are still denying the death; however, it is important to accommodate the dying person as much as possible.

Children should understand that one of the biggest fears of dying people is the fear of being alone. If children understand this and the stages of dying, they may be more inclined to make frequent visits or contacts with a terminally ill relative.

Teaching about Dying, Death, and Grief to Elementary and Middle-Level Students

When teaching death and dying, it is important not only to identify teaching activities that are useful to elementary teachers, but to identify the reasons to teach this topic, to understand guidelines for teaching death and dying education, and to address how to deal with a student death. The information that follows addresses all of these issues.

Reasons to Include Dying, Death, and Grief Education in Elementary and Middle-Level Schools

Some administrators and teachers feel overwhelmed by the number of subjects and topics they are asked to teach their students during the school year. Dying, death, and grief education has been included in this book as a subject area because it is an important topic to include within the elementary and middle-level health-education curriculum. Seventy to 100 years ago, dying, death, and grief would not have been an important topic to teach children because families, churches, and the health-care delivery system were different than they are today. During that time, it was common for children to experience the death of a sibling, parent, neighbor, or grandparent. Not only did deaths occur more often, but the families were responsible for preparing the body and making all of the funeral arrangements. There were no funeral homes as we know them today, and undertakers did not take care of all of the arrangements. Today, the living are isolated from the dying because the terminally ill are typically in hospitals and nursing homes, whereas in the past dying people stayed at home. The changes have made death mysterious and, for some, more fearful. When someone is ill, he or she is generally removed from the home and taken to a health-care facility. When a person dies, the funeral home takes care of all the details, from preparing the body for the funeral to the burial. Many times parents totally isolate their children from the ill person and the funeral because they want to shelter them from any pain. Many children, therefore, do not have any real experiences with death, but instead are educated by the media. Because children are removed from death and do not understand what it is all about, teachers and other adults need to talk with them about death.

Although death is portrayed in the media, these portrayals are often misleading and confusing. According to Kübler-Ross, the media presents "death in a two-dimensional aspect that tends to make it unreal and devoid of significant emotions."[9] A person is alive and then dead, and emotions surrounding the death are often ignored. Because of these misleading portrayals, children are once again protected from the very real emotions that are connected with death.

Children, even those younger than age 6, are curious about death and typically have many questions about the topic.[10] Many parents do not feel comfortable talking about death, and so they ignore the questions or lie to the child. For example, if a child asks what *dead* means, the parent may tell the child that he or she is too young to understand. The teacher can be an objective resource for answering many of these sensitive questions.

Another reason to include dying, death, and grief education in the elementary and middle-level curriculum is to allow students to express their feelings. Students should be taught the stages of grief so that if they do experience a loss, they will know that they are not alone in how they feel. Students also may have a relative going through the dying process, and if allowed to discuss the stages of dying and the feelings associated with those stages, they may feel less isolated.

In the older elementary and middle-level grades, students may become more interested in death-related issues as a result of technology, such as euthanasia and mercy killing. Students will hear those issues being discussed on television, and they may need a forum to discuss them openly.

Some people might argue that the home or the church is the place to discuss the issues of death and dying. It would be wonderful if all children could discuss this topic openly with their parents; however, it just does not happen. In a *Psychology Today* survey, approximately one-third of the respondents could not remember any discussion of death within the family structure, about one-third of the families discussed death and dying with discomfort, and about one-third of the families openly discussed death and dying.[11] *All* children deserve the opportunity to discuss this very relevant issue openly, which leaves the schools as the most practical place to teach about issues of dying, death, and grief.

Guidelines for Teaching about Death and Dying

Several guidelines are important to consider when teaching about dying, death, and grief. These guidelines can help teachers and administrators not become defensive with parents and students when teaching a controversial topic such as dying, death, and grief.

Be Honest with Students   As mentioned previously, many times parents and other adults try to shield children from any death-related experiences or emotions. Although shielding the children may delay the pain, it will emerge at some point. For instance, while discussing death-related issues in college classes, some students express their anger about not being able to go to their grandparent's funeral when they were younger or not being told about a pet's or a relative's death.

It is important for teachers to be honest and open when answering children's questions about death. If children are capable of asking a question, then they are capable of understanding an answer offered at the same level. If teachers avoid questions about death, then children often associate death with fear.[12] Sometimes teachers may not know the answer to a child's question. Instead of making up an answer, teachers should not hesitate to say "I don't know, but I will try to find an answer for you." As soon as the answer is obtained, it is important to relay that information to the students.

When teachers are answering students' questions, it is important to be as factual as possible. For instance, if a student asks, "What makes people die?" an appropriate response might be, "A person's heart stops beating." Although this seems concrete, it is important to remember that most elementary students are concrete thinkers.

If a teacher does not understand a question, it may help to refer the question back to the child. For instance, if a child asks, "Do children die?" it might be a good idea to find out what the child thinks and why he or she asked the question. The teacher might respond by asking, "Do you think children die?" or "What made you ask that question?" The responses to these questions may give the teacher more information and provide a framework to best answer the question.

Avoid Providing Personal Values on Controversial Issues Related to Death   Parents become uncomfortable when teachers voice their views on controversial issues related to death. For instance, a teacher should not suggest that dead people go to heaven, that euthanasia should be legalized, or that reincarnation is possible. These are values that should be discussed within the family unit. Dying, death, and grief education should focus on facts and feelings surrounding grief and death, and not on a teacher's values. Children, however, will ask teachers their opinions about value-related issues, such as, "What happens to people when they die?" The safest way for a teacher to respond to that question is to simply state, "There are many ideas about what happens to people when they die, and the best thing to do is ask your parents what their beliefs are about this question." Because there are numerous religious viewpoints about death, it is important for teachers not to promote any one viewpoint. Remember, teachers should not impose their philosophy of death on children, no matter how comforting they think it may be.[13]

Be an Especially Good and Supportive Listener when Children are Discussing their Feelings about Death   Many children will have already experienced the death of a pet or a relative by the time they reach elementary school, but may not have been given the opportunity to express their feelings about death. During a death education unit, many children want the opportunity to express their feelings about the death of someone they knew. It is important for teachers to listen and encourage the sharing of feelings so that students understand that other classmates have felt the same way in similar situations. It is also acceptable for teachers to share their feelings about grief that they have experienced.

Students need to be listened to when someone close to them dies.

Ask Children to Explain What They Have Learned about Death during Class Because the developmental attributes of young children are consistent with concrete thinking, adults tend to use metaphorical explanations about death. It is important to ask students to explain what they have learned about death during class. Many teachers do not realize they are using metaphors or euphemistic language and can innocently confuse children. For example, if a euphemism such as *gone away* is used instead of *died,* children may view death as a person leaving for a while.

Sentence stems can be used at the end of a lesson to summarize what each student has learned. Sentence stems include:

> I learned . . .
>
> I was surprised . . .
>
> I feel . . .

The Teacher's Role when a Student or a Student's Relative Is Dying or Dies

If a person teaches long enough, he or she will probably experience the death of a student or the death of a student's close relative such as a parent or sibling. Although it is best to teach death education before a death occurs, sometimes this is not possible. Regardless of whether dying, death, and grief has been taught before a death occurs, several guidelines should be remembered when discussing the death of a classmate or the death of a classmate's relative with elementary and middle-level students.[14]

1. Teachers should be prepared to deal with a child in the class who is dying. For example, there may be frequent absences, or hair loss, due to therapeutic regimens. Children should participate in discussions of their feelings about dying as well as death. The class may vote to all wear hats and to get a special hat for the child who lost his or her hair through cancer treatment.
2. Teachers should feel comfortable in expressing their grief openly after the death of a child. When teachers share their grief with the class, students are able to see that it is acceptable to cry or feel sad. Many teachers are scared they will say something wrong or act inappropriately, but the most important thing to children is the sincere care and concern their teachers exhibit toward them.
3. Acknowledge and discuss guilt feelings. As mentioned previously, guilt is a common emotion felt by survivors of a loved one. A teacher can be helpful by acknowledging the guilt and helping children understand that the death was not their fault. It may be helpful for older elementary and middle-level students to write about their feelings if they are having a difficult time discussing them.
4. Encourage students to write personal sympathy cards to the parents or to a student who has had someone close to him or her die. This helps students

deal with their grief and it is also appreciated by the survivors. Teachers can instruct students to emphasize their fond memories of the deceased and their sorrow. Teachers can also ask students how they want to commemorate a student who has died. They may create a memorial book, collect money for a charitable donation, or plant a tree to help remember their friend.

5. Allow children to express their grief and sadness. Because grief always surfaces at some point, it is important for children to be "allowed" to grieve. Many times, adults tell children to "be brave" and "be strong," but this causes students to repress their grief. Because the school may be the only place that children are allowed to express their sadness, teachers should give the students time to openly express their feelings.
6. If a classmate dies, don't force a "typical" day on grieving students. It is important to still have structured and planned activities; however, part of the day should revolve around sharing feelings and discussing death. For example, students should help decide what to do with the "empty chair" and possessions of a classmate who dies. Some daily routines should be maintained because children may become agitated and disoriented when boundaries disappear in times of crisis.
7. Expect unusual behavior for several weeks or months after the death of a classmate or relative. Students may become aggressive, exhibit a lack of concentration, be withdrawn, have mood swings, become nervous, or experience headaches and nausea. These are normal behaviors for persons who are experiencing grief. If teachers are concerned about a student's excessive behavior, it is important to refer him or her to the school counselor.
8. Do not focus on the details of death. For example, it is not important to describe an automobile accident or a deteriorating disease to students. This may frighten the child needlessly and cause unwarranted stress.
9. In talking with students, use the words "dead" or "death." Avoid using phrases that soften the blow such as "went away" or "God took him." These phrases can be confusing and scary.
10. A touch can sometimes communicate more than words can to children who are experiencing grief. If it is appropriate, ask permission to give a child a hug.
11. Plan nonverbal activities to allow expressions of grief. For example, listening to music, drawing pictures, and writing journal entries allows nonverbal students an opportunity to express grief.[15]

These guidelines can help teachers who are faced with the death of a student or a student's relative. If teachers have other concerns, funeral directors and school counselors are typically good resources on how to deal with children after a death has occurred.

ACTIVITIES

Death, Dying, and Grief Awareness Activities

Death and Dying

Several activities can be conducted with elementary and middle-level students to give them a better understanding of death and the emotions that surround death. All of these activities can be conducted with a variety of age groups with minor modifications to make them developmentally appropriate. Following are some of those activities and a selection of children's books that include a death theme.

Teachable Moment/Magic Circle

Although teachers do not know when they will be able to use this activity, this lesson should be prepared in advance. This activity can take place when a class pet dies, a student's pet dies, or a prominent public figure dies. When conducting this activity, have the class sit in one circle so that every student can make eye contact with his or her classmates. Prepare discussion questions that are appropriate to the age of students and how attached students were to the animal or person who died. This is a good opportunity for teachers to allow students to express their feelings, to ask questions, and to clarify any misconceptions students may have about death. Many teachers are scared to do an activity like this because they feel students will not want to express their feelings about death. In fact, most students are eager to talk because they have not been given this opportunity at any other time.

Students have an opportunity to discuss their feelings about death in the magic circle.

Memory Book

The Memory Book activity can be used as a class activity if a class pet or a classmate dies. Adults and children can find comfort and sometimes even pleasure in sharing memories of the deceased. Memories reaffirm that the people and pets we loved go on living in our minds and that they will always be an important part of who we are now and who we grow up to be. Provide students with a blank book made from pieces of construction paper stapled together. Then instruct students to write notes and draw pictures that remind them of the deceased. Have students share their memory book with the rest of the class. Encourage this as an individual project for students who recently experienced the death of a pet or a loved one.

Discovering Emotions

Early elementary students sometimes do not understand what emotions are and how people express them. To teach about emotions, show the class large pictures of people expressing different emotions such as happiness, sadness, anger, confusion, excitement, and shock. Ask students to describe what each person is feeling, and to explain how they know that the people feel that way. For example, a student may look at a picture and say, "He is happy because he is smiling." After the class has identified all of the emotions shown in the pictures, ask students to think of examples of when people might express these emotions. Many times, death will be mentioned as a time when a person might feel sad, angry, or shocked. If a student does bring up the topic of death, continue the discussion about why people are sad or angry when a person or pet dies. Also ask them if they have ever felt that way before. Even if death is not mentioned, students need to understand these emotions when death is discussed in the future.

An additional project for younger elementary students is to have them to cut out pictures of people in magazines who are displaying different emotions, or write a story about a specific emotion. Have them share their projects with the rest of the class. Have upper-elementary and middle-level students role-play situations in which people may feel different emotions, and brainstorm ways that people can react to or help someone who is feeling sad, angry, or depressed. Again, many students will associate sadness or depression with death.

Body Systems

When older elementary students are learning about the body systems, it is important to discuss how to keep the body systems healthy and appropriate to discuss some diseases associated with those systems. Explain further that sometimes there are no cures for diseases, and that people can die from them. Then discuss feelings and issues related to death.

Alive versus Dead

Many early elementary students have a difficult time knowing the difference between the concepts *alive* and *dead,* and distinguishing what will and can die. Discuss the characteristics of living and nonliving things with students and then instruct them to make a collage of things that live and die. Plant seeds and nonliving things, such as a rock, and then compare the results. Students can see from this experiment that some things are not living, cannot grow, and, therefore, cannot die.

Life Cycle

It is important for early elementary students to understand that living things go through a life cycle. Bring in plants in different stages to demonstrate a life cycle, such as buds, seeds, dried flowers, leaves, and dead plants. If there is a class pet, discuss the life cycle information for each animal with the class. Ask older elementary and middle-level students to diagram the life cycle of a plant or animal for an art project.

Planning a Funeral

Many students have questions about funerals, wakes, and other types of services associated with death. Explain the purpose and procedure of these services to the class, and then allow students to discuss their experiences of these services with the rest of the class. If a class pet dies, students may want to plan a funeral for it, but it should be a generic service without any specific religious affiliations. An appropriate focus for the service would be to allow students to share memories of the class pet with one another. The program may include a song performed by a group of students, memory sharing, the burial, and another music selection.

Survey Family Members

Ask older children to survey their family members regarding their cultural traditions and family practices for commemorating death. Have students then share what they learned with the rest of the class. It is important to inform the administrator about this activity, because religious traditions may be discussed by the students.

Sentence Stems

When discussing death and dying with upper-elementary students, use sentence stems, which are a good way to get students to express their feelings about death. Write the following sentence stems on the chalkboard or on newsprint and ask the students to complete them:

> Death is like . . .
> A good thing about death is . . .
> The scariest thing about death is . . .
> When someone dies, I usually feel . . .
> A bad thing about death is . . .

After students complete their sentences, ask students to share them with the rest of the class. These statements can act as a springboard for discussing some of the issues and feelings related to death.

Children's Literature with a Dying, Death, or Grief Theme

Numerous children's books have a death theme that can be used to teach about dying, death, and grief. Some of these books can be used to teach an entire lesson on dying, death, and grief, while others would be more appropriately used to reinforce or support a lesson. For instance, before introducing the memory book activity to students, it would be appropriate to read a book that discussed the importance of memories during the grieving process.

When reading a children's book with a dying, death, or grief theme, the teacher should pause and ask questions. For instance, it would be appropriate to ask students to describe how they think certain characters are feeling or how they would feel in that same situation. This gives students the opportunity to identify with the characters.

Some books may not be ideal to read to an entire class, but they still are good books. Teachers should make these books available to students to read during free time. Some dying, death, and grief books may not be appealing to the teacher, but it should be remembered that the books are written to respond to the developmental needs of the students. For instance, some dying, death, and grief books describe what a dead animal looks like. Some teachers might find this disgusting and, consequently, not make this book available to their classes. When you listen to young children describe a dead animal, however, they typically describe it in a "disgusting" way. Although teachers might not relate to the book, their students might. Before reading a children's book with a dying, death, or grief theme to the class, teachers should evaluate the book to make sure the information is presented appropriately. For instance, a book may describe death as a sleeplike state, or it may discuss heaven and God. Teachers need to be sure that the information that is being presented is accurate and also avoids controversial issues.

A list of several children's books that have a death theme is included after the Suggested Readings at the end of this chapter. Teachers can go to their local public library to find these and other children's books that have a death theme.

SUMMARY

Dying, death, and grief education is an important topic to be included in the elementary and middle-level health-education curriculum because, in many cases, school is the only place where children can ask questions and discuss the topic freely. Many parents do not know how to discuss these topics with their children, or they feel uncomfortable in doing so. This lack of information can increase children's fears and misconceptions about aging and death.

Teachers should have some background information about dying, death, and grief before they begin teaching it. Children go through three developmental stages of understanding death. Children in Stage One do not understand that death is final, but instead view it as a sleeplike state. Children in Stage Two understand that death is final, but personify death as a "bogeyman" or "death man." Children in Stage Three understand that death is final and inevitable.

Adults and children also typically experience stages of grief following a death. Stage One includes feelings of denial, shock, and disbelief and generally lasts up to 2 weeks. Survivors in Stage Two experience feelings of despair, numbness, and apathy for up to 12 to 15 months after a death. Recovery and resolution characterize the third stage of grief. Children should be allowed and encouraged to grieve, and should be provided extra support after the death of a loved one.

It is also important for children to understand the stages that a terminally ill person may experience. Although many dying patients go through all of these stages, many go through only some of these stages, and not necessarily in order. The stages of dying are denial, anger, bargaining, depression, and acceptance.

Teachers should understand why it is important to include dying, death, and grief in the elementary and middle-level curriculum. Reasons include changes in how society and the family are involved in and view illness, dying, death, and funerals; the inaccurate media portrayal of death; the increased risk of suicide with young people; the effect of technology on dying and death; and because all students deserve an opportunity to learn about death and dying.

Several guidelines are important to remember when teaching a controversial topic such as dying, death, and grief. First, be honest with students when presenting information or answering questions about death. Second, avoid providing personal values on controversial issues related to death. Third, be a good listener when students are discussing their feelings about death. Fourth, make sure students summarize the death and dying information presented in class.

There also are several guidelines to remember when a student or a student's relative dies. First, be prepared to deal with a child in the class who is dying. Second, feel comfortable in expressing grief after a death. Third, acknowledge and discuss guilt feelings. Fourth, encourage students to write personal sympathy cards to the survivors. Fifth, allow children to express their grief and sadness. Sixth, don't force a "typical" day on grieving students. Seventh, expect unusual behavior from students for several weeks or months after a death. Eighth, do not focus on the details of the death. Ninth, use concrete terms such as "dead" or "death" with students. Tenth, if appropriate, ask permission to give a child a hug. Lastly, plan nonverbal activities to allow expressions of grief. These guidelines can help teachers when faced with the death of a classmate or a classmate's relative. If teachers have other concerns, funeral directors and school counselors are typically good resources on how to deal with children after a death has occurred.

There are several activities to use with elementary and middle-level students to help them understand the issues and the feelings associated with aging, dying, and death. Children's literature with a death theme can be incorporated into many lessons to help children better understand dying and death.

DISCUSSION QUESTIONS

1. Why should dying, death, and grief education be included in an elementary and middle-level health-education curriculum?

2. Describe the three developmental stages of understanding death.

3. List and describe the three stages of grief that adults typically experience with the loss of a loved one.

4. Do children and adults grieve differently? If so, what are those differences?

5. Why is it important to teach children about the stages of dying?

6. What are the stages of dying?

7. What are some reasons to include death and dying education in the elementary and middle-level school curriculum?

8. What are some of your fears about teaching death and dying, and how can those fears be eliminated?

9. What are some guidelines to follow when teaching about death and dying?

10. What are some guidelines to follow with elementary and middle-level students when discussing the death of a classmate or the death of a classmate's relative?

11. Describe several activities that can be used when teaching about death and dying.

12. What are some children's books that have a death theme, and how can they be incorporated into a death and dying unit?

ENDNOTES

1. V. Clay, "Children Deal with Death," *The School Counselor* 23, no. 3 (1976).

2. M. Nagy, "The Child's View of Death," *Journal of Genetic Psychology* 73 (1948).

3. G. Fulton and E. Metress, *Perspectives on Death and Dying* (Boston, MA: Jones and Bartlett, 1995).

4. J. R. Averill, "Grief: Its Nature and Significance," *Psychological Bulletin* 70 (1968).

5. J. Eddy and A. Wesley, *Death Education* (St. Louis, MO: C.V. Mosby, 1983); R. Schulz and D. Aderman, "Clinical Research and Stages of Dying," *Omega* 5 (1973).

6. American Hospice Foundation, *Grief at School: A Guide for Teachers and Counselors* (Washington, DC: American Hospice Foundation, 1996).

7. J. Oaks and D. Bibeau, "Death Education: Educating Children for Living," *The Clearinghouse* 60 (1987).

8. E. Kübler-Ross, *On Death and Dying* (New York: Macmillan, 1969).

9. Kübler-Ross, *On Death and Dying*.

10. Fulton and Metress, *Perspectives on Death and Dying*.

11. E. Schneidman, "You and Death," *Psychology Today* 5, no. 1 (1971).

12. J. Ketchel, "Helping the Young Child Cope with Death," *Day Care and Early Education* (Winter 1986).

13. American Hospice Foundation, *Grief at School: A Guide for Teachers and Counselors*.

14. W. Yarber, "Where's Johnny Today?: Explaining the Death of a Classmate," *Health Education* 8, no. 1 (1977); C. Postel, "From My Perspective: Death in My Classroom," *Teaching Exceptional Children* (Winter 1986); S. Seibert, J. Drolet, and J. Fetro, *Are You Sad Too? Helping Children Deal With Loss and Death* (Santa Cruz, CA: ETR Associates, 1993), 105–109.

15. American Hospice Foundation, *Grief at School: A Guide for Teachers and Counselors*.

SUGGESTED READINGS

American Hospice Foundation. *Grief at School: A Guide for Teachers and Counselors*. Washington, DC: American Hospice Foundation, 1996.

Fulton, G., and E. Metress. *Perspectives on Death and Dying*. Boston, MA: Jones and Bartlett, 1995.

Gordon, A., and D. Klass. *They Need To Know: How To Teach Children about Death.* Englewood Cliffs, NJ: Prentice-Hall, 1985.

Kart, C. *The Realities of Aging: An Introduction to Gerontology.* Needham Heights, MA: Allyn & Bacon, 1994.

Ketchel, J. "Helping the Young Child Cope with Death." *Day Care and Early Education* (Winter 1986).

Kübler-Ross, E. *On Death and Dying.* New York: Macmillan, 1969.

Leming, M., and G. Dickinson. *Understanding Dying, Death, and Bereavement.* Fort Worth, TX: Harcourt Brace College Publishers, 1994.

Lomardo, V., and F. Lomardo. *Kids Grieve Too.* Springfield, IL: Charles C. Thomas, 1986.

McGuire, S. "Aging Education in Schools." *Journal of School Health* 57, no. 5 (1987): 174–176.

Nelson, R., and B. Crawford. "Suicide Among Elementary School-Age Children." *Elementary School Guidance and Counseling* 25 (1990).

Rofes, E. *The Kids Book about Death and Dying.* Boston: Little, Brown, 1985.

Seibert, S., J. Drolet, and J. Fetro. *Are You Sad Too? Helping Children Deal With Loss and Death.* Santa Cruz, CA: ETR Associates, 1993.

Sternberg, F., and B. Sternberg. *If I Die and When I Do: Exploring Death with Young People.* Englewood Cliffs, NJ: Prentice-Hall, 1980.

Wass, H., and C. Corr, eds. *Helping Children Cope with Death: Guidelines and Resources.* New York: Hemisphere Publishing, 1984.

Woodard, N. "Helping Children Cope with Death: The Role Educators Can Play." *Journal of Health Education* 28 (1997).

CHILDREN'S LITERATURE WITH A DEATH, DYING, OR GRIEF THEME

Grades K–2

Aliki. *The Two of Them.* Greenwillow, 1979.

Buscaglia, Leo. *The Fall of Freddie the Leaf.* Henry Holt, 1982.

Carick, C., and D. Carick. *The Accident.* Seabury Press, 1976.

Clifton, L. *Everette Anderson's Goodbye.* Holt, Rinehart, and Winston, 1973. (Multicultural)

Cohen, M. *Jim's Dog Muffin.* Greenwillow, 1984.

Fox, Mem. *Tough Boris.* Harcourt Brace, 1994.

Fox, Mem. *Sophie.* Harcourt Brace, 1989. (Parent's Choice Honor) (Multicultural)

Powell, S. *Geranium Morning.* Carolrhoda, 1990.

Viorst, J. *The Tenth Good Thing about Barney.* Atheneum, 1971.

White, E. *Charlotte's Web.* Harper Junior Books, 1952.

Zalben, Jane. *Pearl's Marigolds for Grandpa.* Simon and Schuster, 1997.

Zolotow, Charlotte. *My Grandson Lew.* Harper & Row, 1974.

Grades 3–5

Bahr, Mary. *The Memory Box.* Albert Whitman, 1992.

Coleman, H. *Suddenly.* Morrow, 1987.

Ellis, S. *A Family Project.* McElderry, 1988.

Fox, Mem. *Wilfred Godon Mconald Partridge.* Kane Miller, 1985.

Mann, P. *There Are Two Kinds of Terrible.* Doubleday, 1977.

Munsch, R. *Love You Forever.* Firefly Books, 1989.

Patterson, K. *Bridge to Terabithia.* Avon Books, 1972.

Rylant, C. *Missing May.* Orchard Books, 1992.

Silverstein, S. *The Giving Tree.* Harper & Row, 1970.

Smith, Doris. *A Taste of Blackberries.* Crowell, 1972.

Thomas, J. *Saying Good-Bye to Grandma.* Ticknor and Fields, 1988.

White, E. B. *Charlotte's Web.* Harper, 1952.

Wild, M. *The Very Best Friends.* Harcourt Brace, 1989.

Wilhelm, H. *I'll Always Love You.* Crown Publishers, 1985.

Grades 6–8

Hesse, Karen. *Out of the Dust.* Scholastic, 1997. (Multicultural)

Creech, Sharon. *Walk Two Moons.* Harber Collins, 1998. (Newbery Medal)(Multicultural)

Rylant, Cynthis. *Missing May.* Orchard, 1992. (Multicultural)

INTERNET INFORMATION

DEATH, DYING, AND GRIEF WEBSITES

For additional information on dying, death, and grief education, please refer to the following website.

American Hospice Organization
http://www.americanhospice.org

PERSONAL HEALTH: A MATTER OF CONCERN TO ALL

O U T L I N E

CONCEPTS TO TEACH ABOUT PERSONAL HEALTH IN ELEMENTARY AND MIDDLE-LEVEL SCHOOLS

Grades K–2

- Demonstrate practices to keep the body clean,
- Know the importance of the senses,
- Know proper care of the eyes and teeth,
- Practice health measures that relate to disease prevention (i.e., hand washing, not sharing brushes or drinking cups, etc.),
- Explain procedures to protect the teeth from decay,
- Explain how a person is responsible for his or her well-being,
- Describe common childhood illnesses,

- Understand special adaptations of children with chronic conditions (i.e., asthma, diabetes, epilepsy),
- Demonstrate proper dental care,
- Explain the importance of regular health and dental check-ups,
- Identify resources in the community that relate to positive personal health (physicians, dentists, etc.),
- Practice care around chips of paint in old houses,
- Identify situations observed during school day in which health is a concern (asthma attack, diabetic shock, etc.), and
- Understand ways to improve and maintain positive personal health.

Grades 3–5

- Practice behaviors of good personal hygiene,
- Practice behaviors common to good dental hygiene,
- Understand the value of cleanliness and personal health,
- Be aware of signs of vision and hearing problems,
- Explain the relationship between personal hygiene and prevention of disease,
- Desire to have regular dental, medical, and visual examinations,
- Be familiar with growth differences common to preadolescence,
- Have knowledge of problems associated with asthma, diabetes, epilepsy, and other chronic conditions,
- Know the different types of teeth and their purposes,
- Be familiar with dangers associated with lead poisoning,
- Know basic facts about epilepsy, diabetes, and asthma,
- Use resources in the community that provide health information and services, and
- Be familiar with measures on how the body protects itself from disease.

Grades 6–8

- Identify physical changes of males and females during puberty,
- Identify reasons for having periodic examinations (dental, orthopaedic screening, physical examinations),
- Practice appropriate care of skin, nails, hair, etc.,
- Analyze environmental factors associated with lead poisoning,
- Identify health services and products available to middle-level school-age children,
- Outline a personal program to be healthy,
- Know symptoms of chronic diseases (asthma, diabetes, epilepsy, etc.),
- Explain various problems associated with dental health (caries, gum diseases, malocclusion),
- Identify community resources for providing positive personal health services, and
- Analyze influences on personal health decisions (family, peers, media).

INTRODUCTION

As we look in the mirror each day, the condition of our skin and teeth, and our overall level of physical fitness, are apparent. Our basic personality and the initial impressions we make on others are influenced by the status of our personal well-being.

Throughout life, each person invests significant effort in caring for personal health. Personal grooming involves making oneself presentable and attractive. Well-groomed individuals are clean and neat, and they exemplify poise and self-confidence. It is in the early childhood years, at elementary school age, that many personal health behavioral patterns are established. Although many such learning experiences take place in the home, children sometimes do not learn basic grooming patterns from their parents and families. Children need to be taught, encouraged, and reinforced about activities that establish and maintain a healthful personal appearance and lifestyle.

Some people believe that basic health is too personal a matter to discuss as part of an educational curriculum. They say that children are too embarrassed to discuss such matters publicly. However, elementary and middle-level schoolchildren have many questions and concerns about skin care, hair care, dental hygiene, and other personal health matters. Apart from the formal learning and experiences that take place in a health instructional program, children and young people often turn to other, less reliable sources of information, such as popular young people's magazines, product advertisements on radio and television, and peers.

The basic physical well-being of the body is referred to as *fitness*. There is much a person can do to maintain a high level of physical well-being, such as regular exercise, good dietary behavioral patterns, and cleanliness. Failure to take certain actions to maintain physical fitness can result in numerous chronic health problems later in life. There is increasing evidence that such chronic conditions as cardiovascular diseases, diabetes, malignancies, and arthritic problems may begin early in life.

Interplay with the surrounding environment is largely carried out by the activity of the various senses. Understanding personal health as it is related to sensory health promotion is important for elementary and middle-level schoolchildren. Sensory problems can interfere with learning, attention span, and other factors associated with the learning process.

A number of allergy-related problems can affect a schoolchild. One of the most prevalent is asthma. When left unattended, this condition can be most debilitating. Even small children must be aware of allergies and how their lives are affected.

Elementary and middle-school teachers need to understand all of these matters relating to personal health so that they will be better informed about the health conditions of their students. Much can be done in educational settings to help children develop good personal hygiene. Students should establish behavioral patterns early in life that they will practice through their adult years. Teaching about personal health in the elementary and middle-school curriculum should have not only immediate value, but positive lifelong effects. For these reasons, personal health is an important component of any comprehensive school health program.

THE INTEGUMENTARY SYSTEM

Our initial impression of a person is of his or her integumentary system, which includes the skin, the hair, the glands, and the nails. Much of one's self-concept, attitudes, and basic personal outlook on life are influenced by the appearance of these structures. When we rise in the morning, we prepare our skin and hair before we go out to encounter our world. We look for defects in the skin, such as pimples, dirt, cuts, bruises, and wrinkles. The length and appearance of our hair also have a major impact on overall presentation. Most people spend a significant amount of time, money, and effort caring for, and improving, the structures of this body system.

The integumentary system is the largest organ of the human body and is designed to carry out several important physiological functions. For example, the skin, nails, and hair protect the internal body systems.

Among children of school age, appearance has an important impact on social acceptance as well as their personal sense of self-identity. It is not unusual for an unkempt, dirty child to be rejected by classmates. All too often, this child is not looked upon favorably by the teachers either. Such children are often lonely and without friends, and they develop a serious lack of self-esteem.

The Skin

Human skin varies in thickness. For example, the eyelids are the thinnest of skin structures, while some of the thickest parts of the body are found on the soles of the feet and the palms of the hands.

Human skin contains three layers: epidermis, dermis, and hypodermis (figure 17.1). The epidermis, or outer layer, serves principally to protect the other layers. The epidermal layer consists of several rows of cells, all but the deepest of which are made up of dead cells, which are shed and replaced by additional new cells. This shedding of the top cell layer takes place continually, as we rub clothing against the skin, as we rub a towel over our body after showering, or as we simply rub our hands over a part of our body. Skin color is determined by varying amounts of the pigment *melanin,* which is found in the lower rows of the epidermis.

The dermis, or second layer of the skin, is deeper and much thicker than the epidermis. Blood vessels in the

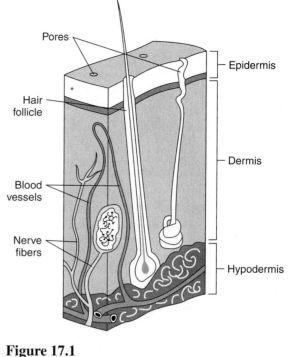

Figure 17.1
The skin.

dermis provide nourishment to the living cells of the epidermis, as well as to the dermal layer. These blood vessels also play an important role in regulating body temperature. Involuntary constriction or dilation of the vascular system in the skin's dermal layer occurs in certain circumstances. Constriction of these blood vessels causes the skin to pale—one of the most obvious signs of traumatic shock. Involuntary dilation of the dermal blood vessels also results in blushing, a reddening of the skin. Sensory nerve fibers are also found in the dermis. They provide the sensations of touch, pain, temperature, and pressure. Some areas of the body are more sensitive to touch, such as the palms of the hands and the lips. The hair follicles and sebaceous glands are also located in the dermal layer.

The third layer of the skin, and the deepest, is the hypodermis, which is often referred to as the subcutaneous layer. It is composed primarily of loose connective tissue and cells interlaced with blood vessels that bind the dermis to underlying structures of the body.

Purposes of the Skin

The skin has a variety of functions. The most obvious is its protective function against disease and external environmental factors. The skin keeps the numerous microorganisms that cause disease from entering the body. Only when the skin is cut or damaged can the organisms enter through the skin.

The skin plays an important role in regulation of body temperature. Body heat is generated from cellular metabolism. When there is increased body activity, particularly of the muscles, body temperature rises. This excess heat is released from the body through excretion and evaporation of sweat or by conduction of heat. Minute waste products are removed from the body through perspiration.

Another important function of the skin is as a receptor to external stimuli. The various sensations of hot, cold, pressure, touch, and pain are received through nerve receptors, called cutaneous receptors, which are located in the hypodermal layer of the skin.

Problems that Affect the Skin

A number of problems can affect the skin, particularly among elementary and middle-level schoolchildren. There are several communicable diseases of the skin that must be understood by the elementary and middle-level schoolteacher because they occur among young children and can easily spread at school.

Contact Dermatitis *Contact dermatitis* is an inflammation of the skin, usually the result of direct contact with substances that cause irritation. There are numerous substances to which a person might be sensitive: poison plants (ivy, sumac, oak), cosmetics, or perfumes. Contact dermatitis initially presents itself with a reddened skin, fluid-filled blisters, and itching and burning sensations. This skin problem is prevented by keeping the irritating substance away from the skin. However, once the irritation has occurred, it can be treated with various prescription and nonprescription medications that are applied to the skin. Antihistamines are sometimes prescribed to help relieve the pain and itching.

Bacterial Infection Staphylococcal bacteria infection of the hair follicles or sebaceous glands results in the formation of a *boil* or *carbuncle*. The basic difference between these two is that a carbuncle usually spreads into the subcutaneous tissues, whereas a closed boil does not spread. Infection can also enter the skin through a small wound or a break in the skin.

These bacteria multiply and grow in the glands or hair follicles. To counter this infection, the blood vessels bring blood serum and white blood cells to the infected area. Pus begins to drain from the core of the infection. The pus contains contagious bacteria, which is why one must use care in wiping the pus from a boil or carbuncle. One should not squeeze a boil or a carbuncle. This accumulation of pus can cause pain by placing pressure on the surrounding nerve endings.

Often, boils and carbuncles need to be opened by a physician to remove the pus. Healing occurs once the pus has been removed. Antibiotics can be helpful in treating this bacterial infection, and hot, moist applications are sometimes effective in causing the pus to dissipate more readily. However, school personnel are wise to encourage a child with a boil or carbuncle to see a physician.

Another skin disease of bacterial origin that is often seen among elementary and middle-level schoolchildren is *impetigo.* This contagious disease usually begins with small, itchy red spots. As the itching persists, impetigo is characterized by pustules that rupture and become covered with loosely held crusts and scabs. This condition is most commonly found around the mouth and on the hands. It can spread easily over other parts of the body when another person comes into contact with the infected individual or with articles of clothing worn by a person with impetigo. Because of its communicable nature, students with impetigo must be removed from school until a physician assures that they are no longer contagious. Usually this disease will heal within 2 to 3 weeks without leaving scarring.

Medical care is necessary in most impetigo cases. Antibiotics are useful in countering the infection, and antihistamines relieve the itching. If left medically untreated, impetigo is likely to spread to other areas of the skin as well as to other people.

Viral Infections Viral infection of the skin results in a variety of problems. For example, warts are a common viral infection caused by the human papillomavirus

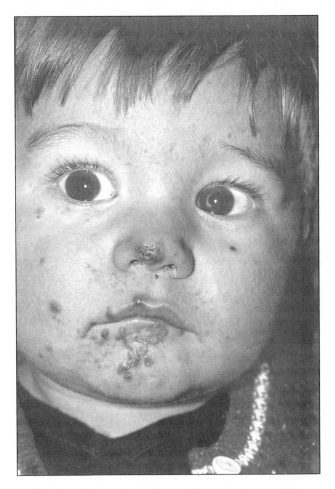

Impetigo is a highly contagious skin infection often observed among elementary schoolchildren.

(HPV). They can appear on any part of the body but are usually found on the hands, fingers, feet, or genital organs. The HPV is a hardy virus; over sixty different types have been identified. When located on the soles of the feet, they are referred to as *plantar warts*. Warts come in a variety of different shapes and sizes. Some are flat, while others are cone-shaped. They appear as firm papules—small, hard, elevated, cone-shaped structures with rough surfaces—and can spread easily through contact with another person.

It is interesting to note that the viruses that cause warts can be found in cells of the epidermal layer of the skin. They cause a problem only when they infect the deeper layers. Two-thirds of warts spontaneously regress over a period of time, usually up to 2 years.[1] Treatment of warts involves surgical removal by physicians. X-ray treatment and laser are also useful in removal. In addition, there are some effective over-the-counter, nonprescription medications for warts.

Warts tend to recur in some persons. For this reason, medical treatment, not home remedies, should be obtained.

Skin Rash *Eczema* is a skin rash that is noncontagious. It is chronic and is often associated with allergies. Substances to which an individual becomes sensitive cause the inflammation. The student with eczema usually has a red skin rash, blisters, pimples, and scaling and crusting of the skin. Curing this condition is difficult, because the cause must be identified and treated many times before the skin problems can be eliminated.

Fungal Infections *Ringworm* refers to several different kinds of skin diseases caused by fungi. Common ringworm noted among elementary and middle-level schoolchildren first appears as a small red area on the skin. As it becomes larger, the inside of the area clears. The surrounding ring takes on a red, scaly appearance. Ringworm is very infectious; however, it is usually easy to

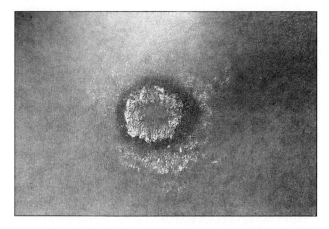

Ringworm first appears as a small red area on the skin, which progresses to a red, scaly ring with a clear center.

identify and can be treated effectively with fungicidal compounds obtained from a physician.

Ringworm is found on the hairy parts of the body in children. This is a particular concern in schools when ringworm is found on the scalp of students who share caps and other types of clothing.

Another type of ringworm found among schoolchildren is *athlete's foot.* This infection is usually located on the skin between the toes and the soles of the feet and results in itching and cracked and scaly skin. It often results from failure to maintain clean and dry skin between the toes after bathing, swimming, or participating in activities that cause wet feet.

Insects *Pediculosis,* or lice infestation, is a condition caused by small parasitic insects. These insects, called *lice,* are about the size of a sesame seed and feed by sucking blood. They can cause numerous problems for schoolchildren. They tend to be without wings, have a flattened, almost transparent body, attach themselves to hair, and are able to pierce the skin and draw blood. The lice that affect people are not transmitted by animals. Although everyone can be affected by lice, females between the ages of 5 and 12 are most commonly affected.

There are three different types of human lice: body lice, pubic lice, and head lice. Body lice are relatively rare. They lay their eggs in clothing and only come into direct body contact to feed. Body lice are easier to treat than head lice. Bathing with soap and water will usually remove these lice from the skin. Washing clothing in hot water that is at least 131 degrees Fahrenheit will kill body lice.

Pubic lice infest mainly the pubic hair, although they can be found on short, coarse hair on other parts of the body, such as the armpits or eyelids. This type of lice is usually transmitted through sexual contact and can live only about 48 hours without a host.

The most prevalent type of lice found on schoolchildren is head lice. Millions of schoolchildren get head lice each year, with the 5- to 12-year-old age group being most commonly affected. Lice infestation is a major contributor to school absenteeism among elementary and middle-level schoolchildren. The National Pediculosis Association recommends that children should be screened for head lice three times each school year: the first week of school in the fall, the week following the Christmas/New Years break, and near the end of the school year.[2]

Adult lice lay oval eggs called *nits*. The lice attach their eggs to the hair shaft close to the scalp. The nits hatch in a period of about a week. Full-grown lice result in about 18 days.

Head lice, which are transmitted by direct contact (they do not fly, leap, or jump from person to person), are diagnosed by identifying either the adult lice or nits (eggs) in the hair. The lice have a short, flattened body

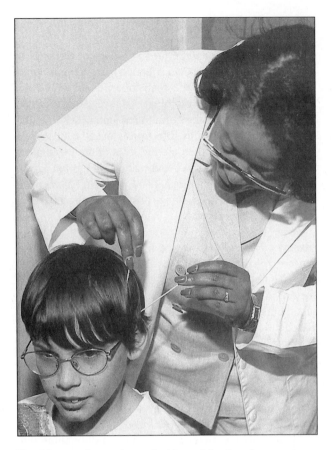

Head lice are the most prevalent type of lice found on schoolchildren. The school nurse must often examine children for the presence of head lice.

and are capable of living anywhere on the human scalp. Nits are very small, are a pearly white color, and attach firmly to the hair shaft close to the scalp. They are easy to see and are prevalent at the nape of the neck and behind the ears.

Adult head lice are killed by washing with a medicated shampoo called a pediculicide. There are both prescription and over-the-counter medications available that provide effective treatment. There is increasing evidence that head lice are developing a tolerance and resistance to some of the pediculocidal treatments, particularly the over-the-counter preparations.

After the hair is dried, special nit combs should be used to remove the nits. This entire procedure should be repeated in a week or 10 days.

Current research has shown that olive oil can be used to treat head lice. It smothers and kills the active head lice and also makes nit removal easier. Olive oil kills the lice by covering holes through which the lice breathe.

The most effective way to prevent the development of lice is to maintain body and hair cleanliness. It must be understood that any child can get lice. In many instances in which students must share lockers at school, lice can spread. Since body lice lay their eggs in clothing, children should not use another child's hat, coat, or garment.

Children at school often need to be inspected for the presence of lice.

Special measures are necessary to clean objects that have been in contact with lice. Personal clothing, bedding, and towels need to be washed in very hot water and dried with a hot iron. Combs, brushes, and other objects that have been in contact with lice and the nits should be soaked in shampoo for lice or in a pan of hot water (150 degrees F) for at least 10 minutes. Hats and clothing that cannot be washed should be dry cleaned.

Acne   When the pores of the skin or the sebaceous glands become blocked, *acne* develops. Since the glandular openings become clogged, the oil secretions cannot escape. Clogging of the sebaceous glands occurs when normal drainage of the oil substance, sebum, is interrupted by dirt, bacteria, dead skin cells, and physical clothing that fits tightly over the skin. The gland then swells and becomes infected. This results in the formation of pimples, blackheads, and whiteheads. Adolescents often refer to these as "zits."

Acne is most likely to occur on the skin of the face, the neck, the shoulders, the chest, and the back. The exact cause of this clogging process is not known. There seem to be several contributing factors. Certain cosmetics may aggravate acne. In addition, bacteria plays a role in the inflammation process. Increased levels of the male sex hormones increase activity of the sebaceous glands. There is also some evidence that stress increases sebaceous gland activity and so affects the development of acne.

Acne is not caused by eating greasy foods or chocolate. However, eating a balanced diet is considered an effective preventative measure. The physiological developments of adolescence, the increased activity of the oil glands, as well as changes in the outer layer of skin, make this age group more susceptible to acne.

In some instances, large abscesses form in the skin. These should be treated by a physician. Because of the destruction of surrounding tissue, scarring often results.

Most dermatologists suggest that it is important to keep the skin clean with frequent washing with soap and water. There is some evidence that balanced eating patterns can help relieve serious cases of acne. For serious cases of acne, antibiotics can be helpful in controlling the condition. Tetracycline, an antibiotic prescribed by physicians, is one such drug. Females need to be informed that vaginal yeast problems can accompany antibiotic treatment for acne. Accutane is another effective drug; however, this drug has several potentially dangerous side effects that make it a less than perfect solution to acne.

Care of the Skin

Care of the skin is very important for everyone, particularly elementary and middle-level schoolchildren. Good grooming starts with cleanliness. Basic cleansing of the body will keep the pores and glands clean. Daily cleanliness—washing with soap and water—removes dirt, oil, and other substances on the skin. Special lotions, cosmetics, and creams are not needed. All too often these substances, which are marketed as having special cleaning agents, cause irritation. In addition, they contain substances that can cause clogging of the pores.

Eating a balanced diet is important for healthy skin care. For example, a change in hair texture may result from vitamin deficiency.

Injury to the Skin

Injury to the skin can require emergency first-aid care, and in many instances, medical care. Among elementary and middle-level schoolchildren, injuries that result from exposure to heat or cold are a special concern.

Heat   Burning of the skin results from exposure to hot items such as flames or hot moisture, or from touching hot structures such as irons, stoves, or furnaces. Burns are classified as first degree, second degree, and third degree, depending on the depth of the injury. A *first-degree burn* occurs when the injury causes a reddening of the epidermal layer of the skin. This type of burn does not lead to tissue damage, but can be rather painful. This is because nerve endings are present in the layer of skin that is burned.

When the burn results in a blistering of the epidermal layer of skin, a *second-degree burn* is present. With this type of burn, it is important not to puncture the blister and permit dirt and other contaminants to enter the wound. Infection can result.

A *third-degree burn* occurs when exposure to heat damages the underlying structures in the dermal layer of the skin. This type of burn is particularly dangerous in that contamination and infection often occur. This leads to the need for long-term care. Damage to surrounding tissue may cause lasting scarring of the skin.

The basic emergency care procedure for burns involves immersing the burned part of the skin in cold water. Care must be taken to cover any breaks in the skin resulting from the burns so as to protect against the spread of infection.

Cold   Exposure to an extremely cold environment can damage the skin. The principal damage is called *frostbite*. When exposed to particularly low temperatures, the body's blood circulation is reduced in the affected skin areas. This lack of blood results in damage to the skin. The appropriate first-aid measure for frostbite involves warming the frostbitten part of the body as quickly as possible. Care must be taken not to immerse the body part in hot water—high temperatures can cause burning. It is important not to rub frostbitten skin in an attempt to stimulate blood flow to the area. Rubbing can cause further damage to the affected skin.

CONSIDER THIS

1. Brushing the hair stimulates circulation of blood to the scalp.
2. Brushing the hair distributes natural oils over the hair, keeping it from drying out.
3. Brushing the hair removes dirt from the hair.

Related Structures

Hair, nails, and certain glands are a part of the integumentary system and come from the epidermal layer of the skin.

Hair

Human hair is found principally on the scalp, the face, the pubic area, and the extremities. The basic purpose of human hair is protection. For example, hair on the head provides protection against sunlight and extreme cold. Eyelashes and hair in the nostrils protect against airborne microorganisms and external particles. Body hair on the skin assists in regulation of body temperature.

Each human hair consists of a shaft, a root, and a bulb. The shape of the hair shaft determines whether hair is curly, straight, or wavy. Hair from a round shaft is straight; the flatter the shaft, the curlier the hair. Nutrients are received from the dermal blood vessels within the bulb.

Dried, dead epidermal layer cells are shed by the scalp. The dead cells clump into white flakes and are often present in the hair as *dandruff*. Dandruff is unsightly and is considered by many a sign of uncleanliness, and can be seen on the affected person's clothing. Keeping the hair clean and well groomed is the main way to eliminate dandruff. Personal care of the hair involves several actions. See the Consider This box above.

Nails

On each finger and toe is a nail, a hardened structure that originates from live roots within the inner epidermal layers. The fingernails and toenails protect the fingers and toes; fingernails help one to grasp objects.

Care of the nails is important. Dirty, unkempt nails indicate poor personal hygiene. Many people chew their fingernails while experiencing stress and tension. The status of the nails also indicates other basic health conditions. For example, persons suffering from nutritional deficiencies often have split nails. A nail that appears pinkish indicates rich vascular capillaries beneath the nail, a sign of good health. Nails should be cleaned regularly and kept free of dirt. The soft skin at the base and sides of the nails, the cuticle, needs to be kept soft and pushed away from the nail.

Both fingernails and toenails need to be trimmed periodically. Toenails should be trimmed by cutting straight

(continued on page 311)

ACTIVITIES

Skin Care

Following are activities that can be incorporated to teach skin care concepts.

- To teach students about the various kinds of hair, have each student remove a couple of hairs from his or her scalp and examine them under a microscope. Look at the shape of the shaft of the hair. Discuss this as it relates to the structure of the individual's hair.

- Draw a family tree as far back as possible, noting the type of hair each family member had. Obtain this information by talking with family members about their parents, grandparents, and so on, or by looking at old family photographs. (Take into account that some students may have problems with this activity due to being adopted, living with stepparents, etc.) Take particular note of the structure of the hair—curly, straight, wavy; the color of the hair—blond, brown, black, and so on.

- Teach the effects of different kinds of washing procedures on the removal of dirt. Have the students immerse their hands in:
  a. a pail of mud.
  b. a pan of dirt and oil.
  c. a plate covered with fat and grease from bacon.

Then provide different washing combinations for the students to wash their hands. Wash the hands with:
  a. plain tap water.
  b. water and hair shampoo.
  c. water and soap (soft soap).
  d. water and laundry soap (hard soap).

Discuss the effectiveness of each procedure. Let the students draw appropriate conclusions.

Note: The wisdom of handwashing activities cannot be overstated. However, many schools will not reinforce classroom lessons with behavioral practices. Lessons should be followed up with handwashing reinforcement following trips to restrooms and prior to snack and lunch time. Also, some schools have spring-loaded spigots that will not allow children to use soap and manage rinsing in an appropriate time.

- Conduct a discussion of such questions as:
  a. Why is there no pain when you cut your nails?
  b. Why do some people have curly hair and others have straight hair?
  c. What are appropriate measures to protect against the spread of lice?

- Teachers of primary students should take students on "field trips" to the rest room to reinforce appropriate behaviors. Whether visiting male or female rest rooms, emphasize respect for privacy, flushing protocol, hand washing using soap, and disposal of paper products.

- Cross-age tutoring suggestions:
  a. Have older children develop posters about hand washing for display in rest rooms and cafeterias.
  b. Have students develop public service announcements about hand washing for morning announcements.
  c. Have older children develop maps of all handwashing areas in the school and share their maps in sessions with primary-grade students.
  d. Have middle-level schoolchildren (in other buildings) prepare transitional resource materials and pair in "buddy" or mentorship activities with counterparts in the upper-elementary grades.

- Assign children to work with a partner to develop a plan, through a drawing, for the appropriate storage of personal possessions at school (coats, hats, boots, scarves, gloves, etc.) and present these drawings to the class.

across to prevent nails from growing into the soft cuticles. This prevents damage to the skin, which can occur if the nail is rounded.

Glands

There are three kinds of skin glands: sebaceous (oil glands), sudoriferous (sweat glands), and ceruminous glands. The sebaceous glands are connected to hair follicles and secrete a substance (sebum) that lubricates the hair, preventing it from becoming brittle and splitting. This oily substance also keeps the skin from becoming too dry. Blockage of these glands can result in infection, the basic physiological process that creates acne. Because sex hormones regulate the production and secretion of sebum, hyperactivity of these glands can result in acne.

The sweat glands secrete perspiration onto the surface of the skin. This process is important as a cooling mechanism of the body and as a regulator of body temperature. Cooling is accomplished by evaporation of the sweat, and is important in preventing heat-related problems. Certain wastes are excreted in this manner. Sweat glands are found in greatest abundance on the palms of the hands and the forehead.

The ceruminous glands are found in the ear canal, where they secrete cerumen, or earwax, which keeps the eardrum from drying out. Excessive buildup of cerumen in the ear canal can diminish hearing.

THE SENSES

Human beings interact with their environment, both external and internal, through the activities of the various sensory organs. These organs are an extension of the nervous system. Various sensory stimuli are picked up by receptors in these organs and are transmitted by way of the nervous system to the brain, where the sensations are interpreted. Numerous sensations are identified in this way: touch, sight, hearing, smell, and taste.

1. *Touch.* The receptors for sensations of touch are located in the skin. Various sensations such as tickling, heat, cold, and pain are commonly identified by most schoolchildren. There are two different kinds of receptors: tactile receptors and pressure receptors. The tactile receptors generally respond to light touch, while the pressure receptors respond to deeper touch.

2. *Sight.* The receptors for sensations of sight are located in the eyeball. These receptors are the rods and cones. The cones identify different colors, while the rods indicate white and black colors. As light rays enter the eye, they come to focus on the retina, where the rods and cones are located. From here the nerve impulses are transmitted to the brain by the optic nerve. (The structure of the eye is discussed in detail in chapter 2.)

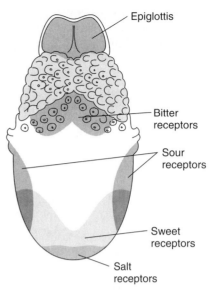

Figure 17.2
Pattern of taste receptors on the tongue.

3. *Sound.* Sound waves are transmitted through the outer and middle ears to the inner ear. Here, the impulses are picked up by the cochlea and transmitted to the brain. (Hearing and the structure of the ear are discussed in detail in chapter 2.)

4. *Smell.* The receptors of smell are known as the olfactory receptors, and are located on both sides of the roof of the nasal cavity. The olfactory system is used principally for detecting the presence of odors in our environment.

5. *Taste.* The receptors for the sensations of taste are located on the tongue (figure 17.2). Four types of taste are identified by humans: sour, bitter, salty, and sweet. The receptors are located in particular regions of the tongue: sourness (on the sides of the tongue), bitterness (at the back of the tongue), saltiness (over various parts of the tongue), and sweetness (at the tip of the tongue). These taste buds respond to chemical stimuli and transmit the sense of taste to the cortex of the brain, where interpretation is made.

The Senses and the Elementary Health Curriculum

Human beings depend on the sensory system to gather information about their environment. Children, particularly preschool and primary-grade children, need to receive instruction about these five senses of the human body. They need to understand the meaning, uses, and purposes of the various information that the sensory system can provide to a person. Young children may not understand the importance of the senses in everyday activities; however, they can be taught that the senses are helpful to us in a variety of ways.

ACTIVITIES

The Senses

Following are activities that will help students learn about the senses.

Sense of Taste

- Introduce children to the appearance and structure of the tongue. Have them look closely at the tongue with a small mirror. Discussion can follow as to which part of the tongue is the location of the taste buds for sweet, sour, salty, and bitter. Then have the children draw a picture of the tongue on a sheet of paper and outline the locations of the receptors for each sense of taste.

- Have the children identify the different types of taste sensations by bringing several different kinds of foods to class. Make paper plates available with the words *salty, sour, sweet,* and *bitter* written on them. Have the students sample the food and indicate which taste they perceive. Place the food on the appropriate paper plate based on the predominant taste.

Sense of Touch

- Help students become familiar with the texture of several different types of objects through the sense of touch. Present several objects having the characteristics of smoothness, roughness, scratchiness, hardness, softness, and so on. Have the students brush the various objects against their skin on various parts of their body. Then encourage discussion of what the students feel.

- Children should learn to identify different types of texture by the sense of touch without seeing the object. Place a number of objects in sacks. Have the students reach in, find, and present to the teacher specific objects, such as a hard object, a smooth object, a rough object, and so on. This exercise encourages and develops the sense of touch without seeing what one is handling.

Sense of Smell

- Present several objects with different odors in boxes or in bags to the students. (Squirt bottles used for condiments in restaurants work well for this activity.) Have the students describe the smell—is it good, bad, appetizing, terrible, or what? What words do they use to describe each odor? Examples of objects that can be used are flowers, a fish, a medicine, gasoline, and various kinds of foods.

Sense of Sound

- To encourage the students to be aware of the many kinds of sounds in the environment, have them sit quietly for a brief period of time, about 2 to 3 minutes. Have them list all of the sounds they heard during this time.

- Tape-record several different sounds. Have the students identify, describe, and discuss each sound.

Sense of Sight

- To show the students the importance of sight, blindfold the students and have them sit at their desks for a brief period of time. What kinds of thoughts do they have when they are unable to see their surroundings? Follow this exercise by having the children attempt to walk a short way with the blindfold on, simulating blindness. Be sure to assist the child so that he or she will not become injured. Partner trust walks are helpful to reinforce this concept. Discuss the importance of being able to see.

- Take an old pair of eyeglasses and place a substance on them that will impair vision. Various substances may be used, including charcoal, oil, egg white, and paper. Have the students put on the glasses and attempt to perform tasks such as reading, writing, and playing.

Sensory Activities

- Have the children write a letter to a literary character who has a sensory deficiency, such as loss of sight, hearing, touch, or taste. Encourage the use of descriptive language to define or explain an event or experience beyond their grasp.

- Introduce eyeglasses or other corrective apparatus (such as a hearing aid) to students through a family tree experience. Have the students develop a "genealogy" of family members with sensory impairments and the corrections or adaptations that help them function effectively.

- Explore with the students the relationship between smell and taste and sensory interactions:
    a. Use nose plugs and blindfolds with taste treats.
    b. Last time I had a cold or allergic reaction, I couldn't taste certain things as well. Discuss.
    c. Explain steps in eating to a partner wearing a blindfold.
    d. Teach a physical skill (such as shoe tying) to a partner wearing ear plugs or wearing a sling.
    e. Process all station work through discussion and/or journal writing.

In addition to providing instruction about vision, schools also provide vision screening to identify children with visual problems.

DENTAL HEALTH

The teeth serve a number of important purposes in humans. One's initial impressions about a person are often influenced by the condition of his or her teeth. The teeth help to give form and structure to the mouth by supporting the cheeks and the lips. Teeth also come into play while speaking. The tongue touches the teeth in the pronunciation of different sounds and words. Some words are almost impossible to form without the teeth. Thus, the absence of teeth can result in poor speaking patterns.

The most commonly identified function of the teeth is chewing food and aiding in the digestive process. There are four different kinds of teeth in the permanent set (three in the primary set), and each has different purposes in the preparation of food for passage through the esophagus into the stomach. The teeth reduce food to a size that can be handled by the digestive system.

Dental problems are commonly noted among elementary and middle-level schoolchildren. At the time a student enters school, he or she has, on the average, three decayed teeth. The Department of Health and Human Services set as a goal to be achieved by the year 2000 that dental caries in permanent teeth be reduced to a level of no more than 60% of all adolescents 15 years or younger.[3] Special target groups for achieving this objective are children from lower socioeconomic backgrounds and African American and Native American children.[4] Also, the Federal National Health Objectives for the Year 2000 Initiative has established a goal that at least 90% of all children in elementary schools should know the primary methods for preventing and controlling dental caries, gingivitis, and periodontal disease.[5] This goal highlights the importance of school oral health instruction activities during the elementary and middle-level school years. Establishment of good dental practices should begin early in life and should be a lifelong practice.

Anatomical Structure and Physiology

There are two different sets of teeth: the primary, or deciduous teeth, and the secondary, or permanent teeth. There are twenty primary teeth, which begin to form in the fetus before birth. They begin to appear in the mouth about the sixth month after birth. By the time a child is 2 years of age, all of the deciduous teeth have erupted through the gums.

Between ages 6 and 12, the child's primary teeth are replaced by the secondary teeth, which have been submerged in the jaw (tables 17.1 and 17.2). There are thirty-two permanent teeth.

In the primary set of teeth, there are eight *incisors,* which cut the food. Four *cuspids* tear food, and the eight *molars* grind food. These primary teeth are replaced by a full set of secondary teeth that include twelve *molars,* eight *incisors,* four *cuspids,* and eight *bicuspids.* The bicuspids, located between the molars and cuspids, crush food and are not present in the primary set of teeth.

TABLE 17.1	Eruption and Loss of Primary (Deciduous) Teeth		
	Average Age of Eruption		Average Age of Loss
TYPE OF TOOTH	LOWER	UPPER	
Incisors	6–7 mo.	7–9 mo.	6–8 years
Cuspids	16 mo.	18 mo.	9–11 years
Molars (1st)	12 mo.	14 mo.	10 years
Molars (2nd)	20 mo.	24 mo.	10–11 years

Source: Ohio Dental Association, *Dental Health Guide for Teachers,* Columbus, OH.

TABLE 17.2	Eruption of Secondary (Permanent) Teeth	
	Average Age of Eruption	
TYPE OF TOOTH	LOWER	UPPER
Incisors	6–8 yrs.	7–9 yrs.
Cuspids	9–10 yrs.	11-12 yrs.
Bicuspids	10–12 yrs.	10–12 yrs.
Molars (1st)	6–7 yrs.	6–7 yrs.
Molars (2nd)	11–13 yrs.	12–13 yrs.
Molars (3rd)	17–21 yrs.	17–21 yrs.

Source: Ohio Dental Association, *Dental Health Guide for Teachers,* Columbus, OH.

Tooth Decay (Dental Caries)

Decay of the teeth (dental caries) affects many people. Dental caries are a primary personal health concern among elementary and middle-level schoolchildren.

Tooth decay is caused by bacteria on the tooth. When foods that contain carbohydrates (sugars and starches) are on the teeth, bacteria thrive, and produce acids. Acids destroy tooth enamel, resulting in cavities forming on the teeth.

Bacteria are always present in the mouth. Alone, they do not cause problems for the teeth; however, bacteria in the mouth attach to the teeth and form a sticky, colorless deposit, which is called dental *plaque.* Plaque is composed of saliva, cells from tissues of the mouth, and bacteria, which form a sticky film that clings to the surfaces of the tooth, particularly near the gum line.

The bacteria in the plaque convert sugars into acid. These acids are held against the tooth surface, which then dissolve the enamel covering the tooth. Since enamel cannot replace itself fast enough, the decay seeps into the tooth and damages the dentin and, eventually, the pulp area. For this reason, it is necessary for dental caries to be filled by the dentist as early in the decay process as possible. Eating foods with high sugar content, such as candy, cookies, pastries, presweetened foods, and soda pop con-

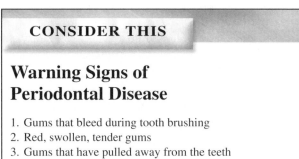

CONSIDER THIS

Warning Signs of Periodontal Disease

1. Gums that bleed during tooth brushing
2. Red, swollen, tender gums
3. Gums that have pulled away from the teeth
4. Pus between the teeth and gums

tributes to the development of acid formation and related tooth decay.

A major protective measure against tooth decay involves regular cleaning of the teeth to remove the plaque. Daily tooth brushing and dental flossing helps in reducing the incidence of plaque and associated decay. In addition, the teeth should be cleaned by a professional dental hygienist twice a year.

Periodontal Diseases

There are diseases that affect the bone that supports the teeth and the soft tissues surrounding the neck of the teeth, the gums. These diseases are referred to as *periodontal diseases.*

An inflammation of the gums (the gingiva) is known as *gingivitis.* This disease is caused by a number of different factors: however, it is most commonly the result of bacteria growing along the gums at the neck of the teeth. Bacteria tend to accumulate, which may result in painful inflammation.

Periodontitis, or *pyorrhea,* often resembles gingivitis at the start. However, in time, the tooth and the gum become separated, and a pocket that is filled with bacteria may form. The bony support of the tooth is destroyed, and the tooth has to be removed.

The most helpful measure to prevent either of these periodontal diseases is to keep bacterial formations from occurring on the gums. Regular tooth brushing and flossing are effective as preventive measures. Good nutritional patterns, including a reduction of sugar-sweetened foods, also will serve as strong prevention.

Malocclusion

In some schoolchildren, the upper and lower teeth do not meet properly. This improper bite is termed *malocclusion.* This condition may be caused by improperly positioned teeth or poor spacing between the teeth.

Malocclusion can result in poor functioning of the teeth, improper chewing of the food, and difficulty in speech. Distortion of facial features is prevalent among

Prevention of Tooth Decay

Brush two times a day with fluoride toothpaste.
Floss the teeth daily.
Eat nutritious and well-balanced meals.
Visit the dentist on a regular basis.

some children with malocclusion. Distorted facial appearances can result in numerous psychological maladjustments.

This condition can be corrected with orthodontics, a procedure that braces the teeth and returns them to a more normal positioning. If the problem is the result of space complications, dental surgical procedures may need to accompany the bracing.

Oral Hygiene

Dental disease is preventable. However, it is necessary that individuals take appropriate measures to care for the teeth.

Bacteria must be removed from the teeth and the gums. This is most effectively accomplished by regular tooth brushing and flossing to clean the spaces between the teeth. Dental health professionals recommend that the teeth be cleaned at least once a day, preferably twice a day.

The procedure of cleaning the teeth is relatively easy. It does take time and one should be sure to brush all sides of the teeth, the front and back, along with the chewing surface, and the surfaces between the teeth.

The use of dental floss is effective in removing plaque and bacteria from between the teeth. Unwaxed floss is usually recommended in that it will eliminate the possibility of leaving a deposit of wax on the teeth.

Fluoridation is effective in reducing the incidences of tooth decay, and it also increases the fluoride content of the teeth. Fluoride helps the teeth to be more resistant to decay, particularly during early childhood years.

Fluoride is used in three different ways as a tooth decay preventive measure: (1) direct application to the teeth, (2) fluoridation of the community water supply, and (3) in tablets. Some suggest that the use of fluoridated dentifrices can be useful; however, evidence suggests that this is the least effective procedure. The importance of fluoridation of community water supplies was noted by the Department of Health and Human Services with its stated objective that by the year 2000 at least 75% of the American population should have access to fluoridated public drinking water.[6] The recommendation was sup-

ported with the statement that "community water fluoridation is the single most effective . . . means of preventing dental caries in children . . . , regardless of race or income level."[7]

Dental Health Professionals

There are two dental health professionals with whom the schoolchild should be familiar: the dentist and the dental hygienist. (Some children also become familiar with the orthodontist.) Dentists fill cavities that develop in the teeth, and they treat the various gum diseases. (Children should see their dentist twice a year.) The first dental visit for a child should be by the first birthday. At this time it is possible to check for early problems. Starting visits to the dentist at this time also help to develop trust with the dentist before a problem develops.

The dental hygienist performs three specific oral services. He or she takes X rays of the teeth, which identify tiny cavities and new decay under old fillings that cannot be seen visually, cleans the plaque from the teeth, and applies topical fluorides to help protect against tooth decay. The orthodontist, a specialist of the dentistry profession, braces the teeth to correct problems of malocclusion.

Dental Health in the Elementary and Middle-Level School Curriculum

Because of the widespread presence of dental caries in elementary and middle-level schoolchildren and the fact that caries are preventable through certain individual behaviors, it is important to include instruction about the teeth and oral hygiene in the health curriculum. There are many materials available to the classroom teacher to use in this instruction. Several suggested sample class activities for the dental health unit follow.

SELECTED HEALTH CONCERNS

Within the context of this chapter it would be impossible to discuss every health problem that children bring to school with which the classroom teacher should be familiar. Three particular problems that are seen in many elementary and middle-level school classrooms are diabetes, epilepsy, and asthma.

Diabetes

The past decade has seen a change in the management of diabetes. The emphasis has shifted more to self-care by the individual, including self-monitoring of the glucose levels and self-administering of multiple daily insulin injections. Under supervision of the school nurse or classroom teacher, the diabetic child in elementary or middle school can manage his or her condition with a minimum of disturbance.

ACTIVITIES

The Teeth

- Children need to be shown the proper way to brush their teeth. Obtain a model of a tooth and show the students proper brushing techniques as recommended by the American Dental Association:

    a. Hold the brush at a 45-degree angle to the gum line.

    b. Using short brushing strokes away from the gum line, move the brush with gentle, scrubbing motions.

    c. Brush the outside, inside, and chewing surfaces of the tooth.

    d. To clean the inside surface of the front teeth, tilt the brush and make several up and down strokes with the brush.

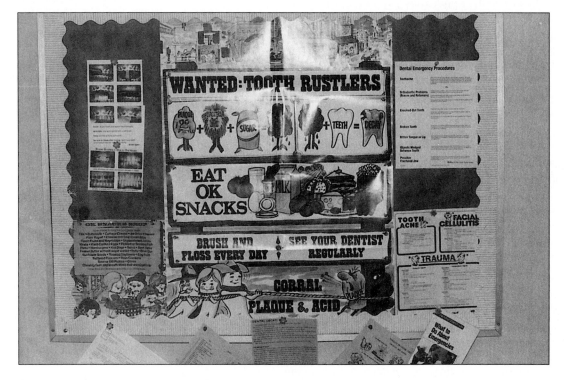

Classroom bulletin boards often serve as information sources about dental health for elementary schoolchildren.

Most children of elementary and middle school age have Type 1 (Immune-Medicated Diabetes, formerly called insulin-dependent diabetes). In this condition, there is a deficiency of insulin that results in metabolic disturbances. The body destroys cells in the pancreas that produce insulin. This can lead to total failure to produce insulin. Without insulin, the body cannot control blood sugar levels. The condition typically starts during childhood or among young adults. Diabetes cannot be cured, but can be successfully controlled. The basic treatment is provision of insulin, proper diet, and exercise.

Most children with diabetes need to be given insulin at least twice a day, usually before breakfast and before dinner. Generally, children can be taught to administer the insulin subcutaneously. The insulin must be injected under the skin, in the fat, for it to work. Insulin cannot be taken orally. There is current research seeking insulin provision by spray. If the diabetic child is on a multidose regimen, he or she will have to take the insulin while at school.

Self-monitoring of the blood glucose level may mean school involvement. The procedure involves taking a blood sample from the tip of the finger. A small drop of the blood is placed on a chemical strip. A reading, involving identification of certain colors, will indicate the level of glucose in the blood.

Normally this procedure is carried out four times a day, before each meal and at night. If the child is at school, particularly during the lunch period, it may be

e. Brush the tongue gently. This will help to keep the breath fresh and to remove bacteria from the mouth.

- Encourage children to brush their teeth both at home and at school following lunch or other eating experiences. Develop a chart as depicted below on days when a child brushes his or her teeth, place a smiley face on the calendar. If the child brushes at night before going to bed, place a moon on the calendar.

Sunday	Monday	Tuesday	Wednesday	Thursday	Friday
☺	☺	☺ ☺	☺ ☽		

- Show how acid affects the enamel of the teeth. Place an egg in a large glass container filled with vinegar and have the students note how the vinegar affects the egg. This depicts how the acid formed by dental plaque affects the teeth.

- Have the students make a tooth out of construction paper. They should be taught to label the various parts and then explain how decay forms.

- Obtain a large model of the teeth. Taking dental floss, demonstrate the proper procedure for flossing the teeth. Have each student perform the procedure, noting how flossing can remove plaque from the teeth. Teach the children how to reach the teeth at the back of the mouth.

- Many primary-grade students are without teeth, which have come out to make room for permanent teeth. Use this time for learning experiences about the roles that teeth can play.

   a. Discuss how the loss of a tooth can affect speech.
   b. Discuss family customs when teeth come out.

Children's health examinations at school can include looking at the mouth and teeth.

necessary to provide an environment in which the individual can carry out the procedure without embarrassment. Usually this can best be done in the school health room. Also, should a child with diabetes develop a headache, or become dizzy or weak, the glucose level should be monitored. The school nurse, or other appropriate personnel, should be available to monitor and assist during these circumstances.

Hypoglycemia, or low blood sugar, is a risk for students with diabetes. School personnel must be aware of the signs and symptoms of hypoglycemia, including hunger, dizziness, pale skin, sweating, headaches, and shaking. During these situations, the child is in need of glucose tablets, snacks, juice, crackers, or other previously identified foods.

Exercise is important for the diabetic in that exercise helps the body use blood sugar. Children who are diabetic usually have no exercise restrictions. However, following vigorous activity, such as a gym class or recess, it may be necessary to provide a snack to the student.

It is important that schools have available a written plan for every diabetic student. Information about the symptoms of hypoglycemia should be included in this plan. Also, the physician's instructions as to when the individual is to eat and what is appropriate for eating should be included. The written plan must also include instructions on how school personnel are to notify parents and medical personnel in case of an emergency. This written plan must be known by every teacher in the school who is responsible for the diabetic child.

Epilepsy

There are children who are epileptics in nearly every elementary and middle-level school. The classroom teacher must have a basic understanding of this chronic disorder of the brain. Teachers should understand, for example, that epilepsy is not a communicable disease, one that can be spread from one person to another.

The principal indicator of epilepsy is sudden, uncontrolled seizures. The teacher must be familiar with the measures to be taken when a student undergoes such seizures while at school.

There are a number of different causes for epilepsy. In many cases, the basic cause may not be known. Problems during fetal development, during the birthing process, and problems during early infancy, such as infections and low calcium or low blood glucose levels, have all been associated with epilepsy. Injuries to the head as well as tumors of the brain are other possible causes. Infectious diseases such as meningitis and encephalitis and, in some cases, severe cases of measles, have been associated with this chronic disorder.

There has been much discussion and study as to whether epilepsy is an inherited condition. The general conclusion is that individuals do not actually inherit epilepsy, but they may inherit a genetic predisposition toward its development. It has been shown that children with one or both parents who are epileptics have an increased risk for the condition.

There are basically two types of seizures that the classroom teacher is likely to see in his or her students. The convulsive seizure formerly was referred to as a grand mal seizure. Today it is referred to as a *generalized tonic-clonic seizure*. During this generalized seizure, the individual will usually lose consciousness and fall to the floor. The body begins jerking movements. Saliva may appear around the mouth, and the person may have difficulty breathing. This type of seizure will usually last for a minute or two, after which the individual will return to consciousness. At this time, he or she will feel confused, sleepy, and in need of rest.

In a second type of seizure, the individual does not go into the convulsive seizures but has nonconvulsive seizures. The individual may have a short period of brief staring spells in which body movements cannot be controlled. The individual may look as though he or she is in a trance, completely unaware of the surroundings. A return to full consciousness occurs shortly, without the individual losing consciousness and falling. It is not unusual for the teacher or child's parents to think that the child is simply being inattentive or daydreaming when, in fact, he or she is having a seizure.

Because of a lack of understanding of the condition and fear of being around individuals who experience seizures, an epileptic seizure may cause a traumatic situation in the classroom setting. For this reason, every teacher should understand what he or she can do to assist the child who experiences a seizure, and the other students should be taught basic information about this condition.

It is important that the teacher and students remain calm. The epileptic should be protected from further injury. This can be accomplished by helping the individual to lie down on the floor and then placing something soft under the head. Glasses should be removed, as should any objects in the immediate vicinity with which the person might hit and injure himself. No effort should be taken to restrain the movements, nor should any attempts be made to force the mouth open. Turning the person onto his or her side will help to protect the individual by allowing saliva to drain from the mouth. Despite what many have been taught previously, a person who is having a seizure cannot swallow the tongue. Efforts to hold the tongue down can injure teeth or the jaw.[8] Nothing should be placed in the person's mouth.

After the seizure is over, the individual should be permitted to rest. An ambulance is usually not needed, but if the seizure lasts for a lengthy time, and/or if the individual experiencing the seizure is not known to be an epileptic, it is important to obtain medical and emergency care assistance.

It is important for schools to be informed when a child is epileptic. Then teachers who have this child in their classes can be instructed about the condition and act in a quiet, calm, professional manner when the seizure occurs. Epileptic children should not be taught that they will outgrow the condition. While such might occur, it is not common for the condition to go into remission as one grows older.

Medically, epilepsy can be treated with drugs, surgical procedures, and special diets. The most common is drug therapy. A number of antiepileptic drugs are prescribed for different types of seizures. The principal purpose of drug therapy is the control of the seizures. It is not unusual for children with epilepsy to need their medication during the school hours. The classroom teacher and school nurse must be informed by the child's parents and physician when there is a need for such medication. Surgery and special diets involving a high intake of fat are methods of treatment for a very small percentage of epileptics.

In most cases of epilepsy, the epileptic can participate in physical activities while at school. Research indicates that epileptics who are active are likely to have fewer seizures.[9] The school district must receive direction and counsel from the student's physician as to what level of physical activity the child can participate in while at school. Such decisions should never be made without consulting the parents and doctors in each individual case.

Asthma

One of the major chronic diseases affecting elementary and middle-level schoolchildren is asthmatic disease. Asthma is a major contributor to school absenteeism, accounting for as much as 10 million lost school days annually—25%

of all school absences. This problem affects nearly 5 million schoolchildren, and is not limited to any single population or age group. Asthma has been observed as early as the first month of life in some infants. Although there is a tendency for asthma to appear in families, no genetic, inherited cause is identifiable. In recent years, the greatest increase of asthmatics has been among the young elementary-age child.

Asthma is a respiratory disease in which the person has trouble breathing. Difficulty in breathing tends to occur in episodic circumstances that are referred to as "asthmatic attacks." Breathing becomes difficult because of several physiological developments at the time of an attack. Under certain circumstances, cells in the lungs become sensitized to an outside agent. A defensive reaction takes place in the bronchial tubes, causing them to constrict and making it difficult for air to move through the bronchial tubes of the lungs. Muscles in the walls of the bronchial tubes tighten, and the inner linings become swollen. The swollen walls of the bronchial tubes give off an extra amount of mucus, which tends to further clog the already constricted airways. As a result, it is difficult to force air through the narrower air passageways. As the person breathes, he or she makes a wheezing or whistling sound. This is accompanied by coughing and spitting of the mucus (phlegm).

The asthmatic attack may be a very mild occurrence or it may be very severe and serious. It may last for a few minutes or occur over a period of several days. However, whenever the attack occurs, the person must learn how to cope with the episodes. By taking certain measures and medication, a person can control the character of the asthmatic attack. Parents and school personnel must be acquainted with the procedures necessary to assist asthmatic children. While there are measures to control the disease, no medications are currently available that will cure it.

Causes of Asthmatic Attacks

One may become allergic to a number of agents that cause an asthmatic attack. In some situations, the allergen is obvious. In other situations, much effort and time are needed to identify the triggering agent. People have been known to be allergic to something as simple as ordinary dust around the home or school. Other potential agents include chocolate, eggs, orange juice, animal skin, hair, dander, and cats.

Asthma attacks can be initiated by weather changes. Breathing cold air or extra humid air can trigger an asthmatic attack by constricting the bronchial tubes. The attack can also be worsened by infections and common colds. Virus infections are particularly known to be a trigger of asthmatic attacks. Sore throat, tonsillitis, and bronchitis can complicate an asthmatic attack.

The increase in asthmatic cases has been associated with the increase in construction of energy-efficient houses in recent years. These houses have a lower exchange of indoor-outdoor air. Indoor air is recycled, resulting in higher concentrations of airborne particles, such as dust, mold, and other allergens, which can trigger an asthmatic attack. Carpeting in homes is another contributing factor, in that carpets and curtains tend to accumulate allergens. Another factor of great concern is exposure to mothers who smoke.[10]

Emotional conditions may cause an attack. Emotional circumstances resulting in stress can stimulate the rapid breathing and wheezing associated with asthma. However, it must be noted that asthma is not a mental disease, but a physical occurrence.

Controlling the Asthmatic Attack

It is impossible to cure the asthmatic. However, control of the attack episode is possible. To cope with the attack effectively, the person needs to be aware of the early warning signals.

Although they vary, certain warning signals usually occur at the beginning of an attack. The individual may have an anxious or frightened look on the face, accompanied by unusual paleness and sweating. There is usually a feeling of tightness in the chest, accompanied by wheezing and difficulty in breathing. Coughing and spitting of mucus follow. Breathing is accelerated, and other signs of restlessness are evident.

When these early signs appear, the individual should be prepared to take certain actions. It is important that asthmatics follow a protocol that is developed with their physician. Most often the physician recommends an appropriate medication, known as a bronchodilator. These medications are helpful in controlling the symptoms of the attack and enable the person to live a more normal life. Since no one drug is effective for all circumstances, a physician should prescribe the appropriate medication.

Two different classes of medications are regularly prescribed for asthma: bronchodilators and anti-inflammatory agents. The bronchodilators dilate the airways by relaxing the bronchial smooth muscle, which helps the individual to relax and helps to open the constricted bronchial tubes. It is possible to tell that bronchodilators are having an effect within 5 to 10 minutes of administration. Within this time, the child should begin to feel better.

The anti-inflammatory agents interrupt the development of bronchial inflammation. These agents have a prophylactic, or preventative, action by reducing the swelling in the lining of the airways and by helping to reduce mucus, which can keep the episodes from starting.

Medications for asthma are given as pills, powders, injections, and as liquids. They are prescribed according to the individual situation. The person must follow the physician's directions carefully, because some medications used to treat asthma cause drowsiness, nervousness, and irritability.

A portable, inexpensive, hand-held device, the Peak Flow Meter, is used to measure how air flows from the lungs in a "blow." Several different types are available. They are useful where the person needs to adjust daily medication. Preschool-age children have been able to use these meters to manage, monitor, and control their asthma.

There are powerful over-the-counter medications that are sold as asthma treatments. However, these drugs may produce unwanted and dangerous side effects, both short and long term. Some over-the-counter drugs may actually stimulate an asthmatic episode.

Feelings of fear and anxiety are natural at the beginning of an attack. However, the person should learn how to relax, breathe more slowly, and control coughing spells. The asthmatic should be given fluids to drink during the course of an attack. This removes the mucus that has developed. The physician should indicate what types of fluids are appropriate and helpful. Water is usually considered the best, but in some instances, juices and other drinks are recommended.

There is no curative value in special dietary treatments or multivitamin tablets for asthmatics. Many are advertised to be useful, but one must not be misled. Good nutrition will help to maintain good body structure and function but will not have a curative affect.

Coping at School

The schoolchild with asthma must learn to cope with the disease. Asthma causes no permanent damage to the lungs. So as long as the person controls the attack episode, there is little reason for most schoolchildren to limit their activities during nonepisodic times. Most asthmatic children should be able to participate in all school functions, including physical education activities, provided the instructor understands any limitations. Children should be encouraged to participate in physical activity within their limits. There is usually no need for modified activities unless so indicated by the physician. Swimming is the least likely activity to provoke asthma symptoms.

Children with asthma need to feel comfortable about taking care of their condition. Elementary children often feel ashamed of their asthma because it makes them feel different than their classmates. These youngsters need to be provided with encouragement and support.

The teacher must be aware of certain mannerisms of the asthmatic child, such as sniffing, sneezing, and coughing. Communication is important among school personnel, parents, and the child's physician concerning the asthmatic condition. Teachers often need to remind these children to take their medicine. However, the teacher should have written directions from the physician and the child's parents.[11]

Research is inconclusive as to whether the asthmatic child's academic performance is affected.[12] Because these children are often absent from school due to the health problem, school performance may be hindered. However, no cognitive or emotional factors should adversely affect school performance. To help asthmatic children cope with the problem at school, schools must permit these youngsters to receive medication while at school, when needed.

Agency Activities

The American Lung Association has been active in providing programs for families and children with asthma. Group counseling sessions are worthwhile. Also, family members and children are helped through the American Lung Association Better Breathers Club or their *Family Asthma Education* program.

Some chapters of the American Lung Association assist children through summer camp programs. These programs help asthmatic children learn physical skills and also teach them how to cope with asthmatic attacks in a variety of different situations.

The American Lung Association has developed curriculum material about asthma for use among children in grades 4 through 6.[13] This program, *Open Airways for Schools Program,* was designed by the Department of Pediatrics of Columbia University's College of Physicians and Surgeons. It is designed to help children with asthma learn how to cope with the disease and to educate nonasthmatic children about the disease. The program is composed of six lessons and includes material for both the teacher and the student. There are nineteen handouts that can be reproduced when teaching the program. In addition, there are activities for elementary schoolchildren. Included are cut-out activities, a board game, and crossword puzzles as well as drawing and coloring activities. Although the program is designed specifically for asthmatic children, it has value in teaching all children about this very important chronic illness.

Lead Poisoning

Lead is a very valuable and useful natural resource. This metal, which is found in the earth's rocks, has been used since early history. The Greeks and Romans used lead in their manufacture of utensils, ornaments, water ducts,

---

CONSIDER THIS

Popular Beliefs about Asthma

1. Asthma is all in the patient's mind.   (False)
2. Asthma is a psychological problem.   (False)
3. Children can turn asthma on and off, if they want.   (False)
4. Tension between parent and child can cause a child to become asthmatic.   (False)
5. Children develop asthma because of their personalities.   (False)

(a)

(b)

The American Lung Association conducts summer camping programs for asthmatic children. In these camp programs, children are taught about asthma and provided with skills to help them cope with this chronic disease.

and numerous other objects of value. Lead has been used in more recent times as an additive in gasoline and in paints, as a metal in water pipes, and in the manufacture of certain ceramics.

Although widely used, lead presents a number of dangerous health-related problems. In small amounts, lead is very toxic and dangerous to the human body. Medical scientists believe that many Americans have low-level lead poisoning. The extent of this problem in the general public is unknown. What is known is that at certain levels in the body, lead can cause very serious problems, particularly among children.

Among children of elementary and middle-level school age, lead poisoning is the most prevalent disease related to environmental factors.[14] Children seem to be much more susceptible to lead poisoning than adolescents and adults in that their bodies do not totally and completely rid themselves of lead. As a result, continual exposure over a long time results in a buildup of high concentrations of lead in the body.

The major source of lead poisoning is the home. This is predominantly a problem in inner-city areas in older, usually blighted, neighborhoods. Children living in old, deteriorating homes where lead-based paint has peeled from walls, floors, hallways, and other parts of the building are particularly at risk.

Children who are exposed to high levels of lead are at risk for developing behavioral problems, learning disabilities, seizures, and even death. Between 3 and 4 million children have toxic levels of lead in their

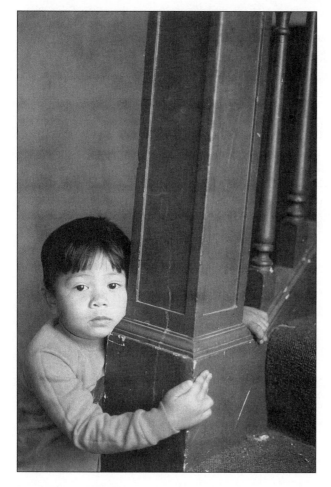

Lead poisoning has become an increasing problem for young children who live in older, blighted neighborhoods. Eating paint chips containing toxic lead can lead to death if the child does not receive treatment.

bodies. The Centers for Disease Control and Prevention recommends that all primary grade children should be screened for lead exposure.

Lead is ingested and absorbed in soluble form into the bloodstream. It is eliminated from the body through the feces and urine and by perspiration. Lead affects primarily the nervous system, blood cells, and the metabolism of vitamin D and calcium. Some lead accumulates in the bones and tends to replace badly needed calcium.

Lead poisoning in the early stages produces signs of anemia. The person experiences headaches, weakness, fatigue, and pain. Low-level exposure can impair the central nervous system, reduce learning capacity, and impair hearing. The kidneys can be affected, often by nephritis, an inflammation of the kidney. If the person is left untreated, coma, convulsions, irreversible mental retardation, and death can result. Blindness, paralysis of muscles, and other neurological conditions may be observed.

Absorption of lead into the bodies of young children can affect their intellectual development and behavior. Studies have shown that IQ and developmental test results are lower in children who have greater recorded lead levels. Hyperactivity, irritability, and aggressive behavior have been associated with lead exposure. Reading disabilities have also been associated with increased levels of lead exposure.

Lead poisoning is a particular problem among children who suffer from pica, which is the behavioral habit of ingesting materials that normally are considered inedible. There are two theories about the cause of pica. One maintains that the child has some specific nutritional deficiency and searches for compensation by ingesting inedible substances. The other theory asserts that pica is primarily the result of psychological factors—that the child has an unmet oral need that is probably connected with an inadequate affective relationship with the mother.

Elementary and middle-level schoolchildren should understand that putting paint chips into their mouths can be harmful to their health. This is a particularly important concept to present during the early preschool and primary-school years. Families that live in houses where childhood lead poisoning might be a risk should have their homes tested for lead paint. Unfortunately, the cost of removing lead from older homes is high, and many people living in these settings cannot afford to have the paint removed.

Exposure to small amounts of lead in the home environment can be dangerous for young children. Children of lead-exposed construction workers were six times more likely to have a dangerous lead blood level than were children of neighbors employed in nonlead industries.[15]

Lead poisoning can also result from exposure to lead outside the home. For example, lead is found in soil and water. Lead does not tend to percolate into the ground; instead, it settles in the top few inches of the dirt. Children playing in dirt or dust around the yard or the house can be exposed to dangerously high levels of lead.

There is also concern about lead exposure through drinking water. Many localities have lead in their water pipes. The solder used in the joints of copper water pipes contains lead. The Safe Drinking Water act requires that states enforce bans on the use of materials containing lead in drinking water plumbing. However, many older pipelines still contain lead. Drinking fountains are another source of lead poisoning, since many have lead-lined tanks or lead-solder red pipes.

Pottery and ceramic dishes are other sources of lead. Cooking utensils such as lead pots and pans contain highly toxic lead, which has been shown to leach from the glaze of dishes and cups of ceramic dishware. If purchased outside the United States, such objects are particularly likely to be a problem.

Children with lead poisoning can be treated medically. A procedure known as *chelation therapy,* in which lead is removed from the body, is available. Also, nutrition is important in the prevention of absorption of lead within the body. The school nurse has an important role to play in helping children to be screened for lead. The schools can also play a role in informing parents about measures to be taken to prevent exposure to lead.

SUMMARY

Elementary and middle-level school age is a time when numerous personal health behavioral patterns are established. The child learns the importance of caring for the skin, the hair, the nails, and the teeth. Many concerns and questions arise during these early school years that necessitate instruction and attention. Without some kind of appropriate instruction, the child is likely to go to questionable sources for information.

Skin care is of great importance because the appearance of one's skin tells much about one's overall physical condition. Numerous disease conditions can occur, many that are contagious.

Dental care is important during all of one's life, but particularly so during the early years. This is because lifetime dental care habits are established during this period. Without proper preventative measures, tooth decay and accompanying inflammation of the gums and surrounding tissues will likely develop.

Several chronic health concerns that affect children must be understood by school personnel. Children with diabetes, epilepsy, asthma, and lead poisoning are most commonly seen in elementary and middle-level schools. Each of these diseases requires care, prevention, and medication that may involve the schools.

Asthma is a major chronic disease that affects many elementary and middle-level schoolchildren. This respiratory disease can be a major debilitator of schoolchildren. Although it is impossible to cure asthma, there are procedures to control the attack episodes. All classroom teachers must be knowledgeable and competent in how to cope with asthma attacks.

DISCUSSION QUESTIONS

1. Explain the basic structure and function of the three layers of skin.
2. How does the skin help to protect against disease?
3. What is dandruff and how can it be prevented?
4. Identify several different bacterial and viral infections that affect the skin.
5. Describe how impetigo differs from eczema.
6. What are the three different types of human lice?
7. What can be done for the care of head lice among schoolchildren?
8. What are pediculicides?
9. Explain the factors associated with acne.
10. Explain the factors associated with warts.
11. What are the differences among first-, second-, and third-degree burns?
12. Develop an activity that would be useful in teaching about the skin.
13. Where are each of the receptors for the sensations of taste located on the tongue?
14. Explain the difference between the primary and secondary sets of teeth.
15. Explain several factors that result in tooth decay.
16. Explain the characteristics of malocclusion.
17. What has been the position of the federal government regarding fluoridation of community water supplies?
18. What is Type 1 diabetes?
19. Discuss factors that relate to diabetes in children that classroom teachers should be aware of.
20. What factors are associated with epilepsy?
21. Discuss factors that relate to epilepsy in children that classroom teachers should be aware of.
22. Explain the basic features of asthma among elementary schoolchildren.
23. Identify the basic indications of an asthmatic attack.
24. Identify measures that can be taken to control an asthmatic attack.
25. What activities has the American Lung Association introduced to assist the student with asthma?
26. How are children exposed to lead?
27. Explain why lead poisoning is a particular problem for children.
28. What behavioral and learning difficulties among children have been associated with lead poisoning?

ENDNOTES

1. John B. Lampe, "Peau-pourri of Skin Conditions in Children," *Health and Disease in the School* (Cleveland, OH: Cleveland Clinic Foundation, November 1992), 89.

2. Ellen Rudy Clore and Leah Ann Longyear, "Comprehensive Pediculosis Screening Programs for Elementary Schools," *Journal of School Health* 60, no. 5 (May 1990): 212–214.

3. Department of Health and Human Services, Public Health Service, *Healthy People 2000: National Health Promotion and Disease Prevention Objectives* (Washington, DC: U.S. Government Printing Office, 1991), 352.

4. Ibid., 359.

5. Ibid., 357.

6. Department of Health and Human Services, *Healthy People 2000*, 357.

7. Ibid., 357.

8. Epilepsy Foundation of America, "Questions and Answers About Epilepsy," 7, n.d.

9. Ibid., 14.

10. Information brochure about asthma from the American Lung Association.

11. Michelle Walsh and Nancy M. Ryan-Wenger, "Sources of Stress in Children with Asthma," *Journal of School Health* 62, no. 10 (December 1992): 462.

12. Warren, Richards, "Allergy, Asthma, and School Problems," *Journal of School Health* 56, no. 4 (April 1986): 151.

13. American Lung Association, 1740 Broadway, New York, NY 10019.

14. Department of Health and Human Services, Public Health Service, *Healthy People 2000*, 319.

15. Waldman, Steven, "Lead and Your Kids," *Newsweek,* July 15, 1991; 42–48.

SUGGESTED READINGS

Arvidson, Cathy R. and Pat Colledge. "Lead Screening in Children: the Role of the School Nurse." *Journal of School Nursing* 12, no. 3 (October, 1996): 8–13.

Bouchad, Jo M. et al. "Oral Health Instructional Needs of Ohio Elementary Educators." *Journal of School Health* 60, no. 10 (December 1990): 511–513.

Brozena, Stephen J. "Scabies: Update on Diagnosis and Treatment." *Journal of School Nursing* 8, no. 4 (December 1992): 15–19.

Clore, Ellen Rudy, and Leah Ann Longyear. "Comprehensive Pediculosis Screening Programs for Elementary Schools." *Journal of School Health* 60, no. 5 (May 1990): 212–214.

Krasner, Paul. "Management of Dental Injuries." *Journal of School Nursing* 8, no. 4 (December 1992): 20–29.

Krasner, Paul. "Management of Tooth Avulsion in the School Setting." *Journal of School Nursing* 8, no. 1 (February 1992): 20–26.

Meng, Anne. "An Asthma Day Camp." *The American Journal of Maternal/Child Nursing* 22, no. 3 (May/June 1997): 135–141.

Reilly, Elizabeth A., and Patricia B. Davis. "Diabetes Mellitus: Management in the School Setting." School Nurse 7, no. 1 (February 1991): 22–30.

Sciarillo, William G. et al. "Lead Exposure and Child Behavior." *American Journal of Public Health* 82, no. 10 (October 1992): 1356–1360.

Walsh, Michelle, and Nancy M. Ryan-Wenger. "Sources of Stress in Children with Asthma." *Journal of School Health* 62, no. 1 (December 1992): 459–463.

Whelan, Elizabeth and others. "Elevated Blood Lead Levels in Children of Construction Workers." *American Journal of Public Health* 87, no. 8 (August 1997): 1352–1355.

CHILDREN'S LITERATURE WITH A PERSONAL HEALTH THEME

Following are some of the many books available to teachers related to the topic of personal health. This is not a complete list, nor are these the only good books. They are simply examples of children's books that can be used with material presented in this chapter.

Grades K–2

Aliki. *My Five Senses.* Harper Collins, 1989.

Arnold, Tedd. *Parts.* Dial, 1997.

Berger, Melvin. *Germs Make Me Sick.* Harper Collins, 1985.

Brazelton, T. Berry. *Going to the Doctor.* Addison-Wesley, 1996.

Brown, Marc. *Arthur's Chicken Pox.* Little, Brown and Company, 1994.

Brown, Marc. *Arthur's Eyes.* Little, Brown and Company, 1979.

Davison, Martin. *Maggie and the Emergency Room.* Random House, 1992.

DeSantis, Kenny. *A Dentist's Tools.* Photographs by Patricia A. Agre. Dodd, Mead, 1988.

Linn, Margot. *A Trip to the Dentist.* Illus. Catherine Siracusa. Harper & Row, 1988.

London, Jonathan. *The Lion Who Had Asthma.* Albert Whitman. 1992.

MacDonald, Amy. *Rachel Fister's Blister.* Houghton Mifflin, 1990.

Miller, Margaret. *My Five Senses.* Simon and Schuster, 1994.

Munsch, Robert. *Andrew's Loose Tooth.* Scholastic, 1998.

Pirner, Connie White. *Even Little Kids Get Diabetes.* Albert Whitman, 1991.

Silverstein, Alvin, and Virginia R. Silverstein. *Itch, Sniffle, and Sneeze: All About Asthma, Hay Fever and Other Allergies.* Illus. Ray Doty. Four Winds, 1978.

Wise, William. *Fresh as a Daisy, Neat as a Pin.* Illus. Dora Leder. Parents, 1970.

Grades 3–5

Barner, Bob. *Dem Bones.* Chronicle, 1996. (Parent's Choice Silver Award)

Betancourt, Jeanne. *Smile! How to Cope With Braces.* Illus. Mimi Harrison. Knopf, 1982.

Cobb, Vicki. *Keeping Clean.* Illus. Marylin Hafner. Harper, 1989.

Doss, Helen. *Your Skin Holds You In.* Messner, 1978.

Krisher, Trudy. *Katy's Hats.* Albert Whitman, 1992.

Shannon, David. *A Bad Case of Stripes.* Scholastic, 1998.

True, Kelly. *I've Got Chicken Pox.* Penguin, 1994.

Ward, Brian R. *Body Maintenance.* Watts, 1983.

Grades 6–8

Blume, Judy. *Blubber.* Bradbury, 1974.

Lowry, Lois. *The Giver.* 1994. (Newbery Medal Book)

PERSONAL HEALTH WEBSITES

For additional information on personal health, please refer to the following websites.

National Pediculosis Association
www.headlice.org

American Head Lice Information Center
www.headliceinfo.com

Pfizer Pharmaceutical Corporation
www.pfizer.com/chc/licerid

American Academy of Dermatology
www.aad.org

Epilepsy Foundation
www.efa.org

American Diabetes Association
www.diabetes.org

National Diabetes Information Clearinghouse
www.niddk.nih.gov

The American Lung Association
www.lungusa.org

National Health Education Standards for Students Organized by Grade

GRADES K–4

Health Education Standard 1

Students will comprehend concepts related to health promotion and disease prevention.

Performance Indicators

As a result of health instruction in Grades K–4, students will:

1. describe relationships between personal health behaviors and individual well being.
2. identify indicators of mental, emotional, social, and physical health during childhood.
3. describe the basic structure and functions of the human body systems.
4. describe how the family influences personal health.
5. describe how physical, social, and emotional environments influence personal health.
6. identify common health problems of children.
7. identify health problems that should be detected and treated early.
8. explain how childhood injuries and illnesses can be prevented or treated.

Health Education Standard 2

Students will demonstrate the ability to access valid health information and health-promoting products and services.

Performance Indicators

As a result of health instruction in Grades K–4, students will:

1. identify characteristics of valid health information and health-promoting products and services.
2. demonstrate the ability to locate resources from home, school, and community that provide valid health information.

3. explain how media influences the selection of health information, products, and services.
4. demonstrate the ability to locate school and community health helpers.

Health Education Standard 3

Students will demonstrate the ability to practice health-enhancing behaviors and reduce health risks.

Performance Indicators

As a result of health instruction in Grades K–4, students will:

1. identify responsible health behaviors.
2. identify personal health needs.
3. compare behaviors that are safe to those that are risky or harmful.
4. demonstrate strategies to improve or maintain personal health.
5. develop injury prevention and management strategies for personal health.
6. demonstrate ways to avoid and reduce threatening situations.
7. apply skills to manage stress.

Health Education Standard 4

Students will analyze the influence of culture, media, technology, and other factors on health.

Performance Indicators

As a result of health instruction in Grades K–4, students will:

1. describe how culture influences personal health behaviors.
2. explain how media influences thoughts, feelings, and health behaviors.

This represents the work of the Joint Committee on National Health Education Standards. Copies of the *National Health Education Standards: Achieving Health Literacy* can be obtained through the American School Health Association, Association for the Advancement of Health Education, or the American Cancer Society.

3. describe ways technology can influence personal health.
4. explain how information from school and family influences health.

Health Education Standard 5

Students will demonstrate the ability to use interpersonal communication skills to enhance health.

Performance Indicators

As a result of health instruction in Grades K–4, students will:

1. distinguish between verbal and non-verbal communication.
2. describe characteristics needed to be a responsible friend and family member.
3. demonstrate healthy ways to express needs, wants, and feelings.
4. demonstrate ways to communicate care, consideration, and respect of self and others.
5. demonstrate attentive listening skills to build and maintain healthy relationships.
6. demonstrate refusal skills to enhance health.
7. differentiate between negative and positive behaviors used in conflict situations.
8. demonstrate non-violent strategies to resolve conflicts.

Health Education Standard 6

Students will demonstrate the ability to use goal setting and decision-making skills to enhance health.

Performance Indicators

As a result of health instruction in Grades K–4, students will:

1. demonstrate the ability to apply a decision-making process to health issues and problems.
2. explain when to ask for assistance in making health-related decisions and setting health goals.
3. predict outcomes of positive health decisions.
4. set a personal health goal and track progress toward its achievement.

Health Education Standard 7

Students will demonstrate the ability to advocate for personal, family, and community health.

Performance Indicators

As a result of health instruction in Grades K–4, students will:

1. describe a variety of methods to convey accurate health information and ideas.

2. express information and opinions about health issues.
3. identify community agencies that advocate for healthy individuals, families, and communities.
4. demonstrate the ability to influence and support others in making positive health choices.

GRADES 5–8

Health Education Standard 1

Students will comprehend concepts related to health promotion and disease prevention.

Performance Indicators

As a result of health instruction in Grades 5–8, students will:

1. explain the relationship between positive health behaviors and the prevention of injury, illness, disease, and premature death.
2. describe the interrelationship of mental, emotional, social, and physical health during adolescence.
3. explain how health is influenced by the interaction of body systems.
4. describe how family and peers influence the health of adolescents.
5. analyze how environment and personal health are interrelated.
6. describe ways to reduce risks related to adolescent health problems.
7. explain how appropriate health care can prevent premature death and disability.
8. describe how lifestyle, pathogens, family history, and other risk factors are related to the cause or prevention of disease and other health problems.

Health Education Standard 2

Students will demonstrate the ability to access valid health information and health promoting products and services.

Performance Indicators

As a result of health instruction in Grades 5–8, students will:

1. analyze the validity of health information, products, and services.
2. demonstrate the ability to utilize resources from home, school, and community that provide valid health information.
3. analyze how media influences the selection of health information and products.
4. demonstrate the ability to locate health products and services.
5. compare the costs and validity of health products.

6. describe situations requiring professional health services.

Health Education Standard 3

Students will demonstrate the ability to practice health enhancing behaviors and reduce health risks.

Performance Indicators

As a result of health instruction in Grades 5–8, students will:

1. explain the importance of assuming responsibility for personal health behaviors.
2. analyze a personal health assessment to determine health strengths and risks.
3. distinguish between safe and risky or harmful behaviors in relationships.
4. demonstrate strategies to improve or maintain personal and family health.
5. develop injury prevention and management strategies for personal and family health.
6. demonstrate ways to avoid and reduce threatening situations.
7. demonstrate strategies to manage stress.

Health Education Standard 4

Students will analyze the influence of culture, media, technology, and other factors on health.

Performance Indicators

As a result of health instruction in Grades 5–8, students will:

1. describe the influence of cultural beliefs on health behaviors and the use of health services.
2. analyze how messages from media and other sources influence health behaviors.
3. analyze the influence of technology on personal and family health.
4. analyze how information from peers influences health.

Health Education Standard 5

Students will demonstrate the ability to use interpersonal communication skills to enhance health.

Performance Indicators

As a result of health instruction in Grades 5–8, students will:

1. demonstrate effective verbal and non-verbal communication skills to enhance health.
2. describe how the behavior of family and peers affects interpersonal communication.

3. demonstrate healthy ways to express needs, wants, and feelings.
4. demonstrate ways to communicate care, consideration, and respect of self and others.
5. demonstrate communication skills to build and maintain healthy relationships.
6. demonstrate refusal and negotiation skills to enhance health.
7. analyze the possible causes of conflict among youth in schools and communities.
8. demonstrate strategies to manage conflict in healthy ways.

Health Education Standard 6

Students will demonstrate the ability to use goal setting and decision-making skills to enhance health.

Performance Indicators

As a result of health instruction in Grades 5–8, students will:

1. demonstrate the ability to apply, a decision-making process to health issues and problems individually and collaboratively.
2. analyze how health-related decisions are influenced by individuals, family, and community values.
3. predict how decisions regarding health behaviors have consequences for self and others.
4. apply strategies and skills needed to attain personal health goals.
5. describe how personal health goals are influenced by changing information, abilities, priorities, and responsibilities.
6. develop a plan that addresses personal strengths, needs, and health risks.

Health Education Standard 7

Students will demonstrate the ability to advocate for personal, family, and community health.

Performance Indicators

As a result of health instruction in Grades 5–8, students will:

1. analyze various communication methods to accurately express health information and ideas.
2. express information and opinions about health issues.
3. identify barriers to effective communication of information, ideas, feelings, and opinions about health issues.
4. demonstrate the ability to influence and support others in making positive health choices.
5. demonstrate the ability to work cooperatively when advocating for healthy individuals, families, and schools.

GRADES 9–11

Health Education Standard 1

Students will comprehend concepts related to health promotion and disease prevention.

Performance Indicators

As a result of health instruction in Grades 9–11, students will:

1. analyze how behavior can impact health maintenance and disease prevention.
2. describe the interrelationships of mental, emotional, social, and physical health throughout adulthood.
3. explain the impact of personal health behaviors on the functioning of body systems.
4. analyze how the family, peers, and community influence the health of individuals.
5. analyze how the environment influences the health of the community.
6. describe how to delay onset and reduce risks of potential health problems during adulthood.
7. analyze how public health policies and government regulations influence health promotion and disease prevention.
8. analyze how the prevention and control of health problems are influenced by research and medical advances.

Health Education Standard 2

Students will demonstrate the ability to access valid health information and health promoting products and services.

Performance Indicators

As a result of health instruction in Grades 9–11, students will:

1. evaluate the validity of health information, products, and services.
2. demonstrate the ability to evaluate resources from home, school, and community that provide valid health information.
3. evaluate factors that influence personal selection of health products and services.
4. demonstrate the ability to access school and community health services for self and others.
5. analyze the cost and accessibility of health care services.
6. analyze situations requiring professional health services.

Health Education Standard 3

Students will demonstrate the ability to practice health enhancing behaviors and reduce health risks.

Performance Indicators

As a result of health instruction in Grades 9–11, students will:

1. analyze the role of individual responsibility for enhancing health.
2. evaluate a personal health assessment to determine strategies for health enhancement and risk reduction.
3. analyze the short-term and long-term consequences of safe and risky or harmful behaviors.
4. develop strategies to improve or maintain personal, family, and community health.
5. develop injury prevention and management strategies for personal, family, and community health.
6. demonstrate ways to avoid and reduce threatening situations.
7. evaluate strategies to manage stress.

Health Education Standard 4

Students will analyze the influence of culture, media, technology, and other factors on health.

Performance Indicators

As a result of health instruction in Grades 9–11, students will:

1. analyze how cultural diversity enriches and challenges health behaviors.
2. evaluate the effect of media and other factors on personal, family, and community health.
3. evaluate the impact of technology on personal, family, and community health.
4. analyze how information from the community influences health.

Health Education Standard 5

Students will demonstrate the ability to use interpersonal communication skills to enhance health.

Performance Indicators

As a result of health instruction in Grades 9–11, students will:

1. demonstrate skills for communicating effectively with family, peers, and others.
2. analyze how interpersonal communication affects relationships.
3. demonstrate healthy ways to express needs, wants, and feelings.
4. demonstrate ways to communicate care, consideration, and respect of self and others.
5. demonstrate strategies for solving interpersonal conflicts without harming self or others.

6. demonstrate refusal, negotiation, and collaboration skills to avoid potentially harmful situations.
7. analyze the possible causes of conflict in schools, families, and communities.
8. demonstrate strategies used to prevent conflict.

Health Education Standard 6

Students will demonstrate the ability to use goal setting and decision-making skills to enhance health.

Performance Indicators

As a result of health instruction in Grades 9–11, students will:

1. demonstrate the ability to utilize various strategies when making decisions related to health needs and risks of young adults.
2. analyze health concerns that require collaborative decision making.
3. predict immediate and long-term impact of health decisions on the individual, family, and community.
4. implement a plan for attaining a personal health goal.
5. evaluate progress toward achieving personal health goals.
6. formulate an effective plan for lifelong health.

Health Education Standard 7

Students will demonstrate the ability to advocate for personal, family, and community health.

Performance Indicators

As a result of health instruction in Grades 9–11, students will:

1. evaluate the effectiveness of communication methods for accurately expressing health information and ideas.
2. express information and opinions about health issues.
3. utilize strategies to overcome barriers when communicating information, ideas, feelings, and opinions about health issues.
4. demonstrate the ability to influence and support others in making positive health choices.
5. demonstrate the ability to work cooperatively when advocating for healthy communities.
6. demonstrate the ability to adapt health messages and communication techniques to the characteristics of a particular audience.

CREDITS

PHOTOS AND ILLUSTRATIONS

Chapter 2

Page 30: © Kathy Sloane/Photo Researchers, Inc.; Figure 2.3: From the National Scoliosis Foundation, Belmont, MA. Reprinted with permission; Page 37: Courtesy of National Scoliosis Foundation; Page 38: Courtesy of National Scoliosis Foundation; Figure 2.5: Centers for Disease Control and Prevention. Recommended Childhood Immunization Schedule, 1998. Internet: www.cdc.gov.

Chapter 3

Pages 52 and 60: © PhotoDisc/Education.

Chapter 5

Page 89: © PhotoDisc/Weekend Living; Page 96: © PhotoDisc/Education.

Chapter 6

Pages 110 and 111: © PhotoDisc/Education; Page 113: © PhotoDisc/Education 2.

Chapter 7

Page 120: © Michael Siluk; Page 122: © Susan McCartney/Photo Researchers, Inc.; Pages 128 and 133: © James L. Shaffer.

Chapter 8

Page 138: © PhotoDisc/Business Today; Page 147: © PhotoDisc/Health and Medicine; Figure 8.1: Children's Safety Network Adolescent Violence Prevention Resource Center. *A Comprehensive Approach to Violence Prevention in Schools*. Newton, MA: Education Development Center.

Chapter 9

Pages 164 and 170: © PhotoDisc/Education.

Chapter 10

Page 177: © PhotoDisc/Government and Social Issues; Pages 180 and 181: © Michael Siluk.

Chapter 11

Page 196 © PhotoDisc/Government and Social Issues; Page 209: © PhotoDisc/Weekend Living; Page 213: © PhotoDisc/Education 2; Figure 11.1: U.S. Department of Agriculture and U.S. Department of Health and Human Services.

Chapter 12

Figure 12.1: Reprinted from *Physical Activity for Children: A Statement of Guidelines* (1998) with permission from the National Association for Sport and Physical Education (NASPE), 1990 Association Drive, Reston, VA 20191-1599.

Chapter 13

Page 243: © PhotoDisc/Education; Page 247: © PhotoDisc/Education 2.

Chapter 16

Page 292: © David Wells/The Image Works.

Chapter 17

Page 306: © Dr. P. Marazzi/SPL/Photo Researchers, Inc.; Page 307: Biophoto Associates/Photo Researchers, Inc.; Page 321: Photos courtesy of American Lung Association of Northwestern Ohio; Page 322: © Nita Winter/The Image Works.

INDEX

A

Academic achievement, 20
Acne, 308
Active aerobics, 224, 227
Adolescent pregnancy, 235
Advertisements
    techniques used in, 108
    tobacco, 177, 179, 185
Advocacy skills
    importance of, 112
    promotion of, 112–113
    suspected child abuse and, 147
AIDS, 256, 258. *See also* HIV/AIDS
Air bags, 120
Alcohol
    absorption of, 156, 158
    effects of, 154–157
    explanation of, 154
    guidelines for use of, 210–211
    pathways of, 157
Alcohol abuse. *See also* Substance abuse
    activities for prevention of,
        168–171
    family history of, 163
    long-term side effects of, 158–159
Alcohol Misuse Prevention Project, 166
All About You, 77
All Fit with Slim Goodbody, 77
American Academy of Pediatrics, 120
American Automobile
        Association, 131–132
American Heart Association, 214
American Lung Association, 320, 321
American Optical Hardy-Rand-Rittler
        Pseudo-isochromatic plates, 34
American Red Cross, 42, 131
American School Health Association
        (ASHA), 144
Amphetamines, 155
Anonymous Cards Strategy, 83
Antagonism, 156
Appliances, electrical, 127
Asthma
    causes of attacks of, 319

control of attacks of, 319–320
explanation of, 318–319
programs for families and children
        with, 320
students with, 320
Astigmatism, 32, 33
Athlete's foot, 307
At-risk students, 20
Audiometer screening, 35
Automatic safety belts, 120

B

Bacteria
    in mouth, 314
    on skin, 306
Barbiturates, 155
Basic Aid Training Program (American
        Red Cross), 131
Bathtub accidents, 122
Bean, Reynold, 276
Bedworth, A., 3
Bedworth, D., 3
Better Breathers Club (American Lung
        Association), 320
Bicycle Safety (American Red Cross), 131
Bicycling safety, 128–131
Bicycling Visual Skills (American
        Automobile Association), 132
Blood-Alcohol Concentration (BAC),
        156–158
Blood glucose levels, 316–317
Blood handling, 261, 265
Boat safety, 122
*Body Awareness Resource Network
        (BARN),* 74
Body fluids, 261, 265
Boil, 306
Breakfast, 212–213
Bronchitis, 182
Buchwald, Art, 282
Buckle Up Game, The (National Safety
        Belt Coalition), 132
Burns
    from cigarettes, 182

prevention of, 124
types of, 309

C

Cancer
    marijuana use and, 160
    tobacco use and, 180, 182
Carbohydrates, 197–198, 202
Carbuncle, 306
Cardiovascular disease, 182
Carousel Activity, 84
Catch Somebody Doing Something Good
        Activity, 283
CD-ROMs, 72–73
Centers for Disease Control and
        Prevention (CDC), 5
    Division of Adolescent and School
        Health, 62–63
    nutritional guidelines and, 193–195
    physical activity recommendations
        and, 230–231
    problem areas targeted by, 11
    tobacco use prevention and, 178–179,
        182–183
Chelation therapy, 323
Chewing tobacco, 180
*Chief Combo's Fantastic Adventures in
        Tasting and Nutrition* (National
        Dairy Council), 213
Child abuse
    disclosures to teachers of, 146–147
    indicators associated with, 146
    making referrals of, 147–148
    observation of children and, 147
    overview of, 144, 146
    prevention and education strategies to
        avoid, 148–149
Child Protective Services, 147
Children
    at-risk, 20
    with disabilities, 28, 29
    growth and development
        characteristics of, 57–60
    guidelines for physical activity in, 222